MANAGING SOFTWARE PROJECTS

Books and Training Products From QED

Database

Data Analysis: The Key to Data Base Design
The Data Dictionary: Concepts and Uses
DB2: The Complete Guide to Implementation and Use
Logical Data Base Design
DB2 Design Review Guidelines
DB2: Maximizing Performance of Online Production Systems
Entity-Relationship Approach to Logical Data Base Design
How to Use ORACLE SQL*PLUS
ORACLE: Building High Performance Online Systems
Embedded SQL for DB2: Application Design and Programming
Introduction to Data and Activity Analysis
ORACLE Design Review Guidelines
Using DB2 to Build Decision Support Systems
IMS Design and Implementation Techniques
SQL for DB2 and SQL/DS Application Developers
Using ORACLE to Build Decision Support Systems
Database Management Systems: Understanding and Applying Database Technology
Effective DSS Processing with Teradata

Systems Engineering

Handbook of Screen Format Design
Managing Software Projects: Selecting and Using PC-Based Project Management Systems
The Complete Guide to Software Testing
A User's Guide for Defining Software Requirements
A Structured Approach to Systems Testing
Storyboard Prototyping: A New Approach to User Requirements Analysis
The Software Factory: Managing Software Development and Maintenance
Data Architecture: The Information Paradigm
Advanced Topics in Information Engineering
Software Engineering with Formal Software Metrics
Data Architecture: An Information Systems Strategy (Video)

Management

CASE: The Potential and the Pitfalls
Strategic and Operational Planning for Information Services
The Management Handbook for Information Center and End-User Computing

Management (cont'd)

Winning the Change Game
Information Systems Planning for Competitive Advantage
Critical Issues in Information Processing Management and Technology
Developing the World Class Information Systems Organization
How to Automate Your Computer Center: Achieving Unattended Operations
Ethical Conflicts in Information and Computer Science, Technology, and Business
Mind Your Business: Managing the Impact of End-User Computing
Controlling the Future: Managing Technology-Driven Change

Data Communications

Data Communications: Concepts and Solutions
Designing and Implementing Ethernet Networks
Network Concepts and Architectures
Open Systems: The Guide to OSI and its Implementation

IBM Mainframe Series

How to Use CICS to Create On-Line Applications: Methods and Solutions
DOS/VSE/SP Guide for Systems Programming: Concepts, Programs, Macros, Subroutines
Systems Programmer's Problem Solver
VSAM: Guide to Optimization and Design
MVS/TSO: Mastering CLISTS
MVS/TSO: Mastering Native Mode and ISPF
Advanced VSE System Programming Techniques
REXX in the TSO Environment
DOS/VSE: Introduction to the Operating System

Self-Paced Training

SQL as a Second Language
Building Online Production Systems with DB2 (Video)
Introduction to UNIX (CBT)
Building Production Applications with ORACLE (Video)

Programming

C Language for Programmers, Second Edition
VAX/VMS: Mastering DCL Commands and Utilities

For Additional Information or a Free Catalog contact

QED Information Sciences, Inc. • P. O. Box 82-181 • Wellesley, MA 02181
Telephone: 800-343-4848 or 617-237-5656

MANAGING SOFTWARE PROJECTS

Selecting and Using PC-Based Project Management Systems

LOIS ZELLS

QED Information Sciences, Inc.
Wellesley, Massachusetts

Library of Congress Catalog Number: 89-10655
International Standard Book Number: 0-89435-275-X

Printed in the United States of America
90 91 92 10 9 8 7 6 5 4 3

Library of Congress Cataloging-in-Publication Data

Zells, Lois.
    Managing software projects: selecting and using
pc-based project management systems / Lois Zells.
        p.   cm.
    ISBN 0-89435-275-X
    1. Industrial project management—Data
processing.   2. Industrial
project management—Computer programs.   I. Title.
HD69.P75Z45   1990
658.4′04′028553—dc20

This book is dedicated in loving memory of
my mother and father,
Eva B. and Albert Steinman,
and my aunt, Dorothy E. Cohen,
and to
D.J. and Mike,
my shining stars.

Contents

Foreword

Not so long ago, a manager called me for advice on a software project with a crucial delivery requirement. I was told the project, which was approaching the critical design review, was only about two months behind the predicted schedule. My analysis, using one of the tools presented in this book, showed the project was at risk and action to correct the environmental problems needed to be taken immediately. The manager's classic reply was "We're not really in trouble yet. If we can't make up the schedule slip by working a little harder, we'll add more programmers." I wondered why I was called in the first place. Needless to say, the project ended up several months late, with a considerable cost overrun. The added load on a development team already working 50-hour weeks was counterproductive; adding the "programming horde" at the last minute was devasting. The manager's factory mentality, still a mindset of a majority of software managers, led him to believe that if you want more widgets, you need more widget makers. The manager refused to heed Brooks' law and other metrics available to him to guide him through the development. The results added up to yet another software failure.

This is the same problem we faced in the 1960's, when the need for a radically different approach to management and development of software became apparent. Unfortunately, the result of the evaluation of existing development practices was the narrow observation that the problems could be solved simply with more advanced engineering tools and methods. Several new software design approaches were introduced with limited success.

We are all familiar with structured methods, interactive development systems, Ada, 4GLs, and end-user programming. Since the introduction of these development improvements, productivity in the aerospace world has improved from approximately 55 delivered source lines of code per person-month (DSLOC/PM) of effort in 1965 to only 95 DSLOC/PM.

This lack of productivity gain does not negate the importance of using these new tools and methods during the development of increasingly large and complex software systems. In fact, we would have reached our maximum systems size limitation years ago without the modern methods and development systems available today. In 1965, we considered 50,000 source lines of code to be large; today, we think of 5,000,000 source line systems in much the same light.

Now that the dust from the initial scramble to solve the world's software problems has settled, we can look objectively at the sources of the problems plaguing software developers and formulate organized means of solving these problems. We are good at learning technology, but not good at applying it effectively. Structured methods haven't done it, 4GLs haven't done it, end-user programming hasn't done it, and CASE won't do it. Management, or the lack thereof, has always been the major obstacle in improving software productivity and quality. Lois Zells' book, *Managing Software Projects*, recognizes this and goes a long way in providing management guidance within the framework of the techniques.

Management in this country has been, and still is, problematical. As a science in general, it is still immature and relatively few managers make effective use of it. There has been little organized thought or direction, and little effort devoted to the understanding of the people-oriented, creative enterprise. Throughout management science, both in the literature and in practice, the emphasis has been on technique rather than principle, and on technical details rather than managerial decisions.

If management science is immature, then we can expect software management science to be especially immature, since the software industry itself is so new and expanding so quickly. The probability, then, of finding effective software managers would seem small. It is.

The rapid expansion of software-related activities combined with software's brief history are enough to cause a definite shortage of management talent. There are not enough people with adequate experience to go around. The shortage of experience is not the only problem. The shortcoming of emphasizing efficiency of the mechanics of producing the line of source code rather than the performance of the development team permeates the software management state of affairs today. There is much attention on the individual phases and functions of the software development sequence, but little on the whole life cycle as an integral, continous process—a process that can be optimized.

The value of Lois Zells' book is that it provides the experience you may not get on the job, while at the same time makes one of the first reasonable attempts at removing the mist (or should I say fog) that surrounds the management and optimization of the software development process. The text provides a fresh viewpoint of management techniques and their application of software projects.

Managing Software Projects focuses on the procedural aspects of the development process and leaves the people issues out of the discussion. At first I was concerned that ignoring the psychological side of the process would be a disservice to the reader. However, after reading the manuscript, I agreed that an attempt to cover both sides of the management problem would dilute the effectiveness. The people issue will have to be the topic of another independent work.

This text deals with the *realities* of software project management. The process is not simple and there are no "silver bullets" that make the complexity of the task disappear. Lois promises no miracles, but establishes an order to the multitude of things that must be done to make the creation of a successful software system possible. The clearly stated guidelines, techniques, and tools contained in the following pages are giant steps in the right direction. The time you spend here will be a sound investment.

Randall Jensen

Acknowledgments

Many years ago, when I was a fledgling project leader, I was given the job of managing my company's largest project. Other than my intuitive skills, I had no project management training. Fortunately, the budget was hefty and I was able to attend several classes. I always went with high hopes. Nevertheless, I came away very disappointed, because, while I expected to be told *how* to manage projects step by step, instead, I only received lots of good advice on *what* to do.[1] I vowed, even then, to someday write a "How To" book on project management.

In the early years, I was fortunate to work with some very fine people. I owe my thanks for the help I received from Phoebe Sharkey, Joyce Little, Jerry Smith, Donald Evans, Larry Campbell, Tom Smith, Dave Bergford, Dick Picard, W. D. Goldsmith, Karen Groseclose, Mary Kay Holtrop, Bob Boyle, Wayne Smith, Ray Strecker, and Merle Fajens. A special thank you goes to Barbara Gates.

My luck was good; and, ultimately, I was able to transform my ideas into my own courses. This book is based on the numerous versions of systems development and project management courses I have developed and have been teaching for many years.

Teaching alone, however, would have limited the evolution of these concepts. During this time, I also did lots of consulting, frequently implementing and refining the concepts. I received many good ideas from Don Shiflett, Peggy Foerstchbeck, Jinni Jeffers Ciruli, Dave Ciruli, Joe Dormady, Mart Hanna, Jack Murphy, Harry Johnson, Roxanne Stoutner, Terry and Steve Sapp, Debbie and Jeff McCauley, Kathy Sharman, Julie Wilson, Larry Proctor, Paul Ward, Marie Martz, Pat Selsor, Gary Austin, Mercedes Lopez, Richard Zultner, Ken Orr, Capers Jones, and Barry Boehm. My special thanks go to Sandi Rapps, Judy Martin, and Randy Jensen.

Sometimes when writers believe that they have a new way of viewing old ideas, they invent new names, hoping to attract attention and give visibility to the new concepts. In naming the phases in the life cycle in this text, I, too, have tried to use different names. I did this because the popular names have so many different meanings that I was concerned about propagating confusion. I hope that, in using the new names, I have not simply added to the disorder.

In many parts of this book, I go into excruciating detail. This is especially true when describing how to implement a concept in each particular product. I have done so because I sincerely tried to help position readers to be able to wisely choose the package they want *or* to make the most productive use of the package they already own.

---

[1] I am sure that there were some very good seminars out there on project management. I just wasn't lucky enough to find them.

On the other hand, time constraints have prevented this from becoming an exhaustive study of each of the products. As a consequence, some of the subtle nuances of using each package may have been overlooked. Furthermore, some of the vendors are continually, and on an ad hoc basis, updating their software —albeit not through formal releases. (They simply include the latest modifications in the current systems being sold.) The implication for this text is that problems that still exist at press time may disappear by the time the user reads about them. At the bottom line, the final authorities on each product are, obviously, the vendor documentation and its technical support departments.

Speaking of the packages, a special thanks is owed to the product vendors—for without them, this book could *never* have been written. Similarly, I owe a debt of gratitude to *all* of the valiant men and women on the vendor's technical hotlines, especially because of their patience and clear explanations.

I would also like to take this opportunity to state that the procedures and concepts presented in this book are based on *my* personal experiences. This book has been written from only one person's view—my own. Furthermore, this book is interwoven with *my* opinions and judgments. These procedures, concepts, opinions, and judgments do not necessarily represent the views of other consultants in the industry. As a matter of fact, I am sure we could all have many interesting "discussions" over the thoughts presented within.

The vendors frequently share my opinions about product features. They may even sincerely want to be able to make their products be all things to all people. But sound business decisions preclude this possibility. Consequently, the vendors may not be able to incorporate all of the features *I* would like to see in a product. They often let their users help prioritize the release enhancements. And, naturally, different sets of users establish different sets of priorities.

I must state that it has *not* been my intention to favor any product over the others; nor have I tried to single one product out for more criticism than any of the others. I have tried to treat all of the products fairly and objectively.

Many of the pictures in this text could not be drawn using conventional desk-top publishing systems. Corel Draw has been used to complete the more difficult illustrations. I want to thank Corel Systems Corporation for their generous assistance in this area. Corel Draw runs under Microsoft Windows. Maureen Holt of Microsoft Corporation was very helpful in expediting the process required to get me the correct version of Windows.

The material in Chapters 6, 7, 8, and 10 that references the Wiest and Levy text and the material in Chapters 5, 10, 14, and 15 that references the Boehm text has been included with the permission of the publisher, Prentice-Hall. The material in Chapters 7, 8 and 10 that references the Moder, Phillips, and Davis text has been used with the permission of the publisher, Van Nostrand Reinhold. The description about Function Point Analysis in Chapter 5 has been included with the permission of the IBM user's groups, Guide and Share; Melissa Colangelo and Theresa Johnson were especially helpful in expediting the permission process. Certain material in Chapter 14 originally appeared in 1985 in *Computerworld* and *Government Data Systems*. These articles are both referenced in the bibliography.

Finally, no book gets on the shelf without its publishers and editors. To Ed Kerr, my thanks for believing enough in the premise of the book to agree to publish it—What a gentleman! I would also like to thank my technical editor, Richard Zultner and the production coordinator, Beth Roberts. Last, but not least, Dianne Wood put out an effort that was beyond belief—her patience and perseverance made this book syntactically and grammatically correct.

Lois Zells

CHAPTER 1 AN INTRODUCTION

1.1 INTRODUCTION

This is a book that teaches the principles of project management and also evaluates and teaches the readers how to use seven popular project management packages. More specifically, it is about planning, managing, and controlling software projects that use the company's computer(s) for part of a solution and incorporate other organizational resources (such as personnel) to solve the rest of the problem. These projects can be for developing brand-new systems or they might be for enhancing existing systems—from a project management perspective, there's no difference!

A project is a group of interrelated jobs taken on to achieve a specific goal. While this may also be said of departments, managing departments is different from managing projects. Departments may go on forever but projects should have a definite beginning *and* a definite end. Hopefully, they also produce a clearly identifiable and verifiable end-product—the newly developed system or the enhanced existing system. The two questions that project members hear most frequently are:

- How much will the project cost (in terms of time, people and/or money)? and
- Are we on schedule?

This book shows practitioners how to develop a plan that provides the data to answer the first question. Moreover, readers will find simple-to-follow steps for statistically determining the likelihood of making (or missing) the project completion date. Then, too, the text will tell exactly what data is needed—and how to get it—in order to answer the second question.

While data processing people traditionally write software so that other members of the company can work more efficiently, they have not, until recently, been able to *use* software to increase *their* productivity. Now, because organizations have begun to recognize the advantages of a systematic approach to project management, there has been an acceptance and, in some cases, an enthusiastic embrace of the many computer-aided software engineering and project management software packages available in the marketplace.

In addition to teaching practitioners the principles of project management, this text will also evaluate seven popular project management software packages and will tell readers how to use these products. Consequently, some practitioners will want the book to help them learn how to more effectively use the package they've already bought. On the other hand, those who are about to select a package will find it helpful for picking out the product they want to purchase.

This choice may initially be driven by the kind of users they are. For example, some groups manage very large projects and so plan size is an essential feature for any package they will consider. In other circles, simple user interfaces are the most vital consideration. In project management environments that are driven by resource availability, the key selection criterion is how the system supports resource assignment from a multiproject perspective. Then there are those to whom the type of graphics support is critical.

Finally, people are always interested in the features, flexibility, and complexity of each product. This book may aid in (1) deciding what features are important; (2) determining how easy they are to implement; and (3) evaluating the software based on organizational priorities.

1.2 THE ORGANIZATION OF THIS BOOK

The subject matter is divided into two main sections: a project management tutorial and an appendix of the project management software packages.

Providing the steps a practitioner will want to execute in order to do project management, the tutorial describes the Project Management Process and is partitioned into five large categories. The first four are: (1) The Systems Management Process; (2) Sizing the Effort; (3) Producing Alternative Plans; and (4) Managing the Project. Each of the chapters in these groups explains the details behind the practices that are employed in project management. A fifth category, Implementing Project Management, is the concluding chapter in the tutorial. It addresses the cultural factors that will affect success.

In order to describe how each package supports each of the covered practices, in-depth discussions of the software products will be presented. The bulk of each of these reviews is cross-referenced back to the corresponding tutorial discussion that covers the point being discussed. Conversely, inasmuch as many of the tutorial sections are addressed again in the appendices, these corresponding tutorial sections are flagged with a *knowledge indicator*:   ◆

1.3 WHY IS THERE A NEED FOR PROJECT MANAGEMENT BOOKS?

In the last few years alone, project expenditures have risen significantly. The rising costs of data processing salaries and benefits are certainly contributing to this increase. Furthermore, in this era when many companies are project oriented, their systems management efforts are becoming more and more complicated. Less and less often do we encounter single-purpose, stand-alone development (or enhancement) efforts. Nowadays, systems integrate across functional boundaries, raising complex interface and security problems. Much of the work may even be done outside of the data processing environment, requiring project management skills to be taught to nontechnical employees. And, as the pace of technology continues to pick up speed, the need for more proficient coordination will rise as well.

Naturally, organizations can not afford the luxury of unprofitable project ventures; therefore, we are seeing an accelerated awareness of the need for project management techniques that work.

1.4 WHO WILL WANT TO READ THIS BOOK?

This text has been written for anyone who is involved with systems projects. Naturally, this includes data processing professionals like project managers, DP directors, and their supporting staffs. Systems projects, however, affect the entire organization! Consequently, it is essential for user project managers, user directors, and their supporting staffs to learn about projects as well! This is a palatable book for users because data processing expertise is not required for most of the topics.

Quality assurance groups and data processing auditors will find the book's policies, standards, and guidelines invaluable. Finally, students and career-minded data processors who ultimately want to move into management will also find this text highly informative.

1.5 WHAT THIS BOOK IS ABOUT

This is a text about the procedural side of systems management. (See Figure 1.1.) Practitioners like knowing that they can follow a set of predefined steps and the results will always be the same. Because people are more comfortable when the fundamental processes have been mechanized, these guidelines are essential. They are the tools and techniques of our trade and indeed are cornerstone components of the Project Management Process.

Figure 1.1 The project management process.

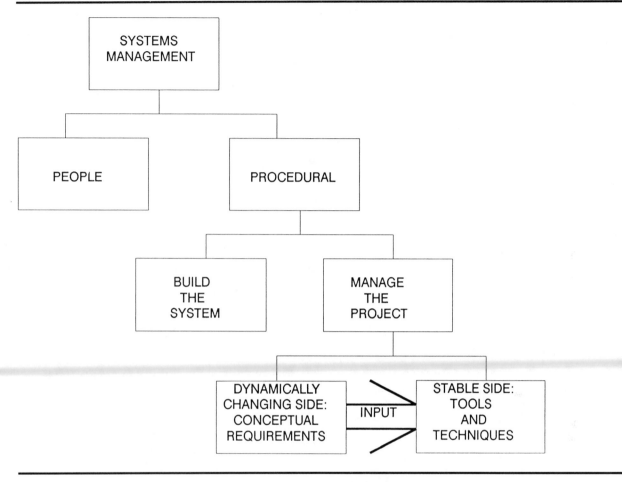

Actually, the Process may be partitioned into: the *stable* side—the commonly agreed upon tools and techniques of project management; and the *dynamically changing* side—the conceptual requirements that serve as input to the use of the tools and techniques.

If teams want to insure the highest probability of success, they must concisely describe the conceptual requirements of the environment (for example, the roles and responsibilities) before proceeding too far into the project. The term, *conceptual requirements*, will be used throughout the book to indicate all of the subtle nuances of project management that people assume they may take for granted—until they are slapped with the realization that not everyone has taken these concepts as much for granted as they have. There will be several references in the book to these fuzzy areas as well as suggestions for how to clear up the misunderstood expectations surrounding them.

1.6 THE REALITIES

In closing, it is necessary to recognize that this book is not the ultimate solution to successful project management. It is not intended to be a panacea, nor is it to be regarded as the final word. In just a few years, there will be marked improvements in project management, and in ten years there will be a whole new horizon of tools. And one of these days, state-of-the-art expert systems will give us "mindless" project management techniques. For the present, though, this is a synthesis of the best ideas around. So be it!

CHAPTER 2 DIVIDE AND CONQUER

2.1 INTRODUCTION

It is unfortunate that, in some organizations, people are performing in an undirected work environment. While it is true that they may work hard throughout the entire day, their efforts often do not produce meaningful results that contribute much to enhancing the bottom line of the corporation. That is because so many people are busily working at doing *stuff*. They don't intentionally waste time; they're just not sure about exactly what they're supposed to be doing. As a consequence, they do a lot of "make-work", often simply defaulting to the stuff they do best, the stuff they're most comfortable doing—not necessarily the work that will move them closer to their goals.

The stuff syndrome might be eradicated if each person's day could be efficiently planned. *The goal, then, is to arrive at a place where every project participant has a personal plan for every day of every week of the project.* If the time that is about to be spent will not result in a meaningful deliverable that can be justifiably put in some plan, workers should question whether or not they should be doing that job. At the very start, it is important to acknowledge that:

1. Any individual (or group)—in or out of the organization—that can impact the installation date must be part of the planning process; that is, providing input to the plan, getting weekly assign-

ments, reporting weekly status, etc. If such is not the case, the group must determine just exactly what it is they *are in control of—certainly not the whole project*; and

2. Every individual (or group) who can impact the date must avoid wasting time on *stuff*. The project is not under total control until all of its participants can know, on every Monday morning, just exactly what work they must accomplish during that week in order to keep the project on schedule.

To achieve these two goals is not an easy trick.

2.2 QUESTIONS THAT MUST BE ANSWERED TO GET CONTROL OF THE PROJECT

Organizations are looking for a believable date. For a variety of good business reasons, they want and need to know when the system will be implemented. On the other hand, developers want the rest of the company to understand the varying degrees of accuracy in the numbers they publicize.

To make matters worse, many people (in and out of DP) rebel at any hint of regimentation. As a consequence, they may challenge any disciplined process. They may state, "Why bother with project management at all? It's such an overhead in an already overcrowded schedule! Besides, I don't have time to do all of this *Manage the Project* effort, especially when

I have so much other important work to do—like *Build the System.*'' (See Figure 1.1.) They may add, ''Just teach us how to get control of the project—without changing the way we do things now and without giving us any extra work. And whatever you do, don't ask us to proceduralize anything.''

These are common statements heard from the uninitiated. In response to these comments, expert project managers wisely advise:

''Do only what makes sense and provides the information essential for control!''

So what does makes sense? And what information is necessary? The two questions that project members hear most frequently are (1) How much will the project cost (in terms of time, people, and/or money)? and (2) Are we on schedule?

In response to these challenges, this text presents what may be considered *generally accepted project management principles.* These fundamentals may be viewed as a huge menu of everything that can be implemented. Organizations may then customize their own bill of fare, doing what makes sense to them. A note of caution, however, is in order as well. The cost of leaving processes out is often greater than the cost of including them, a fact that is not always intuitively obvious at the time. It is important to take care that projects don't suffer from project management malnutrition, in much the same way that people get scurvy without vitamin C. The following list of questions should be addressed *and answered correctly* in order to get control of the project.

2.2.1 How Much Will It Cost (Time, People, Money)?

1. What do organizations need to do in order to increase their confidence in the *accuracy* of their estimates?
2. How small does the estimate have to be to put the team in a strong position to resist the inevitable pressure to reduce it?
3. How reliable does the estimate have to be?
4. How can people measure the reliability?
5. What can the teams realistically accomplish—given

the number and skills of the resources they have available?
6. How can people tell when the project will be finished?

2.2.2 Are We On Schedule?

1. How can the managers measure progress?
2. What information do organizations need in order to know if the project is on time and within budget?
3. How often do they need this information, and how long can they afford to wait for the data, before taking corrective action?
4. How reliable does the data have to be?
5. Is there some psychological benefit (to project participants and the rest of the organization) of completed jobs frequently ''rolling off the assembly line''?

What is the company willing to do to reach its goals? Each organization must use these questions and the respective answers to make its own decisions about what makes sense: what information is needed, how often it's required, and what risks can afford to be taken. This chapter is intended to help make those decisions.

2.3 IT'S DIFFICULT TO MANAGE BY PHASES

Early project management concepts introduced the idea of gaining control by partitioning the project into phases. Because it was moving in the right direction, this was a good step; but, it didn't solve the total problem. As practitioners have come to recognize, using the disciplines, methodologies, and development techniques did not automatically guarantee project success. Those early project developers found that the phases could be very long and that they still couldn't determine if they were on schedule. So they tried breaking the phases into major milestones, with each milestone representing a significant project event.

2.4 MILESTONES

Again, this was a move in the right direction; but still not the total answer. The significant events were hard to identify, and progress was hard to monitor. What really happened was:

- Milestones were very far apart, and estimators had a difficult time sizing up the effort it took for completion;
- Long periods elapsed before the project manager could evaluate status; and consequently valuable time would be wasted before the problems were recognized and corrective action could be taken;
- There was no really effective way to evaluate progress, so status was reported as a function of percentage against hours used (e.g., if a job was estimated at 40 hours and the worker had spent 20 hours on it, the job was reported as 50 percent complete). This is one of the ways projects got to be 90 percent complete so quickly while the last 10 percent took another 90 percent of the time.

Figure 2.1 shows time plotted against expectations of progress towards the completion of a milestone. As seen on the heavy solid line, after the passage of 16 weeks, x progress was expected. The thin broken line illustrates the actual progress made. After 8 weeks, regardless of progress, the teams commonly reported status at 50 percent completion. Unfortunately, although they intuitively knew something was amiss, project managers often had difficulty determining or even validating the accuracy of this report. At about the 12-week mark, an uneasy feeling would begin to invade the team's consciousness, and they would realize just how much they would need to accomplish in order to make up the deficit. Panic often ensued, and everyone would then usually put in long hours of overtime. Unfortunately, they would often still miss the target date.

2.5 INCH-PEBBLES

The circles on the progress line in Figure 2.4 show partitioning the same milestone into smaller pieces. Commonly referred to as inch-pebbles, these bits and pieces afford better control of the unknowns and easier monitoring of progress. The milestones are now planned and executed by cycles. Here is how it works:

1. In the first step, the small jobs that can be identified and estimated—*by each of the project members*—with confidence (usually only those jobs in the immediate and short-term future) are scheduled. In Figure 2.2, these Step 1 inch-pebbles are represented by the hollow circles next to number

Figure 2.1 Milestones.

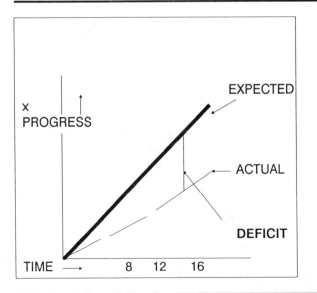

Figure 2.2 Inch-pebbles.

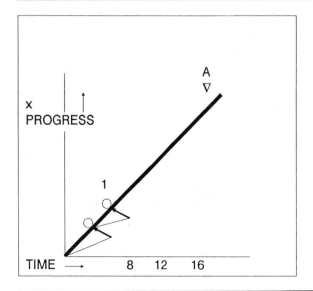

1. The team is committed to making these Step 1 dates. At the same time, the first guess at the finish of the milestone is made (perhaps at 16 weeks). In Figure 2.2, this is represented by the upside-down delta symbol A.

2. As before, actual progress may not correspond to expected progress. Similarly, this is noted in Figure 2.2 by comparing the arrowed lines going back to the heavy solid line. As always, if there is a deficit in progress, some extra effort may be required to catch up, as reflected in these corrective lines being brought back to target.

3. At the completion of the first series of inch-pebbles (represented by the gray circles next to Number 1 in Figure 2.3), a *replanning exercise* is held (represented by the "Replan Box" above Number 1 in Figure 2.3). At that time, Step 1 is repeated: that is, the next series of small jobs are identified, estimated, and scheduled (represented by the white circles next to Number 2 in Figure 2.3) and the milestone is reassessed (represented by the upside-down delta symbol now at B in Figure 2.3).

4. And so the process continues: replan (represented by the "Replan Box" above Number 2 in Figure 2.4), estimate and schedule (step 3 inch-pebbles being represented by the white circles next to 3 in Figure 2.4), work, manage, replan, and so on.

This approach has been implemented in many enlightened companies. Those that accept this concept buy into certain *givens*: It is agreed that the project team members will be allowed the time to plan, in the first place. Then, after completion of a preselected and limited number of inch-pebbles, it is agreed that the team members will be allowed to use their newly acquired knowledge (and be given the time) to replan the rest of the milestone effort. It is also agreed that this process may be repeated more than once for each milestone—depending on its size and complexity.

Furthermore, it is also accepted that, during each replanning exercise, the new knowledge that is gained may necessitate the implementation of one or more of the following project management strategies:

- Extending the finish date;
- Adding more resources;
- Eliminating features;
- Risking (sacrificing) some degree of quality and/or reliability and/or performance;
- Finding a low-risk method of improving productivity. (There are efficiencies to be gained in both the project management process and in the development techniques. The introduction of new methodologies and/or technologies may, in the long run, improve productivity. However, in the short term, the asso-

Figure 2.3 Inch-pebbles.

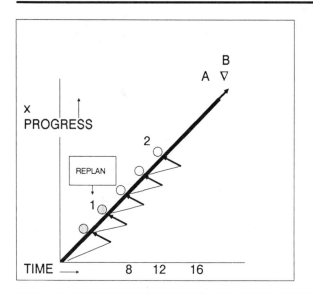

Figure 2.4 Inch-pebbles.

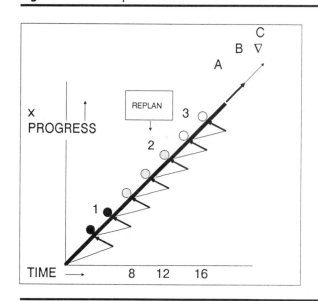

ciated learning curve may actually appear to reduce productivity and will certainly extend the dates. On the other hand, this learning curve may be offset by "buying the expertise"—either by reassigning in-house experts or by hiring outside consultants.); or

• Even canceling the project.

These appear to be the only six choices. For example, the date may be locked in and the project must not be cancelled (because of a valid business requirement); but then, some combination of the second through fifth choices must be selected.

Moreover, there's no free lunch! If, in order to save time during the project, quality, reliability, and/or performance are sacrificed, operational costs are likely to be increased later during maintenance. Many organizations are either not aware of this obvious state-of-affairs or they just refuse to acknowledge it. The result is that, unwittingly, they often choose unrealistic strategies that, by default, simply lead to the ultimate sacrifice of quality (performance, reliability). There are enough sorry practitioners around (who remember burning the midnight oil while trying to maintain a poor-grade system) who can attest to the results of such choices.

2.5.1 The Value of Inch-Pebbles

The sum of many small estimates is more reliable than one large estimate and is also harder to shave down during scheduling negotiations.

To begin, because the rigor of partitioning to this level and the corresponding visibility encourages planners to seriously assess the value of the entry, *stuff* is easier to identify.

Then, inch-pebble jobs can be assigned to one person, making status easier to determine. Similarly, status is easier to report when the state of a job can only be binary—the job is either 100 percent complete or it's 0 percent complete. No other status is meaningful. This approach diffuses the impact of the subjective reporting of fractional percentages of completion, which are often expressed simply as a function of how much of the original effort has been consumed. Using smaller estimates and reporting binary status also reduces the possibility of the last 10 percent of the project taking another 90 percent of the time.

With smaller jobs, status is reported more frequently. If progress is poor, the manager knows it right away. Corrective action may be taken sooner, thus helping to avoid the wide differential between expected progress and actual progress. And, finally, the smaller the estimate, the smaller the confidence interval. The smaller the confidence interval, the higher the level of accuracy in the estimate.

Although the accumulated sum of each of the corrective inch-pebble efforts in Figure 2.4 may sometimes exceed the total deficit effort in Figure 2.1, the total inch-pebble effort is still less detrimental to the organization. The benefit of added control certainly makes the expenditure worthwhile. Furthermore, there is an added psychological advantage of improved morale when participants can see frequent and tangible results of their efforts.

But what is the size of an inch-pebble? How small is small?

2.6 WORK BREAKDOWN BASICS

The secret to successful project management is to partition the phases and their milestones into small and manageable inch-pebbles. The effort is broken into pieces of pieces of pieces. It is easy to demonstrate this concept when it is illustrated graphically. This kind of partitioning is referred to as a work breakdown structure. Figure 2.5 shows a sample work breakdown structure. The project is, of course, the highest level.

Then, for example, the project is divided by phase deliverables. The phase deliverables, in turn, are separated into their significant milestone deliverables. The milestone deliverables are then partitioned into major deliverables; and the major deliverables are broken into individual deliverables. Inch-pebbles are usually found at the individual deliverables level.

It takes the completion of a significant number of inch-pebbles to produce a major deliverable. A fair number of major deliverables contribute to the completion of a milestone. And, of course, every phase has a certain number of milestones.

2.7 HOW SMALL IS SMALL?

Each of the inch-pebbles must be small enough so that (1) a reasonable estimate may be figured for its com-

Figure 2.5 A sample work breakdown structure.

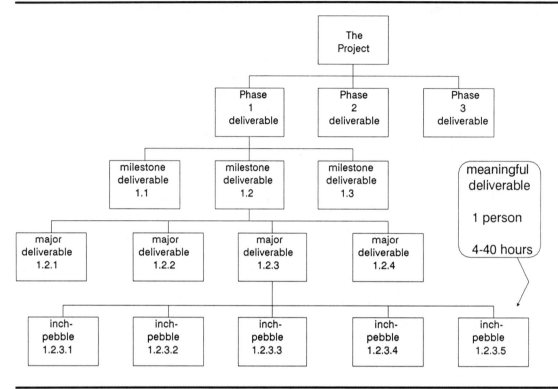

pletion; (2) the estimate reflects reality; (3) the confidence interval will be small; (4) the organization may be comfortable about the level of "accuracy"; (5) it will be hard to intimidate the estimator into reducing the estimate; (6) 100 percent completion can be reached rather quickly; (7) managers know they're in trouble before disaster descends upon them; and (8) when the job is done, there is a meaningful and verifiable deliverable. An inch-pebble represents a work-unit that can not be meaningfully subdivided and is best completed without interruption.

> **To afford effective partitioning, estimating, scheduling, and status reporting, a unit of work (inch-pebble) produces a meaningful and tangible deliverable that can be verified, is commonly assignable to one and only one person, and is usually completed in from 4 to 40 hours.**

Meaningful deliverables go far in helping to eliminate *stuff*. Identification of meaningful deliverables is an area that causes lots of confusion when trying to partition the development of specifications. For example, if an analysis specification is to be produced across the span of several phases, it may be prepared at a high level in phase 1, an intermediate level in phase 2 and a detailed level in phase 3. One could then say that it will not be completed until the end of phase 3. However, this would make status reporting and management of each phase very difficult. A better approach would be to partition the development of each specification into a job that can be worked on as an inch-pebble (whatever the size for an inch-pebble the organization chooses) and later designated as *100 percent completed* when it is finished. For example, a deliverable could be (1) the high-level specification of payment processing; (2) the intermediate-level specification of payment types; or (3) the detailed specification of backdated payment processing.

The implementation of the inch-pebble concept will allow organizations to achieve many of the goals they are attempting to satisfy. It also helps them to recall that many small estimates added together have less margin for error than a single large estimate; therefore, they may more quickly realize their ambition for ''accurate'' estimates. Additionally, ''one job–one person'' combined with status of ''done–not done'' dramatically simplifies status reporting and thus the management of the project. Remember: ''one job–one person'' is a ''rule of thumb''. And, as such, there are always exceptions. For example, group development workshops and reviews are inch-pebbles that, obviously, are assigned to more than one person.

Setting a 40-hour maximum on inch-pebbles creates an environment in which a number of jobs are being completed every week. As a result, crises are frequently identified soon enough to avert disaster. Not every inch-pebble, however, will be exactly 40 hours long. Many will be be less than that and some may even be greater. Therefore, not every job starts on Monday morning and finishes on Friday evening.

And last, since most organizations have few to no experts in estimating, the discipline of getting down to the 4–40 hour confidence intervals goes far to diffuse the novice effect.

2.7.1 Many Groups Will Rebel!

Agreed! To identify 4–40 hour inch-pebbles is not a trivial task. Although they are never faced at the same time, there may ultimately be as many as 2,000 inch-pebbles in a medium-sized project. Frequently, people balk at what appears to be just so much overhead. It is important to determine what makes sense in the organization, what information is needed, how often it is required, and how reliable it must be. Organizations should decide (1) how much estimating expertise is on the team—and its effect on the accuracy of the total plan; (2) if the range that is selected is small enough to support a high degree of confidence in the accuracy of the estimate; (3) if the range that is selected gives the status data soon enough (that is, how long the group can comfortably wait before knowing if they're in trouble?); and (4) how much risk can be borne. This text is intended to help make these decisions.

2.8 CHASING THE ELUSIVE RAINBOW

Just to start, organizational acceptance of inch-pebble partitioning should become part of the conceptual requirements for project success (See Figure 1.1.). And that may initially appear to be easy enough to implement. Yet, in spite of this enlightened approach, certain members of the organization will still want an immediate answer for how long the project will take, how much it will cost, and how many people will be needed. These very numbers become a function of being able to identify just how many inch-pebbles must ultimately be completed and how many people will actually be available to do the work, given the other priorities these people must also address.

Similarly, let's not forget that when the idea for a new medium-sized project blossoms, it is no small effort to identify all of the 2,000 or more 4–40 hour jobs that must eventually be done in order to deliver the system. As a matter of fact, to try to do so in the early phases is often an impossible feat and one that simply courts disaster. It is something like searching for the pot of gold at the end of the rainbow. People think it's there, but they can't quite reach it. Organizations chase the rainbow of date commitments, not quite reaching them yet pretty much unwilling to sacrifice the myth.

2.8.1 The Myth of the Quick Appraisal

The request for a quick appraisal is often overheard in DP shops:

> ''Oh, Lois, I know you're busy working on project [X] but can you give me a few minutes? We worked these requirements out at lunch yesterday (specs are on the back of the napkin). Give me a rough idea of what it'll take to do it. Take as long as you need (as long as you have an answer for me by tomorrow morning). I just need it for a quick appraisal. Don't worry. No one will hold you to it!''

How many practitioners have heard these famous last words: ''We won't hold you to it . . . .''? And then their feet become locked in concrete, to dates, money, and/or resources.

Important decisions are made based on these numbers: projects are approved; resources are committed; completion dates are set; business decisions are made—all depending on these quick appraisal numbers. Later, resources may be overextended; dates may be missed; costs may be exceeded; quality may be sacrificed; and the failure syndrome may set in.

Then the rest of the company becomes dissatisfied with DP and DP becomes critical of them. Polarization between groups gets wider and wider. And, most important, the organization loses its ability to capitalize on its DP expenditures. This scenario doesn't do much to raise the bottom line and many people become very unhappy.

Yet, the realities are that those numbers are needed. *The Need For A Quick Appraisal Will Never Go Away!* So, if it will always be here, what *will* change?

2.9   CAPTURING THE MOVING WINDOW OF COMMITMENT

Organizations that are looking for a more enlightened approach to handling their project environment are willing to acknowledge that the management of a data processing project is often an attempt to manage in total and absolute uncertainty. Teams are rarely developing the same system over and over again. Consequently, this type of effort is closely akin to research and development work. Thus, organizations are willing to recognize that planning should not be a onetime exercise at the beginning of the project. It must be an iterative process, and constant reassessment is necessary to determine, based on the current data, the value of the project. Additional replanning often requires that one or more of the six project management strategies be employed: dates extended; resources added; scope reduced; quality, and/or performance, and/or reliability sacrificed; productivity measures introduced; or projects cancelled. The teams accept that their payoff comes from better distribution of resources, higher-quality systems, lowered maintenance costs, and control of an otherwise often unmanageable situation.

Those that accept this premise understand that, as a result, the interpretation of the numbers (time, people, and/or money) must continuously be redefined. Called *THE MOVING WINDOW OF COMMITMENT*, these new definitions also become part of the conceptual requirements for successful project management.

Furthermore, the group needs to be reminded that the implementation of this concept will not overcome deficiencies in *Building the System*. Although this is not a text on how to *Build the System*, Chapter 3 will describe the major deliverables of each of the phases.

If the work that is described in Chapter 3 has not been done correctly, even the best project management will do little to make the project a success.

2.9.1   The Rapid Survey Number

The quick appraisal of the requirements (in terms of time, people, money) to get from day 0 to installation day will be called a *RAPID SURVEY NUMBER*. (See Figure 2.6.) In other words, this number represents—based on what is currently known—what it's going to take to do the *whole* project. The Rapid Survey Number *is not based on any plan*.

It is agreed that the Rapid Survey Number is an inexact number, one that is based on "gut feel". As team members get more experienced, *and* as organizations build up their project history data, this number gets better and better. By comparing the request to past projects, assumptions are made about the number, size, and complexity of features, programs, code, hardware, etc. These are *gross* assumptions and, as such, are subject to change. Consequently, any figures that are presented are given in ranges, confidence levels, and orders of magnitude. For example, ranges may be given as best case and worst case. The larger the project, the more the uncertainty; and the more the uncertainty, the wider the range. As for orders of magnitude, it is rare that the project winds up costing significantly less than originally anticipated. On the other hand, it is not unusual to find projects in which the final costs (assuming accurate records are kept) are two to ten times the costs originally anticipated at this time.

2.9.2   The Committed Numbers

A quick appraisal is of particular value in helping to determine if the project is worth pursuing, but usually only through the first phase. Therefore, the quick appraisal should also contain a detailed plan for Phase 1. (Since its purpose is only to gather slightly more information than is provided by the Rapid Survey, Phase 1 in a medium-sized project may often be completed in one to four weeks.)

Consequently, a detailed plan with the 4–40 hour inch-pebbles for Phase 1 is presented along with the Rapid Survey Number. Since they are based on the 4–40 hour inch-pebble details, the date, costs, and

Figure 2.6 Quick appraisal.

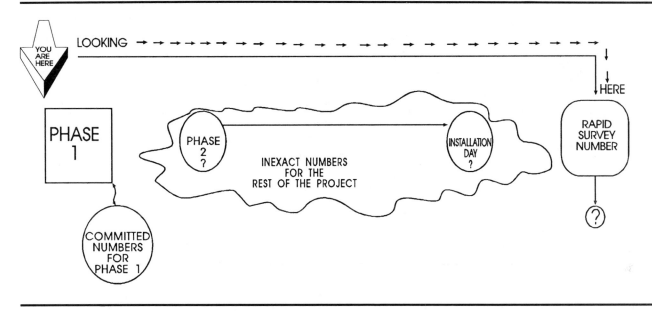

people requirements for this first phase are considered to be *COMMITTED NUMBERS*; and there is no range. If the first phase is approved, the team is then, as the name implies, committed to make these numbers. (See Figure 2.6.)

Finally, the Rapid Survey Number is useful any time an analysis of alternatives is performed.

2.9.3 The Actual Numbers

During the execution of Phase 1, the status data (about completed work) that is gathered from the status reports will provide information on resource utilization, effort, and costs. The total accumulation of this exact data will be called the *ACTUAL NUMBERS* for Phase 1 (See Figure 2.7.). At the conclusion of the first phase, a detailed plan with the 4–40 hour inch-pebbles for the second phase will also be completed, and these will be Committed numbers for Phase 2 (See Figure 2.7.).

2.9.4 Inexact Plans for the Rest of the Project

A rough, high-level estimate for the work from Phase 3 through Installation is also made at the end of the first phase (See Figure 2.7.). Once again, assumptions are made about the number, size and complexity of

features, programs, code, hardware, etc. Representing a combination of mostly milestones and major deliverables with some degree of inch-pebbles, these numbers are now referred to as *INEXACT NUMBERS* for the rest of the project. Because they are based on the additional knowledge gained during the Phase 1 effort, these numbers are better than the RAPID SURVEY NUMBERS. However, they are still only based on assumptions. Therefore, they are given as a range and may be plus or minus a percentage value or, in some complex projects, still within orders of magnitude.

2.9.5 The Assessment Number for Total Project Effort

The organization will always be interested in the current outlook for the Installation date. This number is now called the *ASSESSMENT NUMBER* for total project effort and is computed as the sum of the Actual Numbers, the Committed Numbers, and the Inexact Numbers (See Figure 2.7.). Assessment Numbers are provided at the end of Phase 1, Phase 2, and Phase 3 and are always given as a range with a confidence level and within percentage values or orders of magnitude. Furthermore, organizations should remember—if the Assessment Numbers are too high, they may, at any time during the project, reconsider adding resources,

Figure 2.7 Status of the plan at the end of phase 1.

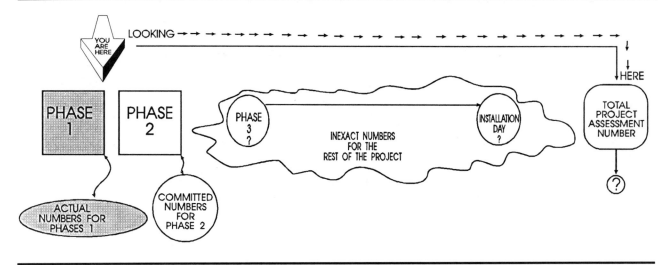

descoping, sacrificing quality (etc.), introducing productivity measures or canceling the project.

2.9.6 The Scheduled Numbers

At the end of Phase 2, the team will have actual numbers for the first and second phases. (See Figure 2.8.) A detailed plan with the 4–40 hour inch-pebbles for the third phase will be also be prepared. The discussions in Chapter 3 address how difficult it is to estimate

the third phase and why committed numbers for the end of this phase may be risky. For now, suffice it to say that on a medium to large project, hundreds (or even thousands) of hours may be expended during Phase 3. Consequently, the numbers for the third phase will be called *SCHEDULED NUMBERS*. (See Figure 2.8.) These numbers are a little less firm than the Committed Numbers; but, they are not given in a range. The team is still required to attempt to make them— just as if they were Committed Dates. However, it is

Figure 2.8 Status of the plan at the end of phase 2.

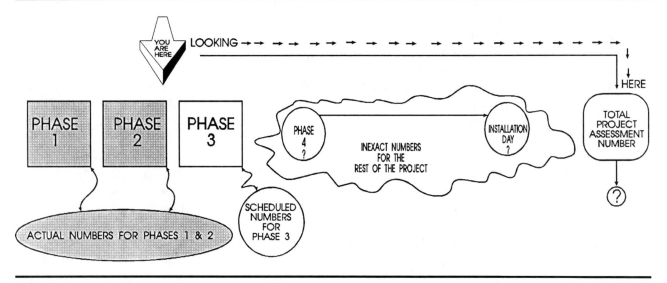

Figure 2.9 Status of the plan at the end of phase 4.

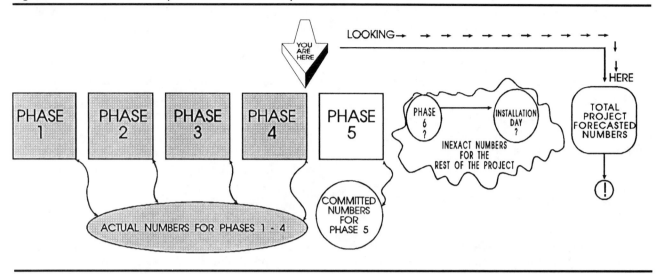

understood that if the scope is greater than the team was able to anticipate when the estimates were given: (1) the numbers may slide; (2) more people may be required; (3) the project may be descoped; (4) quality (etc.) may be risked and/or sacrificed; (5) measures for increasing productivity may be introduced; or (6) the project may be cancelled. The Assessment Number at the end of the second phase will be the sum of the Actual Numbers from the first and second phases, the Scheduled Numbers for the third phase, and the Inexact Numbers for the rest of the project.

2.9.7 The Forecasted Numbers

If users continue to follow this process through the end of the fourth phase, they will have Actual Numbers for these four phases. They will also have the detailed 4–40 hour inch-pebbles for the completion of the fifth phase. (See Figure 2.9.) These are, once again, Committed Numbers for Phase 5. And now, they must also recognize that there has been a change in the constitution of the Inexact Numbers. By this stage in the project, there are only two phases left and it becomes easier to predict the amount of work left to be completed. The Inexact Numbers for Phases 6 and 7 are still composed of milestones and major deliverables, but they also contain many inch-pebbles. As a result, the sum of the Actual Numbers for the first four phases, the Committed Numbers for the fifth phase, and the

Inexact Numbers for the rest of the project can be presented with a higher degree of confidence. This sum will now be called the *FORECASTED NUMBER* and is given within percentage values.

2.9.8 The Projected Numbers

At the end of the fifth phase, users will have Actual Numbers for five phases, Committed Numbers for the sixth phase, and Inexact Numbers for just the last phase. The sum of these numbers can be presented with a high degree of confidence. They are call *PROJECTED FIGURES* for project completion and are given with percentage values.

2.9.9 The Committed Date for Installation

It is during the last phase, and once the team has a good "handle" on how well the testing is going, that the date to go live is confirmed.

2.10 THE CONSTRAINTS *CAN* DRIVE THE PROJECT—A FINAL WORD ABOUT FIXED DATES AND RESOURCES

Sometimes, projects must be managed with a fixed date for completion (for example, regulatory requirements and strategic product development). In this situation, practitioners need not think that the moving window approach will be of little use to them. On the contrary, many groups who do not have the luxury of moving the date simply integrate the moving window with the other management strategies of (1) adding more resources, (2) descoping, (3) sacrificing quality, (4) introducing productivity measures, or (5) cancelling the project.

If cancelling the project is not an alternative in either of the scenarios, then teams are, obviously, left with the first four choices.

2.11 SMALL PROJECTS AND THE MOVING WINDOW

Similarly, others who manage small projects may think that they cannot effectively use these techniques. The only difference between small and large projects is that on smaller projects there are fewer phases, fewer "continue/cancel" decisions, and an easier and faster transition from Rapid Survey to Assessment to Forecasted to Projected numbers.

2.12 HOW TO PICK A PROJECT PLAN

First, the system features must be partitioned into subsystems. Similarly, all of the potential installation locations must be identified. This is an analysis process, part of *Building the System*. Providing all of the features in all of the locations is referred to as *total functionality*. Next, two plans for introducing total functionality should be created.

- An Optimal Plan: a plan for implementing total functionality is produced—assuming that there will be as much time and as many people as is necessary. When there are no limitations on time and resources, the plan is referred to as the *optimal plan*. The probability of success—based on percentage tolerances selected that are by the organization—is then computed.

- A Resource-Constrained Plan: a second plan for implementing total functionality is produced—reflecting the known resource constraints. Naturally, adding in resource constraints has the effect of extending the project duration. Rarely, does it help to get the project finished sooner.

The probability of success for this second plan is also computed. The value of the first plan is realized when it is compared to the second plan to demonstrate the effects of limited resource availability.

- Once these two plans are produced, it usually becomes apparent that the likelihood of providing total functionality, by the requested dates, with the available resources is not very high.
- At this point, subsets of any combination of features and locations are selected as candidates for additional alternatives. Optimal plans and resource-constrained plans (both adjusted for probability of success) are developed for each of the alternatives.
- The alternatives (their costs, advantages, disadvantages, opportunities, risks, and the recommendation) are presented, and the choice is made.

It is also important to remember that this process is repeated at the end of every phase, producing a detailed plan for the next phase and an inexact plan for the rest of the project.

2.12.1 Planning Is Hard Work

As students delve into the subject of project management, they realize that planning is not a trivial process. This is true. But, they might also want to refer back to the earlier discussion that acknowledged that project management isn't simple and also pointed out that it isn't necessary to employ every practice on every project. To emphasize this point, earlier in this chapter users were also advised that they will only want to do what makes sense to them and gives them the information that they feel they need to have. They simply need to pick and choose what they will—reminding their organizations that if they, the users, are not able to do the work, the important data might not be available.

2.13 A PARTITIONING APPROACH FOR THE PROJECT MANAGEMENT PROCESS

Figure 2.10 demonstrates the planning process (i.e., Sizing the Effort and Producing Alternative Plans). It is important to note that some work is done in parallel and other work may be repeated several times before

Figure 2.10 The planning process.

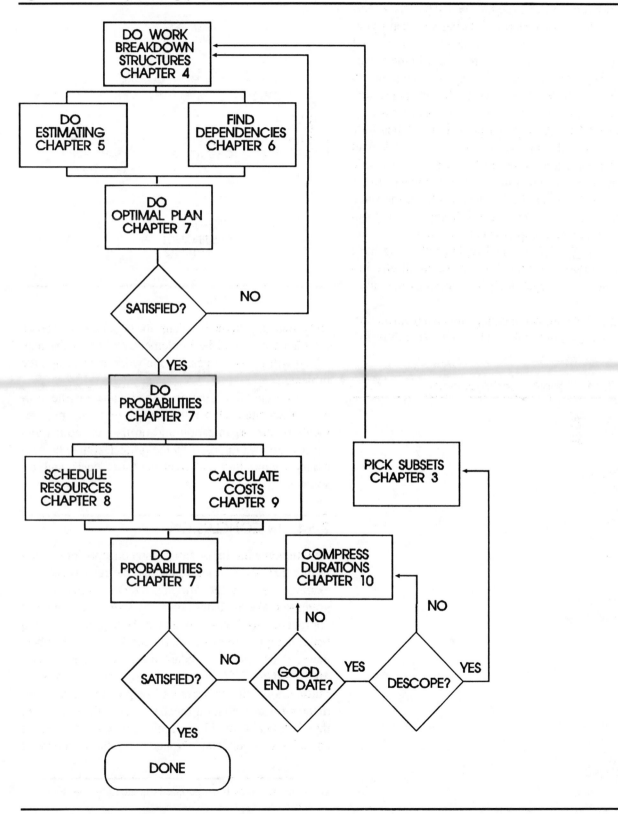

the finished plan is produced. For example, when some of the work breakdown structure (WBS) has been completed, the group may start estimating and identifying dependencies. Then, they may develop an optimal schedule for the work they've approved. In the meantime, if they are not satisfied, they may continue to expand the initial WBS, estimates, dependencies, and schedule. They keep repeating these steps until they are satisfied with the optimal plan. Later, when they want to assess the probability of success, calculate costs, and constrain the optimal plan by the available resources, they may enter into another looping process. This second loop may be invoked while, at the same time, the team is extracting and refining subsets from the work that was completed earlier. Now, they may also repetitively descope and replan until they have exhausted that possibility. Finally, when all else has failed, they may repetitively try compressing durations.

The whole project planning and management process is illustrated in Figure 2.11. After sizing the effort

Figure 2.11 Planning and managing.

Figure 2.12 Managing the project.

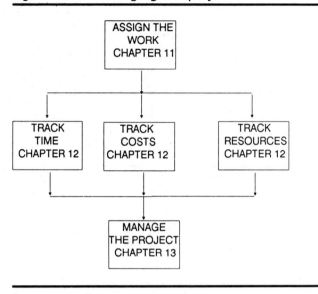

and producing alternative plans, the organization chooses the plan which will be implemented. This is the plan which will be used to assign the work and manage the project.

In Figure 2.12, the process of managing the project is illustrated. Depending on the reporting requirements of the organization and on the constraints and success criteria imposed on the project, it may be necessary to monitor and manage time, costs and resources.

2.14 IN CONCLUSION

The implementation of any of the concepts introduced in this text is not going to change the real world. For example, use of the *Moving Window* concept isn't going to make the dates come any sooner. Using these approaches *will* make managers better informed and better equipped to make intelligent decisions. The best news, if organizations adapt these new ideas, is *NO MORE SURPRISES!* (or at worst, fewer surprises). Furthermore, this process will help to recognize candidates for cancellation much earlier in the operation, thus helping to avoid the innumerable cost overruns and missed target dates.[1] Nonetheless, those who insist

---

[1] How many times have people lamented, "If we had only known then, what we know now!"

on ''price-to-win''[2] numbers may attack the process and/or its proponents—or simply ignore the situation altogether.

On the other hand, the implementation of these concepts is a vital cornerstone to successful project management. As such, they need the visible, demonstrable, and sustained support of all levels within the organization. Furthermore, if the key managers do not visibly and continuously show that they sincerely want success, they may not reach it! A memo supporting the ideas which is then followed by contradictory directions or noticeable absence from the program, serves only to defeat the operation, often demoting the implementation into a meaningless drill in uselessness. In these situations, it is often better to do nothing at all.

---

[2] A term coined by Barry Boehm. It implies that the estimators give a bid that, while not necessarily realistic, is likely to win the contract.

CHAPTER 3 THE PROJECT LIFE CYCLE

3.1 INTRODUCTION

The study of systems management is broken into the people side and the procedural side, with the procedural side being further divided into work that is done to *build the system* and work that is done to *manage the project*. (See Figure 1.1.) Another view shows that, if organizations wish to excel in the systems management process, it is essential that they develop expertise in the building disciplines, the project management process, the written procedures, quality assurance, and the automated tools that support development and maintenance. (See Figure 3.1.)

3.1.1 The Disciplines

Effective systems building (and maintenance) requires expertise in *the disciplines*—the work that relates to the building techniques that must be applied as part of the development and maintenance process in order to produce quality products:

- Analysis of the data *and* the business functions that use the Data
- Design—systems application and/or data base
- Programming
- Testing

3.1.2 The Project Management Process

Effective project management requires expertise in a *project management process* that is defined to include:

- Business planning (long-range and operational)
- Systems planning (information [data] driven, business function [business policy] driven)
- Project planning (partitioning, estimating, scheduling, resource management, costing, and status reporting)

3.1.3 Quality Assurance

The implementation of a *quality* program addresses:

- Reviews and inspections
- Verification and validation
- Independent testing (testing strategies and test case types)
- Configuration management (versions of source code and corresponding test cases; versions of documentation; versions of features descriptions)
- Phase reviews and continue/cancel check points
- Quality assessments
- Risk assessments
- Consulting assistance

Figure 3.1 The systems management process.

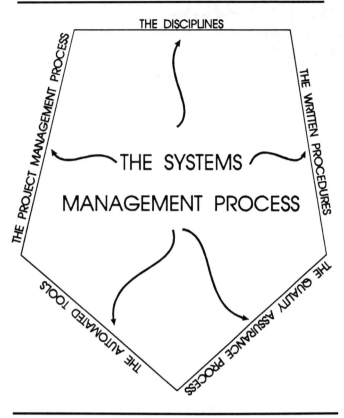

3.1.4 The Written Procedures

The *written procedures*—job aids, methodologies, steps, and checklists—for the techniques, skills, and tools that support *Building the System* and *Managing the Project* include:

- Systems planning
- Information planning
- Analysis, design, programming, testing
- Quality assurance and productivity improvement
- Methodologies for phase management
- Rapid development approaches

3.1.5 The Automated Tools

Some examples of *computer-aided software engineering (CASE)* tools are:

- Computer-aided analysis tools
- Computer-aided design tools

- Computer-aided data base management systems
- Programmer Workstations
- Computer-aided application generators, fourth-generation languages, and other rapid development tools
- Computer-aided project management systems
- Computer-aided project scheduling tools
- Computer-aided estimating tools

3.1.6 Equal Importance

On many smaller projects, it may be possible to do ad hoc project development and still achieve acceptable results—because the worker already has a clear understanding of what the customer needs and because the consequences of decisions are easy to foresee. Even on larger, more complex projects, an informal approach may also work—when there is a high degree of technical expertise, business application expertise, project management expertise, few people on the project (i.e., restricted interpersonal communication), and few people who need to be satisfied.

However, most organizations do not have this level of proficiency, nor do they enjoy such simplistic project participation. Then, lack of structure often leads to highly unacceptable results and serious deficiencies in project management success as well as system development.

Careful consideration shows that each of the five components of the Systems Management Process (See Figure 3.1.) are very closely intertwined and that *total project success demands the effective application of each unit*. As a consequence, *properly managed projects should use all five components*. Not only do the disciplines, the project management process and the written procedures define the phases and activities that must be carried out in the project, they also introduce standardization and consistency among all of the projects in the company. Second, the project management process and written procedures also furnish intermediate checkpoints for determining whether the project is behind, whether more resources need to be added, or whether the project should be continued or abandoned. These checkpoints provide an opportunity to gain control of the project and to act on the environment rather than blindly react to it. Last, the use of the proper development techniques gives practitioners the tools they need to correctly build their systems.

Nevertheless, many companies fall prey to the misguided belief that, if they can develop expertise in one area, it will negate the need to attend to the others. Unfortunately, this is a fallacy. As a case in point, automated tools are productivity aids; they do not teach or replace the concepts of the disciplines or techniques. For example:

• Providing writers with the latest in word-processing software does not enable every author to compose Dickensian classics.

• Providing analysts with the latest state-of-the-art computer-aided analysis tool will not do very much good if the analyst does not know how to do analysis.

• Providing planners with project scheduling software does very little to improve the group's ability to meet its target dates, if the planners do not know what jobs to enter into the software system.

3.1.7 The Project Life Cycle

Before the discussion of the tools and techniques of managing the project is continued, the conceptual requirements of building the system should first be briefly explored because these, too, will influence the use of software packages and they are the input to the tools and techniques of planning. (See Figure 3.2.) Ideally, this chapter will help the organization to appreciate that the best project management skills alone will do little to overcome deficiencies in the systems management process—without a corresponding level of expertise in *Building the System*. If the project is on-time and within budget and it solves the wrong problem, it is not likely to be of much use to anyone. While this chapter is not intended to teach *HOW* to do the work, it does address *WHAT* must be done correctly in order to ensure project success. Furthermore, until planners understand the deliverables that are produced while

Figure 3.2 The systems management process.

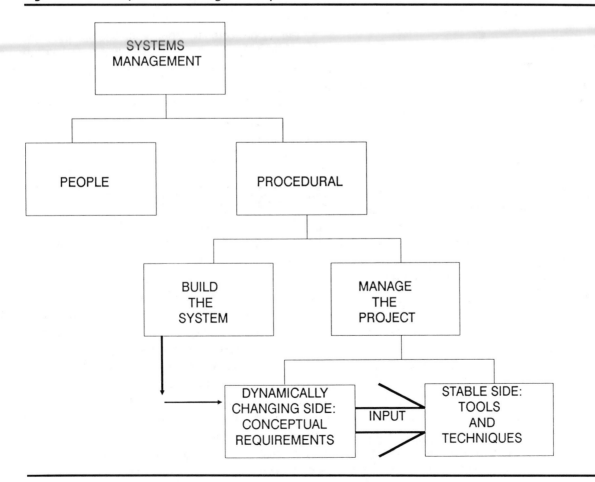

building the system, they will have difficulty developing a complete and comprehensive plan.

3.1.8 The Life Cycle of Systems

In project management, it is important to remember that the phases in the development stage are actually repeated in projects that also occur later during maintenance of the system. For example, in enhancement projects, the team should still complete analysis, design, and so forth. Therefore, project management activities cross all of the life cycle stages. In other words, the material in this book is pertinent whether the project is new systems development or modification of an existing system.

3.1.9 Traditional Development Phases

In any kind of a project—even a project to build a simple bird house—there are at least four phases:

1. Analysis—the builders must determine what is to be constructed.
2. Design—the builders must then create a blueprint for construction.
3. Construction—the product must actually be built.
4. Installation—the product must be tested and accepted.

3.1.10 Building a House

In choosing to build a dream house, the winner of the million dollar lottery must first find a trusted builder. Later, at the initial conference, most likely the winner will not be able to ask the builder to immediately commit to a fixed price and schedule. (The winner can try, but without either a prototype model house or a completed set of specifications, reputable builders will not usually agree to such terms.) In construction projects, fixed commitments are not generally made until the blueprint or design phase has been completed. Sometimes, the price isn't even fixed until the end of installation!

Furthermore, in construction projects, it is important to remember that the work being done in the phases listed above is work that is being done to build the product. And, although the tasks that are done to manage the project are usually transparent to the customer, they are jobs that, nevertheless, are also being performed. Work effort must be estimated. Materials must be ordered. Inventory must be controlled. Work must be scheduled. Milestones must be selected. Status must be assessed. Costs must be reported.

Finally, the majority of work is done *after* the blueprint has been approved. By comparison to the later phases, there are few people involved in the first two stages and completion of these phases is achieved rather quickly.

3.1.11 Building a System

Software projects must also complete the Analysis, Design, Construction, and Installation phases. Even when working in a multiproject environment on several small projects at once, the chances for success are greatly increased if each of the projects is addressed individually, informally broken into the four phases mentioned above, and managed accordingly. This maxim is true even if each project is only three to four weeks long.

Larger projects are more manageable if they are formally broken into more phases—the larger the project, the more phases that are necessary. Each phase must be a manageable size and produce a meaningful deliverable. The time between the beginning and the end of a phase cannot be too long or it will become hard to manage. Conversely, making a phase too short is merely overkill.

3.2 A NEW LOOK IN PHASES

In larger systems projects, analysis as a single phase is simply too big. It should be divided into three separate phases—a high-level analysis, an intermediate-level analysis, and a detailed analysis. In order to have a frame of reference for this text, these phases may be called (1) the Kickoff phase, (2) the Sizing phase, and (3) the Data Gathering phase. (See Figure 3.3.) Each analysis phase is driven from the user's business perspective. Therefore, answering the question ''What would be the problem if this were 1901 and there were no computers?'' helps to identify the correct requirements. There will also be, during this process, some technical aspects which need to be taken into consideration. Thus, it would be useful to think of analysis as 90 percent business and 10 percent technical. Since

Figure 3.3 Building the system.

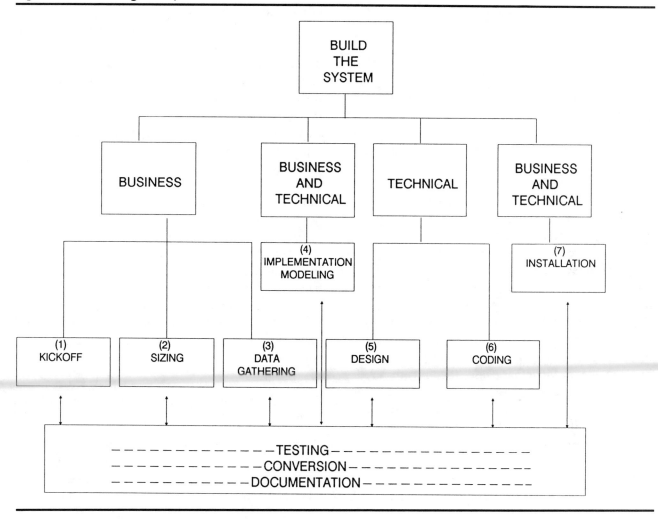

the business perspective drives the effort, the three analysis phases may be grouped under that type of work category. (See Figure 3.3.) On the other hand, the Design and Coding phases are driven from the technician's perspective. For these two phases, the heuristic can be reversed—about 90 percent technical and 10 percent business. So they are put in the technical category. But what about Phase 4 and Phase 7?

3.2.1 The Transition Between Analysis and Design

It helps to remember that in the analysis phases, decisions are being driven to answer the question "What

business problem are we trying to solve?" On the other hand, during Design and Coding, people are answering the question "What computer solution are we implementing?" Sometimes, the effort to answer these questions is performed by separate teams from a business area and a technical area; but frequently, project members simply switch hats back and forth between analyst and technician.

Nevertheless, there has always been a gap between analysis and design, causing a great deal of confusion in the data processing community. How does the team make the transition from analysis (which produces a business problem model) to design (which produces a technical specification)? In order to make this great leap forward, certain decisions must be made about the data gathered during analysis:

- What features will remain manual operations? What will be automated? What will be batch? What is the batch processing window? What will be on-line? What will be distributed? What will be on the host? What will be resident? What language(s) will be used? Can any (or all) of the systems requirements be satisfied with the purchase of software packages?

It is obvious that these are technical decisions. However, the choices will also be driven by the budget; and money considerations are surely driven from the business perspective. Therefore, the decision making in the gap is shared as much by the business representatives as by the technicians. This gap is also very important because it is here that the *SOLUTION* to the problem is chosen! During this phase, the team is finally answering the question *"How* are we going to solve the problem?"* It is for these reasons, therefore, that a separate and distinct phase is created, called the Implementation Modeling phase. (See Figure 3.3.)

The Installation phase, when everything is put together to ensure that the system is operational, is also part business and part technical.

3.2.2 Testing and Conversion

It is important to remember that the procedural side of Systems Management is divided into work to: (1) build the system, and (2) manage the project. Building the system may be further partitioned into (A) phases such as those just described (that is, The Project Life Cycle); and (B) The Support Components. The Support Components represent certain major categories that contain jobs that are very familiar to developers, but that also cause confusion when managers try to integrate them into the process and subsequently try to control them.

Representatives of these groups are Testing, Conversion, Training, Documentation, and so on. For example, it is not unusual to see certain phases in the life cycle called the testing phases. While it is true that the code is tested in the latter phases of the project, the total testing effort actually begins in the early phases—with the development of testing plans, the

identification of acceptance criteria, and the creation of early test cases.[1]

Figure 3.3 shows the support components of testing and conversion as a separate foundation group under the Project Life Cycle and also illustrates that these components are active for almost all of the project. They weave their threads so intricately through the tapestry of the phases that it's easy to get lost. The best way to get control of testing and conversion is to separate the components into their own work groups, clearly identify the work units that must be completed, and then carefully disperse the work across the phases. This concept of weaving testing and conversion into the fabric of effective project management will be developed later in this chapter.

Similarly, the support components will also have important involvement from other parts of the company. Examples of these may be marketing, customer service, manufacturing, distribution, and so on. While these areas are certainly important and project teams must include them in their plans where appropriate, they are not within the scope of this book.

3.2.3 Understanding the Objectives of Each Phase

Control of the project is gained by breaking it up into phases, milestones, and major deliverables. In order to complete the plan, the major deliverables must ultimately be partitioned into inch-pebbles. This implies that somewhere on the project team, there must be members who know enough about each of the phases and support components (See Figure 3.3.) to complete the partitioning. Although not intended to go down to the inch-pebble level, this chapter in presented as a guide to identifying the major deliverables of each phase.

---

[1]One excellent way to demonstrate that the requirement is defined correctly is to determine if it is testable—and if it tests correctly. Therefore, the specification may be tested (with its own customized set of test cases) long before any test scripts are written for the code. A second benefit to early and continued testing is realized when, because they are able to isolate when and where the errors occur, the group can identify the skills areas that need to be improved.

There are seven phases described in this text, but that number is not cast in concrete. Teams may use any number of phases and/or names that are appropriate for their project. What's important is that the work is partitioned, that each member of the team has a clear understanding of the purpose, objectives, and outputs of each partition, and that the team has identified all of the jobs that must go into the plan.

3.2.4 Traditional Phased Development Versus the Innovative Approaches

Initially, this chapter will present the traditional phased approach to systems development. This is the most systematic technique, one with a lower risk in environments where there is not a lot of building and/or management expertise. On the other hand, there are innovative techniques to development—such as incremental implementation, prototyping, and rapid development—that may be used individually or in concert. Before project teams can embark on any of these more innovative methods, it may be advisable that they master an understanding of the objectives of each phase in the development process. Then, depending on the learning curves involved and the risks that can be borne, the group can choose a strategy that integrates some (or all) of the innovative techniques with the traditional approaches. Incremental implementation, prototyping, and rapid development will be addressed at the end of this chapter.

3.3 THE KICKOFF PHASE

The Kickoff, an orientation and screening phase, evaluates the justification for data processing services. A *quick assessment* is made to determine the justification of the request. Many projects, perhaps 50 percent, do not survive this initial screening.

To start with, the organization ought to have an existing set of procedures by which requests for projects are submitted. Assuming that the request has been authorized and that the department is the appropriate one to act on the request, the analyst(s) must first be sure that the requestor information is complete and that the contents are clear. Usually, some additional investigation is necessary to clarify the request.

The early phases of a project are typically some-

what chaotic. People may not know one another and may be unsure of themselves; users may have a hard time conveying what they want; meetings may go astray; and the whole project may seem ungovernable. The most common obstacle encountered at this point is that the request often states a solution rather than a description of the problem. For example, a request for a group of rotating, high-resolution color-graphics terminals is a solution to a problem—NOT its definition. The problem may have stemmed from a need for more current, easier to access sales information about the company's XYZ product. Furthermore, the issue may even be solved in a more cost effective manner than a DP project. This phase begins to crystallize these problems.

One of the concepts that continues to plague systems developers is getting a clear understanding and agreement on the definition of *scope*. To many people, scope implies the description of the areas subject to *study* or analysis. To others, it connotes a clear definition of the *features* of the system that will ultimately be automated. This text will differentiate between the two by calling the areas subject to study or analysis the *domain of study* and then calling the definition of the features of the system that will ultimately be automated the *scope of the system*. System scope will not be finalized until later in the project. However, it is essential that the domain of study be clearly identified *before* going any further.

It is a good idea to interview a good cross section of more than one representative from the domain of study—in more than one level of user management, operations, and data processing. Since managers and supervisors have a good conceptual understanding of the business perspectives and may provide a good constraint to over-expansion of system scope, it is appropriate that they participate in this phase (and later in the second and fourth phases).

The Kickoff phase is an analysis phase and as such should be driven from a business perspective. A high-level analysis is completed, and a project objectives matrix that describes the priorities and value of each required feature should be produced and verified. (In *Software Engineering Economics*, Boehm's ''GOALS Approach to Software Engineering'' is an excellent source of guidance on how to prepare a project objectives matrix.) Approval of the project objectives also refines the domain of study and initiates the definition of the success criteria. It is often the case that it will not be possible to satisfy all of the project objectives of all of the interested groups. Therefore, the project team is well advised to institute some type of conflict resolution process and to identify the decision makers who will serve as the designated conflict resolvers. And last, a small amount of technical representation is also advisable, simply to insure that the project is not flying off into a direction for which there will be no technical support.

3.3.1 Analysis of Alternatives

Sometimes, it is advantageous to gather sufficient information as soon as possible to enable the early *elimination* of unfeasible solutions. Each time the project team refines the project objectives matrix, it is appropriate for them to use this information to examine potential alternatives. Even though they want to continue to remember the judicious postponement of design decisions until the Design phase, it is also necessary to do a limited amount of high-level design as they go along. This work, which is done by the analysts and designers with input from the end-user client, will take the form of evaluating possibilities for automation boundaries, equipment types, and/or the purchase of software packages.

Choices are not usually made at this point, other than to drop the unfeasible solutions from further consideration. Premature decisions could prejudice the design, only to lead to the later discovery that the selection is unworkable to some degree, causing the need for rework, wasted effort, and missed target dates.

3.3.2 Managing the Expectations of the Analysis of Alternatives

It is necessary to emphasize that, in the early phases, the presented alternatives are based on a *conceptual understanding* that may *change* during the subsequent phases. Therefore, it is important to stress to management that these early analyses are for comparison and elimination only. With the increased knowledge gained in the subsequent phases, some (or all) of the assumptions may be disproved. But the desire for increased knowledge is, after all, one of the reasons the subsequent phases are conducted!

3.3.3 Defining the Criteria for Success

It is essential to know, right from the start, the criteria by which the project will be judged successful. Furthermore, it is important to know who should be making the decisions. Success may be described from varying perspectives and to varying levels of detail.

Management, users, operations, project members, and anyone else who may be affected by the installation of the system all have their own criteria for success. As in setting project objectives, all of the views must be concisely defined, the conflicting requirements identified, the conflicts resolved, and the remaining subset determined. This subset becomes a subset of the criteria for success and must be approved by all key project participants.

3.3.4 A Record Frozen in Time

Although the decisions from all subsequent phases will be documented and will migrate from one phase to the next, the information from the kickoff phase may also be archived—as a record of the original intentions.

3.3.5 The Continue/Cancel Decision

With the completion of each phase, more is known about the project than was known previously. It is not unusual to provide the group with the opportunity to reflect on the new information and to use this knowledge to make a conscious decision regarding whether to continue or cancel the project. Occurring at the end of each of the early phases, the choice is usually made at a phase review meeting. (Not every project can afford the luxury of the ''continue/cancel'' decision. For example, various types of regulatory requirements and strategic product developments can not usually cancel.) Some individuals may be skeptical about the value of the cancellation process and may also be concerned about the losses that are suffered when a project is cancelled. Nevertheless, it appears that savings are realized by:

• Earlier elimination of projects that used to get shelved later in the life cycle (and after significant revenue expenditures); and

• Earlier elimination of systems that become very costly to maintain.

These savings more than make up for the cancellations.

3.3.6 The Major Objectives of the Kickoff Phase

The major objective of the Kickoff phase is the development of a quick, high-level assessment. Because the ''project'' may end at the completion of this phase, a minimum number of days is spent on this effort. Also, the work is accomplished with a minimum number of people. The goal is to determine how big the effort will be (in orders of magnitude, *NOT* to three decimal places); what the priority is; and if the company really wants to do it. Remember, even though there are many questions to answer, the answers are to be brief. The purpose is simply to gather a little more information than the team had when they started. So statements ought to be kept simple and to the point. The next phase, if it is approved, will provide the opportunity to dig deeper. The main deliverables of this phase are:

1. An executive summary
2. The Project Charter (including the project objectives matrix and the domain of study)
3. The high-level analysis
4. An impact assessment (including the identification of risks and show stoppers)
5. The evaluation
6. A high-level analysis of possible alternatives
7. A sign-off of the success and completion criteria
8. Detailed plans and a committed date for the second phase
9. Inexact plans for the rest of the project
10. Assessment plans for the total project
11. Assessment level cost/benefit analysis
12. Phase review meeting (i.e., the continue/cancel decision)
13. Phase assessment report (including what was right, what was wrong, what was learned)

This is the first opportunity in the project to become familiar with the requirements. Deliverables 1–7 of this phase are the specifications for *Building the System*. They will be repeated, in one form or another, in each of the subsequent phases in order to verify, validate, and elaborate on the results.

Deliverables 8–13 are planning and management. They are usually repeated at the end of every phase, becoming more and more detailed as the project progresses.

3.4 THE SIZING PHASE

During the second phase, the Project Charter is expanded, a Project Agreement is written, the analysis is reworked, and the team drives to get a ''handle'' on how big the project really is. Similarly, if the group is able to ascertain that the risk is too high to try the project as it is currently defined, they may reduce the domain of study *and* the system scope before proceeding any further.

In this phase, and before the *real* job of analysis in the third phase, developers have often produced what has been traditionally called the Statement of Work, Feasibility Study, Project Charter, or Survey. In its simplest form, a statement of work may be an economic evaluation such as a cost/benefit analysis based on some high-level assumptions. A more complete definition recognizes that an intermediate analysis of existing system deficiencies and new system objectives is also required.

3.4.1 The Purpose of the Sizing Phase

Like the Kickoff phase, this phase should also be driven from a business perspective. And, as before, a small amount of technical representation is also advisable, to insure that the project is not flying off into a direction for which there is no supporting technology.

3.4.2 The Project Agreement

One of the deliverables from the statement of work may be an approved charter to proceed with the development of a data processing project. However, it is also essential to get everyone to agree on how the project will be managed. Consequently, it is important to also define the conceptual requirements of building the system and managing the project! (See Figure 3.2.) Those undefined and assumed cultural attitudes and expectations still need to be crystallized, the success and completion criteria reevaluated and reconfirmed, and the conflicts resolved. This information ought to be documented in the Project Agreement and distributed to anyone who can affect or who will be affected by the project. This is the time to assess the project's impact, determine if the organization is committed to successful completion, and decide if the effort ought to go forward or be abandoned.

If a project methodology (for example, guidelines and procedures) already exists in the organization, this is the time to customize it to fit the project. However, although every project is unique and the development approach needs to be modeled to specific needs, care should be taken not to plunge into the time-consuming and expensive development of a new methodology.

The Project Agreement is a living document and is not cast in stone. It is reviewed at the end of every phase, and, if necessary, it is modified to reflect current needs and thinking.

3.4.3 Intermediate-Level Analysis

Although the Sizing phase is a pre-analysis step, it is nevertheless necessary to initiate some moderate investigation at this time. The work should not be made unreasonably complex at this preliminary level because the real job of analysis will be done in the next phase—if the project gets approval to proceed. While preparing the intermediate-level analysis, however, the project team will want to keep an eye to the future, always remembering that the ultimate goal in the next phase will be to completely and concisely define what is to be built, what should not be included, how much the organization is willing to spend, and how long they are willing to wait.

Both the manual and automated parts of the system should be reviewed. Therefore, the managers and supervisors responsible for end-user client departments, major sections, and major business functions should be interviewed.

A rare exception may occur when the team is specifically chartered to perform a one-to-one rewrite of an old set of code. Even then, they may want to consider looking beyond the current code for opportunities to improve the business processes.

The intermediate-level analysis explains the current system's deficiencies. Key features of the new system are identified and new functions are described.

The major inputs and outputs are defined and outside system interfaces are declared. Performance requirements may be included, and pertinent information about existing hardware and software is provided.

Many organizations also require that the end-user client areas prepare an independent requirements definition. After resolving any inconsistencies and/or conflicts with the data processing group's findings, both documents are then merged.

REMEMBER: THIS IS JUST AN INTERMEDIATE-LEVEL ANALYSIS! There is a natural tendency, at this stage, to forget that this process is only a moderate investigation and to want to plunge to the detail level. Discipline ought to be exercised to constrain the outputs to simple lists and descriptions. It is unwise to spend a great amount of effort on analysis before it is known if the project will continue beyond this phase.

3.4.4 The Third-Phase Effort Will Be Difficult to Estimate

At the end of the second phase, the team will be estimating the effort for the third phase. Also, in large projects, the team must be continuously reassessing their estimates. Furthermore, in the early phases, the numbers may often be very difficult to predict. For example, in the third phase, the team will be attempting to completely, concisely, and accurately determine the requirements definition. Yet, in this second phase, total understanding of the requirements is usually still very rudimentary. Since, in most development efforts, the final form of the product is not crystallized until the completion of the third phase (or even into the fourth phase), this wreaks havoc on prior committed completion dates. As a consequence, providing accurate commitments (in the second phase) for how much time and how many resources will be needed to complete the third phase as well as the rest of the project is a significant challenge and, at best, a risky business.

3.4.5 Sizing the Effort and Reducing the Domain of Study and the System Scope

Current state-of-the-art practitioners have adapted an approach that softens the blow of these poor estimates. They have discovered that the ''80/20'' rule holds true in systems specification—80 percent of the requirements may be specified in 20 percent of the time. It is the crystallization of the last 20 percent that takes 80 percent of the effort.

If teams keep this in mind, they may employ the concept in a *depth-sounding* process, which is intended to quickly specify that 80 percent. Because only 80 percent is defined, the goal is not completeness or perfection. Therefore, these specifications may be viewed as planning models. (It should be stressed that they are *not* building models!) Group dynamics workshops are an excellent environment in which to quickly achieve the objectives. They will be addressed later in this chapter. Furthermore, the exercise *requires* that accurate records be kept of all effort expended during the high- and intermediate-level analyses (the first and second phases).

After the intermediate-level analysis has been completed, the known requirements should be grouped by some partitioning scheme—for example:

• Relatively trivial
• Simple, straightforward
• Middle-of-the-road
• Moderately difficult
• Hard
• Very complex

For smaller projects, this number of categories will likely be lower; the larger projects, naturally, may have an even higher number.

Next, a representative sampling of requirements within each of the categories should be selected for further specification, making sure to include some hard and/or very complex requirements in the selection. To enable completion of the exercise within a meaningful timeframe, the hard and very complex requirements may sometimes require additional partitioning.

It's a good idea to look for requirements that touch as many of the affected departments as possible, especially where there is overlapping processing. In a depth-sounding exercise, these interdependent requirements are good candidates for added specification—because they will give the group a good opportunity to gauge unknowns, conflicts, and unresolved issues.

The analysis of this finite number of conditions is to rapidly be driven to "completion," keeping accurate records of effort and of any conflicts and unresolved issues.

Each depth-sounding exercise is considered finished when the group can *confidently* and *accurately* estimate how long it will take to exhaust that part of the study to perfection.

The team should then assess how effectively they classified the known requirements, making any necessary recategorizations. Then the actual numbers and their corresponding estimates are applied to each of the remaining features in the chosen categories; the other categories and features are estimated using some selected method of extrapolation. All of these estimates are totaled to provide an estimate for the next phase.

If the estimates gathered during the sizing effort indicate that the project is too big or unmanageable, the data is then used to help make descoping decisions.

3.4.6 Analysis of Alternatives

In the fourth phase, the Implementation Modeling phase, the project team will perform *in-depth* evaluations of several implementation alternatives. For the lowest risk of failure, the actual implementation approach ought to be selected only *after* the Data Analysis of the fourth phase has been completed! Thus, it is inappropriate to go that level of detail in the first phases. However, some foundation work for the identification of alternatives does begin during these early phases. As a consequence, project teams often find themselves in a precarious balancing act—trying to descope, trying to identify releases, trying to do enough implementation modeling—all in an effort to get the project pared down to a manageable size. Yet, all of the requirements have not been completely specified. Until the business specifications have been nailed down, premature design decisions could prejudice the technical solution, leading to the discovery later that it is unworkable to some degree, causing the need for rework, wasted effort, and missed target dates. Therefore, if risk containment is important, the project team ought to be cautioned not to get trapped into doing a premature detailed design.

3.4.7 The Major Objectives of the Sizing Phase

The main deliverables of this phase are:

1. The updated Project Agreement
2. The updated Project Charter (including the updated project objectives matrix and the domain of study)
3. The intermediate-level analysis
4. The updated impact assessment (including the identification of risks and show stoppers)
5. The current evaluation
6. The sizing effort results
7. The descoping findings
8. An intermediate-level analysis of possible alternatives
9. A sign-off of the success and completion criteria
10. Detailed plans and a scheduled date for the third phase
11. Inexact plans for the rest of the project
12. Assessment plans for the total project
13. Assessment level cost/benefit analysis
14. Phase review meeting (i.e., the continue/cancel decision)
15. Phase assessment report (including what was right, what was wrong, what was learned)

The planning and managing deliverables (10–15) are usually repeated at the end of every phase, becoming more and more detailed as the project progresses.

3.5 THE DATA GATHERING PHASE

The third phase is the time to completely dissect the business problem. It is during this phase that the real job of analysis is completed. The most significant deliverable of this phase is the verified requirements definition, which establishes the specifications for *Building the System*. It describes in thorough detail what the system must do in order to be deemed a success. Emphasis, then, must be on the document's completeness and accuracy. Most failures to deliver the correct system can be traced to the fact that even by this stage there was still no unambiguous agreement between the developers and the users about the system's requirements.

3.5.1 Good Analysis Is Not Easy

Proper analysis, then, is crucial to correctness of the system. Yet many systems experts agree that, in the whole Systems Management Process, analysis is probably the single most difficult technique to master. And until the organization has developed this expertise within their environment, there will be a downside effect on systems quality as well as any estimates of the analysis effort.

3.5.2 Why the Analysis Effort Is So Difficult to Estimate

Whenever an *in-depth* analysis of the problem is occurring for the first time in a project, the team can expect to uncover requirements that were missed in the preliminary studies. This can simply be due to the natural process of refining the specification or the group may discover major flaws in the current domain of study and system scope. In either case, the analysis effort may be extended in terms of time, resources, and, naturally, money. It seems logical, then, for the organization to be willing to make the necessary accommodations. However, because of the pressure to meet the impending dates, there is usually a reluctance to consider slipping commitments. This causes a great deal of tension and frustration for both the project team and management. As a result, one or more of the following can occur:

- The organization becomes disenchanted with the project team and its capabilities
- The domain of study and the system scope are enlarged, but the time and resources remain the same. Analysts work overtime and/or quality may suffer. The project team becomes disenchanted with the organization and its capabilities
- Analysis is viewed to be finished when the time that was earmarked for it has been used up and no more analysis is done—until the system is tested and found to be lacking, or worse: until after installation
- Analysis is reported to be finished when the time earmarked for it is up but its actual completion is planned to occur during design. (This is one of the ways a project quickly gets to be 90 percent com-

plete, but the last 10 percent expands to take another 90 percent of the time.)

None of these options is particularly appealing and not one needs to happen. Companies may be helped to *rethink* their expectations so that they may become aware that the project team cannot always accurately estimate what the analysis effort will be.

3.5.3 More Changes to the Domain of Study and System Scope May Occur in This Phase

When new requirements are uncovered, the organization may simply choose to document them and delay any action or, more commonly, choose to enlarge the domain of study and system scope. When the domain and scope are enlarged, the amount of time, money, and resources ought to be enlarged proportionally.

On the other hand, if the domain and scope are growing disproportionately, another descoping exercise may be indicated.

3.5.4 Good Analysis Can Be Partitioned Into Three Subphases

If analysis is so difficult to estimate, the secret to getting control of the process is partitioning this third phase into more manageable chunks. The first step in this direction is to create three subphases: (1) getting to know the problem; (2) isolating the real business requirements; and (3) modeling the new business requirements. The use of the term "business" is not restricted to commercial applications. Even scientific applications have their "business"; that is, the "business" of whatever scientific application is being studied.

These subphases are often done sequentially. However, depending on the analysis expertise, the application knowledge, the complexity of the project, and/or the level of acceptable risk, these subphases may be done, to some degree, in parallel.

Getting to know the problem. The analyst(s) should know the environment of the system. If there is already a high degree of familiarity, this may be a limited effort. However, this is not usually the case, and it will be necessary for the team (which by now has probably been enlarged) to review any existing system documentation, procedures, guides, and the information from prior phases. It is often also appropriate for the new analysts to schedule some *getting-to-know-you* interviews with their users.

Isolating the real business requirements. After the teams have been assigned, they will perform in-depth analyses of the various subsystems, departments, etc. in order to document the true nature of the system. Care ought to be exercised not to get trapped in describing data and functions that are not within the domain of study and scope of the system, that are scheduled for elimination, or are simply present because of some obsolescent technology (or way of doing business) that should not be carried into the new system.

Both the manual and the automated systems that are within the domain and scope should be studied.

All of the business data *and* the corresponding business policies for using this data must be described. It is helpful to complete a census of data to insure that (1) any data that must ultimately be reported can be extracted from the system or can be derived from other data in the system; and (2) any data that is stored in the system will ultimately be extracted or used to derive reporting data. Data that does not pass the second test should be considered for elimination. Until these processes have been completed, analysis is *not finished!*

Modeling the new business requirements. The new requirements should be modeled and integrated into the existing system model. After approval, this model becomes the guide for development of the new product.

3.5.5 The Major Objectives of the Data Gathering Phase

The main deliverables of this phase are:

1. The updated Project Agreement
2. The updated Project Charter (including the updated project objectives matrix and the domain of study)
3. The detailed-level analysis
4. The updated impact assessment (including the identification of risks and show stoppers)

5. The current evaluation

6. An updated intermediate-level analysis of possible alternatives

7. A sign-off of the success and completion criteria

8. Detailed plans and a committed date for the fourth phase

9. Inexact plans for the rest of the project

10. Assessment plans for the total project

11. Assessment level cost/benefit analysis

12. Phase review meeting (continue/cancel decision)

13. Phase assessment report (including what was right, what was wrong, what was learned)

Deliverables 8–13 are usually repeated at the end of every phase, becoming more and more detailed as the project progresses.

3.6 THE IMPLEMENTATION MODELING PHASE

Emphasis is now placed on exactly what the system will do as well as what it will not do. It is during this Phase that the data from Phase 3 is analyzed and the alternatives for automation that were *invented* during the earlier phases are finalized and presented to the organization. And, in ideal circumstances, if a package is to be implemented, the final selection is not made until this fourth phase.

The integrated model of existing and new business requirements that was produced in the prior phase serves as the baseline universe of the new system. Using this integrated model, it is now necessary to designate which features (or parts of features) will be automated and which will remain as manual operations. Then, the parts elected for automation should be mapped into hardware and software requirements.

First, the team determines if it is possible to automate the entire system. If so, they use this as the highest alternative. However, it is not usually practical to consider full automation; therefore, the project team picks the largest reasonable subset as the first alternative. Other scenarios are chosen from different or smaller subsets.

This procedure may be very simple in projects that are exact rewrites of an existing automated system. However, when organizations use the opportunity (of new projects) to improve old systems by also automating new functions, the issue then becomes one of deciding how many features can be automated while still justifying the expenditure.

In choosing the automation boundary, it is necessary to decide what features (or parts of features) would be more reasonable and/or economical if carried out by the computer. When allocating the remaining procedures to manual processors, they must be grouped together by the department or job function that makes most sense. The team may also identify support functions such as data entry preparation, audit procedures, and reporting media as well as the procedures that enable user interaction with the computer. It is also appropriate at this time to decide (for example) whether the automated system will be a straight batch system with overnight processing; an on-line data entry and/or inquiry system with overnight batch file updates; a distributed on-line data entry system with overnight uploading of data, batch processing, and downloading of refreshed files; an on-line real-time distributed database system; any combination of the above; or any other technical approach. The alternative finally selected will serve as input to the selection of one or more packages or the design of the automated portion of a new system.

3.6.1 Implementation Costs

The determination of costs is needed for informed decision making, evaluation against benefits, budgeting, and establishing the yield on the investment. Costs to date and projected costs to completion for each potential alternative ought to be reported. Development costs may be weighed against the benefits of anticipated savings in operations, high returns, improved service, or tax savings.

The payback period for return on investments and discounted cash flow techniques, such as net present value and internal rate of return, may be used to compare the yield on the investment against other potential ventures. It will also be necessary to do a high-level comparative analysis of costs, resource requirements, and completion schedules for each alternative.

At this point, the amount of work involved seems considerable, but it is necessary for an honest analysis. Although there's no denying that this does require effort, teams should realize that—if the alternative scenarios have been developed as subsets—there will be some degree of overlap between the tasks, so it won't be as bad as it initially appeared.

3.6.2 Other Considerations

It is during this phase that the hardware configuration is confirmed and new equipment is ordered. If position orders were placed during the earlier phases, this is the time to confirm the choice. Now that the automation boundaries have been established, the decision whether to develop the system in-house or to buy a software package is made and the selection of software packages and/or usable existing in-house software may be completed. Choosing the hardware and software involves specifying either the make and model of hardware (CPU, memory upgrades, auxiliary storage devices, terminal types, distributed processors, data communications requirements) or the name and release for the software (communications protocols, control programs, program products, development aids, and, last but not least, applications packages). The software package evaluation and selection techniques discussed at length later may now be employed. If incremental implementation is selected, the releases ought to now be clearly packaged.

A separate individual (or group of individuals) within the development team ought to be charged with overseeing the control of the interfaces between man and machine (e.g., procedures for using terminals and reports), machine and machine (e.g. distributed processor and mainframe), machine and software, software and machine, and software and software (e.g., compatibility of databases or input and output interfaces whether on same machine or on different machines). While the time to start developing these procedures is during this phase, they will be refined during the Design phase, and completed during Coding and Installation.

In order to complete the plan for the Design phase, a portion of the system's technical architecture (which is described below) will need to be initiated during this phase.

3.6.3 When Will the System Scope Be Defined?

Although the domain of study must be specified at the beginning of the project, it is not until the process of carving out the boundaries for automation has been completed that the final decisions regarding scope are made. Therefore, the scope[2] is not truly defined until the end of the Implementation Modeling phase. Subsequent changes to the scope of the system will be subject to the change management procedures described later in the book.

3.6.4 The Major Objectives of the Implementation Modeling Phase

The main deliverables of this phase are:

1. The updated Project Agreement
2. The updated Project Charter (including the updated project objectives matrix and the domain of study)
3. A few completed alternatives
4. The chosen alternative
5. The initial system technical architecture
6. The updated impact assessment (including the identification of risks and show stoppers)
7. The current evaluation
8. A sign-off of the success and completion criteria
9. Detailed plans and a committed date for the fifth phase
10. Forecasted plans for project completion
11. Forecasted cost/benefit analysis
12. Phase review meeting (continue/cancel decision)
13. Phase assessment report (including what was right, what was wrong, what was learned)

Deliverables 9–13 are usually repeated at the end of every phase, becoming more and more detailed as the project progresses.

3.7 THE DESIGN PHASE

This phase provides the transition from the selection of a solution to the ability to construct a reliable, high-

---

[2] The true definition of scope being the part of the system, in a data processing project that will be committed to automation.

quality product. The objective is achieved through systematic software design methods and techniques that are applied to the chosen automated portion (from the prior phase) in order to obtain an implemented computer system. For example, the design may be completed using traditional structured design techniques and/or the newly popularized object-oriented design techniques.

Always remembering that the secret of successful project management is the continued partitioning of labor, the team may divide the design phase into three types of work: (1) the design of the technical architecture of the system; (2) the external design; and (3) the internal design.

This treatment facilitates scheduling, work assignments and status reporting. For example, to a large degree, the design of the system's technical architecture and the external design can be scheduled concurrently; and, ideally, the internal design would wait until these first two subgroups have been completed. Nevertheless, many developers may want to start internal design as soon as the technical architecture of the system identifies some modules or functions. Naturally, waiting extends project duration, while starting sooner, theoretically leads to an earlier finish—and this may sometimes be true. The risk is, however, that as the design of the technical architecture progresses, concepts may change that subsequently affect the internal design, often requiring substantial rework. This situation, of course, negates any time savings and, what's worse, may also affect the quality of the finished product. The strategy selected will depend on the potential risk and the corresponding level that the group can reasonably tolerate.

3.7.1 The Technical Architecture of the System

The system is partitioned into pieces that will ultimately become groupings of source code instructions. These groupings, usually called subsystems or programs, are in turn divided into modules, routines, subroutines, etc. How these groupings interface with one another is called the technical architecture of the system, and may be graphically represented in a hierarchy diagram similar to an organizational chart (called a structure chart), or it may be drawn as an object-oriented design diagram.

Names given to the groupings vary from instal-lation to installation. Organizations will most likely have their own names and want to use them; however, it is essential that the team declares the meanings of the terms when the project starts so that everyone can understand the definitions.

The technical architecture declares the basic system design, the control subsystems, and the data structure control interfaces for intermodule communication. It illustrates what functions will be batch, how they are grouped, and when they will be processed; what functions will be on-line and how they are grouped; and what on-line modules will be resident in the computer's main memory and which will be on auxiliary storage. Similarly, the specifications for linkage editing, loading, and job control language are completed.

Technical design also includes preparing of specifications for software development tools (e.g., drivers, stubs, formatted and snapshot dumps, miniature files, preprocessors, post-processors, test data generators, cross-reference reports, conversion aids, etc.).

At this time, the development team will also want to allocate the support computer areas (sometimes called libraries) for testing, training, integration, etc. These support subsystems are needed for providing convenient storage, retrieval, and correction of design units, test units, and training units, as well as for providing the overall assessment of status and progress against objectives.

3.7.2 External Design

External design, so-called because it considers design from the outside of the system (that is, the user perspective) without regard to the internals of the modules, programs, etc., addresses such issues as hierarchy of menus; design of input screens and forms; design of output reports; the definition of their purpose, data content, format, frequencies, volumes, origins and/or dispositions; and the identification of transaction types and codes. In a prototyping environment, some of the external design may have been done much earlier in the project. If so, the external design (to the extent that it was not completed in the earlier phases) is finished now. Production schedules (e.g., frequencies, run times, and cycle durations) are identified, and the projected operating costs are reviewed and revised. Data security, legal, and audit policies; procedures for balance and control (e.g., input, output, run-to-run, and other systems or file interfaces); and the steps for reentry of rejects are included. The performance criteria are reviewed and refined, and the system is evaluated to determine if it meets the stated objectives.

Many of the deliverables in this subphase will be direct input to user procedure guides and manuals. Therefore, since external design is so closely related to the documentation factors, these tasks must be closely coordinated with the individual(s) responsible for user documentation.

3.7.3 Internal Design

The internal design completes the specifications for module design, program design, database design, and so on. These internal specs will be used, during the Coding phase, to create source code in one or more compiled programming languages. Team members are assigned the responsibility for designing each module (generally less than or equal to 100 source code instructions), or program (group of modules, routines, or subroutines). The specifications will include the name, purpose, language, calling parameters, calling sequence, error routines, algorithms, module logic, and restart and recovery procedures. The data base design—complete with names, descriptions, values, size and format of fields, data usage statistics, the distinction between stored and derived data, keys, access relationships and methods, backup and retention criteria—will also be finalized.

3.7.4 The Major Objectives of the Design Phase

The main deliverables of this phase are:

1. The updated Project Agreement
2. The updated Project Charter (including the updated project objectives matrix and the domain of study)
3. The technical architecture
4. The corresponding internal design
5. The external design
6. The updated impact assessment (including the identification of risks and show stoppers)
7. The current evaluation

8. A sign-off of the success and completion criteria
9. Detailed plans and a committed date for the sixth phase
10. Projected plans for project completion
11. Projected cost/benefit analysis
12. Phase review meeting (continue/cancel decision)
13. Phase assessment report (including what was right, what was wrong, what was learned)

Subsequent changes to the design of the system will be subject to the change management procedures described further on.

3.8 THE CODING PHASE

It is during this phase that the code is actually written from the internal design specifications that were developed for the program modules and data bases. Programming considerations are influenced by the type of language (e.g., third or fourth generation), the choice of language itself (e.g., COBOL, C), and the installation of productivity aids (e.g., code optimizers, application generators). The units coded during this phase will also be tested.

3.8.1 The Major Objectives of the Coding Phase

The main deliverables of this phase are:

1. The updated Project Agreement
2. The updated Project Charter (including the updated project objectives matrix and the domain of study)
3. The completed program modules and data bases
4. The updated impact assessment (including the identification of risks and show stoppers)
5. The current evaluation
6. A sign-off of the success and completion criteria
7. Committed plans for project completion
8. Committed figures for the cost/benefit analysis
9. Phase review meeting (continue/cancel decision)
10. Phase assessment report (including what was right, what was wrong, what was learned)

By this phase, it is usually the case that the decision (in Deliverable 9) is to continue; although in cases of disaster, projects may be canceled this late in the game.

3.9 THE INSTALLATION PHASE

During the Installation phase, all of the activities carried out during the project finally come to a climax. Characterized by the integration of software development, hardware installation, documentation, testing, training, and conversion, this last phase of the Project Life Cycle marks the ultimate joining together of all of the deliverables from each of these efforts. During system testing and acceptance testing, the successful integration of these outputs and the smooth operation of the system are verified and the final decisions regarding implementation are made.

It is not surprising, then, that the big question at this point is "When are we going to push the button and go live?" Well-managed projects can, at the appropriate time, answer this question with confidence!

3.9.1 Herein Lies the Essence of Project Management

The ideal project seems to glide in effortlessly: there is no disruption to daily business operations; the turnover occurs without a hitch; the users have no difficulty using the product; and the system functions with no failures. The users are joyous in their acceptance of the product and brag about the wonderful job done by the project members and the white knights of project development ride off into the sunset—to do yet more good deeds another day.

Unfortunately, the scenario just described doesn't usually happen. Many projects end on a downnote. But they don't have to end dismally. Knowing how to coordinate all of the groups and pull them together into a homogeneous entity, which enables everything to fall into place at the prescribed time, is the key to success.

A project is truly under control when the project manager is in possession of a project plan—containing *every job that must be completed by every person (in and out of the organization) who can affect the ability to push that button and go live*. Yet, this very process exerts a major impact on the organization and without

supreme cooperation and meticulous control, the results can have disastrous consequences. Nevertheless, if there is no project plan with every job that can affect the installation date, then the project is just not under control! It is the very need for this meticulous control that drives the search for effective project management techniques and the software to support them.

3.9.2 The Major Objectives of the Installation Phase

The main deliverables of this phase are:

1. The final Project Agreement
2. The final Project Charter (including the updated project objectives matrix and the domain of study)
3. An implemented system
4. The final impact assessment (including the identification of risks and show stoppers)
5. The final evaluation
6. A sign-off of the success and completion criteria
7. Perfect plans for project completion
8. Perfect figures for the cost/benefit analysis
9. Phase review meeting
10. Phase assessment report (including what was right, what was wrong, what was learned)

3.10 TESTING

From a management perspective, it is essential to acknowledge that quality cannot be tested into a system. Since the fastest way to build the system is not having to do any job more than once, it is a good idea to do it right the first time. Thus, good development techniques (and reviews and inspections) are essential requirements for improved quality, and they should not be ignored.

3.10.1 Analysis, Design, and Testing

Proper analysis and design, then, are crucial to effective testing of the system. Not fully appreciating this, participants in traditional project development rushed through the early phases in order to insure that they would have enough time for testing. At a maximum, they spent 25 percent to 40 percent of the software development effort on analysis and design (with hardly any test effort at the beginning of the project). Consequently, programmers spent the majority of their time fixing errors that were carried over from the early phases. Of course, what they were really doing was the analysis and design that ought to have been done earlier in the project. Sooner or later, analysis and design must be done, so why not do it in the beginning—when it's more cost effective? Errors discovered during testing cost 15–75 times more to fix than those that are discovered during analysis.

Simply stated, this means front-loading the effort for analysis and design, as well as developing and executing test cases in these early phases. Enlightened project managers are (1) concentrating on developing expertise in analysis, design, and testing; and (2) dedicating 65 percent to 75 percent of their efforts to these activities. They are seeing the payoff later in reduced testing efforts. Organizations that are interested in another view of just how much their errors are costing them should record the execution time for just one pass through the test data. All additional test runs (and the attendant expenses) are the costs to the organization of poor quality during development.

3.11 CONVERSION

Conversion is the act of changing property of one nature into property of another nature. For project development, this can mean the modification of procedures, the renovation of office space, and/or the exchange of data in a file system. Requirements such as the modification of procedures and office renovations are certainly nontrivial. However, this section will only address the translation of data from a file (manual or automated) into a machine-readable format which a new DP system can accept. More specifically, this means:

- The exchange of data that currently exists in the old system in some kind of manual processing form (e.g., index cards, rolodex files, carbon copies and original data entry forms).

- The exchange of data that currently exists in the old system on some kind of machine readable medium.

- The identification of additional data not currently being provided by the old system and the resolution of the source of this new data (e.g., will this new data be provided at the conversion or will it simply be introduced when new records are added?).

- The resolution of differences in data content between the old and new files.

- The creation of a Conversion Acceptance Testing Plan.

- The creation of test programs (e.g., snapshot dumps, formatted record dumps, and file compares) and test files to test the conversion programs.

- The potential merging of separate files into an integrated data base.

- The creation of procedures and manuals that will support the conversion effort.

3.11.1 Conversion is a Project Unto Itself

Regardless of whether it's a big effort or a small effort, conversion should be viewed as though it were a project in and of itself! Although conversion is one of the last events that occur before Installation, the actual preparation begins early in the Project Development Process and continues through the whole Project Life Cycle.

3.12 INCREMENTAL IMPLEMENTATION

Often, the timeframe for completion of the whole project may be so long that (1) the customer may lose interest; (2) the original specifications may radically change before the system is delivered; or (3) the system may be too complex to deal with at one time. In such cases, the project team might consider partitioning the development effort into a series of increments (also referred to as releases or versions). Incremental implementation assumes that it is possible to isolate a meaningful subset of the whole system and to develop, test, and implement that piece. Using this approach, customers can receive a usable working model of the system (or a subset of the system), albeit with limited capabilities, early in the process. As each subsequent increment is implemented, more and more functionality is added.

Project teams often rapturously embrace this concept as a means of *doing some magic quickly* and sometimes select versions prematurely. It is no mean feat to try to keep new pieces of the system that are in various states of development in synchronization with old pieces of the system that are in various states of maintenance and replacement. The packaging of versions must be done in such a way as to:

- Organize each version to insure that it stands on its own and each function within the version is independent of the other functions.

- Structure the release of versions to minimize modifications to production versions that result from requirements that are needed in subsequent versions, and to minimize the impact (on the new and old pieces) of maintenance changes.

- Implement procedures to support careful control of any modifications that are made to new and old production versions in response to problems found during testing of new versions.

- Structure the new versions so that control of their interfaces is kept to a minimum (e.g., the extra ''black box'' code needed to interface from version to version; or the additional customer procedures and training that, because of their complexity, might negate user friendly interfaces).

It is unwise to select increments until enough of the total analysis has been completed to allow team members to insure that they have maintained the integrity between the subsystem interfaces, can deliver a meaningful piece to the users, and can stay within the prescribed budgets. Difficulties may also arise when trying to reconcile the tradeoffs regarding the extra costs, time, and resources associated with this approach. For example, additional resources are often needed to supplement the development team when existing resources are diverted to maintain newly implemented versions.

3.13 RAPID DEVELOPMENT

This text defines *rapid development* as an approach in which, after having identified manageable candidates for incremental implementation, the team rapidly proceeds through all of the high-level analysis, intermediate-level analysis, detailed analysis, implementation modeling, design, coding, and testing for the selected piece. There are many strategies for invoking this approach. As illustrated in Figure 3.4, each piece may be completed before embarking on the next piece (Example 1); they may all be done at the same time (Example 2); or they may be done in a step-wise fashion, where later increments lag slightly behind the initial tasks (Example 3).

An excellent example of this approach to developing an effective strategy would be one in which, as part of the depth-sounding effort described for the Sizing phase, the team takes the candidate pieces through the implementation modeling phase or, sometimes, all the way to completion.

3.14 PROTOTYPING

The strategies of incremental implementation and rapid development have been enhanced in recent years by prototyping tools. Prototyping (basically a throwaway concept) stems from engineering principles which advise that a mock-up model of the product be built and tested before costly full-scale manufacture. This technique acknowledges that the development experience is often the only tool that the builders have for even beginning to understand the problem. There are many advantages of prototyping:

- It provides a fast and inexpensive approach to testing a working mock-up of the final product. The traditional approach often makes the time between the recognition of a problem and the implementation of its solution simply take too long. Furthermore, it assumes that the users know *all* of their requirements at a given point in time, that the requirements won't change, and that new requirements won't surface. There is a lot to be learned by experimentation— and the many changes that usually occur can be made quickly and easily to throwaway models. There are many people who argue that paper throwaway models are less expensive than technically-developed throwaway models. This may be true—if only one model is to be built. The advantage to technically-developed models is that, in a mature prototyping environment, fewer of them may be needed.

- The beauty of prototyping is that complete specifications are a by-product of the experience—not a prerequisite.

Figure 3.4 Rapid development.

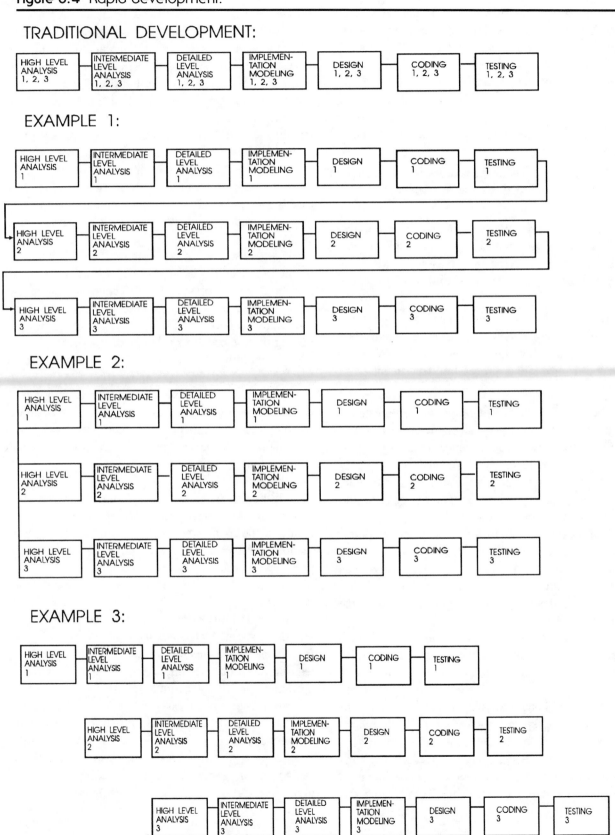

TRADITIONAL DEVELOPMENT:

EXAMPLE 1:

EXAMPLE 2:

EXAMPLE 3:

- The use of incremental prototyping provides a way of allowing users and developers to get early feedback on the system's idiosyncracies and subsequently build a series of successively more enhanced versions, incorporating user experience into each enlarged subset of the product—until the whole problem has been solved. Major misunderstandings, errors, omissions, ambiguities, and inconsistencies are easily discovered—and then eliminated during subsequent refinements.

- Because of immediate and sustained involvement by the customers, there exists a sense of ownership and, therefore, commitment to success.

- It provides an opportunity to capitalize on the positive benefits of group dynamics by allowing the team to learn to work together in a reasonably low-pressure environment while they build team spirit and confidence.

- In an effective data base environment, users can sometimes independently create and maintain their own systems; other times, they can do so with assistance from the data processing department.

The ability to do prototyping has been enhanced in recent years by technological improvements in data base technology, application generators, fourth generation level languages, sophisticated user-friendly screen and report generators, sophisticated user-friendly query languages, easy-to-use graphics packages, and parameter-driven applications packages.

Prototyping, as a formal development discipline, is still in its evolutionary stages. There are many definitions of the term itself, and just as many ideas on how to implement its concepts. (Simply calling the development strategy prototyping does not *make* it prototyping.)

One popular school does not do much, if any, formal analysis and design and believes that the entire system is built by continued refinement of disposable prototypes until the product is completed. An alternate school believes that prototyping is not a replacement for the traditional specification phases. While recognizing that conventional analysis is still necessary for identifying the core of data base requirements and internal data manipulation, these practitioners capitalize on the new technologies by using them *during* the

analysis and design phases to do *hands on* prototyping (modeling and testing) of the screens and reports.

Another common approach is to develop the prototype using a very high level language or application generator along with a sophisticated relational data base. The user may then use the prototype for a trial period. Any necessary improvements are made to the existing or new prototype; and, if the performance of the finished product is satisfactory, it is put into production. However, if performance improvement is necessary, the sluggish portion of the system will be rewritten, using a more efficient language and the prototype as the specification for the finished product.

The tradeoffs of improved machine performance should be measured against the increased costs of maintaining code written in the more efficient but harder to maintain procedural language. Hearty advocates of applications generators and fourth generation languages strongly believe that all such prototypes should become production versions of the system. Believers of optimizing the use of CPU cycles favor rewrites.

In building the first prototype, developers only need to concern themselves about what they currently know of the system's behavior. As they work with this first subset (and subsequent versions), they figure out the necessary enhancements and go forward from there. Ideally, the development of each prototype should take no longer than a few weeks to, at most, a few months.

If the group chooses to prototype during the analysis phase(s), they may quickly capture the business data and the associated business rules as well as the man/machine interfaces. They may also develop the prototype incrementally. For example:

Increment 1: Naive screen menus and simple screen layouts.

Increment 2: Fully populated screens; simple editing; and more sophisticated menus.

Increment 3: All business functions; fully populated data base; all on/line functionality.

Increment 4: All batch functionality.

While this most assuredly reduces the analysis time and may replace design with simply revising the prototype, the risks are that some important business functions may be missed or, what's worse, premature design decisions may be made; decisions which may ultimately force rework of earlier deliverables.

If the prototyping is initiated during the Implementation Modeling phase, the scope has already been clearly defined and the data base structure has been largely stabilized. On the other hand, uncovering new requirements at this stage may exact a significant amount of analysis rework.

The ability to develop large systems faster and cheaper is certainly a benefit. But it is essential to insure that the system is really solving the right problem and that the team has not chosen this method simply because it's new and state-of-the-art. In novice environments, the project effort may be shortened but may negatively impact operating costs, reliability, service and morale.

3.15 DISTRIBUTION OF EFFORT ACROSS PHASES

In the early and unsophisticated days of systems development, projects were often on time and within budget all of the way through the project—until testing. Somehow these projects got to be very, very late during the testing phase. As a result, it only took getting burned once before the smart participants realized that falling behind in testing was not such a good idea. Their solution was simply to hurry through the early phases so they'd have more time during testing. (The sooner teams fall behind, the more time they have to catch up.) They'd frequently wind up spending 40 to 60 percent of the project on the testing phase. As a result, the traditional resource loading curve looked something like Figure 3.5. Note the heavy buildup of resources during the later part of the project.

However, these people weren't actually testing

in that dubious phase. They were actually completing the unfinished analysis and design (the omissions, ambiguities, errors, and conflicts) that had been dragged along from the uncompleted early phases.[3] (See Figure 3.7. below.)

3.15.1 Software Projects Are Not Like Construction Projects

Experts in systems management now acknowledge that 40–65 percent of requirements errors may arise from poor analysis and design. Furthermore, the cost to fix errors discovered during testing may be 15–75 times more to fix than if they are found during analysis. It seems logical, then, to ask: why not front-load the effort and spend 40–65 percent of the operation during analysis and design—that is, shift the distribution of effort to the beginning of the project? (See Figure 3.6.) Analysis and design will be done! It's just a question of when they will be done and how much the organization is willing to pay for them. Why not do the job right in the first place, especially when what's being done in testing is mostly analysis and design anyway, and at a higher premium?

But what a change in the mindset of the organization this kind of an approach requires—because many people believe, "Project teams are not doing

---

[3] Think about it! When an error is discovered during testing, the programmer must (1) analyze what's wrong; (2) analyze what's right; (3) design the solution; (4) rewrite the code; and (5) carry on. There is more analysis and design going on during testing than anything else.

Figure 3.5 Traditional resource curve.

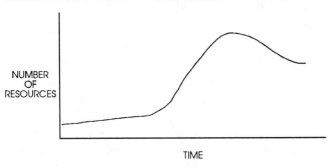

Figure 3.6 Suggested resource curve.

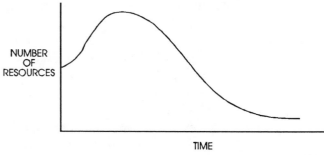

Figure 3.7 Poor analysis and design.

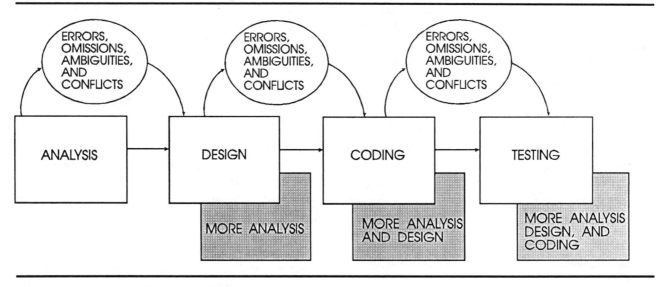

anything meaningful until they're writing code.'' People are not used to spending 40 percent to 65 percent of the project before they start building the product—but that's what it takes to build quality systems. Similarly, to provide quality software project management, organizations will have to divorce themselves from their construction project notions and embrace new ways of addressing the management issues. This text will address many of these concepts.

Experience indicates that a good percentage distribution of effort over the project life cycle might be 1, 10, 30, 10, 10, and 15 for the first six phases respectively, with the rest of the effort allocated to Installation, project management, and other miscellaneous activities. Notice that, unlike construction projects, which seem to breeze through the early phases, in a systems project, 60 percent of the effort may be expended before any coding starts!

As a final suggestion, participants are advised NOT to use these percentages to gauge time and money to completion. In other words, a one-month effort for Phase 2 does not necessarily imply that the rest of the project (''the other 90 percent'') will take 9 more months. The fallacy in that assumption catches up with its users in the later phases—stemming from a common misunderstanding regarding what level of detail constitutes completion of those phases, how long it should take to get to that level of detail and how many people should be employed to reach the goals. Traditionally,

project teams are either overly optimistic in their estimate of where they are, or worse, are pressured by the organization into reporting that they are much further along than they really are. Of course, when this situation occurs, project teams find themselves spending another 90 percent of their effort finishing up the last 10 percent of the project.

Project managers are cautioned to adapt (not blindly adopt) the application of these percentages to their particular project. In projects that are exact rewrites of existing systems, allocating 65 percent to analysis and design may be overkill. On the other hand, if the project is a first-time effort to develop an on-line, distributed processing system that also incorporates a new database management system, it may be necessary to increase the percentage.

3.16 GROUP DEVELOPMENT DYNAMICS

Effective systems development and maintenance is no small feat. Trying to get a group of individuals (with often wildly divergent goals and objectives) to agree on a single definition of the business and technical features of the system is, at best, difficult and, at times, nearly impossible. The problem (and project time and costs) is exacerbated when team members go around and around in one-on-one interviews, trying to nail down requirements.

There are no simple solutions to this problem.

However, the implementation of group development workshops has been of significant benefit in easing the pain.[4] The premise is so simple that it's startling: simply get everybody in one room (at the same time) to discuss the requirements, to resolve conflicting opinions, and to develop a specification that is understood and accepted. For example, in any project with a size that warrants it, a group dynamics workshop is a very effective arena in which to identify the domain of study.

A number of group development workshops may be conducted, each for several days at a time. Ideally, the workshops are held in an isolated environment where interruptions are eliminated or, at least, kept to a minimum. The participants are selected based on the type of specifications being addressed: for example, users in analysis workshops, systems technicians in design workshops, etc.

Group development workshops can be repeated many times in each of the phases, with the agenda of each workshop being directed to the type of specification being addressed. There are several key factors to success:

- The project participants must understand the objectives of each phase and what type of specification is supposed to be produced during each phase. Otherwise, the work may be done at the wrong time, requiring rework, missed target dates, and perhaps resulting in the group development workshop being blamed for the failure.

- The right participants must be matched to the corresponding workshop. For example, the users who attend an analysis workshop must know the data and business policies of the feature being specified.

- The participants must be available for each workshop. This often requires significant commitment from the organization, because large projects often require many workshops.

- The agenda must be precise or the meeting will be undirected. Accomplishment will be limited. The process will lose credibility and be abandoned.

- No workshop should be held without an agenda and a clear statement of the objectives to be achieved and deliverables to be produced.

- The facilitator must be accomplished in application knowledge, specification techniques, and the management of group dynamics. Such superpeople are not easy to find, but without a good facilitator, the workshops often deteriorate into apathetic meetings or nonproductive shouting matches. Furthermore, without enough qualified facilitators, workshop scheduling backs up significantly.

- There must be an accepted process for resolving conflicts that arise during the workshop and procedures for documenting and subsequently answering issues that can not be resolved during the workshop.

An organizational commitment to develop expertise in this approach appears to have a high payback and significant improvements in productivity.

3.17 IN CONCLUSION

The project team must objectively assess the pros and cons of any development approach, evaluating the potential selection against its ability to meet their project objectives. Consequently, developing an extensive understanding of the process of *Building the System* is one of the essential components for mastering project success.

---

[4] IBM's *Joint Application Design*, Boeing Computer Services Co.'s *Consensus*, Western Institute of Software Engineering's *WISE*, Performance Resources, Inc.'s *The Method*, and M. G. Rush Inc.'s *FAST*.

4 WORK BREAKDOWN STRUCTURES

4.1 INTRODUCTION

When managers try to plan a project without being able to reference an internal corporate project history file, a methodology checklist, or even a book, they may simply draw a blank and be stymied about where to start. Unless they have some preexisting template of project plans, this first step may initially be very hard. Conversely, if there *is* an existing template, and it is comprehensive and correct, this first step may be very abbreviated, or even non-existent.

In either case, there's no such thing as a single project plan that will work on every project, in every corporation, every time. Therefore, even in the simplest and most rudimentary projects, there must be some effective way to develop and verify the goals, objectives, major milestones and deliverables, and the individual jobs that must be accomplished in order for the project to be a success.

Consequently, the project management masters designed, among other things, Work Breakdown Structures, Network Charts, and Bar Charts. The work breakdown structure (WBS) is an extension of an organizational chart. However, in this case, it is drawn to depict the essential components of the project. Initially, WBSs are developed because they help to identify the major project deliverables and break them into

individual workunits (the inch-pebbles), insuring that the work gets done and that people don't waste their time doing "stuff." The process is rigorous enough to drive practitioners to remembering the essential components; yet, at the same time, it streamlines an otherwise intricate planning effort by partitioning the project into manageable pieces. Thus, it is possible to work on only one phase (or milestone) at a time.

In spite of the value of WBSs, people frequently try to begin the planning effort with a network chart or a bar chart. On smaller projects, this strategy may suffice—especially when the participants have an excellent understanding of the environment and the application. However, on larger and more complex projects, there ought to be some kind of conceptual preplanning process. Otherwise, when project teams are faced with conjuring up the data to use as input to the drawing process, they may hit a brick wall. If they can develop a global view of the project—what their objectives are, what major deliverables must be completed in order to achieve these objectives; and what groups of individual achievements will be necessary to produce the major deliverables—the wall often crumbles. The WBS provides us with this perspective. It lends itself to any view of project organization that the group deems appropriate, and becomes the foundation for partitioning the project into governable units that can be reasonably planned, tracked, and managed.

4.2 WORK BREAKDOWN STRUCTURES: A VIEW OF PROJECT ORGANIZATION

At the highest level, the team ought to start with the project's major objective. (See Figure 4.1.) The second level represents significant achievements to be met. The third level provides visibility for the management milestones. Then, the structure is continuously divided into levels and sublevels until the lowest level, the inch-pebble, is reached. Each lower level represents a natural set of work that must be completed in order to produce the deliverable from which it descends. The naming conventions for the levels vary from organization to organization.

The development of a WBS is iterative. It is important to remember that, during the first pass at creating it, the WBS will not necessarily be complete. This first pass is done at a high level and is not intended to take the whole project—or even the current phase—down to the inch-pebble level. Some of the high level is done, then some estimating, then some dependencies are identified, and then some scheduling is done. And while all of this is going on, the work breakdown structure is continuously refined, each time going further down and into more detail—until the inch-pebble level is finally reached. Ideally, this operation is completed with graphics software; however, if there is no software or no support in the available software for WBSs and if the organization has accepted the moving window concept, manual completion may not be too difficult.

4.3 REFINING THE WBS PARTITIONING

When drawing the WBS, it's a good idea to just let it evolve rather than try to force it into a preconceived structure. The first draft may be created partially top-down and partially bottom-up, subsequently connecting the two somewhere in the middle. In this manner, practitioners will find that not all of the inch-pebbles will be reached at the same level. In other words, at any given level there may be a mixture of major deliverables, intermediate deliverables, inch-pebbles, etc. Similarly, it is sometimes advantageous to go part of the way down the structure, then to regroup upward, repeating this up and down exercise until satisfied that the best partitioning has been achieved.

4.4 CHOOSING A WBS PERSPECTIVE

Later on, during the management of the project, various groups within the organization will want to receive information about the project. Each area may want their own customized view of the data. It is important to establish the reporting structure *before* the project begins—so that the WBS will support these views. Also, once the partitioning has started, it is not unusual to find that there's more than one way to divide the WBS, and they may all be correct. The choice that's selected may be driven by how the group wants to report costs (often related to the financial chart of accounts), status, or by the technical allocation of work. It may designate the way the organization wants to allocate the management of certain pieces of the project (and, therefore, show control levels for project management), or the way the group wants to give visibility to success criteria. Furthermore, when trying to allocate resources, WBSs may help to distribute the work units across resource pools. This is especially true when the work may cross more than one department boundary or when some of the participants may only spend part-time on the project.

4.4.1 Work Breakdown Structures Support Rollup Totals

Similarly, the project team will usually be required to report summary totals of money, durations, and people expenditures. These accounts are recaps based on several levels of intermediate totals, where each of the tallies is progressively rolled up to the next level into aggregate totals. This reporting structure is defined via an encrypting scheme (the WBS code) that supports the desired rollup totals.

Thus the length and structure of the WBS code is very important, since it determines the number of levels and reporting views that will be used in sorting the project data. Similarly, it provides direct access to any project record, instead of scanning sequentially through the file looking for a particular work unit.

Users[1] are frequently advised to number the jobs in ascending order by multiples of 5 or 10, so they

---

[1] From now on, the term *user* will be used interchangeably with project management practitioner.

can insert additional jobs as they are identified. However, it is not unusual to run out of the intervening numbers as well and then begin a frenzied renumbering exercise. Rather than fall prey to this timewaster, it is preferable to simply view the numbers as part of the rollup scheme (do they support it or not?) and if they get out of sequence, just don't worry!

A cursory evaluation of the rollup features supported in each of the software packages is provided in the sections that relate to Chapter 4 in each appendix. More specific uses of the rollup feature may be found in the chapters on managing the project.

4.4.2 Sample Work Breakdown Structures

The work breakdown structure lends itself to describing any view of project organization that the group deems appropriate. Here are several ways of partitioning the *same* project:

Example 1 (Figure 4.1). A common approach to partitioning the WBS is by phase deliverables. It is traditional to then divide the phases by major milestones, the milestones by major deliverables, the major deliverables by intermediate deliverables, and so on until the inch-pebbles are identified. Note the coding scheme used in each level.

Example 2 (Figure 4.2). Sometimes, it is important to divide the phases by the work that is done to *Build the System* and *Manage the Project.* Also illustrated is the desire to differentiate, at the major deliverable level, between software development and the support components. Notice, at the bottom level, the introduction of a coding scheme.

Example 3 (Figure 4.3). In some projects, there

Figure 4.1 The standard work breakdown structure (example 1).

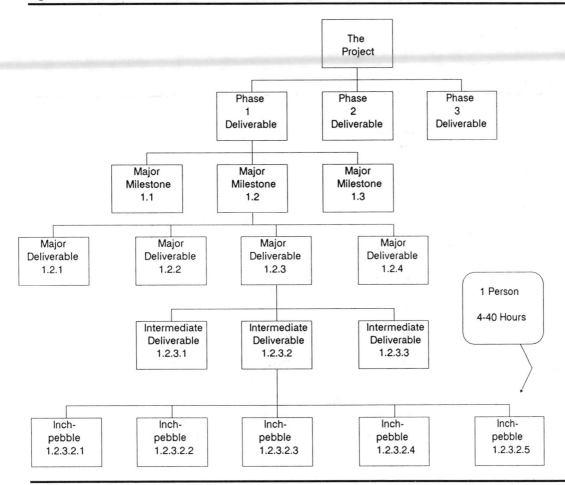

Figure 4.2 Example 2.

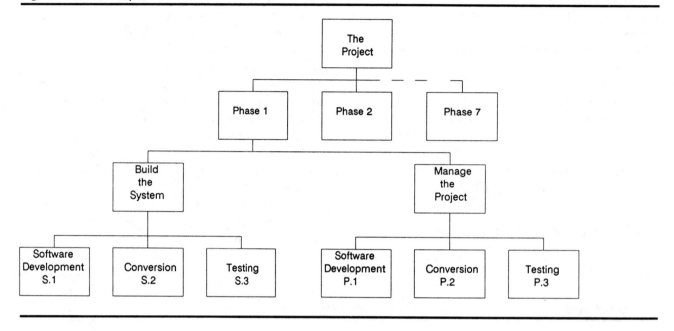

Figure 4.3 Example 3.

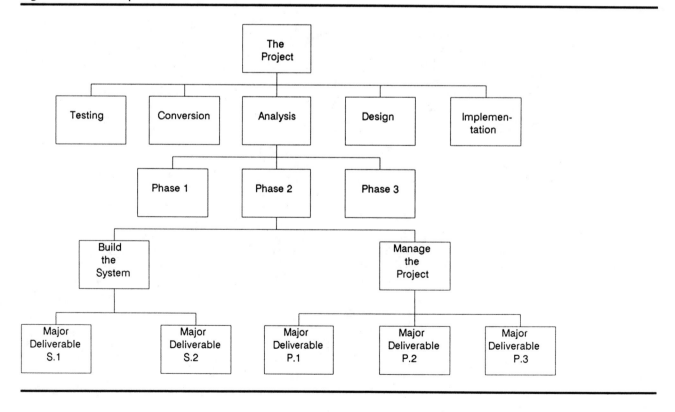

is a desire to roll up all of a support component effort into one total, the business analysis effort into another total, the technical design into a third total, and the installation costs into a fourth total. The next level down represents each phase in which the corresponding work is done.

Example 4 (Figure 4.4). If measurement of project management is an important part of the success criteria; the highest levels may be partitioned into *Build the System* and *Manage the Project*.

Careful examination of the lowest level in Figure 4.4 will show the planning activities in the *moving window of commitment* that occur at the end of every phase. (Note the continuation of the coding scheme.) The plan is done (1) in detail for the next phase; (2) at a high level for the rest of the project; and (3) with the totals added together to come up with a current assessment number. This illustration demonstrates that certain groups of jobs may be repeated over and over again in the project. These jobs may be called the *template* tasks. Ideally, the *template* tasks are set up once (perhaps in a stand-alone unit) and then inserted

whenever and wherever they are needed. Users will not have to rekey these jobs every time they are needed. Saving these frequently used portions of a workplan in a separate file and then recalling them whenever necessary can significantly reduce the time and cost of planning. When *template* tasks are repeated in each phase, their WBS codes must be unique in each occurrence. This is done in order to support the unique rollup tallies. In this text, it will be assumed that the *template* jobs have been stored in a separate plan.

Users who work with an existing methodology may find that it may drive the WBS—either explicitly or implicitly. If so, they should certify that it is the WBS they truly want.

4.4.3 Work Breakdown Structures: Reporting, Communicating, and Negotiating

It is easy to see that the number of permutations is truly varied. When the group has finally agreed on the view that best satisfies their need, they ought to devise a numbering scheme for the WBS that allows them to

Figure 4.4 Example 4.

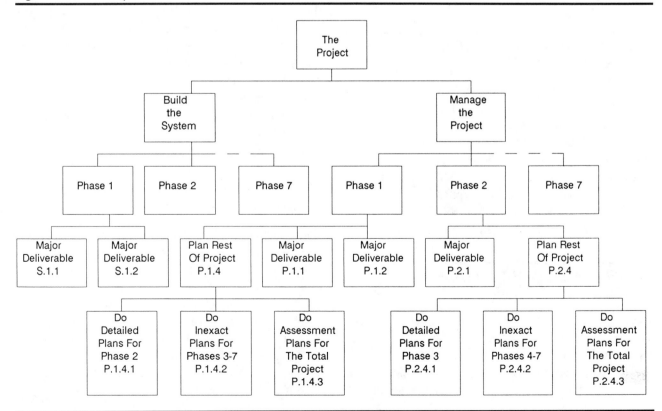

sort on various fields and extract the data from many different views. Thus, the reporting possibilities are infinite.

One of the many graphic aids of the Project Management Process that support effective communication, the WBS is valuable in the negotiation process. It allows the group to pick from various levels of detail for presentations on a need-to-know basis. For example, presentations to executive management may show the highest levels. On the other hand, workers find satisfaction in also seeing the lowest levels.

4.5 ELIMINATING THE UNNECESSARY *STUFF* FROM THE WORKDAY

Work breakdown structures are aids in the crusade to eradicate *stuff* from the daily activities. To begin with, it is hard to find a place to put the *stuff*. On the other hand, when these unrelated items are somehow wedged into the WBS, they often stick out like a sore thumb. If the team can't justify making the entry into the WBS (i.e., justify putting it in a plan in which the jobs produce *necessary deliverables*), they should question if they really want to be doing the work represented by the entry.

4.6 WEAKNESSES IN THE WORK BREAKDOWN STRUCTURE

While the work breakdown structure is very helpful in getting started with the planning effort, its users sometimes become frustrated because of its weaknesses. The WBS does not show the order in which the jobs are executed, nor does it show the dependencies between the jobs. Another picture is still needed to give this perspective; and this is where the network chart will come in. Nevertheless, this tool won't be thrown away simply because it doesn't do *everything*.

4.7 WEAKNESSES IN THE PLANNING PROCESS

Regardless of which graphic aid is selected, it is very difficult to illustrate decision points (and their respective branches) pictorially. Similarly, there is no way to say "do these four jobs ten times" or "do this set of jobs until they are right." In this last example, users

must put each group of jobs into the plan the required number of times.

Other problems in the planning process come in the form of overcompensation. In the beginning, many novices have a tendency to overfragmentize their plans and to add too many inch-pebbles. However, in the short run, to err on the detailed side is much better than to miss some important jobs that do not become part of the plan. (Besides, the smaller the estimate, the better the confidence level and the lower the margin of error.) On the other hand, omitting work is a more serious problem, of course, since it may cause the team to miss target dates. And in the long run, overfragmentation is still not as serious as it sounds. If given the support to proceed with learning the process, the workers will soon develop the feel for when to stop partitioning and will produce much better plans.

4.8 WORK BREAKDOWN STRUCTURES AND PROJECT MANAGEMENT SOFTWARE

Even though the project management community acknowledges the value of using WBSs to plan and manage the project, many software products do not feature work breakdown structures as a significant element of their systems. However, it is not unusual to find products that do refer to the necessity of initializing projects by using WBSs to identify objectives and goals, but then mysteriously gloss over their creation. Work breakdown structures definitely seem to take a back seat compared to bar charts and networks. Nevertheless, in the sampling, there are a few highly acceptable products, and several relatively satisfactory products. None were rejected.

4.8.1 Does the System Support Work Breakdown Structures At All?

The packages were initially separated into two categories—those that feature graphic work breakdown structures as a component of the product and those that do not.

Two of the products feature work breakdown graphics: Harvard Project Manager 3.0 and Super-Project Expert. The other systems allow the user to designate the WBS according to indentations in an outline style or by simply using a WBS code to establish a rollup sequence.

Figure 4.5 A partitioning scheme for evaluating WBS features.

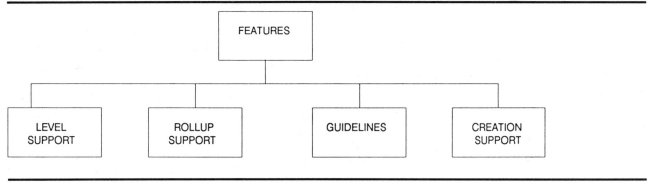

The products were then further partitioned into evaluations of their level support, rollup support, guidelines, and creation support. (See Figure 4.5.)

4.8.2 Graphics Support   ♦ [2]

Does the package graphically illustrate work breakdown structures? How easy is it to continue to create entries at the same level?

How easy is it to create a new level? People who truly wish to use the WBS approach, and who also use packages without WBS graphics support, will often discover that it may be necessary initially to manually draw some (or all) of the WBS—in all but the simplest projects.

4.8.3 Level Support   ♦

Is there a limit on the number of levels within a WBS? Is it possible to have four or five levels? Is there a limit on the number of entries at each level? Is it easy to modify and update the WBS? Is it easy to move entries from level to level?

The number of levels is often related to the identification number that is assigned to the job. That is, the number of levels is directly dependent on the pattern that can be derived from the number of positions in the identifier. Some products require that a special character (such as a period) be used as a delimiter

---

between the levels. Other products ask the user to create a WBS template that tells the system where the breaks are. One product relies on a one-character entry to tell the system which of its three levels to apply. Another class of products simply relies on rollup patterns that are entered at report time. The most serious limitation here occurs in those products that require delimiters *and* also only have a small number of characters with which to work. Then, the number of levels and the number of entries within each level may be sorely constrained.

All of the packages allow any mix of levels. The number of entries per level is driven by the total number of records per project.

4.8.4 Data Entry Requirements   ♦

Are the options described in level support easy to implement, or must the user try to *work-around* the software? In other words, does the software require an additional system identification number that is not part of the WBS for each job? As a result, must users do a second entry (double data entry) of identification numbers if they want to use the WBS feature? How many identification numbers are there?

4.8.5 Durations and Dependencies   ♦

The WBS approach supports a true top-down development philosophy that does not require durations and dependencies to be identified at planning initiation. Mandatory durations require that estimates be com-

---

[2] The ♦ indicates that the corresponding section is discussed in each appendix.

pleted when planning begins. Entering *fake estimates* is a *work-around* alternative; but this requires extra data entry later on when the estimating process has been completed and the true estimates are known. Keeping track of those jobs with *fake estimates* versus those with valid estimates is time consuming, labor intensive, and subject to errors.

Drawing the work breakdown structure ought to be a flowing-type operation. That is, each level (or entry on the same level) should evolve, one to the other. Since a WBS doesn't normally show dependencies, requiring dependency connections complicates the process. Mandatory dependencies require that the network be completed when planning begins. Having to create a network or bar chart first in order to draw the WBS defeats the purpose. Furthermore, when dependencies are mandatory, unless they are completely and perfectly laid out, starting top down through the WBS sometimes creates a tangled mess of dependencies that may later require a frustrating and tedious effort to unravel.

Can the work breakdown structure be created without durations and dependencies?

4.8.6 Random Sequence of Data Entry ♦

If project data is added with the outline or bar chart modes, can it be added in random sequence, and then reorganized into the right position? This is an important feature, because not all levels (or parts within a level) of a plan have been identified when the planner starts developing the plan. Therefore, the support of random data entry becomes an advantage as the plan becomes more detailed.

Network driven systems, by nature, do not allow the random placement of workunits. However, if finding the correct position and the subsequent introduction of the job are easy enough, this may not be a terrible detriment—even though it does not support WBSs.

Can project data be added in alternative modes (e.g., via outline, bar chart, or networks)? If random data entry is not supported, how rigid is the structured data entry?

Will the system support random data entry while maintaining the correct WBS reporting structures *and* the correct and natural inter- and intraproject dependencies?

4.8.7 Using the Copy Features with the *Template* Tasks ♦

The copy feature and its use with the *template* task is given a cursory introduction in this chapter. Its deeper implications will be discussed in more detail later.

Is it easy to copy the *template tasks* repetitively—in order to avoid duplicating data entry—and insert them in several different branches of the structure?

Regardless of which product is chosen, when the identification number is used for the WBS recognition and when that same identification number is a mandatory field to originally create the *template* tasks, the user may be faced with significant re-entry of this field.

4.8.8 Rollup Support ♦

When planning to use the project management software, project teams should take care to first fully specify their rollup reporting requirements and the WBS numbering scheme that will support them. Then, the reporting capabilities of the software package ought to be evaluated to insure that it will support the required numbering scheme and rollup requirements. Some modifications to the user's numbering scheme may be necessary. Then, and only then, can the WBS be created with the system.

Remember, the goal of a WBS is to help partition the project into manageable pieces with manageable deliverables, and the goal of the rollups is to be able to report on and manage those small pieces and deliverables. If these goals are not satisfied, if the modifications to the rollup specifications and numbering scheme are excessive, and if the purchase of the package has not been finalized, it may be advisable to reconsider the choice.

In graphics and outline mode, if the rollup reporting is to be accurate, the users must often insure that the jobs are inserted into their correct positions in the WBS scheme. As discussed earlier, they may not always be entered in a random pattern. On the other hand, when the rollups are driven simply by the WBS code, regardless of where in the plan the job was placed, random entry is acceptable. What level of key structure (in either the system identification number or the WBS field) is supported for reporting on the desired rollups? Will the key structure support the WBS and the required rollups? Does the product provide standard reports that satisfy the rollup reporting requirements? If not, will the system support customized reporting on the desired rollup views? How easy are the standard and customized reporting features to use? In a WBS similar to Figure 4.2, is it possible to report on all of the support component activity (e.g., all of testing)—even when it occurs in two branches of the structure (e.g. *Build the System* and *Manage the Project*)? Sometimes report selection is completed by extracting the data that matches a string of characters. The character string can be set up so that some of the positions can take any value (for example, ''&'' means any value is correct) or so that other positions will not be compared at all (for example, ''#'' means don't look at that character). When this occurs, the character string is often referred to as a *wildcard*. Several products support wild-card selection.

A virtue not to be found in many of the products reviewed is the feature where, with no extra effort on the part of the user, the rollup on the duration field computes—not the total work effort—but rather the total timespan of the level entries below the selected level. This rolled up timespan is based on the cumulative time-spans of any sequence of tasks on the corresponding lower level. For example, it is possible to see, at a glance, the duration of a major deliverable —based on the sequence and durations of the intermediate deliverables under it. Naturally, the application of this feature requires the completion of the network (and dependencies) first. Consequently, its value is fully realized later in the planning process, making this a very helpful feature.

4.8.9 Guidelines ♦

Are there project management guidelines in the user's manual? Is there any documentation in the user's man-

ual to describe the process of using work breakdown structures in project management (e.g., describing what a WBS is and why to do it)? If the product supports a complex WBS, does the documentation provide clear instructions on how to optimize its use? (Instructions on how to use the system to achieve the implementation of a feature are not considered guidelines.)

4.9 COMPLETING THE WORK BREAKDOWN PROCESS

After the team has finished the partitioning of the project (or phase) down to the inch-pebble level, they still have a *very important* job to perform. This operation pertains to the gathering and recording of data, much of which will become *essential* when the job is actually assigned to the individual who is designated to do it. Work packages will be prepared for each assignee. Some of the information that should be entered by the project team follows:

- A brief narrative describing the job;
- The tools and skills required to complete the job;
- The identification of the deliverable that is to be produced by the effort;
- The criteria for completion, success and acceptance;
- A list of reviewers and approvers;
- A list and description of any sub-tasks; and
- A list of potential consultants or advisors to the job.

Now is the time to prepare this data. Ideally, the information may be entered into the ad hoc notes in the record for each job.

CHAPTER 5 ESTIMATING

5.1 INTRODUCTION

To estimate, according to Webster, is to calculate *approximately* the value, size, or cost of something. It is a rough judgment or opinion based on thought or research. An estimate, acknowledging Burrill and Ellsworth, is a prediction "based on a probabilistic model, *not* a deterministic one—that is, the quantity being estimated can take not just one value but several values, with some more likely [to be correct] than others." Be that as it may, in spite of these conservative definitions, organizations have ambitious hopes for their estimates and what they represent.

5.2 DISPELLING ESTIMATING MYTHS

As a consequence, estimators should recall, at this point, how important it is to manage everyone's expectations—in this case, it's necessary to explain the estimating process in the Project Agreement. If people don't accept the premise that estimates provide approximations and, therefore, may not be cast in stone, then the whole planning process may become a charade.

5.2.1 Can Software Developers Esitmate Well?

Some people would insist that "accurate estimates" in the software industry are impossible. It even seems contradictory to put these two words together. To the contrary, in some organizations, there are groups that consistently give good estimates. Yet, the skill does not seem readily transferable. Sadly, many people do give very poor estimates. However, careful investigation has surprisingly shown that it isn't the estimate that has been so wrong. The problem often stems from the fact that the bulk of the effort required to complete the job is simply *overlooked* during the estimating process. In other words, it's what is left *out* of the estimate that usually gets the estimators into trouble.

5.2.2 When Can Software Developers Provide Reliable Estimates?

In this chapter, practitioners are reminded that, after the rapid sizing number, they may concentrate on producing primarily two kinds of estimates—the detailed estimates for the next phase, and the inexact plan for the rest of the project. For example, in the detailed plan for the next phase, the numbers will all be at the inch-pebble level, which is why that part of the plan is so reliable. But in the inexact plan, although the estimates may sometimes be at the intermediate level with an occasionally light sprinkling of inch-pebbles, they are often only at the major deliverable level and are, as a consequence, less accurate.

5.2.3 Can Estimating Be Done Procedurally?

It is not unusual to find groups that are looking for some universal estimating model or formula that will work in all companies in all projects all of the time. They are looking for a way to get the numbers without thinking (unreasonable) and to be assured that they will get the same results every time no matter who is doing the estimating (reasonable). Each company has unique people, skills, procedures, and (frequently) projects; and any use of formulas should be adjusted by these variables. Furthermore, these formulas should also be tempered by internal observation, experimentation, and practical experience. After the group has accumulated a history of results and the history represents a satisfactory population of a statistical database, it may be used, with confidence, to make predictions. Until that time, any numbers will be subject to the effects of the normal learning curve. That is, there will be some miscalculations and when they occur, there will be false starts, rework, and missed target dates.

Boehm[1] feels his project managers are doing well if they can come to within 20 percent of actual costs 70 percent of the time. However, it is important to recognize that *this accuracy is not expected until the end of* the phase that corresponds to Phase 3 in this text. His statistical database demonstrates that this goal can be accomplished.

Here again, it is important to recognize that Boehm's results were compiled from efforts using highly qualified project teams. How many estimators are experts or have experts doing the estimating? The disappointing reality is, unfortunately, that many organizations are not lucky enough to have an unlimited supply of superstar estimators. And when the average novice or intermediate is asked to use new estimating techniques, the organization ought to modify its expectations accordingly.

In the same vein, Jones (in personal correspondence) maintains that the historical data collected by many of the organizations he has observed is incomplete, and has omitted from 30 percent to 70 percent of the real costs of building the system. These over-

sights may include unpaid overtime (about 15 percent), user involvement, documentation, systems integration, quality assurance, and so on. Some companies do not even include the costs of project management. As a result of all of these omissions, a large number of organizations do not realize how bad their estimates really are.

Jones believes ±5 percent for effort and schedules, and ±15 percent for staffing to be good results. He further asserts that it is very easy to match historical data to within a few percentage points once projects are finished and all of the unknowns have surfaced. In a recent experiment against data published for 15 completed projects, his group came to within 9.2 percent for schedule accuracy and 0.56 percent for effort accuracy. Staffing data was not available in the original data set. On the other hand, Jones defends that it is much harder to achieve accurate results when estimating forward from some early point in the project, when many uncertain events are not yet clear.

5.2.4 Why Are Software Developers So Poor At Estimating?

To begin with, competent estimators, based on their superior performance, often get promoted to positions where their skill is no longer required. Then, newly elected estimators rarely find adequate procedures or sufficiently available skilled consultants from whom they can learn. This is compounded by the fact that there is rarely a project history file available for reference. Furthermore, in organizations where there is a generally inadequate understanding of the planning process and its value, lack of commitment for time and resources also affects estimating results. At least one of the advantages of using project management software is that it provides the foundation for just such a database.

5.2.5 Do Systems Projects Have Definitive Boundaries?

Estimates should reflect reality. But unless the group is developing the same system (or type of system) over and over again, the management of systems projects may turn into an attempt to manage in chaos and uncertainty. Consequently, it is difficult to hit the esti-

---

[1] B.W. Boehm, *SOFTWARE ENGINEERING ECONOMICS*, (New Jersey: Prentice-Hall, 1981).

mating numbers right on the button, so estimators look to come within some "likely range." Similarly, they look for strategies that will reflect their uncertainty and work effectively in climates of unpredictability. This will be explained in more detail later in the chapter.

5.2.6 Is There Anything Else That Can Be Done to Compensate for the Drawbacks?

From a scientific perspective, trust in the quality of an estimate increases when the size of the range of the estimate (the confidence interval) is small. The smaller the range, the higher the degree of confidence and the higher the probability that the estimate will be close to the actual result. The sum of these many small estimates has a higher likelihood of being close to actual than one large estimate. Inch-pebbles that are 4 to 40 hours in duration go far to support this premise.

5.2.7 When Should Software Developers Estimate?

No matter what phase of the project the team is currently working in, if there is no plan, they should produce one for the remaining effort. Nevertheless, it is not unusual to hear "Well, we're so far into this project that it doesn't pay to plan for this one. We'll plan the next one." To the contrary, *IT IS NEVER TOO LATE TO PLAN!*

5.2.8 Who Should Provide the Estimates?

Planning a systems project is not the exclusive property of the DP department. It's a good idea to get the group who will ultimately be responsible for producing the deliverable to provide the estimates for its completion. In other words, the estimate should be furnished by either a candidate who could actually do the work or the supervisor of a group of candidates, with input from the group. Similarly, if the work is to be completed by a group outside of the DP department, then the estimates should be contributed by that group. The two most significant benefits of this tactic are (1) involvement of the estimators, thus generating their sense of ownership and, therefore, commitment to success; and (2) a more reliable appraisal of the influencing variables that can affect the outcome.

5.3 ESTIMATING STEPS

The following set of steps may prove to be a valuable guideline to estimating:

Step 1: select the estimating technique(s). If the participants are not experienced in the technique(s), allow extra time for the learning period.

Step 2: determine the data requirements.

Step 3: define the planning process.

Step 4: automate as much as possible.

Step 5: produce the estimates.

Step 6: save the results in an accumulated history file, recalibrate as necessary, and make the data available to everyone in the company.

5.4 STEP 1: SELECTING THE ESTIMATING TECHNIQUES

As a group, the data processing community has been unable to agree upon one commonly accepted estimating technique. Because this discipline is still so new, no models have yet progressed into becoming the standard. Nevertheless, two basic approaches to software estimating have evolved: a macro approach and a micro approach. Using a top down perspective, macro techniques first apply equations which will compute the *total* project effort and then invoke supplemental methods for distributing the results across a discrete set of phases or milestones. The micro techniques use a bottom up approach: (1) partitioning the project according to a predetermined work breakdown structure, (2) estimating each job in the WBS separately, and then (3) summing all of the estimates to derive total project costs.

Since there is no single estimating approach that is better than all of the others all of the time, it may be beneficial if organizations use more than one appraisal technique. Using several of these approaches in combination can compensate for the inherent weaknesses of each of the stand-alone pieces. The results could then be compared, necessary adjustments made (based, for example, on experience and/or levels of expertise), and the process repeated until satisfied. Employing several methods and comparing the results is especially important if accuracy is essential.

Various macro methods are based on estimating lines of code, which are in turn used to derive measurements of time, resource requirements, and costs. The more technical of these approaches have evolved from early contributions popularized by Norden and Putnam.

Norden of IBM concluded that, in research and development projects, there are well-defined and predictable manpower loading patterns which fit the mathematical formula for a Rayleigh distribution. He also demonstrated that each phase in a project does not completely finish before the subsequent phase begins. With respect to the work effort, the phases actually overlap each other.

Putnam (later with Wolverton or Fitzsimmons) applied Norden's concepts to macro-level estimating for the code generation aspect of software development projects, describing consistent patterns for staffing levels in the corresponding project phases. This approach allowed estimators to specify the project size (in lines of code) as well as to also independently factor in the impacts of technical complexity and technical ability. It also applied the PERT micro estimating techniques, described later in this chapter.

Interestingly, neither the Norden nor the Putnam and Fitzsimmons[2] estimates address the work that is done in the phases that are equivalent to Phases 1 to 3 in this text. Although Putnam and Fitzsimmons do acknowledge the need to do a systems requirements definition, their estimates for development are presumed to start somewhere in the phase that corresponds to Phase 4.

Furthermore, these approaches are driven by Norden's assumption that the manpower distribution curve is based on a Rayleigh distribution which allocates the greatest percentage of effort to coding, testing, and internal system integration—processes which are equivalent to part of Phases 4 and 7 and all of Phases 5 and 6 of this text. It is important to bear in mind that the macro methods are based on historical data and that these measurements reflect projects which have used traditional development practices. Current experiences in software engineering have shown that more time should be spent during analysis and design, therefore suggesting that these rates may no longer be wholly satisfactory in organizations using state-of-the-art development techniques.

Two well-known lines of code estimating techniques that are based on Norden's and Putnam's concepts will be discussed in this chapter: Boehm's Constructive Cost Model[3] and Jensen's Macrolevel Software Development Estimation Model.

Lines of code estimating techniques are not the only way to go, however. As a matter of fact, they have certain limitations—which will be discussed later in this chapter. Two prominent micro estimating alternatives—Function Point Analysis and the Program Evaluation and Review Technique—will also be presented here. However, they, too, are not infallible; and their weakness will also be addressed.

5.4.1 COCOMO

One of the more popular estimating approaches, Barry Boehm's Constructive Cost Model (COCOMO), is as much intended as a costing model as it is an estimating tool. Centered around estimating the final count of delivered source code instructions (DSIs), the formulas in the technique are based on an historical data base of 63 projects—e.g., business, scientific, interactive, operating system software projects and so on. Instructions, job control language, format statements, and data declarations are considered part of the count while comments and unmodified utility software are not. The majority of the systems in Boehm's were written in FORTRAN or ASSEMBLY language.

To begin, Boehm categorizes projects into three different types—organic, embedded, and semidetached. For each of these types of projects there are subsequently three separate respective sets of COCOMO models—basic COCOMO, intermediate COCOMO, and detailed COCOMO. These sets of respective models are applied at different points in the project, with the exponents and coefficients in the for-

---

[2] L.H. Putnam & A. Fitzsimmons, *Estimating Software Costs*, Datamation, (September, 1979. Continued in October, 1979 and November, 1979.)

[3] Ibid

mulas varying according to whether the system is classified as organic, semidetached, or embedded.

Organic projects. An organic project is highly manageable, one with limited numbers of people who are ideally experienced with the application and the environment. These projects are done in mature and stable development climates where there is not too much external pressure to meet imposed target dates. These are usually medium- to slightly larger than medium-sized projects.

Embedded projects. On the opposite extreme are embedded projects, research and development type projects in which, at the start, there may be many unknowns and undefined variables. They have large numbers of participants and therefore exact rigid interpersonal communications procedures. Embedded projects have highly structured requirements, little or no flexibility from rules, and are greatly constrained by time and budgets. These are usually large to very large projects.

Semidetached projects. A semidetached project falls somewhere between the two extremes of organic and embedded, exhibiting some characteristics of each type.

The formulas. There are three sets of formulas (basic COCOMO, intermediate COCOMO, and detailed COCOMO) for each of the three project types (organic, embedded, and semidetached). The basic COCOMO formulas yield results that are within 20 percent of actuals 25 percent of the time. Basic CO-COMO can be employed any time the team feels that they can estimate the final count of DSIs. In the early phases of the project, this may simply be based on intuition, past experience, or some other confidence source.

The remaining two sets of formulas are used in the *later* phases—those that approximate Phases 4 to 7 of this text. With intermediate and detailed CO-COMO, Phases 1 through 3 are each estimated independently and not as part of the whole project. This is an admirable implementation of the moving window concept! Intermediate COCOMO falls within 20 percent of actuals 68 percent of the time, while detailed COCOMO falls within 20 percent of actuals 70 percent of the time.

None of the COCOMO models include estimates for installation planning, user training, documentation and conversion; nor do they include computer operations, administrative support, upper management, and other such indirect costs. Additional formulas, however, are provided later in Boehm's book. All CO-COMO models assume that business requirements do not change substantially after the phase that corresponds to Phase 3 in this text; otherwise, it is also assumed the numbers will likely need to be revised.

The tables that Boehm provides are the key to application of these formulas. They contain values derived from smoothing the results of his 63 projects across a series of Rayleigh curves. The answers the users get (from running their numbers through the formulas) are then matched to the tables. If an exact match is not possible, the user is provided with formulas for interpolating the answers.

Basic COCOMO. Based on being able to make an educated guess early in the project on how many delivered lines of source code will be produced, basic COCOMO will give the total man months of effort, the total elapsed time, and the number of full time staff needed. It will also give an estimate and schedule of the distribution (i.e., percent) of effort across the phases. Boehm employs Norden's traditional manpower distribution curve in all of his formulas; i.e., he allocates a maximum of 6 to 8 percent of the total project effort to the first three phases and the greatest percentage of effort (48 to 68 percent) is spent on programming (defined as program design and coding —which are equivalent to part of Phase 4 and all of Phases 5 and 6 of this text).

At the beginning of the phase that corresponds to Phase 2 in this text, the application, with an 80 percent confidence range, of the basic COCOMO formulas provides results that are within 256 percent to 400 percent of final actuals (a factor of 4). The results, when basic COCOMO is applied at the beginning of Phase 3, match final actuals within 85 percent to 130 percent (a factor of 1.3) only 29 percent of the time and come to within 128 percent to 200 percent of the costs 60 percent of the time. Understandably, at these stages of the project, estimators shouldn't expect to get any better. While it may be very helpful for the rapid survey numbers or assessment numbers, basic COCOMO is not accurate enough for definitive budget negotiations or detailed project planning. This is primarily due to the fact that it only addresses DSIs and not the many other variables that can affect estimates. To quote Boehm:

> Basic COCOMO is good enough for early, rough orders of magnitude estimates, but its accuracy is necessarily limited because of its lack of factors to account for differences in hardware constraints, personnel quality and experience, use of modern tools and techniques, and other project attributes, known to have a significant influence on software costs.

Basic COCOMO also assumes average skill levels and no discontinuities of staff.

Intermediate COCOMO. Intermediate COCOMO takes into account 14 additional predictor variables that basic COCOMO does not address (e.g., type of application, experience of workers, number of inputs and outputs, computer configuration, number of approvals required, and so on). These cost-driver variables actually represent the averaged values of the multipliers used in the more detailed COCOMO model. Executed at the end of the phase that is equivalent to Phase 3 in this text, the intermediate COCOMO formulas provide estimates that come within 20 percent of actuals 68 percent of the time, the results being roughly equivalent in all three project types.

Like basic COCOMO, intermediate COCOMO will give the total man months of effort, the total elapsed time, the number of full-time staff needed, and an estimate of the distribution of effort across the phases.

Detailed COCOMO. When using intermediate COCOMO on very large projects, however, the distribution of effort across phases may be inaccurate. Therefore, detailed COCOMO is the suggested alternative when more specific information is required. For example, with this set of formulas, the project may be partitioned into significant milestones and these milestones may be charted against time and effort. Furthermore, detailed COCOMO weights specific cost drivers by phase. These phase sensitive multipliers are then driven by a three-level system hierarchy: module (and numbers of DSIs per module), subsystem (target dates, skills, tools, etc.), and system (overall project considerations). From Phase 4 until the end of the project, it will be helpful to identify the major milestones and then use detailed COCOMO to develop the

estimates for the remaining assessment numbers. It will certainly help to make the inexact plan far less inexact.

Work breakdown structures in COCOMO. With regard to work breakdown structures in the detailed COCOMO, Boehm takes the WBS for detailed COCOMO down to a fourth level, referred to as the module level. The completion of a module may take from 2 weeks to 15 man-months. Boehm's element (the lowest level) ranges from small projects: .5 man-months; to medium projects: 3 man-months; to very large projects: 15 man-months. This level appears to relate to this text's major or intermediate deliverable level, which, again, makes it useful for assessment planning.

Intermediate COCOMO only goes down to the third level.

From the end of the product design phase (equivalent to Phase 4 in this text) until project completion, he suggests that the supervisors create unit folders. A unit is defined as "a specific, well-defined deliverable, assignable to one person, and testable." It has all the earmarks of an inch-pebble, with the exception of size. Therefore, a unit is not assumed to be an inch-pebble; rather, it is presumed to be a major or intermediate level deliverable.

It is necessary to also establish procedures for (1) how to determine the start and finish dates of the jobs in the earlier phases that don't use unit folders; and (2) how the project is managed without unit folders in the earlier phases (that is, how status is reported and collected).

Project planning and control with COCOMO. This is an estimating chapter, and project control is slated to be discussed later in the book. However, since COCOMO has been addressed at this point, it is appropriate to add a word about using COCOMO for project management. Boehm suggests that "if you want to plan and control, you should use detailed COCOMO." Furthermore, after the supervisors create the unit folders described above, Boehm also indicates that they then meet with the worker to negotiate a start and end date of each unit. Thereafter, it is up to the worker to determine the start and end dates of the inch-pebbles within the unit. Since unit dates are driven by a COCOMO schedule, it may also be a good idea to provide procedures to determine what happens if, during the "negotiation," the workers feel that they are unable to meet these dates.

5.4.2 The Jensen Model for Software Development Estimation

The Jensen model provides estimates that reflect the effort to develop the *software* for the system. As such, it addresses the phases that are equivalent to Phases 5, 6, and the first part of Phase 7 of this text. Jensen also provides formulas for schedule extensions to account for Phases 1 through 4 and the remaining portion of Phase 7. Like Boehm, he adds approximately 8 percent up front to account for Phases 1 through Phase 4. To represent the integration part of Phase 7 that occurs after acceptance testing has been completed, an additional 17 percent is tacked on to the end of the project.

There are four components to Jensen's software estimating model: (1) size—the number of lines of source code, excluding comments; (2) the inherent complexity of the problem; (3) the technical ability of the organization to produce the system; and (4) the ability of the organization to staff the project. Using the fourth component to find the shortest schedule and the optimum staffing rate will be addressed in detail later in the book. However, for now suffice it to say that the model may assume that initially there is a known, predetermined staffing size and rate. By applying different staffing values against the model and then using the accompanying Jensen chart (a parametric graph which supports the model), the minimum development time (in elapsed years) for each staffing rate may be determined.

In the Jensen model, a major relationship is established between a software equation and a source code complexity equation. The software equation is a computation that relates the effective size of the system, an effective development technology constant, and the life cycle effort (in total person-years) to the development cost and time (in elapsed years). The source code complexity values are presented in a table. They have evolved from Putnam's original data and from more recent experimental results.

The Jensen model is primarily intended to be used in critical projects, where there are more than 5 team members and the elapsed time is less than 5 years. In these types of projects, the results often come within 12 percent of schedule and 20 percent of costs.

The minimum development time (in elapsed years) is shown in Formula 5.1.

Jensen says that in small maintenance projects (for example, 5,000—10,000 lines of code) where there are 2—4 people and 2—3 months elapsed time, the software equation presented above will not consistently yield acceptable values. This is especially true in a multiproject scenario. To reflect the smaller project environment, Jensen also provides several factors for modifying the primary equation.

The effective size. The effective size of a system is measured in lines of source code. In new development projects, the actual software development size and the effective size are equal. However, in maintenance projects, this measurement should include, not only the modified existing source code and the newly developed source code, but should also account for any already present software. The count should also reflect the coding effort required to adapt the design to fit into the new system, the coding effort required to interface the new code to the new system, and the coding effort required to test the system.

The formula for the effective size is:

Total size × the size factor;

Formula 5.1 Using Jensen's software equation to calculate the minimum development time.

$$\left[\frac{\text{the effective software size (in source code lines)}}{\text{the effective technology constant} \times \sqrt{\text{the source code complexity}}} \right]^{.4}$$

where:

Total size = the estimated original size + the optional[4] estimated modification size;

and

In new development projects:

The size factor = 1.

In maintenance projects

The size factor is = (.4 × a design complexity factor) +
(.25 × an implementation complexity factor) + (.35 × a testing complexity factor).

For maintenance projects, Jensen provides directions for computing the design complexity factor, the implementation complexity factor and the testing complexity factor. They are used to reflect the state of the current system. For example, where the system is well-structured, where there is good documentation, and where the application is well-known, the implementation complexity factor and the testing complexity factor will usually be less than 1. The design complexity factor may also hover around 1. Thus, the size factor will frequently be less than 1. On the other hand, where the system is not well-structured, where there is not good documentation, and where the application is not well-known, the design complexity factor could be significantly greater than 1 and the size factor will increase proportionally.

The development team should regard a complexity factor of greater than 1 as a signal that the technical solution may be risky. When this occurs, wise developers will mold an alternative set of more desirable implementation strategies. They will then use each of the corresponding complexity factors during negotiations that are intended to choose a technical solution that has a higher probability of success.

The effective technology constant. The effective technology constant is a factor that allows users to reflect technical complexity and technical ability in the project cost and the corresponding development time. It is a measure of the organization's technical ability to implement the project under a set of technical constraints and conditions that have been imposed by their requirements for the project. For example, the team may have already been directed to implement the system on a given computer, using a given language and a given data base management system—even though there is not a great deal of team expertise supporting any of these requirements.

The effective technology constant is influenced by two sets of factors: a group of seven *basic* capability parameters and a second group of twenty-four *environmental* parameters (analogous to Boehm's cost drivers).

The basic technology constant accounts for variations in the underlying computing environment for projects which have similar size and scheduling constraints. The first six basic capabilities include an analyst component (skill levels, motivation, and working conditions), a programmer component (skill levels, motivation, and working conditions), application experience, automated tool support, the level of established quality development techniques, and the average required transaction response time. There is a seventh category, the average turn-around time for programming tasks. Unique ratings are provided for each of the seven categories that allow users to reflect "very low, low, normal, high, and very high" scores.

The ratings for each of the first six categories are multiplied together. The result may be called *X*. Then, the following formula is applied:

$$-3.70945 \times \text{(the natural log } (\frac{X}{4.11}) \div 5 \text{ times the value for the seventh rating)}$$

[4] In maintenance projects.

This answer is used as the exponent to raise 2000 to a given power. The basic technology constant usually ranges between 2,000 and 20,000—with, according to Jensen, higher values being characteristic of higher productivity environments.

The environmental parameters are then used to adjust the basic technology constant. They take into account such concerns as language experience, language complexity, quality assurance level, verification and validation requirements, CPU time constraints, practices and methods experience, development system complexity, real-time operations and so on. Here, too, specific factors are provided for the twenty-four categories that allow the user to reflect "extra low, very low, low, nominal, high, very high, and extra high" ratings or number of months of experience.

The ratings for each of the environmental adjustment factors are multiplied together and divided into the basic technology constant. This answer is used as the effective technology constant.

The source code complexity. The source code complexity, a measurement that is size and environment independent, is a rating that is inversely proportional to complexity. The least complex source code (for example, simple sequences, simple straightline code, loose coupling, and few decisions) is scored with a 32. On the other end of the scale, the most complex source code (for example, extremely complex control logic, internally interactive, extremely complex interfaces) measures at 4. Jensen also provides guidelines for rating systems that fall in between the two extremes. These values have been verified for a variety of development projects.

Jensen models and COCOMO. Jensen has also provided formulas for converting the common COCOMO parameters to the corresponding Jensen parameters or the common Jensen parameters to the corresponding COCOMO parameters. Using the parameters or Jensen's conversion data, cost prediction correlations have been consistently obtained.

5.4.3 Function Point Analysis

Function points are used to measure system size as a component of productivity measurement. Users count the number of inputs and outputs, the number of internal files, the number of inquiries, and the number of interfaces (people and subsystem). Starting the process at a point when a comfortable amount of analysis and design has been completed, the estimators classify and count raw function points.

Raw function points. First, the raw function points that will be used for measurement are listed and approved. (See the Categories column in Table 5.1. There may be dozens of components in each of the raw function point categories.) Next, the number of times that each function point being used for measurement occurs in the system being evaluated is recorded.

Each incidence of inputs such as data entry forms, on-line transactions, optical character readers, mass storage interfaces from other applications, and so on, is counted. The number of outputs (e.g., reports, online messages, optical character readers, mass storage devices) is noted. The occurrences of internal files (e.g., master files, file structures [flat files versus inverted versus hierarchical versus relational, etc.], control files, audit files) are listed. The number of interfaces to other applications (passed back and forth or shared by both) are also itemized. And, finally, the total of inquiries (inquiry transactions versus decision support systems versus error messages versus help/selection menus) are counted.

Raw function points: weighting factor. In Step 3, for *each* occurrence of a raw function point that was identified in the prior step, a value that rates it as simple, average or complex is provided. (See Table 5.1 for a set of commonly accepted values.) This value is multiplied by the number of occurrences in that category. Thus, if 5 complex outputs were counted, the weighted score would be 35.

Unadjusted raw function points. In Step 4, the weighted scores are added up to give the total of the unadjusted raw function points.

Level of influence adjustment. Finally, this unadjusted raw function point total is tuned—by the effect that 14 different complexity factors exert on the system. Each of these 14 factors is evaluated according to its level of influence, a number that ranges from 0 to 5. From a global system perspective, a level of influence (0 = not present; 1 = trivial influence; 2 = moderate influence; 3 = average influence; 4 = significant influence; 5 = strong influence throughout) is assessed for each of the following factors:

- Data communications
- Distributed processing

Table 5.1 Raw function points weighting factors.

Table 5.1 Raw Function Points Weighting Factors			
CATEGORIES	SIMPLE	AVERAGE	COMPLEX
EXTERNAL INPUTS e.g., number of data elements,* complexity of screens	3	4	6
EXTERNAL OUTPUTS e.g., number of columns, subtotals, data manipulation complexity	4	5	7
INTERNAL FILES e.g., media type, number of record types, hierarchy levels	7	10	15
EXTERNAL INTERFACES e.g., search criteria, record types, number of shared databases	5	7	10
EXTERNAL INQUIRIES e.g., activity, balances, menu types, control transfers	3	4	6
* A data element is the smallest atom of stand-alone data, when to further divide it would serve no useful purpose			

- Performance objectives
- Computer configuration capacity
- Transaction rate
- On-line data entry
- Interactive on-line update
- Human ergonomics
- Complex processing
- Reusability requirements
- Conversion and installation ease
- Operational ease
- Number of sites
- Ease of modifications

After each of these 14 influencing variables has been rated, the scores are added together. Last, the score is processed to give an adjustment factor of ± 35 percent (.65 to 1.35) This is done by executing the following steps:

1. Take the sum (of the scores of each of the 14 influencing variables) and multiply it by .01.
2. Take this answer and add it to .65.
3. Multiply the answer in Number 2 by the original unadjusted raw function point total.
4. The final answer will be the total adjusted function points for the system.

A medium- to large-scale system may have a score of 500–900 function points.

The relationship between function points and influencing variables might be enhanced by the application of additional unknowns that also influence developmental productivity. Many of these supplementary variables have been identified by C. E. Walston & C. P. Felix.[5] They weight 29 additional variables

[5] C.E. Walston and C.P. Felix, *A Method of Programming Measurement and Estimation*, IBM Systems Journal, Volume 16, Number 1, 1977

and use them as correction factors to adjust their estimates—e.g., user participation (none, some, much), programming skills (minimal, average, extensive), application complexity (below average, average, above average), and so on. Based on 60 projects that range from 12 man months to 11,758 man months, with 28 different languages and 66 different computers, their results fall within reasonably good tolerances.

Scheduling with function points. Ideally, the organization has an historical database of projects that includes a record of the effort that was expended in producing each of the corresponding systems. If so, project teams can run each of these systems through the function point analysis, determining each of the respective function point scores. Next, the group may sort each of the systems into related groups (e.g., very large COBOL mainframe applications of high quality and reliability, or moderately sized PL/1 mainframe applications of average quality and reliability), and they may calculate the average number of hours per function point for each of these categories. Later, these hours per function point can be used for developing assessment numbers (e.g., staffing and elapsed time) of future project estimates. Barring the presence in the organization of a personalized database, there are vendors who have large statistical samplings and are able to help organizations to "customize" the data for use in their own installation.

5.4.4 Function Points and Lines of Code

If there's one thing the experts in the software industry are good at, it's their willingness to offer opposing views while maintaining or improving (1) the balance of perspective for their own ideas and (2) respect for their adversaries. This is certainly evident in the controversy and polarization between lines of code advocates and proponents of function points.

The most obvious dissimilarities stem from differences over how to count lines of code. For example:

- The number of lines of code can not be effectively predicted until late in the project (when a considerable amount of the design has been done) and is not accurately measured until after the project has been completed.
- It's difficult to determine what to count as a line of code—job control statements, comments, a line of a source code listing, a complete statement (no mat-

ter how many lines of a listing it takes), data declarations, and so forth.

- Lines of code are not technology independent and therefore, the number of lines of code may differ significantly from language to language.
- The higher level languages may get penalized in the counting process—because they provide more functionality with fewer lines of code. Therefore, according to Jones, the cost per line of source code goes up.
- Quality as a function of lines of code may not be an effective metric. Jones also says "In higher level languages, it seems that, even when the total number of defects goes down, the fewer the lines of code, the higher the number of defects per lines of code (therefore the higher the cost per defect)."

Another problem is encountered when trying to deal with all of the extraneous, non-code-related work that is now such an integral part of most software projects.

Lines-of-code models might only effectively be used from approximately the middle of the project (when the team has an idea of how many lines of code will be produced). Yet, from that time on, they may be a valuable aid in producing estimates that converge to actual more than a respectable number of times.

On the other hand, one of the soft spots in function point analysis is the wide variance (sometimes 10 to 30 percent) in resulting scores—even from members of the same application. This is usually the case when the estimators have not been properly trained to understand the rating scheme. However, many of the vendors and user groups have refined the guidelines and if the function point analysis is supervised by trained and experienced personnel—working with the project team—this problem is largely diffused.

From another perspective Symons[6] questions (1) whether the function point weights will be valid in all circumstances and (2) whether the restriction to 14 factors will be satisfactory for all time. Furthermore, he presents some scenarios in which the resulting scores are counter-intuitive. For example, in one setting, a

---

[6] C.R. Symons, "Function Analysis: Difficulties And Improvements," *IEEE TRANSACTIONS ON SOFTWARE ENGINEERING*, Volume 14, Number 1 (January, 1988).

single new system that replaced three old systems linked by interfaces and that duplicated identical transactions against an integrated database scored lower than the old systems—even though it managed the data more efficiently. (Three interface files get more credit than one integrated file.) In spite of the difficulties just mentioned, if the organization has been wise enough to save the records of development effort, both lines of code and function points will prove to be valuable aids in estimating maintenance projects. Similarly, productivity improvement programs will get precious assistance from the lines of code and function point statistics.

5.4.5 Managing Projects in Uncertainty

When some of the estimating myths were dispelled at the beginning of this chapter, the need for strategies that deal with managing projects in uncertainty (and sometimes chaos) was recognized. The following sections are based on accepted mathematical concepts and deal specifically with managing the unknown.

The normal distribution. A well-known statistical theorem, the Central Limit Theorem, states that the distribution of a set of results will approach an approximately normal distribution as the size of the statistical population increases. (See Figure 5.1.) This theorem supports the planner's ability to calculate the probability that any chosen result will fall within a given interval, if the sample population's mean and variance are known. This concept will become increasingly important, and is essential for determining

the probability of success, as will be explained later in the book.

In estimating in certainty, it may be possible to derive acceptable results by using just one estimate. For example, when customers take their car into a repair shop to replace the rear quarter panel, the mechanic is likely to consult the ''blue-book'' for repairs and give you an estimate. But, if it is not apparent that replacing only the quarter panel will complete the job, the customer may only receive a range of estimates instead of one predictor—to compensate for the uncertainty.

The mathematics of uncertainty. In systems projects, team members are usually trying to estimate within the same type of uncertainty. Therefore, it may be advisable to provide a range of estimates to compensate for their lack of knowledge. If three estimates are provided:

- The optimistic—(given that everything falls smoothly into place and there are no unforeseen problems, what is the shortest period of time?)
- The pessimistic—(given that the most difficult problems to overcome are encountered, what is the longest it will take?)
- The most likely—(given normal circumstances, how long will it take?)

it is possible to derive an acceptable range for the effort. In analyzing these three estimates, it is expected that the most likely estimate would, as its name implies, occur most often, and the pessimistic and optimistic estimates would occur least often. In terms of a probability distribution, then, the most likely estimates would occur at the peak of the distribution. But this peak can be affected by the two extremes; and, therefore can move back and forth. This skews the distribution either to the left or to the right. These curves are called a beta distribution. (Figure 5.2 and Figure 5.3) The optimistic (''O'') and pessimistic (''P'') estimates are at both extremes of the X axis. Note how the most likely (''ML'') falls in the peak range. Furthermore, the beta distribution can be used to calculate an expected effort (''EXP'') that incorporates all three estimates and can be used very effectively as the effort that will be required to complete the task. The formula for expected effort (''EXP'') is:

Figure 5.1 Normal distribution.

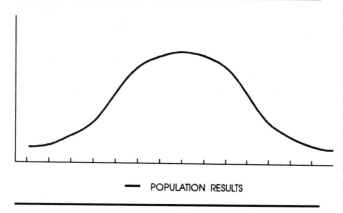

— POPULATION RESULTS

Figure 5.2 Beta (skewed left).

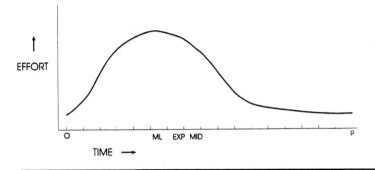

Figure 5.3 Beta (skewed right).

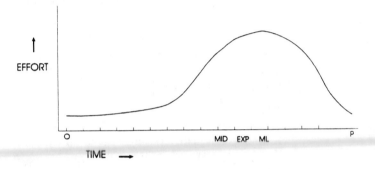

$$\frac{(1 \text{ times the optimistic estimate}) + (4 \text{ times the most likely estimate}) + (1 \text{ times the pessimistic estimate})}{6}$$

In frequency distributions that—like the beta distribution—are moderately curved, the mean in the formula can be weighted so that the expected effort will fall one-third of the way between the most likely estimate and the mid-range. This weighted average simply gives more importance to the estimate about which the estimator is most certain (the most likely). At the same time, it biases the result so that the expected effort falls closest to the side of the greatest uncertainty (either optimistic or pessimistic). Thus it also allows for some compensation due to that uncertainty.

Finally, the formula lends itself excellently to any level in the work breakdown structure as well as supporting the calculation of probability of success. Computed using this formula, the expected effort represents the 50 percent probability point in the distribution. To increase the probability of successfully finishing a particular job, the number of standard deviations from the mean may be increased. For a 68 percent proba-

bility of success, 1 standard deviation is used to compute the 3 values. For 95 percent, 2 standard deviations are used. For 99.7 percent, 3 standard deviations are used. The result derived from 3 standard deviations does not necessarily portray all of the values for the absolutely best and worst cases but rather values beyond which there is a rare likelihood of occurrence. With each increase in the number of standard deviations, however, the range gets broader and the expected effort increases accordingly. Rather than attempt to do this on a task by task basis, there is, perhaps, a more pleasing way of accomplishing the desired result, that will also be covered later in the book.

The pert method of estimating. The Navy Special Projects Office employed the concept of uncertainty, the beta distribution, and the formula for expected effort in estimating and managing the POLARIS missile submarine project in 1958. They called their process the Program Evaluation and Review Technique

(PERT). The PERT technique was quickly adapted in many commercial sectors (e.g., the construction industry). Similarly, it was suggested in 1979 by Putnam and Fitzsimmons that the PERT concept could be especially useful in systems projects, although they suggested its use at a higher level in the work breakdown structure than the inch-pebble level of this text.

5.5 STEP 2: DETERMINE THE DATA REQUIREMENTS

After the organization has completed Step 1, having selected the estimating technique(s) that will be used, its next step is to itemize the data requirements for each method and the respective formulas that will massage the data. Additionally, the estimating units (money, people, time) must be approved; the estimating objectives, constraints, and assumptions must be identified; and the estimating success and completion criteria must be identified. Then, each of these items must be endorsed by the project champion and other significant stakeholders. These covenants should be documented in the Project Agreement.

5.6 STEP 3: DEFINE THE PLANNING PROCESS

Assuming that the planning effort will be participative (i.e., those that are closest to the job will provide the estimates, etc.) it will be necessary to develop some guidelines. This is done in order to ensure consistency throughout the operation. Completing this activity is a three-step application: (1) develop the guidelines; (2) develop the procedures; and (3) produce the planning materials.

5.6.1 Develop the Guidelines

Although each group may want to customize its own guidelines, the following lists, which have been successfully adapted by many organizations, may be combed to extract kickoff sets.

• General management considerations

  (1) True work effort is easier to estimate than duration.
  (2) For reliable estimates, the estimators can't be coerced to provide the answer that the organization wants to hear. The estimators can't be pressured to "price-to-win." An unattainable target remains unattainable—no matter how much pressure is put upon the estimators.
  (3) The whole is equal to the sum of its parts. If the estimators can't reduce the parts, they ought not to be influenced to reduce the whole.
  (4) The people side should not be ignored, i.e., the effect of experience (or lack thereof) of the team members. If there are no superstars, not a lot of estimating experience or project management experience, learning periods should be factored into the plan.
  (5) Planning is participative: (1) a candidate for doing the work or (2) the supervisor of a group of candidates gives the estimates. Participative estimates are based on a better understanding of the work and create self-fulfilling prophecies of success.
  (6) What teams spend their time on ought to be scrutinized. One way to weed out *stuff* is to ensure that everyone is working from a plan. If no one can justify putting it in the plan, then perhaps the job shouldn't be done.
  (7) The main objective of estimating is not the estimates! The purpose of estimating is to enable the development of a plan. Since one purpose of a plan is to enable workers to know—in any given week—exactly what they are supposed to be working on, important projects must have a plan.
  (8) Because a secret to successful estimating is finding the inch-pebbles, managers who insist on accuracy in the plan must be willing to work with smaller numbers.
  (9) Inch-pebble estimates do wonders to compensate for lack of experience. However, it is also essential to understand that beginners sometimes have a tendency to overfragmentize the plan, thereby including more estimates in the 4-hour range than in the 40-hour range. This situation is often disconcerting to upper management. Nevertheless, in the long run, having many small assignments is infinitely better than overlooking duties, underestimating, and consequently missing targets. Furthermore, small estimates go far in compensating for lack of estimating expertise, because the smaller the

interval, the higher the degree of accuracy. This inclination dissipates with experience so, in the meantime, the organization ought to be forgiving.

(10) Managers who insist on accuracy must be willing to accept ranges—until such time in the project that sufficient information that can support detailed planning is known.

• General planning considerations

(1) An inch-pebble may be called an activity or a task. If the term *task* is selected, the level above the inch-pebble (intermediate deliverable or major deliverable) may be called an *activity*. (Figure 5.4) These terms may be used in reverse. In this chapter, the task is the inch-pebble and the activity is the intermediate or major deliverable.

(2) Activities and tasks produce meaningful deliverables that can be tested and verified.

(3) Activities and tasks will be named with an action verb followed by the name of the deliverable (e.g., design packaging; analyze feature x; code module n).

(4) An inch-pebble produces one and only one deliverable. In other words, an inch-pebble cannot be designated as ''Produce A and Review A.'' These are two separate inch-pebbles.

• Specific planning considerations

(1) Included in this section are the instructions for implementing the estimating technique(s) that the organization has selected.

(2) Inch-pebbles can be completed in 4–40 hours. They produce a meaningful deliverable that can be verified and they are generally assignable to one person. Group development workshops, reviews and meetings, and some limited technical design tasks are exceptions to the one-person maxim. An inch-pebble represents a unit of work that can not be subdivided and is generally best completed without interruption.

Figure 5.4 Breaking milestones into activities and tasks.

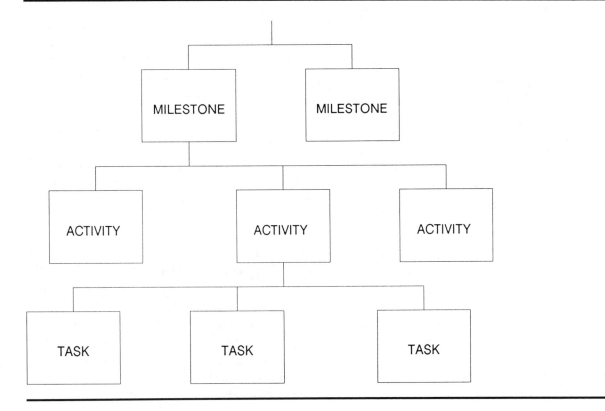

(3) Milestones give visibility to significant events in the project. When they are entered into the project plan, they may be introduced with zero duration. Their start and end dates are then determined by rolling up the sequential durations of the activities and tasks that occur before or under them. Hammocks and summaries may also be used for milestones.

(4) When an activity is introduced into the project plan without lower level tasks, rough estimates for its completion should be provided as well.

(5) Once the tasks for an activity have been introduced, its rough estimate should be erased. Its start and end dates are then determined by rolling up the sequential durations of the tasks that occur under it.

(6) It is possible to have activities or tasks that represent lead or lag time. While these are entered with a duration, they do not represent any actual project cost or effort.

(7) The Protected Environment concept implies that the productivity level will remain constant from the moment the task is started until its completion. Furthermore, it assumes no coffee breaks, interruptions, lunch, meetings, fires, earthquakes, labor strikes, vendor problems, etc. Everyone accepts that these assumptions are unrealistic and that productivity levels are not constant. However, individual subjectivity is diffused and consistency is achieved by (1) removing the adjustment for non-creative time from individual estimates, (2) the group choosing one constant approved factor for non-productivity; and (3) factoring it in after the estimates have been accepted. The factor for non-productivity will be referred to as *broad-based overhead*. Common factors for *broad-based overhead* range from 20 percent to 35 percent of each day.

(8) When estimating tasks, assume the resource who completes the job will be working in a Protected Environment and will be 100 percent dedicated to the task during its execution. Also assume the resource will have average qualifications. Similarly, assume everything required to start the job will have been received prior to task initialization.

(9) Unless it is guaranteed that the estimator will also be completing the work, the estimator should be very careful not to reflect his or her own abilities in the estimate. The estimate is made assuming normal qualifications.

(10) When estimating tasks, do *NOT* add time into the estimate to compensate for contingencies or for the possibility of changing requirements. (They will be handled separately, when they occur.)

The above assumptions are essential for development of the optimal plan. This plan will be adjusted for resource constraints later on.

5.6.2 Develop the Procedures

Don't forget a planning exercise is held at the end of every phase, to develop the detailed plan for the next phase and the inexact plan for the rest of the project.

1. Hold a Group Development Workshop(s) to generate a first-cut plan—The first-cut plan includes two work breakdown structures: (1) down to the activity level for the next phase; and (2) somewhere between the milestone and activity level for the rest of the project. It also includes high-level networks. The first-cut plan is frequently developed by the project leaders (i.e., those individuals one level below the project manager).

2. Hold a planning initiation for the estimating candidates—Explain the planning and estimating process; present an overview of the first-cut plan; and distribute the estimating packets. Estimating packets are turn-around documents. For example, estimating packets for detailed planning of the next phase may provide one turn-around document for each activity. This activity planning packet is usually required to be completed by the estimator and will be given to the individual charged with partitioning the activity into its tasks and with providing the estimates for the tasks. For each task, the estimator should enter a task name, a task identifying number, the estimate(s), the assumptions, and a list of predecessors. (Predecessors will be covered later in the book.) Finally, the packet must also contain instructions for filling out the forms.

3. Estimate the work effort—This is completed by the estimating candidates. If they are new to estimating, the candidates may initially not know where to begin. Plan to provide these people with sample project plans and/or some qualified consultants.

4. Collect and validate the estimates—Using heuristic guidelines, organizational experience, or historical information, *carefully* and *painstakingly* scrutinize the estimates for completeness and reasonableness.

5. Repeat Steps 3 and 4 until satisfied with the estimates.

6. Have a grand review of the estimates—This is a review that should be attended by *all* planning participants. Their charter is to look for *missing* jobs and *unreasonable* estimates.

7. When the estimates have been approved, factor in the broad-based overhead. The estimate is now called the *true work effort*.

5.6.3 Produce the Planning Materials

Identify and produce the required planning reports and forms. Ideally, the data entry of estimating information may be an on-line interactive operation, a procedure which is completed by each of the estimating candidates. However, this would require multiple workstations and multiple copies of the package—as well as a software architecture which supports multi-threading. In lieu of such sophistication, it may be necessary to resort to hard-copy turn-around forms—for example, lists of milestones, activity estimating packets, approval forms, etc.

5.7 STEP 4: AUTOMATE AS MUCH AS POSSIBLE—ESTIMATING AND PROJECT MANAGEMENT SOFTWARE

In spite of the fact that estimating is a crucial aspect of project planning and management, it is a process that gets very little recognition from most project management software products. *There are, however, several estimating software products available—but they are not within the domain of study for this text.* With the exception of one product, SuperProject Expert, each of the software packages evaluated assumes that estimating has been completed off-line. SuperProject Expert supports the PERT approach to estimating.

The comparative analysis will investigate (1) if the product supports estimating; and (2) the intricacies of *entering a duration*, the number that results from the application of an estimating process.

5.7.1 Estimating Support and Estimating Guidelines ♦

Does the system support estimating at all? Does the package support the introduction and use of any of the estimating formulas described earlier? Is there any documentation in the user's manual to describe the process of estimating in software project management—e.g., describing what estimating is and how to do it? If the software supports an estimating technique, are the knowns and the unknowns in the formulas interchangeable, so that users can try various *what-if* scenarios?

5.7.2 *Work-Arounds*

If the product being evaluated does not support estimating, is there a *work-around* process? Will the software support the Protected Environment broad-based overhead approach? Will it support producing the estimating packets—for example, the activity planning worksheets and the directions for their completion?

Many of the products support ad hoc reporting capabilities which can be used to produce the planning packets. The ad hoc feature will be discussed later and then addressed in detail in each of the product appendices.

None of the packages support a data manipulation process which provides "free fields" and then allows the user to "customize" the software to support an estimating process. However, if the vendors chose to supplement their features, the macro facilities of SuperProject Expert and Viewpoint may be candidates for expansion to accommodate this enhancement.

On the other hand, the best solution to supporting the estimating approach may be to write a separate program (or series of programs) with a spreadsheet package, a word processor, report writer, COBOL, etc. Using the earlier questions as specifications, this adjunct software can create the planning packets, do the estimating computations, factor in the Protected Environment *broad-based overhead* and so on. Then, if the record layouts of the files in the project management software are available, the results can be programmatically moved into the *duration* field of the appropriate record(s).

Some of the products provide a function for importing data, but only on a complete record basis.

Since only one field within the record is at issue here, this import function may prove to be impractical—unless there is some more efficient means for off-line entering of the complete record. When this is not constructive, the programmatic approach described above may be the best alternative.

Primavera Project Planner, Project Workbench, SuperProject Expert, and Microsoft Project all provide record layouts as part of their documentation.

5.7.3 Durations and Project Management Software

This chapter presents a cursory evaluation of duration issues that commonly arise at this point in the planning process. To complete the evaluation of how the package totally supports the use of durations, it will also be necessary to consider how duration will be used later—in scheduling and in resource allocations. This final evaluation can not be completed until the user has finished studying "Identifying Dependencies," "Developing the Optimal Schedule," and "Scheduling Resources."

For example, consider networks. Some packages' networks are drawn scaled to time. If the user follows the 4–40 hour estimating approach but the smallest network time scale in the system is weeks, the task, when illustrated in the network, may only be represented as a fraction of the week. When this happens, the task is seen as a tiny vertical line or a box. Furthermore, some products place the plan data inside the node; when this occurs, there is little or no accompanying text. Consequently, the network may be difficult to understand, hard to verify, and frustrating when trying to connect or verify dependencies. Thus, a conflict between the estimating (or durations) concept and some networking approaches has been discovered. This will be discussed in more detail in the next chapter.

5.7.4 Estimates of *True Work Effort* Versus Resource-Driven Elapsed Time ◆

There are two numbers people usually find confusing: the *true work effort* and the *elapsed time*. True work effort is the amount of time it *actually* takes to complete the job while elapsed time is the number of calendar days that might pass by until the work is finished. A football game actually takes 60 minutes of true work effort, but the match might last 3 elapsed hours. Because of resource constraints, 5 hours of true work effort may need to be spread over 4 days of elapsed time. The true work effort estimate is 5 hours, not 4 days.

In following the natural planning process, it should not be necessary to designate resources when entering estimates. This is because frequently the workers have not yet been matched to the jobs. Furthermore, estimates of true work effort are needed to develop the optimal plan, to do cost/benefit analysis, and manage status reporting. Resource driven scheduling and leveling will be addressed later.

For effective planning, the system should support both types of numbers: the true work effort and the elapsed time. If the elapsed time is extended, it should *not* automatically change the true work effort.

Does the system support the use of the true work effort it takes to do the job? Or are the estimates made on resource driven elapsed time? Are the estimates driven by resource availability (e.g., an 8 hour effort, when the resource is only available halftime, will have an elapsed calendar time of 2 days. The true work effort estimate should be 8 hours, not 2 days.)? Are estimates changed by the application of resources? If the estimates *ARE* based on elapsed time or resource availability, how is true cost of effort computed (e.g., when the amount of time worked equals the actual cost, but may not equal elapsed time)? And how is status reported (e.g., when the amount of time worked equals the actual effort but may not equal the elapsed time)?

5.7.5 Warnings and Overrides

Will the system signal tasks:

- That have more than one person assigned?
- That are greater than 40 hours?
- That produce more than one deliverable?

Will it also allow users to override these options, if necessary? Since none of the systems have been developed to follow this philosophy, none supports such warnings and overrides.

5.7.6 Durations and Units of Measurement ◆

What is the smallest unit of measurement (hours, days, weeks, etc.)? If the product is to support the 4–40 hours task size, then the product should support hours or fractional days. What is the default unit of measurement? Will the product allow mixed units of measurement (within different WBS levels—not within the same entry) and subsequently convert them all into a globally selected unit of measurement? How easy is it to change units, if the group should decide to use a different one?

5.7.7 Zero Duration Milestones ◆

Zero duration milestones are very helpful in giving visibility to key deliverable points in the project as well as for summary reporting. Will the software support zero duration milestones?

5.7.8 Lead and Lag Times with Duration But No Effort ◆

Usually, each job in a series of jobs starts as soon as the one before it finishes. In Figure 5.5, Jobs B and C may start as soon as Job A is finished. But what if a delay is necessary between Job A and the other job(s)? This delay is referred to as lead or lag time and must be estimated along with other durations in the plan. Lead and lag are terms that have a variety of meanings to different users. In this text, unless describing terminology used specifically by one of the products, lags will mean a delay is attached to the end of a job, and leads will mean the delay is inserted before the beginning of a job. Lead and lag times may be used, for example, for fixed time periods such as

Figure 5.5 Lag and lead times.

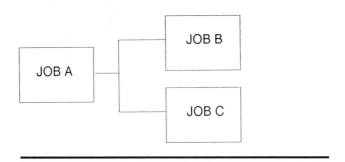

legal minimums. They are especially useful in situations such as waiting for delivery of hardware, printed forms, advertising copy, and so on. In these cases, it may be desirable to have the delay times show up as line items on the management reports to allow tracking of the vendor status. There are many ways to show lag and lead times. The key factor now is simply whether the product supports lead and lag times with durations but no cost of effort. The concept of delay times has been introduced in this chapter and will be developed further later on.

Can a job have lead or lag time with duration and no effort, so that, while waiting, it adds the time but not the costs to the schedule? Can it be tracked through the reporting system?

5.8 STEP 5: PRODUCE THE ESTIMATES

Estimates are provided using the elected estimating technique(s).

5.9 COMPLETING THE ESTIMATING PROCESS

After the team has produced the estimates, they still have a *very important* job to perform. This operation pertains to the gathering and recording of data, much of which will become *essential* when the job is actually assigned to the individual who is designated to do it. Work packages will later be prepared for each assignee. Some of the information that proves very helpful to workers is:

- The assumptions that were used in estimating the effort; and
- An update to the data that was created during the preparation of the work breakdown structures.

  Now is the time to prepare this data. Ideally, the information may be entered into the ad hoc notes in the record for each job.

5.10 STEP 6: CREATE A PROJECT HISTORY FILE

The more empirical data that organizations have to draw from, the greater their confidence can be in their estimates. If it is important to base decisions on organizational experience, this information is only obtained with the passage of time, with the saving of the data, and with making it available to everyone.

Once a group has an accumulation of results, they will be able to use the data to produce better estimates on future projects. As they keep repeating the process, organizations will improve their estimating skills, identify opportunities to streamline their procedures, and thus increase productivity, and justify efforts in relationship to improved system quality.

Furthermore, other mathematical concepts may also be used to help make intelligent predictions. For example, regression analysis may be used to summarize the past experience, to analyze the range of accuracy of the results, and then to make predictions by translating from past to present (in much the same manner as the estimating techniques discussed in this chapter were formulated). Similarly, a project post-mortem (in which the estimators compare how close they've come, what they've done right, what they've done wrong, what they would do differently, etc.) is essential to building project management expertise within the company. Without the post-mortem, team members miss a wonderful opportunity to sharpen their skills.

5.11 IN CONCLUSION

Although, to the extent that they are based on formulas, all of the estimating techniques are rigorous— they are also highly subjective, to the extent that opinion is the input to the formulas. Similarly, function point analysis may even be slightly more subjective —because it relies on the most opinions.

5.11.1 Can the Organization Rely on an Estimate?

Many people have expectations of estimating that are not in line with reality. However, consider these words of wisdom from Burrill and Ellsworth:[7]

> Some people look upon an estimate as a prediction of what will be. The estimate will either be right or wrong, and obviously it must be right to be of any use. The fact is if anyone *could* predict the future, he would never use this skill to determine the cost of a DP project. Las Vegas, Wall Street or the nearest race track would offer far greater rewards for such a priceless gift.

Estimating techniques are intended to provide data for input to a decision-making process; they are not intended to make the management decisions for any organization.

What organizations are looking for are suitable, practical, and functional estimates, for which the merit would be determined by (1) the group who will be using them and (2) the employment of the operation. Finally, it is always necessary to remember that the caliber of the estimate depends on what estimates are actually being addressed.

---

[7] C. Burrill and L. Ellsworth, *Modern Project Management*, (Tenafly, NJ: Burrill-Ellsworth Associates, Inc., 1980).

CHAPTER 6 IDENTIFYING DEPENDENCIES

6.1 INTRODUCTION

If readers consider the traditional activities of building a house, the concept of interdependence between jobs is not hard to comprehend. For example, the roof cannot be started until the sides have been put into place. The sides cannot be started until the cement in the foundation has been cured. Furthermore, these steps and their dependencies are more easily understood if they are illustrated graphically. (See Figure 6.1.)

Producing the plan, therefore, requires at least three steps: (1) the identification of what jobs will need to be completed (as in a work breakdown structure); (2) the estimates of how much effort will be required to complete each job; and (3) the resolution of the order in which each job gets executed. The third step, this sequencing of work and the accompanying determination of the relationships between work units is subsequently completed by identifying and illustrating the dependencies. In the world of project management, the pictures used to convey these relationships are called network diagrams. While many people agree that the other graphics are very important tools for *managing* the project, they also believe that they can only effectively complete the *planning* process with network diagrams. This text supports that premise.

Since the average project is usually a series of complex interrelationships, these interrelationships must be illustrated and verified during preparation of a corresponding plan. Network diagrams certainly make it easier for everyone involved with the project to understand this plan and to verify its components. Like work breakdown structures, they help to partition the project into manageable pieces. Once again, by dealing with smaller pieces of the project, more of the uncertainty is diffused. Furthermore, at the end of the planning effort, when scheduling the resources and compressing the schedule, the effects of these constraints on the plan will be evaluated more easily. Finally, while managing the actual project, these networks help to communicate proposed modifications to the plan.

6.1.1 Parallel and Sequential Execution

Jobs that are being done at the same time are described as being completed concurrently or in parallel. In Figure 6.2, Task A and Task B are parallel jobs. On the other hand, operations that occur one after the other are described as being executed sequentially. In Figure 6.2, Task C and Task D are sequential jobs. During the planning process, it important to ask:

- What other jobs (activities or tasks) can be done while this job is being performed?

- What jobs are done one after the other?

Figure 6.1 Building a house.

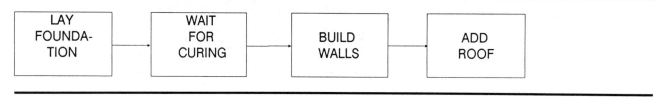

Figure 6.2 Predecessors and successors.

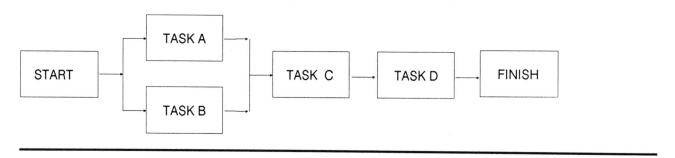

6.1.2 Predecessors and Successors

Dependencies indicate which work units must be completed before others can begin. The earliest jobs are called predecessors (in Figure 6.2, Task C is the predecessor to Task D—and Start is the common predecessor to both Task A and Task B); the later work is referred to as successors (in Figure 6.2, Task D is the successor to Task C—and Task C is the common successor to both Task A and Task B). During the planning process, it is important to ask:

- What other jobs must be completed so that this job may begin?
- What other jobs may not start until this one has finished?

When designating work units as predecessors or successors, only those jobs that immediately precede or follow the current position are named. It is traditional to draw the network so that the predecessors are always on the left of the successors. Furthermore, in a true-to-life environment, there should be no limit to how many predecessors or successors an activity or task may have.

6.1.3 The Criticality of Dependencies

This part of the planning process must be rigorous enough to drive the flow of the work units so that they follow one another in the proper sequence, and so that the dependencies are *correctly noted*. Surprisingly, identifying all of the dependencies and getting each of the connections correctly noted is one of the most difficult parts of project planning. Yet, if the dependencies are *not* complete and correct, the whole project plan may be askew. It is also essential to recognize that the process will not be completed in one try. It may take several passes through the plan to (1) identify all the predecessors and (2) clean up the wrong dependencies. Consequently, this process is an ideal candidate for a series of group dynamics workshops.

6.2 METHODS OF DRAWING NETWORKS

The methods for drawing network dependency diagrams vary according to artistic or functional preferences. Although there are many variations on network types, two or three common approaches seem to prevail.

6.2.1 Arrow Diagrams

Arrow diagrams (sometimes called activity-on-the-arrow networks [AOA] or the arrow diagram method [ADM]) are dependency drawings with the name, duration, and other pertinent information written above and below each line that represents a job. In Figure 6.3, Start, Task A, Task B, Task C, Task D, and Finish are work units. At either end of each line that represents a job, there are number annotations (often within circles), which are referred to as nodes or events. The earlier node is sometimes referred to as the "I" node, while the later one may be called the "J" node. Each of the jobs may be identified by their beginning and ending node numbers. The "I" node of Task D is 5, and its "J" node is 6. Therefore, Task D may also be referred to as "5-6."

When two or more jobs can be completed concurrently, they may be illustrated as Task A and Task B in Figure 6.3. However, if the "I-J" node concept is to be used, the network must be drawn so that no two work units have the same pair of nodes. Consequently, in Figure 6.3 the identifications of Task A and Task B are no longer unique. That is why the broken line connection was inserted between nodes 3 and 4 in Figure 6.4. Now Task A and Task B have unique "I-J" nodes—"2-4" and "2-3" respectively. Broken line connections such as "3-4" are called *dum-*

Figure 6.3 Activity-on-an-arrow.

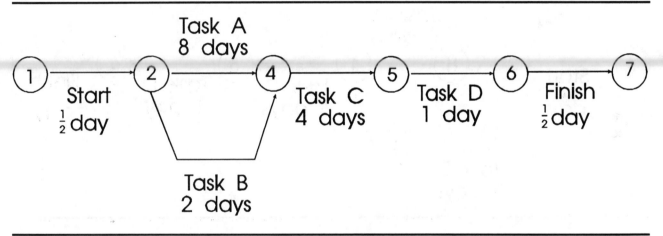

Figure 6.4 Activity-on-an-arrow.

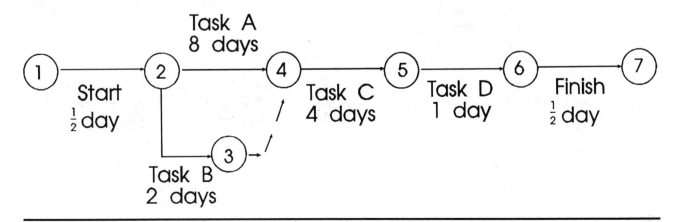

mies. Dummy jobs have no duration and may be used to illustrate precedence relationships when unique "I-J" identifiers are needed.

Similarly, dummy dependencies may be used to simplify complicated relationships such as the addition of Task X in Figure 6.5. Task X and Start may both be done in parallel and must both be completed before Task A may start, but the start of Task B is only dependent upon the completion of Start. Without the "2-8" dummy, the unique "I-J" node illustration of these relationships may have been impossible.

Sometimes, arrow diagrams may be drawn in *free form*, as illustrated in Figure 6.6.

6.2.2 Activity-on-a-Node Diagrams

The desire to satisfy the unique "I-J" node requirement sometimes leads to the creation of very cumbersome networks with an inordinately high number of dummy jobs generated. This problem fathered the development of the activity-on-a-node [AON] approach. (See Figure 6.7.) The job name, duration, and

Figure 6.5 Activity-on-an-arrow.

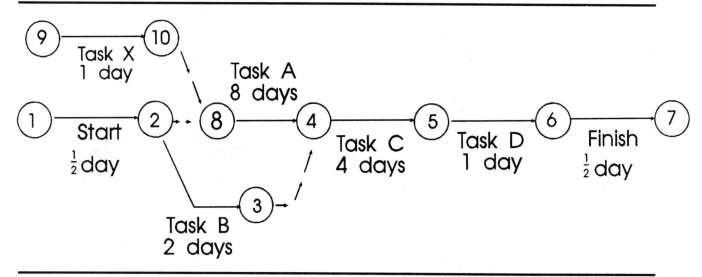

Figure 6.6 Activity-on-an-arrow.

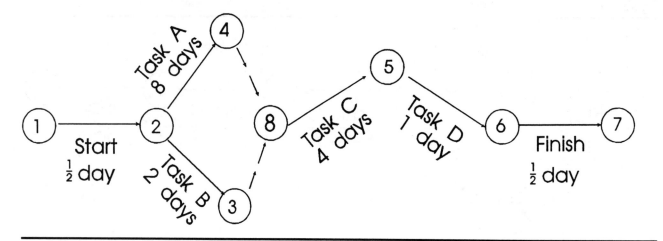

Figure 6.7 Activity-on-a-node (AON).

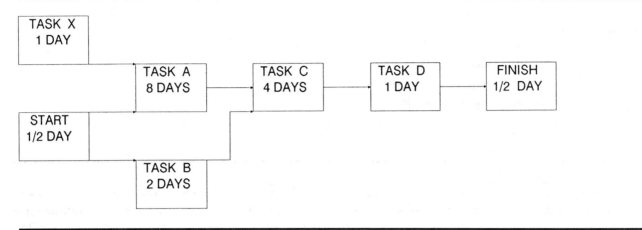

other pertinent information are placed *inside* the node. Nodes are usually circular or rectangular. The arrows begin at the end of each job and point to the start of each succeeding job. This is referred to as a "finish-to-start" relationship; i.e., the start of the successor is dependent upon the finish of its predecessor.

In Figure 6.7, once again, Task A can not begin until both Start and Task X have been completed; but Task B only has to wait until the completion of Start.

6.2.3 Precedence Diagrams

An objection to AON diagrams is that they are limited to finish-to-start relationships. And although for many

project plans, this is not a serious drawback, it has inevitably sparked some creative elaboration on networking techniques. In Figure 6.8, A and B have the traditional finish-to-start relationship. All of A must be completed before B can begin. But what if B can begin when only part of A is done? (See Figure 6.9, left side.) Using AON, A can be split up and drawn as two tasks (as illustrated in the right half of Figure 6.9). That A must now be treated as two separate jobs is often seen as a drawback. However, a start-to-start connection solves this problem. D (in Figure 6.8) may not start until so many days *after* C has started—and is so noted on the arrow. Similarly, finish-to-finish and start-to-finish dependencies may also prove useful. For

Figure 6.8 Precedence relationships.

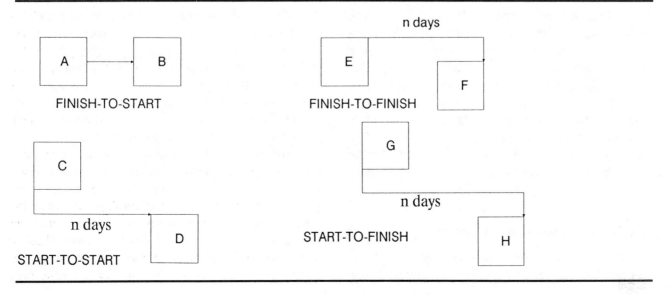

Figure 6.9 Overlapping tasks.

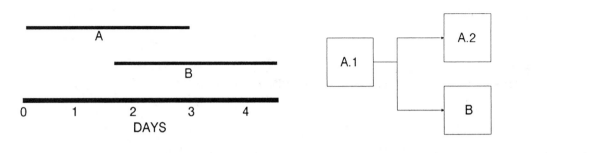

example, F (in Figure 6.8) may not finish until so many days *after* E is done. On the other hand, H (in Figure 6.8) may not finish until so many days *after* G has started.

Adding these three new dependency types is an extension of the activity-on-a-node approach. It is called the precedence-diagramming method [PDM]. The PDM is very popular in the construction industry, because of its usefulness in demonstrating lead and lag times.

6.2.4 Using PDMs for Inexact Planning

Some people believe that the additional relationship types of the PDM may also be convenient while creating the inexact plan. For example, start-to-start relationships may be helpful for overlapping high-level jobs like the milestone and large activity estimates that are so common in the inexact plan. These high-level jobs are the types (1) that have indeterminate estimates, and (2) where intuition directs that the first job doesn't have to be 100 percent complete before the next starts. For example, if the project is currently in the Sizing phase and the team is preparing an inexact plan that includes the later phases of Design and Coding, they may decide that, for lack of more specific data, some of the Coding can begin five weeks after Design starts. Thus, the two jobs in question may have a start-to-start relationship. This subjective evaluation of what percentage of the first job must be finished before the next job can start is acceptable in inexact plans; however, it is very risky in detailed plans.

6.2.5 Networks and Status Reporting

For the greatest majority of systems projects, the AOA and the AON approaches are both highly satisfactory

for planning *and* managing. Furthermore, it is important to note that the AON "drawback" of splitting Job A may even become an advantage during status reporting in the systems world. In other words, if the team implements the status reporting philosophy of 0 percent done or 100 percent done, AOA and AON easily support this reporting approach. On the other hand, by trying to subjectively insert a relationship somewhere inside of a workunit, the three additional PDM dependency types conflict with implementation of this status reporting philosophy. Moreover, if this approach makes assessment of completion harder, it may even conflict with effective management of the systems project.

6.2.6 A Further Warning About Using Precedence-Type Relationships

In performing network analysis, the importance of the critical path will be stressed. For now, suffice it to say that the critical path consists of a series of the plan's milestones, events, activities, and tasks, and it will equate to the length of the project. These jobs on the critical path may be connected with one of the four types of relationships illustrated in Figure 6.8. It is commonly accepted that lengthening the duration of any of the jobs on the critical path will usually extend the duration of the project and vice versa.

In certain PDM scenarios, two jobs may have *two* sets of relationships—instead of the usual one set. For example, B and C in Figure 6.10 have both start-to-start and finish-to-finish relationships; and while the jobs may start at different times, they must finish at the same time. A real-life example is when Testing may start after Coding, but both must finish at the same time. Furthermore, when one job is longer than

Figure 6.10 Precedence diagrams.

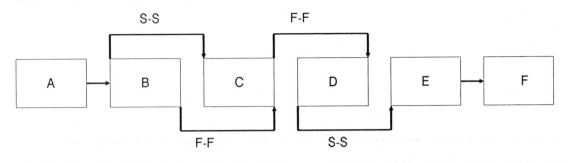

the other, the work in the shorter job can not start and continue without interruption to its completion. If that were allowed, it would finish before the longer job and sometimes that should not happen. Consequently, the work in the shorter job is interrupted and stopped from time to time.

There may also be times when there will be a series of jobs in which there is a mixture of start-to-start, finish-to-start, and finish-to-finish relationships. In certain combinations of these relationships types, a scenario occurs that is totally counter-intuitive. Whenever a job on a critical path has a finish-to-finish relationship with its predecessor (See D's relationship with C in Figure 6.10) *and* a start-to-start relationship with its successor (See D's relationship with E in Figure 6.10.) *and* the work inside of that job may not be interrupted, shortening the duration of that job *will extend the duration of the project (and vice versa)!* There is an excellent discussion of this phenomenon in Wiest and Levy.[1] The user is advised to proceed with caution when using these types of relationships. On the other hand, this is not to be confused with changing the lead or lag times on the dependencies (shorter or longer), an action that produces the expected effect.

6.3 PROGRAM EVALUATION AND REVIEW TECHNIQUE (PERT)

The PERT Method was developed in the late 1950s as a joint effort between the Navy Special Projects Office, Lockheed Aircraft, and Booz, Allen, and Hamilton for the POLARIS Ballistic Missile Project. A variation on the activity-on-a-node method, it was developed to aid in the management of research and development projects.[2] Because it was originally intended for top-management presentations, PERT gives greater emphasis on the major deliverables; that is, the milestones or events. These major events are placed in the nodes, while the less important activities or tasks may (or may not—at the user's discretion) be illustrated on the arrows. It is also possible to put the three estimates, the computed duration, and other pertinent information on the arrow. (Figure 6.11)

6.4 CRITICAL PATH METHOD (CPM)

The Critical Path Method (CPM), developed by duPont and Remington Rand Univac, was originally intended as an aid in equating costs to time during the management of large construction projects. A CPM network is an arrow diagram that looks like Figure 6.4 and Figure 6.5.

6.5 THE PERT/CPM DIAGRAM

Over the years, the term PERT/CPM has come to mean any variation on the different types of networks, as well as whatever the user wants it to mean. Any of the drawing methods are used in combination with any of the calculation methods. Consequently, the best features of each may be selected and used to improve

---

[1]J.D. Wiest & F.K. Levy, *A MANAGEMENT GUIDE TO PERT/CPM* (New Jersey,: Prentice-Hall, 1977).

[2]R & D projects, as mentioned in Chapter 5, have a high degree of uncertainty—much like many systems projects.

Figure 6.11 PERT network.

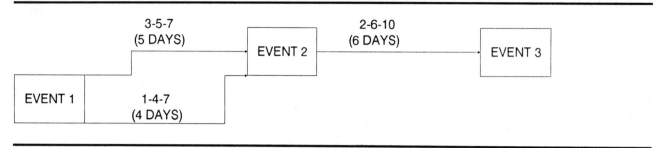

Figure 6.12 PERT/CPM network.

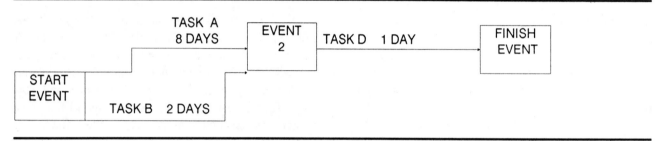

the networking process. Figure 6.12 is an illustration of one type of PERT/CPM network.

6.6 LOOPS IN THE NETWORK

A loop in the network occurs when a successor to one job is subsequently designated as the predecessor to its predecessor (or to one of the earlier predecessors of its predecessor). (See Figure 6.13.) This type of logic cannot be tolerated in the traditional scheduling algorithms. Nevertheless, this is a common error. There may be times when there is a strong desire to employ this logic approach (e.g., when trying to demonstrate that Design, Code, and Test may have to repeat several iterations before the process has been completed). Viewed in the network world as an endless loop, it is

Figure 6.13 Incorrect looping.

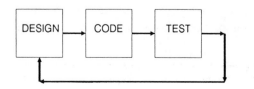

important to resist the temptation to use this approach. If three iterations of the process are needed, then three unique iterations of the jobs must be included. (Figure 6.14)

6.7 DECISIONS PATHS IN A NETWORK

When there may be one or more alternative paths through the network for producing a given deliverable—and only *one* of these paths should be selected, given certain conditions—decision-making logic is required. Like looping, the popular network scheduling algorithms have not been designed to accommodate choosing and executing only one path from many while traveling through the network. Any time a group of jobs has been implanted within the plan, it is assumed that these jobs must always be completed in order to finish the project.

6.8 NETWORKS AND PROJECT MANAGEMENT SOFTWARE

This section deals with the mechanics of drawing networks with the project management software. The important issues deal with how user friendly the system

Figure 6.14 Iterations in the network.

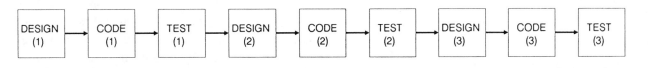

is and whether it satisfies the requirements for establishing and verifying the relationships between jobs in a plan.

6.8.1 Types of Networks ◆

Networks may be drawn as activity-on-the-arrow, activity-on-a-node, or precedence diagrams. What type of network does the product support?

6.8.2 Types of Relationships ◆

There are four types of dependencies: finish-to-start, start-to-start, finish-to-finish, and start-to-finish. What type of relationships does the product support?

6.8.3 Number of Dependencies ◆

When there is more than one predecessor (or successor) to an activity, there exists the condition of multiple relationships. In each software product, the number of dependencies allowed per job affects how the user may capitalize on these multiple relationships. Ideally, there will be no limitation to the number of predecessors and successors that a job can have—or, at least, the limit should be high enough to allow for the majority of cases.

If the project management software product is of the type that handles the plan data on a hard disc, there is usually no reason to limit the number of relationships.

In the *variable-length, main memory* products, the maximum number of jobs, resources, and dependencies is limited by the total size of remaining memory. In other words, the total number of dependencies per plan is directly related to the sum of the memory storage requirements for each job times the total number of jobs—plus the memory requirements for each of their respective resources and dependencies. With

these products, it is important to remember that the more resources and dependencies there are, the fewer the total number of jobs per plan will be available. The fewer the number of jobs per plan available, the greater the number of subprojects will be required—assuming the product also supports subprojects.

6.8.4 Establishing Dependencies ◆

How easy is it to enter the dependency information? Can the relationships be entered while in network mode? How easy is it to interactively enter the relationships and immediately see the results?

Dependency data entry in Gantt mode is certainly satisfactory in smaller projects and projects with a limited number of interconnections; but, ideally, the process of entering relationships can be performed in network mode. This is because plans with the complex interdependencies associated with several parallel subnetworks, many tasks, and many relationships are not as easy to follow during Gantt mode data entry. As a consequence in Gantt-driven products, it is often necessary to work from a hand-drawn, hard copy network and do the data entry while alternating between the Gantt and the PERT. Dependency data entry while in WBS mode has the same limitations. Forms entry, of course, is even more difficult.

Many of the products that support WBSs allow users to establish relationships at any level in the work breakdown structure. When the start of one task may be dependent upon the completion of all of the tasks within another group of tasks, it is advisable to designate the summary task of the group as the predecessor rather than the last detail task in the group. In this manner, additional ending detail tasks may later be inserted into the group without the need to modify relationships. This concept will be addressed in this section and again later in this chapter.

It is important to recall, when developing the optimal plan, that a job is not dependent when it is waiting for an available resource. This type of constraint will be addressed later.

6.8.5 Special Considerations for I-J Mode Multiple Relationships ◆

Next, the user must consider the effect limitations on multiple relationships will have on the planning effort. Normally, beyond noting how many dependencies are permitted per job, multiple relationships are not very significant. The exception enters when discussing activity-on-the-arrow networks [AOA or ADM] and their "I-J" nodes. Most important, when in AOA or ADM, the user must be concerned when trying to enter groups of parallel jobs that have the same starting node and the same ending node. As noted earlier, entering multiple parallel relationships in an ADM network is traditionally prohibited. "Dummy" entries are usually used to overcome the problem with a unique "I-J" number when there are parallel multiple relationships. However, in AOA/ADM products where the total number of jobs, relationships, and resources is limited, having to use valuable memory on "dummies" is an undesirable constraint. Primavera Project Planner (which supports "I-J" mode) maintains its plans on the hard drive; therefore, storage limitations are not an issue. However, even in products where there is unlimited storage for project files, the labor and time consumed in entering the extra "dummies" might be a consideration when choosing the network mode.

6.8.6 How Easy It Is to Enter Dependencies? ◆

How easy is it to enter the dependencies? If a number for the dependency must be entered (rather than pointing with the mouse or cursor), how many keystrokes are required and how difficult is it to keep track of the values that must be entered? (When the numbers aren't displayed on the screen at the same time the dependency number must be entered, a copy of the project plan must be in hand before the dependencies may be entered.) Is the dependency number also the WBS number? If not, must the user do double data entry— and how hard is it to keep track of two sets of numbers (one the WBS number and one the dependency number?)

6.8.7 Inserting Jobs Into the Middle of the Plan ◆

How are new jobs added to the plan? When inserting a new job into the middle of the plan, must the user then go in and manually resolve all the new relationships? How easy is it to resolve the new relationships?

6.8.8 Subnetwork Dependencies ◆

Does the product support dependencies between the nodes in multiple parallel subnetworks?

6.8.9 Moving Jobs in the Network ◆

There are two approaches to implementing the "Move" feature. One is actually to change the position of the job in the network, thus changing the relationships. The second is to be able to move the job and maintain dependencies. This latter approach is useful when trying to clean up the aesthetics of the network.

6.8.10 Removing Dependencies ◆

How easy is it to remove or change dependencies?

6.8.11 Deleting Jobs in the Plan ◆

When an intervening job is removed, is there automatic resolution of dependencies? In other words, if the user eliminates a job in the middle of the network, will the product delete it and connect the jobs that are adjacent to the deleted job, or must the user do this manually?

Some products automatically reconnect adjacent dependencies. More often than not, the new relationships will be correct. While there may be some additional effort to correct those relationships that are in error, this approach is more desirable than being left after a delete with many dangling jobs.

When the delete does remove all traces of the activity and leaves dangling jobs, rather than directly deleting the job, a better approach is to reestablish all of the new relationships first. When this process has been completed, the activity can then be deleted leaving no dangling effects. Often, this operation cannot be completed unless all of the old and new connections have been written down first. Given that all of these steps must be done for every delete, the process of removing jobs becomes tiresome indeed.

Figure 6.15 Lag and lead times in software.

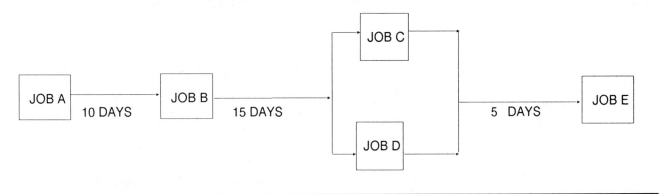

6.8.12 Lag and Lead Times ◆

The user may desire to insert several types of delays between jobs. In Figure 6.15, there is a 10-day delay between Jobs A and B. Delaying the finish of Job A is causing its finish to lag. Delaying the start of Job B is adding a lead time to its start. But what about the 15 days after Job B? If it is to affect both Job C and Job D, the lag of 15 days ought to be added to Job B. Otherwise, the lead of 15 days is to be added to either Job C or D—as the case may be. If both Job C and D are to delay Job E by 5 days, then this lead is added to Job E. Otherwise, the lag of 5 days is added to either Job C or D—as appropriate.

Does the product support lag or lead times? Does it support lag or lead times with all relationship types?

6.8.13 Copying Jobs in the Plan ◆

In this section, the process of making duplicate copies of *entire* plans is addressed. Similarly, the steps for the occasional need to replicate a small number of jobs within a plan will be addressed. On the other hand, when activities or tasks must be used over and over again, they may be classified as part of the *template* tasks. For more on how to complete the *template* copy process, see the discussion in the next section on the *template* tasks. It is important to note that all copy features may be limited by the size limitations of the product.

6.8.14 Copying the *Template* Jobs ◆

The need for a *template* application occurs when certain groups of jobs must be used over and over again— within the same project *or* across several projects. (See Figure 4.4.) Ideally, users will not have to rekey these jobs every time they are needed. For the purpose of the discussion in this section, it is assumed that the *template* jobs have been stored in a separate plan.

Can the *template* plan be copied at all? How easy it is to repetitively copy *template* plans? How easy is it to copy and *keep* the dependencies *within* the *template* plan?

There are two ways to get *template* plans into a master plan: (1) copy them in; or (2) "attach" them as a subproject. It is important to recall that the copy (also known as combine or include) features may be limited by the size restrictions of the product. On the other hand, when subprojects are "attached" to a master project, they don't always copy in *all* of the associated data and therefore are not usually restricted by the size limitations.

Unfortunately, some products support the subproject feature, but limit the use of the subproject to one time per project or one time per system. The workaround for this limitation requires making multiple copies of the *template* plan and saving it under different names. The disadvantage, of course, lies in the additional bookkeeping effort.

Some products also require that the job names in

the subprojects as well as the master project be unique. When duplicate names are prohibited, it will again be necessary to make several copies, under different file names, of the same group of *template* tasks. Then the name fields of the activities in each subproject will need be edited by adding a unique version number to the beginning or end of each job. Although this process definitely represents additional effort, it is not as hard as individually keying in all of the repetitive activities.

How easy is it to copy the *template* plan and then *insert* additional dependencies *into* it?

Sometimes, it is necessary to establish relationships between jobs in the master plan and those that are inside of the *template* plan. If such is the requirement, and the product's subprojects can't have inside dependencies, their usefulness in a *template* application is further restricted.

Although many of the products do indeed support subproject functions, the feature is so limiting in its relevance for *template* application that the file copy (alias combine or include) is a preferred alternative. However, it, too, has its drawbacks. When getting the *template* jobs into the plan via the previously mentioned subproject ''attach'' function, *any changes made to the subproject are automatically reflected whenever the master project is newly invoked.* But, after the file has been imported into a master project using the file combine or include, *it loses the automatic update advantage.* From then on, any changes made to the *template* plan must also be made in the master project, in each occurrence of the *template* tasks. The danger here is that the other data sets will get out of synchronization with the *template* plan and will often not reflect current changes.

The bottom line is that the requirements of this feature are not often successfully met.

6.8.15 Loops in the Network ◆

Will the software prevent loops? How easy is it to debug loops?

6.8.16 Dangling Jobs ◆

In this sense, a dangling job is one that is found somewhere in the plan and has no successor, implying that the job can go on forever—or at least until the end of the project. Ideally, the product will prevent dangling and flag the nodes in question.

6.8.17 Verifying Dependencies Are Correct ◆

How easy is it to follow the links between the nodes and to be able to confirm that the plan has been correctly entered?

The network-drawing algorithms of some products seem to have difficulty mapping out the nodes in a logical manner. Jobs that sequentially follow one another within a subnetwork are instead frequently scattered around the network. When this occurs, verification may sometimes not take place until the jobs have been moved to their correct positions.

If the subnetworks are vertically distanced from each other, their subnetwork connections may spread across more than one screen. As a result, the dependencies become very hard to follow. When this occurs more than a few times (as is usually the case), there will be many open-ended crossed lines on the screen, and interactive network verification becomes next to impossible.

If the product has a ''Move'' feature that maintains relationships, these problems can often be minimized by repositioning the nodes so that they are closer together. Assuming that the product supports this kind of move, it is still a process that may take a long time—even in only an average-size project (with several subnetworks, many tasks, and many relationships).

When the possibilities of the ''Move'' have been exhausted, or when there is no ''Move'' at all, other tools such as dependency reports and trace facilities must then be used for certification. The trace facilities will be evaluated in the next section.

6.8.18 Highlighting Dependency Paths ◆

The user may only wish to see *all* of the predecessors and successors attached to a designated job in the network. This application is especially helpful in the verification process. Several products support this requirement.

6.8.19 Network Aesthetics ◆

Are the networks easy to read? Is the network simple, straightforward, and uncluttered? For example, how are overlapping lines treated? Are there dotted lines? solid lines? How are they used?

6.8.20 Scaled to Time? ◆

Some packages' networks are drawn scaled to time. This is a fine feature when it does not conflict with the estimating approach. If the user follows the 4–40 hour estimating guidelines, yet the smallest time scale in the network is weeks, the task, when illustrated, may only be represented as a fraction of the week. When this happens, the task is seen as only a tiny vertical line or a box. Furthermore, some time-scaled products place the plan data inside the node; when this occurs, there is little or no accompanying text. Consequently, the network may be difficult to understand, hard to verify, and frustrating when trying to connect or verify dependencies.

6.9 NETWORKS AND WORK BREAKDOWN STRUCTURES ◆

If the first level of the WBS is called the major milestone level, the initial network may be entered as a milestone network and have milestone-to-milestone dependencies.

As the WBS expands and the planning process progresses to an activity-level network, there will be many activity-to-activity dependencies. In cases where the milestones have yet to be partitioned or where there are subnetwork dependencies, there may also be milestone-to-activity dependencies or activity-to-milestone dependencies.

By the time the WBS and the network have descended to a task level, there may be mixed dependencies, such as task-to-task, task-to-activity, activity-to-task, task-to-milestone, and so on.

Because not all levels of the WBS and not all jobs within a level have been identified when the planning process begins, work units have to be added into their respective niches as the planning process progresses.

Ideally, when a lower level is being expanded

and jobs are being added at the end of the sequence of tasks at that level, it should not be necessary to undo/redo predecessor-successor relationships for the "latest last job." Some products handle the resolution for the user.

• These products create duplicate beginning and ending nodes for each level except the lowest level. Relationships between these nodes and other beginning and ending nodes do not have to be changed when the lower levels are expanded with the "latest last jobs."

In those that do not, resolution must simply be done by the user. All of the dependencies must be changed as the lower levels are developed. This is not only more labor-intensive, but also subject to errors. However, this problem can be avoided by simply creating a matching ending job for each level above the lowest level. (Of course, this also consumes memory.)

6.9.1 Limiting Relationships to the Lowest Level ◆

Some products demand that relationships can only be created at the lowest level. SuperProject Expert and Project Workbench fall within this category.

6.10 CONVERGING AND DIVERGING TASKS

Parallel tasks within an activity may converge (that is, come together) at a starting point for a next set of tasks that may, in turn, diverge (that is, separate) to another set of parallel tasks. (See Figure 6.16.)

Having a place for these convergence and divergence points to meet simplifies the plan. Although the date computations are not affected, without this meeting point, there may be many crossed and confusing connections. "Dummies" satisfy the need to indicate the end of one set of parallel tasks and the beginning of the following set. Unfortunately, this use of the "dummy" tasks not only requires additional data entry, but also reduces the total number of jobs available in the plan. In all of the products evaluated, these "dummy" tasks must be created by the user.

Figure 6.16 Converging and diverging tasks.

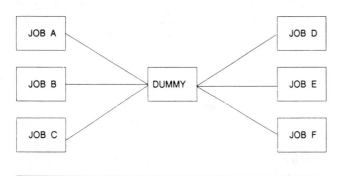

6.11 SETTING UP HAMMOCKS ♦

A hammock is a special kind of activity or task that may be connected to both the beginning and the end of a group of jobs. It provides a synopsis of information pertaining to the group, rolling the data into a single reference point. After the dependencies between the hammock and the group have been established, the hammock summarizes the dates and durations of the jobs it encompasses. Two products support this feature: Primavera Project Planner and Viewpoint.

6.12 DEPENDENCIES IN A MULTIPROJECT ENVIRONMENT ♦

A common source of contention in a data processing shop is caused by trying to plan in a multiproject environment. In many multiproject environments, the same pool of resources may be shared by several simultaneous projects, some big and some small; while, at the same time, these exact resources are also expected to work on maintenance jobs, some big and some small. The challenge arises from attempting to effectively schedule shared resources across all of these endeavors. Although resource issues will not be addressed until later in the book, the concept of dependencies in multiprojects will be introduced in this chapter.

The projects in a multiproject environment may be independent projects that simply share a common

resource pool but are otherwise unrelated. (Figure 6.17) On the other hand, they may be interdependent. (Figure 6.18) Although not illustrated, the relationship may take the form in which the only interdependency between two subprojects occurs when the start of Project 2 is dependent only on the finish of Project 1.

Determining the most efficient distribution of resources is facilitated when managers can set up all of the projects under one plan. Ideally, a master project (also called a superproject) can be created that will show all of the associated projects. Each of these associated projects may be called subprojects and are, of course, complete projects in their own right. The master project shows the parallel subprojects that are going on at the same time, as well as all of the sequential subprojects. It also illustrates the interdependencies between the subprojects. This global view shows, at a glance, where the resources are overscheduled and later demonstrates the effects of eliminating these conflicts. Furthermore, in products that operate on project data in main memory, partitioning the project into subprojects is also an excellent way in which to overcome limitations in project size. Finally, the subproject concept lends itself beautifully to the Moving Window approach.

A complete understanding of the multiproject implementation may be achieved by dividing the pertinent discussions into their respective topics. This section will deal with creating the master project and its interdependencies. Scheduling and resource planning in a multiproject environment will be covered later in the book.

The products fall into two classifications: (1) those systems that "attach" the subproject to the master project but do not import its activities or tasks; and (2) those products that merge the subprojects into a single grand plan.

In the systems that "attach" to the subprojects, only one version of the subproject plan is ever produced. Modifications are made to the subproject and are automatically reflected in the master project. There is no need to do double data entry. Attached subprojects are usually represented by a single one-line entry on the master project Gantt chart and in the network. This makes it very easy to get the global perspective of all of the projects at once. Subprojects may be nested one within another. Nesting will be addressed later in the book.

Figure 6.17 Independent multiprojects.

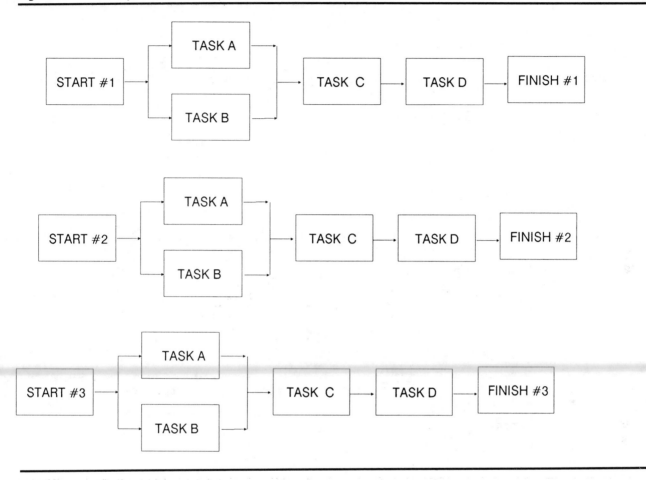

Merged master-project plans copy in all of the activities and tasks from the subproject. All of the jobs from the subproject will be seen in the network and in the Gantt chart of the master project. Modifications to the plans ought to be made in the master project. If there is a need to work with a separate subproject and the current schedule is to be reflected in both plans, maintaining the original *and* the merged copies of a subproject plan will often later require some degree of double data entry. The danger here is that the subproject sets will get out of synchronization with the master plan, and one of them will often not reflect current changes. One way to avoid this problem is to update at the subproject level, delete the master project, and remerge it. Of course, this operation must be performed frequently if the merged sets are to reflect reality. Furthermore, this is not always an easy operation—especially when there are subproject interdependencies. In the worst scenario, the user would need to do double data entry and still worry that the data will be out of synchronization.

As a final comment, there is one strong advantage to merging subproject files. With merged plans, reports can be produced with any level of detail. (For example, all of the jobs within each subproject *and* all of the subprojects within the master projects.) With the exception of SuperProject Expert, the products that ''attach'' the subprojects will *not* produce reports with the details of each of the subprojects within the master project. This limitation may prove troublesome later on, when trying to assign the work and when trying to manage the project.

Figure 6.18 Interdependent multiprojects.

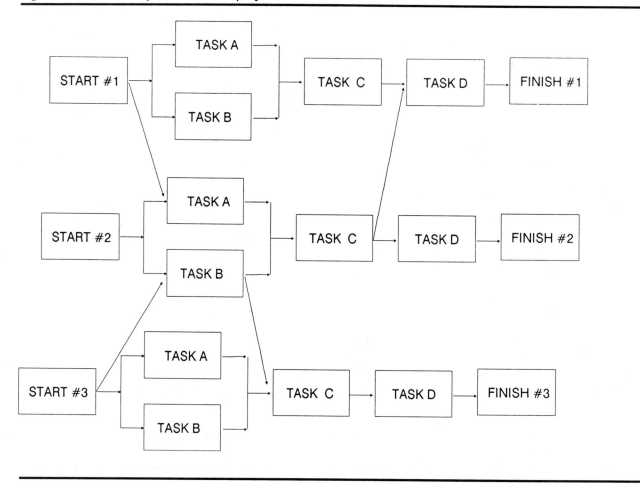

6.13 PRINTING AND VIEWING NETWORKS ◆

How easily does the system allow the user to print hard copy versions of the networks? Is there a special print function or does the system rely on the computer's print-screen key. Is the process of invoking the on-screen display of the network easy?

6.14 COMPLETING THE DEPENDENCY PROCESS

After the team has produced the networks, they still have a *very important* job to perform. This operation pertains to the gathering and recording of data, much of which will become *essential* when the job is actually assigned to the individual who is designated to do it. Work packages will be prepared for each assignee. Some of the information that proves very helpful to workers is:

- The inputs and prerequisites to each job
- Any constraints imposed on the completion of the job
- An update to the data that was created during the preparation of the work breakdown structures and estimates.

Now is the time to prepare this data. Ideally, the information may be entered into the ad hoc notes in the record for each job.

6.15 GUIDELINES AND DOCUMENTATION ◆

Is there any documentation in the user's manual to describe the process of using networks and dependencies in project management? (Instructions on how to use the system to achieve the implementation of a feature are not considered guidelines.)

CHAPTER **7** DEVELOPING THE OPTIMAL PLAN

7.1 INTRODUCTION

Having prepared the work breakdown structure, the estimates, and the network, the user must now direct attention to computing an optimal plan. This is the plan that represents the time it would take to complete the venture—if all of the resources were dedicated to the project and were qualified to do the work (neither trainees nor experts), and if the Protected Environment *broad-based overhead* had been factored into each estimate of expected effort.

Furthermore, this plan is not constrained by desired completion dates, nor is it constrained by the known limitations on the number of available resources. Finally, it is the plan whose network shows only the true and natural dependencies.

In other words, the optimal plan is not being forced to retrofit into anyone's preconceived notions about its outcome. *The optimal plan is the rock bottom, best schedule that can be developed.*

Although many people are concerned about the effort involved in the development of an optimal plan that is not likely to be implemented, it is an essential part of project planning. Its real benefit will become especially apparent later on, when actually demonstrating the effects that date constraints and/or resource limitations may have on the project goals. (Naturally, when the traditional restrictions are factored into the

optimal plan, the schedule gets extended rather than compressed. The optimal plan *then* becomes a powerful negotiating tool.)

7.2 THE CRITICAL PATH

A map of the United States will show many routes going across the country from New York to Los Angeles. In a race between these two cities, the shortest route would obviously be chosen. But what if every route had to be traveled at least once? Then, the duration of the race would be directly related to how fast the longest route could be crossed.

A project network has many paths that are each like the routes across the country. In other words, there are many routes from the beginning of the project to the end of the project. If someone wanted to know the length of a particular route from New York to Los Angeles, he or she would add up all of the mileage designations from a map that shows that route. If that person wanted to know the length of a path through the network, he or she would add up the durations of each of the jobs on that path. If he or she wanted to know the length of the project, the longest path through the network would need to be found. This longest path is sometimes referred to as the critical path. When there are multiple parallel jobs on a critical path, they are all considered to be part of the critical path.

When two or more paths are equal and they also equal the longest duration, then there is more than one critical path.

The critical path is the path where, if any job on that path is late, the whole project may be late. Therefore, an activity is also critical when it lies on the critical path. Jobs on the critical path must be managed very closely.

Sometimes there is a path (or more than one path) that is very nearly as long as the critical path. This type of path is called a near-critical path. When a near-critical path is very close to the critical path, it must also be managed very closely so that it does not become *the* critical path and inadvertently cause the project to be late.

In a project with many paths, adding up the durations of each job on each separate path is time-consuming and may even be error-prone. Therefore, finding the critical path and near-critical path(s) may be very difficult. There is a shortcut to uncovering the critical path, and it will be presented later in this chapter.

7.3 THE IMPORTANCE OF THE CALENDAR

The proper calendar is essential to computing the correct dates. It signifies (1) all observed holidays, both legal ones and those that are unique to the organization; (2) workdays and non-workdays; (3) workhours and non-workhours; and (4) vacation closings, if applicable.

It is also important to prepare the calendar so that there is consistency in the setting of dates. For example, if the workday ends at 5 P.M. and a job also ends at that time, its successors either begin at 5:01 P.M. or they begin at the start of the next working day. For successors that represent normal, run-of-the-mill jobs (durations greater than zero), either implementation is correct, as long as the same one is consistently invoked.

On the other hand, a zero duration milestone is preferably designated as occurring at the *instant* when all of its predecessors have *finished*. Otherwise, it will have the effect of scheduling the end milestone one day later than expected—or three days later in the case of a weekend.

Finally, some scheduling algorithms try to give each job as long as possible to be completed. They assume that even though a job is scheduled to finish at 5 P.M. on one particular day and its successors begin at 8:00 A.M. the next working day, the predecessor will be scheduled to finish at 7:59 A.M. of that next working day. Thus, its finish is not scheduled until immediately before the start of the successors. Unfortunately, this has the effect of scheduling the end of the project one day later than expected—or three days later in the case of a weekend.

If the *broad-based overhead* has previously been factored into the individual jobs, then they have already been expanded to account for the nonproductive time in every workday. Therefore, if, for example, eight hours is the normal working day, an eight-hour day will be scheduled into the calendar. If the *broad-based overhead* has *not* been factored into each estimate and the group still wants to account for the nonproductive time, they could use the calendar to accomplish this. In other words, if two hours of an eight-hour day are considered to be the nonproductive rate, then a six-hour day is scheduled into the calendar. Either alternative is acceptable—as long as it is consistently applied.

The hours per day and days per week should be realistic. If the calendar starts off by including extra time at night or on the weekends, then one of the options available when late—(working overtime)—is gone before the project even starts. Even when the team is intentionally choosing to sacrifice this alternative, they are employing risky business.

7.4 PICKING THE START DATE

It is also important that the start date of the phase (or project) that is currently being planned be far enough into the future to allow time to prepare and approve the plan. Similarly, when using the Moving Window concept, planning for the next phase occurs at (or near) the end of the current phase. Picking the start date of this next phase can be tricky, especially in those situations when the team is still unsure about the end date of the current phase.

7.5 PICKING THE END DATE

While developing the optimal plan, the end date is allowed to evolve. Because it is essential to know the true end date of the phase (or project), given the legitimate dependencies and unlimited, qualified resources, the end date is not forced. (A date-constrained, resource-constrained plan *may* subsequently be developed, but not at this point.)

When organizations insist on picking an end date first and retrofitting the project into the resulting timeframe, they sooner or later discover that they will need to (1) descope, and/or (2) add more resources and/or (3) sacrifice some degree of quality, reliability, performance, and/or maintenance. Even when they also introduce measures for increasing productivity, they may often also wind up late and over budget anyway.

7.6 TWO SETS OF DATES

While developing the plan, two sets of dates are usually computed: a set of early dates and a set of late dates. For the early dates, there will be a date computed that shows the earliest each job can start, and a date computed that shows the earliest each job can finish. For the late dates, there will be a date for the latest that each job can start (and still not affect the end of

the project), and one for the latest that each job can finish (and still not affect the end of the project).

These dates are computed by following each path through the network and entering the respective dates for each job in the plan. The early dates are established in a forward pass through the network and the late dates are determined with a backward pass through the network.

7.6.1 The Forward Pass

The first strategy is called the forward pass because dates are computed by starting at the beginning of the project and moving forward into the future. The early finish of any job is computed by adding its duration to its early start.

This is most easily illustrated when the relationship between the tasks is the traditional finish to start, as seen in Figure 7.1. In this example, predecessor jobs are assumed to finish at the *end* of a workday and successor jobs are assumed to begin at the *start* of the

Figure 7.1 The forward pass.

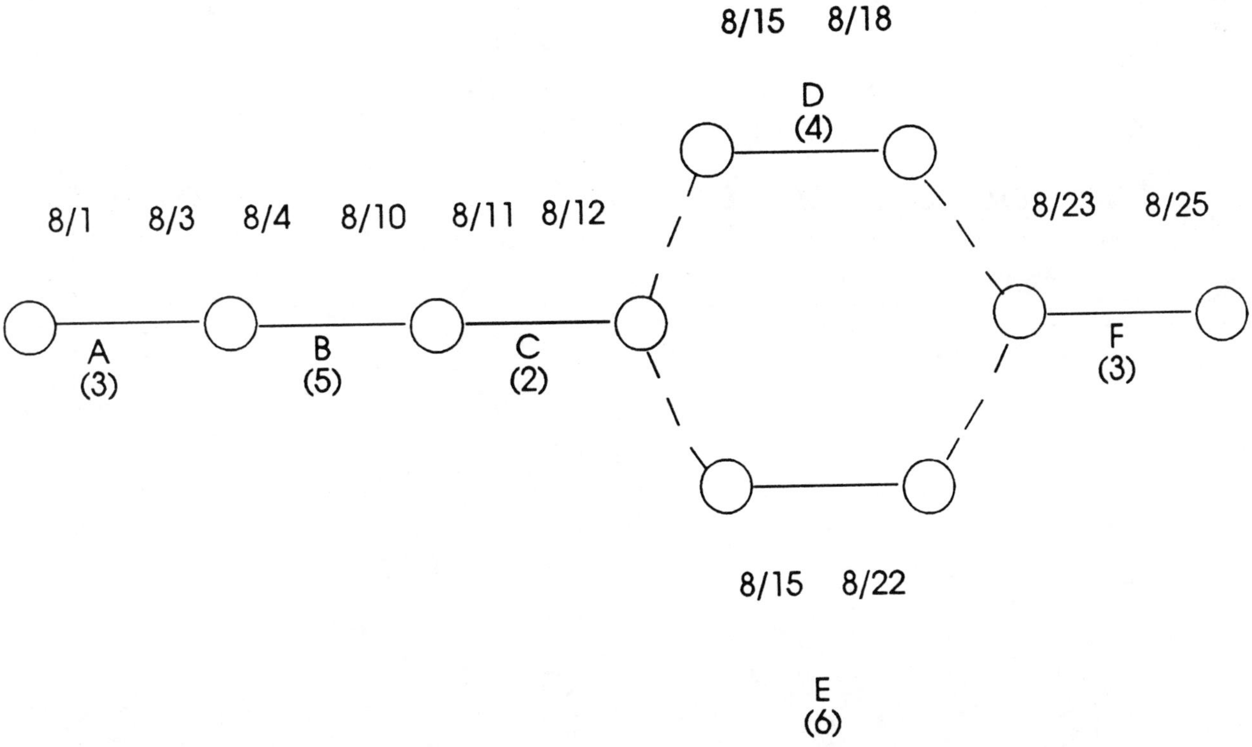

next workday. The project starts on 8/1 and the weekends fall on 8/6–8/7, 8/13–8/14, 8/20–8/21, and 8/27–8/28.

Jobs A, B, and C are serial activities, each in a finish to start relationship, with no lead or lag between them. Their respective durations are three days, five days, and two days. If the phase (or project) starts on August 1, then the early start and finish dates for job A are 8/1 and 8/3, respectively. Job B then starts at the earliest on 8/4 and the earliest it can finish, acknowledging the intervening weekend, is 8/10. The early start and finish dates for job C are 8/11 and 8/12, respectively.

Jobs D and E are parallel jobs, and neither may start until C has finished. Allowing for the weekend, jobs D and E will start, at the earliest, on 8/15. A four day job, D's early finish is 8/18. E, a six day job that spans another weekend, may finish, at the earliest, on 8/22.

F, the successor to both D and E, *may not start until* both *D and E have finished.* This does not occur until 8/22; therefore, F may not start until, at the earliest, 8/23. It finishes on 8/25.

- During the forward pass, no job may begin until *all* of its predecessors have been completed. When two or more parallel jobs converge to one job, an easy way to remember how to determine the successor's early start date is to have it start only after the *latest* early finish date of all of its predecessors.

7.6.2 The Backward Pass

The second strategy is called the backward pass because dates are computed by starting at the end of the last job in the project and moving backward in time to the present. The late start of any job is computed by subtracting its duration from its late finish.

In Figure 7.2, if the phase (or project) may end, at the latest, on August 31, then the late finish and the late start for job F are 8/31 and 8/29, respectively.

As a result, jobs D and E, which are both parallel

Figure 7.2 The backward pass.

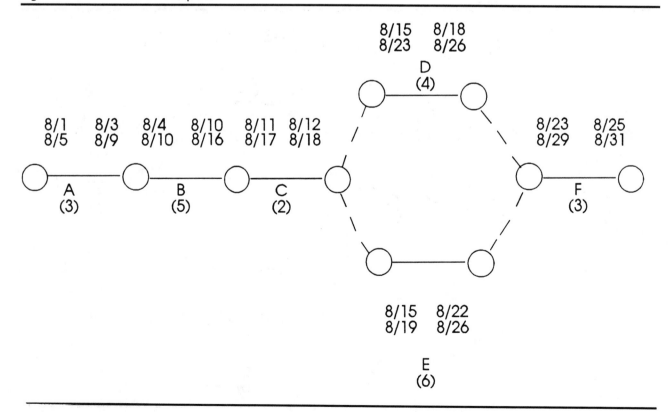

jobs, must both finish before F can start. Furthermore, F must start, at the latest, on 8/29. So that this may happen, jobs D and E must finish, at the latest (acknowledging the weekend, on 8/26).

A 4 day job, D must then start, at the latest, on 8/23. E, a six-day job that spans another weekend, must start, at the latest, on 8/19.

Job C *must end in time for* both *D and E to start.* This means that C must finish, at the latest, by 8/18. It must start, at the latest, by 8/17.

- During the backward pass, no job may end *after* the beginning of any of its successors. When two or more parallel jobs converge to one job, an easy way to remember how to determine the predecessor's late finish date is always to have it finish before the *earliest* late start date of all of its successors.

Acknowledging the weekends, the late start and late finish dates for jobs A and B are 8/5 to 8/9 and 8/10 to 8/16, respectively.

7.6.3 Annotation of Dates

After both passes have been completed, there will be two sets of dates for each job. It is traditional to put the early dates above the late dates. (See Figure 7.2.)

7.6.4 Alternative Time Units or Dependencies

When the duration units are measured in hours or fractions of a day, then predecessor jobs may finish and succeeding jobs may begin sometime between the start and end of each workday. Furthermore, they may also start near the conclusion of one workday and span to the beginning of the next workday.

When there are finish-to-finish relationships and zero lead or lag time, the same date is used for the end of each job. When there are start-to-start dependencies and zero lead or lag time, the same date is used for the start of each job. When there is a specified number for the lead or lag time, then the affected dates are modified accordingly.

7.7 SLACK (OR FLOAT)

Slack (sometimes referred to as float) is the difference in time between the two dates at the beginning of a job or the two dates at the end of the job. In other words, slack is computed by subtracting the early start of any job from its late start, or subtracting its early finish from its late finish. The answer is the same for both sides of any job. (Weekends are not included in the count.) *Slack is not fluff; therefore, it is* not *doctored in any manner!* This type of slack is also sometimes referred to as *total* slack. At any point in time, the *total* slack associated with any path in the network will remain constant for that path. There is another type of slack, *free* slack. *Total* slack and *free* slack will both be addressed again. In this text, if slack is not specifically designated, then the reference is intended to mean *total* slack.

In Job A, there are five working days between its early start date of 8/1 and its late start date of 8/5. (Figure 7.3) When any of the dates cross a weekend, the computation for slack must also cross the weekend. Therefore, there are also five working days between Job A's early finish date of 8/3 and its late finish date of 8/9. Note that the slack (seen in brackets) in Job D is 7. The significance between slack of 5 and slack of 7 will be explained in the next section.

7.8 SLACK AND THE CRITICAL PATH

In the example in Figure 7.3, it is easy to find the critical path. With the exception of the point where Jobs D and E are parallel, there is always only one path from which to choose. Between Jobs D and E, it is also easy to discern the longest: Job E is on the critical path.

When attempting to analyze a complex network with many subnetworks, many tasks, and many parallel paths, the critical path is not so readily apparent. Furthermore, trying to find the longest path by adding up the durations of each job on each separate path is time-consuming and even may be error-prone. Therefore, finding the critical path and near-critical path(s) may be very difficult.

Following the path in the network that has the *least amount of total slack* will reveal the critical path. At any point in time, this number will remain constant across the critical path and through the whole plan. The path(s) with the next highest amount of *total* slack will be the near-critical path(s). In Figure 7.3, following the path with slack 5 reveals the critical path.

Figure 7.3 Slack and the critical path.

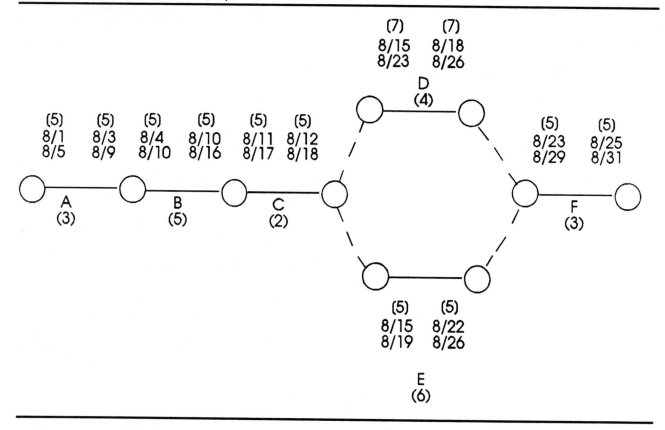

7.8.1 The Trouble with Zero Total Slack

In the past, many managers have believed that the critical path is the path with zero *total* slack. Therefore, they have believed that, when doing the backward pass, the late finish date of the project ought to be the same as the early finish date of the project. When this approach is used, the critical path will indeed have zero *total* slack. For now, suffice it to say that when there is zero *total* slack on the critical path, the probability of finishing the project on time is only 50 percent. The odds for success increase above 50 percent in relationship to the amount of slack added to the critical path.

> *The Critical Path, Then, Is Defined As The Path Through The Network With The Least Amount Of Total Slack, And Not Necessarily The Path With Zero Total Slack!*

Using probability theory to (1) determine the chance of successfully meeting the late finish date of the project and (2) pick a late finish date with better odds for success will be covered later in this chapter.

7.8.2 A Warning About Using Precedence-Type Relationships

Earlier, the critical path was equated to the length of the project and was described as consisting of a series of the plan's milestones, events, activities, and tasks. Furthermore, the jobs on the critical path may be connected with one of the four types of PDM relationships. PDM networks—that have combined the four types of relationships and also have lead or lag times between the jobs—result in networks that are often hard to analyze. Finding the critical path in these networks is not always an easy chore.

Similarly, the normal bounds of intuition are strained. For example, it is commonly understood that lengthening the duration of any of the jobs on a critical path will usually result in extending the duration of the project and vice versa.

There may also be times when there will be a series of jobs in which there is a mixture of start-to-start, finish-to-start, and finish-to-finish relationships. In certain combinations of these relationships types, an abnormality occurs that is totally counter-intuitive. Whenever a job on a critical path has a finish-to-finish relationship with its predecessor *and* a start-to-start relationship with its successor *and* the work inside of that job may not be interrupted, shortening the duration of that job *will extend the duration of the project (and vice versa)!*

The user is advised to proceed with caution when using these types of relationships. On the other hand, this is not to be confused with changing the lead or lag times on the dependencies (shorter or longer), an action that produces the expected effect.

7.8.3 Negative Slack

When picking a target date for project completion and attempting to retrofit the plan into it, the target date becomes the late finish date of the project—no matter what the project early finish date is computed to be, even if the early date is later than the late date. Remember that slack is computed by subtracting the early start from the late start or the early finish from the late finish. When the early date is later than the late date, the application of this formula causes what is known as a negative slack condition. Consequently, the phase (or project) is already late before it starts! *And the more negative the slack, the closer the plan gets to 0 percent probability of success.*

7.9 DEVELOPING THE OPTIMAL SCHEDULE

Developing the optimal schedule requires iteratively (1) drawing the network (2) removing artificial dependencies and retaining only the true and natural dependencies (3) entering the estimates (4) calculating dates (needed to assign the work) (5) finding the slack (needed to identify the critical path) and (6) finding the critical path (needed to manage the project). This is the crucial juncture where work breakdown struc-

tures, estimating, networking, and scheduling all converge. (See Figure 2.10.)

7.10 ZERO DURATION MILESTONES

Zero duration milestones are very helpful in giving visibility to key summary points in the project. There may be occasions when there are many jobs that are scattered in several subnetworks, and the completion of all of these jobs has a special significance as well. Making them all predecessors to a single zero duration milestone gives visibility to an important date. Similarly, the user only has to look in one place in the plan for the information about the current status of the end date of all of these jobs. Furthermore, when there are many zero duration milestones of this type, it is advantageous to group them in a family of related milestones.

7.11 SCHEDULING LAG AND LEAD TIMES

Lag times or lead times may be inserted between jobs in the network. They are usually associated with finish-to-finish, start-to-start, and start-to-finish relationships although they are also sometimes used with traditional finish-to-start dependencies.

Lead and lag times are especially useful in situations such as waiting for delivery of hardware, printed forms, advertising copy, and so on. However, they are not usually significantly illustrated in many of the products. In these cases, it may be desirable to insert the lead or lag times as separate jobs with zero-cost resources so that they become line items on the management reports, thus allowing tracking of the status. With respect to the software, this topic will be explored again later in the chapter.

7.12 SCHEDULING WITH GANTT CHARTS

A Gantt (or bar) chart is an alternative graphics tool that, in lieu of a network, may be used to develop schedules. The Gantt chart is a matrix of rows and columns. The first few columns may be reserved for the job name, duration, resource name, dates, and so on. All remaining columns are then divided according to a predetermined timeframe. For example, the project may be scheduled in days and, therefore, the columns will each represent one day. In Figure 7.4, with

Figure 7.4 Gantt chart.

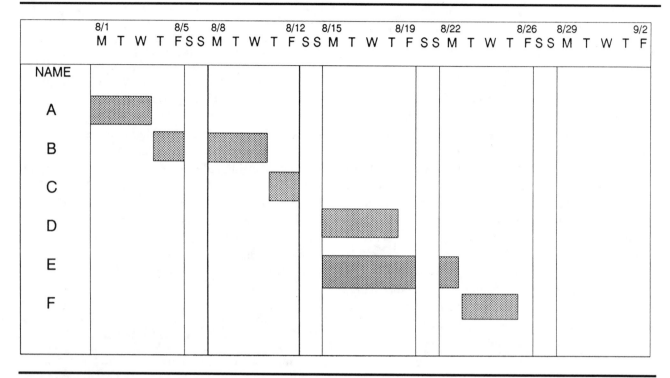

the exception of the first column that has been used for the job name, all of the columns have been divided into days and further grouped by workdays and weekends. A primary advantage of the Gantt chart is its ability to graphically show the optimal plan, the resource-constrained schedule, and progress all on one chart. Initially, it shows what tasks must be done, when they should start, when they should finish, and how long they should take. Note that this application of the notation leaves gaps in the bars to illustrate that there is no work done on the weekends. Other types of notation use one solid bar that crosses the weekends. Generally speaking, this is simply a personal preference decision.

Many people begin the planning effort with a Gantt chart. On smaller projects, this strategy may suffice—especially when the participants have an excellent understanding of the environment and the application. Data entry in Gantt mode is certainly satisfactory in smaller projects and projects with a limited number of interconnections.

On the other hand, in an average plan with several parallel subnetworks, many tasks, many parallel paths and many relationships, the bar chart does have its limitations:

- Estimates must be completed and approved before the chart can be drawn.

- Dependencies between jobs are not effectively illustrated. Frequently, a job winds up in a time slot, not because of a predecessor/successor relationship, but because that is simply where it best fits or because that is when a resource is free.

- Dependencies are hard to verify. For example, it is not intuitively obvious that the plans in Figures 7.3 and 7.4 are exactly the same. This is especially true when trying to visualize the relationship between D and F. These difficulties become even more of a factor in a larger plan.

- It is difficult to show two sets of dates without drawing two bars for the job or adding additional notation. In either case, the chart may become cluttered.

- It is difficult to show slack and the critical path without even more additional notation.

- Changes to the schedule require redrawing the bar

chart, thus losing one historical perspective of the impact of the changes.

- The optimal plan is harder to produce.
- Several scheduling alternatives can not be presented on the same Gantt chart.
- Resource assignments are not easy to illustrate. (This is also an inherent problem with networks.)

Gantt charts excel as presentation tools for effectively illustrating groups of milestones and for demonstrating individual resources scheduled to time. Finally, they are very useful in status reporting—to show how much of the plan has been completed. Gantts will be covered in more detail later.

7.13 NETWORK AESTHETICS

Figure 7.5 shows the network from Figure 7.3 in activity-on-a-node [AON] notation. No matter which type

of network is used, plan to throw several away before developing one that is aesthetically pleasing. At best, it's merely hard to get it right the first time—and sometimes it's even next to impossible.

7.14 SCHEDULING AND PROJECT MANAGEMENT SOFTWARE

While most of the products evaluated immediately compute schedules as new data is entered, Project Workbench and Primavera Project Planner are semi-immediate processors. That is, they do not compute schedules until a special action has been taken by the user. The other systems allow the user to control the automatic calculation feature by toggling it on or off. The topics described in this section will address:

1. How to establish the calendars to be used in the computations;

Figure 7.5 Activity-on-a-node.

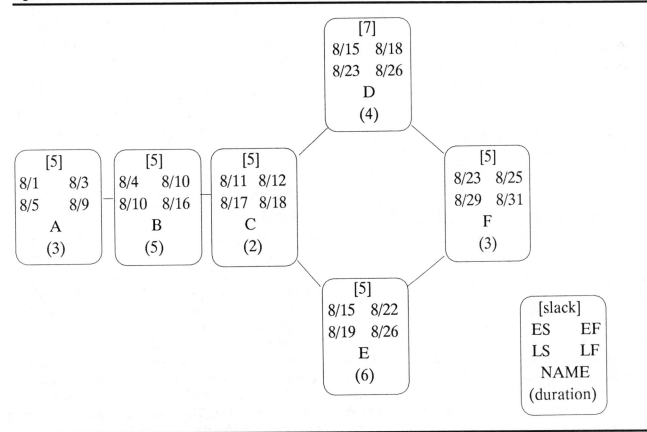

2. How to tell the system the correct project start date to use in the computations;

3. How to insure that resources are not reflected in the optimal plan;

4. How to insure that there are no imposed target dates in the optimal plan;

5. How to compute schedules;

6. How the forward and backward passes are computed;

7. How the product deals with slack, zero duration milestones, and estimates of less than one day;

8. How baseline plans are used as optimal plans;

9. How to control what dates are displayed;

10. How the product schedules subprojects, and lead or lag times;

11. How the critical path is displayed on the screen and how Gantt time frames are managed;

12. How hammocks are scheduled; and

13. Working in a multiproject environment.

7.14.1 Calendars ◆

How easy is it to create the calendar? What kind of calendars does the system use? Does the system support user-defined holidays, user-defined workdays, or user-defined workhours?

If estimates of less than one day are used, the system must be able to schedule around nonworking time such as lunch and regularly scheduled meetings. Will the calendar support scheduling these breaks into each day?

How many different procedures are required to establish the calendar? In how many different places is the calendar information found?

7.14.2 Choosing the Correct Project Start Date ◆

How easy is it to set and save the correct start date for the project (or phase)? It is meaningful to recall that the start date of the project (or phase) that is currently being planned is not likely to be the same date as the current date that the operating system automatically generates. Consequently, it is important to evaluate how easy it is for the user to control the project

start date when this occurs. For example, the *least* desirable alternative would be one in which the user must always alter the operating system date—to coincide with each different project start date—before the software product can be invoked and any scheduling can take place.

7.14.3 Insuring That the Plan Is Not Constrained by Resources or Fixed Dates ◆

The optimal plan is not driven by resource constraints or fixed dates. Therefore, the schedule must be able to be computed based on true work effort, driven by the true dependencies. What must be done to insure that the integrity of the optimal plan is maintained?

7.14.4 Calculating the Schedule ◆

Products fall into three categories: those that compute the schedules immediately, those that are semi-immediate processors, and those that are batch processing systems. What actions must be taken in order to compute the schedule?

When updating large plans with immediate and semi-immediate processors, long delays between entries may occur while waiting for the system to complete the calculations. In this case, it may be helpful to turn off the automatic calculations, thus intentionally making the system a batch processor. How is this done? How easy is it, then, to recalculate the schedules?

7.14.5 The Forward Pass: Calculating the Early Dates ◆

Does a job get scheduled with the workday ending at 5 P.M. and its successor(s) scheduled beginning at 5:01 P.M.? or is its successor scheduled beginning at the start of the next working day? Alternatively, is a job (that can be scheduled to finish at 5 P.M. one day) not scheduled until immediately before the start of the successor(s) and therefore not scheduled to finish until the start of the next working day? The traditional scheduling algorithm will be defined as the following:

If a job may finish at the end of a working day, it is so scheduled. The scheduled start time of any successor(s) is the start of the next business day. The project finish date is computed as the end of the day on which the last job finishes.

All of the products computed the forward pass correctly.

In Harvard Project Manager 3.0, each job is scheduled to finish at the exact instant of the scheduled start of its successor(s) and is thus not scheduled to finish until the start of the next working day. Even considering this difference in the finish dates, the forward pass was computed correctly.

7.14.6 The Backward Pass: Verifying the Late Dates

All of the products computed the backward pass calculations correctly.

7.14.7 Verifying Slack

All of the products computed slack correctly.

7.14.8 Zero Duration Milestones ◆

A zero duration milestone is preferably designated as occurring on the *same* date at the *instant* when all of its predecessors have *finished*. If the zero duration milestone is then scheduled at the *end* of a business day, all of its successors ought to ideally be scheduled at the start of the following business day.

Alternatively, but not as desirable, the zero duration milestone is scheduled at the start of the next business day following the completion of all of its predecessors, with all of its successors also being scheduled at the same start of the same business day. Unfortunately, this approach is particularly distressing when the predecessors end on a Friday and the milestone isn't scheduled until Monday. Naturally, when the predecessors end on the Friday before a three-day weekend, the scenario gets even worse.

7.14.9 Verifying Schedules with Units of Measurement Less Than One Day ◆

Schedules with durations in hours and schedules with mixed durations of hours and days were computed for Harvard Project Manager 3.0, Microsoft Project, Time Line 3.0, and SuperProject Expert. They all checked out correctly.

7.14.10 Products That Do Not Report Hours

Although it supports estimates of less than one day, Time Line 3.0 does not provide any reports that show times. Time Line 3.0 does, however, report the time on the task edit form. (See Figure A4.4.) Understandably, Project Workbench does not show time on any reports.

7.14.11 Retaining a Baseline Record of the Optimal Plan ◆

Many of the products provide the user with a useful feature—the ability to save a snapshot of the plan *before* any resources are factored into it or any progress is posted to it.

This snapshot serves as a yardstick or a standard against which to measure the effects of any constraints that must ultimately be added to the plan. Often, the snapshot view of a project is called the *Baseline* plans, allowing the user to compare the original values to the future affected values in various reports. (Those products that do not support some form of baseline, naturally, do not feature comparative reports.)

The use of baselines will be discussed again further on in the book.

7.14.12 Interpreting the Dates on the Screen ◆

In the process of interactively developing the plan, it is often necessary to see the dates displayed on the screen during the planning process. For example, on the Gantt chart, some products only display a time-scaled bar to indicate where the jobs occur. They do not display the actual dates that correspond to the beginning and end of each job. Sometimes it is difficult to tell the exact data for either of these two positions. Those products that also automatically report the dates in a separate column or on the job itself provide a more useful function. Finally, those products that allow the user to customize which dates are displayed provide the ultimate in functionality.

7.14.13 Annotating the Critical Path ◆

How does the system display the critical path on the Gantt chart and the network? Several products use the color red to show the critical path.

7.14.14 Verifying Lag and Lead Time ◆

There were two methods of computing dates for lag and lead times: the traditional method (Method 1) and an alternative method. Method 1 is used by all of the products—except Time Line 3.0.

The traditional method (Method 1). The clock starts ticking for the duration of the lag time at the *start of the first business day following the completion of its predecessor(s).* In Figure 7.6, Job 2 can not start until 10 days after Job 1. If, for example, Job 1 is finished at the end of the day on February 3, the 10-day period starts on February 4. Each business day of the duration of the lag time is then added to the schedule. In Figure 7.6, the 10 days are up at the end of the day on February 17. (These dates reflect weekends.) The successor is then scheduled at the *start of the first business day after the lag has been added into the schedule.* Thus, in Figure 7.6, Job 2 is scheduled to start on February 18.

7.14.15 Gantt Chart Time Periods ◆

Is there a limit to the number of time periods that can be seen on the Gantt chart screen? What are the units of measurements that can be displayed on the Gantt chart screen? Is there a break in the bar where the weekends and holidays occur, or are jobs that cross weekends and holidays represented by a continuous bar? This will become an issue later on when trying to resolve resource conflicts.

7.14.16 Hammocks and Dates

The two products that feature hammocks (Viewpoint and Primavera Project Planner) both summarize the spanned duration of the activities within the group. The hammock's early and late start as well as its early

and late finish dates will represent the respective dates of the first and last activity in the group.

7.14.17 Scheduling in the Multiproject Environment ◆

Once more, this is the scenario in which the same pool of resources may be shared between several simultaneous projects and maintenance jobs while attempting to effectively plan resource sharing across all of these endeavors. A plan that will show all of the parallel and sequential subprojects that are going on at the same time will provide the global view at a glance. (See Figures 6.17 and 6.18.) Furthermore, in products that operate on project data in main memory, partitioning the project into subprojects is also an excellent way in which to overcome limitations in project size. Finally, the subproject concept lends itself beautifully to the Moving Window approach. (See the discussion in the next section.)

The issues of concern in this section are centered around how the master project deals with the project calendars in the subprojects and whether the starting and ending dates of the subprojects are computed correctly in the master project.

When the master project does not automatically import the calendar information with the subproject, additional actions must be taken to insure that the schedules will be computed correctly. This is true especially since those products that do not automatically import the calendar information do not read the calendar from the subproject either. When this scenario occurs, users must either import the calendar information in a separate action or, in the worst case, re-key it.

The master projects are created by following the directions outlined in the multiproject environment discussion in Chapter 6. Calendars may be created following the directions outlined earlier in this chapter.

7.14.18 Nesting Subprojects in a Multiproject Environment ◆

The first set of numbers given to management is the rapid survey number. It consists of a quick appraisal for total project effort and committed numbers for Phase 1. (See Figure 2.6.) At this point, the detailed plan for Phase 1 has been entered into the software and will ultimately be used to manage Phase 1.

Figure 7.6 Verifying lag and lead time.

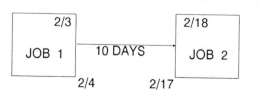

At the end of Phase 1, the team will produce the detailed plan for Phase 2 and an inexact plan for the rest of the project. Furthermore, they will now have the actual numbers from Phase 1. (See Figure 2.7.) Finally, the three plans must be totaled in order to give management the data pertaining to the whole project effort. It may be useful to keep these four sets of data separated: (1) managing the plan for Phase 1 requires one set of actions and the corresponding data; (2) developing the detailed plan for Phase 2 requires a different set of actions and the corresponding set of data; (3) an inexact plan with less detailed data requires a third set of actions and the corresponding set of data; and (4) adding up the first three plans to determine the total effort requires a fourth set of actions.

Ideally, the software will allow the user to create and maintain the three *separate* sets of plans *and* link them together at other times to create a fourth set of data that corresponds to the total project plan.

With the exception of the first and last phases, there will always be four data sets: (1) the actual numbers to date; (2) the plans for the next phase; (3) the plans for the rest of the project; and (4) the sums of the first three plans—the plans for total project effort. The first three plans are often called subprojects, and the fourth plan is often referred to as the super project or the master project. The development of the super project is usually accomplished with the multiproject (or subproject) feature.

Furthermore, in products that operate on project data in main memory, it is also an excellent way with which to overcome limitations in project size—assuming that the fourth plan is not a permanently merged data set that is then subject to the size limitations.

Finally, in a true multiproject environment there may be several projects going on at the same time and each of these projects may have its own master plan of the four subplans. To complete the picture, the system must be able to support nested subprojects (projects within projects within projects) and roll the information up into one project notch at a time. This section addresses the nested subproject feature.

7.14.19 Subprojects and Their Dates ◆

All of the products were tested to verify that the correct dates were computed when subprojects were *attached* to master projects or when files were included into master files. With the exception noted for Project Workbench, all of the dates were computed correctly—without the need for additional operations.

7.14.20 Guidelines and Documentation ◆

All but two of the products did not have any documentation on how to compute the dates in the schedule. (Instructions on how to use the system to achieve the implementation of a feature are not considered guidelines.)

7.15 THE PERT METHOD OF ESTIMATING

The Navy Special Projects Office employed the concept of uncertainty, the beta (β) distribution, and the formula for expected effort to estimate and manage the POLARIS missile submarine project in 1958. Because of the value of the beta characteristics for project management, it was selected by the developers of the PERT technique of estimating. Wiest and Levy[1] describe that they believed that the beta (β) distribution was a close enough similarity to how the estimates of activity or task effort would have been broadcast across a frequency distribution. This choice was a subjective decision and not based on any experiential data. Since projects are rarely repeated *many* times, *and, most significantly,* since people rarely save their data, frequency distributions may not easily be recreated from historical information. (See Figures 5.2 and 5.3.) As a result of analyzing the characteristics of the beta (β) distribution, the standard deviation and variance are used to measure the degree of uncertainty in the original estimates. The formula for the standard deviation of a given activity or task has been written as:

$$\sigma = \frac{\text{the high end of the interval } - \text{ the low end of the interval}}{6}$$

[1] Op. cit.

The formula for variance is:

$$\sigma^2 = \left(\frac{\text{the high end of the interval } - \text{ the low end of the interval}}{6} \right)^2$$

Earlier, it was suggested that three estimates be provided: the optimistic, the pessimistic, and the most likely. These formulas may only be used when there are the *three* estimates for each job! Now, the standard deviation and the variance are written as:

$$\sigma = \frac{\text{the pessimistic } - \text{ the optimistic}}{6}$$

$$\sigma^2 = \left(\frac{\text{the pessimistic } - \text{ the optimistic}}{6} \right)^2$$

Thus, two sets of estimates that result in the same expected effort may not be equal. For example, when both 7, 8, 9 and 6, 8, 10 are respectively used as optimistic, most likely and pessimistic estimates, the expected value is 8–in both cases. However, the standard deviation and variance in the first set of estimates computes to .33 and .11, respectively; while in the second set, the answers are .66 and .44, respectively. This simply means that there is more uncertainty in the second set of estimates than in the first.

Furthermore, if the expected effort is 8, then, using one standard deviation from the mean, the optimistic and pessimistic values would be 5 and 11 respectively. To be 68 percent certain that the job would be completed in time, 11 may be used as the duration in computing schedules. In the example above, the expected effort is the constant, 8, and the other values are the variables. Conversely, it is possible to leave the expected effort as the variable. When this occurs along with increasing the number of standard deviations, the expected effort increases accordingly. To increase the probability of successfully finishing a particular job, the number of standard deviations may thus be increased. For 95.45 percent, 2 standard de-

viations are used. If the expected effort is 8, then, using two standard deviations, the optimistic and pessimistic values would be 2 and 14 respectively. To be 95.45 percent certain that the job would be completed in time, 14 may be used as the duration in computing schedules.

For 99.73 percent, 3 standard deviations are used. If the expected effort is 8, then, using three standard deviations from the mean, the optimistic and pessimistic values would be 0 and 18 respectively. To be 99.73 percent certain that the job would be completed in time, 18 may be used as the duration in computing schedules. The result derived from 3 standard deviations does not necessarily portray all of the values for the absolutely best and worst cases; but rather values beyond which there is rare likelihood of occurring.

In an ideal scenario, the durations that relate to 3 standard deviations may be used for every job in the project. However, this obviously has the effect of extending the project duration beyond a time that most organizations may be able to accept. As a result, the theories and formulas are normally used in a different manner that will be described in the following sections. The process starts by *having the estimators provide the three estimates for each job*. It is also dependent on the critical path(s) and the dates that are computed during scheduling. Finally, one of the most important properties of this strategy revolves around the *independence* of the estimates (as discussed earlier).

7.16 THE STANDARD DEVIATION AND THE VARIANCE OF THE CRITICAL PATH

The above formula may be used to compute the standard deviation for *every* activity or task *along the critical path*. Thus:

$$\sigma \text{ (Critical Path)} = \sigma(A) + \sigma(B) + \ldots + \ldots + \sigma n$$

Then the variance for *each job on the critical path* is computed and added together to get the variance of the critical path:

$$\sigma^2 \text{ (Critical Path)} = [\sigma(A)]^2 + [\sigma(B)]^2 + \ldots + \ldots + [\sigma n]^2$$

Finally, the standard deviation of the critical path may be computed as the square root of the variance of the critical path:

$$\sigma \text{ (Critical Path)} = \text{the square root of } [\sigma^2 \text{ (Critical Path)}]$$

7.17 THE PROBABILITY OF MAKING A GIVEN DATE

In project management, using the normal probability distribution function, a value called Z may be computed as:

$$Z = \frac{\text{pessimistic} - \text{optimistic}}{\sigma}$$

The probability of finishing the project by its *late* finish date *without having to make any additional corrective action* is determined by using the formula:

$$Z = \frac{\text{late finish date of the project} - \text{early finish date of the project}}{\sigma \text{ (critical path)}}$$

where the σ (CRITICAL PATH) is computed as described in the foregoing section.

Since three estimates were used to compute the durations of each of the jobs on the critical path, Z now reflects the cumulative uncertainty of these jobs. Table 7.1 has been extracted from a normal probability distribution table and, based on the resulting value of Z, is used to find the percentage value for the probability of successfully meeting the *late* finish date of

the project—without encountering any *unexpected* obstacles. (*Expected* obstacles are reflected in the three estimates.)

7.18 THE TROUBLE WITH ZERO SLACK

Earlier, users were advised that, when doing the backward pass, the late finish date of the project should not be the same date as the early finish date of the project. If it is the same date, the critical path will

Table 7.1 Finding the probability of success.

Table 7.1 Finding the Probability of Success							
Z	%	Z	%	Z	%	Z	%
3.0	99.87	1.4	91.92	−0.1	46.02	−1.7	4.46
2.9	99.81	1.3	90.32	−0.2	42.07	−1.8	3.59
2.8	99.75	1.2	88.49	−0.3	38.21	−1.9	2.87
2.7	99.65	1.1	86.43	−0.4	34.46	−2.0	2.28
2.6	99.53	1.0	84.13	−0.5	30.85	−2.1	1.79
2.5	99.38	0.9	81.59	−0.6	27.43	−2.2	1.39
2.4	99.18	0.8	78.81	−0.7	24.20	−2.3	1.07
2.3	98.93	0.7	75.80	−0.8	21.19	−2.4	0.82
2.2	98.61	0.6	72.57	−0.9	18.41	−2.5	0.62
2.1	98.21	0.5	69.15	−1.0	15.87	−2.6	0.47
2.0	97.73	0.4	65.54	−1.1	13.57	−2.7	0.35
1.9	97.13	0.3	61.79	−1.2	11.51	−2.8	0.26
1.8	96.41	0.2	57.93	−1.3	9.68	−2.9	0.19
1.7	95.54	0.1	53.98	−1.4	8.10	−3.0	0.14
1.6	94.52			−1.5	6.68	−3.1	0.10
1.5	93.32	**0.0**	**50.0**	−1.6	5.48	−3.2	0.07

have zero slack. When the slack is equal to zero, the value of the "Late Finish Date of the Project — Early Finish Date of the Project" (in the above formula) is also equal to zero. When there is a zero in the numerator (the top) of any fraction, the value of the fraction will always be zero as well—no matter the value in the denominator (the bottom). This will also cause the value of Z to be zero as well. When Z is equal to zero, the probability of making the late finish date of the project is only *50 percent*.

7.19 NEGATIVE SLACK

When picking a target date for project completion and attempting to retrofit the plan into it, the target date becomes the late finish date of the project—no matter what the project early finish date is computed to be, even if the early date is later than the late date. When the early date *is* later than the late date, the value in the numerator of the fraction is negative. This causes the value for Z to be negative as well. *And the more*

negative the value of Z, the closer the plan gets to 0 percent probability of success. Consequently, in this scenario, the phase (or project) is already late before it starts!

7.20 PICKING A REASONABLE LATE FINISH DATE

After completing the forward pass, users are frequently in a dilemma regarding how to pick the date that *should* be used as the late finish date of the project. Earlier, it was suggested that three late dates be chosen: (1) the late date that will give a 50 percent probability of success; (2) the late date that will give a 75 percent probability of success; and (3) the late date that will give a 95 percent probability of success. As soon as the forward pass has been completed, the late date for 50 percent is known. (It is the same as the early date. See the above discussion.) The big question revolves around how to get the other two dates. The solution lies in readjusting the formula for Z:

$$Z = \frac{\text{late finish date of the project } - \text{ early finish date of the project}}{\sigma \text{ (critical path)}}$$

and

$$\text{late finish date of the project} - \text{early finish date of the project} = \text{slack}$$

Therefore:

$$Z = \frac{\text{slack}}{\sigma \text{ (critical path)}}$$

Multiplying both sides of the equation by σ (CRITICAL PATH) yields:

$$\sigma \text{ (CRITICAL PATH)} \times Z = SLACK$$

The σ (CRITICAL PATH) is already known. Now, choosing the desired percentage and finding its corresponding value for Z will complete the left side of the equation. When the σ (CRITICAL PATH) is multiplied times Z, the resulting value for slack may be added to the early date in order to determine the late date that should be used for the backward pass in order to achieve the desired probability of success.

7.20.1 Managing Organizational Expectations

It is a good idea to summarize at least three values for the potential late finish date. The percentage values may be selected by the group (for example, 50 percent, 75 percent, and 95 percent) or they may be selected from Table 7.2. Furthermore, it must be emphasized that based on these computations, expectations of project completion are matched to the late date *and not the early date!* Work will generally be assigned using the early dates and not the late dates; but completion expectations will be matched to the late date. Finally, recipients of this data should be reminded that the results are based on probability theories and, therefore, are not guarantees.

7.20.2 A Short-Cut Reluctantly Presented

Although it is in direct contradiction to the scientific principles presented in this chapter, there is a *work-*

Table 7.2 Values of "Z" matched to desired success rate

TIME NOW: January 1, Year 1

%	Z	COMPLETION DATE[2]
99.9	3.00	June 1, Year 2
97.7	2.00	April 1, Year 2
84.1	1.00	February 1, Year 2
50.0	0.00	December 1, Year 1
15.9	−1.00	October 1, Year 1
2.3	−2.00	August 1, Year 1
0.1	−3.00	June 1, Year 1

around alternative to using three estimates and to computing the standard deviation of the critical path. Users may simply substitute a 1, 2, or 3 for the standard deviation (68 percent, 95 percent, or 98 percent) in the above formula, choose their Z, and proceed from there.

7.21 PROBABILITIES OF OTHER PATHS IN THE NETWORK

The computations presented thus far have been applied to what is recognized as the official critical path(s) of the project. However, some other path(s) through the network may have a higher degree of uncertainty. When the near-critical path is very close in length to the critical-path, its probability should also be computed as well. Furthermore, if users wish to know the probability of finishing *both* the critical path *and* the near-critical path, *their percentages must be multiplied together!*

[2]The dates in this table are for illustrative purposes only.

Percentages are fractional values of 100 percent—and when fractions are multiplied, the answers get smaller. Thus, when a critical path has a 72.57 percent probability of finishing by its late date, and the near critical path has an 84.13 percent probability of finishing by its late date, there is a 61.05 percent probability of finishing them both by their late dates.

7.22 THE PROBABILITY OF BEING LATE SOMEWHERE IN THE PROJECT

If the probability for every path in the network were computed and all of the probabilities multiplied together, then the answer would rapidly approach zero! Therefore, it is easy to assume that somewhere, someday in the project, some job will be late. Nevertheless, since there is usually slack on the other paths, corrective measures may be taken to prevent these jobs from becoming *the* critical path. Consequently, it is not necessary to compute the probability for every path in the network. It is essential, however, to manage the critical path(s) and the near critical path(s) very closely.

7.23 CONFIDENCE INTERVALS

One of the advantages of using three estimates is that they are classified as *interval estimates*. Interval estimates indicate the precision or accuracy of the estimate and are preferable to estimates of a single point. The smaller the interval, the higher the accuracy will be. This is another reason for estimating at the inch-pebble level! Small intervals are called *confidence intervals*.

Using formulas found in most business statistics texts, confidence intervals may be used to pick the "best case–worst case" ranges when providing management with the Rapid Survey, Assessment, Forecasted, and Projected Numbers.

7.23.1 Confirming the Value of Inch-Pebbles Once More

The credibility of confidence levels confirms the value of using three estimates at the inch-pebble level (4–40 hours). The smaller the range of the estimates, the higher the accuracy will be. One delightful advantage of entering three estimates at the inch-pebble level is

that the resulting standard deviation and variance for each job is frequently very *low*! As a result, the standard deviation of the critical path is correspondingly low and the amount of slack that needs to be added to the critical path to increase the probability of success is surprisingly low.

7.24 CRITICISMS OF THE PERT STATISTICAL APPROACH

From the many detractors of the PERT statistical approach come several very valid concerns.

For example, there may be several parallel paths that are almost identical in length to the critical path and/or that may also demonstrate a high degree of uncertainty. Unless the manager factors in the probabilities for *all* of the critical and near critical paths, he or she may grossly overestimate the probability of successfully meeting the project's late completion date. Conversely, if all of the respective probabilities *are* multiplied together, this approach will perform acceptably. Similarly, if the critical path is much longer than any of the other paths, there is not as much need for concern.

The concept of safety in a longer critical path has been given credibility by Wiest and Levy[3] as well as Moder, Phillips, and Davis[4] in describing studies performed by MacCrimmon and Ryavec on what they designated as the bias of the point of merged events. They found that the PERT-calculated mean and standard deviation veritably *deviated* from the actual mean and standard deviation. Furthermore, the differences were "quite large when the paths were about equal in length, but decreased substantially as the path lengths became farther apart". There is also an excellent discussion in Moder, Phillips, and Davis and they have also presented several very interesting correction procedures.

In another vein, if there are any activities or tasks that have a very high degree of uncertainty, but are not on any of the paths just mentioned, they may

---

[3]Op. cit.

[4]J.J. Moder, C.R. Phillips, E.W. Davis, *Project Management with CPM, PERT, and Precedence Diagramming* (New York,: Van Nostrand Reinhold Company, 1983).

ultimately cause serious damage to timely completion. These jobs must also be closely managed.

With regard to estimating, providing three estimates at a small inch-pebble level does much to defray many potential problems. However, many organizations shy away from such detailed estimating. Consequently, this situation, combined with a general lack of estimating expertise, may result in estimates that are, of themselves, overly optimistic. This scenario is especially true when people feel coerced to price the estimates to win. In the same vein, purists in the application of PERT concentrate on managing the major composite events (or what is referred to in this text as major milestones). In such a scenario, the important details are again often overlooked. This book assumes that estimating at the inch-pebble level is always the preferred estimating technique.

Then there are the many people who believe that using three estimates tends to result in durations that are frequently longer than it should really take to complete the job. Furthermore, when considering Parkinson's Law which satirically states that "Work expands so as to fill the time available for its completion," they feel even more justified in their objections.

7.25 MONTE CARLO SIMULATION

Another deceiving aspect of the PERT approach is the implication that, if the procedures are followed correctly, they should always yield the same critical path(s) and near critical path(s). And this is true. However, studies have shown that critical path(s) and near critical path(s) are *not* necessarily unique.

Wiest and Levy[5], as well as Moder, Phillips, and Davis,[6] describe experiments performed by R. M. Van Slyke in which, by using a Monte Carlo simulation sampling technique, random values for activity durations were selected as the estimates to be used in the standard PERT calculations. This was automated programmatically and then repeated thousands of times. The critical path was recorded each time. At the conclusion of the experiment, the cumulative data was used to calculate the average project length and the standard deviation. One of the most surprising findings

(although, given the random selection of values for the estimates, it shouldn't be) was that the critical path(s) and near critical path(s) are *not unique!*

This experiment may be repeated for any project. Each of the individual jobs in the candidate project may then be managed according to the number of times it winds up the simulated critical paths. As a matter of fact, if such a count were made for each job, and the results were then divided by the total number of simulated runs, this answer would be called a criticality index. For example, a criticality index of 0.4875 for Job 73 means that, in 4,875 out of 10,000 runs, Job 73 wound up on the critical path. Users may then rank the jobs so that those with the higher criticality indices are tagged for special attention during the management of the project. Moder, Phillips, and Davis go on to describe an empirical study completed by K. C. Crandall that indicated that "the sample size can be reduced to 1000 or less and still obtain an adequate level of confidence in the final estimates." Other uses of this technique believe that the sample size may safely go as low as 400.

Several mainframe packages support the Monte Carlo simulation feature.

7.26 PROBABILITIES AND PROJECT MANAGEMENT SOFTWARE

When evaluating the software products for their implementation of the concepts presented in this chapter, two areas have been considered: (1) whether or not the product supports computations for the variance of the task and for the standard deviation of the critical path; and (2) how to set a reasonable late project completion date while maintaining the correct early project start date.

7.26.1 Products That Support the Statistical Approach ♦

SuperProject Expert is the only product that supports standard deviations and variances.

7.26.2 *Work-Arounds* for Determining the Standard Deviation of the Critical Path

Earlier in this chapter, users were reluctantly advised of a short-cut in the formula for computing a reason-

[5]Op. cit.

[6]Op cit.

able late finish date of the project:

> **Instead of computing the standard deviation of the critical path, users may simply choose 1, 2, or 3 standard deviations for the value in the formula and proceed from there.**

But what about those people who *want* to use the formulas but have products that do not support this feature?

The best solution for implementing the estimating computations and for factoring in the Protected Environment *broad-based overhead* is simply to write a separate program (or series of programs). If the record layouts of the files in the project management software are available, this adjunct software may extract the jobs on the critical path from the project management software file. Then, using the formulas in this chapter as specifications, this new software can compute the results. Finally, the results can be programmatically moved back into the corresponding field(s) of the appropriate record(s) of the project management software file.

Some of the products provide an import data function, but only on a complete record basis. Since only one field within the record is at issue here (i.e., duration), this import function may prove to be impractical—unless there is some more efficient means for off-line entering of the complete record. When this is not constructive, the programmatic approach described above may be the best alternative.

7.26.3 Using the New Reasonable Late Finish Date of The Project ◆

Ideally, the system will allow the user to maintain the original early start date of the project and also allow the user to enter the new reasonable late finish date of the project. Then, the system should also automatically compute the correct dates for both the forward and backward passes. Furthermore, the system should still recognize the critical path—even though it is no longer a zero slack critical path. When the system does not recognize critical paths that are greater than zero, some products allow the user to extract data based on least slack. This will be covered later.

When the product does not allow *both* the early start date of the project *and* the late finish date of the project to be set, there is a *work-around*:

> **Users may enter a milestone that is a successor to *all* of the last jobs in the network and make it a fixed date job. If the additional milestone is required, users will also need to connect it to each of the last tasks in the project.**

Most of the products will correctly compute both sets of dates. The problem is that when slack is greater than zero, many products no longer recognize the critical path. Therefore, users must be working with 2 sets of plans: one with the two sets of new dates and one with the original set of dates and the zero slack critical path. One may be made a baseline, but then the options for other types of baselines are lost.

CHAPTER 8 CONSTRAINING BY RESOURCES AND DATES

8.1 INTRODUCTION

In software projects, resources usually mean people. However, computer time may also be measured as a resource, in order to determine its costs to the project or to see if it can be scheduled at a specified time. Finally, resources can mean the materials or the equipment used to complete a task. Ideally, each of these categories can be managed separately.

8.2 RESOURCES AND THE OPTIMAL PLAN

By now, the optimal plan has been developed—to the extent that it shows how *long* the project will take under ideal circumstances and how *many resources* it would take—given an unlimited source of supply. However, management is also interested in obtaining other information about the optimal plan, such as how much it will cost and what the *optimal* resource requirements will be. Optimal resource requirements include information such as how many analysts are needed, how many programmers will be required, when the computer will be needed, and so on.

To wrap up the compilation of data for the optimal plan, resources are added to the plan by job skills or classifications, *not yet by individuals' names*, always assuming that the number of people required (in that job group) will be available no matter what the required number is. The cost per job skill or classifi-

cation may be whatever is determined by the organization's designated cost accountants to be the going rate for that group. This, then, becomes the optimal resource baseline. It states how many people in each resource category are required.

8.3 ADDING REAL-WORLD CONSTRAINTS

From this point, project teams are faced with responding to one or more of the following scenarios: limitations on people, limitations on money, and/or limitations on time.

- Limitations on people usually imply the need to extend the date or eliminate features.
- Limitations on money usually imply the need to reduce the number of resources or eliminate features.
- Finally, limitations on time require that the number of resources be increased, the costs be increased, or features be eliminated.

The one common alternative in all three scenarios is eliminating features (descoping). When reducing scope, the user must choose subsets of the system, and then the team must apply the planning techniques all over again.

However, aside from eliminating features, each of the other alternatives is definitely in conflict. It is not surprising, however, to discover that many organizations get into a hopeless situation—wanting to impose *all* of the limitations while, at the same time, being unwilling to make any of the sacrifices.

It is not possible to invoke *all three* scenarios, but teams can develop many optional plans.

- Even when projects are not constrained by resources, these concepts help to allocate the best distribution of skills, to assess the costs of resources in several alternatives, to assess costs of resources within the project as well as across multiple projects, to control costs of resources within the project as well as across multiple projects, and, basically, make the most cost effective use of resources.

- When projects *are* constrained by resources, they may be restricted by the *number* of people available, by the *skills* they possess or by the *time* each person is available. The time each person is available can be further partitioned as (1) available, but only on limited days; (2) available, but only at certain hours; or (3) available a set percentage of the time.

8.4 DISTRIBUTION OF RESOURCES

It is necessary to avoid overutilization (when resources are overcommitted) and underutilization (when resources are idle). The goal is to uncover the most effective deployment of resources so that the best project schedule can be selected. This procedure is based upon using the number of hours per day that each resource is planned to be available, as well as their respective skill levels.

The operation starts with the optimal plan, the plan that assumes that *all the skills that are required have been provided, and that all the skills are equal and that people and jobs are interchangeable.* The reality is that the project teams don't always get *all* of the required skills, not everyone has the *same qualifications*, and people and jobs are *not interchangeable.* Users cannot always write code and technicians are not always the best business analysts.

8.5 BONA FIDE RESOURCE PLANNING

Now is the time to match the right people to the right jobs. A list of available people ought to be compiled.

These resources should be grouped under the job skills or classifications that were prepared for the optimal plan. The list should then be expanded to include each individual's skill level. As before, the costs to be used for each resource will be determined by the organization's designated financial analysts.

8.6 ADDING RESOURCES WITH PROJECT MANAGEMENT SOFTWARE

When adding resources to a project plan, several operations must be performed. To begin with, the resource pool and the resource calendars should be created. Then, resources who will be part-time throughout the entire project must be flagged and their level of participation must be noted.

The next step, assigning resources to jobs, is a very complex effort. It will be addressed later in this chapter. After matching the resources to jobs, users have the option of executing one or more of several different transactions. Initially, these involve flagging resources that have differing degrees of task-level part-time participation and/or assigning more than one resource to selected jobs.

Special attention is needed for fixing certain immovable dates and/or adjusting jobs in which the *true work effort* may need to be less than the elapsed calendar days.

Finally, resource conflicts may be identified and resolved by using the system's automatic leveling feature, by user-driven interactive leveling, or by a combination of both.

Each of these topics will, in turn, be covered later in this chapter.

8.7 RESOURCE CALENDARS

To start, individual calendars for each resource should be produced, in addition to the project calendar. Resource calendars are needed because it is important to see who is working each day of the project and how many hours per day they will be available. These figures will also be necessary later on—for comparison against how many hours per day the resource is actually scheduled.

Initially, it is important to designate who will be working part-time; when vacations and personal days will be taken, known travel plans, and known training classes. Sometimes, resources will even be allocated for different levels of part-time on different days for different tasks.

Furthermore, when resolving resource over-scheduling and, later, during management of the project, there may be times that it will be necessary to schedule one resource (but not the whole project team) to work on a weekend day.

Finally, there is also a need to allocate time in certain individuals' calendars for known management overhead or overhead for individuals with a high need for meetings and other types of communications. Many of these individuals are part-time project leaders, part-time systems developers, part-time maintenance managers, and part-time maintenance workers. It is essential to designate what percentage of each day or week is allocated to each of these categories. Each type of work should be prioritized in case there's not enough time to complete them all. (Figure 8.1)

At the highest level there's a global project calendar indicating the weekends, the workweek, the company holidays, other nonbusiness days, and the daily work hours. Ideally, individual resources can have personal calendars as well; and it is also nice if, into the bargain, departments can have their own calendars. The more flexibility a product gives the user in these areas, the more the user will be able to model the real world and get a truer picture of potential schedules.

8.8 CREATING THE RESOURCE CALENDARS ◆

Resource calendars are created at the *project level* to provide the system with resource values that will affect *all* of the tasks in the project. Project-level resource values include information such as special resource-specific holidays, vacations, business trips away from the project, special project training classes, nonworking days, part-time at the *project level*, nonstandard shift working hours, nonworking hours during each day (for example lunch, coffee breaks, regularly scheduled meetings), nonworking hours on a specific day, and so on. This information is to be differentiated

Figure 8.1 Allocating and prioritizing work.

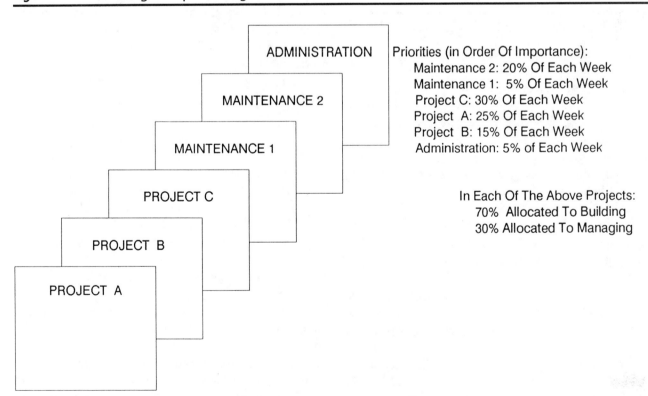

Priorities (in Order Of Importance):
Maintenance 2: 20% Of Each Week
Maintenance 1: 5% Of Each Week
Project C: 30% Of Each Week
Project A: 25% Of Each Week
Project B: 15% Of Each Week
Administration: 5% of Each Week

In Each Of The Above Projects:
70% Allocated To Building
30% Allocated To Managing

from resource calendar information for an *individual* task, a topic that will be covered later in this chapter.

Not only is it important to designate the resource's unique nonworking days, it may also become essential to set unique working days. For example, certain weekend days may need to be designated as workdays for a specific resource. This occurs later in the planning process (when trying to resolve resource overscheduling) and in the management process (when trying to catch up on late tasks). Without unique resource calendars, most systems will not support the respective date changes that reflect the overtime. To get the correct dates into the schedule, the project-level calendar must be modified, an action which, in turn, has an undesirable effect on the scheduling of resources who are not supposed to work overtime on that weekend. Obviously, this is a catch-22.

From a reporting perspective (for example, costs, impact evaluation, or status reporting), when resource-specific values are entered into a calendar, they often lose visibility. There is an alternative approach to entering this data, one that requires creating separate high-priority, fixed date jobs in the plan. Fixed dates and priorities will be addressed later in this chapter.

8.9 CREATING THE RESOURCE POOL ♦

Before resource management may be initiated, a list of available resources needs to be created. This list, which may be called the resource pool, ought to include pertinent data such as the resource identifier, resource costs, and work group category.

The work group category is often essential for reporting. In the case of job skills or classifications, it will also be necessary to tell the system how many of each job type will be available.

Under certain scenarios, the costs per resource may vary. For example, when projects last a long time, the resource rates may change over time. Systems that support variable billing rates are closer to real-life situations.

Frequently, information about part-time participation is added to the system while the resource pool is being created. However, since designating part-time participation can be such a knotty problem, it will be treated separately—in two sections. Part-time at the project level and part-time at the job level will be individually discussed later in this chapter.

8.9.1 The Resource Identifier

Ideally, the resource identifier field is long enough to allow a meaningful name to be entered. Shorter fields require cryptic codes that are often difficult to remember. The resource identifier will be especially important later on—when resources must be assigned to jobs. Subsequently, during the assignment process, some products invoke lists of resources from which to choose. In that case, short codes become a non-issue. On the other hand, in some products, the only way to remember the short codes is to have a hard copy report available before starting the assignment process.

8.9.2 Staff and Nonstaff Resources

Resources may be added to a plan as individuals, groups of individuals, equipment, or materials. Costs of individuals and groups of individuals are easily classified as staff costs. However, when the costs are materials costs, overhead costs, travel costs, rental costs, and so on, they are usually classified as nonstaff costs. Nonstaff costs may be based on usage, fixed costs, or onetime costs. In some products, they may be entered separately as costs, thus bypassing the resource pool entirely. In several other products, however, entering nonstaff costs requires two operations, creating a resource in one record and then adding the costs to a different record. Finally, they may simply be entered as part of the resource pool and treated as any other resource.

8.9.3 NUMBERS OF RESOURCES PER PLAN

Ideally, there will be no limitation on the number of resources that projects (and the jobs within projects) can have—or, at least, the limit should be high enough to allow for the majority of cases.

If the project management software product handles the plan data on a hard disk, there is usually no reason to limit the number of resources per plan or per job.

In the *variable-length, main memory* products, the maximum number of jobs, resources, and dependencies is limited by the total size of remaining memory. In other words, the total number of resources per plan is directly related to the sum of the memory storage requirements for each job times the total number of jobs—plus the memory requirements for each of their respective resources and dependencies. With these products it is important to remember that the more resources and dependencies there are, the fewer the total number of jobs per plan that will be available. The fewer the number of jobs per plan that are available, the greater the number of subprojects that will be required—assuming the product also supports subprojects. In this section, discussions pertaining to the number of resources indicate *total number of resources per plan*.

8.9.4 Numbers of Resources Per Job and for Leveling

In another vein, the number field for any given resource is used in two ways: as the maximum number of resources that can be assigned to each job *or* as the number used when leveling resources. How the number field is to be used in these scenarios will be covered in more detail later in this chapter—in the section on assigning resources and in the section on leveling resources.

8.10 ASSIGNING PART-TIME RESOURCES AT THE PROJECT LEVEL ◆

Frequently, resources are working on many projects at the same time. (See Figure 8.1.) Furthermore, this situation is often compounded by the fact that they must also be maintaining existing systems. As a consequence, it is of great interest to many people in the organization to be able to see the impacts of this part-time resource disbursement.

To begin with, each of the projects and maintenance systems that a given resource will be involved with must be identified and organized in order of importance. Then, the amount of time that the resource may allocate to each area must be determined. Ideally, this level of participation may be designated at the project level. (Part-time participation at the activity level will be discussed later in this chapter.) After part-time allocation has been entered at the project level, all subsequent resource assignments should be automatically scheduled according to the designated resource availability.

Users ought to be advised that this does not automatically eliminate all overscheduling. A combination of leveling and prioritization will also be required. If the resource is being assigned in a multiproject environment, the system will also need to level and prioritize across all projects. (Leveling and prioritization will be addressed later in this chapter. Resources in the multiproject environment will also be covered later in this chapter.)

Example 1 in Figure 8.2 represents the values for an activity in the optimal plan *before* constraining for resource limitations.

In Example 2, the same activity becomes resource driven because the resource is only available halftime.

Figure 8.2 Part-time resources at the project level.

	TRUE WORK EFFORT × *RESOURCE HOURS/DAY* = *CALENDAR DAYS ELAPSED TIME*		
JOB	TRUE WORK EFFORT	AVAILABILITY	ELAPSED CALENDAR DAYS
1.0	24 HOURS	8 HOURS PER DAY	3 DAYS
2.0	24 HOURS	4 HOURS PER DAY (part-time)	6 DAYS (resource driven)

8.10.1 Assigning Part-Time Resources

The implementation of part-time participation is expected to result in the total amount of the true work effort being spread over a corresponding number of elapsed business calendar days that reflects the part-time participation. As in Example 2, if the true work effort is three days and the resource is allocated for 50 percent participation, the resource would be assigned four hours per day for six days. Thus, the scheduled dates should show six calendar days to complete the job.

> **It is important, when resources are part-time, to insure that, while the elapsed calendar days may change, *the true work effort should not be modified*. In some products, these types of resource-driven applications often obscure the original value of the true work effort. Except for the data in the baseline version (which the user may even soon overlay), the record of true work effort may even be obliterated!**

8.10.2 Varying the Amount of Part-Time Participation at the Project Level

Under certain circumstances, a resource's level of part-time participation may vary. For example, in a multiproject environment, it is very helpful for project managers to allocate resources at varying levels of participation in each project to which they are assigned—each percentage decision often depending upon the priority of the project.

For example, the resource may be generally allocated to a project at 25 percent participation. During the majority of the project, this may even be an acceptable level of participation. However, because of the 25 percent limitation at one point in the project, this resource's jobs may become *the* critical path. On the other hand, if the resource were available for 50 percent participation during this finite period, the constraint would disappear. When negotiations for this exception have been successful, users will want to be able to reflect this condition in the project plan. Ideally, the system will allow these types of varying levels of part-time participation to be modeled.

8.11 DELETING AND CHANGING RESOURCES AT THE PROJECT LEVEL ♦

With regard to deleting resources from the project resource pool, systems are divided into two categories.

Into the first class fall those products that require that all corresponding resource assignments at the task or activity levels be eliminated before the resource may be deleted from the pool. (Eliminations at the job level may be completed with a reassignment or a simple delete.) This approach prevents removal by mistake, but also requires more work *before* the delete. It also helps to avoid jobs with no resource assignments.

The second group of products, when a resource is eliminated from the pool, will also wipe out all corresponding resource assignments at the job level. With this type of delete, the work of reassignment must still be done, but it can be done *after* the delete. The likelihood of jobs with no resource assignments may also be increased.

On the other hand, there will be times when one resource is taken off a project and another resource is assigned to take his or her place. Ideally, if the user *changes* the name in the resource pool, the system should automatically change all corresponding resource assignments at the task or activity level.

8.12 RESOURCE LOADING

After completing the resource calendars and adding the resources to the plan, it is time to assign people to jobs. This is called *resource loading*. Temporarily, this operation ought to be done without concern over the effects of any known constraints. In a subsequent step, the objective will be to find out where resources are overscheduled.

When assigning the work, it is important to remember to allocate *one person per job*—barring exceptions like reviews, meetings, and group dynamics workshops.

Unless the organization has a reliable and in-depth history of personnel records, it will be very difficult to plan for illness or attrition. Even when there are exhaustive records, the factor that is added to the plan to represent these obstacles is often little more than an educated guess. Special tasks (called "contingency tasks'') are added to the plan. The assumptions used in establishing the contingency are documented. When it is likely that the contingency will affect the project completion date, the task is put on the critical path. On the other hand, project teams are often better advised to leave them out and deal with them when, and if, they occur. In either case, it is advisable to notify management of the approach that *will* be employed *and* its ramifications.

Resource loading is the time to add task-related travel, task-related classes, and task-related management overhead. Sometimes, grouping jobs under a supervisor eases the management of the plan. Often, this is accomplished by adding a budget code to the system for each team and/or group of teams. Most commonly, several jobs that have been assigned to different resources are allocated to one supervisor. However, it is also possible to have a job assigned to one resource for completion and another resource for supervision, where the job is the only one for which the supervisor is responsible. When a resource is a supervisor of a group of jobs, a portion of his or her time should also be allocated for this effort.

8.13 ADJUSTING ESTIMATES TO REFLECT SKILL LEVELS

When the original estimates were produced, the appraisers were instructed to assume that the person who would actually complete the job would be a qualified individual, not a novice or an expert. Now, it is time to adjust the estimates to reflect the actual skill levels.

Remember, it is essential that the true work effort be archived in some manner! Ideally, it is left unchanged in the project plan, and the new estimates are saved separately. An additional storage unit can even be created, the *skill-level* duration.

When experts are assigned to work, *all* of the associated estimates may be shortened. On the other hand, when novices are assigned to work, learning time is usually only added into the *initial* jobs in the associated skill category. More effort is allocated to the very first jobs in the group and less and less effort is allocated as time goes on.

Having initially assumed that the person who would actually complete the job would be a *qualified* individual, it may sometimes be safe to now assume that

he or she will learn quickly. Other times, the amount of extra time added into each job and the number of jobs that are affected by this learning curve are related to the complexity of work being performed. For example: surprisingly, many technical jobs, by comparison, have a shorter learning curve than analysis. Unfortunately, there is no foolproof method for estimating the durations of learning curves.

8.14 MATCHING RESOURCES TO JOBS ◆

After the resources, their calendars, and their project-level part-time participation have been added to the system, the resources may be matched to jobs.

The issues of interest now deal with whether resources may be added to all levels of the work breakdown structure,[1] how easily resources may be assigned to jobs, and what data is required. Minimally, the data required at job assignment consists of the resource name and the assigned number of resources.

8.14.1 What Data Is Required: The Number

One of the key pieces of data in project planning is the number of resources. However, talking about numbers of resources per job can become really confusing—because the term *number* may refer to five very different figures.

1. The first definition refers to a number that has already been determined and is called the *number of resources per project plan*. This number was addressed earlier in this chapter.

2. The second definition also refers to a number that has already been determined and has been entered into the resource pool—that is, the maximum number of one type of resource that will be *available* (from the resource pool) for assignment. This is

---

[1]In some systems, resources can be assigned to summary jobs in the work breakdown structure as well as to tasks. This is very helpful when trying to assign management costs to a group of jobs, allocating a portion of secretarial assistance to a group of jobs and so on. Computer time, on the other hand, should be allocated to each job that it individually affects.

called the resource *availability number*. For example, from a pool of five programmers, three documentation specialists, and two trainers, the numbers of *available* resources are five, three, and two respectively. The resource *availability* number was also addressed earlier in this chapter.

3. The third definition refers to a potential system limitation—that is, how many resources may be *assigned to a particular job*. To enable the differentiation between all of these terms, this is called *resource names* per job, where names refers to the names in the resource pool. For example, if the system is said to allow three resource names to be assigned to each job, then, from the previous scenario, programmer, documentation specialist, and trainer may be assigned.

4. The fourth definition refers to *assigning numbers* to the resource names in the job assignment (just described above)—that is, how many units of the named resource will be required (from the available number in the pool) to be assigned to the job. For example, from the pool of five programmers, three will be *assigned* to the job. This is called the resource *assignment number*.

5. The last number refers to the *total* number of resources who may ultimately work on a job. If three programmers, one documentation specialist, and one trainer are assigned to a job, the *total* number of resources on that job is five.

Attention ought to be paid to what happens when the *assigned* number of resources exceeds the *available* number from the resource pool. Ideally, the system will prevent inconsistencies between these two numbers and will reject the transaction when the assigned number exceeds the available number. However, in some products, the resource availability number (established in the resource pool) is not checked when resource assignments are made. It is a number used *only during leveling*. (See the discussion on leveling later in this chapter.) Alternatively, some products will (1) send a message that the number assigned has exceeded the number available or (2) prevent the number assigned from exceeding the number available, sending a message and aborting the process. Other systems simply allow the number assigned to exceed the number available and do nothing about it.

8.14.2 What Data Is Required: The Name

People are interested in how many resource names may be assigned to a job (that is, how many resources per job the system will allow).

People are also interested in how many times a resource name can be used in one job assignment. From this perspective, the products are then divided into (a) those that only allow a resource name to be assigned to a given job one time, and one time only—regardless of the resource availability number in the pool and (b) those that allow any resource name to be assigned to one job as often as the user desires—regardless of the resource availability number in the pool. A third group of products does not require the resource availability number to be established in the resource pool; they have alternative procedures for establishing the number of resources.

Similarly, the system will either reject an *unknown* resource name (one who has not been added to the resource pool) or provide a mechanism to add it to the pool whenever a new resource is recognized.

Finally, the issue of how to maintain the integrity of the true work effort must be explored. As discussed earlier, this field should not be modified when assigning resources. *If* the resource effort must be greater than the task effort, it stands to reason that the task effort has not been correctly estimated and, consequently, must be changed.

8.15 ASSIGNING PART-TIME RESOURCES AT THE TASK OR ACTIVITY LEVEL ◆

Many products that do not support part-time participation at the project level do support it at the activity or task level. Even when the system does support part-time participation at the project level, there may be situations in which the resource is part-time on certain selected jobs, but not others.

There may also be circumstances in which there is a need to vary the level of participation—either from job to job or within one job itself. For example, varying from job to job may occur when the resource is assigned 50 percent on one job and 25 percent on another. Varying *within* the job enables the user to designate a *different number of part-time hours for each day of the task*.

In those products that do support varying part-

Figure 8.3 Assigning multiple resources.

TRUE WORK EFFORT × RESOURCE HOURS/DAY = CALENDAR DAYS ELAPSED TIME

JOB	TRUE WORK EFFORT	AVAILABILITY	ELAPSED CALENDAR DAYS
1.0	24 HOURS	8 HOURS PER DAY	3 DAYS
2.0	24 HOURS	12 HOURS PER DAY	2 DAYS time driven
3.0	48 HOURS	8 HOURS PER DAY	6 DAYS incorrect estimate
4.0	24 HOURS	8 HOURS PER DAY	3 DAYS multiple resources
	24 HOURS	8 HOURS PER DAY	3 DAYS
5.0	12 HOURS	8 HOURS PER DAY	1.5 DAY resource driven
	12 HOURS	8 HOURS PER DAY	1.5 DAY (*double-up*)
6.0	8 HOURS	8 HOURS PER DAY	1 DAYS resource driven
	16 HOURS	8 HOURS PER DAY	2 DAYS (longest time)
7.0	4 HOURS	8 HOURS PER DAY	5 DAYS

time participation from job to job but do not support varying the amount of part-time participation within the job (either at the job level or in the resource calendar hours), there is a *work-around*, albeit not a great one: users may create a series of smaller jobs, with each one equivalent to the part-time constraints.

8.16 ASSIGNING MULTIPLE RESOURCES TO A JOB ◆

It may be required to demonstrate how much sooner a job can be finished if more people are added to it. On the other hand, assigning more than one resource to a job is counter to the *one person, one job* philosophy suggested earlier. Furthermore, this only works in limited situations. Many years ago, Brooks[2] observed that adding more resources to a late project will only make it later. Some jobs just can't be finished sooner by adding more people. For example, if it takes eight days for an ocean liner to cross the Atlantic from Liverpool to New York, eight ocean liners can't do it in one day. Similarly, some work simply cannot effectively be divided, no matter how many people are available.

Multiple resource scheduling is another of project management's confusing and misunderstood concepts. The following examples will be used to explore just what is meant when people talk about resource driven assignments.

Example 1 in Figure 8.3 represents the values for an activity in the optimal plan *before* constraining for resource limitations.

Example 2 represents what happens when the same job is time constrained and must be finished in 2 days. The resource becomes overscheduled. Time constrained plans will be explored in more detail later.

In Example 3, while the original estimate (in

---

[2]F.P. Brooks, Jr., *Mythical Man Month*, (Reading, MA: Addison-Wesley, 1975).

Example 1) was 24 hours, it is now realized that the resource must actually complete 48 hours of true work effort. This implies that the original *true work effort* estimate was incorrect and must be modified to reflect the current knowledge.

Sometimes a workunit must be performed twice; and it may be done by two separate people, at the same time. This scenario is illustrated in Example 4.

Example 5 simply shows that the work in Example 1 may be divided; therefore, two resources are assigned to the job and it gets done in half the time. This may be referred to as *doubling up*—even when more than two resources are added to shorten the calendar days.

In Example 6, however, the work can not be evenly distributed. One resource works longer than the other resource.

Example 7 is a horse of a different color. Here the true work effort is small and it does not have to be completed in one sitting. Furthermore, the work can be spread out over a number of days. This is a different scenario than is being addressed here, and it will be covered in the next section.

In Examples 5 and 6, the longest elapsed calendar days will drive the schedule. This section deals with implementing Examples 5 and 6. If the system will automatically choose the resource with the longest duration as the elapsed calendar days, this can be very helpful when there is more than one resource assigned to a job, each with different durations.

Users also ought not to forget that resource-driven applications often obscure the original value of the true work effort. Except for the record in the baseline version (which the user may likely soon overlay), the record of true work effort may even be obliterated!

8.17 WHAT TO DO WHEN THE RESOURCE EFFORT MUST BE LESS THAN THE ELAPSED CALENDAR DAYS ◆

Sometimes, the resource effort is equal to the true work effort but is less than the elapsed calendar time. Furthermore, the true work effort may not have to be completed in one sitting and it can be spread out over a number of days, anywhere within the task *candidate time slice*. The term *candidate time slice* has been coined to represent elapsed time, total slack, or free slack. This will be explained in detail later in the chapter. In Example 1 of Figure 8.4., a four-hour preparation time for a walkthrough can extend over a five-day period.

At other times, a specified percentage of the resource's time may be allocated to one job that lasts for a finite period of time. Example 2 illustrates that 20 percent of the resource's available time has been allocated for one month for supervision.

Occasionally, there might be the need to create a delay between the scheduled start of the job and the time that the resource begins the work. In Example 3, the work may not be started until the last afternoon of the fifth day of the job.

Figure 8.4 Resource effort less than elapsed days.

	TRUE WORK EFFORT × RESOURCE HOURS/DAY = CALENDAR DAYS ELAPSED TIME		
JOB	TRUE WORK EFFORT	AVAILABILITY	ELAPSED CALENDAR DAYS
1.0	4 HOURS	8 HOURS PER DAY	5 DAYS
2.0	20% OF EACH DAY	8 HOURS PER DAY	30 DAYS
3.0	4 HOURS	8 HOURS PER DAY	worked on the 5th DAY

8.18 IMPOSING TARGET DATES

Now is the time to enter the known fixed dates such as vendor deliveries, funding meetings, and so on. Entering these fixed dates is the issue that will be covered in the following section.

But first, in another vein, on occasion, a job may be scheduled for completion many months before its successor is due to start and it may be advisable to reschedule this job. (See Figure 8.5.) Applying Job A's early dates causes it to finish several months before Job C. Furthermore, it is not advisable to let the finished Job A sit too long before using it. Applying Job A's late dates, however, makes Job A finish too late for Job C to start on its early dates.

Sometimes, the new date for Job A simply must be selected at random. When this occurs, caution ought to be exercised not to choose dates that leave too little slack, creating the potential of missed target dates and even a new (or additional) critical path.

Figure 8.5 Rescheduling.

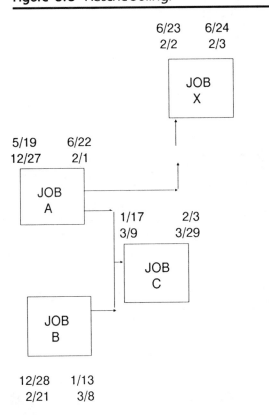

8.19 FIXED DATES FOR ACTIVITIES OR TASKS ◆

During the creation of the optimal plan and the optimal resource baseline, the system was directed to compute the earliest dates: As Soon As Possible (ASAP). Each time the schedule is recalculated, these dates can dynamically change, depending on new constraints such as the resource leveling that will be addressed later in this chapter.

Now is the time to enter immovable dates such as vendor deliveries, seminars, and such special project deadlines as funding meetings. Fixed dates are used to fasten an activity or task to a specific date.

In both main memory resident products and permanent-save products, a copy of the unaltered plan should be saved under a separate name (or saved as one of the baselines). Then, the results of the fixed dates may be evaluated without having to continuously erase and reenter data. (None of the products evaluated had a feature that supported saving both the system-generated dates *and* the fixed dates, along with a way to signal to the system which dates should be used in the schedule computations.)

There are several types of fixed dates: As Late As Possible (ALAP), must start *by* the prescribed date, must start *on* the prescribed date, must finish *by* the prescribed date, must finish *on* the prescribed date, can't start until the prescribed date, start no earlier than the prescribed date, start no later than the prescribed date, finish no earlier than the prescribed date, and finish no later than the prescribed date. While most of these may be critical for other industries, software development projects can easily manage with fewer of these options.

It is important to note that if fixed dates are added to the plan, they should be attached to jobs whose names declare what they are. For example, the vendor delivery date should be attached to a job that says ''vendor delivery'' and not to a job that says ''start coding''.

As discussed earlier in this chapter, vacations, personal days, training classes, and other fixed tasks could have been added to a resource calendar. However, from a reporting perspective (for example, costs, impact evaluation, or status reporting), when resource-specific values are entered into a calendar, they often lose visibility. There is an alternative approach to entering this data, one that requires creating separate fixed-date jobs in the plan. If vacations, personal days, training classes and other fixed tasks have not been added to a resource calendar, they are added to the plan at this time. Ideally, these types of fixed-date jobs can be grouped together under unique summary groups. For example, there could be one summary group for vacations, one for training classes, and so on.

It is advisable to always start with a plan of system-generated dates. Then, the fixed dates may be added to the appropriately designated activities or tasks. During these operations, it is also important to maintain the proper dependencies so that the computation of the correct dates will remain a dynamic part of the schedule. Removal of these dependencies obliterates the true relationships and can impair management of the project (or phase).

Ideally, if jobs are delayed due to the fixed date, the system ought to flag the delay.

8.19.1 Fixed-Date Scheduling Algorithms

Because a fixed date may be viewed as the absolute latest time that the job can be scheduled, many traditional scheduling algorithms reasonably follow the strategy of putting the values for the fixed dates into the late-date fields.

Example 1 of Figure 8.6 shows five tasks. Task 1 is followed by Tasks 2 and 3, both in parallel and both of the same duration. Tasks 2 and 3 are followed by Task 4. Task 4, in turn, is followed by Task 5. The early start and finish dates of each task are in the respective top lines; the late dates are in the respective bottom lines. (Because the purpose of these examples is to simply show how the dates are shifted, durations and the year have been omitted in an effort to simplify the illustration.) In the following scenarios, the start date of Task 4 will need to have a *fixed* date.

As illustrated in Example 2, when using this tech-

Figure 8.6

Example 1: System-generated dates.

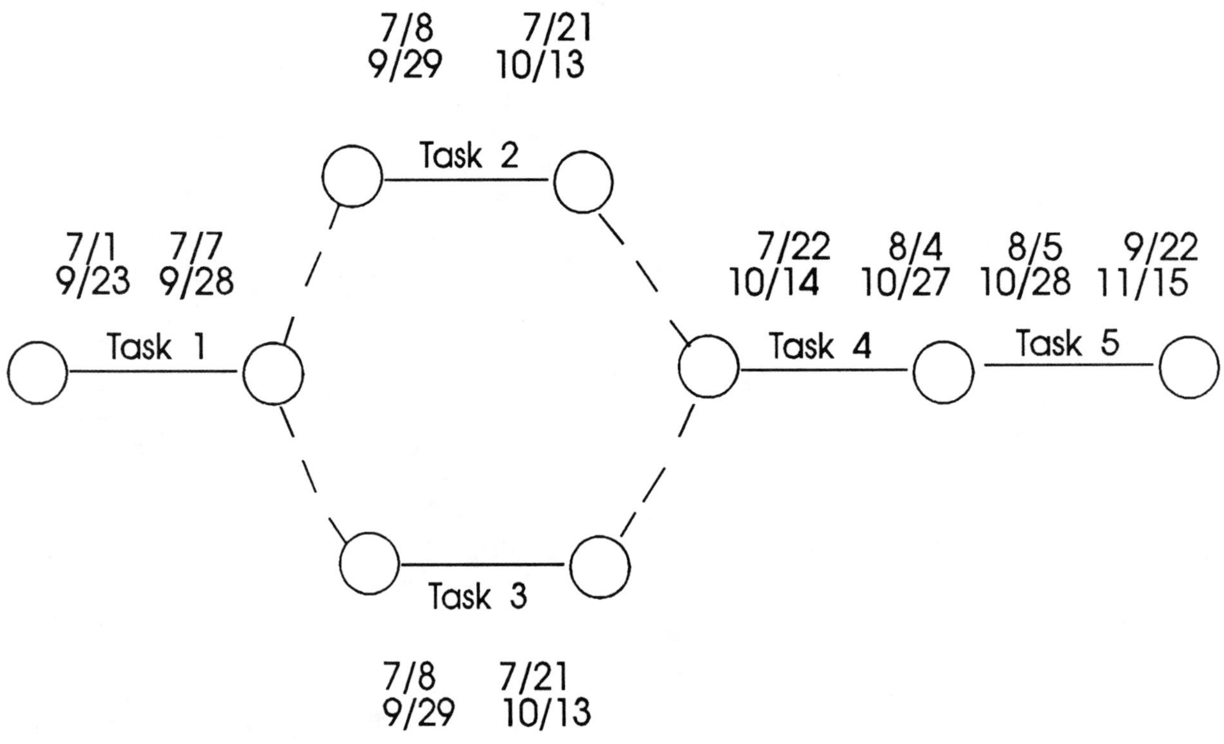

Figure 8.6 Continued.

Example 2: Fixed date equals system-generated date.

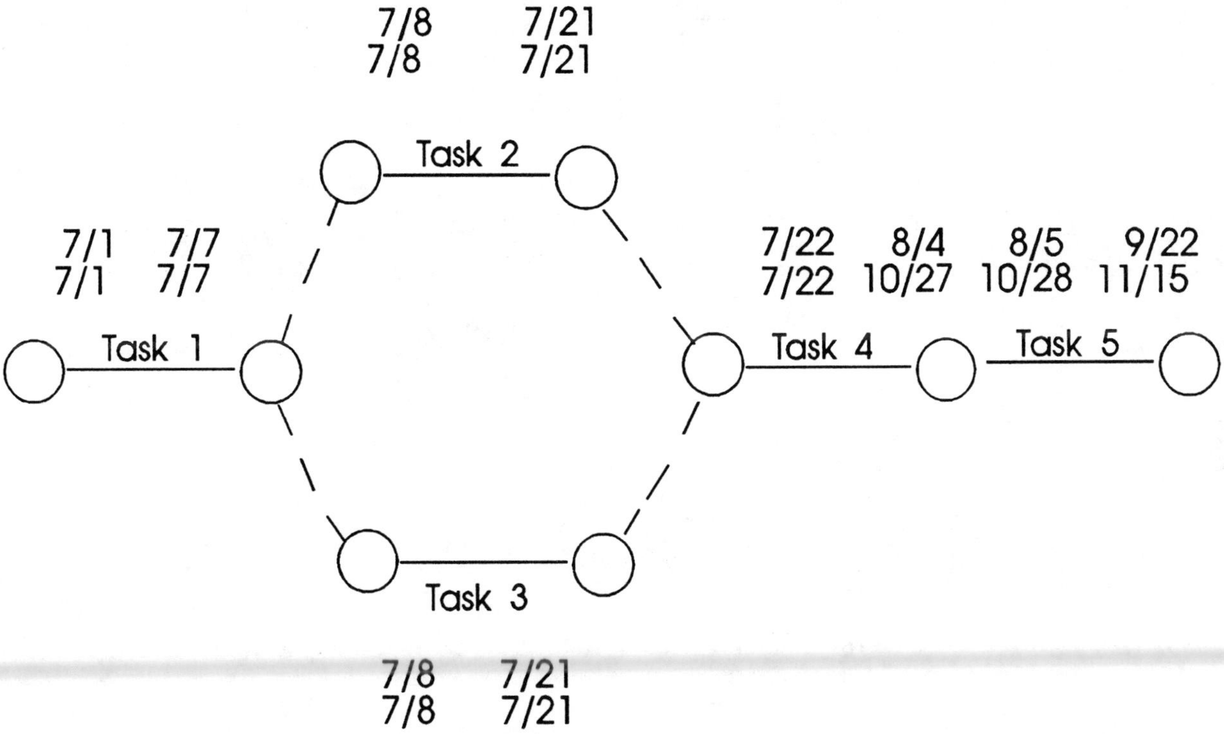

Example 3: Fixed date later than system-generated early start date.

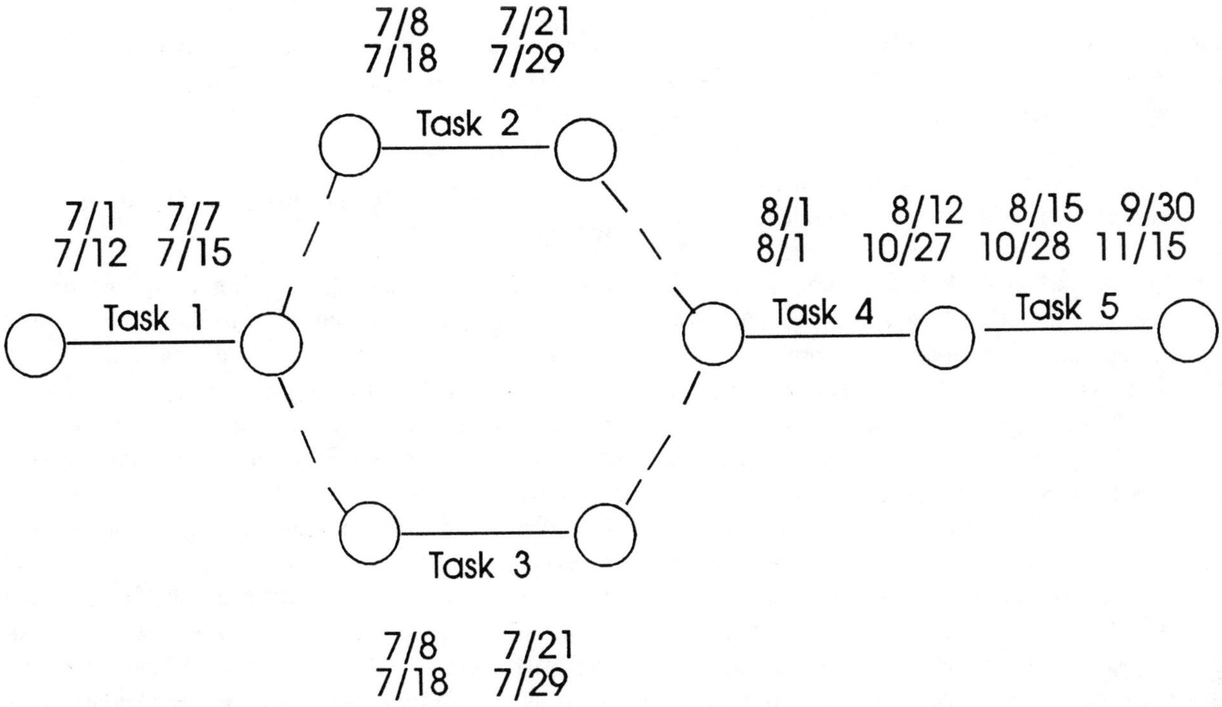

Example 4: Fixed date later than system-generated late finish date.

7/8   7/21
10/5   10/19

Task 2

7/1   7/7   10/20 11/2   11/3   11/21
9/29   10/4   10/20 11/2   11/3   11/21

Task 1   Task 4   Task 5

Task 3

7/8   7/21
10/5   10/19

nique to fix the start of Task 4 to its *system-generated early start* of July 22, its late start of October 14 is replaced with July 22. Although the subsequent late dates are not affected by this action, the late dates of all of the predecessors do need to be recalculated.

Example 3 shows that the fixed date is later than the system-generated start date. When using this technique to fix the start of Task 4 to a date that is later than its system-generated early start (for example, August 1), its late start of October 14 is replaced with August 1; its early start of July 22 is also replaced with August 1; and all of the successor's early dates must be recalculated. Although the subsequent late dates are not affected by this action, the late dates of all of the predecessors also need to be recalculated.

On the other hand, when, as illustrated in Example 4, the fixed start date is so much later (for example, October 20) that it also affects the late finish of the task, both the early dates and the late dates of the affected task and its successors will need to be

recomputed. Similarly, the late dates of all of the predecessors will also need to be recomputed.

8.19.2 Highlighting Projects That Are Late Before They Start

When using the strategy of putting fixed dates in the late-date fields, if the new date in the late-date field is earlier than the current date in the early-date field, the resulting slack will be *negative*! Furthermore, since the job then becomes late *before* it starts, the late dates show the user just exactly when the job *should* have been started.

Ideally, the system should use this approach and recompute the affected late dates. Negative slack should show up where jobs are so affected and if necessary the negative slack in the starting job(s) of the project should show users when the project should actually have started. Those products that ignore the late dates

Figure 8.7

Example 5: Fixed date earlier than system-generated early start date.

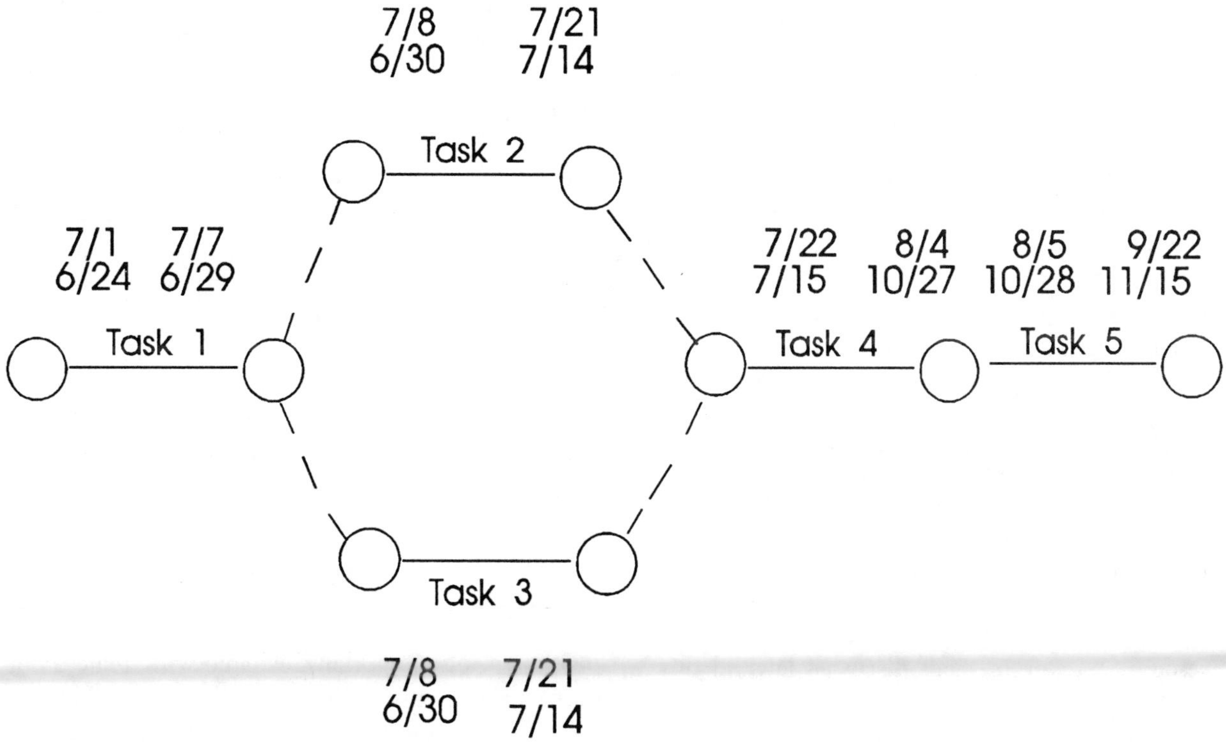

or obscure the earlier dates are overlooking an important aid to users.

As illustrated in Example 5 of Figure 8.7, if the fixed date is earlier than the current system-generated date (for Example, July 15), it affects the late start of the job, but not its early start. Neither the finish dates of the affected job nor any dates of the successors will need to be recomputed. However, the late dates of the predecessors do need to be recalculated. Furthermore, the new late dates show the user just exactly when the affected task and its predecessors should have been started. The resulting slack will be negative and frequently ripples all the way to the beginning of the project. This negative slack in the jobs at the *beginning* of the project shows just when the project should actually have started as well as how late the project is —before it even starts!

Harvard Project Manager, Viewpoint, and Primavera Project Planner use this scheduling algorithm for fixed dates.

8.20 COMPLETING THE RESOURCE ASSIGNMENT PROCESS

After the team has assigned the resources, they still have a *very important* job to perform. This operation pertains to the gathering and recording of data, much of which will become *essential* when the job is actually assigned to the individual who is designated to do it. Work packages will subsequently be prepared for each assignee. Some of the information that proves very helpful to workers is:

- The assumptions used in assigning any resources or fixed dates; and
- An update to the data that was created during the preparation of the work breakdown structures, the estimates, and the networks.

Now is the time to prepare this data. Ideally, the information may be entered into the ad hoc notes in the record for each job.

8.21 INTRODUCTION TO RESOURCE LEVELING

The next goal in the planning process is to see how the current resource assignments work out. *The original optimal resource baseline should, of course, be archived before proceeding!* At a minimum, two plans can be initiated at this point. They will provide the basis for beginning the process of *resource leveling*, which basically means adjusting the plan to accommodate resource limitations.

In the first plan, the end date of the optimal resource baseline ought to be locked into place and the scheduling of resources should have *no* constraints. Naturally, certain resources are likely to be overscheduled. Furthermore, a new critical path may even emerge. The negative effects of these new constraints must be alleviated. Before the advent of project management software, this could be accomplished, to some degree, with manual leveling techniques. Today, the plan may be massaged using both the system-generated and the user-driven resource leveling methods discussed later in this chapter.

In the second plan, the trigger levels for resource availability constraints ought to be set and the end date should be released. It is likely that this date will go farther away into the future, but it will also show what can be done within the current resource constraints. This plan will still have negative effects and they must be alleviated as well. Before the advent of project management software, this new schedule would have been developed solely with manual resource leveling techniques, a difficult and time-consuming process. Today, this plan will be developed using both the system-generated and the user-driven resource leveling methods discussed later in this chapter.

8.21.1 Leveling for Time Constraints

When the end date of a project must remain fixed, leveling is directed towards meeting the time constraints. Furthermore, if features cannot be eliminated, *there can be no limit on the number of available resources*. Since the project is date driven, resources are also likely to be overscheduled in several situations. It will be necessary to even out resource requirements

by reducing these peak areas. This is accomplished by smoothing out assignments in selected time slices—through shifting overscheduled jobs that also have slack to time periods where there are available resources. However, the constraint is on time rather than people.

8.21.2 Leveling for Resource Constraints

Leveling for resource constraints, on the other hand, is an attempt to even out workloads, staying within a *fixed* number of available resources. The goal is to find the shortest viable schedule, reassigning resources where necessary, and meeting the original dates to whatever degree possible. However, any and all jobs may be delayed in order to accommodate the resource limitations. This may require delaying the scheduled dates of individual jobs, and even slipping the project completion date itself.

8.21.3 Allowing Resources to Remain Overscheduled

Sometimes, one important resource will create a bottleneck. Frequently, this individual is *the* technical expert needed for many key tasks. If a person is assigned to do too many tasks in one time frame, the dates may ultimately slip, the quality may ultimately suffer, or both may occur. Since this is an undesirable option, overscheduling should not be allowed to remain in place. Ideally, resource leveling will eliminate most, or all, of this problem. Nevertheless, there may be occasions when a resource *will* need to be permitted to remain overscheduled. Naturally, teams are advised not to let this happen too often!

8.21.4 Using Priorities for Resource Leveling

Some jobs in a plan are more important than others. Obviously, the user will want to insure that jobs on the critical path get first priority to resources. This would also hold true in certain other situations such as jobs that are on any near-critical path(s), jobs that have high management visibility, key jobs that are predecessors to those jobs on the critical path, and so on. A prioritization scheme ought to be developed that will identify the required levels of importance for each corresponding job.

8.21.5 Using *Total* Slack and *Free* Slack for Leveling

During the process of adjusting for resources, jobs may be shifted using *total* slack or *free* slack.

Earlier, *total* slack was defined as the difference (not counting weekends) between the early and late dates at the start of a job or between the early and late dates at the finish of a job. It may be shown in brackets above the two dates for Job A. (See Figure 8.8.)

In a plan with a zero slack critical path, the *total* slack is the amount of time by which jobs on the noncritical paths can be shifted without affecting the *early* start of any job on the critical path. Thus, the integrity of the *early* finish of the project is maintained. Jobs on the critical path *cannot* be shifted—unless the organization is willing to accept an extended finish date.

In a plan with a critical path that has slack factored into it, the *total* slack is the amount of time by which a job can be shifted without affecting the *late* start of any of its successors. Thus, the integrity of the *late* finish of the project is maintained. Jobs on both the critical and noncritical paths can be shifted.

In either of these two cases, when any job on a path is shifted within any part of the related slack, the amount associated with all of the remaining jobs on that path is reduced by that same part. This may cause new critical and/or near-critical paths to emerge and necessitate new calculations for probability of success.

In both of these two cases, jobs on the noncritical paths may be adjusted by *total* slack; but they have the added advantage of also being responsive to *free* slack. *Free* slack is the period between the early finish of any predecessor and the earliest of all corresponding early start(s) of its successor(s). (Figure 8.8) The 4 in

the circle represents the period between EF1 and ES3. *Free* slack is not affected by any changes to the early finish or the late finish of the project. Thus, modifications made to increase the probability of success will not affect *free* slack. Because *free* slack will *not* affect any other jobs in the network, it may be used to adjust for resource constraints without the same concerns about the end date that are associated with *total* slack.

Primavera Project Planner is the only product that allows the user to choose between using *free* float or *total* float during leveling.

In a zero or positive slack critical path, *free* slack may never exceed *total* slack. However, when the project is late before it starts and thus has negative slack, the *free* slack may be greater than the *total* slack.

The term *candidate time slice* has been coined to represent either *total* slack or *free* slack.

When leveling for resource constraints, as in leveling for time constraints, it is also necessary to even out resource requirements by reducing peak areas. Once again, this is accomplished by smoothing out assignments in selected time slices—through shifting overscheduled jobs that also have slack to time periods where there are available resources.

Jobs with a *candidate time slice* are ideal delegates for shifting. Since scheduling is usually initiated by using early dates, assignments may be shifted down the *candidate time slice*, calendar unit by calendar unit, to a later time, using up the slack. Since using slack from the noncritical paths will not affect the end date of the project, the first jobs to be selected are those with the most slack.

It is important to note again that, as jobs are shifted along the *candidate time slice*, slack is being consumed. A new critical path may emerge, or more jobs may wind up on the current critical path. As a last resort, the end date of the project is slipped.

8.21.6 True Work Effort and Resource-Leveled Durations

It is necessary to recall that the duration that was used to create the optimal plan was the figure represented by the *expected effort*, which, in turn, was adjusted by the Protected Environment *broad-based overhead*. This number is called the *true work effort*. When a

Figure 8.8 Using slack for leveling.

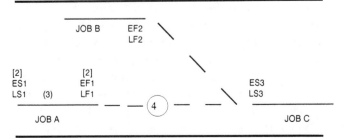

job is shifted for rescheduling and/or reassignment, *the true work effort must not change!* The true work effort may be shifted in its entirety to another point in time or it may be spread out across the *candidate time slice*. But, no matter how it is used during the resource leveling process, *the integrity of the value of true work effort must always be preserved.* It must never be replaced by the new duration number which reflects the results of resource leveling. This new duration number is called the *resource-leveled* duration and should be stored separately. While the true work effort only changes when users have recognized that the estimate was incorrect, resource-leveled durations may change each time a different resource is assigned to the job.

8.22 DISTRIBUTION PATTERNS FOR LEVELING TRUE WORK EFFORT ACROSS A CANDIDATE TIME SLICE

There are several ways in which a resource's allocation to true work effort may be distributed across a *candidate time slice*. The following formulas are applied to jobs, always using any remaining resource availability. Resource availability is, in turn, based on a respective resource calendar.

8.22.1 No Interruptions—Working the Job to Completion

Optimal plans have a set of scheduled early dates and scheduled late dates. If the early dates are used in assigning the work to the resource and no other jobs are allowed to conflict with the assignment, the effect is *uninterrupted front-loading* of resources to the true work effort. On the other hand, if the true work effort is shifted to the very end of the *candidate time slice* and no other jobs are allowed to conflict with the assignment, the effect is *uninterrupted back-loading* of resources to true work effort. Since uninterrupted front-loading and uninterrupted back-loading are both leveling techniques, these assignments may only be allocated when they stay within the known daily resource availabilities.

The advantage to either of these two leveling options is that the job, once started, is not interrupted and is worked from its start until its completion. This

also means that, after the momentum gets going, productivity usually does not get seriously disturbed.

8.22.2 Splitting the True Work Effort

When there is not enough resource to work the job, without interruption, from its start to its completion, it must be split and spread across a *candidate time slice*. The three ways described in this section are the third through fifth leveling patterns.

In the third type of resource leveling, the number of hours of true work effort may be divided by the number of days (not including weekends) in the *candidate time slice*. In this manner, the *true work effort* will be evenly distributed across the *candidate time slice*. This pattern uses up slack and may create a new critical path.

The fourth pattern, on the other hand, uses left-over time and jobs. After allocating resources to *true work effort* according to job priorities, some of the remaining unallocated jobs may be assigned by spreading their *true work effort across any remaining resource hours of any qualifying day. These days may even extend beyond the candidate time slice.* This pattern uses up slack and may create a new critical path. Naturally, this pattern ought to be avoided for jobs that are already on the critical path and near-critical path(s).

Finally, there may be occasions when users choose to allocate true work effort according to their own predetermined pattern. For example, the resource may be assigned to complete a 10-hour job by working 2 hours on Monday, 1 hour on Tuesday, 5 hours on Wednesday, no time on Thursday, and 2 hours on Friday.

It is important to remember that splitting jobs interrupts momentum and thus affects productivity. In most cases, there will be a time lapse between the occasions when the resource is actually working on the job. As a result, the resource cannot be instantly productive when the work is resumed. Sometimes, in order to compensate for this reduction in productivity, a little extra time ought to be factored into the work time on the working days after the first day. Other times, the job itself is so technically complex that productivity really suffers. When this occurs, larger chunks of time must be added to the days following the first day.

Figure 8.9 Leveling matrix.

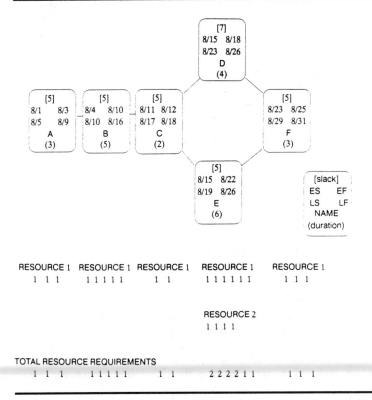

RESOURCE 1   RESOURCE 1   RESOURCE 1   RESOURCE 1   RESOURCE 1
 1 1 1   1 1 1 1 1   1 1   1 1 1 1 1 1   1 1 1

RESOURCE 2
1 1 1 1

TOTAL RESOURCE REQUIREMENTS
 1 1 1   1 1 1 1 1   1 1   2 2 2 2 1 1   1 1 1

8.23 GRAPHIC AIDS TO LEVELING

A matrix may be drawn to represent the number of people required in a given time slice. (Figure 8.9) The jobs depicted in this matrix may be limited to those assignments for an individual resource, a selected department, all of the jobs in a particular subnetwork, all of the jobs in the entire plan, and so on. The key to this matrix is the bottom line, the line that shows, at a glance, the total number of people required for each time period.

When the number of entries in the matrix gets large, however, users may find it very difficult to get a reasonably accurate idea of how the resources are actually distributed. A more useful kind of graph is a histogram. (Figure 8.10) Like the resource matrix, histograms may be drawn to depict assignments for an individual resource, a selected department, all of the jobs in a particular subnetwork, all of the jobs in the entire plan, and so on. Since the height of each column shows the level of resource commitment, they are par-

ticularly useful in showing overutilization and underutilization of resources as well as significantly aiding in the process of leveling individual resource assignments. (In Week 3 of Figure 8.10, one resource is assigned for five days and a second resource is assigned for four days.)

Figure 8.10 Resource histogram.

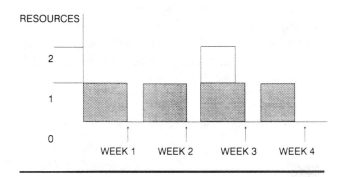

Figure 8.11 Repackaging.

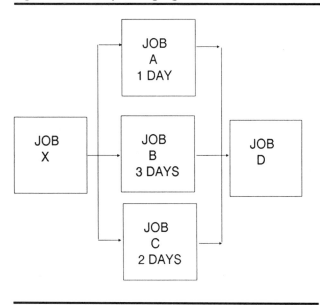

8.24 SUPPLEMENTARY AIDS TO LEVELING

In addition to resource leveling, users ought to look for opportunities to apply the following supplementary aids to eliminating resource constraints.

8.24.1 Repackaging

In Figure 8.11, A, B, and C are all the true and natural predecessors to D. Furthermore, they cannot start until X has been completed. If three resources were available during the period from the end of X until the beginning of D, there would be no resource contentions. If only two resources were available, A and C could be *repackaged* together into one three-day assignment without affecting the start of D. The slack will have been consumed, however, and the new package will have become part of the critical path. If only one resource is available, all three jobs may be repackaged into one long assignment and the start of D will be delayed by three days.

8.24.2 Reordering Dependencies

Until now, the team has been working with a plan that is built upon the true and natural order of dependen-

cies. When there are resource conflicts that are difficult to resolve, dependencies may sometimes need to be reordered. Imagine a system that is to be developed so that all of its users find it easy to use, and whose users will be the clerical staff and the computer data entry clerks. Ideally, the clerical forms will be designed before the data entry screens and the data on the forms will be placed in approximately the same area as it ultimately appears on the screens. Consequently, forms design comes before screen design. (See Figure 8.12.1.) However, if the forms designers cannot be available at the appointed time and the screen designers can be available, the order of dependencies may be reversed. (Figure 8.12.2)

8.24.3 Delaying or Eliminating Features

The value of the benefits of each feature is measured against the cost of the resources required to provide it. Depending on the answer, features may be included, deferred, or completely eliminated.

8.24.4 Negotiating for Full-Time Participation

It is not unusual for a job that is nowhere near the critical path to become *the* critical path after part-time resources have been assigned to it. (See the part-time discussions earlier in this chapter.) Project teams are advised to evaluate the impacts of part-time scheduling and look for opportunities to negotiate for full-time participation whenever necessary and possible.

Figure 8.12.1 Reordering dependencies.

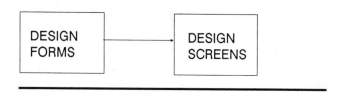

Figure 8.12.2 Reordering dependencies.

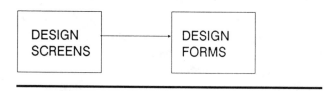

Figure 8.13 Schedule dates.

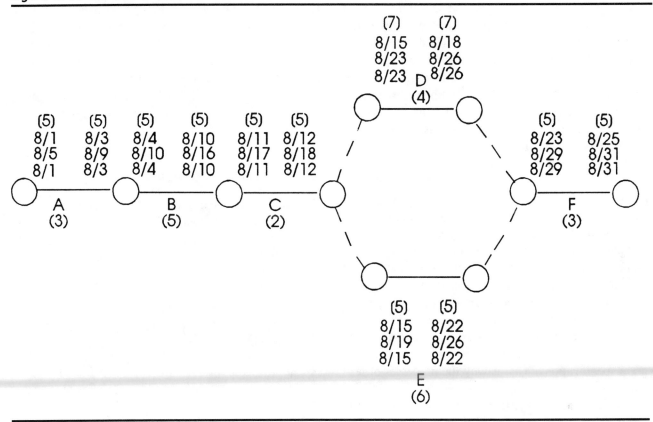

8.24.5 Replanning

When all else fails, the team may enter into a replanning exercise. The replanning effort is supplemented by planning and estimating experts (either from within the company or outside), with individuals who have a higher degree of application knowledge than the original planners, and with individuals who have a fresh perspective. This means redoing the WBS and, perhaps, the network, both of which are very labor-intensive and time-consuming operations! When applying this approach, users also ought to be cautioned not to impact any important WBS rollup reporting structures.

8.25 SCHEDULED DATES AND RESOURCE PLANNING

Most of the leveling approaches start by using the early start, early finish schedule. At the conclusion of resource leveling, there will be *three* sets of dates, the set of early dates, the set of late dates, *and* the set of

scheduled dates. New dates may be used for the scheduled dates, dates that may be the same as the early dates, the same as the late dates, or entirely different dates. (See Figure 8.13.) The early dates go on the top line; the late dates go on the second line; and the scheduled dates go on the third line.

8.26 RESOURCE LEVELING ALGORITHMS

This is often regarded as one of the less stimulating aspects of project management. Yet, it is not the kind of work that can easily be resumed after an interruption. For an average-size project, manually applying these concepts is labor-intensive, time-consuming, and, often, error-prone. Fortunately, the current software products are a real boon to the resource leveling effort.

8.26.1 The Challenge of Identifying Solutions

Calculating the number of possible solutions for allocating resources is done using mathematical formulas for combinations of arrangements. Basically, this means that (1) the order of the selections is fixed (that is, the order of job execution is dependent on the relationships between the jobs) and (2) there is a finite number of resources available for each job.

For the first job in any subnetwork, the total number of solutions is equal to the number of resources available for that job. Thereafter, the current solution total is *multiplied* by the number of resources available for the next job in the series. It is easy to see how quickly this number can increase—for only one subnetwork. For a whole project of average size, this number can rapidly become very high. Consequently, current technology for personal computers is not sophisticated enough to support this type of mathematical complexity. Most software products use some commonly accepted, empirical heuristics—empirical meaning based on experience and heuristics being synonymous with rules of thumb. Even so, it is important to note that the complete set of mental deliberations that the scheduler exercises during this operation is still not easily distilled down to comprehensive program specifications. That is why the processes of leveling and loading are still so interactive.

There are many different options for leveling the resources assigned to each task. If this number is limited to the uninterrupted leveling pattern and the four splitting patterns discussed earlier in this chapter, it now means that the number of possible alternatives for any plan is equal to five raised to the power of the number of jobs in the plan. The number of alternatives could easily be in the thousands. Obviously, it is not necessary to present so many scenarios. Furthermore, to develop a software system that could provide the optimum plan for the user requires expensive and extensive dynamic programming algorithms in an environment that is not yet available in the current micro computer software platforms (or on many mainframes, for that matter). Once again, here is justification for the processes of leveling and loading still being so interactive.

8.26.2 The Basic Strategies

There are two basic strategies used in the leveling algorithms: leveling by available slack or leveling by established priorities. Many algorithms tackle the jobs with slack first, initially using the noncritical path(s).

Others allocate resources according to priority, with, for example, the jobs on the critical path having the highest priority. There may, of course, be variations on these basic strategies. For example, the plan may be leveled by priority, then by department, then by the jobs with the most slack, then by the jobs on the near-critical path, and last by the jobs on the critical path. In any event, the strategies also usually start by using the early dates.

8.26.3 Leveling by Slack

Starting on day one of the project (or phase), resources may be assigned *serially* job by job and then day by day. If there are two jobs competing for resources, preference is given by assigning resources to the job with the least amount of slack. Jobs with the most amount of slack are rescheduled in order to free up resources for those jobs with the least slack. The rescheduling is initiated by moving the candidate to the next available time period and starting again. Sooner or later every job will become *the* job with the least amount of slack.

8.26.4 Leveling by Priority

Starting on Day 1 of the project (or phase), candidate jobs are considered in *parallel*. All of the jobs in a selected time slice are prioritized, then resources are assigned in order of job priority until the supply of resources is exhausted. As each new time slice is selected, the priorities are resorted. Sooner or later every job will rise to a priority level that will insure resource assignment.

8.26.5 Leveling By Slack and Priority

Starting with Day 1 of the project (or phase), all of the jobs within a time slice are organized by the least amount of slack first, and within this group, the job with the shortest true work effort duration gets highest priority. Resources are scheduled in this order. This formula works as well in a multiproject environment as on single projects. Categories other than slack may be used for the ordering. For example, the jobs may be prioritized according to those jobs that have the highest resource requirements, according to those jobs that result in the least amount of idle time, according to random number selection, and so on.

8.26.6 The Burgess Algorithm

The Burgess algorithm is particularly good for those situations when there is slack and when there is not a severe limitation on the number of resources. It was originally intended for use with arrow diagramming networks, but it also works with precedence networks. This algorithm is based on computing variations on the total resource requirements.

> **If each day's resource requirements are added to an accumulator, the final total for the whole project will always be the same—regardless of how the resources are redistributed. On the other hand, if the number of each day's resource requirements is squared and the answer is added to an accumulator, the answer will decrease as resources are redistributed across the peaks and valleys, and will start going back up after the optimal schedule has been achieved.**

This algorithm can also be employed very effectively as a reasonability check during the resource leveling operation.[3]

8.26.7 The Spar-1 Algorithm

Many years ago, Wiest developed a scheduling algorithm for resource-constrained projects called SPAR-1 (Scheduling Program for Allocating Resources). It is a software program that, in addition to the normal scheduling data, requires that three other resource numbers be provided for each job: the maximum number of people that can be applied to get the specific job done in the shortest possible time, the number of people who would normally be assigned to the job, and the minimum number of people that can be assigned and still get the job done. Jobs are randomly selected from the critical path and then assigned resources in order of maximum, normal, or minimum availability.

There are other subroutines included in this program. For example, there are subroutines that continuously go back and look for jobs that still do not have the maximum number of resources, wherever possible augmenting resources, or that handle variable resource types such as people, machines, or money.

SPAR-1 works well on small to very large projects, in a single or multiproject environment, with few or many resources and under other circumstances such as varying workshifts or splitting job assignments. It is especially helpful in large projects with few resources.

Because of the random selection of jobs, different schedules are often developed—even with exactly the same input. As a result, several alternatives may be created for consideration.

8.27 SELECTING ALTERNATIVE PLANS

There is no one correct way to go about developing options. Consequently, the following discussion is only intended to provide the user with a general feeling for how to develop alternative resource-constrained plans. Users ought to always keep in mind that there's still no free lunch! Introducing resource constraints often reduces total plan slack which, in turn, may reduce the probability of success. It may also create new resource-limited dependencies in addition to the natural dependencies.

8.27.1 Alternative 1

Starting with the optimal resource baseline, the end date of the project is fixed and known resources are assigned, wherever possible, to jobs on the critical path. When there are resource conflicts, people are matched to jobs according to priorities, leaving the unfulfilled jobs with resources representing the original job skills or classifications instead of actual assignments.

Choosing the near-critical path(s) next, people are matched to these jobs. At the same time, resource conflicts are reduced where possible by using slack, but not by delaying the project. This is repeated until the slack possibilities have been exhausted. There will still be some job skills or classifications, instead of people, assigned to jobs—where there were conflicts but no available resources or slack.

Names are added to all of the remaining jobs, still maintaining the optimal plan end date. It is likely

---

[3]Users who are interested in this algorithm will find directions in the Moder, Phillips, and Davis text.

that there will be scenarios in which resources are overcommitted. Some of these will actually be impossible (for example, one person who is scheduled 27 hours in one day). When this occurs, the plan is *not* a good candidate for an alternative! Nevertheless, a copy of this plan should be set aside as a starting place for Alternative 2.

Continuing with the Alternative 1 plan, overcommitted resources must be eliminated by assigning different people or by adding new people to the plan. If new (or additional) critical paths arise, the probability of success will need to be recalculated.

Alternative 1 is driven by the optimal plan end date; therefore, it is still a time-constrained plan. As such, it ought to be completed working on the assumption that, where necessary, there are unlimited numbers of resources. This is the plan that represents meeting the optimal end date, having identified the total number of real resources that are required. It may be used as input to a time/cost tradeoff analysis. (See chapter 10.)

8.27.2 Alternative 2

Needless to say, rarely are the exact number of *required* resources assigned to the project. Alternative 2 uses the partially completed Alternative 1 plan that was set aside. Now, the end-date constraints are removed and a new schedule is computed. This plan gets smoothed and leveled so that no resources are overloaded, but all available resources are fully maximized. A new end date evolves, demonstrating what can be accomplished given the number of known resources. If new (or additional) critical paths arise, the probability of success will need to be recalculated.

Two similar alternatives ought to be developed for each of the subsets that evolve from the planning process.

8.28 LEVELING WITH PROJECT MANAGEMENT SOFTWARE

Users may opt to turn the job of eliminating resource conflicts entirely over to the system, invoking the automatic leveling feature. Conversely, they may opt to do all of the conflict resolution themselves, using the features provided for user-driven interactive leveling

such as priority setting, resource loading histograms, resource loading reports, date shifting, and so on.

On the other hand, many users generally employ *all* of the tools at their disposal. Ideally, they will use all of the system's automatic leveling features as a template to initiate the leveling process. Then, they will go back to the plan before leveling and do their own user-driven interactive leveling, using the product's user-driven leveling tools with the automated leveling results as a reference.

8.29 SPECIAL LEVELING PATTERNS IN PROJECT MANAGEMENT SOFTWARE ◆

To begin the leveling process, several products allow the user to choose the manner in which the resource's available time will be allocated to jobs. These are Project Workbench, Viewpoint, Primavera Project Planner, and SuperProject Expert. SuperProject Expert, Viewpoint, and Primavera Project Planner each offers users two ways to level:

1. Assigning resources and, if necessary, delaying jobs until the resources that can complete them are available. Of course, this will often extend the project completion date.

2. Alternatively, only leveling resources on tasks with positive slack. This process will, to the degree possible, minimize sharp differences between resource utilization from one day to the next. Its purpose is to achieve a more uniform distribution of resource usage. However, much as this process might change the critical path, it will not extend project duration.

Alternative 1 is an ideal way to explore the possibilities of what can be achieved through leveling and by limiting the project to the available resources. Then, although Alternative 2 leaves several conflicting resource assignments, it is a good kickoff point for the user-driven interactive leveling described later in the chapter.

8.30 AUTOMATIC RESOURCE LEVELING ◆

In the interest of maintaining a control sample in which each of the products could be evaluated on the same basis, identical optimal project plans were used. All dates and dependencies were matched across all of the plans. All jobs were activity driven rather than resource driven. Resource values, availabilities, and assignments were also identical in each of the plans. There were no part-time resources, no special calendars, no special leveling patterns, and no priorities set. Resource assignments were also limited to one resource per job. Resources were assigned in an identical manner that would intentionally create overscheduling. The first leveling approach (described in the previous section) was the approach that was used on the control sample. Although the second approach was not used for the control sample, it can be very helpful as a starting point during user-driven interactive leveling. (See the discussion later in this chapter.) Finally, all jobs were open to leveling; none were flagged for exclusion from the leveling process. Each plan was then automatically leveled according to the vendor specifications.

From seven different packages, seven different schedules resulted. There was not one duplicate. Five products came up with the shortest leveled (resource-constrained) schedule, the same new project end date, the same critical path, and the same dates for the jobs on their critical path. However, there was no similarity in any of the jobs on the noncritical paths—either in the arrangement of jobs or in the scheduled dates. These five systems were: Super-Project Expert, Harvard Project Manager 3.0, Viewpoint, Project Workbench, and Time Line 3.0. Primavera Project Planner also came up with the same new project end date as the five products listed above. Therefore, it, too, had the shortest resource-constrained schedule. However, it had a slightly different critical path.

On the other hand, Microsoft Project only supports the second leveling approach described earlier in this chapter. It restricts leveling solely to those activities with slack; therefore, it retained the original project end date. Although it also left several conflicting resource assignments, this is a good kickoff point for the user-driven interactive leveling described later in this chapter.

The product discussions explain how to invoke the automatic leveling process, the contents of the various dates fields at the end of automatic leveling, and how the system flags delays that are caused by leveling. (For example, if the product levels on a zero slack critical path and plans have been created which reflect probabilities greater than 50 percent, the zero slack plan must be used for leveling.) Furthermore, since leveling is often only part of the *what-if* process, the process of restoring to the preleveled plan will be explained. Finally, if the product documentation gave the rules for its leveling process, these policies have been summarized.

8.31 SETTING SPECIAL LEVELING PRIORITIES ON TASKS OR ACTIVITIES ◆

The ability to set priorities gives users the opportunity to control some of the leveling process themselves and thus assign levels of influence to certain jobs. The priority number establishes the significance of a job in relationship to all of the other jobs in the plan. Then, when there are resource conflicts *during the automatic leveling process*, these jobs get scheduled in order of importance.

For example, setting priorities for each task tells the system that when there are resource conflicts, the task priority may be more important than slack. On the other hand, setting priorities for each resource assignment tells the system that when there are resource conflicts, scheduling one particular job that uses that resource may be more important than scheduling an alternate job that uses that resource. In yet another example, the system can be instructed so that the early start date has the highest priority during resource leveling.

Since setting these priorities often requires working on a task-by-task basis, this process requires more effort from the user. However, it also transfers more control over which jobs will be delayed when resource availability is limited.

The significance of the priority number may be set so that the priority increases in ascending order (the higher the number, the higher the priority), or so that the priority increases in descending order (the lower the number, the higher the priority). In some systems, this order may even be selected by the user.

Setting priorities may be very useful in multiproject environments, where the same resources are working on many jobs in several small projects. Resources in a multiproject environment will be addressed later in this chapter.

Information about special resource-specific holidays, vacations, business trips away from the project, special project training classes, and so on, may have been put into special resource calendars. (See the discussion earlier in this chapter.) From a reporting perspective (for example, costs, impact evaluation, or status reporting), when resource-specific values are entered into a calendar, they often lose visibility. On the other hand, once the plan is stabilized, users may instead choose to create separate highest-priority, fixed-date jobs and place them in the appropriate positions in the plan. (See the discussion earlier in this chapter.) Then, putting all of these jobs inside of one work breakdown structure provides the higher visibility.

Users ought to be advised that setting priorities during leveling often adversely extends the end date of the project—much more so than using slack. Therefore, caution should be exercised when invoking this feature.

Harvard Project Manager 3.0 and Viewpoint do not support priorities.

8.32 USER-DRIVEN INTERACTIVE LEVELING ◆

The process of resolving resource conflicts may be initiated by producing two versions of the plan, one of each of the two automated leveling patterns described earlier in this chapter. Of course, users may often then discover that they are not totally satisfied with the results of either of the system-generated leveling solutions. Keeping in mind that an optimal leveling solution is not always possible, even from automated leveling operations, users may instead want to tweak the system-leveled version.

They may even opt for finding the resource conflicts and making the adjustments themselves. For example, although Alternative 2 from the discussion earlier in this chapter still leaves several conflicting resource assignments, it may prove to be a good kickoff point for the user-driven interactive leveling process.

Also as part of the kickoff process, it will be necessary to decide how to prioritize the rescheduling effort. The degree of importance to place on leveling by excess slack, task priority, resource priority, and so on, ought to be determined before starting. For example, conflicts may be resolved first for the tasks with the least slack or for the tasks with the longest duration or for the tasks with the greatest resource requirements.

Most leveling techniques try to provide a reasonable buildup of resources at the beginning of the project (or phase). Then, they try to maintain a constant level of commitment during the majority of the plan, smoothing resource utilization so that there are no excessive periods of overutilization or excessive periods of underutilization. Finally, they complete the leveling process with a sensible tapering off at the end. This is a good approach for users to employ.

With the height of each column in the histogram representing the level of the resource's commitment, histograms become especially useful in illustrating overutilization as well as underutilization. Since one of the goals of the leveling operation is to redistribute the periods of overutilization to periods of underutilization, the histograms are very helpful visual aids. Certainly, they make the process of pinpointing periods of resource conflicts significantly easier. However, the histogram only shows that the resource is overscheduled during a particular time period. It does *not* tell what jobs are causing the overcommitment. The only way to identify the source of the conflict for certain is to move the cursor:

1. Horizontally across the histogram, watching to see where resource availability has been exceeded; then

2. Vertically through the Gantt chart on that date, looking for task bars that relate to that resource.

But now another problem surfaces. When the Gantt is cluttered with the whole project plan (all of the tasks for all resources), moving vertically up and down the Gantt to find the offending tasks for a particular resource can become difficult and frustrating. It is much easier to work with a Gantt chart that is limited to one set of resource tasks at a time. Products that provide this feature make user-driven interactive leveling much easier than those that do not.

Then, too, there is a problem when the histogram does not show weekends and holidays. Sometimes, the only solution to resolving a resource conflict occurs when the team member willingly agrees to work on a nonworking day. Histograms that cannot show weekends and other nonworking days are more limited in their functionality than those that do.

In addition to the histograms and Gantts, several products mark the tasks that have overscheduled resources with some type of highlighting flag. But these flags only warn that there is a resource scheduling conflict somewhere in the task; it could be through the whole task or on just one day of the task. Furthermore, the Gantt chart itself only shows the elapsed calendar days of the task; it does not show the amount of true work effort that is scheduled to be done on each of these days. Microsoft Project is the only product that lists, on a daily basis, the offending activities that are contributing to resource overscheduling. The user does not have to go poking through the Gantt to find them.

The bottom line is that there is no one tool that suffices for the whole job of interactive leveling. An ideal user-driven interactive leveling process would enable the screen to be split into three crucial windows. These windows would allow the user to see: (1) a Gantt of the whole project highlighting the critical path; (2) a resource histogram window showing the corresponding occurrences of overscheduling; and (3) a list of the resource's jobs that are causing the overcommitment. *From this windowed screen,* modifications may be made to the plan by invoking the corresponding data entry forms, which would be superimposed on the windowed screen. Impacts of the modifications would be seen immediately in the three windows—*without requiring any special action to get back to the windowed screen.*

Once users have identified the offending tasks and have pinpointed the days on which the overcommitment actually occurs, they can set to work to resolve the resource conflicts. Although each of the systems evaluated does feature some form of resource-leveling graphics, using the criteria above, none were ideally interactive. For this section, systems are classified into three groups: (1) those that are fully-interactive, (2) those that are semi-interactive, and (3) those that require manual intervention. All of the systems display one or more of the crucial three windows described above.

- *Fully-interactive* leveling systems enable all of the possible modifications to the plan to be made by superimposing windows for each of the corresponding data entry forms. The impacts of these modifications are seen immediately, and do not require any special action to get back to the windowed screen. Time Line 3.0 is a fully-interactive leveling system.

- *Semi-interactive* leveling systems enable most of the modifications to the plan to be made by superim-

posing windows for the corresponding data entry forms. Most of the impacts of the modifications are seen immediately, and do not require any special action to get back to the split screen; but the rest of the modifications can only be made by leaving the windowed screen, making the modifications, leaving these screens and *recalling* the windowed screen. SuperProject Expert, Microsoft Project, Project Workbench, and Viewpoint are semi-interactive leveling systems.

- *Manual* leveling systems always require that the users *leave* the windowed screen, go to the data entry screens, make their modifications, leave these screens and *recall* the windowed screen so that they may see the results of the modifications. Harvard Project Manager 3.0 and Primavera Project Planner are manual leveling systems. With these products, the leveling process is facilitated when the user is working along with hard copy reports. Furthermore, it is not unusual to experience the need to reproduce current versions of the reports often during the leveling process.

During the user-driven interactive leveling process, conflicts may be resolved by reassigning resources, deleting resources, adding new resources, moving dates, splitting jobs, assigning overtime, making resources part-time, and adding resource lags.

In conclusion, the most important feature for this process is being able to do it interactively and immediately see results. The next most important feature is being able to see where a resource is overloaded (for example, in the histogram) and what tasks, on a day-by-day basis, are causing the overload (for example, in the Gantt). Finally, it is important to know where the project critical path is so that the project is not unintentionally extended by creating a new and longer critical path. Armed with this information, users may then proceed to interactively level the plan.

As a closing note, it is important to moderate expectations regarding the ease with which this process may be executed. *It is not an easy chore. Flipping back and forth can quickly become frustrating. Furthermore, the process requires creativity and ingenuity. It also takes patience and perseverance. It is not unusual to find people who give up and just let the system do it!*

8.33 COMPLETING THE RESOURCE ASSIGNMENT PROCESS TO REFLECT LEVELING

If the team has changed any of the assigned resources, they still have a *very important* job to perform. This operation pertains to the gathering and recording of data, much of which will become *essential* when the job is actually assigned to the individual who is designated to do it. Work packages will be prepared for each assignee. Some of the information that proves very helpful to workers is:

- The assumptions used in reassigning any resources; and

- An update to the data that was created during the preparation of the work breakdown structures, the estimates, the networks, and the original resource assignments.

Now is the time to prepare this data. Ideally, the information may be entered into the ad hoc notes in the record for each job.

8.34 BASELINE PROJECT PLANS FOR RESOURCE LEVELING ◆

Ideally, at the beginning of each project (or phase), there can be at least two baselines: one pure optimal resource baseline (with unlimited resources) and the resource-constrained plan for the project (phase). Later in the project, after posting progress to the resource-constrained plan, project management decisions will need to be made. The more data the project manager has, the better the decisions will be. Ideally, users may be able to save a baseline version of the optimal plan *and* a baseline version of the resource-constrained plan that is selected for implementation. These two plans can then be compared to the plan with the posted progress. In lieu of two baselines, the final resource-constrained plan becomes the new baseline, the original optimal resource baseline is archived, and the status is reported against the new baseline.

8.35 RESOURCES IN A MULTIPROJECT ENVIRONMENT

When resources are assigned across multiple projects, one way of adjusting their overcommitment is to start by prioritizing each project. Then, based on each project's standing in this classification scheme, it is possible to control the number of hours per week that each resource may be assigned to each job. This is accomplished by using priorities at the job level *and* by varying the resource's part-time participation at each project level. (See the discussions about part-time earlier in this chapter.)

Unfortunately, these procedures do not entirely eliminate overscheduling. Frequently, it will still be necessary to pinpoint the places in each subproject that are contributing to the global overcommitment and to then resolve the conflicts. To initiate this process, it is necessary to be able to see:

- All of the subprojects grouped together in one place (the master project);

- The interdependencies, if present, between the subprojects;

- The start and finish dates of each subproject; and

- Where each resource is overcommitted—across all of the subprojects.

8.35.1 Modeling Resource Availability

Certain data in the resource pool and in the resource calendars may often need to be replicated from one master project (or subproject) to the next—for example, the resource's workweek, normal working hours, normal billing rate, vacations, etc. In this case, the *template* concept can be applied to create a "project" that has no activities or tasks, but is replete with all of the global resource data. The *template* may include, as well, the standard calendar information addressed earlier. When users subsequently create their master projects, it ought to be possible to start by importing all of the respective *template* resource data.

On the other hand, the subprojects may also need to have individualized resource data and individual resource calendars. (For example, if the resource may only work on the subproject certain days of the week or certain hours of each day.)

Since the calendar in the master project has the global view, it should rule over global resource commitments. If the system later detects a resource in a subproject that is not defined in the master project, the irregularity may be handled simply by incorporating the new resource into the master file or by flagging it for a decision that may be made by the user.

8.35.2 Leveling in a Multiproject Environment

Ideally, system-generated resource leveling may be done top-down from the master project tier across all of the related subprojects, bottom-up from each subproject layer or by a combination of both—depending on the user's needs and preferences. On the other hand, some or all of the leveling may be done interactively, as described earlier in this chapter.

If a product does not support the ability to level across the subprojects from the master project downward, the leveling of each rung in the nest of subprojects must subsequently be initiated by users. In this situation, users are advised to create a hard copy tree of the nested groups and check each one off as it is leveled. This is important because, if only one subproject is overlooked, all of the subsequent schedules may be incorrect. There is no alternative to this procedure.

8.35.3 Finding the Resource Conflicts

During the leveling processes, users ought to be able to see, from the master project tier, the impacts of the resource leveling on the dates across the subprojects, along with any remaining overcommitments—without the clutter of all of the jobs in each subproject. Therefore, each entire subproject should be able to be represented by a single one-line entry in the master project Gantt chart and a single node in the PERT chart. Furthermore, the master project histograms ought to show —by individual resource in each subproject—the source of each overcommitment. Then, it ought to be possible to flip between each of the subprojects to see the dates of their particular tasks and activities, to see the cor-

responding resource commitments, and to make any necessary modifications. All changes at the subproject level should automatically be reflected upward to the master project.

8.35.4 Resources, Multiprojects, and Project Management Software ◆

The master projects have been created following the multiproject directions given earlier. Project level calendars and rolling up data in nested subprojects have both been handled also as addressed earlier. The issues of interest in this section deal with (1) how the resource *templates* are handled; (2) how to import resource pool and calendar data into the subprojects and the master project; (3) how (and if) data is distributed downward and/or rolled upward in the nest of subprojects; (4) how the subproject is represented on the Gantt chart and the PERT chart; (5) how to determine which project within a group of several subprojects is causing the overcommitment; (6) whether it is possible to switch back and forth between the master project and the subproject; (7) whether it is possible to level across the subprojects from the master project level; (8) how duplicate resources are handled; and (9) scenarios under which merging the subprojects may require double data entry.

8.36 GUIDELINES AND DOCUMENTATION ◆

Is there any documentation in the user's manual to describe the process of creating resource calendars, allocating resources, leveling algorithms, and resolving resource conflicts? (Instructions on how to use the system to achieve the implementation of a feature are not considered guidelines.)

Chapter **9** CALCULATING PROJECT COSTS

9.1 INTRODUCTION

Many years ago, I was in charge of my company's major DP project of the year. My performance review of that year was to be based on my ability to complete the project within plus or minus 15 percent of the forecasted costs. I was thus highly motivated to get accurate numbers for costing. Many was the night I burned the midnight oil trying to balance my budget. The most difficult part of the whole process was learning what costs should be counted and how to quantify the benefits. This chapter and the other chapters in this book that deal with costs should help users to have an easier time than I did, but they are not intended to be a gospel on cost accounting. The final word on this subject must come from the organization's financial and legal departments.

9.1.1 Describing Resource Costs

Generally, the use of a resource is associated with expenditure commitments and thus has a direct bearing on the costs of the project.

Resource costs are affected by the amount of time the resource actually spends working on the project. On the other hand, a resource may even have different rates—depending on the type of work being performed. Other times, when the length of the project is protracted, the rates per resource will vary over time. Thus, resource costs also vary with their rates.

To lower resource costs, the team may try using less costly resources to perform the job. For example, they may use an *internal* forms designer rather than a more expensive *outside* graphics design company. The decision may be based on whether the job can still be done in the same (or less) time. If it will be less expensive but take longer, the group will also need to complete a time/cost tradeoff analysis.

9.2 IDENTIFYING COSTS

After developing the schedule and assigning the resources, costs for the project must be calculated. This chapter is concerned with identifying what expenditures are candidates for being included in the project costs and how to use this data.

There are many ways to illustrate the breakdown of costs. To attempt to list them all would fill a single book alone. One popular approach is to break the costs into two major categories: (1) development costs; and (2) recurring or ongoing operational costs.

9.2.1 Development Costs

Figure 9.1 lists a series of items that can be considered as costs of constructing DP projects. Furthermore, costs for each functional group could also include:

1. Personnel

   Inhouse (including overtime and benefits)

   Consulting

2. Materials and supplies (typewriters, word processing equipment, telephones, copiers, paper, ribbons, etc.)

3. Space and Power (rental, electricity, janitorial, insurance, security, etc.)

4. Recruitment and relocation

5. Publication and Support

6. Other miscellaneous costs (postage, periodicals, books, etc.)

The costs of all of the details that are illustrated in Figure 9.1 can then be itemized for each phase and listed on a spreadsheet by weeks, months, or years—as illustrated in Figure 9.2.

In other cases, project teams may further divide their phases into major milestones using the details in Figure 9.1 to develop costs for each of the milestones. These figures can also be listed on a spreadsheet, as illustrated in Figure 9.3.

A third method may be to simply itemize major

categories for each alternative. (See Figure 9.4.) For example, the team may group all costs for personnel, all costs for materials, all costs for publication, all costs for equipment, etc., ignoring the management, software development, conversion categories, etc. in Figure 9.1.

Last, some project teams sort and report on all of the above. Others also present several scenarios for each alternative (e.g., best case, worst case, and most likely).

The amount of effort the project team expends is dictated by the corporate reporting requirements of your organization, the availability of the information, and the time they are willing to invest to get the data.

9.2.2 Ongoing Operational Costs

Before the project team begins the assessment of ongoing operational costs, they are faced with the dilemma of determining whether these costs will be calculated assuming:

- A static activity base (i.e., the same information volume processed in future years as in the current or some chosen past year); or

Figure 9.1 Development cost details.

```
SOFTWARE DEVELOPMENT
CONVERSION
TRAINING
TESTING
DOCUMENTATION
USER PARTICIPATION
PROJECT MANAGEMENT
EQUIPMENT
    Existing (portion allocated to new development)
    Purchased (payments, maintenance charges, and insurance)
    Leased/rented
    New (acquired payments, maintenance charges, and insurance)
    Purchased (payments, maintenance charges, and insurance)
    Leased/rented
    Allocated costs of computer time
    Power
HARDWARE AND COMMUNICATIONS (SELECTION AND SUPPORT)
SYSTEM INSTALLATION (FIVE-WEEK INSTALLATION PERIOD)
```

- Certain values that represent some anticipated growth (or reduction) in business volume.

The second approach is usually the more popular choice, especially in organizations that anticipate an increase in business volume. It is also the most difficult to assess because it demands that the cost accountants respond as though they had a crystal ball at their disposal. Sometimes, the team may be able to start the process with projections from the company's long-range business plan. However, like as not, there are often no long-range plans and the information must be gathered in a series of interviews. A framework for a simplified version of a six-year long-range business projection is illustrated in Figure 9.5.

Using the predictions from either the business plans or interviews, costs for each of the items in Figure 9.6 should be calculated. Worksheets such as the one illustrated in Figure 9.7 may be used to calculate the costs for each year for each group in Figure 9.6. The yearly totals should then be transferred to a spreadsheet similar to the one illustrated in Figure 9.8.

Ongoing operating expenses are calculated for the current system and for each of the alternatives chosen for presentation. The project team may also choose to present several scenarios (best case, worst

Figure 9.2 Alternative 1: Monthly costs by phase.

	MONTH 1	MONTH 2	MONTH 3	● ● ● ● ● MONTH N
KICKOFF PHASE				
all of the details from Figure 9.1				
SIZING PHASE				
all of the details from Figure 9.1				
DATA GATHERING PHASE				
all of the details from Figure 9.1				

Figure 9.3 Alternative 2: Weekly development costs by milestone within phase.

```
                          WEEK 1   WEEK 2   WEEK 3  ● ● ● ● ● WEEK N

KICKOFF PHASE
    MILESTONE 1
              . . . . . .
              . . . . . .
              . . . . . .
        all of the details from Figure 9.1
              . . . . . .
              . . . . . .
              . . . . . .

    MILESTONE 2
              . . . . . .
              . . . . . .
              . . . . . .
        all of the details from Figure 9.1
              . . . . . .
              . . . . . .
              . . . . . .

    MILESTONE 3
              . . . . . .
              . . . . . .
              . . . . . .
        all of the details from Figure 9.1
              . . . . . .
              . . . . . .
              . . . . . .



SIZING PHASE
    MILESTONE 4
              . . . . . .
              . . . . . .
              . . . . . .
        all of the details from Figure 9.1
              . . . . . .
              . . . . . .
              . . . . . .
```

Figure 9.4 Alternative 3: Quarterly development costs by major category.

	QUARTER 1	QUARTER 2	QUARTER 3	• • • • • QUARTER N
PERSONNEL				
EQUIPMENT				
MATERIALS				
SPACE AND POWER				

Figure 9.5 Six-year long-range business projection of yearly anticipated growth.

YEAR	BEGINNING NUMBER OF ACCOUNTS	NEW ACCOUNTS	PAY- MENTS	DRAFTS	ACCOUNT MAINTENANCE	INQUIRIES	TRANSACTION TOTALS	ENDING NUMBER OF ACCOUNTS
				TRANSACTIONS BY TYPE				
YEAR 1								
YEAR 2								
YEAR 3								
YEAR 4								
YEAR 5								
YEAR 6								
TOTALS								

Figure 9.6 Items for calculating ongoing operational costs.

USERS
MAINTENANCE SUPPORT
  Programming
  Technical Systems
  Documentation
  Training
EQUIPMENT
COMPUTER ROOM
  Allocation of computer usage
PRODUCTION CONTROL
DATA ENTRY
MANAGEMENT

Figure 9.7 Worksheet for calculating ongoing operational costs.

DEPARTMENT	MONTH 1	MONTH 2	MONTH 3	MONTH 4	MONTH 5	MONTH 6	MONTH 7	• • • • •	MONTH 12	YEAR* N
USERS										
MAINTENANCE SUPPORT										
EQUIPMENT										
COMPUTER ROOM										
PRODUCTION CONTROL										
DATA ENTRY										
MANAGEMENT										
TOTAL OPERATING EXPENSES										

* The figures in this column are to be transferred to the corresponding year in the spreadsheet illustrated in Figure 9.8.

Figure 9.8 Forecasted ongoing operational costs.

DEPARTMENT	YEAR 1	YEAR 2	YEAR 3	YEAR 4	YEAR 5	YEAR 6
USERS						
MAINTENANCE SUPPORT						
EQUIPMENT						
COMPUTER ROOM						
PRODUCTION CONTROL						
DATA ENTRY						
MANAGEMENT						
TOTAL OPERATING EXPENSES						

case, and most likely) for each of the alternatives *and* for the current system.

9.2.3 Other Cost Considerations

In pure accounting, there are additional factors to costing other than the ones presented in the previous sections. If these areas pertain to the organization's policies, it is advisable that the team research the cost accounting literature *and* solicit guidance from their finance department.

Costs and benefits can be seen as having tangible and intangible characteristics. The term *tangible* denotes substance and describes items that can easily be identified and measured. Equipment and supplies are tangible articles. *Intangible* suggests no physical substance and therefore these items are harder to identify (for example, the benefits of obtaining trademarks or copyrights). The organization needs to decide how and if they will distinguish between the two.

Looking at direct and indirect figures provides a second perspective. *Direct* costs can be readily connected to departments, products, or projects. They are costs that are incurred solely to further the cause of the project. *Indirect* costs are external to the project, are incurred for the benefit of the business as a whole, and are allocated in part to various departments, products, or projects. An example of an indirect cost is the expense for the switchboard operators' handling of messages for the project members. In a second example, consider the problem of how to allocate the costs of a piece of equipment acquired for the current project for use with future projects as well. The team must determine whether or not they will distinguish between direct and indirect costs.

Dollar expenditures that are *controllable* and *noncontrollable* provide a third consideration. A company can control the number of personnel it employs and the amount of equipment it buys. It has no control over the salary marketplace or inflation that raises equipment prices. The project team must decide how to determine the figures that will be used for noncontrollable items.

Some figures are fixed; others are variable. *Fixed* costs are those that do not change from time period to time period. A company knows exactly how much it will pay for rent each month of the current rental agreement. However, *variable* costs change directly and proportionally with changes in volume. Costs for paper, copy services, power, and communications vary with each period. As in each of the previous types of costs, the team must decide what figures they will use for variable items.

To better understand the next example, users may consider the following scenario:

> The team has completed the cost/benefit analysis and their recommended alternative has been approved. Two months into the project, an unanticipated expenditure surfaces. Obviously, it wasn't included in the budget. What can they do?

It is advisable to include a certain amount in the budget to cover such unanticipated costs. This may be referred to as a *bucket for uncertainties*, and the project manager may negotiate for a dollar range that can be spent from this *bucket* at his or her discretion.

In a final case, perhaps the team will also be required to factor in the effects of certain *tax regulations*. Depreciation of equipment, capitalization of software, and accrual or cash basis of accounting will all increase the complexity of the costing process. For example, a common cause of concern stems from the confusion over choosing where to count costs incurred after implementation. Some of these costs may really have been part of development costs. This and other similar questions should be answered by the organization's tax department.

9.3 CLASSIFYING COSTS

Cost accounting categories are used for rolling up summary data of costs according to a preselected group. These rollups may be achieved by using work breakdown structures. The work breakdown number may be a unique identifier, or accounting codes may be used to designate the rollup requirements. Hammocks and summary records may also be used for rollup reporting.

9.3.1 Rollup Totals

Rollup totals can be accumulated from several perspectives: for example, by resource totals, by job totals, or by project totals. Resource totals may equal the sum of all of the hours spent by a given resource on all of his or her assigned tasks. Activity or task totals equal the sum of all of the hours spent by all of the resources assigned to the given job. Also added into this value are any fixed or overhead costs. Project totals are equal to the sum of all of the resources on all of the jobs for each day during the project. Again, also added into this value are any fixed or overhead costs.

It is usually necessary to view the costs from several perspectives. Some common reporting structures are: resource totals by period; activity or task totals by period; milestones by period; or projects by period. Periods may be chosen based on time or project deliverables. Another view of costs may be from the project perspective: resource costs per project; activity or tasks costs per project; milestone costs per project; support component costs per project; or phase costs per project. Some of these groupings are illustrated in the work breakdown structures pictured in Chapter 4.

Figure 9.9 Fixed costs and overhead costs.

ONE TIME COSTS		USAGE (OR ONGOING) COSTS	
SINGLE VALUE	QUANTITY X UNIT PRICE	SINGLE VALUE	QUANTITY X UNIT PRICE
OVERHEAD	OVERHEAD	OVERHEAD	OVERHEAD
FIXED	FIXED	FIXED	FIXED
PENALTY	PENALTY	PENALTY	PENALTY
BONUS	BONUS	BONUS	BONUS

9.3.2 Accounting Codes

Accounting codes are often used to classify the rollup views. For example, they may designate the name of an outside consulting company. Or, they may categorize resources according to the type of skills required for the job or by the type of work. Cost accounting categories may be used to group resources together and indicate the particular department that is supplying the resource. Furthermore, one resource may be assigned to different accounting codes—depending on how the organization wishes to report the costs associated with that resource.[1] Separate accounting codes may be used, or the code for the work breakdown structure may be used.

9.3.3 Fixed Costs and Overhead Costs

If a cost that is to be charged to the project will always be the same specified amount, regardless of the duration of the work with which it's associated, the cost is referred to as a *fixed* cost. As an example, when it's only necessary to track the costs of equipment, the values may be entered as fixed costs *or* as costs associated with allocated overhead. (Figure 9.9) Furthermore, these costs may be onetime costs, or they may be ongoing and charged to the project according to usage. Fixed and overhead costs may be entered as a single dollar value or by a cost per unit price.

Ideally, fixed and/or overhead costs may be entered at the activity or task level where they apply *or* at the project level—depending upon the requirements.

Sometimes, teams are unsure about how to treat computer time—whether it is an allocated overhead cost or if it needs to be a separate job. When it is necessary to *schedule* the use of the equipment, it may be easier to manage if it is entered as a separate job in the plan, with dependencies, costs, an assigned supervisor, etc.

The final example in this section addresses the scenario in which outside vendors or subcontractors may be paid a bonus for completing their deliverables early or at least on time. (Figure 9.9) Conversely, they may be levied with a penalty fine if they are late. A penalty fine may be added to represent an amount per time unit, starting on a particular day, of cost per delay (for example, retributive fines, lost revenues, increased operating costs.) These values may also be entered as fixed costs.

9.3.4 Formulas for Costs

The team will also be required to determine what formulas are to be used and how to identify the variables in each of these formulas. For example, there are many ways to simply compute the costs per day:

1. The hourly rate times the hours per day
2. The weekly rate divided by the number of defined days per week

---

[1] For example, the programmer who is classified as a coder in one situation and as a tester in another situation.

3. A predefined daily cost

4. The monthly rate divided by 22 days

Occasionally, there will be a requirement to be able to enter costs, have them included as part of the project totals, but prevent them from being charged to any particular group. This requirement may be met by establishing a separate accounting code for these costs. For example, these costs may simply be entered in an accounting category called *nonbillable*.

9.3.5 Setting Up the Correct Distribution of Costs

Traditionally, the costs that are associated with resources will ultimately get charged to the project as the corresponding work progresses and will be distributed evenly across the duration of the *true work effort*. However, under certain situations, users may wish to set the costs up so that all (or a portion) of the costs are paid at either the start or finish of the respective job. This may be called front-loading or back-loading the costs. For example, subcontractors may only get paid at the completion of their work. On the other hand, some purchases require that a down payment be made when the order is signed. When these situations occur, special actions may be necessary.

Initially, it may appear that front-loading or back-loading the entire resource assignment will accomplish the costing goals. And this is true. However, this action will also cause the wrong dates to be used for assignment of the work. Consequently, the project (or phase) will be harder to manage and the subsequent status reporting will be incorrect.

Ideally, the system will provide a cost distribution mechanism (such as the one provided by Viewpoint) which is independent of the resource assignment. In lieu of this feature, users will need to complete two operations:

- Add an additional dummy resource to the task, at $1 per unit. This dummy resource assignment is front-loaded or back-loaded, as the case may be, for as many units as necessary to equal the charge. A *fixed* cost type may be used to front-load the charge. A *unit* or *per use* cost type may be used to back-load the charge. When available, resource loading patterns may also be used to distribute these costs.

- Make the actual resource a no-cost resource. In this way, the assignment hours will be correct, but no charges will be incurred by the assignment.

9.4 COSTS AND PROJECT MANAGEMENT SOFTWARE ◆

Each product was initially evaluated to determine its accuracy in computing total costs. In every product, total costs per resource, total costs per job, total costs per milestone, and total costs per project all checked out correctly.

When certain types of costs must be entered as separate project-level resources (for example, *fixed* project overhead), the number of costs per project will be restricted by the number of resources per project. When they are entered as task- or activity-level resources, they are limited to the number of resources per job. On the other hand, some of the products have a nice feature—separate fields for entering these types of costs. In that case, the number of costs is limited to the corresponding number of fields.

Besides the number of cost fields, the other features that were evaluated were: (1) how the system supports the use of accounting codes for rollups; (2) whether the costs may be viewed on the screen; (3) if the system provides graphic displays of project-related costs; and (4) whether the system supports fixed costs, overhead costs, bonuses, and penalties. If descriptions of the formulas for determining the costs have been provided in the product documentation, a summary will be provided in this section. Finally, exporting cost data to spreadsheet packages often allows users to manipulate cost data more effectively. These capabilities will also be explored.

9.5 COSTS IN A MULTIPROJECT ENVIRONMENT ◆

The details of working in a multiproject environment have already been addressed. Since, in most cases, the costs are rolled up into the master project without additional actions on the part of the user, these products will not be readdressed in this section. On the other hand, Time Line 3.0 and Microsoft Project have subtle nuances that pertain to costing in a multiproject environment.

CHAPTER 10 COMPRESSING PROJECT DURATIONS AND ANALYZING THE EFFECTS

10.11 INTRODUCTION

So far, the group has produced a *real-world* plan, one that reflects how long the project will take and how much it will cost—given the available resources. The team may have also created more than one version of this plan: one with dates that reflect the 50 percent probability (that is, the plan with zero slack on the critical path) and one or more plans with late project finish dates of varying probabilities. For the purpose of discussion in this chapter, this set of plans will be referred to as the *normal* set of plans. The respective durations are called *normal* durations. Furthermore, it is possible to make a correlation between these durations and costs. Thus, one could say that the project costs $X per month and that any given job costs $Y per day. These costs may be referred to as *normal* costs. (Figure 10.1) Now is the time to try to retrofit the plan into a predetermined finish date (if there is one);[1] and to evaluate the effects of such a strategy on the normal durations and costs. Finally, the strategies described in this chapter may also be employed in optimizing the normal set of plans.

---

[1]When the project is constrained by time, leveling Alternative 1 may be used along with the techniques in this chapter.

10.2 TIME-COST RELATIONSHIPS

Starting from the normal time and costs, there may be a direct relationship between shortening or lengthening the project and correspondingly increasing the costs. (Figure 10.2) There is usually a period of time during which the normal costs are likely to remain constant, regardless of how the probabilities vary. Within that range of time and probabilities, costs do not significantly change. This can be seen in the flat part of the curve—which represents the costs associated with the 50 percent to 95 percent probability range. With the higher probability, the costs rise slightly because of the extended involvement of the project team. (When the confidence intervals are small, the difference in time between 50 percent and 95 percent is not that great.) Then, if there are delays (frequently unexpected), the final costs of the project start to creep up insidiously. This is commonly due to overtime and rework by the existing team members as well as to the costs associated with adding resources. Sometimes, if the delays are long enough, the costs rise to such a high point that *the project is no longer justified and should be cancelled*!

Working overtime and adding resources may be used as a strategy for finishing sooner—especially when there is an imposed target date. More experienced resources may be reassigned to the jobs in order to expedite completion. When experts can finish the work

Figure 10.1 Normal plan and costs.

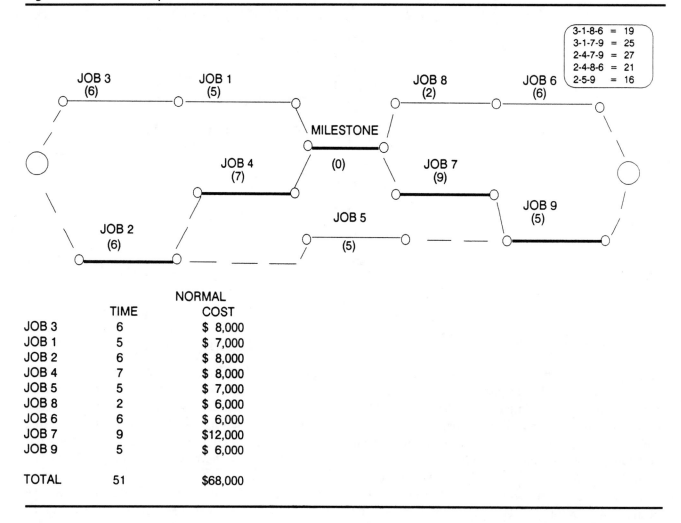

	TIME	NORMAL COST
JOB 3	6	$ 8,000
JOB 1	5	$ 7,000
JOB 2	6	$ 8,000
JOB 4	7	$ 8,000
JOB 5	5	$ 7,000
JOB 8	2	$ 6,000
JOB 6	6	$ 6,000
JOB 7	9	$12,000
JOB 9	5	$ 6,000
TOTAL	51	$68,000

even sooner than experienced workers, they may also be recruited. As these strategies are employed, the duration of the project may be decreased; but the costs will, in turn, be increased. Of course, there comes a point where, no matter how many people are added, the project just can't be shortened anymore.

The shortened durations are referred to as *crash* times. All estimates for crashing ought to be made with the agreement that a job's completion may *only* be expedited if quality is *not* sacrificed. The associated costs are called *crash* costs. Also included in the crash costs are the costs attributable to replacing any personnel who are transferred to the project with substitutes for their original commitments.

In Figure 10.1, the critical path (highlighted) is

through Jobs 2, 4, 7 and 9. Path durations are noted in the inset. The normal project duration is 27 days long. The normal cost of this group of jobs is $68,000. The total manpower effort is 51 days.

10.3 CRASHING THE PROJECT

In Figure 10.3, all of the jobs have been crashed, as noted by the second number inside of the parentheses. Using the crash durations, the critical path is still through Jobs 2, 4, 7 and 9. The crash project duration is 15 days long. The total crash cost of this group of jobs is $123,000. The total manpower effort is 25 days. For an extra $55,000, 12 days have been eliminated from the project duration. In a hypothetical project

Figure 10.2 Time-cost relationship.

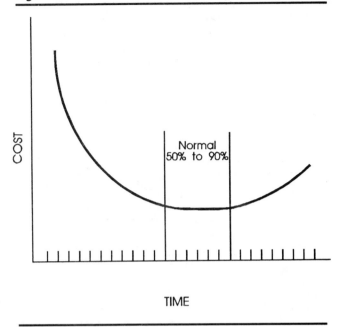

where $5,000 is saved for every day the duration of the project is shortened, $4,583 per day to crash may be viewed as a real bargain.

A closer look at Job 5 in relationship to Job 4 and Job 7, however, reveals that there is no value to crashing Job 5. (Since the total crash duration of Job 4 and Job 7 is 10 days, using a normal time of 5 days for Job 5 is satisfactory.) Recognizing these situations allows managers to understand that, to begin with, jobs should only be crashed when there is a net reduction in time. Since this is not the case for Job 5, it is a candidate for completion in normal time.

This leads to the next problem—one in which users may question how to proceed with this process. Is there a simple way to uncover the shortest schedule that also minimizes total project expenditures—i.e., those costs of development plus the costs due to an extended completion date? These crash costs are weighed against the value of getting the system completed earlier—for example, the operational savings that accompany a faster implementation or a bonus paid for expediting delivery. The secret lies in balancing the value of the time saved against the cost of saving it. To start, users may opt to crash the critical path, the place they are likely to get the best return on the additional investment. In the example in Figure 10.3, Jobs 2, 4, 7, and 9 are the initial jobs to be considered

for crashing. Since 2, 7, and 9 have the best effect for the least cost, they will be crashed first. At $6,000 per day to crash, Job 4 will be bypassed for the time being. (See Figure 10.4.) Similarly, there is no value to crashing Job 5; so, it will be scheduled for normal time and costs. By stopping at this point and also using the normal time and costs for Jobs 3, 1, 8, and 6, the critical path will be 19 days long and the total costs will be $85,000. This amounts to saving 8 days at a crash cost of $2,125 per day.

There are many variations on this theme. Furthermore, as the process progresses, it is not unusual to find new critical paths emerging. Similarly, just when users think they have finished with the exercise, they may then notice that several near-critical paths have emerged. Of course, when the near-critical paths are very near to the critical path, the probability of success may be reduced. This scenario has occurred in the example in Figure 10.4. Two of the paths were 18 days and one was 17 days. After careful consideration, a second scenario was developed. (Figure 10.5)

Job 1 and Job 3 are crashed in order to reduce the near-critical paths. Now, the project may be completed in 18 days for $95,000 or the project duration may be reduced by 9 days at $3,000 per day to crash. Although this is a more costly option than the prior one, this is also a lower-risk scenario, since there are fewer near-critical paths that are so close to the critical path. Management may prefer to choose the lower-risk option, even though it is more costly.

This process may continue to be repeated, developing new scenarios as long as the project duration can be crashed while also yielding a net reduction in development costs, factoring in the operational savings. The options may be compared and ranked using the format in Table 10.1.

As illustrated, the results of this exercise are often very surprising. Consequently, this information may be very useful in presentations to management.

10.4 PROLONGING THE PROJECT

It is not uncommon for organizations to be faced with the dilemma of having more candidate projects than the personnel required to complete them. Therefore, they may also be interested in what happens when they reduce the assigned workers and therefore prolong the project duration.

Figure 10.3 Total crash plan and costs.

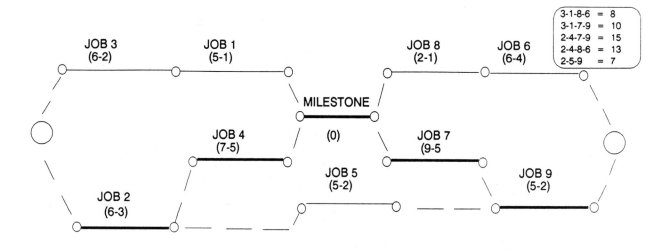

	NORMAL		CRASH		CRASH	
	TIME	COST	SAVED TIME	COST PER DAY	TIME	COSTS
JOB 3	6	$ 8,000	4	$1,500	2	$14,000
JOB 1	5	$ 7,000	4	$1,000	1	$11,000
JOB 2	6	$ 8,000	3	$ 667	3	$10,000
JOB 4	7	$ 8,000	2	$6,000	5	$20,000
JOB 5	5	$ 7,000	3	$2,000	2	$13,000
JOB 8	2	$ 6,000	1	$4,000	1	$10,000
JOB 6	6	$ 6,000	2	$3,000	4	$12,000
JOB 7	9	**$12,000**	4	$2,500	5	$22,000
JOB 9	5	$ 6,000	3	**$1,667**	2	$11,000
TOTAL	51	$68,000			25	$123,000

Table 10.1 Crash Options.

PROJECT DURATION	NORMAL DEVELOPMENT COSTS	PLUS	TOTAL CRASH COSTS	MINUS	OPERATIONAL SAVINGS	EQUALS	TOTAL PROJECT COSTS
27 DAYS	$68,000						$68,000
15 DAYS			$123,000		$60,000		$63,000
19 DAYS	$42,000		$ 43,000		$40,000		$45,000[*]
18 DAYS	$27,000		$ 68,000		$45,000		$50,000[*]

[*]Between these two options, the 18-day option is shorter and more costly, but it is also a lower risk.
The 19-day option is less costly but it is a higher risk.

Figure 10.4 Partial crash plan and costs.

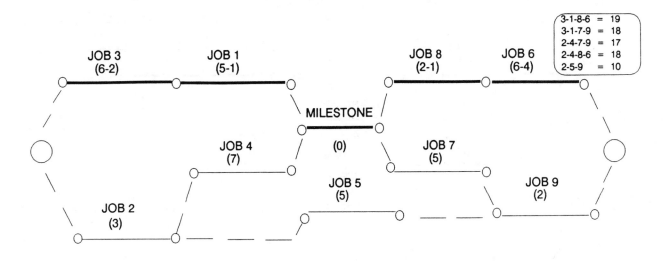

	NORMAL		CRASH		CRASH	
	TIME	COST	SAVED TIME	COST PER DAY	TIME	COSTS
JOB 3	6	$8,000	4	$1,500		
JOB 1	5	$7,000	4	$1,000		
JOB 2			3	$ 667	3	$10,000
JOB 4	7	$8,000	2	$6,000		
JOB 5	5	$7,000	3	$2,000		
JOB 8	2	$6,000	1	$4,000		
JOB 6	6	$6,000	2	$3,000		
JOB 7			4	$2,500	5	$22,000
JOB 9			3	$1,667	2	$11,000
TOTAL	31	$42,000			10	$43,000

Thus far, the concept of speeding up the project has been explored. These concepts may also be applied in the opposite direction. That is, when elongating the project does not result in a serious decrease in quality and productivity, this process may be used to evaluate several options of stretching project duration.

10.5 PRACTICAL CONSIDERATIONS OF CRASHING

The procedures that have thus far been outlined in this chapter are based on a trial and error application of the crash concepts.

Without a mathematical basis, such trial and error applications may not necessarily uncover the optimal compression schedule (that is, the lowest possible duration) along with the corresponding project expenditure (that is, the lowest possible costs).

Furthermore, the sample project that was presented had only five possible paths open for consideration. In reality, even only an average-sized project will have many more candidate paths than five. As the procedure progresses and more and more jobs are crashed, the number of critical paths and near-critical paths increases. Similarly, the number of potential alternatives also increases. Thus, the identification of all possible paths is, at best, a tedious and labor-intensive

Figure 10.5 Partial crash plan and costs.

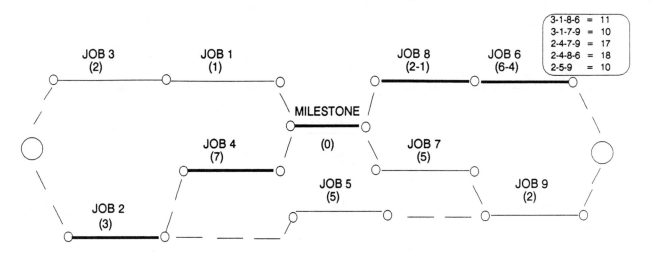

	NORMAL		CRASH		CRASH	
	TIME	COST	SAVED TIME	COST PER DAY	TIME	COSTS
JOB 3			4	$1,500	2	$14,000
JOB 1			4	$1,000	1	$11,000
JOB 2			3	$ 667	3	$10,000
JOB 4	7	$8,000	2	$6,000		
JOB 5	5	$7,000	3	$2,000		
JOB 8	2	$6,000	1	$4,000		
JOB 6	6	$6,000	2	$3,000		
JOB 7			4	$2,500	5	$22,000
JOB 9			3	$1,667	2	$11,000
TOTAL	20	$27,000			13	$68,000

activity. At worst, it is also highly error-prone in that a crucial path may be overlooked.

Because of these problems, project management practitioners have searched for some practical approach to identifying the correct subset of alternatives. Over the years, some excellent operations research has been performed in this area, research that has resulted in the development of several linear programming algorithms.

Although hand computation of these formulas is impractical, they may be computed programmatically. On the other hand, on all but the most trivial projects, these algorithms produce a large number of constraints and variables. Consequently, they require computer resources that are greater than that available on a microcomputer platform. For those readers who are interested in exploring this topic further, there are excellent presentations in Moder, Phillips, and Davis *and* in Wiest and Levy. (See the bibliography.)

In the absence of a programmatic solution, users may use manual computations to help achieve their goals. While the application of these types of formulas (that are based on empirical observations) does not always produce the universe of optimal solutions, they do come close enough to perform satisfactorily in the software development environment.

10.5.1 Using COCOMO to Find the Shortest Schedule[2]

Along with the COCOMO model, Boehm provides additional formulas that allow users to compute an accelerated schedule. Even if all of the COCOMO models have not been applied, at a minimum these formulas can be used for a reasonability check against the trial and error crash results. It follows that the corresponding costs may also be determined. Starting with Phase 4 (in this text) through the end of the project, the COCOMO value that has computed for total man-months is increased by a schedule acceleration rate that ranges from 4 percent to 25 percent. Then, three more formulas are used that raise the accelerated man-months to a unique exponent, one for each of the modes, and then multiply the result times 2.5.

According to Boehm, accelerating a schedule that is below 75 percent of normal is considered impossible by COCOMO. He presents a very convincing case for this position and has some excellent data to back it up.

On the other hand, in projects that are 15 total man-months or less, that do not have high requirements for reliability, that have highly qualified personnel, and that are using high quality development techniques, the organization may be able to justify taking the risk. But, how many projects meet these conditions?

10.5.2 Using the Jensen Model to Find the Shortest Schedule and the Optimum Staffing Level

The development time and costs are coupled together in the Jensen software equation. It is not possible to obtain one without the other. This is not unusual—since it has already been established that time and costs are usually directly related.

Using Norden's manpower loading concepts, Jensen's model is a composite of two overlapping Rayleigh curves which build from zero personnel at a point in what is equivalent to phase 4 of this text to the peak staffing size at the time when the group is ready to start coding. Variations on the Putnam equations are used for confirming the initial staffing rate and the minimum development schedule. The Jensen chart (a parametric graph) is used to determine the optimum staffing rate and the optimum schedule. Because this work is based on Norden's Rayleigh distribution curve as well as historical data, the results will closely assume the traditional manpower loading scheme. Nevertheless, Jensen's rate of personnel staffing does increase more rapidly during Phases 4—6 than other similar approaches. The initial staffing rate is equal to:

$$\frac{\text{the life cycle effort (in total person-years)}}{\text{development time }^2 \text{(in elapsed years)}}$$

where, the life cycle effort (in elapsed years) is equal to the source code complexity factor (See Chapter 5.) times the development time[3] (in elapsed years).

By simplifying the above equation, the initial staffing rate is equal to the source code complexity factor times the development time.

The initial staffing rate is independent of system size. Its value becomes important later in determining the optimum staffing rate.

The source code complexity is also used in determining the optimum staffing rate. It may also be used as a limiting parameter in determining the minimum development time that an organization can achieve for a given project. Putnam observed that the source code complexity can be used to classify projects into distinct categories. Similar projects tend to maintain a natural equilibrium so that as the system size increases, the minimum development schedule increases accordingly. The initial staffing rate is also maintained.

In the Jensen approach, the software equation, the source code complexity, and the initial staffing rate are all functions of the life cycle effort (in total person-years) and the development time (in elapsed years). Therefore, each of the equations may be plotted using parametric representations of their curves, with all of the curves being drawn on one graph. This parametric graph is the Jensen chart.

Next, Jensen provides a formula for reflecting

---

[2]Boehm, Op. cit

the project's technical constraints. This rate is computed by dividing the effective technology constant into the effective size of the software. Finally, an adjusted development cost is computed as 40% of the life cycle cost. (This reflects Putnam's view that only 40% of the total system's life cycle effort is actually associated with software development while the remaining effort is expended during system operation.)

The source code complexity, the initial staffing rate, and the rate of the project's technical constraints are each calculated—in terms of varying the development time and the adjusted development time. All of the other parameters are fixed. These three curves are superimposed onto the Jensen chart. They may form the boundaries, on the graph, of a region which represents feasible development options. Alternatively, the perimeter of the feasible development re-

software projects, Putnam demonstrated that there is a definite inverse relationship between productivity and the rate at which people are added to the project. Obviously, too few people can delay the completion of the project. Similarly, too many people often only serve to create chaos and wreak havoc.

10.5.3 Moder, Phillips, and Davis' Modified Siemens Algorithm[3]

Moder, Phillips, and Davis have modified a time/cost trade-off approach first developed by Siemens. To start with, they find all of the paths through the network that have a duration that is greater than the desired crash duration.[4] Then, they make a column listing all of the jobs that occur in each of these paths. (See Figure 10.6.) For each job in the list, they apply three formulas:

---

(1) The candidate time that may be saved = Time Available = Normal time − Crash time

(2) The costs savings/duration unit (Crash Costs − Normal Costs) ÷ Time Available

(3) The *effective* savings = (savings/duration unit) ÷ Number of Paths, With Duration Greater Than Crash Time, In Which The Activity Occurs

---

gion may be completed by substituting a vertical line which represents desired development time for one of the other three boundaries.

For example, the project's technical constraints and the source code complexity may be superimposed on the Jensen chart along with a desired development time—leaving the staffing rate unspecified. In this case, the *minimum effort* solution will be the point of intersection, in the feasible region, of the project's technical constraints and the desired development time constraint. For the trade-off analysis, this point will show how to reach the desired delivery date with the lowest number of resources and the least cost. Conversely, the *earliest delivery* solution is the point of intersection, in the feasible region, of the project's technical constraints and the source code complexity constraint.

Using the same parameters, the *optimum staffing rate* is then interpolated between low end and high end values for the initial staffing rate. Also referred to as the *minimum development time*, this solution provides the shortest schedule boundary for the trade-off analysis.

The importance of the correct staffing rate can not be overstressed. In analyzing the data from several

This procedure requires that users choose to crash the jobs with the most effective savings from the path with the largest path time available. (See Figure 10.6.) In the example, when a number appears in one column in brackets, it represents the results of crashing a job that was selected from another path. Figure 10.7 shows the results of reducing the project to eighteen weeks.

Sometimes, there will be more than one path with the same path time available. This calls for some tie-breaker rules:

(1) The user may look for an activity that falls on two or more of the paths in the tie—and crash it; or

(2) The user may choose an activity which gives the most reduction in time for the least cost. Other times, when the crashing operations have caused severe acceleration on a given path, it may be possible to reverse a transaction and return a job to its normal time and costs. This may be

---

[3]Moder, Phillips, and Davis, Op. cit.

[4]Sorting the project activities and tasks on the value of slack will provide a list of the jobs. Users will have to match this list to a network in order to find the paths. (See the discussion at the end of this chapter on sorting on slack.)

Figure 10.6 Moder, Phillips, and Davis' modified Siemens algorithm.

JOBS IN PATHS ≥18 DAYS	EFFECTIVE SAVINGS	CANDIDATE PATHS				CRASH COSTS	NORMAL COSTS
		3-1-8-6	3-1-7-9	2-4-7-9	2-4-8-6		
JOB 1	$ 500	X	X			$11,000	
JOB 2	$ 333			X	X	$10,000	
JOB 3	$ 750	X	X				$8,000
JOB 4	$3,000			X	X		$8,000
JOB 6	$1,500	X			X		$6,000
JOB 7	$1,250	.	X	X		$22,000	
JOB 8	$2,000	X			X		$6,000
JOB 9	$ 833		X	X		$11,000	
INITIAL PATH LENGTH		19	25	27	21		
DESIRED PATH LENGTH		18	18	18	18		
PATH TIME AVAILABLE		1	7	9	3		
PATH LENGTH₁				24	[18]	$10,000	
PATH TIME AVAILABLE₁				6	[0]		
PATH LENGTH₂		[15]	21			$11,000	
PATH TIME AVAILABLE₂		[–3]	3				
PATH LENGTH₃			[18]	21		$11,000	
PATH TIME AVAILABLE₃			[0]	3			
PATH LENGTH₄			[14]	17		$22,000	
PATH TIME AVAILABLE₄			[–4]	–1			

JOB 5 (NOT A CANDIDATE) | $ 7,000 (NORMAL COSTS)

TOTAL CRASH COSTS AND NORMAL COSTS — $54,000 $35,000

TOTAL PROJECT COSTS — $89,000

PROJECT COMPLETION: 18 WEEKS FOR $89,000 — $45,000 SAVINGS = $44,000 TOTAL COSTS

Figure 10.7 Moder, Phillips, and Davis' modified Siemens algorithm.

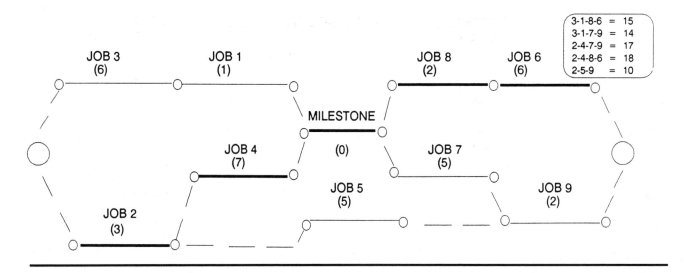

acceptable—as long as the second transaction does not create any new paths that violate the desired project duration. Users should also be wary of creating too many near critical paths.

While the results of this operation would, at first blush, appear to be less satisfactory from a management perspective than the manually devised examples presented in this chapter (because the near critical paths are nearer to the critical path), users should remember that, in both cases, the example which was used is an oversimplification of the real world. In an average-sized project, this approach is usually much more beneficial than *eye-balling* it.

10.6 OTHER APPLICATIONS

Earlier, the potential of using less costly resources to perform a job in order to lower resource costs was introduced. For example, teams may use an internal forms designer rather than a more expensive outside graphics design company. The decision may be based on whether the job can still be done in the same (or less) time. If it will be less expensive, but take longer, the group will also need to complete a time/cost tradeoff analysis. The techniques presented in this chapter will aid in the development of the data that is used for the analysis.

Later, during management of the project, applying more resources (either in the form of adding new people or working overtime) is one form of making up time in a late project. Using the data from a time/cost tradeoff analysis may aid in choosing management and/or recovery strategies.

10.7 CRASH TECHNIQUES AND PROBABILITIES

At the conclusion of these operations, users should remember to recalculate probabilities for new critical and near-critical paths.

10.8 CRASH TECHNIQUES AND PROJECT MANAGEMENT SOFTWARE

None of the products evaluated provide a feature for crashing projects.

10.9 TIME-CONSTRAINED PLANS AND PROJECT MANAGEMENT SOFTWARE ◆

Developing time-constrained plans requires that a fixed end date be assigned to the project; that priorities and fixed dates be set where necessary on certain jobs; and that resources be leveled only within the time constraints of the project.

Setting a fixed completion date for the project has been covered earlier as has assigning priorities and fixed dates to jobs. The guidelines found in those discussions hold true for time-constrained plans as well as for the optimal plans and resource-constrained plans.

However, in addition to the directions found earlier for leveling resources, there are certain nuances that need to be be covered now, because leveling in a time-constrained environment is not the same as leveling in a resource-constrained environment. Sorting on slack will also be covered in this section.

10.10 GUIDELINES

None of the systems provide any directions on crash techniques. Harvard Project Manager has a little information on critical path adjustments and Project Workbench has a little information on scheduling against a fixed end date.

CHAPTER 11 ASSIGNING THE WORK

11.1 ASSIGNING THE WORK ♦

After management has selected the plan they want to implement for the coming phase (or project), the next jobs that are performed complete the assignment process.

11.1.1 Picking the Scheduled Dates

The scheduled start and end dates should most often be taken from the calculated early start date and the early finish date of the job. However, when the early date is much too early and the late date is too late, the user may need to pick an arbitrary date. By sorting on *free slack* in descending order, these kinds of conditions may be easy to spot. When the system does not have a separate field for holding distinct scheduled dates, this date must be entered as a fixed date. Unless otherwise noted, the date fields that are displayed on the reports described in this section are the fields that correctly reflect any assigned dates—fixed or otherwise. Ideally, the system will allow the user to limit the displayed dates to just the scheduled dates, suppressing the late dates. Although this is not essential, not showing the late dates does reduce confusion.

11.1.2 The Assignment Report

For each resource in the plan, an assignment report may be created. This report lists *all* of the jobs that have been identified to date and that have been assigned to the designated resource.

The heading of the report may include the date of the report, the name of the project, and the name and identifier of the resource.

Then, there may be a detail line entry for each job. The line entry may include the following information: the name and identifier of the activity or task, the scheduled start and end dates of the activity or task, the original estimated *true work effort*, a list of the predecessors, and a list of the successors. On an assignment report, it is not necessary to display the costs per resource or the costs per job. As a matter of fact, it is often desirable to limit this data to the manager's reports.

Since the assignment information is a subset of the turn-around data that will ultimately be used for status reporting, the turn-around status collection document may often double as an assignment report. The assignment report will be a component of the work package (described later in this chapter.)

11.2 THE AD HOC INFORMATION ♦

During the development of the work breakdown structures, the team was advised to record ad hoc information (pertaining to each activity or task) about:

• A brief narrative describing the activity or task;

- The tools and skills required to complete the activity or task;
- The identification of the deliverable that is to be produced by the effort;
- The criteria for completion, success, and acceptance;
- A list of reviewers and approvers;
- A list and description of any sub-tasks; and
- A list of potential consultants or advisors to the activity or task.

During the development of the estimates, the team was advised to record ad hoc information (pertaining to each activity or task) about:

- The assumptions that were used in estimating the effort; and
- An update to the data that was created during the preparation of the work breakdown structures.

During the development of the network, the team was advised to record ad hoc information (pertaining to each activity or task) about:

- The inputs and prerequisites to each activity or task;
- Any constraints imposed on the completion of the activity or task; and
- An update to the data that was created during the preparation of the work breakdown structures and estimates.

During the assignment of resources, the team was advised to record ad hoc information (pertaining to each activity or task) about:

- The assumptions used in assigning any resources; and
- An update to the data that was created during the preparation of the work breakdown structures, the estimates, and the networks.

During the leveling of resources, the team was advised to record ad hoc information (pertaining to each activity or task) about:

- The assumptions used in reassigning any resources; and

- An update to the data that was created during the preparation of the work breakdown structures, the estimates, the networks and the original resource assignments.

Now is the time to pull all of this ad hoc information together into a packet of supporting documentation that will be included in the work package that is distributed to each person assigned to perform the work.

The data for these reports may have been entered using features provided by the system, or they may have been produced using a word processor. (A complete description of the ad hoc information storage capabilities of each package comes later.)

11.3 WORK PACKAGES

The concept of grouping data—that is pertinent to the performance of a job—into a stand-alone packet of information was popularized by a *DOD* and *NASA* guide on cost accounting for project management. Their goal was (1) to simplify the management of many small deliverables by grouping them into a major deliverable that costs about $100,000 and lasts about three months; and (2) to be able to equate the work effort to different cost centers. These work packages relate to specific entries in a predetermined work breakdown structure to which the project adheres, where each entry in the work breakdown structure relates to a job that has a clearly identifiable and unique deliverable along with agreed-upon start and finish dates. The group to whom the package is assigned may then subdivide it in a manner that seems manageable to them.

It was not very long before some practitioners of project management began to realize that packages of three months' duration were difficult to manage during the execution of the plan (for example, in interpreting status reports). Several articles in the literature referred to the need for smaller, short-term work packages. A more difficult dilemma came from trying to define what *short-term* actually meant.

In keeping with the concepts of this text, work packages may be completed for each activity or task that is assigned to each individual in the plan. If the organization chooses to follow the guidelines outlined in Chapter 2, then for each activity or task:

1. A reasonable estimate may be figured for its completion

2. The estimate will reflect reality

3. The organization may be comfortable about the level of *accuracy*

4. It will be hard to intimidate the estimator into reducing the estimate

5. 100 percent completion can be reached rather quickly

6. Managers will know they're in trouble before disaster descends upon them

7. When the job is done, there will be a meaningful and verifiable deliverable

8. The job can not be meaningfully subdivided

9. The job is best completed without interruption.

> **To afford effective partitioning, estimating, scheduling, and status reporting, a unit of work (inch-pebble) produces a tangible deliverable that can be verified, is commonly assignable to one and only one person, and is usually from 4 to 40 hours long.**

An inch-pebble represents the basis for a work package. If the project members have been producing a tangible plan and its corresponding ad hoc information as they progress through the operations of producing estimates, networks etc., there should be little or no special action required to produce these components of the work packages.

11.4 THE CONTENTS OF A WORK PACKAGE

Ideally then, there ought to be a work package given to each individual who has been assigned to each job in the plan. Work packages equate to the department or job title where the work is performed. Therefore, they include any desirable work breakdown codes and/or accounting codes. They also include the job identification number—if it is not the same as the work breakdown number. As a suggested format, the work package may consist of:

1. A cover sheet

2. A responsibility grid

3. An assignment report

4. Supporting documentation

5. The corresponding system specifications

6. A problem log

7. A blank work notes form.

With the exception of the cover sheet, the components of the work package should be by-products of the management effort that would be expended anyway—even if there were no work packages. In other words, aside from the time needed to assemble the pieces, there should still be no extra effort required for producing a work package. Each of the components will be addressed in the following sections.

Although much of the literature pertaining to the management of systems projects suggests that the work package include various forms of test specifications, this text assumes that the test specifications are separate deliverables, and form their own unique work packages.

11.5 THE WORK PACKAGE COVER SHEET ◆

The work package cover sheet may contain the name of the project, the name of the resource, the date that the package was assembled, and a sign-off place for the signatures of the reviewers and approvers.

11.6 THE RESPONSIBILITY GRID ◆

Management of the project is streamlined when everyone knows their roles. Responsibility grids clearly define control points, speed up decision making, and identify bottlenecks and areas of conflict. Because they are such helpful communications tools, they also go far to improve productivity. These charts are initiated by listing each job in a column. Next to this column are columns for who assigns the work, who manages the work, who is responsible for the outcome, who expedites problems, who reviews the work, who approves the work, who audits the work, who decides the work is completed, and so on.

If the project is large enough, it is advisable to group the jobs according to a meaningful subset of work—for example, by support component.

11.7 THE ASSIGNMENT REPORT

The assignment report that was described earlier in this chapter is included in the work package.

11.8 THE SUPPORTING DOCUMENTATION ◆

For each of the jobs listed in the assignment report, a packet of supporting documentation is assembled. If there is to be a long time span between the assignment point and the time that the work actually commences, including the supporting documentation in the work package should either be delayed until it is needed or continuously updated.

The supporting documentation includes the accumulated ad hoc information that has been developed throughout the planning process.

Added to this section will be as many hard copy reports (for example, resource Gantts and histograms) from the project management software system that the manager deems appropriate. Since they have been illustrated elsewhere in this text, bar charts and histograms will not be pictured in this chapter.

Because of the graphic appeal of the histograms, nowadays one type of report is often overlooked. The tabular resource loading report is a simplified nongraphic view of the histogram. It displays columns relating to time periods. In each column, there is a figure that tells the resource commitment for that time frame. While it is not intended as a replacement for the histogram, it is frequently viewed as an enrichment to the packet of supporting documentation.

11.9 THE SYSTEM SPECIFICATIONS

For each of the jobs listed in the assignment report, a set of the corresponding specifications developed to date is included in the work package. For example, at the end of Phase 1, the work package given to the analyst who will develop the intermediate-level specification will include the corresponding high-level analysis specification. At the end of Phase 5, the work package given to the programmer will contain the corresponding analysis specifications, the corresponding implementation modeling specifications, and the corresponding design specifications.

If there is to be a long time-span between the assignment point and the time that the work actually commences, including the system specifications in the work package should be delayed until they are needed.

11.10 THE PROBLEM LOG ◆

The problem log is a blank form that is included in the work package so that the resource may record problems encountered and the corresponding solutions.

11.11 THE WORK NOTES FORM ◆

The work notes form is a blank form that is included in the work package so that the resource may record any pertinent information that he or she wants to pass on about the activity or task.

11.12 VIEWING THE DATA ON THE SCREEN ◆

Some of the products allow the user to choose between sending the report to the printer or viewing it on the screen. At a minimum, it is nice to be able to check the output before wasting time and paper. When there are many available work stations, the best scenario occurs when the team members have access to both hard copy and on-line data. Then, the on-screen reporting feature becomes a real bonus.

11.13 LARGE PROJECTS

If, in spite of the proactive project management philosophies presented in this text, the project manager or the project team have been "encouraged" to produce the *whole* plan for a very long project in one single operation, it is advisable to postpone the development of work packages until just before they are to be assigned. Of course, another one of the advantages of phase-limited planning is realized during the assignment process—in that it is only necessary to step up to jobs (and their work packages) that can be more easily assessed, assigned, and managed in the short term.

11.14 ASSIGNING WORK IN A MULTIPROJECT ENVIRONMENT

Discussed earlier in the text, there are two basic approaches to incorporating subprojects into the master plan: (1) *attaching* the subprojects and (2) *merging* the subprojects. There is one strong advantage to merging subproject files. With merged plans, reports can be produced with any level of detail. (For example, an assignment report may be produced, for each resource, that has all of the resource's assigned jobs within each subproject within the master project.) With the exception of SuperProject Expert, those products that *attach* the subprojects will *not* be able to produce reports with the details of each of the subproject within the master project. This limitation is troublesome now—when trying to assign the work—and will become troublesome again later on—when trying to manage the project.

11.15 IN CONCLUSION

Years ago, people thought that the project started with the coding. This approach usually led to disastrous consequences. The concept of front-loading the project so that more time would be spent doing analysis and design was introduced earlier in this text. A case was presented for spending approximately 40–65 percent of the project effort—before writing any code—in order to get the payoff in the later phases of the project.

All of the work that has gone into the development of the project plan is analogous to this approach. By front-loading the effort into building a sound plan, the organization reaps the benefits through an easier-to-manage project. Similarly, just like the fact that the longer the team waits to do analysis, the more the analysis costs, the longer the team waits to develop a good plan, the more the project will cost.

People also used to think that project management began with status reporting of time, people, and costs. If the size of this text so far is any indication of how much work needs to be done before project management can start, then, clearly, at least 40–65 percent of the effort goes into producing the plan. The rest of the effort goes into tracking time, costs, and people utilization, and into status reporting and management of the project.

CHAPTER 12 TRACKING TIME, COSTS, AND RESOURCES

12.1 INTRODUCTION

Tracking is the process of collecting data about the progress of the project. Essentially, there are three different types of tracking data that flow through the management process: time and schedule tracking data, cost tracking data, and resource utilization data. Since there are these three different and unique types of data, this chapter is divided into three main topics that deal, respectively, with (1) collecting data on time, (2) collecting data on costs, and (3) collecting data on people utilization. The next chapter describes what to do with the data once it's gathered—that is, how to manage the project.

Initially, this chapter will address time data about *actual work effort to date* and *estimated work effort to completion* that is collected to aid in the management of the project. In reporting time, there are three characteristics of actual and remaining work effort: when the actual and remaining work effort equals the original estimate; when the actual and remaining work effort is greater than the original estimate; and when the actual and remaining work effort is less than the original estimate.

12.1.1 Clarifying the Purpose of Status Reporting

In spite of understanding the three characteristics of progress data, organizations frequently do not allow project participants the opportunity to report the truth about actual and remaining work effort. Sometimes, it is simply a matter of participants having to prove that they have worked their 40 hours. Other times, it's because their performance objectives state they must meet the estimates. These are double-edged swords. Not only does the opportunity to develop estimating expertise suffer, but quality of the end product may also be sacrificed—in order to meet the estimate. The effects that this type of coercion has on status reporting may be called *coloring* and takes many forms. For example, bogus jobs may be added to the plan; time may be reported to unrelated jobs that have excess time left in them; descriptions of jobs may be changed to allow the estimates to be revised and increased; or work may be charged to a general overhead category.

The bottom line, however, doesn't change. If employees are prevented from reporting the truth about the actual and remaining work effort, the project may

173

prove unmanageable, and the organization's estimating expertise is not likely to improve.

Rather than encounter the problems described in the above section, the group should insure that there is a clear understanding of the progress reporting goals—before embarking on the management phase of the project. All decisions should be documented in the Project Agreement.

12.2 BASELINES ◆

If the group has not saved a baseline version of the chosen plan, they should do so before going any further. Furthermore, the team should be sure about where the baseline values are stored.

12.3 FREQUENCY OF REPORTING ◆

The next step in the management process involves the determination of how often the status reports will be collected. Although the data that summarizes time, costs, and people utilization may be prepared and distributed at the same time, it is also possible that the corresponding summaries will be reported at different intervals.[1] Therefore, some of the corresponding data may also be collected at different intervals.[2] It is advisable that the group obtain the necessary approvals for the status reporting periods, before embarking on the management phase of the project.

12.3.1 Two Ways to Gather Status Data

There are two popular approaches to gathering the status data: by an *As-of* date or by time periods.

In the former, the operation has no restrictions other than rejecting the entry of data about work that occurs *after* the *As-of* date. Of the two types, this is the less demanding and easier to use. All of the products support this approach. With this approach, there are no special requirements pertaining to the setting

---

[1]For example, time may be collected weekly but summarized and distributed biweekly; cost data may be summarized and distributed monthly; resource utilization may be summarized and distributed quarterly.

[2]Thus, while the status data is collected weekly, accrued project overhead costs may only be entered once a month.

up of reporting periods. The user simply chooses an *As-of* date (See the next section.) and proceeds from there.

Gathering data by time periods provides the ability to be more specific with regard to exactly *when* the work was performed and the corresponding costs were incurred. However, this approach is also more rigorous—in that it insists that only data about work that occurs between the *start* and the *end* of the period may be entered. All other data will be *rejected*, forcing the user to exit the current time period and go to an appropriate one. In addition to the first type described above, Project Workbench also has a subsystem that supports this approach which, in turn, requires the establishment of designated reporting periods.

12.4 TYPES OF TIME REPORTS

There are basically two types of hard copy status reports: the narrative form and the preformatted turn-around document.

12.4.1 Narrative Status Reports

These reports are prepared using the ad hoc information reporting features of the product or using a word processor.

Since the goal of the project is to produce the system and not to spend an inordinate amount of time preparing status reports, the objective is to keep any narrative reporting brief and to the point. A good way to control the proliferation of excess data is to:

A. Divide an $8\frac{1}{2} \times 11$ piece of paper lengthwise into 8 sections, each $1\frac{1}{4}$ inches high; and

B. Head each section respectively with the following topics:[3] (1) List all late jobs; (2) Describe all new problems; (3) Describe any outstanding unresolved problems; (4) Describe *your* planned solutions; (5) Describe any actions required by management; (6) Describe any conflicting non-project work; (7) Describe accomplishments for this period; and (8) Describe plans for next period.

---

[3]It is a good idea to maintain the order as shown as well. Then, the important information is at the top of the report.

If all of the pertinent data cannot be entered on this form, then, perhaps the time between the reporting periods is too long. This may also be true if the group finds they are taking too long to complete the form. On the other hand, if the group is taking longer because they are being coerced into "inventing" justification for being present and not accounted for, that is a different matter altogether.

12.5 EXTRACTING THE JOBS FOR THE TURN-AROUND DOCUMENT—ON A RANGE OF DATES ◆

To start, the assignment reports from Chapter 11 become the foundation for the turn-around document. However, whereas *all* of the jobs in the project (or phase) were printed on the assignment report, the jobs that are printed on this report may be limited to just those *in progress* plus those that are *about to start* in the next one or two reporting periods.

The concerns addressed in this section deal with how easy it will be for users to extract data on a range of dates.

12.6 SETTING UP AN *AS-OF* DATE ◆

The *As-of* date is the date up to and including the day for which actual work effort is to be entered. This date is also important because it affects the date from which the new schedule is generated; that is, the new schedule that should result from recalculating dates that reflect progress to date.

If the progress data is to reflect the status as of the close of a particular calendar day, it would seem logical to enter an *As-of* date that is equal to that calendar day. This is true for some of the products. Yet, several systems require that the *As-of* date be set to *one day later* than the actual status date.

12.7 ENTERING PERCENT COMPLETE ◆

Many people also want a place to enter the percent complete, particularly when they are employing the earned value analysis that is described later in this chapter. On the other hand, if the group subscribes to the binary theory for completion,[4] this field may be-

come superfluous. The *meaningful* data will be entered in other operations—that is, "*how many hours are remaining*" and "*what is the revised completion date?*" When the job is 0 percent complete until it is 100 percent complete, the percentage method is referred to as the *Zero-One Hundred percent method*.

On the other hand, many times *payment* schedules have been linked to the start or completion of a job (or group of jobs)—for example, when an outside company has been contracted for services performed. As an outgrowth of the original work-package concept of three months or $100,000, both the employer and the contractor wanted an equitable method for reimbursement. Consequently, four payment patterns that were based on percent complete were devised:

- Linear progress—that is, percent as a portion of the original or currently projected estimated time (for example, if the job is estimated at 40 days and 10 days of work have been done, the job is considered to be 25 percent complete)
- The *One Hundred-Zero* percent method—as soon as the job is started, it is considered 100 percent complete
- The *Fifty-Fifty* percent method—as soon as the job is started, it is considered 50 percent complete. Then, the status doesn't change until completion, when, of course, the job is marked as 100 percent complete
- Subjective progress—that is, percent as estimated by the worker (for example, if the job was estimated at 40 days and 10 had elapsed, but the worker only felt that the job was 15 percent complete).

Percentages and Costs. Ideally, the system can be set up so that the accrual of costs and the earned value of work are both dependent on the respective actual time worked but are isolated from percentage complete. If such is the case, then the group may use the Zero-One Hundred percent method and can disregard the percentage field.

Cost accrual and earned values will be covered in more detail later in this chapter. Suffice it to say, at this point, that earned values and other types of cost accrual methods rely primarily on the percentage of completion. Thus, if cost accrual or earned value cannot be separated from status, but the group has agreed upon an inch-pebble length that supports the Zero-One

---

[4]"0 percent or 100 percent" complete—see Chapter 2.

Hundred percent method, they can temporarily disregard the percentage field, until the work is 100 percent complete. If the project is an internal project and cost accrual or earned value are not issues, *this* group may also choose to disregard the percentage field.

If (1) none of the foregoing three cases are true or (2) either the software or the payment plan *requires* the use of the percentage field, then one of the last four percentage methods may need to be employed.

The Fifty-Fifty Rule. The Fifty-Fifty rule to some degree eliminates the unrealistic status of linear and subjective progress reporting. It is especially useful when the job does not extend beyond the next one or two reporting periods. This means that it can easily be adapted to the inch-pebble philosophy espoused in this text. Even if the size of the inch pebble is larger than 4–40 hours but less than 80 hours, the 50-50 method will still be satisfactory.

The Milestone Method. This is an alternative method that is used when the work extends over several reporting periods and a faster payment schedule is required. Payments are linked to a series of completed deliverables that are considered a prerequisite to a designated milestone. These milestones are placed at key payment intervals and a percentage of the total is paid at these times. This application lends itself nicely to the Zero-One hundred percent method and, other than agreeing upon the intervals and payment ratios, requires no additional actions.

From a software perspective, the issues of concern pertain to:

1. Whether the percentage is a required or optional field
2. How many different percentage fields exist
3. If, and how, the user may enter percentages into the system
4. Whether the system automatically computes the percentage based on the presence of the start date
5. How the system computes percentages
6. If it is possible to override the percentage value computed by the system
7. If the system automatically enters 100 percent when the user enters the actual finish date
8. Which of the four percentage types the product employs

9. Whether the percentage may be totally under the control of the user
10. What fields are automatically updated by an entry into the percentage field
11. If the system-computed percentage reflects elapsed calendar time or *true work effort*.

12.8 HARD COPY TURN-AROUND DOCUMENTS ◆

There are two methods of collecting status data: via hard copy reports and via on-line work station data entry. On-line data entry will be covered in the next section.

The report heading of a hard copy status collection report may include the date of the report, the name of the project, and the name and identifier of the resource.

Then, there may be a line-entry for each job. From the assignment report, the line entry may include the following information: the name and identifier of the activity or task, the scheduled start and end dates of the activity or task, the original estimated *true work effort*, a list of the predecessors, and a list of the successors. Now, there must be a place for the worker to enter the actual start date, the actual/revised completion date, the hours spent this period, and the remaining hours. Ideally:

- The system will compute the time-to-date when the data is entered into the system. (See the discussion in the next section.)
- If the remaining time is left blank, the system will assume that it is equal to the difference between the original hours and the time-to-date.

Space must be provided for workers to add new jobs. It is not necessary to display costs on the status turn-around document.

12.9 ENTERING THE STATUS COLLECTION DATA ◆

Now is the time to enter the actual start date, the actual/revised completion date, the actual time spent this period, and the remaining time. It will be helpful if the system automatically computes for each activity or task for which status is entered:

- The time-to-date by continually adding in the time-this-period—that is, the user shouldn't have to do the arithmetic each time new status data is entered
- The remaining time if it is not entered or modified by the user—as the difference between the original time and the time-to-date
- A new duration—based on the sum of the time-to-date and the remaining time
- A new finish date—based on the new duration.

Finally, a new project schedule—based on the new finish date of each activity or task—should automatically be computed.

While almost all of the products support the entry of time-to-date, most products do not support the entry of time-this-period. This limitation may be offset by collecting and reporting status in a speadsheet package.

The project manager may want to be in control of permanent changes to the schedule. Opening on-line updates to all of the resources in the project may require that data entry be limited to a temporary copy of the plan. Otherwise, a hard copy collection of the status data (which is followed by review and approval *before* the data entry) is likely to be the preferred approach. The implications associated with on-line data entry and networking work stations will be addressed in the next chapter.

Several types of updating transactions were tested. They are illustrated in Figure 12.1.

1. The activity started on time and finished on time. The original duration was correct. (See A, J, F, K, and T.)
2. The activity was scheduled to start in this reporting period but it didn't; it still needs to be done. The duration hasn't changed but the dates need adjusting. (See N and O.)
3. The activity was scheduled to start; it did start on time; progress has been linear;[5] there is no change to the finish date. (See B and Y.)

4. The activity was scheduled to start; it did start on time; progress has been linear but the job will take more time to complete. The duration must be increased and the end date must be adjusted. (See C.)
5. The activity was scheduled to start; it did start on time; progress has been linear but the job will take less time to complete. The duration must be reduced and the end date must be adjusted. (See S.)
6. The activity started on time and finished early, but the same duration was expended.[6] (See G.)
7. The activity started on time and faster progress was made. The duration did not change, and there is an earlier end date. (See X.)
8. The activity started on time, progress was delayed.[7] The duration doesn't change, but the end date must be extended. (See I.)
9. The activity started on time and progress has been greater than the linear rate. The end date must not be extended but it can be shortened. (See L.)
10. The activity started on time; progress has been linear but the end date must be extended. (See M.)
11. The activity started on time; some progress was made. The duration has been reduced but the end date must be extended. (See H.)
12. The activity did not start on time. The duration does not change; the dates must be adjusted. (See P and Q.)
13. The activity will not start on time. The duration does not change; the dates must be adjusted. (See D and E.)

In all of these transactions, caution must be exercised to insure that while elapsed calendar time may change, the integrity of true work effort will be maintained. (If it is not, the resulting project costs may be invalid. Costs will be addressed in more detail later in this chapter.)

The products were evaluated first with respect to what screens and *how many different* screens must be invoked in order to enter the status data. Then each

---

[5]That is, if a job has a duration of 4 days and has been worked on for 2 days, it is 50 percent complete.

[6]For example, when the resource works overtime to finish early.

[7]For example, the resource was diverted.

Figure 12.1 Status collection transactions.

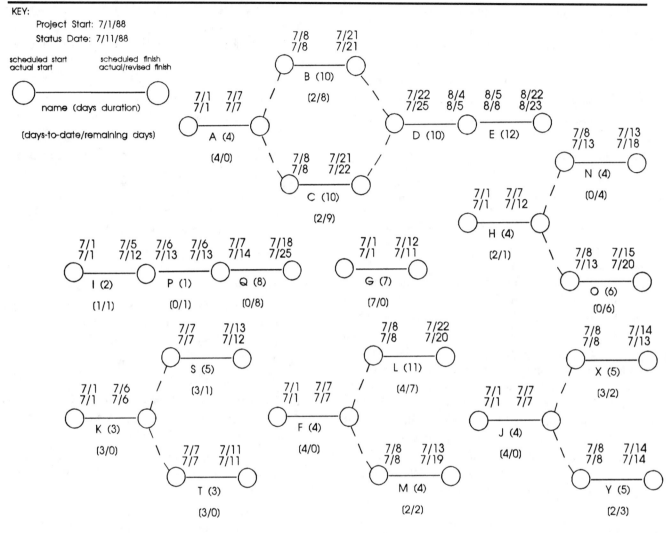

of the transactions in Figure 12.1 was tested in each of the products. With the exception of SuperProject, all of the products required special processing actions in one or more of the transactions. Some of the products were unable to handle *all* of the transactions.

12.10 PERFORMANCE STATUS REPORTING ◆

There are two kinds of status data collected: data about the *actual performance to date* and data about the *estimates to completion*. While the historical data is certainly meaningful, from a management perspective the most important and significant information is the data used to predict the outcome of the rest of the project.

For each job in the project, it is necessary to report and identify the slack position relative to the critical path, original duration, new duration, remaining duration, revised finish date, and the original finish date. Ideally, the system will also display a list of successors and their relationships to the critical path, so that it is possible to tell at a glance where the potential problem areas are. When the successors cannot be listed, it is always possible to refer to the network.

Users may wish to be able to see different views

of the status. For example, to see where the project has been, they may want to report on:

- All jobs on the critical and near-critical paths that are late in finishing by the *As-of* date;
- All jobs on the critical and near-critical paths that are late in starting by the *As-of* date;
- All other jobs that are late in finishing by the *As-of* date; and
- All other jobs that are late in starting by the *As-of* date.

To see where the project is going, they may want to see:

- The current projected end date of important milestones and the projected end date of the project;
- All revised estimates, especially those on the critical path and near-critical paths;
- All jobs that are late and scheduled to finish in the next reporting period, especially those on the critical and near-critical paths; and
- All jobs that are late and scheduled to start in the next reporting period, especially those on the critical and near-critical paths.

To measure status from a deliverables perspective, they would report by period on:

- All deliverables for which the current estimate to completion varies from the original estimate;
- All deliverables due for completion in the current reporting period;
- All deliverables due for completion in the current reporting period that will be late;
- All deliverables in the current reporting period that are in progress;
- All deliverables in the current reporting period that should have started but haven't;
- All deliverables due for completion in the next reporting period; and
- All deliverables due for completion in the next reporting period that will be late.

See the discussion earlier in this chapter about selecting data based on a range of dates. See the discussions in Chapters 7 and 10 about identifying the critical path when the slack is greater than zero.

When the system does not directly identify late jobs, users may select jobs that (1) are scheduled to finish by a certain date and have started (that is, have actual time reported to them); and (2) are scheduled to finish by a certain date and have not started (that is, have no actual time reported to them). Within each of these categories, the work may be sorted by percent complete to aid in finding the worst trouble spots and flagging them with the top visibility. Sorting on slack is then helpful for devising recovery strategies. Even when the system *does* flag late jobs, this type of report is very helpful.

In order to show the user where the project is deviating from the norm, the system should be able to compare the current values (actuals-to-date plus estimates-to-completion) against the baseline values. This data may be presented in a tabular report or on a comparison Gantt chart.

It is also helpful to know where the project is running out of slack (especially on the critical and near-critical paths) and where the estimates to completion are exceeding predefined tolerance levels. Users may want to report on:

- All jobs that are late and have low percent complete and low slack;
- All jobs whose current estimates to completion vary from the original estimates by more than 5–10 percent;
- All jobs that are less than a designated percentage complete (for example, 50 percent) and are scheduled to finish in the next reporting period; and
- Percent complete and/or slack in descending order.

When the system does *not* support selection of jobs whose estimates have been revised, but *does* allow selection based on a combination of relational (Boolean) and arithmetic operators, users may sometimes get around the limitation by selecting records where the difference between the original estimate and the current estimate to completion is greater than zero. If that doesn't work, then perhaps the data can be selected based upon variances on durations.

Finally, many people would like to know the number of planned finishes (or starts) versus the number of actual finishes (or starts), especially for those jobs on the critical and near-critical paths. Since this data represents only what is known in the past, its usefulness for project management is limited. It does not reflect revised estimates to completion or the addition of new jobs to the plan. Consequently, judgments based on this kind of past history may be unduly optimistic. Reports that pertain to revised estimates to completion, new end dates, and variances give a more realistic picture of status.

Each of the products was evaluated based on its ability to satisfy these requirements.

12.11 HIGHLIGHTING PROGRESS ◆

This is when time-scaled PERT charts come in handy. It is helpful to look at the PERT, see a time line that represents the *As-of* date, and then be able to look to the left of the time line to get an impression of what jobs have been done. Similarly, it is useful on the Gantt to be able to draw a time line that represents the *As-of* date, look to its left and be able to tell if everything's on time. In both cases, a glance to the right of the line should show the user where the project is going.

The Gantt is useful but to be ideally beneficial it also needs to show dependencies—so users can follow the chain of jobs while planning their recovery strategies. When the dependencies cannot be illustrated with connecting lines, the requirement could be met if the Gantt had dependencies listed in columns. None of the products supports the ability to show Gantts and dependencies on the same report.

The products were evaluated based on (1) if there is special highlighting on the network to show progress; (2) if there is special highlighting on the Gantt to show progress; (3) if there is special highlighting on the other graphics to show progress; (4) if, and how, the *As-of* date is shown on the network; (5) if, and how, the *As-of* date is shown on the Gantt; (6) whether the highlighted progress relates to elapsed calendar time or *true work effort*; and (7) whether delays are highlighted.

12.12 INTRODUCTION TO TRACKING COSTS

Earlier in the chapter, tracking was defined as the process of collecting data about the progress of the project. Three different types of tracking information are collected: time and schedule tracking data, cost tracking data, and resource utilization data. In addition to collecting this information so that the organization will know the *final costs* of the project, there are three other important reasons for collecting progress data: (1) to be able to charge for project services performed; (2) to be able to manage the project; and (3) to accumulate historical data for developing future estimating and project management expertise. The last two objectives are very compatible. However, it is not unusual to discover that they are often in conflict with the first.

12.12.1 Charging for Services

There are many situations in which an organization would have cause to charge for the project. When this occurs, the group is usually dealing with an accounting function and not a project management function. For example, if the project will be completed by an outside consulting group, the consulting company will need to know how to charge for their services, and the hiring company will need to be able to reconcile the charges. On the other hand, if internal projects have been funded through a charge-back system, or if the project has been classified as a Research and Development project, some or all of the project costs will be based on employee costs. Furthermore, if an employee gets paid for a 40-hour work week, regardless of how many hours he or she works, then the organization may only be interested in what percentage of that individual's salary is attributable to each project and not the actual hours worked. In these types of scenarios, employees are not required to report overtime hours. (As a matter of fact, in some organizations, they are actually *discouraged* from reporting overtime.) Needless to say, while this type of data is necessary for accounting functions and charge-back systems, it is not always very helpful in meeting the last two project management objectives that were described above.

When the system supports the differentiation between regular hours and overtime hours, it is possible to use the project management system for the accounting function *and* for the project management function. As the group was advised in the introduction to this chapter to insure that there is a clear understanding of the progress reporting goals *before* embarking on the management phase of the project—they are also advised to do the same for the cost reporting goals. This is especially true when only one of the costing objectives is achievable.

12.12.2 Tracking Project Cost Information

The type of costing information that is tracked relates to direct labor costs, fixed costs, overhead costs, and penalty or bonus costs. Direct labor costs are captured as a result of gathering the information on the turnaround documents; overhead costs, etc., must be independently tracked and recorded at preselected times by a designated individual—frequently the project manager.

12.13 COSTS AND PROJECT MANAGEMENT SOFTWARE ◆

Each product was initially evaluated to determine its accuracy in computing total costs after actual time and remaining time had been reported to the project. In every product, the resulting total costs per resource, total costs per job, total costs per milestone, and total costs per project all checked out correctly.

With the exception of Microsoft Project, the actual-costs-to-date checked out correctly for each product. Due to its dependency on percents that are linked to *elapsed calendar times* rather than *true work effort*, Microsoft Project's actual costs are not always correct. This will be addressed later in this section.

In all of the products except for SuperProject Expert, reporting time to tasks automatically resulted in new costs being calculated. However, this is not true for SuperProject Expert.

While almost all of the products display costs-to-date, several products do not display actual-costs-this-period.

Changes that are made to the unit rates of resources were *not* considered part of the above accuracy check. Since these kinds of changes affect the end costs of the project in a different manner than time reporting, they were evaluated separately. In all of the products except for SuperProject Expert, changes to

unit rates of resources are automatically reflected in new costs being calculated. This is not true for SuperProject Expert.

Several products report variances. When this field is negative, the task or project is in an overrun state. When it is positive, the task or project is in an underrun state.

The products were initially evaluated based on where to find actual costs; what happens to costs when time is reported to a job; and what happens to costs when the resource rate is changed.

12.14 PERCENTAGES AND THEIR EFFECTS ON COSTS ◆

Earlier in this chapter, concern was expressed regarding how the use of percentages affects the accrual of costs and earned values. (Earned values will be addressed later in this chapter.) This concern is centered on the case when (1) the system *requires* the use of percentages during progress reporting; (2) the Zero-One Hundred Percent Method can't be used; (3) cost accrual cannot be isolated from percentages; and (4) the job is only partially complete. If the percentages are, in turn, linked to elapsed calendar time rather than true work effort, the costs of the corresponding jobs and of the project may *not* be correctly reflected—until all of the jobs are 100 percent completed.

The use of percentages in Microsoft Project has special significance in how they affect costs.

12.15 COST STATUS REPORTING ◆

For each job in the project, it is necessary to report and identify the original costs, the actual costs this period, the actual costs to date, the remaining costs, the revised (or projected) total costs, and the amount by which the projected total costs will vary from the original costs. Users may also wish to be able to report on:

- All jobs that are over budget;
- All jobs that are under budget;
- All jobs that are more than a selected percentage over budget (percent variance over budget);
- All jobs that are more than a selected percentage under budget (percent variance under budget);

- The histogram of costs per period;
- The graphic view of cumulative costs; and
- The graphic view of cash flows based on early starts versus late starts.

When they can show the costs for both an early date schedule and a late date schedule, graphs of cumulative costs are helpful in demonstrating the range of feasible costs. (See Figure A5.24.) To get the desired distribution of costs, start and finish dates may be adjusted anywhere within the range.

The histogram of costs, the graphic view of cumulative costs, and the graphic view of cash flows are all useful in management presentations. However, they do not provide the discrete data values that are required for accurate cost management. This information may only be obtained from tabular reports. Consequently, those products that are limited in their support of cost graphics need not be judged harshly if they are strong in the other reporting capabilities.

With the exception of Primavera Project Planner, none of the products report on actual-costs-this-period. And in Primavera Project Planner, the period data may only be entered from batch or import mode.

SuperProject Expert is the only product that will select jobs that are over or under budget. None of the products will select jobs based on percent variances over or under budget. If users wish to see this view of the cash status of the project, they will have to export the data to a spreadsheet package.

Ideally, the cost histogram will show two bars for each period: the originally planned costs for that period and the current total forecasted costs for that period. The current total forecasted costs equal the amount of actual costs for the periods on or before the report date plus the projected total costs for the periods after the report date. With the exception of Harvard Project Manager 3.0, all of the products that do support cost histograms only show the second bar, the total costs for that period. Harvard Project Manager 3.0 has a cost histogram that shows both bars.

Ideally, the graphic view of cumulative costs will show both the original costs and the revised costs. With the exception of Primavera Project Planner, all of the products that do support cumulative costs only show the revised costs. Primavera Project Planner shows both types of costs.

Several products do not support graphic views of cash flow reporting; but they do show cash flow in tabular reports by printing the costs of each job across a designated time period. Where the products do not support either approach, the user can still get cash flow reports by exporting the data to spreadsheet packages.

Each of the products were evaluated based on the foregoing discussions. Reporting on costs per resource will be covered later in this chapter.

12.16 EARNED VALUES AND VARIANCES

The early project managers who used the PERT method to estimate or to schedule discovered that it was not very helpful in the areas of project management, especially in the area of cost control. For example, it was difficult to relate cost consumption to time expended. Furthermore, when projects were contracted to outside developers, it was difficult to develop an acceptable payment schedule. For example, from the customer perspective, payments based only on actual time spent were unsatisfactory.

Finally, because in the defense industry so many outside contractors may be involved at one time, the Department of Defense established a standard by which they could initially screen candidate contractors *and* by which they could later effectively manage the contractors once they were selected.

This standard is called the C/SCSC (Cost/Schedule Control System Criteria)—also known as Earned Value Analysis. Before the implementation of C/SCSC, project management control systems concentrated on (1) the amount of time that had been spent; and (2) the amount of money that had been spent. C/SCSC integrates cost and time reporting by adding a third dimension: called the *earned value*. The basis behind C/SCSC is that payment is matched, *not* to elapsed calendar time or to the actual time spent, but to (1) the amount of the deliverable that was actually completed for the amount of resources that were actually spent; (2) the amount of *true work effort* that will ultimately be required to finish the job; and (3) the proportion of that *true work effort* that has been earned to date. By invoking this third dimension, project managers are better able to forecast the final costs and end dates of the project.

It is assumed that the comparisons are made against the stored baseline values. Earned value analysis techniques rely on the existence of this baseline plan, against which status is reported and performance may be assessed. To effectively apply this concept, users are expected (1) to have developed a work breakdown structure, (2) to have assigned work at the work package level, (3) preferably to have designated individuals (or, if not designees, then specific organizational groups) accountable for the completion of the package, and (4) to manage the project by a schedule and a budget.

There are 10 terms that are applied in earned value analysis:

1. B%C (Budgeted Percent Complete). This is calculated from the stored baseline values. It is the percent of the elapsed calendar time, starting from the baseline scheduled start of the job to the *As-of* date.

2. BAC (Budget At Completion). This is the total baseline cost (or time) allocated to the job.

3. BCWS (Budgeted Cost for Work Scheduled). This is the value determined by multiplying the B%C by the BAC. In essence, this represents the progress that *should* have been made to date—if the project had proceeded according to the baseline plan.

4. ACWP: (Actual Cost of Work Performed). This is independent of the value and status of the work. It is simply the costs associated with the effort expended to date.

5. A%C (Actual Percent Complete). This is the result from the formula:

$$\frac{\text{Actual Duration To Date}}{\text{Actual Duration To Date} + \text{Estimated Remaining Duration}} \times 100.$$

6. BCWP (Budgeted Cost for Work Performed). This is the proportion of that true work effort that has been earned to date. Independent of actual *cost* of the work effort, it is determined by multiplying A%C by BAC. In essence, this represents the progress that has *actually* been made to date. It is an important measure because it excludes both the schedule variance and the unit price variance in its calculation.

7. CV (Cost Variance). This is a comparison of the value that *has been earned* against what *has actually been spent*. The formula is BCWP − ACWP.

8. SV (Schedule Variance). This is a comparison of the value that *has* been earned against what *should* have been earned. The formula is BCWP − BCWS.

9. % Overrun (Underrun) is the value of:

$$\frac{\text{ACWP} - \text{BCWP}}{\text{BCWP}} \times 100.$$

10. Delay (Advancement). On any given day this is the difference between the BCWS and the BCWP.

The schedule variance and the cost variance are used in combination. If either variance is positive, the project is ahead of schedule or under budget; if either is negative, the project is behind schedule or over budget. If the schedule variance is negative in proportion to the amount that the cost variance is positive, the project may be behind schedule but it is not likely that it will be over budget. If the schedule variance is zero and the cost variance is negative, the project may be on time, but it is likely that it will be over budget. If both the schedule variance and the cost variance are negative, the project will be both late and over budget. This last scenario requires prompt action by the project manager.

The formulas used above may be modified to reflect the data based on the current forecasted project values instead of the baseline values.

Proponents of earned value analyses believe that the total variance (BCWS : ACWP) may be an interesting statistic albeit not a useful one. This is because it does not shed light on the differences between planned work and accomplished work.

At the end of the day on July 11 in the project in Figure 12.1, the BCWS is $8,760, the ACWP is $8,920 and the BCWP is $9,008.40. There is a cumulative schedule underrun of $248 and the percentage value is 1 percent. There is also a delay of 6.75 days.

After several reporting periods, each of the earned values may be plotted on a graph. (Figure 12.2) These illustrations are very helpful in portraying the *current* scheduling status of the project at a glance. When the value curve falls below the scheduled curve, this indicates that the project is experiencing a delay.

For example, as of a current reporting date of September 12, the dollar progress that has *actually* been made (BCWP) is $9,400. This same amount of dollar progress *should* have been made (BCWS) by September 6; therefore, the project is 6 working days behind schedule. Similarly, the project has a cumulative schedule overrun of $1,562 (or 21 percent). Although the group has significantly stepped up their level of effort, they are still behind.

From this data, projections to completion may then be drawn directly from the baseline's remaining durations, from the status report's remaining durations, or from a combination of both. (Figure 12.3) These illustrations are very helpful in portraying the *final* scheduling status of the project at a glance. At the current rate, the project will actually cost $17,562—against a scheduled cost of $14,693 (BCWS). They will fall progressively behind, finishing nine days late at a cumulative schedule overrun of $4,341 (or a 17 percent overrun).

This type of exercise may be applied at the project level, in which case the results may clearly signal the existence of cost or scheduling problems. However, the results will not pinpoint the source of the problems. On the other hand, when the same exercise is limited to a support component level, a department level, and so on, it may be possible to isolate the source of the overrun.

Users are cautioned to note that earned value analysis is not a panacea for project management. Earned value analysis surely measures the labor costs and their effect on the schedule; however, unless careful attention is also paid to recording the indirect costs, the overhead costs, and the materials costs, the status picture will be distorted.

12.17 EARNED VALUES AND PROJECT MANAGEMENT SOFTWARE ◆

Some of the systems support the full application of earned value analysis; some partially support it; some do not support it at all. When the system's export is being used for financial analysis, the data for earned value can be sent along. Therefore, for those systems with limited or no support for this feature, users may not view the limitation as a serious drawback.

With the exception of Project Workbench, all of the products support earned value analysis, although some products do an excellent job and others do a questionable job.

12.18 COSTS IN A MULTIPROJECT ENVIRONMENT ◆

For most of the products, no special actions are required when rolling costs upward in a multiproject environment. However, for Microsoft Project, the user will need to give the system some additional instructions regarding how to accrue costs.

12.19 INTRODUCTION TO TRACKING RESOURCE AVAILABILITY AND RESOURCE UTILIZATION

Unlike time tracking and cost tracking, *collecting* resource tracking data does not usually require any special actions on the part of the user. However, there are three additional views of the status reporting data—other than those already covered earlier in this chapter—that are of interest during the project management process: reporting on information about resource *availability*, reporting on information about resource *utilization*, and reporting on information about resource *productivity*.

12.20 REPORTING ON RESOURCE AVAILABILITY ◆

Project managers need to be able to track the status of resource availability so that they will be able to readjust the plan by reassigning resources. To begin with, this type of reporting is simply a continuation of the reporting that took place during the work assignment process and during the resource allocation and leveling processes. Resource histograms are helpful in demonstrating the available resources compared to the required resources. However, they do not show the tasks to which the resource is assigned. Therefore, although

Figure 12.2a Earned values.

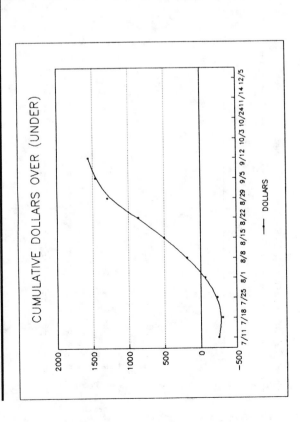

CUMULATIVE DOLLARS OVER (UNDER)

Figure 12.2b Earned values.

CUMULATIVE DAYS OVER (UNDER)

Figure 12.2c Earned values.

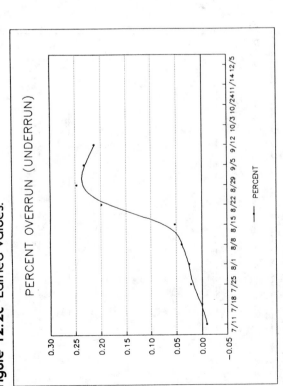

PERCENT OVERRUN (UNDERRUN)

Figure 12.2d Earned values.

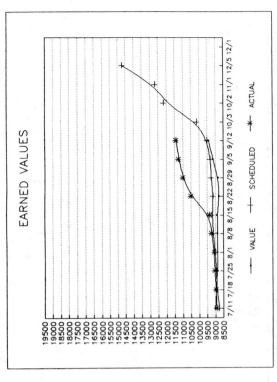

EARNED VALUES

Figure 12.3a Earned values.

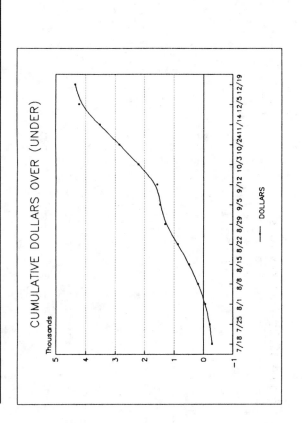

CUMULATIVE DOLLARS OVER (UNDER)

Thousands

5
4
3
2
1
0
-1

7/18 7/25 8/1 8/8 8/15 8/22 8/29 9/5 9/12 10/3 10/24 11/14 12/5 12/19

— DOLLARS

Figure 12.3b Earned values.

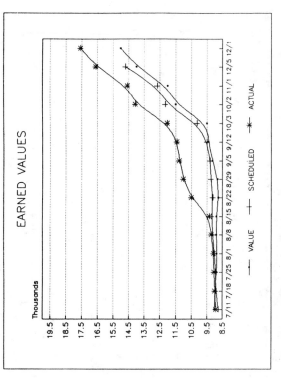

CUMULATIVE DAYS OVER (UNDER)

10

8

6

4

7/11 7/18 7/25 8/1 8/8 8/15 8/22 8/29 9/5 9/12 10/3 10/2 11/1 12/5 12/1

— DAYS

Figure 12.3c Earned values.

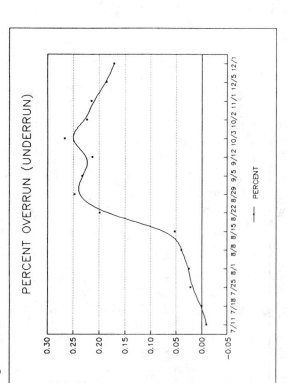

PERCENT OVERRUN (UNDERRUN)

0.30
0.25
0.20
0.15
0.10
0.05
0.00
-0.05

7/11 7/18 7/25 8/1 8/8 8/15 8/22 8/29 9/5 9/12 10/3 10/2 11/1 12/5 12/1

— PERCENT

Figure 12.3d Earned values.

EARNED VALUES

Thousands

19.5
18.5
17.5
16.5
15.5
14.5
13.5
12.5
11.5
10.5
9.5
8.5

7/11 7/18 7/25 8/1 8/8 8/15 8/22 8/29 9/5 9/12 10/3 10/2 11/1 12/5 12/1

— VALUE   + SCHEDULED   * ACTUAL

186

Figure 12.4 Resource availability by resource name.

RESOURCE NAME: LEADER

	JULY 1			JULY 5			TOTAL		
	REQ'D	AVAIL	OVER (UNDER)	REQ'D	AVAIL	OVER (UNDER)	REQ'D	AVAIL	OVER (UNDER)
TASK 1	2	1	(1)	3	1	(2)	3	1	(2)
TASK 2	1	1		1	1		1	1	
TASK 3	1	1		1	1		1	1	
TOTAL	4	1	(3)	5	1	(4)	5	1	(4)

they are very valuable during the leveling process, they are not quite as helpful during the management process. Used with a resource Gantt chart, they do give the complete picture, especially when the Gantt chart also displays actuals to baselines and actuals to current forecasts. However, this process requires moving from graphic to graphic; and the transition is not always smoothly accomplished.

When the system does not provide a feature for producing a hard copy of its histograms and such, the user may transfer the screen image to a graphics printer with the "print screen" key.

Tabular resource loading reports provide an alternative approach to resolving resource availability problems, since it is possible to put all of the data on one report. These reports need to be formatted so that, for every resource, there is a list of that resource's assignments. (See Figure 12.4.) The resource's commitment to each assignment needs to be distributed across the time periods (for example, by day or by week). Ideally, each time period is, in turn, broken into columns for required resources, available resources, and a flag that highlights that the required number doesn't match the available number.

When the system does not support this type of true periodic reporting, the user may display the start and finish dates of the task and work the problem from that perspective. (This is not always an easy solution to implement but it is better than no solution at all.)

None of the products supplies a tabular report that provides all of the data required to complete this

process. Nevertheless, they are all still evaluated in this section.

12.21 REPORTING ON RESOURCE UTILIZATION ◆

Reporting on resource utilization has to do with displaying data on how much of the resource has *already* been used and not about displaying data on how much of the resource is scheduled for the *future* or is *available* for scheduling in the future.

Information about resources often seems limited to a sorted view of the time reporting described in the previous section and earlier in this chapter, *or* of the cost reporting also described earlier in this chapter. For example, it is not unusual to find that resource reporting is simply a reformatting of the existing time and cost data into differently formatted reports, all still pertaining to the future use of the resource.

Resource utilization information is a by-product of *capturing* the time that the resource actually spends on a particular job. However, given the amount of time that is spent adjusting plans for resource *constraints*, it is surprising how little emphasis is given to monitoring resource *utilization*. This is probably because (1) no special actions are required to capture resource utilization data; (2) evaluating resource utilization is sometimes considered outside the scope of project management; and (3) people are unsure about what kind of data to collect and what to do with it.

Three views of the resource utilization data may

Figure 12.5 Resource utilization by resource by period.

RESOURCE NAME	RESOURCE TYPE	PERIOD 1			PERIOD 2		
		PLANNED	ACTUAL	VARIANCE	PLANNED	ACTUAL	VARIANCE
BOSS	MANAGER	1	1		1	1	
LEADER	MANAGER	2	2		2	1	−1
SENIOR	ANALYST	3	2	−1	3	4	1
WORKER	DESIGNER	2	2		4	2	−2

Figure 12.6 Resource utilization by resource dollars, by tasks, by time periods.

RESOURCE NAME: BOSS

TASKS	THIS PERIOD			TO DATE			PROJECTED			COMMENTS
	PLANNED	ACTUAL	VARIANCE %	PLANNED	ACTUAL	VARIANCE %	PLANNED	NOW	VARIANCE %	
TASK 1	2,000	2,000		4,400	4,500	−2	4,400	4,500	−2	
TASK 2	2,200	2,200		2,200	2,200		3,000	3,000		
TASK 3	2,500	2,800	−12	2,500	2,800	−12	4,000	4,000		EARLY START
TOTALS	6,700	7,000	−4	9,100	9,500	−4	11,400	11,500	−1	

Figure 12.7 Resource utilization by resource hours, by tasks, by time periods.

RESOURCE NAME: BOSS

TASKS	THIS PERIOD			TO DATE			PROJECTED			COMMENTS
	PLANNED	ACTUAL	VARIANCE %	PLANNED	ACTUAL	VARIANCE %	PLANNED	NOW	VARIANCE %	
TASK 1	40	40		88	90	−2	88	90	−2	
TASK 2	44	44		44	44		60	60		
TASK 3	50	56	−12	50	56	−12	80	80		EARLY START
TOTALS	134	140	−4	182	190	−4	228	230	−1	

be of interest to project managers: the information about head counts (Figure 12.5), the information about the costs spent per resource (Figure 12.6), and the information about the hours spent per resource (Figure 12.7). In these illustrations, the term "Planned" refers to the baseline values.

Used in conjunction with the time status reports, the head count can be matched to jobs that are late.

This is one way of discovering a source of problems related to meeting the schedule.

Costs spent per resource and hours spent per resource may be of interest to project reporting, in general, and to the resource's manager, in particular. Many groups require that an explanation be provided when the actual figures vary from the planned figures beyond a designated tolerance—for example, ± 10 percent.

Sometimes, users also like to add columns to Figures 12.6 and 12.7 that will show the scheduled and actual start and finish dates for each task, as well as the remaining hours and costs.

When a product does not support periodic reporting, users may satisfy some of the requirements by selecting the report data on a range of dates. (See the discussion earlier in this chapter.)

Although Viewpoint is the only product that features reports that provide all of the required data, the other systems are also evaluated in this section.

12.22 EARNED VALUE PRODUCTIVITY REPORTING ◆

Although not specifically aligned with resource data, the information that is developed during earned value analysis may be used to report on productivity cost and schedule ratios. Positive values for these ratios indicate completions ahead of schedule, and negative values indicate lateness.

The two formulas are:

$$\text{schedule performance index} = \frac{\text{BCWP}}{\text{BCWS}} = \text{SPI}$$

$$\text{cost performance index} = \frac{\text{BCWP}}{\text{ACWP}} = \text{CPI}$$

Time Line 3.0 supports this type of reporting.

12.23 COMPLETING THE TRACKING PROCESS ◆

The work packages include the problem log and a work notes form. These two documents were inserted into the work package so that the resource may (1) record problems encountered and the corresponding solutions and (2) record any pertinent information that he or she wants to pass on about the activity or task. Now is the time to capture this information.

13 MANAGING THE PROJECT

13.1 MEETING ORGANIZATIONAL EXPECTATIONS

Throughout the management process, it is important to continually reassess where the project stands in relation to the approved project objectives, the approved success and completion criteria, and the approved acceptance criteria:

- It may be necessary to remind many people in the organization that requirements for finishing by a pre-selected end date *and* finishing within a designated budget *and* completing the project with resource limitations may not be feasible—unless the success criteria also specifically excludes requirements for a quality system that is also reliable and maintainable.

- On the other hand, there may be occasions in which, if the team makes the target date, the project will be considered successful—even if it exceeds the budget and the resource allocations.

- Conversely, the project may only be considered successful if the team manages to stay within the budget for people and/or costs—regardless of the end date.

Since project management success is likely to be judged by one of these scenarios or by a similar scenario, *it is essential that the project manager always maintain a clear and constant vigilance on the objectives and criteria of the project.*

13.1.1 Publicizing the End-Date of the Project

Another area essential in managing organizational expectations concerns the perceived project end date. If the techniques for calculating a reasonable late project finish date have been applied, the late finish date of the project will be sometime later than the early finish date of the project.[1] Although most of the activities and tasks are *assigned* using the *early dates* of each job, it is advisable that the organization be persuaded to expect *project completion* by the *late date*. After all, that is the date on which the computations for probability were based.

Since the work is assigned using the early dates, the project is being managed to meet the early dates. Therefore, if any of these early dates should be missed, the expectation of late date completion of the project gives the project manager the leeway that is necessary to manage to successful completion.

13.2 INTRODUCTION TO PROJECT MANAGEMENT

Project *management* is defined as a five-step process: (1) feedback, (2) contrast, (3) assessment, (4) deter-

---

[1]Hopefully, the late finish date is not earlier than the early finish date—causing a probability of success that is less than 50 percent.

mining corrective actions, and (5) project control. During this management process, a loop is created in which the status data that has been gathered is fed back into an exercise that contrasts actual results against the planned results. There are two kinds of status data being collected: data about the *past* accomplishments of the project and data about the *future* of the rest of the project. While historical data is certainly meaningful, the most important and significant data, from a management perspective, is the information used to predict the final outcome of the project.

Thus, the study of the status data is made in order to assess the impacts of any deviations from or changes to the project's end dates and costs as well as from the resource utilization. The output of the comparison is used to determine what corrective actions, if any, must be applied.

Without a comprehensive plan and without this feedback loop, satisfactory control of any project is questionable. During the project control step, the project team reverts back to the planning and assignment procedures outlined earlier.

13.3 THE TWO PERSPECTIVES OF PROJECTS

Although considerations about costs are certainly not neglected, DP projects basically fall into two general management categories: time-driven projects and resource-driven projects. Diametrically different in nature, both categories use the same management data. But in time-driven projects, the management emphasis concentrates on gathering information about the end date, and then, within the end-date analyses, collecting data about resources. In resource-driven projects, the manager needs to concentrate more on resource utilization and resource availability than on end dates—while, secondarily, keeping an ever-watchful eye on the end dates. In both cases, managers must always remember to maintain the value of the *true work effort* and to maintain the *true and natural dependencies* between jobs.

13.4 THE IMPORTANCE OF THE CRITICAL PATH—RETRACING THE PLANNING PROCESS

Where does the plan now stand, in relationship to the planning process? Ideally, the project team started with an optimal plan, a plan with *true and natural depen-*

dencies and with its own unique critical and near-critical paths. The team may then have added resources and developed a set of resource-constrained alternatives, each with its own unique critical path and near-critical path. This set of plans may be regarded as the *normal* set of plans. The project duration may have then been compressed by partially *crashing* the alternatives. The results of this exercise may have evolved into a second set of plans, again each with its own unique set of critical and near-critical paths. Management has chosen *the* plan that will be implemented for the coming phase or project.

The *chosen* plan is the source of the critical path that will be used to initiate management of the project. However, it is quite likely that the critical and near-critical paths will change during the execution of the plan. It is always advisable to closely manage to the *most current* critical path(s) during project management! Of course, in acutely time-constrained plans, it is also possible to drive the project so that it will deviate as little as possible from the baseline critical path.

In some situations, the team may have been unable to follow all of the above steps faithfully, either because the size of the project didn't warrant the effort or because of some other consideration, reasonable or unreasonable. Even if this occurs, teams shouldn't give up. The bottom line goal is to get a plan selected, a plan that can be implemented, a plan with the critical and near-critical paths *clearly identified.*

13.5 TWO VIEWS OF THE STATUS DATA

Surprisingly, people are often confused about what to do with the knowledge gained during status reporting: what the data is collected for, what to do with the data, who needs what information, and how detailed the information should be. The importance of status data is twofold: (1) for *managing the project downward*, with unique types of management data required; and (2) for *reporting upward*, with different types of reporting data required at each level. For managing downward, the project managers and project leaders need all of the detail, because they must assimilate this data in order to make strategy decisions about the direction of the project. But upper management usually only wants to see summary reports that give a broad perspective of the status of key milestones. This is especially true in large projects and in a multiproject environment where summary reports are based on groups of projects. In addition to the details that the activity leaders in large projects need for decision making, they have also found that the broad perspective provided by the upper management summary reports is helpful at their level as well. On the other hand, it's not safe to assume that upper management doesn't want the details. Therefore, it's wise to get an agreement up front with regard to what level of detail upper management actually does want to see.

13.6 STATUS REPORTING: WHAT DATA IS REQUIRED AND WHERE WILL IT BE FOUND?

The following section is driven from the perspective of what data the project manager really needs in order to report status upward as well as to manage downward. Several pertinent questions have been presented. These are the questions that usually need to be answered in order to satisfy the organization's interest in the status of the project. The answer to the foregoing question "Where will it be found?" has, for the most part, been addressed in the earlier chapters. The remaining issues will be addressed in this chapter.

13.6.1 When Will We Be Done?

What is the current finish date of the project? The answers to this question are found in the various types of status reports. If the project has slipped, *Why? ! ?* What happened since the last report that caused slippage? The answers to these questions are found in the narrative reports, the ad hoc information, and the work notes form.

13.6.2 What's Going On with the Critical Path and the Key Milestones?

What is the status of jobs on the critical path? Is there more than one critical path? Where are the near-critical paths? Some products provide standard critical path reports. Others allow the user to extract data based on the system's identification of the critical path, simply requiring users to choose an entry called *critical path*. When neither of these features are present, critical path reports may be generated by sorting and selecting on slack. When the techniques for choosing a reasonable late finish date have been applied, the system may no

longer recognize the critical path. Then, users will need to extract data based on the lowest value for slack. Special attention is also given in the next section to creating PERTS and Gantts which are limited to just the jobs on the critical path.

What is happening to the key milestones? When the system supports summary tasks or hammocks, specialized reports may be produced. These hammock or summary jobs may be chosen to be separately displayed on any of the reports described in the tracking chapter. Special attention is given later in this chapter to extracting graphic views of summary jobs.

What's happening with the fixed tasks? Special attention is given later in this chapter to extracting jobs based on fixed dates.

Dummy tasks (such as the one illustrated in Figure 6.16) are also very helpful for isolating and highlighting important dates such as the current status of the end of analysis, the start of coding, the beginning and end of implementation, and so on. Then, it's even nicer if all such tasks are grouped with a higher-level WBS summary task so they, too, are all in one place.

13.6.3 Where Are We in Relation to Where We Thought We'd Be?

It is helpful to compare the current position (the sum of the actuals to date plus the estimates to completion) to the original baseline values. PERT charts are totally helpful in this application. A Gantt is certainly very valuable for satisfying this requirement but to be truly beneficial, it also needs to show dependencies, so that it can be used to follow the chain of jobs while planning recovery strategies. When it is not practical to put connecting lines on the Gantt, dependencies listed in columns are satisfactory. None of the products supports the ability to show Gantts and dependencies on the same report. As a consequence, a combination of Gantt and PERT is necessary to identify trouble spots and plan strategies for recovery.

Where is the project going? This is when time-scaled PERT charts truly come in handy. It is helpful to look at the PERT, see a time line that represents the *As-of* date, and then be able to look to the left of the time line to get an impression that all the jobs are done. Similarly, it is useful on the Gantt to be able to draw a time line that represents the *As-of* date, look to its left and be able to tell if everything's on time.

In both cases, a glance to the right of the line should show the user where the project is going.

13.6.4 What Does the Future Look Like?

What work is outstanding, and why? Narrative reports, ad hoc information and the work notes forms may provide the answers to "why?" Where are there new estimates, and why? Extracting data based on variances may provide this information. Where are there new jobs, and why? This data is especially crucial for jobs on the critical path and near critical path. Special attention is also given in the next section to creating PERTS and Gantts which are limited to just the jobs on the critical path.

Trend analyses such as those described in the earned value discussions are also very helpful in analyzing the project's future. *What-if* analysis (described later in the book) is helpful in trying out new strategies.

13.6.5 What Can Be Done to Recover?

Where's the available slack? Where are the available resources? What can be crashed? It is advisable to consider, not just the jobs that are causing the current difficulties, but to look for recovery opportunities further along in the project (or phase) as well. PERTS that are limited to critical and near-critical paths expedite this operation.

13.6.6 Is Resource Utilization Being Maximized?

What's happening to the resource utilization and the resource availability? Do we have the best distribution of resources? Where are the available resources? Are they working on the highest priority jobs? What are resource limitations doing to the end dates of projects and subprojects?

13.7 WHO PRODUCES PERTS AND GANTTS THAT MAY BE RESTRICTED TO CRITICAL PATH JOBS? ◆

Traditionally, the critical path has zero slack. On the other hand, if a new reasonable late finish date has been computed, the critical path will have slack greater than zero. The easiest way to extract the data for the uses described in the previous section would be when the system recognizes the critical path—whether it has zero slack or not. When the system does not recognize critical paths where slack is greater than zero, users may search through the plan data to discover the value of the lowest slack. Then, if the system allows selecting on slack, the critical path graphics may be produced. Primavera Project Planner will display a network that is limited to just those activities on the critical path. Project Workbench always recognizes the critical path—even if slack is greater than zero. Although they do not support networks limited to the critical path, several products do support Gantts limited to the critical path. Other products can be made to report on critical paths or slack, but *not* on the PERT or Gantt. Time Line 3.0 cannot be made to recognize any jobs of greater than zero slack as being on the critical path.

13.8 WHO PRODUCES REPORTS THAT MAY BE RESTRICTED TO FIXED DATE JOBS? ◆

Entering a fixed project end date was discussed earlier as was creating fixed dates for jobs. This section explains how to extract data based on fixed dates. Two products will not support extraction of report data based on fixed dates: Microsoft Project and Harvard Project Manager 3.0.

13.9 WHO PRODUCES PERTS AND GANTTS THAT MAY BE RESTRICTED TO SUMMARY JOBS? ◆

High-level, summary PERTS and Gantts are helpful aids for the upper management presentations described earlier. Most products support the feature that allows graphic reports to exclude all data save for the summary data. Those products that can*not* perform this useful function may overcome the limitation by using the subproject features—if the system supports the subproject attach and does not merge the subprojects.

13.10 PREVENTING UNAPPROVED CHANGES TO THE PLAN

There are two methods of collecting status data: via hard copy reports and via on-line data entry. In an on-line environment, status data may be entered by each project participant. Consequently, the project manager may want to be in control of permanent changes to the schedule. Opening on-line updates to all of the resources in the project compromises that control, with regard to allowing indiscriminate changes to estimates and adding jobs to the plan . To prevent corruption of the master plan, project managers may want to require that on-line data entry be limited to temporary copies of the plan. Otherwise, a hard copy collection of the status data (which is followed by review and approval *before* the data entry) is likely to be the preferred approach. In either case, permanent changes should only be made to the master *after* they have been approved by the project manager. Organizing projects and managing file security in a local area network on-line environment will be covered later in this chapter.

13.11 MANAGING CHANGES TO THE DOMAIN OF STUDY AND THE SYSTEM SCOPE

The organization must have a way to respond to changes in the *domain of study* and/or the *scope* of the system. Many people try to freeze the specifications but that often only leads to (1) discovery that people change their minds anyway; (2) animosity when the system users feel they didn't understand what they were signing off to; or (3) resulting in an "on-time" system that doesn't fulfill the system users requirements.

It is not possible to control change but it is possible to manage it. Yet, before an organization attempts to institute any change management procedure, they must first understand the systems management process with respect to change management. If the following conditions are not an accepted part of the culture, the success of the change management process is questionable:

1. Changes to the *domain of study* are almost immediately subject to the change management process. However, the organization needs to accept that, while it is possible to identify the domain of study at the *outset* of the project, the *system scope* will not be fully defined until the *end* of the Implementation Modeling phase. Until that time, *changes* made to the specifications are being made because of what may be termed the *process of refinement* and *not* because of increases to the system

scope. As a result of gaining more knowledge about the system, changes because of the process of refinement do often cause the *size* of the project to be enlarged. On the other hand, the scope is *not* actually being enlarged, merely better defined. If the size of the project must then be reduced, practitioners are directed to the guidelines for reducing size and/or invoking increments given earlier in the book.

2. Good specification techniques are vital. If the system users cannot understand and verify the specifications, it is likely that they may misunderstand the specifications and agree to the wrong interpretation of system requirements. It is necessary to develop expertise in the disciplines of analysis and design. Furthermore, until this expertise is perfected, it will be difficult to distinguish the difference between changes resulting from the process of refinement and changes resulting from enlargement of the scope. The organization should be patient and forgiving in the interim.

3. Verification and validation and testing must be performed from the start of the project. Otherwise, errors, omissions, ambiguities, and contradictions may slip through the cracks. This condition wreaks havoc when problems *are* discovered and causes confusion when trying to distinguish the difference between changes resulting from the process of refinement and changes resulting from enlargement of the scope.

4. It is imperative to do reviews and inspections. They are essential requirements for improved quality and should not be ignored. Furthermore, if the system specifications are *not* carefully and consistently reviewed during their development, it will be next to impossible to recognize a change when it occurs. People will surely be confused about whether or not the request is for something new or for something that they expected to be there in the first place.

5. While the practitioners are developing expertise in new technologies and management concepts, they will be surmounting a learning curve. During this time, they may not be able to make the best judgments about recognizing changes. This skill does improve with time but if personnel are not given encouragement to enhance their skills, it will take longer—or it may never even happen.

13.11.1 The Change Management Request

The following data is necessary:

Table 13.1   The Change Request Data

FROM THE REQUESTOR:
REQUEST DATE: REQUESTOR'S NAME:
REQUESTED COMPLETION DATE: REQUESTED PRIORITY: APPROVAL SIGNATURE
PROBLEM
JUSTIFICATION:
IMPACT (APPROVED/NOT APPROVED):
REQUESTOR'S ALTERNATIVE SOLUTION:

FROM THE DECISION MAKERS:
PRIORITY (ACCEPTED, REJECTED, POSTPONED):   APPROVAL SIGNATURES:
PLANNED START: PLANNED COMPLETE: INFORMEES:
COMMENTS:

FROM THE CURSORY EVALUATION:
TIME: DOLLARS: PEOPLE:
CLASSIFICATION (TRIVIAL, WORK IN PROGRESS, SIGNIFICANT):
TYPE (LEGAL, NEW FEATURE, NEW TECHNOLOGY, ENHANCEMENT, OTHER):

FROM THE CHANGE ANALYST:
AFFECTED AREA: ESTIMATES (TIME, MONEY, PEOPLE):   SCHEDULED DECISION DATE:
PROBLEM STATEMENT:

FOR THE LOG:
DATE RECEIVED: LOG NUMBER:

13.11.2 Change Management Procedures

The change request is assigned a number and entered into a change management log that keeps track of the current status of the request.

The request is then assigned to an analyst for a *cursory* review (less than eight hours). A rapid sizing number is given for the request. It is returned to the requester for reconsideration, given the results of the rapid sizing number. If the requestor wishes further consideration for the request, it may be returned for additional investigation. It is not advisable to make any organizational decisions based on this rapid sizing number!

In the second evaluation, the analyst assesses the costs, the benefits, and the impact in terms of time, money, and people. It is then scheduled for consideration by the change management decision makers.

The change management decision makers consider the impact and prioritize the request: accepted, rejected, or postponed until the next release.

The necessary parties are notified of the decision and its impact on the time, money, and resources of the project(s).

13.11.3 Finding the Time to Do Change Analysis

When project team members are busy trying to make the target dates for jobs that are already in the plan, interrupting them to ask for change analysis is often counterproductive. Where is the time supposed to come from, so that change analysis doesn't impact scheduled target dates?

In a large project, a separate team designated for change management analysis is sometimes an acceptable answer. When they are not doing change analysis, this team may be working on noncritical project jobs.

When organizations allocate different personnel for development and maintenance, the maintenance team may be brought in to do change analysis. This will ultimately be their job anyway. Thus, change analysis is a good way to introduce the maintenance staff to the system.

If neither of these solutions may be implemented, then it is simply left to the project team to wear two hats: developers *and* change analysts. *However*, everyone buys into (1) extending the other target dates; (2) overtime; or (3) adding some extra time into each job (to begin with), which will compensate for the added responsibility. When the third alternative is selected, the time spent on change analysis must be tracked. When it is used up, (1) more time is added back in; (2) the other target dates are extended again; (3) people agree to work overtime; or (4) no more requests will be accepted. Whatever strategy is selected should be made part of the Project Agreement.

13.12 STATUS REPORTING MEETINGS

As an adjunct to collecting status reports, status meetings may be held at certain intervals. On a long project that is under control, the meetings may be held monthly. If the project is out of control, the meetings may be held weekly or, in extreme cases, daily. Smaller projects may have weekly meetings or no meetings at all. The Project Agreement should document the agreed-upon period, as well as the criteria for attending and directing the meetings. With the exception of extreme emergencies, meetings should not be held on the spur of the moment. The agreed-upon lead time for meeting notification should be documented in the Project Agreement. The Project Agreement should also ad-

dress procedures for handling *no-shows* and unprepared attendees.

Many organizations also institute a review of a quarterly deliverables plan in addition to the regular status reporting meetings. The quarterly deliverables are reviewed in a progress meeting with a management steering committee, focusing on 90 day deliverables and emphasizing that time frames beyond the 90 days are less definite. In that same vein, where necessary, a new monthly status meeting for *all* projects and all levels of management provides yet an additional level of control. In organizations that are heavily project-oriented, these quarterly reviews and monthly status meetings have been received with enthusiasm.

13.13 MANAGING THE PROJECT

Managing the project is the process of iteratively looping back through the planning operations described earlier in the book. Then, too, a reasonable amount of *What-if* analysis is performed at this time. As a result of all of these exercises:

- The required changes to the plan will be relatively minor and the new end dates, costs, and resource requirements will be within acceptable tolerances.
- There will be significant and extensive changes required for the plan, causing dramatic variances from the original end dates, costs, and resource requirements.

13.13.1 Relatively Minor Alterations to the Plan

When (1) there is a need for relatively minor changes to the plan and (2) as a result of these changes the plan will remain within tolerances that have previously been approved by upper management, the project manager may independently revise the dates, resource assignments, and subsequently, the costs.

13.13.2 Dramatic Alterations to the Plan

When there are significant changes to the plan, the project manager will need to present the options and recommendations to upper management for selection and approval of the new dates, resource requirements and costs.

When they are facing the second scenario, organizations should not deceive themselves into believing that they can get away with the first. Sooner or later, the ugly truth surfaces. It is better to take a *no surprises* stance. The earlier the true facts are presented, the better the recovery position will be. Of course, this is another justification for managing at the inch-pebble level and collecting status on a weekly basis.

13.14 LOCAL AREA NETWORKS ◆

Local area network (LAN) software lets nearby users share hardware devices[2] and data files, in a platform where the hardware is distributed. This is facilitated, using what is called, in a local area network software environment, network servers.

There are many sources of network software, such as: Microsoft MS-NET; Banyan Vines; AT&T Starlan; IBM PC Network or IBM Token Ring Network; Novell Netware; 3COM3+; Ether Series; Ungermann-Bass Net/One; and AST PCNET. These products may also determine and control how many active distributed users can get on to the system at once.

Not every project management software product interfaces with every LAN software product. Therefore, users must carefully coordinate their selections and purchases.

Although the concept of LANs is sometimes intimidating and mysterious to the uninitiated, there is little magic involved in understanding their use. (It *does* involve specialized technical expertise, however, to install LANs. Wise organizations insure that experts perform this activity.)

LANs allow several pieces of hardware to communicate with each other. These pieces of hardware may or may not include their own data storage devices (such as floppies or hard drives). In the traditional *stand-alone* platform, the user enters data into predefined data storage areas—directories and/or subdirectories. This is also true in a *distributed environment*. However, in the distributed environment, effective organization of the data storage areas into directories and subdirectories that have been spread across all of the

pieces of hardware is a key to successful implementation of the LAN concept. This implementation also usually requires special expertise.

LANs also allow users to install one version of the project management software in a main directory that can be accessed by multiple users. This main directory is called the *host* directory. The project data files may also reside in that host directory or other directories spread around the LAN. The project data files may be read and modified in their residing host directory, or imported into and read or modified in the directories on the user's distributed hardware. Similarly, the data from the user's distributed hardware may be moved back up the line to the host directory.

In a LAN, whenever a file is being used it is called the active file. LAN software usually keeps other users out of the active file while it is being used, only releasing the active file so that it may be accessed by other users (1) as soon as it is written back, (2) as soon as the active user accesses a different file, or (3) as soon as the active user exits the system.

There is a second dimension to the use of LANs, which pertains to what kind of security exists that will keep workers out of permanent master files and only allow them access to temporary files. (See the earlier discussions about containing indiscriminate changes to the plan.) When a file should be safeguarded against modifications from unauthorized individuals, it may be called *protected*. In *absolute protection*, no one may read or write a file. On the other hand, if a file is protected by an authorized user, it may alternatively be set up so that the next people who access it can read it but can't modify it. In some systems, people who read a protected file are allowed to save it under a different name. When there is no protection on the file, then anyone can read and alter the permanent version.

The process of adding users and their access rights can be managed by a trained in-house network administrator. Access rights may be set up by specific group titles (for example, all analysts). New users are then simply added to the group by being told the group password. When necessary, users' access rights may later be changed by simply assigning them to a new group and telling them the new group's password. (The negative side to this procedure occurs when there is a need to lock a user out of a group that he or she was formerly a part of. The group password may need to

---

[2]Such as printers, plotters and space on a hard disk.

change, and *all* of the users may need to learn a new one.) An alternative to the group arrangement is to assign each user his or her own password and access rights. (The negative side of this procedure is that it requires more bookkeeping and the additional process of setting up the access rights for each user.)

Used together, the file protection feature and the organization of temporary files in the directories will help the project manager control the modifications to the permanent master file. Workers may update their own versions and the project managers (project leaders) may review the modifications before importing the changes into the permanent version.

Primavera Project Planner does not support LANs. All of the products that do support LANs lock other users out of the currently active file. Some of the products do not provide read/write protection. Those that do not provide this feature depend on the security features provided with the LAN software.

13.15 GUIDELINES FOR TRACKING AND MANAGING THE PROJECT ◆

Documentation that is intended to be used for understanding how to apply the tracking features of the system is not classified as guidelines for tracking.

13.16 MAKING A CASE FOR A HISTORY FILE

Organizations that want to improve their project management skills should be encouraged to save and subsequently reuse the data about their past project experiences. Expertise in estimating time and costs, expertise in anticipating and overcoming obstacles, and expertise in maximizing resource productivity are all more rapidly developed when the new project teams use factual past results to predict future events. (Of course, the value of this information is directly related to the level of (1) completeness to which it is captured; and (2) honesty supported during the collection of the data.)

The estimating portion of this database is populated from the results of the estimating techniques presented earlier. The costs are derived from the costing algorithms also presented earlier. After a large enough statistical sampling has been accumulated, the results may be calibrated using standard deviations, confidence intervals, and regression analysis.

Exhaustive and methodological procedures are necessary to insure that the data will actually be collected. Furthermore, there is a value to merging the collection of projects so that they are grouped by projects with common characteristics. Finally, the set of estimates will need to be continuously merged and culled to insure that they reflect the latest and most correct estimates for recurring jobs. The best successes are realized when a separate function is established and charged with the responsibility of collecting and maintaining this accumulated history of projects. The existence of such a database must also be widely publicized so that all potential project participants are made aware of this source of help. The ability of future teams to make effective use of this database is also dependent upon their being able to equate their current project to a similar sample historical project. This activity will often require that the team be able to examine the specifications of the system as well as the other data described above. Consequently, there needs to be (1) a set of the original specifications included in the history file or (2) pointers to the source of the corresponding specifications.

CHAPTER **14** KEY FACTORS IN SUCCESSFUL IMPLEMENTATION

14.1 INTRODUCTION

People have come to expect that projects should finish on time, be within budget, and solve the right problem. Yet, this is no small feat. As a matter of fact, many projects tend to be regarded as failures. Less than 10 percent finish on time and within budget, and many never finish at all. Why is there such a dismal record?

Organizations have tried to improve their success rate but their efforts often fail unexpectedly. Managers were thrown for a loop because they concentrated on such items as new procedures, methods, and equipment and expected to see real results. These results may only be realized if strategists also concentrate on (1) the people who have control over these items and (2) the cultural conditions that have control over the people.

It is important to recognize that the ingredients necessary to boost project management success are the *practical and common sense methods for:*

- Evaluating the impact of the organizational environment on the probability of success;
- Introducing *proven* turnaround techniques for diffusing the negative repercussions of the corporate culture;
- Establishing organizational standards for effective systems management;
- Understanding the systems management process and the project life cycle; and
- Developing realistic project expectations.

The implementation of these concepts is an essential cornerstone to the establishment of increased performance, productivity, and quality of workmanship.

Yet, many organizations are unable to create an environment that nurtures these skills. As a result, over 90 percent of project attempts fail in some manner. This is primarily due to serious flaws in the existing organizational culture, the most serious flaw being poor communications. As a result of poor communications, organizational expectations are unrealistic, unreasonable, and/or undefined. These situations are exacerbated by insufficient upper management participation; sparse middle management participation; lack of user participation; conflicting organizational objectives; poor project management; poor planning and control; poor software development techniques; and inadequate training strategies.

As these areas are, in turn, explored, practitioners marvel that, given each of the above inhibitors, they see success of any kind. Before any turn around can be affected, organizations must first understand these contributors to failure. Each cause should be examined closely. If it can be eliminated or diffused—so much the better. On the other hand, if organizations can't (or won't) eliminate the problem, they should be honest about the repercussions of their decisions.

14.1.1 Poor Communications

This is the single most significant contributor to project failures. Free and open exchange of information is an essential ingredient of successful projects, but good communication is very difficult to achieve. Initially, there is no sharp understanding of what is to be done and, therefore, no good way of disseminating and validating requirements. In the confusion, the organization overlooks the establishment of a clear-cut network of communication. People who need to know are not informed; people who don't need to know are inundated with useless information; important facts are not conveyed; and misinformation spreads malignantly. Poor organization, the consequence of poor communication, sets up barriers to coordination. When coordination fails, disputes increase, groups polarize, work grinds to a halt, and schedules slip.

14.1.2 Unrealistic, Unreasonable, and Undefined Expectations

In most cases, failure to successfully complete projects is not the fault of the project teams at all. Lack of success often occurs because results simply do not match organizational expectations of the Systems Management Process.

The most highly regarded projects in the company are not always the ones with the biggest budgets or the greatest visibility, but those that truly lived up to their predictions. Deviations from the organization's perceptions of what will be produced and how it will be delivered can therefore be an important cause of failure.

At the outset, these deviations are usually readily apparent to the discerning observer and may range from minor misinterpretations to serious misunderstandings. Present in every organizational effort are many undefined and assumed attitudes. These are the dozens of subtle nuances that float like puffs of smoke over every enterprise, often in conflicting directions and usually clouding the issues. This is because whenever there are 2 to N participants, it is likely that there will be 2 to N views of the project, and they will rarely be in agreement. These conflicting sets of ideas make

up the company's criteria for success but since it may be virtually impossible to satisfy all expectations, this kind of atmosphere wreaks havoc on any enterprise.

Aspirations for systems development are no different. Expectations may be unrealistic and unreasonable and, as usual, it is not likely that they will be in total agreement. It follows, then, that the highest success rates are achieved in endeavors where there have been a minimum number of surprises along the way.

Yet, project teams keep retreading the same treacherous paths to failure over and over again, as if they'd never taken the trip before. Traditionally, they muddle through the process, *hoping* that everyone has identical perspectives and that no conflicting opinions exist. If they encounter sensitive issues, they close their eyes, trudge on, and pray that time and short-term successes will make them go away. To the contrary, such good fortune rarely exists.

Rather than play ostrich, project teams should bring the red flag issues immediately into the open and deal with them objectively—before they become emotional hot potatoes. It is necessary to meet these controversial subjects head-on, assess the impacts to both the company and the projects, clarify the differing views, resolve the conflicts, and disseminate this information to the participants—*before* the project even gets fully underway. If the red flag issues cannot be resolved then perhaps the project should be considered for cancellation.

Managing expectations—that is the foundation of this chapter! Managers cannot control what they cannot define. And if they cannot define what the organization is expecting, then their likelihood of success is a gamble with highly uncertain odds.

14.1.3 The Corporate Culture

Not surprisingly, another cause of project failure is direct conflict between the corporate value system and the group's ability to achieve its goals. Companies that recognize the impact of these opposing forces also realize that marked improvements will be less dependent on instituting procedures than on innovative changes to the personality of the organization.

Corporate personality—the so-called *organizational culture*—is the result of subtly or directly programming people's behavior in given sets of circumstances. Long-term improvements in project success will necessitate the infusion of strong cultures into organizational objectives.

14.1.4 Insufficient Upper Management Participation

Although project teams are chartered with successful completion of the enterprise, upper managers—as important components of the organization's culture—are also key participants in affecting the final outcome. Because management attitudes determine organizational acceptance of any new program, success is directly proportional to the level of management participation and influence. They are responsible for providing the framework for harmonious implementation and for continuously and visibly demonstrating a commitment to the project and to the new system.

Without this apparent and sustained support from all of the management levels above the project leader, the opportunity to achieve total success is in jeopardy. Nevertheless, this degree of backing is not always present. Management commitment is often either limited or completely invisible.

Strategies are often agreed upon, but when the team attempts their implementation, organizational support may not be evident. Similarly, decisions that affect project success may also be made without project team representation, placing the entire effort in an untenable position and weakening all subsequent project development efforts in the company.

- If senior management lacks a clear understanding of what it takes to do a project, they may inadvertently fail to support success-oriented strategies. On the other hand, some managers profess to believe in realistic planning, but when project teams present their requirements for time, people, and costs, these managers try to condense these figures *without reducing scope and complexity of the project.*

- By the same token, while the desire for quality systems is an acknowledged goal, execution is blocked and practice is often nothing more than lip service. Given the choice between a system finished late with higher quality and one finished early with imperfections, the organization often chooses the early one. Project teams become amazed and frustrated at what seems to be an inordinate push for quick and dirty solutions, approaches that appear to demonstrate lit-

tle or no regard for quality or future maintenance costs—in spite of protestations from upper management to the contrary. Later, the high costs of operations cause the company to view the system (and sometimes the project team) with dismay, forgetting the earlier decisions, perhaps poorly made.

- In certain politically charged environments, some senior managers are unwilling to commit their support until they determine that the project will be a success—then they jump on the bandwagon, pretending they've been riding all along.

- Other times, upper management may be rigid in its refusal to add more time and resources or be flexible in their adherence to unworkable standards.

14.1.5 Sparse Middle Management Participation

Improvements to operating results and the corresponding increases in the bottom line are often limited only by the opportunities employees have for becoming involved. This ability of workers to be made available to a particular program is, in turn, proportional to the willingness of their superiors to let them actively participate. Thus, while the tone for a winning outcome is set by upper management, successful implementation of any productivity aid is also directly related to the daily support the practitioners get from their immediate supervisors.

A new corporate policy may dictate that an entire group learn modern concepts or skills, and the organization may establish elaborate goals for training and implementation. Upper management may even subscribe to and actively support the implementation of the new approach. The practitioners may be trained, but the situation may then arise in which circumstances prevent students from exercising the techniques they've learned, and implementation is again unsuccessful. Situations such as these frequently arise because of what is termed the *middle management block*, a condition in which middle managers become the obstacles to success.

The cause of this block may simply be a natural reluctance to change or an innate tendency to guard territorial rights. However, more often than not the problem occurs because middle managers have not been given the opportunity to learn what is being taught to their employees. Yet, studies have shown that a significant cause of program failure is simply because managers did not feel that they were an important part of the management team and, therefore, did little to encourage their workers to become effective members of the company team.

Often, middle managers may have been given little or no chance to understand the long-range goals of the organization. (Perhaps the company doesn't understand their objectives themselves?) Consequently, the middle managers may be unable to evaluate whether the ideas being taught to their employees will meet current objectives or support long-range goals. They may also be unaware of how new technologies can best be exploited to serve the needs of the organization.

These middle managers may have little understanding of the foundations of the new approaches and the requirements for successful implementation. Furthermore, when they have no idea of what is being taught to their employees, only halfhearted support may be given to the new methods. As a result, actual execution of the ideas and practices agreed to by upper management is often distorted or disappears entirely when passing through this barrier.

Often totally unaware that they are doing so, both upper and middle management may be sending out paradoxical messages that only serve to confuse and frustrate their employees. As an illustration, a directorate memo followed by noticeable absence from the program, or by behaviors that send contradictory and conflicting messages, will simply degrade the introduction into a meaningless exercise, leaving participants feeling frustrated and hopeless.

The bottom-line effect of the middle management block is that often there are no plans for implementing the concepts being taught. When students get back to work, they are not given the chance to apply what they've learned. This turns out to be a shameful waste of company resources.

In most situations, the biggest factor influencing operating results is what managers say and do, that is, their managerial behavior. And this is one factor over which we have the most control. Since productivity gains are maximized when students return to a working environment that encourages proper application of the concepts just learned, it is essential that middle managers prepare themselves in the subject matter being

taught to their employees. If it is believed that middle managers are too busy for training or are above the need to continue learning, management will at best suffer a loss of credibility, and at worst the implementation of the new approaches will be doomed to failure.

14.1.6 Lack of User Participation

Lack of user commitment (whether legitimate or unreasonable) leads to reduced communications, which, in turn, contributes to poor definition of requirements. This ongoing communication gap creates a never-ending adversity between users and data processing, a situation that continues to reinforce polarization, hampering productivity and draining important energy— energy that should be rechanneled and made to work productively for the corporation.

Most of us have observed that it is unusual to find a high level of success in projects where there has not been a strong driver at the wheel. Yet, more often than not this driver is required, by default, to be the DP project leader. What's worse, circumstances dictate that the only path to success is the one in which the project leader must bulldoze through the obstacles, leaving a slew of injured egos along the way. This is not a pleasant experience for the leader, nor is it profitable and beneficial for the organization.

By rights, because the system being developed is actually a product for the user, the user should be regarded as the customer. Since the customer usually pays the bill, he or she usually also calls the shots. It follows therefore that the user should be the driver, champion, or sponsor of the project. If the project is big enough, the champion should be a high-ranking individual, and he or she should be answerable to the organization for the success or failure of the project. In some companies, this success has even been made part of the sponsor's performance evaluation criteria.

Nevertheless, in some situations, it is virtually impossible to find a user champion. Lack of this kind of sponsorship leads to user apathy and certainly reduced involvement. When there is reduced involvement, there is a limited feeling of ownership of the product. When there is little or no pride of ownership of the product, user commitment to the project suffers. This comes right back to the polarization problem, and the project circles around and around in this abyss, spiraling downward, driving the probability for success farther and farther away.

14.1.7 Conflicting Organizational Objectives

Typically, company-wide commitment to a project is not thorough, clearly defined, or even understood. In general, this fact results simply from a lack of understanding of the organization—by the organization. As a result, there is inadequate priority setting as business needs shift like eddies of a stream.

- The resolution of conflicting managerial and technical goals and objectives is not usually addressed or completed. Imagine, for example, a project (1) that must be finished within six months; (2) that must be delivered with a particular technical solution; (3) that must use a selected state-of-the-art product or process that has not been perfected; and (4) for which the company has few or no resources with the technical expertise. This project has irreconcilable conflicts and may be doomed to failure before it even starts.

- Companies do too many *Number 1* priority projects. Sometimes, all projects are Number 1, with some being more Number 1 than others. The true importance of each project changes with the latest phone call or meeting. Organizations should assess the priority of each project—in relationship to all other projects and in relationship to existing business. Then, if a project slips, it slips because of the organizational prioritization—and not because of poor project management.

- Resource conflicts often dictate that the most competent participants are not appointed but are instead assigned to some other project or activity. Because of this limited resource availability, those actually assigned to the new project are often the most expendable individuals and are frequently not even wholly qualified. Yet there are often no plans to (1) formally train the new resources and (2) allow sufficient time in the project plan for these trainees to go through the required learning period. Similarly, there simply may not be enough people assigned to the project, yet early target dates are still expected.

- It has become widely accepted that systems people have very strong motivational drives, yet surprisingly high on the list of management problems are failures in personnel motivation. Crisis management that results in extended overtime and burnout, failures to reward good performance, frequent shifts in effort, and changes in scope are all demotivators and causes of high frustrations. The bottom line in this scenario is high incidence of dropouts and/or the ever-haunting adversarial stance of the participants.

- Poor matching of skills and personality characteristics to jobs, or elevating individuals to their level of incompetency can also contribute to project failure. People often wind up in the position of project manager because they want career advancement, and project management seems to be the only avenue leading to that goal. Unfortunately, while a person may be highly creative or the best technician, he or she may lack the skills necessary for effective leadership, organization, and planning.

- The impact of doing the project is not always assessed. Companies rarely determine, going into the project, if they have established an environment that will support success or if the organizational attitudes will in any way obstruct a satisfactory outcome. Moreover, the impact of doing the project *and* delivering the system is not always assessed. If conflicting priorities are frequently encountered, a project can be very late. In order to allow the group to correctly assess the causes of delay, it is essential to rank and prioritize the project in relationship to other projects and to existing business. Conscious choices may then be exercised if conflicts occur. Later, when the contentions negatively impact completion, causing due dates to be missed, participants must then acknowledge that tardiness is due to poor organizational choice rather than poor project management.

- The impact of delivering the product is not always assessed either. Users' concerns are often overlooked, and, consequently, they may unwittingly (or even surreptitiously) sabotage the project because they feel threatened.

Many organizations simply spread themselves too thin in their project implementation efforts. Frequently, companies attempt to do too many projects and wind up completing them all poorly rather than limiting their efforts to a finite number of projects that can be finished successfully. The pity is that this is not usually a conscious business decision on their part. It is rather a default process that results from lack of proper planning and prioritizing of organizational objectives.

14.1.8 Poor Project Management

Why are organizations so poor at project management? They are not new to the arena. Certainly some of them have learned their lessons well. What has happened to all the successful project managers that they have thus far produced?

In many companies, the experienced and proven planners get elevated to higher positions of responsibility while the organization is often left struggling with inexperienced leadership, a situation that often effects project success. Assigning a novice or intermediate as project manager is certainly a legitimate business decision. However, many times this occurs without the group fully considering the risks and tradeoffs.

For one thing, the individual may not fully understand his or her position in the process or what expectations are reasonable. Often, an inexperienced manager may intuitively know the project is a high risk, but may lack the confidence or credibility to convince upper management. Other times, an extended project may have replacements (for example, because of a change in the management structure or because the predecessor has failed). The new manager may naively believe that he or she can succeed where others have labored in vain.

A poor project manager may assign the wrong people (or combinations thereof) to the wrong jobs. He or she may have difficulty delegating work or monitoring progress, which sometimes results in task overlaps, duplication of effort in some areas, and lack of effort in others.

Project managers are required to deliver successful projects, but often have no control over the environment that affects the Project Development Process. They are required to *answer* for the success of the project, but are rarely given the *authority* over all of the participants who have a role in getting the job done.

Orr once told me that he compares the project manager's job to that of the manager of the deck chairs on the *Titanic*: "the person responsible for making everybody comfortable while the ship is going down."

Organizations that place inexperienced personnel in positions of project management should also specify that their long-range goals are to build project management expertise and that, in the interim, they are willing to accept the inevitable mistakes and overruns that may occur while novices are developing their skills.

- The problems resulting from inexperience could be overcome with the proper training programs but, sadly, until recently, the infatuation with keeping current in the technical arenas has overshadowed the less exotic studies in management. Fortunately, the tide has been turning, and the industry is slowly conquering this deficiency.

- For years, the only tools available to project managers were pencil and paper. Later, in the development stage, several methodologies appeared in the marketplace. Nevertheless, while it may be difficult to develop systems without them, methodologies alone were not a panacea.

- Now, the number of automated project management products is on the rise. While several are very, very good, many practitioners are still unhappy. Sometimes, people are disillusioned with the project management tools because they want one tool that is all things to all people. Furthermore, many people want the tool to do their thinking for them. It is not likely that either of these requirements will be met in the immediate future.

Meaningful increases in project management productivity will only be realized when people accept the need to use *all* of the tools at their disposal—*plus their minds*.

14.1.9 Poor Planning and Control

Projects without a formal written plan lead to lost time, misdirected effort, unproductive labor, and squandered dollars. Thus, it is surprising that more companies (1) do not know that a key to successful projects is proper planning and (2) have not implemented formal planning methods. As a result, their experiences in attempting to control projects have been dismal.

- Because there is a generally inadequate understanding of the planning and estimating process, objectives have not been identified, techniques have been poorly developed or non-existent, and tasks have been inadequately defined.

- Some administrators believe that planning *takes time away from producing real product deliverables*, and, therefore, it is *not real work*. These people believe that planning is a nonproductive effort. Because of this limited management commitment for the time and people necessary to produce a viable plan, there is no firm basis for negotiating. Unreasonable budgets and schedules may then be imposed by management, which (1) results in unrealistic and optimistic targets and (2) leads to inevitable overruns and performance compromises.

- Experienced and successful planners get elevated to positions of greater responsibility, and the people subsequently responsible for the planning effort are new to the experience. They lack the knowledge of proper planning methods and the confidence to insist on adherence to the techniques. Unnecessary jobs get assigned; important jobs get overlooked; jobs are done wrong; people are not sure of what to do or when to do it; and assignments overlap. Lateness is combatted with too much overtime and added manpower. The results are poor quality systems and personnel burnout.

- Status is poorly reported because it is difficult to determine when a particular milestone has been attained. Projects rapidly reach the 90 percent complete level; yet, the remaining 10 percent of the project often consumes another 90 percent of the budget. Since quality is not regarded as a criteria for completeness, quantity of deliverables finished is used as an indicator of status, and it is not until the end of the project that the team finds out that the system doesn't work.

The most pernicious effect of poor planning and control is a false sense of accomplishment, which leads the organization to believe that the project is on time when, in reality, *it is out of control before it even starts!*

14.1.10 Poor Software Development Techniques

The traditional approaches to systems software development have poor track records on all but the most trivial projects. Project teams have failed in analysis, design, programming, testing, training, documentation, and so on.

- Analysis, the process of clearly stating the problem to be solved, is the hardest job there is to do! Poor systems analysis leads to confusion as to what the needs really are, user unwillingness to participate, and misunderstandings that result in systems that solve the wrong problems. Poorly defined requirements negate opportunities for successful management of change. Lack of change policy leads to an ever-expanding scope and the inevitable illusive completion date.

- When there are limited design and programming standards, ad hoc techniques lead to solutions that are technically unsound or unnecessarily complex, decisions that are rarely objective, and no firm basis for evaluating hardware/software tradeoffs. Programmers spend the majority of their time fixing errors, most of which are carried over from poor analysis and design.

- Experiences in traditional systems development have proven that testing and debugging take a long time —perhaps as much as 50 percent of the total effort. Therefore, participants rushed through the early phases in order to insure that they had enough time for testing. Closer examination reveals, however, that most of the work being performed during testing is *analysis* of the problem and its solution and *design* and *programming* of the correction. Boehm[1] says that fixing errors during testing can be 20 to 50 times more costly than the same corrections made during analysis. Given that this is true, it is surprising that more organizations don't front-load the effort into

---

[1]Boehm, Op. cit.

analysis and design—doing this work when it actually costs less.

- New state-of-the-art solutions often introduce an added level of technical complexity. As a result, a corresponding level of technical expertise is required, expertise that the project participants may lack. Education and learning periods that allow for the development of these skills are often not factored into the schedule.

- Often hidden costs of systems, maintenance factors cannot be ignored. Boehm[2] reports that maintenance could account for 60 to 75 percent of the cost of a system over its useful life. This means that a system that cost $1 million to develop could have a total cost of $2.5 to $4 million. Lientz and Swanson[3] also reported that maintenance equates to 47 to 53 percent of the total costs of systems, indicating that systems really cost twice as much as people believe.

14.1.11 Inadequate Training Strategies

Surveys of managers often reveal that, in general, training is not considered that important in their organizations. At the same time, however, these very managers have complained that they were also unhappy because their employees have some basic gaps in determining how new technologies and management concepts could increase productivity.

It is unclear how the employees could have been expected to improve their skills when they were unable to ascertain what was expected of them, when they were not given the opportunity to learn the skills that would enable them to satisfy corporate requirements, and when they were not given the chance to go through the learning periods necessary to refine their expertise.

Effective training programs have been linked to better performance and enhanced productivity. Specialists in operations management agree that vocational grooming of the staff is clearly one of the highest leverage functions in which an organization can invest.

Yet, a good understanding and appreciation of the training function is hard to find. It is difficult to

grasp why, when there is such an overwhelming national concern about increasing output, companies fail to use the training process to achieve their objectives.

Many organizations will staunchly defend their training functions and are offended when they are classified as being in the educational Dark Ages. Those that think they are enlightened will point out the number of classes whose training objectives they believe were clearly satisfied. They will produce the rating statistics that unequivocally prove that the classes were successful.

Management will declare that they endorse the idea that the seminars their employees attend are meant to improve the skills of the students and are not just a cover for vacations, a way to break the monotony of routine, or simply a way to substantiate that overall training requirements are being met. They will insist that training programs increase both individual skills and company productivity.

Similarly, most attendees at training seminars regard the opportunity as a genuine employment "perk," not just a break. They recognize that continued education is one road to career advancement. As a matter of fact, many employees are so conscientious that they will only agree to leave the job to attend those classes that they believe will actually help them in their work. Seminar students are usually eager and optimistic, and this attitude is frequently complemented by the enthusiasm of the instructor.

But then something goes awry. Disillusionment sets in—either during the learning session or later on the job. Employees up and down the organization convey feelings of extreme frustration and exasperation. For example, students demonstrate their skepticism in the classroom by asking: "Why are we learning these concepts when it is unlikely that they will really be implemented in our organization?"; "Since *we* can't make any decisions about implementing these procedures, why aren't our managers here to hear this?"; and "Why is there never enough time to do it right, but there is always time to do it over?"

A continuous, voluntary, and tailored training program that is flexible enough to meet both the technical and managerial needs of the organization should be developed. As the company acquires new pieces of equipment, implements new technologies or software, and institutes new management philosophies, related training modules should be provided for employees.

---

[2]Ibid.

[3]B.P. Lientz and E.B. Swanson, *Software Maintenance Management*, (Reading, Mass.; Addison-Wesley, 1980).

A *finite and manageable* number of training programs—ones that support organizational objectives—should be selected. (It is better to introduce 5 new programs effectively than 15 poorly.)

Each new approach should be introduced with a three-tier training program:

- A high level overview to get the senior management endorsement;
- A more detailed introduction to insure the middle management *buy in*; and
- An intensive skills-building workshop for practitioners.

While these seminars are certainly an essential part of the process, training classes by themselves are not enough. The ideal implementation package should be completed by instituting a follow-up program that is presented by the same group that teaches the classes and is directed to the teams who are using the new methods. This program should include review workshops and clinics, drop-in consulting, and teleconferencing.

Figure 14.1 Organizational culture and project failure.

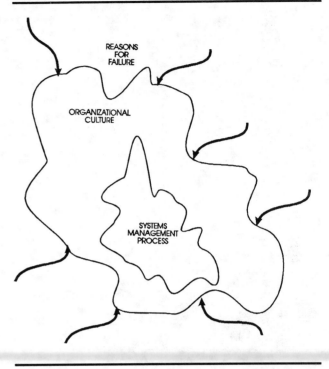

14.2 THE ORGANIZATIONAL CULTURE

Overcoming these contributors to failure, not surprisingly, requires redefining the organizational culture, usually an amorphous and undefined form. The Systems Management Process (similarly an amorphous and undefined form) falls into the organizational culture. And it is the organizational culture upon which all of the agents for failure act. (Figure 14.1)

No wonder projects fail! Obviously, the Systems Management Process needs to be clearly explained. Not surprisingly, groups search for quick and simple ways to attain this objective. They want to treat the process as a cookbook issue, one that should lead to the discovery of step-by-step procedures that are easily implemented. The problem is often solved by adapting mechanical methods such as definitions of the phases, identification of jobs to be done, estimates of durations, procedures for status reporting, etc.

But, will that alone suffice? Probably not. This sort of approach inevitably leads to disappointing results because long-term improvements are less dependent on mechanical procedures than they are on

innovative changes to the personality of the organization. Although a crystallization of the Systems Management Process will certainly represent a marked improvement in many companies, concentrating in that one area alone and ignoring the organizational culture simply maintains the current barriers to success. Participants will continue to butt heads while attempting to complete the endeavor in an undefined culture.

When the emphasis is on overcoming the poor management of organizational expectations, the impact of the other causes of failure can be significantly reduced (and in some cases, completely eliminated). In other words, success is facilitated when organizations (1) pause to crystallize their goals and objectives, (2) consider the alternatives, (3) assess the tradeoffs, and (4) make conscious and informed choices. Referred to as *pro-active* management (acting on the environment) rather than *reactive* management (reacting to the environment), this approach has been employed successfully in other business arenas and can be of great benefit in helping to defeat those inhibitors to project success.

CHAPTER **15** **HOW TO PICK SOFTWARE PACKAGES**

15.1 INTRODUCTION

In the past, when considering a software acquisition, organizations frequently started the process by searching industry directories, journals, and periodicals—in order to find vendors who marketed products that seemed to answer their requirements. After evaluating sales presentations and vendor-supplied literature, they chose the product that seemed to come closest to fulfilling their needs. Then, more often than people would care to admit, they spent many months and workers trying to "fix" the product to work in their environment. Sometimes they even had to modify the business policies of the organization to fit the software package. This unhappy state of affairs needn't have been: the group should have first defined what project management meant to them *before* they chose the software they wanted to purchase.

In order to do this, each organization must decide what facets of the project management conceptual requirements they want to implement in their organizations. They need to broadcast and standardize these concepts across the organization, making them part of the corporate culture. Of course, these concepts need to be visibly and demonstrably supported by upper management. Then, and only then, can the group proceed to identify the software that has the features that will support the chosen concepts.

15.2 OBJECTIVE DECISION MAKING

Sometimes, people feel good merely by making a purchase. But the choices made today so greatly influence the future, sometimes for a very long time. Thus, it is often wise to slow down the rush to spend the money and to make sure that the wisest selection is made.

This decision-making process should involve all affected levels of the organization. There is more sharing of relevant information; the impacts of choices are more quickly recognized; and differing positions may be more easily reconciled. In selecting the software, the emotionalism and subjectivity should be extricated from the process. This exercise may be completed with participation from a software selection committee, perhaps consisting of seniors and managers from DP and the systems users group, the potential users of the software, the technical staff, and the finance and legal staffs. In this manner, the broad representation introduces a degree of objectivity into the choice of values and into the final selection of software.

In selecting *project management* software packages, the group is working with complex systems, often with exceedingly large numbers of capabilities and attributes, and with an increasing number of variables. The question is: how can the process be executed effectively: (1) using the information currently available; (2) providing consistency and standardization in the approach; (3) insuring that the group hasn't overlooked any crucial factors; and (4) preventing the participants from getting overwhelmed with insignificant details? Since it is easy to exceed the human conceptual counting limit, there needs to be some systematic method for evaluating the many judgments that must be made. Breaking the decision-making process into definition, evaluation, and selection follows the principle of partitioning to gain better control of the process.

15.3 DEFINING THE DESIRED FEATURES AND THEIR VALUE TO THE ORGANIZATION

Having chosen the conceptual project management requirements that the organization wants to implement, the next step is to find a software package that supports these requirements. The deliverable from this step should be a Software Selection Specification that outlines the requirements. Weighted sum techniques provide a fairly good approach to developing these documents and solving these sorts of problems. They have been described by Kepner and Tregoe in 1965 (decision analysis)[1]; and Boehm in 1981 (weighted sum analysis)[2]. Using this approach allows practitioners to further partition the technique into two activities: (1) Listing the evaluation criteria; and (2) Prioritizing the criteria. It is advisable that this exercise be completed with participation from the software selection committee described in the previous section. Several iterations of interviewing and revising may be required until final agreements for each part of the specification are reached.

15.4 LIST THE EVALUATION CRITERIA

At the outset, it may be difficult to see any marked advantage of one product over another. The goal is to evaluate the products in detail on how they excel at supporting the feature and also how they compare relative to one another. The first job that needs doing is the listing of the criteria to be used for evaluation. Table 15.1 lists the possibilities for project management software evaluation and Table 15.2 provides the common criteria for vendors.

Before proceeding, however, the following examples in Figure 15.1 may be used to demonstrate how to further distinguish the criteria from Table 15.2, numbers 2 and 16. In other words, it is possible to build as much detail into the evaluation criteria as the team desires.

15.5 BUILDING THE EVALUATION MATRIX

Using the evaluation criteria shown in Tables 15.1 and 15.2, it is possible to develop a matrix that will allow users to weight and note the criteria. The level of complexity can vary. It must be consistent for each product, and the weights given each feature and criteria must be carefully considered. As an example, the categories may be weighted according to the project's *Needs*, *Wants*, or *Wishes*:

- Needs are the criteria that are mandatory, absolutely must be fulfilled to guarantee success and cannot be omitted.

- Wants are the highly desirable criteria where fulfillment is dearly preferred.

- Wishes are the criteria that are often viewed as pie-in-the-sky or the gingerbread.

After the required software features and their value to the organization have been agreed upon, the group must then use this data to compare against each of the alternatives. It is necessary, now, to evaluate the products in detail on how they excel at supporting the feature and also how they compare relative to one another. Three steps may be carried out: (1) it is possible to request the vendors to provide information about their products; (2) it is necessary to evaluate the products; and (3) it is necessary to assess the risks associated with the choice.

15.5.1 Requiring Vendor Proposals

After the criteria have been approved, the evaluation team may start negotiations with vendors. Suitable vendors are those that the organization currently does business with or those that can be found in industry directories, bulletins from research firms, and hardware and software periodicals.

The evaluation may be completed unilaterally, that is, by the group that is planning the software purchase with no input from the vendor. They simply

[1]C.H. Kepner and B.B. Tregoe, *The New Rational Manager* (London: John Martin Publishing, Ltd., 1981).
[2]Op. cit.

Table 15.1 Project management software features.

Products With More Than One Graphic Data Entry Mode	Moving Jobs In The Network
Gantt-driven Products	Removing Dependencies
Network-driven Products	Deleting Jobs In The Plan
Full-screen, Forms-driven Products	Lag And Lead Times
Size And Storage Constraints	Copying Jobs In The Plan
System Structure	Copying The Template Jobs
Global Defaults	Loops In The Network
Adding New Projects	Dangling Jobs
Accessing Plan Data	Verifying Dependencies Are Correct
Immediate Processor Or Batch	Highlighting Dependency Paths
Adding Plan Data	Network Aesthetics
Optional What-ifs Or Permanent Saves	Scaled To Time?
Storing Ad Hoc Information	Networks And Workbreakdown Structures
Exporting Data	Limiting Relationships To The Lowest Level
Products With Shared Data Agreements	Setting Up Hammocks
Graphics Support	Dependencies In A Multiproject Environment
Level Support	Printing And Viewing Networks
Data Entry Requirements	Calendars
Durations And Dependencies	Choosing The Correct Project Start Date
Random Sequence Of Data Entry	Insuring That The Plan Is Not Constrained By Resources
Using The Copy Features With The Template Tasks	Avoiding Imposed Target Dates
Rollup Support	Calculating The Schedule
Estimating Support And Estimating Guidelines	Zero Duration Milestones
Estimates Of True Work Effort Versus Resource-driven Elapsed Time	Verifying Schedules With Units Of Measurement Less Than One Day
Durations And Units Of Measurement	Retaining A Baseline Record Of The Optimal Plan
Zero Duration Milestones	Interpreting The Dates On The Screen
Lead And Lag Times With Duration But No Effort	Annotating The Critical Path
Types Of Networks	Verifying Lag And Lead Time
Types Of Relationships	Gantt Chart Time Periods
Number Of Dependencies	Scheduling In The Multiproject Environment
Establishing Dependencies	Nesting Subprojects In A Multiproject Environment
Special Considerations For Multiple Relationships	Subprojects And Their Dates

Table 15.1 (Continued)

How Easy Is It To Enter Dependencies?

Inserting Jobs Into The Middle Of The Plan

Subnetwork Dependencies

Creating The Resource Calendars

Creating The Resource Pool

Assigning Part-time Resources At The Project Level

Deleting And Changing Resources At The Project Level

Matching Resources To Jobs

Assigning Part-time Resources At The Task Or Activity Level

Assigning Multiple Resources To A Job

What To Do When The Resource Effort Must Be Less Than The Elapsed Calendar Days

Fixed Dates For Activities Or Tasks

Special Leveling Patterns

Automatic Resource Leveling

Setting Special Leveling Priorities On Tasks Or Activities

User-driven Interactive Leveling

Baseline Project Plans For Resource Leveling

Resources And Multiprojects

Costs

Costs In A Multiproject Environment

Time-constrained Plans

The Assignment Report

The Ad Hoc Information

The Work Package Cover Sheet

The Responsibility Grid

The Supporting Documentation

The Problem Log

The Work Notes Form

Products That Support The Statistical Approach

Using The New Reasonable Late Finish Date Of The Project

Viewing The Status Data On The Screen

Baselines

Frequency Of Reporting

Extracting The Jobs For The Turn-around Document—on A Range Of Dates

Setting Up An As-of Date

Entering Percent Complete

Hard Copy Turn-around Documents

Entering The Status Collection Data

Performance Status Reporting

Highlighting Progress

Percentages And Their Effects On Costs

Cost Status Reporting

Earned Values

Costs In A Multiproject Environment

Reporting On Resource Availability

Reporting On Resource Utilization

Earned Value Productivity Reporting

Who Produces Perts And Gantts That May Be Restricted To Critical Path Jobs?

Who Produces Reports That May Be Restricted To Fixed Date Jobs?

Who Produces Perts And Gantts That May Be Restricted To Summary Jobs?

Local Area Networks

Guidelines For Tracking And Managing The Project

Guidelines And Documentation

Miscellaneous Features

Table 15.2 Vendor evaluation criteria.

1. Main business of vendor.

2. Years vendor in business.

3. Private or public company.

4. Financial stability and solvency.

5. Prior experiences with vendor.

6. Purpose for which product was originally developed; period product has been available; its current operational status.

7. Package customer base: first installation and its current status; vendor market share; current number of customers.

8. Delivery statistics.

9. Positive (and negative) references from other customers; (e.g., reports on responsiveness of customer service (hotline) department; ease of getting into the hotline as well as hotline response; hours of hotline availability; knowledge level of hotline representatives; duration of product use; fulfillment of expectations; status of documentation; number of delays; number of errors; vendor assessment (see # 13); recognized need for product improvement; overall performance and throughput levels).

10. State-of-the-art status and forecasted obsolescence.

11. Anticipated extensions to product line and implications of their procurement.

12. Reports from user groups: level of intelligence interchange, extent of vendor's influence, level of vendor's responsiveness.

13. Vendor assessment: instruction, machine time, staffing, conversion support, proximity of vendor service to customer.

14. Documentation requirements (e.g., caliber, clarity, readability, user friendliness, and value/completeness of the index).

15. Implementation requirements.
   ° Limitations on customer staffing levels required to support the product.
   ° Interface requirements for existing systems and procedures and for the product (software or hardware) and production libraries.
   ° Backup and recovery contingencies.

Table 15.2 (Continued)

° Startup and shutdown requirements.
° Performance requirements.
° Benchmark requirements.
° Limitations on changes in procedures, forms, etc.
° Requirements for ease of conversion.
° Factors governing ease of installation.
° Delivery lead time.

16. Procurement Arrangements.
° Sale or lease.
° Price structures: ranges of acceptable costs, what is and is not included in the price (e.g., number of manuals, number of training days or classes, number of your personnel to be trained and number of their support people, percentage of time from their support people, expected response time to service requests, expected fix time), costs for multiple installations.
° Maintenance agreements: maintenance policy, preventative maintenance and warranty requirements (e.g., length, costs, and vendor position regarding modifications); customer requirements for ease and flexibility of modifications and maintenance; duration of maintenance period for (1) duration of contract as well as (2) daily field engineering normal and emergency support service hours; quantity and frequency of maintenance, releases, and other types of vendor support (e.g., initial and ongoing training support for users and technical personnel, trial period before acceptance and recourse if product doesn't pass customer acceptance testing, conversion support, vendor newsletter, users group, trouble reporting procedures, and diagnostic aids); durations of time between releases and vendor policy on mandatory installation of releases.
° Customer requirements for vendor on-site technical assistance, technical qualifications for vendor support personnel, cost limitations for additional assistance.
° Clarification of marketing and earnings rights when customer makes substantial modifications to improve the product (especially pertinent in applications packages).
° Costs incurred by customer to modify product, interfacing systems and procedures, training personnel, converting files, installing and acceptance-testing the product, operating production, and maintaining the product.

do the best job they can interpreting the vendor-supplied promotion material.

On the other hand, it may be possible to complete the evaluation bilaterally, asking the vendor to respond, *in writing*: where their product meets the requirements, where it does not meet the requirements, whether they will modify the product to match the requirements, and how they propose to make these modifications (including the number and qualifications of their resources who will be assigned, target dates and compensation agreements should they miss the target date and/or fail to deliver the promised product). Vendors may also be advised that their written responses will later serve as an addendum to the contract.

Figure 15.1 Expanding vendor detail.

PRICE STRUCTURES
    Ranges of acceptable costs
        $ 300 to $1,000
        $1,001 to $2,500
        $2,501 to $5,000

YEARS VENDOR IN BUSINESS
    Ranges
        2 to 5 years
        6 to 10 years
        11 to 20 years

15.5.2 Evaluating the Responses

When all of the vendor responses have been completed and/or returned, the evaluation team first screens all vendors by eliminating those that do not meet all of the Needs criteria. If a preferred vendor is eliminated at this stage, and the team chooses to retain the vendor for further consideration, the negating item may be changed to the Wants category and *all* vendors reassessed accordingly.

15.5.3 Evaluating the Risks

This is probably the most difficult part of the selection process. Before the final choice can be made, the team might consider the negative consequences of each choice, stretching their imaginations to discover what important factors might have been missed.[3] Risk analysis is also very helpful in breaking ties. Even when the scores are not close, the evaluators may determine a confidence interval and subject all of the products that fall within that range to risk analysis.

In this step, the evaluation team tries to *disqualify* the best alternatives one at a time. The purpose is to assume negative and pessimistic postures and examine

---

[3]Later, after the product has been in use for a year or more, few people will regret the time that was invested earlier in making the decision—providing the right choice was made. Compared to the stress involved in contending with an inappropriate product, the effort that is expended in probing for risks during the decision analysis is minimal.

each tentative choice for probabilities of failure, potential problems, or invalid assumptions that were made during the evaluation process. Because of natural optimism and the psychological commitment to the choices that have survived the evaluation of available alternatives, people are normally attracted toward setting aside and overlooking their negative feelings and instincts. *CAUTION!* This tendency is actually against the tenets of Objective Decision Making: the right choice is the one that will work and can only be made considering *all* of the relevant information—positive *and* negative. Disregarding facts that make an ultimate choice unworkable is diametrically opposed to reaching the goal.

15.5.4 Risk Analysis

Risk analysis is a process that uses probabilities to help rank projects. Assigning a value to the probability that an event will occur can be as simple as making a subjective guess or as complex as employing mathematical probability theory. If a subjective guess is made, the probability that an event will occur can be rated, for example, on a scale of 1 to 10, with 10 being the highest likelihood. Users who are well versed in mathematics may find instruction for determining numerical probabilities in statistics books as well as in texts on operation research.

Each product is considered separately, as a unique strategy. To do a risk analysis on a group of strategies, each strategy is initially evaluated *by itself*.

For each strategy, the group "invents" a set of events that represent the *worst* scenarios that could occur during the project. Each of these scenarios is then also treated separately, and the group assigns (1) a number that represents the probability that the event will occur and (2) the seriousness of the situation should the event really come to fruition. These two numbers are *multiplied* by each other. The results for each scenario in the strategy are then added together. Finally, the strategies are compared, with the lowest totals getting the highest consideration. (See Table 15.3.)

15.6 COMPLETING THE SELECTION

Once a choice has been made, the contract must be negotiated. These written instruments are usually preprinted affairs and may vary only slightly from vendor

Table 15.3 Risk Analysis

	PROBABILITY	SERIOUS	RESULT
PROJECT 1 STRATEGY 1			
SCENARIO 1	8	4	32
SCENARIO 2	5	8	40
SCENARIO 3	7	6	42
SCENARIO 4	8	7	56
TOTAL			170

to vendor. However, negotiations usually lead to agreements that were not stipulated in the document. When this occurs, the cases in point should be written into the contract. There is no substitute for a vehicle that clearly establishes the requirements, responsibilities, and obligations of both the vendor and the purchaser, stating exactly what will happen in case of breach of promise by either party.

Since no contract should be completed without the direction of the organization's legal department, this section is not intended as an advisory for legal negotiations. Expertise in contract law is thus not a discipline that should be required of project members. However, the entire process may be facilitated if the participants have some awareness of the problems involved, since they can often help the lawyers on certain key issues. Consequently, as partners in the contracting process, the evaluation team should be cognizant of the obvious pitfalls: they should involve the legal staff from the very beginning, document all verbal agreements, and make sure that the contract specifies everything that the organization expects to get.

The Software Selection Specification and the vendor's written responses may be included in the contract as an addendum.

It is important to stipulate expectations for: the basic requirements, performance levels, training, and documentation; delivery dates; and version or release levels. Contracts often focus on considerations of the worst case; therefore, ample emphasis should be placed on penalties and/or remedies for: late delivery; substandard performance, quality, and reliability; delayed repairs; failure to meet acceptance criteria; payment schedules; and contract termination criteria. Provisions should also be made for business shutdown of the vendor, reassignment of the vendor's vital personnel, and responsibility for performance of specific tasks. If it is pertinent, it is also necessary to define emergency and normal field maintenance and preventative maintenance in terms of responsibility, hours, promptness of response to requests, and compensation for nonfulfillment. Additionally, it is important to specify who may (should) make improvements to the product, how quickly they should be completed, and how this affects the warranty.

Thorough procedures and test cases for benchmarks should be specified to insure that the installation has been successful. The product should not be accepted until it demonstrates that it can operate at peak efficiency and provide error-free results for a specified period of time. Provisions should be made regarding refund of any earlier monetary deposits should the product fail to perform according to specifications within the selected time period.

15.7 POTENTIAL PROBLEMS WITH THE EVALUATION PROCESS

Boehm[4] talks about a company that selected a piece of hardware based on the highest score in a weighted sum evaluation, only to discover some months later that the product's operating system was plagued by serious overhead problems. Even when the team reassessed the product and gave the operating system a zero rating, the product still ended with the highest score. When this scenario occurs, the cause can sometimes be traced to the wrong factors and weights being used. To solve this problem, the team should develop a more representative set of factors, ratings, and weights.

---

[4]Op. cit.

If faster response time was such a critical consideration, it should have been given more importance in the ranking and weighting. Those products with serious deficiencies could have been given negative evaluations, which in essence would have reduced their bottom line total.

On the other hand, if the analysis doesn't yield *any* good alternatives, the evaluation team should consider the possibility that the objectives are unrealistic and that no product can fulfill them. It is also possible that too many unimportant details are obscuring the process. The software selection committee must then reassess their objectives, making them clearer and more realistic.

At another extreme, if all of the products being evaluated perform equally well on all points, it is entirely possible that the criteria were too loosely stated or that the team had a faulty perception of what is required for success. The software selection committee must simply go back to the list of objectives and make them tighter, more demanding, and more numerous.

Although the values ideally reflect the objective consensus of an experienced managerial staff, the political environment may sometimes affect the outcome of the criteria. Certain special interest groups or influential individuals with vested concerns may govern the factors used for the criteria, ratings and weightings. Requiring that the participation group clarify the rationale behind their choices will, to some extent, balance the subjectivity involved and the temptation to "fix" the scale, but objectivity may sometimes be sacrificed to the lobbyists. Loading the evaluation to guarantee the smooth passage of a certain choice of vendor or product makes a sham of the entire process.

From another point of view, unless there is a standardized approach to assigning values, a whole range of unrelated scores may result, making subsequent analysis of the findings practically impossible. Maintaining a consistent scale may be achieved if the software selection committee initially chooses and adheres to the range. Adjectives such as *none, poor, modest, marginal, adequate, moderate, good, very good,* and *outstanding* may be assigned numeric values and the scale used consistently by all of the participants. However, the sensitivity of the individual as to what constitutes the definition of good, outstanding, etc., can again be subjective and may vary from person to person. Sometimes from one user group to another

there is even an honest difference of opinion about the level of importance that is to be assigned to a feature. When this occurs, it may be necessary to evolve some system of weighting the users themselves.

Finally, the assumptions used in preparing the evaluations are only as good as the knowledge and realistic attitudes of the participants. Any outcome can be suspect and should be taken into consideration when evaluating the risks as defined earlier in this chapter.

15.8 FACING REALITY

Initially, judicious postponement of the work involved in evaluating and selecting software until the completion of the Software Selection Specification was stressed. In practice, it is often the case that certain related work can begin in the earlier phases.

15.8.1 Analysis Activities

During the study of the features requirements, the analysts may be collecting information on software packages, and the technicians may be collecting information on hardware. Both groups will weed out unqualified vendors and/or products. Discipline must be exercised at this point not to submit to vendor pressures (or any other subtle marketing strategies) aimed at consummating the sale.

The analysts, knowing about new software ideas, can introduce these concepts to the study of the new requirements. Care must be taken, however, not to introduce bias into the study.

The technicians study the hardware and may introduce new ideas about hardware features, again taking care not to bias the outcome.

15.8.2 Decision-Making Activities

The software selection committee may begin to identify the criteria, weights, and ratings. The Software Selection Specification is approved. The vendors (products) are evaluated, and the approved selections and contracts are then recorded.

As a last note, it is important that the project team be sure to include in the project plan those tasks that represent the lead times for delivery of the selected product(s), time for any installation activities such as benchmarks and acceptance testing, and, finally, power-up time for each of the users.

15.9 IN CONCLUSION

In the final analysis, several months may be devoted to a detailed study of each vendor offering, concluding with extended testing on each product before acceptance.

Software packages are important because they provide an economical way of obtaining useful functions. When an organization does not have the technical expertise, time, or budget for in-house development, the purchase offers a means of sharing the development costs with other buyers, thus diluting the expenditure. Unfortunately, this approach has presented some major problems to customers. Packages are developed for the mass market and it is rare that a generic approach will work in all companies in all applications. As a result, the organization may need to expend time, money, and resources to modify the product to work in their environment, *or* modify their policies to do business the way the product does. Sometimes, the package winds up sitting unused on a shelf, negating the considerable time and money spent in its procurement. On the other hand, custom development of a project management software package from the ground up may be viewed as an expensive and risky undertaking, especially when considering the required applications expertise and the number of project starts that ultimately fail in spite of the applications expertise.

This approach does not guarantee to eliminate all of the problems associated with software procurement. However, it does insure that surprises and delayed implementations will be reduced and that changes to the business operations or the product will only be made as a result of a conscious choice on the part of management and the rest of the organization.

CHAPTER **16** **PROJECT MANAGEMENT SOFTWARE**

16.1 PROJECT MANAGEMENT SOFTWARE PACKAGES

The following packages will be evaluated:

Table 16.1 The Products

HARVARD PROJECT MANAGER 3.0
Software Publishing Corporation
P.O. Box 7210
1901 Landings Drive
Mountain View, CA 94039
Price: $695

MICROSOFT PROJECT 4.0
Microsoft Corporation
P.O. Box 97017
16011 N.E. 36th Way
Redmond, WA 98073
Price: $495

PROJECT WORKBENCH 3.0
Applied Business Technology Corporation
361 Broadway
New York, NY 10013
Price: $1,275

VIEWPOINT 2.52
Computer Aided Management
1318 Redwood Way Suite 210
Petaluma, CA 94952
Price: $1,995

PRIMAVERA PROJECT PLANNER 3.1 and PRIMAVISION
Primavera Systems
2 Bala Plaza
Bala Cynwyd, PA 19004
Price: $2,500, PRIMAVERA PROJECT PLANNER
          $1,500, PRIMAVISION

SUPERPROJECT EXPERT 1.1
Computer Associates International, Inc.
Micro Products Division
2195 Fortune Drive
San Jose, CA 95131
Price: $695

TIME LINE 3.0 and TIME LINE GRAPHICS
Symantec Corporation
10201 Torre Avenue
Cupertino, CA 95014
Price $595, TIME LINE 3.0
          $195, TIME LINE GRAPHICS

16.2 PRODUCT GROUPINGS BY DATA ENTRY MODE

The products have been grouped according to the manner in which project data is entered into the system. For example, some products are Gantt driven, others are network-driven, and still others are full-screen forms driven. This introductory classification does not endure throughout the appendices that describe each package, however. As each software feature is evaluated, the products will be regrouped according to the manner in which they support that feature. The heading of each section is keyed to the chapter and section number where the respective discussion will be found.

16.2.1 Products with More than One Graphic Data Entry Mode ◆

Many of the products evaluated allow the user to choose from more than one type of graphic data entry mode. However, some of them are more Gantt driven than network driven, or vice versa. These products will be classified separately. On the other hand, in that they are not clearly identifiable as Gantt-driven, network-driven, etc.[1], SuperProject Expert and Harvard Project Manager 3.0 are grouped in this category.

16.2.2 Gantt Driven Products ◆

Although they support data entry in more than one graphic mode, Project Workbench, Time Line 3.0, and Microsoft Project are primarily Gantt driven products.

16.2.3 Network Driven Products ◆

Viewpoint is primarily driven by network graphics.

16.2.4 Full-Screen, Forms-Driven Products ◆

Primavera Project Planner is a forms-driven product.

16.3 PRODUCT FEATURES

When trying to evaluate project management software, it's not easy to devise a scheme that will satisfy everyone's needs. Should the packages be grouped by price? Or should they be categorized by functionality? On the other hand, some users believe that processing speed is the most important criteria.

16.3.1 Size and Storage Constraints ◆

Perhaps the systems should be classified according to the project sizes they support. Some products operate on project data when it has been loaded into main memory. Therefore, the project size (allowing for the memory consumed by the operating system, other memory resident programs, and the product software itself) is affected by the total main memory size of the computer in which the software resides.

These *main memory dependent* products appear to be further subdivided into two groups. In the first group, the record size per job is fixed. Thus, in these products, each job provides for a predesignated number of resources and dependencies. The total number of jobs in the *fixed-length* products is limited, as just described, by the remaining main memory and is usually a constant number.

Other main memory dependent products support *variable-length* job records, where the length of each record is determined by the number of resources and relationships attached to it—the more resources and/or dependencies, the longer the record. In these products, the total number of jobs per plan is directly related to the sum of the basic memory storage requirements per job times the total number of jobs plus the memory requirements for each of the respective resources and dependencies. The more resources and dependencies there are, the fewer total number of jobs per plan.

Limitations in size may be overcome by breaking the project into several subprojects, storing them on the hard disks, and only loading the necessary data into main memory. *This is not viewed as a detractor, since it often follows the Moving Window concept, anyway!* Each subproject may represent a different phase (or group of phases) of the project, with the end date of one subproject serving as the start date of the next subproject in the series. Ideally, the product will allow the user to connect the subprojects in some manner and globally allocate resources, compute schedules, and so on. The use of subprojects has been addressed in many chapters of this book.

Other types of systems that are not main memory

[1]That is, they are equally strong in several graphics modes.

dependent access the project plan data from the disk drives. Working in main memory gives faster response times, albeit limiting the project size. On the other hand, while working on disk drives does extend the limits of project size, it also increases the length of the response times.

Although some of the products allow the user to invoke the system from a floppy disk, all of the software was evaluated in a hard-drive environment. Not all of the application software is required to reside in main memory during system processing. However, the data must be accessible—if the system needs it. Furthermore, the software needs a place to reside when it's not in use. Therefore, when the software is not being accessed, it should reside on the hard drive. With the exception of Primavera Project Planner, all of the products require approximately 1.5 megabytes or less for the application installation. Primavera Project Planner requires 3 megabytes or more.

Regardless of which product is chosen, the total of hard disk storage requirements increases proportionally with the size and number of project plans implemented.

16.3.2 System Structure ◆

There are two basic types of system structure. Some of the products are driven by pull-down menus while others are driven by command lines that are found at either the top or the bottom of the screen. Both types of system structures are very easy to use. In another vein, several of the products allow the user to bypass the menus and command lines and move around the system by entering shortcut keys.

16.3.3 Global Defaults ◆

Several of the products allow users to set system-level default values for calendar information, resource allocation directions, costing directions, and other miscellaneous parameters.

16.3.4 New Projects ◆

Setting up new projects should be a simple, straightforward operation. Furthermore, several products also allow the user to override the global defaults at the project level.

16.3.5 Accessing Plan Data ◆

How easy is it to recall existing plans?

16.3.6 Immediate Processor or Batch ◆

Most of the products evaluated process data immediately. That is, new schedules are computed as soon as each task or resource assignment is added or modified. This is an advantage, since it allows the user to visually verify results while doing the data entry. However, when entering data in large projects, waiting for the whole schedule to be recalculated each time a job is entered can be very time consuming. Most of the immediate processors also provide a toggle to optionally turn off the automatic recalculation. Products that are not immediate processors compute new schedules only when a separate transaction has been invoked—which means that the impact of any change may not be evaluated until the operation has been executed. For want of a better term, these products will be referred to as batch processors. Being a batch processor is *not* a terrible disadvantage, since the plan data will frequently be entered with the ''recalculate'' turned off, anyway.

16.3.7 Adding Plan Data ◆

How easy is it to add data to an existing plan?

16.3.8 Optional *What-If's* Or Permanent Saves ◆

Most main memory dependent products allow the user to enter data into a project plan, manipulate the data and plan, evaluate the results, choose whether or not to save the data, and finally choose the file name under which to save the current version. Other products update the plan each time the user enters data. In these products, when they are just exercising *what ifs*, users are advised to save the original version of the plan *each time before* they work with any plan.

16.3.9 Storing Ad Hoc Information ◆

An important aspect of project planning and management is the ability to record ad hoc information about: assumptions used in estimating; unresolved issues, agreements, reminders, and follow-up dates; lists of advisors and consultants for a particular job; a description of the deliverable, completion criteria for the job; and so on. To have an opportunity to record this data is frequently an important requirement. The ad hoc data requirements were described in several chapters earlier in the text. As an added example, these ad hoc requirements become an essential part of communicating the information requirements in the work assignment packages. Many of the products provide a feature that allows the user to record this data. Some products have special free-form note fields; others provide description fields. Some products provide several levels of description fields: at the project level, at the task and activity level, and at the resource level. Other products only have description fields at the activity level. The term *ad hoc information storage* has been used to refer to this feature. When the product itself provides only limited storage capacity, the user may export the plan to a word or text processor and then expand on the ad hoc data.

16.3.10 Exporting Data ♦

Several applications require that data be exported to word processing packages, spreadsheet packages, and so forth. Does the system export data?

16.3.11 Miscellaneous Features ♦

Several of the products support the micro-mainframe link. Other products have unique features that are of interest to readers. This section serves as a summary piece for these items of special interest.

16.3.12 Guidelines and Documentation

Some products assume a strong working knowledge of project management. As a result, even though they may be packed with instructions on how to use the system, they usually offer little direction on how to do project management per se. Guidelines and documentation are addressed throughout the book.

16.4 EVALUATING THE TECHNICAL SIDE OF SOFTWARE PACKAGES

This is a book which evaluates software product features that support the Project Management Process. It will not delve into such technical considerations as performance benchmarks and *how* to import/export external data bases. Therefore, on-line or batch response times will not be checked. Nor will the book address (1) how to create off-line programs to do estimating computations and import the data; or (2) how to export the data to a mainframe when the local printer carriage isn't wide enough for the report.

16.5 PRODUCTS WITH SHARED DATA AGREEMENTS

Primavera Systems and Microsoft Corporation have formally agreed to link their three products: Primavera Project Planner, Primavision, and Microsoft Project.

APPENDIX 1 HARVARD PROJECT MANAGER 3.0

APPENDIX 1.0 INTRODUCTION

Each section in each appendix is keyed to its corresponding introductory section in the tutorial. Readers will find that the respective tutorial section is noted in italicized parentheses at the end of each appropriate section header line.

APPENDIX 1.1 BASIC FEATURES: PRODUCTS WITH MORE THAN ONE GRAPHIC DATA ENTRY MODE

Appendix 1.1.1 Data Entry Mode (16.2.1)

This product supports six data entry modes: PERT, Gantt, Work Breakdown Structures, Work Breakdown Outline, Task List, and Fast Track.

Appendix 1.1.2 Size and Storage Constraints (16.3.1)

Harvard Project Manager 3.0 also operates on projects loaded into main memory. With 640K, the maximum number of tasks per project is 280. This limit goes down as the number of calendars and resources per task goes up. On the other hand, this number may be increased by creating several subprojects and linking them together under one superproject. Subproject creation is easy and supports a total project size of 78,400 jobs. The vendor suggests that subproject mode should be invoked whenever the "70% full" message appears.

Appendix 1.1.3 System Structure (16.3.2)

The system is composed of eight subsystems that are selected from a main menu that is (1) presented to the user at system start-up or (2) accessed, once work has started, by using the escape key to exit from the current subsystem. (See Figure A1.1.) Each of the subsystems has its own unique command line at the top of the screen. The vendor calls them menu bars. The respective subcommands are in pull-down menus that are accessed with function keys. (See Figure A1.3. below.)

Appendix 1.1.4 Global System Project Data Defaults (16.3.3)

There are no special commands to set global system project data defaults. However, users may designate which of the six data entry modes should be used as the default for creating projects.

Appendix 1.1.5 New Projects (16.3.4)

New projects are initialized with a five-step process: (1) "1. Create a project" is selected from the main

Figure A1.1

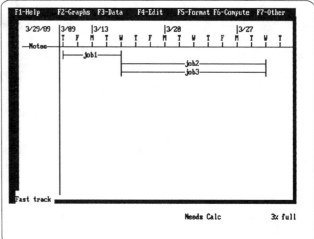

Figure A1.2

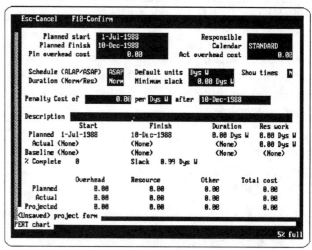

Figure A1.3

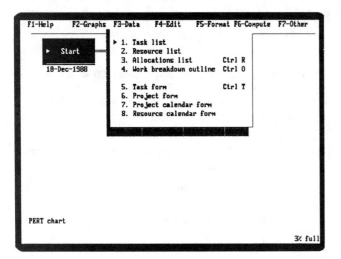

Figure A1.4

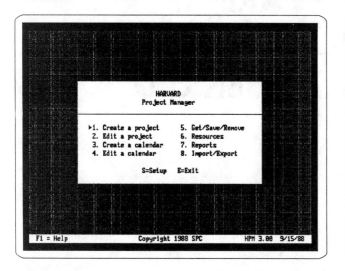

menu; (2) the *Fast Track* window appears on the screen and the name and duration of the task can be entered in a Gantt-type mode (See Figure A1.2.); (3) the F3 Data pull-down menu is accessed with the F3 function key (See Figure A1.3.); (4) ''6. Project Form'' is selected; and (5) the Project screen (See Figure A1.4.) is completed.

Appendix 1.1.6 Accessing Existing Plans (16.3.5)

To load an existing project into main memory, ''5. Get/Save/Remove'' is selected from the main menu and the Project Names window appears. (See Figure A1.5.) When the desired project name is entered, the

Figure A1.5

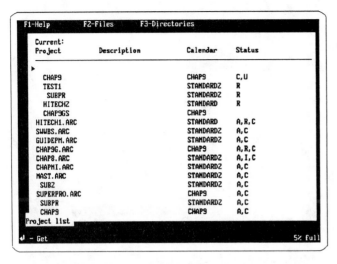

```
F1-Help          F2-Files      F3-Directories

  Current:
  Project        Description        Calendar    Status

▶ 
    CHAP9                            CHAP9       C,U
    TEST1                            STANDARD2   R
    SUBPR                            STANDARD2   R
    HITECH2                          STANDARD    R
    CHAP9GS                          CHAP9
  HITECH1.ARC                        STANDARD    A,R,C
  SWWBS.ARC                          STANDARD2   A,C
  GUIDEPM.ARC                        STANDARD2   A,C
  CHAP9G.ARC                         CHAP9       A,R,C
  CHAP8.ARC                          STANDARD2   A,I,C
  CHAPHI.ARC                         STANDARD2   A,C
  MAST.ARC                           STANDARD2   A,C
    SUB2                             STANDARD2   A,C
  SUPERPRO.ARC                       CHAP9       A,C
    SUBPR                            STANDARD2   A,C
    CHAP9                            CHAP9       A,C
Project list

⏎ - Get                                          5% full
```

project plan is loaded and the "2. Edit a project" subsystem is automatically invoked bringing up the project data in PERT chart mode.

Appendix 1.1.7 Immediate Processor or Batch (16.3.6)

Harvard Project Manager 3.0 is an immediate processor system. The automatic recalculation may be turned off by "F6 Compute; 1. Calc On/Off".

Appendix 1.1.8 Adding Plan Data (16.3.7)

The four graphic entry modes are found with the F2 function key in the Graphs pull-down menu, which is accessed from the "2. Edit a project" subsystem. The task list and work breakdown outline are accessed from the F3 Data pull-down menu.

Appendix 1.1.9 Optional "What-if's" Or Permanent Saves (16.3.8)

Plan data is not made permanent until the user (1) chooses to save it and (2) designates the name under which the plan is to be saved. However, under certain circumstances, changes to resource data and calendar data become permanent as soon as they are made. On the other hand, plans can be *write-protected* with an

archive function (in the 5. Get/Save/Remove subsystem as described later in this appendix—see the ".ARC" extension in Figure A1.5.) If users have performed this function, it can be recalled in its original form when the "What-If" exercise is done.

Appendix 1.1.10 Ad Hoc Information Storage (16.3.9)

The description field in each of the Task screens, Project screens, Milestone screens, and Calendar screens is 254 characters long. The description field in the Resource screen is 57 characters long. The notes field in Fast Track mode is 50 characters long.

Appendix 1.1.11 Exporting Data (16.3.10)

This product exports task and allocation data to LOTUS 1-2-3 in Version 1A and Version 2 format, to dBase II and dBase III, and in Delimited ASCII format.

Appendix 1.1.12 Special Effects: Archiving Projects (16.3.11)

As described earlier and in detail through this appendix, Harvard Project Manager 3.0 enables users to archive plans, thus removing them from the active project list and, consequently, also protecting them from unwanted changes. Users are advised to archive all but the current active project.

Appendix 1.1.13 Special Effects: Separate Subdirectories (16.3.11)

All projects within a subdirectory share the same calendar and resource pool. Thus, they are affected by changes made to the calendar or pool. Furthermore, during the resource leveling process, Harvard Project Manager 3.0 will level across *all* of the projects that are in the same directory as the project being leveled, except for archived projects. Having unrelated projects in the same subdirectory will then significantly slow up the leveling process. Therefore, users are advised to set up separate subdirectories for any unrelated sets of projects. Subdirectory designations can easily be changed from the Project Names window by pressing

''F3 Directories; 4. Change data directory''. (See Figure A1.5.)

APPENDIX 1.2 WORK BREAKDOWN STRUCTURES

Appendix 1.2.1 Graphics Support (4.8.2)

Harvard Project Manager 3.0 supports WBS graphics. It is very easy to learn. In Harvard Project Manager 3.0, entries at the same level may be made with one action, ''Control-A'', which will invoke the Add Task window. (See Figure A1.6.) When starting a lower level, a second function will automatically be invoked and a request for some generalized, yet simple, network directions must be completed. (See Figure A1.7.) At first, because networks do not normally drive the work breakdown structure, this caused some confusion and worry but it actually turned out to be very helpful later on, when entering dependencies. Once a lower level has been created, the upper level is designated as a *milestone*. When the network is generated, each milestone will become a beginning and ending node in the network, thus surrounding the jobs within the group. This can be very beneficial.

Appendix 1.2.2 Level Support (4.8.3)

The system features automatic generation of the 14-character identification number, using an Arabic outlining numbering scheme. Furthermore, even though the numbering scheme is limited, users may continue to create more levels beyond this boundary. The new levels just won't have a WBS complete code.

Appendix 1.2.3 Data Entry Requirements (4.8.4)

Harvard Project Manager 3.0 automatically generates the only required identification number.[1] There is a second 12-character code field, available for notes and pertinent information.

---

[1] A very nice time saver.

Figure A1.6

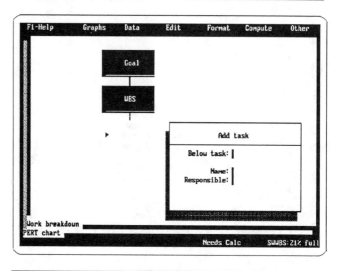

Figure A1.7

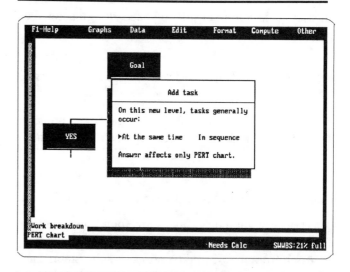

Appendix 1.2.4 Durations and Dependencies (4.8.5)

Harvard Project Manager 3.0 requires no durations, but asks for generalized dependency information (See Figure A1.7.) when creating each new level. The user does not have to complete the network in order to provide this information. While this may represent a few extra keystrokes now, it may be helpful later on, when creating dependencies.

Appendix 1.2.5 Random Sequence of Data Entry *(4.8.6)*

Harvard Project Manager 3.0 supports WBSs, Gantts, Networks, and outlines. With the exception of the networks, each of these modes allows random data entry.

Appendix 1.2.6 Using the Copy Features with the *Template* Tasks *(4.8.7)*

If the *template* tasks have been stored in a separate plan, Harvard Project Manager 3.0 will allow the user to selectively take the *template* plan into other projects. Harvard Project Manager 3.0 limits importing a *template* plan to only once per project; but this can be overcome by making duplicate copies of the *template* plan before starting the operation.

Appendix 1.2.7 Rollup Support *(4.8.8)*

Harvard Project Manager 3.0 allows the selection of rollup reports on any level—for time, resource, and money fields. This is accomplished by choosing the desired fields from the "F4. Sort/Select" from the F2 Options menu for the "Work Breakdown" reports in the Reports subsystem. (See Figure A1.8.)

Figure A1.8

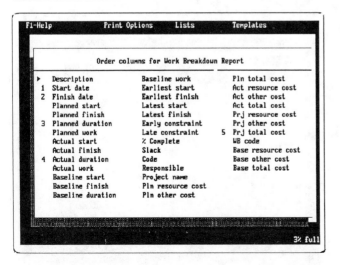

Appendix 1.2.8 Guidelines and Documentation *(4.8.9)*

In their documentation, Harvard Project Manager 3.0 has a few paragraphs at the beginning of the chapter on how to use a WBS with their product.

APPENDIX 1.3 ESTIMATING

Appendix 1.3.1 Estimating Support and Estimating Guidelines *(5.7.1)*

Harvard Project Manager 3.0 does not provide guidelines that support the estimating techniques described in this book. They assume the estimating has been completed and the duration is known. (Instructions on how to use the system to achieve the implementation of a feature are not considered guidelines.)

Appendix 1.3.2 Estimates of *True Work Effort* Versus Resource-Driven Elapsed Time *(5.7.4)*

Before resources are added to the plan, if "duration: normal" and "default units: working" is selected on the Project screen, Harvard Project Manager 3.0 supports *true work effort* in the *duration* field of the Project screen and the Task screen. After resources have been assigned to tasks, the *true work effort* might only be found in the *resource work* field.

Appendix 1.3.3 Durations and Units of Measurement *(5.7.6)*

Harvard Project Manager 3.0 supports minutes, hours, days, weeks, months, and years. Minutes and hours have limited use, however. In most projects, they will generate more time periods than the system can handle; therefore, they can only be used in short projects or phases. In Harvard Project Manager 3.0, the global default is zero days and may be overridden at task and resource level within the project. Harvard Project Manager 3.0 supports mixed units of measurement through its override option.

Appendix 1.3.4 Zero Duration Milestones *(5.7.7)*

Harvard Project Manager 3.0 (See Figure A1.9.) has special Milestone screens.

Figure A1.9

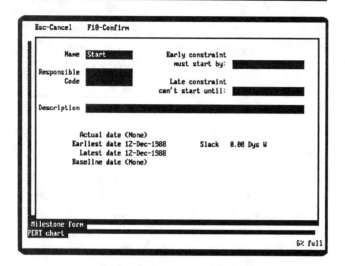

Figure A1.10

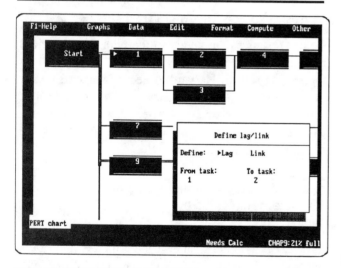

Appendix 1.3.5 Lead and Lag Times with Duration but No Effort (5.7.8)

Harvard Project Manager 3.0 supports lag time through "F4 Edit; 5. Define lag/link; Define:lag". (See Figure A1.10.) Although it shows on the network chart as a different shape than the task node, the lag isn't a task; as such, it does not show on any reports.[2]

---

[2]A better approach is to create a separate task with the corresponding duration and then enter a dummy resource whose cost is zero. Of course, this does consume precious memory.

APPENDIX 1.4 NETWORKS

Appendix 1.4.1 Types of Networks (6.8.1)

Harvard Project Manager 3.0 produces activity-on-a-node diagrams. The system allows users to select up to five pieces of task information to be displayed below the node.

Appendix 1.4.2 Types of Relationships (6.8.2)

All four types of relationships are supported in Harvard Project Manager 3.0. They can be entered via the lag/link choice. Except for the traditional finish-to-start, a new node that describes the relationship type will be inserted on the PERT. (See Figure A1.11.) This will also be addressed later in this appendix.

Appendix 1.4.3 Number of Dependencies (6.8.3)

Harvard Project Manager 3.0 theoretically has no limits on the number of relationships. However, since it is a memory-dependent product, the total number of jobs, dependencies, and resources is determined by the variable-length formula. The information needed to compute the total number of potential dependencies (etc.) is documented in an appendix.

Figure A1.11

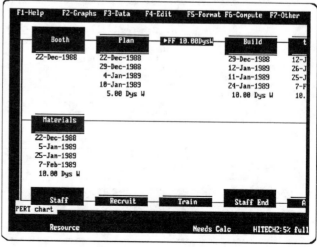

Appendix 1.4.4 Establishing Dependencies (6.8.4)

In Harvard Project Manager 3.0., if tasks have been added in WBS mode, many relationships have already been created. Additions or modifications to the relationships may easily be made in PERT mode. The "F4 Edit; 5. Define lag/link" window is used:

- For those dependencies that are not correctly created from the WBS; and
- For those that are not automatically created in PERT or Gantt mode (e.g., when there is more than one predecessor or successor).

The "From Task" and "To Task" entries are automatically filed in when the cursor arrow is moved to the desired task and return is pressed. Alternatively, the user may also key in the correct predecessor and successor information.

Appendix 1.4.5 How Easy Is It to Enter Dependencies? (6.8.6)

Harvard Project Manager 3.0 does not require number entries to create relationships. All the user need do is position the cursor and press enter. If the tasks are easy to find, there is no need to key in the corresponding name.

In an average-sized project plan, however, the connecting tasks may be far apart, may not show up on the same screen, and may be hard to locate with the cursor.

If this occurs when the dependencies have already been roughly mapped out on hard copy, the user may simply use the "Find Task" function under the F4 Edit menu, by keying in the correct task name—instead of scrolling with the cursor. (Users who are unsure of the task name may flip back and forth between the task list and the PERT chart.)

On the other hand, if the user is attempting to interactively lay out the schedule without a mapped-out hard copy, establishing dependencies may become a trying experience.

Appendix 1.4.6 Inserting Jobs into the Middle of the Plan (6.8.7)

When adding a task from the Harvard Project Manager 3.0 WBS, the request for dependency information (Figures A1.6 and A1.7) asks if tasks at the new level usually occur at the same time or in sequence. The user must then assess which of the two conditions is most likely to happen most frequently within that level. All entries at the lower level are created with this selected choice and will be added accordingly to the network. More often than not, the correct dependency will result. Discrepancies may then be corrected in the separate procedures for entering dependencies, described earlier. This extra effort is usually offset by the elimination of the need to create relationships between those tasks that are automatically and correctly joined.

Adding tasks in PERT mode requires a similar process; however the system makes a "best guess" regarding where in the WBS the task should be placed. In this case, more often than not, the WBS is correctly updated from PERT mode.

Appendix 1.4.7 Subnetwork Dependencies (6.8.8)

In Harvard Project Manager 3.0, subnetwork dependencies are no problem—except for the verification problems described later in this networking discussion.

Appendix 1.4.8 Moving Jobs in the Network (6.8.9)

The move in Harvard Project Manager 3.0 is not intended to be used to clean up aesthetics of PERT (e.g., crossed lines); the user must accept the placement of jobs on the PERT. This move is used to change placement of the job in the plan. It does not carry dependencies because it asks for the new dependencies. A move in WBS mode will not affect the PERT and vice versa. Consequently, a move in one mode may necessitate a duplicate move in the other mode.

Appendix 1.4.9 Removing Dependencies (6.8.10)

Dependencies may be eliminated in Harvard Project Manager 3.0 with "F4 Edit; 6. Remove lag/link".

Figure A1.12

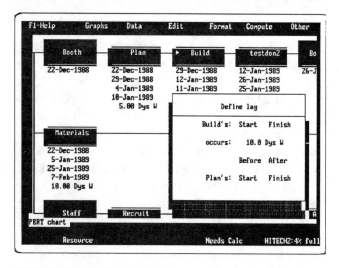

Appendix 1.4.10 Deleting Jobs in the Plan *(6.8.11)*

In PERT mode, Harvard Project Manager 3.0's "F4 Edit; 4. Remove task" eliminates the task and reconnects adjacent dependencies. If these new relationships are not correct, the user may easily fix them by selecting "F4 Edit; 6. Remove lag/link" and "F4 Edit; 5. Define lag/link" or "F4 Edit; 3. Move Task".

Appendix 1.4.11 Lag and Lead Times *(6.8.12)*

Harvard Project Manager 3.0 supports lag time through selecting "F4 Edit; 5. Define lag/link; Define:lag". (See Figure A1.12.) The lag supports all four types of relationships. Although it shows on the network chart (Figure A1.11), the lag isn't a task; as such, it does not show on any reports. A better approach is to create the task with the corresponding duration and then enter a dummy resource whose cost is zero. Of course, this also consumes precious memory.

Appendix 1.4.12 Copying Jobs in the Plan *(6.8.13)*

In Harvard Project Manager 3.0, there is no copy per se but saving a current project under a new name will copy an entire project. It is also possible to link one whole project to a task within a second project by calling it a subproject, and then to expand this task to show all of the tasks in the first project. A project may only be linked once; therefore, the original ought to be duplicated under different names before starting.

Appendix 1.4.13 Copying the *Template* Jobs *(6.8.14)*

Harvard Project Manager 3.0 supports subprojects, a feature that may also be used for the *template* application. Subprojects may be created in Harvard Project Manager 3.0 by (1) grouping tasks that are already in the master plan into a subproject or (2) bringing tasks from another project file into the current plan. Either approach will be bound by the size restrictions of the product.

From the current master project, selecting "F4; 7. Create subproject" will gather in designated jobs and make them into a subproject, creating a single node in the network or on the WBS. Once this action has been taken, these jobs cannot be used a second time.

With "F4. 8. Link subproject", a previously existing *template* plan may be linked to the master project as a subproject. Subprojects may only be copied into a master plan one time.

In either approach, all of the tasks within the subproject may then be opened into the master project with "F4; 9. Expand subproject". In this expanded mode, it is possible to establish dependencies between master project tasks and tasks inside the subproject.

Because subprojects may only be copied into the superproject once, the *work-around* described at the head of this respective tutorial section for copying uniquely named subprojects into the plan must be employed.

Appendix 1.4.14 Loops in the Network *(6.8.15)*

Harvard Project Manager 3.0 prevents loops with the message "You cannot create a circular task sequence".

Appendix 1.4.15 Dangling Jobs *(6.8.16)*

Harvard Project Manager 3.0 flags dangling tasks.

Appendix 1.4.16 Verifying Dependencies Are Correct (6.8.17)

The PERT in Harvard Project Manager 3.0 is very easy to read in a small project with few (or no) subnetworks. In an average-sized project with several subnetworks, many tasks, and many relationships, the nodes are often vertically separated and this makes following the connections a difficult process. There is no "Move" that allows repositioning entries. The system does provide a feature that greatly shrinks the network so that the connections may be followed; but it drops all of the information in the node except a portion of the task name. If the user has printed a hard copy of the network, the reduced PERT may be helpful in the verification process. This product's find feature (described in the next section) significantly aids in the verification process. During the verification process, there is no problem changing dependencies with PERT.

Appendix 1.4.17 Highlighting Dependency Paths (6.8.18)

If the user invokes the find feature (F4 Edit; 1. Find task") for any given task, Harvard Project Manager 3.0 will display a list of predecessors and successors for that task.

Appendix 1.4.18 Network Aesthetics (6.8.19)

In Harvard Project Manager 3.0, the user must accept the PERT as drawn by the system. Although there are very few crossed lines in this network, other aesthetics cannot be improved by the user. In an average-sized project plan, the connecting tasks may be far apart, may not show up on the same screen, and may make following the connections a difficult process.

Appendix 1.4.19 Scaled to Time? (6.8.20)

Harvard Project Manager 3.0 has a very nice function called "time-relative" that will vertically align all of the task boxes in approximately the same timescale. The time-scale units of measurement are minutes, hours, days, weeks, months, and years. Based on the selected time unit, the system determines if the length of the plan will fit into the space allotted for the network. If it does not, the user will be advised to select a larger time unit. An average-sized plan will not be accommodated in units of days. Weeks, however, will usually work.

Appendix 1.4.20 Networks and Work Breakdown Structures (6.9)

Because Harvard Project Manager 3.0 creates beginning and ending milestones for each group of tasks, it is not necessary to undo relationships as the "latest last jobs" are added to the network. This product also allows automatic resolution of relationships when the "latest last job" is added.

Appendix 1.4.21 Dependencies in a Multiproject Environment (6.12)

Although they may be maintained separately, subprojects can never be expanded into a superproject more than one time. The master project is *not* constrained by the sum of its subprojects—unless the user takes a special action to *expand* all of the subprojects in the master project. Needless to say, under most circumstances, this is not an advisable action.

A separate master project is to be created, with one task for each of the subproject plans. Then, each task should, in turn, be linked to its respective subproject.[3] This is very simply accomplished by moving the cursor to the desired task, selecting "F4 Edit; 8. Link Subproject", and entering the subproject name. Dependency connections are made as outlined earlier in this appendix.

The user may easily flip back and forth between the master project and its subprojects by moving the cursor to the corresponding task and selecting "F7 Other; 3. Visit subproject" or "F7 Other; 4. Leave subproject". To speed things up, the calculations may be temporarily stopped by selecting "F6 Compute; 1. Calc on/off". When there is no longer a need to flip back and forth, the calculations ought to be turned back on by repeating "F6 Compute; 1. Calc on/off".

There is no need to do double entry when the subprojects have been linked. When an attempt is made to return to the master project, the system forces the user to save the subproject, whether or not modifications have been made. Consequently, changes made

---

[3]Subprojects may not be linked to milestones.

in visited subprojects are automatically reflected in the master project.

Projects that have been unlinked from a master project are still retained within the master project group and may be accessed from the "5. Get/Save/Remove" subsystem (Figure A1.5). They are flagged with a "U" in the status column.

Appendix 1.4.22 Printing and Viewing Networks (6.13)

To view the network in Harvard Project Manager 3.0, the user must first be in Edit mode. This is achieved by selecting "2. Edit a project" from the main menu. Then, pressing "F2 Graphs ; 2. PERT chart" will bring the network to the screen. To print, select "7. Reports" from the main menu. Then, from the invoked report menu, choose one of (a) PERT, (b) PERT half zoom, (c) PERT full zoom, or (d) PERT time relative. For the last step, enter "F2 Print Options; 2. Run".

Appendix 1.4.23 Guidelines and Documentation (6.15)

In Harvard Project Manager 3.0, there are two pages of documentation on networks and three pages of documentation on types of dependencies. Although there is a whole chapter on subprojects, only one page may be regarded as management guidelines.

APPENDIX 1.5 OPTIMAL PLANS

Appendix 1.5.1 Calendars (7.14.1)

Harvard Project Manager 3.0 comes with a standard calendar from which to start. The system assumes that the user wants to use this standard calendar. If this is not the case, the name of the designated calendar must be entered on the Project screen (Figure A1.4) when the project is initialized.

New calendars are created by copying an old one, modifying it, and saving it under a new name. This process is completed from the F2 Files menu by pressing "7. Copy Calendar" or by selecting "3. Create a Calendar" from the main menu.

While normally Harvard Project Manager 3.0 is

Figure A1.13

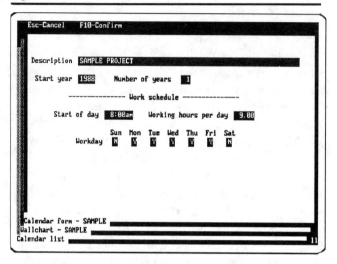

not a permanent save product,[4] this is not true in the case of the project calendars. If one project plan makes any changes to its calendar, the modifications will affect the data in every project plan in which the calendar occurs. Accordingly, unless users want all projects to share the same calendar, they are advised save calendars under a name that is unique to the project.

Furthermore, users are advised to archive all projects that do share a calendar and then remove them from the active projects list. Thereafter, only the current plan should be activated. Archiving, removing, and reactivating are completed in the "5 Get/Save/Remove" subsystem. These operations are documented in the manual.

There are two Calendar screens in this product. The first form may be retrieved from the main menu after selecting "4. Edit a calendar", and then by moving the cursor to the correct calendar name and pressing enter *or* by selecting "2. Edit a project" and pressing "F3 Data; 7. Project calendar form". (See Figure A1.13.) The user may then enter the project start year, the workday starting hour, the number of hours worked per day, and the days worked each week. Although it

---

[4]That is, it usually allows the user to play around with the project plan and exit without saving the plan, without having to worry about retaining the original plan.

allows duration entries in hours, the system does not support scheduling lunch and other nonworking hours into the calendar.

The wall calendar (which contains the days of the month) is accessed by pressing "4. Edit a calendar" in the main menu, moving the cursor to the correct calendar name, pressing return, and then pressing escape *or* by pressing "2. Edit a project; F2 Graphs; 6. Project wallchart". (See Figure A1.14.) Once in the wallchart, holidays are entered moving the cursor to the designated day and pressing "F4 Edit; 2. Make a holiday".

Even though it supports estimates and schedules in hours, the system does not support daily breaks (for example, lunch).

Appendix 1.5.2 Choosing the Correct Project Start Date *(7.14.2)*

The default date used by the Harvard Project Manager 3.0 Fast Track mode is the current operating system date. When in Fast Track mode, however, users may also move the start date; and then the system will use that date as the start date. Alternatively, the start date of the project may be controlled through the *Planned Start Date* in the Project screen which is accessed by selecting "F3 Data; 6. Project form". It is only necessary to take this action one time—at plan initiation.

Figure A1.14

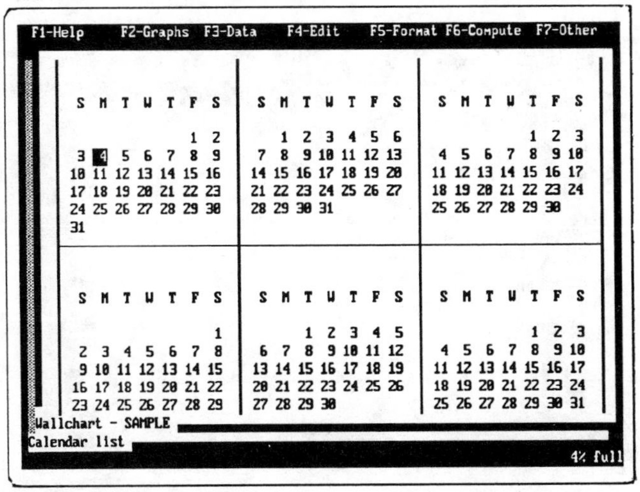

Appendix 1.5.3 Insuring that the Plan Is Not Constrained by Resources *(7.14.3)*

In Harvard Project Manager 3.0, if *Duration: normal* is selected on the Project screen and no resources have been entered into the Task screen, the system will correctly create the optimal plan.

Appendix 1.5.4 Avoiding Imposed Target Dates *(7.14.3)*

In Harvard Project Manager 3.0, there are two choices for date scheduling in this product: ASAP (As Soon As Possible) and ALAP (As Late As Possible). The default may be set in the Project screen. The user is advised to choose *ASAP*.

Appendix 1.5.5 Calculating the Schedule *(7.14.4)*

In Harvard Project Manager 3.0, automatic calculations may be turned on by setting "F6 Compute; 1. Calc on/off" to *Yes*. (The default is *Yes*.) On the other hand, if this slows the system down, it may be set to *No*. Then, schedules may be recalculated on an ad hoc basis by pressing "Control-C".

Appendix 1.5.6 The Forward Pass: Calculating the Early Dates *(7.14.5)*

Harvard Project Manager 3.0 allows as much time as possible to finish each job. Therefore, each job is scheduled to finish at the exact instant of the scheduled start of its successor(s) and is thus not scheduled to finish until the start of the next working day. Unfortunately, this has the effect of scheduling the end of the project a minimum of one day later than expected—at the beginning of the next business day following its actual completion.

Appendix 1.5.7 Zero Duration Milestones *(7.14.8)*

Harvard Project Manager 3.0 uses the alternative approach—it schedules zero duration milestones at the start of the next business day following the completion of all of its predecessors.

Appendix 1.5.8 Verifying Schedules With Units of Measurement Less Than One Day *(7.14.9)*

Although the schedule checked out correctly, Harvard Project Manager 3.0 does not allow for a nine-hour workday with one hour included for lunch. The scheduled times, therefore, were correspondingly offset.

Appendix 1.5.9 Retaining a Baseline Record of the Optimal Plan *(7.14.11)*

In Harvard Project Manager 3.0, selecting ''F7 Other; 2. Set baseline'' saves the original start date, the original finish date, and the original durations, costs, and resources in the baseline fields. The early start and finish dates are used for the baseline dates, which do not change until the baseline is set again. These fields may then be seen (and/or compared to actuals) in various screens and reports.

Appendix 1.5.10 Interpreting the Dates on the Screen *(7.14.12)*

The Harvard Project Manager 3.0 user may choose to display any 5 fields from a list of 30 fields, many of which are the desired date fields. This is true for both the Gantt and the network. From Edit mode, pressing ''F5 Format; 7. Tag PERT chart/Gantt chart'' will invoke the list of fields. (This list is similar to the list pictured in Figure A1.8 and supports most of the fields pictured in that list.)

Appendix 1.5.11 Annotating the Critical Path *(7.14.13)*

Harvard Project Manager 3.0 shows the critical path's Gantt time-scaled bars and the network nodes in red. It also shows the node connectors on the network in red. For users with monochrome monitors, Harvard Project Manager 3.0 shows the critical path with double lines around the nodes.

Appendix 1.5.12 Gantt Chart Time Periods *(7.14.15)*

The number of timeframes displayed in the Harvard Project Manager 3.0 Gantt chart is related to a formula whose two values are entered by the user.

Intervals, the first value, may be in units of minutes, hours, days, weeks, months, or years. This value is selected from the window that is invoked when the user selects ''F5 Format; 4. Timescale display''.

The maximum number of intervals per project is 100. (See Figure A1.15.) This is not documented in the manual but is discovered in an error message that is displayed when trying to pick a unit of measurement that creates more than 100 intervals. Consequently, if the user selects days, the project must be 100 days or less in duration. To get around this limitation, there is a second field in this screen, the *Units Of* field. If the user enters a number higher than 1 into this field, the duration of the project may be increased by multiplying each interval by this number. For example, if the user selects a value of 2 along with intervals of a day, then each interval will be equivalent to 2 days and the project may be 200 days in duration.

The user may move in any direction around the Gantt chart by pressing the arrow keys.

The weekends and holidays may be shadowed behind the bars on the Gantt chart. However, the bars are continuous; they are not broken by weekends or holidays. (See Figure A1.21 below.)

Appendix 1.5.13 Scheduling in the Multiproject Environment *(7.14.17)*

In Harvard Project Manager 3.0, the calendar that is designated on the Project screen when the master proj-

Figure A1.15

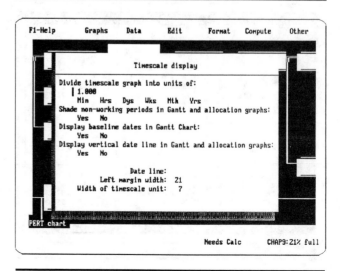

ect is initialized remains the ruling calendar. Its data is retained, and the calendar data in the subproject is dropped.

Once a subproject has been made a part of a master project, it may be accessed from the master project by selecting "F7 Other; 3. Visit subproject".

If modifications have been made, and if the autocalculation has been turned off, the schedule should be recalculated. The return to the project is completed by pressing "F7 Other; 4. Leave subproject". When an attempt is made to return to the master project, the system forces the user to save the subproject, whether or not modifications have been made. In this manner, all changes made in visited subprojects are automatically reflected in the master project.

Appendix 1.5.14 Nesting Subprojects in a Multiproject Environment (7.14.18)

When there are nested subprojects in Harvard Project Manager 3.0, the process of visiting and returning from subprojects may be repeated until the desired subproject is reached. On the other hand, any project within the nest may also be accessed with the "5. Get/Save/Remove" subsystem. If the instructions in the previous section are followed, all date changes are reflected in each rung of the nest. In a complex nest of subprojects, users are advised to create a hard copy tree of the nested groups and check each one off as its schedule is computed. If only one subproject is overlooked, all of the subsequent schedules may be incorrect. There is no other *work-around* to this procedure.

Appendix 1.5.15 Guidelines and Documentation (7.14.20)

Harvard Project Manager 3.0 has several very good pages on schedule computations.

APPENDIX 1.6 CALCULATING A FINISH DATE

Appendix 1.6.1 Using the New Reasonable Late Finish Date of the Project (7.26.3)

In Harvard Project Manager 3.0, all the user need do is enter the desired end date in the project finish date of the Project screen. The correct late dates are computed and stored in each of the latest start and latest

finish fields. The early finish and late finish dates of the project may be found in the project ending milestone (automatically generated by the system). The slack on the critical path may be redefined in the *minimum slack* field of the Project screen. Then, the highlighting of the critical path will not be lost.

APPENDIX 1.7 ADDING RESOURCES

APPENDIX 1.7.1 Creating the Resource Calendars (8.8)

Users of Harvard Project Manager 3.0 ought to recall that, if the calendars are shared by one or more project plans, there may have been global modifications to the calendar—unless all other plans that use the calendar were archived before the modifications.

There are two Calendar screens in this product. (Figures A1.13 and A1.14) Both forms default to the project-level hours and holidays. After pointing the cursor to the desired resource name in the resource list, which is accessed by pressing "F3 Data; 2. Resource list" (See Figure A1.16.), the first Calendar screen may be retrieved by pressing "F3 Data; 8. Resource calendar form". The user may then enter the resource's workday starting hour, the number of hours worked per day, and the days worked each week.

The resource wall calendar (which contains the days of the month) is accessed by pressing "F2 Graphs; 7. Resource wallchart". Holidays are entered into the

Figure A1.16

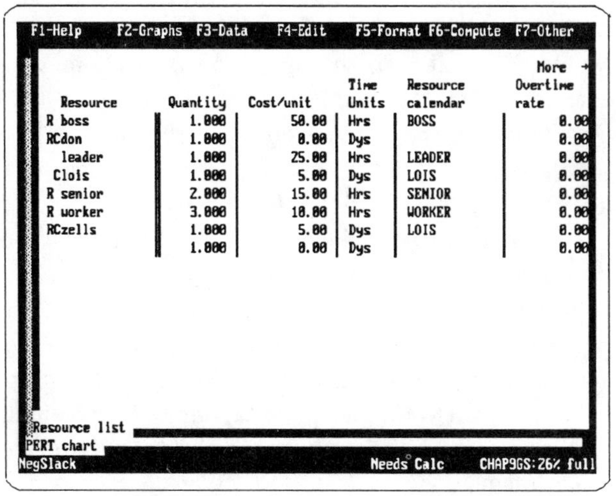

Wallchart screen by moving the cursor to the designated day and pressing "F4 Edit; 2. Make a holiday".

Even though it supports estimates and schedules in hours, the system does not support daily breaks (for example, lunch). Similarly, this system cannot set unique working hours for a single specific calendar day.

If a unique resource calendar is created, the name of this calendar should be entered into the calendar field of the corresponding resource entry in the resource list discussed below.

Setting part-time resources at the project level will be addressed later in this appendix.

Appendix 1.7.2 Creating the Resource Pool (8.9)

While normally Harvard Project Manager 3.0 is not a permanent save product, this is not true in the case of the resource pool. Users ought to be advised that the resource pool in Harvard Project Manager 3.0 is a directory-wide pool. Any changes to the pool from one project plan will affect the resource assignments in every project plan in which the resource occurs. Consequently, users are advised to archive all projects with resources and then remove them from the active projects list. Thereafter, only the current plan should be activated. Archiving, removing, and reactivating are completed in the "5 Get/Save/Remove" subsystem. Unwanted changes to the resource list must be corrected before leaving the system. These operations are not clearly documented.

Resources may be individuals, groups of individuals, equipment, or materials. On the other hand, when the costs that are associated with a task's resource are fixed costs or one time costs, they may be entered into the Task screen fields for "other costs", thus bypassing the resource pool. (See Figure A1.17.) Similarly, costs that are associated with project overhead may be entered on the Project screen.

Harvard Project Manager 3.0 theoretically has no limits on the number of resources per project plan. However, since it is a memory-dependent product, the total number of jobs, dependencies, and resources is determined by the variable-length formula. The information needed to compute the total number of potential resources (etc.) is documented in an appendix of the user's manual.

Figure A1.17

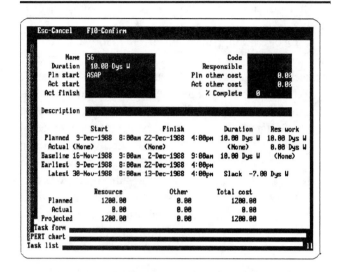

Resource information resides in a directory-wide resource list. In other words, Harvard Project Manager 3.0 only maintains one resource pool—and it contains all of the latest resource information for all resources in all projects. (See Figure A1.16.) It is accessed from the main menu by pressing "6. Resources" (Figure A1.1) or from within the edit subsystem by pressing "F3 Data; 2. Resource list". (Figure A1.3) If users do not wish their projects to share resource pools, they should set up the projects and their respective resource pools in separate subdirectories.

Resources are added to the system by easily keying in one line of data for each resource. The required information is: an 11-character resource name, the number of available resources of this type, the units in which the resource is measured (hours, days, etc.), the cost per unit, the name of the resource calendar to be used, the rate of overtime pay, the resource's supervisor, the work group category of the resource, and descriptive notes.

The number of resources defaults to one. Both hours-per-day fields default to the number determined by the setting in the project calendar. Several of the fields are optional.

Harvard Project Manager 3.0 does not support multiple billing rates for one resource.

Appendix 1.7.3 Assigning Part-Time Resources at the Project Level *(8.10)*

If the part-time value is not to be the same for all of the projects in a subdirectory, then part-time participation should be applied at the task level. (See the discussion later in this appendix.) The vendor describes the following process for creating part-time resources at the project level:

- Resources who will be part-time for all jobs in one or more projects are designated through the resource calendar in the field for number of working hours per day (Figure A1.13); or
- Resources who will be part-time for all jobs in one or more projects are designated with a fractional entry in the quantity field of the resource list. (Figure A1.16)

However, neither of these approaches achieves any changes in scheduling, after normal calculations and even after leveling resources as described later in this appendix. The bottom line, at the project level, is that there is no way to get schedules to reflect the part-time participation scenario described in Example 2.

Appendix 1.7.4 Deleting and Changing Resources at the Project Level *(8.11)*

Users ought to recall that the resource pool is a subdirectory pool. Any changes to the pool from one project plan will affect the resource assignments in every project plan in which the resource occurs. Consequently, users are advised to archive all projects with resources and then remove them from the active projects list. Thereafter, only the current plan ought to be activated. Archiving, removing, and reactivating are completed in the ''5 Get/Save/Remove'' subsystem. These operations are not clearly documented.

Resources are deleted with ''F3 Data; 2. Resource List; F4 Edit; 2. Remove Resource''. If the other projects have been archived, deleting a resource in the pool automatically results in the project-wide removal of all corresponding resource assignments, but it does not affect the other projects. Otherwise, the deletion will be directory-wide.

Names are changed in the same manner as other modifications. If the other projects have been archived, changing a name results in a project-wide replacement of all occurrences of the old name with the new name. Otherwise, the modifications will be directory-wide.

Appendix 1.7.5 Matching Resources to Jobs *(8.14)*

In Harvard Project Manager 3.0, resources may only be assigned to tasks; they may not be assigned to milestones.

The number of allowable resource names per task is determined by the variable-length formula discussed earlier in this text.

The Allocations List screen is used to make resource assignments. (See Figure A1.18.) After recalling this screen by moving the cursor to the designated task and pressing ''F3 Data; 3. Allocations List'', resources are easily assigned to tasks. Many fields on this form default to the preferred values; therefore, much of the keying has already been done. However, the user may override each of the defaults.

The required data is: the 12-character resource name, the number of resources being applied to the task (defaults to one), units of measurement (defaults to the unit—hours, days, etc.—designated in the Project screen), lag start (defined later in this appendix), planned resource effort (defaults to the task duration),

Figure A1.18

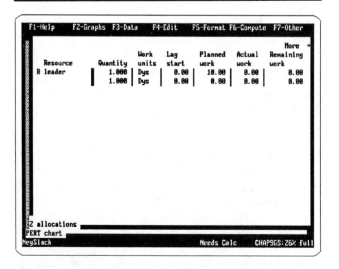

hours per day the resource will be available (defaults to the value in the resource list), hours per day the resource is available to work overtime (defaults to the value in the resource list), a flag to indicate whether the leveling process should be allowed to permanently change the data in this job. (See the discussion on leveling)

In Harvard Project Manager 3.0, the resource assignment number in the Allocations screen is used for leveling. Therefore, a resource name may be assigned to a task as often as the user chooses—regardless of the availability number in the pool. If the assignment number exceeds the available number, it will not be flagged until leveling. At that time, a message will flash on the screen but leveling will not abort.

If an unknown resource is assigned to a task, the system will ask the user if the resource ought to be added to the resource list. If the answer is *Yes*, skeleton information will be added. However, none of the dollar values associated with the resource will be set. The user must remember to enter these values at a later date.

At the project level, duration defaults should have been set to *normal working time (true work effort)*. If the integrity of the duration field is to be maintained, this setting should *not* be changed. When the resource effort is different from the task duration, special actions are required, which will be addressed later.

Appendix 1.7.6 Assigning Part-Time Resources at the Task or Activity Level *(8.15)*

For setting part-time participation at the task level, the vendor suggests that the number of working hours per day in the Task Allocations screen be reduced to reflect the part-time level. (Figure A1.18) However, there is additional work that needs to be completed, that has not been documented:

> **This action causes the planned work field in the Task Allocations screen to also be multiplied by the corresponding fractional percentage value, thus reducing the resource effort. This is artificial and incorrect. However, if, additionally, the user also *resets* the planned work field in the Allocations screen to equal the *true work effort and* sets the duration type in the Task screen (Figure A1.17) to "res" (resource driven), this will achieve the de-**

> **sired scheduling dates (described in Example 2 under assigning resources part-time at the project level). The correct elapsed calendar days will now be in the task duration field. The *true work effort* will not be obliterated, but it will only be found now in either the resource work field of the Task screen or the planned work field of the Allocations screen.**

Appendix 1.7.7 Assigning Multiple Resources to a Job *(8.16)*

If Harvard Project Manager 3.0 users wish to do resource-driven scheduling at the project level, they must set the duration type in the duration field of the Project screen to "res" (resource driven). On the other hand, if this field in the Project screen is left at "normal" (duration driven), individual tasks may become resource driven by setting "res" in the duration field of the Task screen.

In the allocations list, more than one resource name may be assigned to a task, or the assigned number for one specific resource may be increased. (The assigned number of resources, of course, should not exceed the availability number in the resource list. See Figure A1.16.)

Even when more than one resource name is assigned to a task, the system will not automatically adjust durations to allow the job to get finished sooner. It simply assumes that all of the resources will be working in parallel. The user must also accordingly modify the values in each respective resource planned work field. (If there are different values in the planned work field for each resource, the system will use the longest one for scheduling.)

On the other hand, as long as the multiple resources are all the same resource name, the user may (1) increase the available number of resources for that name in the resource pool, (2) make the task resource driven, (3) indicate more than one assigned resource in the allocations list, (4) enter into the Allocations List screen the total planned resource effort to be spent by all of the resources combined. The system will compute correct duration.

In computing the dates during resource-driven scheduling, the duration from the planned work field in the task allocation list (rather than the task duration from the Task screen) will be used. Furthermore, the scheduling algorithms will then use the project calendar and not the resource calendar. Users ought to also remember that when this action is taken, the original record of the *true work effort* is now in the resource work field of the Task screen and the planned work field of the Allocations screen. The task duration field at the bottom of the Task screen will then contain the elapsed calendar days.

APPENDIX 1.7.8 What To Do When the Resource Effort Must Be Less Than the Elapsed Calendar Days (8.17)

In Harvard Project Manager 3.0, when the resource planned work is equal to *true work effort* but is less than the task elapsed time, the resource planned work can be distributed anywhere within the task duration. (See Figure A1.19.) To create the conditions illustrated in Example 1, the task duration is left untouched and the *true work effort* is placed in the resource planned work field.

Harvard Project Manager cannot compute percentages. When the scenario illustrated in Example 2 occurs, the user will need to compute manually the hours or days that equate to the percentage level and then proceed as in Example 1.

The scenario in Example 3 is accomplished by delaying the resource planned work with a corresponding value in the resource lag start time.

Naturally, the sum of the resource planned work and the resource lag start time may not be greater than the task *candidate time slice*.

Remember, also, that when these actions are taken, the original record of the *true work effort* is now in the resource work field of the Task screen and the planned work field of the Allocations screen. The task duration will then contain the elapsed calendar days.

Figure A1.19

task *candidate time slice* = 15 days

resource lag start time 10 days	resource planned work 5 days

Appendix 1.7.9 Fixed Dates for Activities or Tasks (8.19)

Harvard Project Manager uses the scheduling algorithm that highlights projects that are late before they start.

Fixed dates may be entered into milestones or into tasks. All fixed dates drive the late dates of their predecessors, often making them earlier. Of course, this may also create changes in slack for the predecessors. Fixed dates additionally create other date changes (described below) which similarly modify slack. Although these actions may create new critical paths, there is nothing unique about this effect.

Milestones are created by pressing "F4 Edit; 2. Add task" and choosing "M" (for milestone) in the type field. The Milestone screen is then invoked by positioning the cursor to the milestone and pressing "F3 Data; 5. Task form".

Each milestone has two dates, an early date and a late date. Since they are milestones, they also have zero durations and initially take on their dates from the latest of the finish dates of their predecessor(s). There are also two kinds of constraints that may be added to a milestone: the early constraint or the late constraint. Users may choose to enter one or the other or both.

The early constraint is a *must start* constraint. If this date is the same as milestone's system-generated date, the late dates of the predecessors will be modified, but dates in the successors will not be changed. However, if this date is earlier or later than the milestone's system-generated date, the late dates of the predecessors will be modified, and the late dates of its successors may be recalculated to maintain compatibility with its fixed date. Furthermore, when the late dates in the predecessors are recalculated, negative slack may be created in the predecessor(s). Similarly, the message "Negative slack" will appear at the bottom of the screen.

The late constraint is a *can't start until* constraint. If this date is the same as or earlier than the dates of the milestone's predecessor(s), there will be no impact on the schedule. However, if it is later than these dates, the dates in its successor(s) may be recalculated to reflect the fixed date.

When the start date of a *task* (rather than a milestone) is to be fixed, the new value should be placed into the *pln start* field of the Task screen which is invoked by positioning the cursor to the task and pressing "F3 Data; 5. Task Form". (Figure A1.17) When this occurs, the planned start and finish dates of the affected task will change, but the other dates in the task will remain unaffected.

Furthermore, when this new date is the same as the task's system-generated date, the late dates in the predecessors will be modified, but there will be no change to the dates in the successors. When this new date is later than the task's system-generated dates, the late dates of the predecessors will be modified, and the planned and early dates in the successors to the task may also be modified by the system to maintain compatibility with the fixed date. Similarly, when the fixed date is earlier than the task's system-generated dates, the planned and early dates in its successor(s) will be recalculated to reflect its fixed date. Furthermore, the late dates in the predecessors are recalculated; as a result, negative slack will be created in the predecessor(s). Similarly, the message "Negative slack" will appear at the bottom of the screen. This is an excellent signal that the project is late before it starts!

Tasks may also be scheduled with ALAP in the planned start field. This action will cause the task to be scheduled at the very end of a *candidate time slice*. While this does not extend the project end date, it can easily create a new critical path.

If the late finish date of the *project* (rather than task or milestone) is entered onto the planned finish date of the Project screen, the late dates of all of the predecessors will be correctly computed.

Other than showing the negative slack on the Gantt chart, the system does not flag delays caused by fixed dates.

Appendix 1.7.10 Automatic Resource Leveling (8.30)

During any leveling operation, Harvard Project Manager 3.0 *automatically levels each resource, based on all active projects in the subdirectory in which the resource occurs*. This application can produce some very dramatic scheduling changes in the current project. Furthermore, while normally Harvard Project Manager 3.0 is not a permanent save product, this is not true in the case of leveling. Leveling makes permanent changes to some of the fields in the task al-

locations.[5] Therefore, users are advised to save a baseline and then archive a copy of the project to be leveled. Similarly, they ought to archive each of the other projects that contain duplicate resources, a step that should then be followed by removing these projects from the active project queue. Only the current project ought to be activated. Archiving, removing, and reactivating are completed in the "5 Get/Save/Remove" subsystem.

Leveling itself is an easy operation. It is simply accomplished by pressing "F6 Compute; 4. Level resources". Harvard Project Manager 3.0 uses the following rules and sequence of execution for resolving leveling conflicts:

1. Jobs flagged for exclusion, called anchoring, are skipped.
2. If the resource duration is less than the activity duration (See the earlier discussion.), the job may be shifted within the excess time slice.
3. If there is a *candidate time slice*, the job is shifted within that timeframe.
4. Part-time resources will be scheduled for more time per day, up to full-time.
5. Overtime will be scheduled for resources flagged for acceptable overtime.
6. As a last resort, the end date of the project will be extended.

The leveled dates are found in the planned start and planned finish fields. Some of the leveling effects may be eliminated by pressing "F7; 1. Erase; Planned dates" followed by "F7 Other; 1. Erase; Resource leveled dates". However, as described earlier the sys-

---

[5]There is a field in the Allocations List screen called *Anchored?*, which tells the system whether it should be restrained from changing the resource working hours, overtime hours, or lag time for the corresponding resource assignment during the leveling process. This field automatically defaults to *No*. If users want leveling to proceed, they are advised to accept this default. If this value is retained, then the following discussion becomes very important. On the other hand, if this field is changed to *Yes* on every task, then leveling will be aborted. If it is changed to *Yes* on just a few tasks, then the following discussion is still very important.

tem may have also set resource lag times, changed the working hours per day, or assigned overtime. Since it has no record of these original values, the system cannot put them back. Users must manually correct these values or recall the archived project and start afresh.

The system provides no flags to indicate leveling delays.

Because of its file management architecture, this product takes much longer to complete the leveling process than any of the other products. A 6-month project plan with 60 activities and 4 resources took 35 minutes to complete processing—in comparison to other systems that took anywhere from a few seconds to a few minutes.

To some degree, this is because, during the resource leveling process, except for archived projects, Harvard Project Manager 3.0 will level across *all* of the projects that are in the same subdirectory as the project being leveled. Furthermore, so that it does not have to limit the size and number of subprojects, the system leaves the candidate projects on the hard drive rather than bringing them into memory for the operation.

1. Leaving the other projects in the subdirectory in the active state (rather than archiving them) tells the system to factor in the resource availability from these projects into the project being leveled. While this may be a good idea, and while it is also likely that the candidate project being leveled will be in memory, the other projects will likely be on the hard drive. The hard drive access time, of course, slows down response time.

2. Having unrelated active projects (that do not share the same resources) residing in the same subdirectory as the project being leveled will then significantly slow up the leveling process. Therefore, users are advised to set up separate subdirectories for any unrelated sets of projects. Subdirectory designations can easily be changed from the Project Names window by pressing "F3 Directories; 4. Change data directory". (Figure A1.5)

Appendix 1.7.11 User-Driven Interactive Leveling (8.32)

Harvard Project Manager 3.0 provides two key leveling tools: the Resource Histogram screen and the resource-limited Gantt chart. These are display-only screens; there is no way to make modifications from either of them.

The Resource Histogram screen is accessed by selecting "F2 Graphs; 8. Resource loading". (See Figure A1.20.) The height of each column in the histogram shows the level of commitment. With a horizontal line drawn across the histogram at the corresponding vertical axis level, the histogram also implicitly shows available resource levels. Resource utilization within the limits of availability is shown with a blue column. If there is no utilization, the slot is blank. Overscheduling is shown in red.

The histogram in Harvard Project Manager 3.0 does not show weekends or holidays.

The resource Gantt chart is accessed by selecting "F2 Graphs; 9. Resource allocations". If the "shade nonworking periods" in the Timescale Display (accessed by pressing "F5 Format; 4. Timescale display") is set to *Yes*, the weekends and holidays will be shown in the background of the Gantt chart. However, the bars will still be solid lines that cross the nonworking periods. Any jobs on the critical path are automatically displayed in red; slack is also marked. This chart shows both the task and the project that are causing the allocation conflict, since the resource conflicts may stem from other projects.

A helpful aid is the Split-window Display, which

Figure A1.20

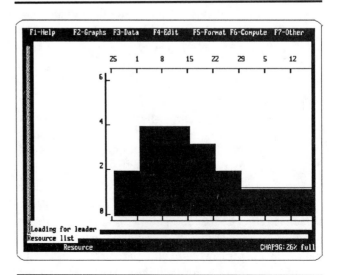

Figure A1.21

Figure A1.22

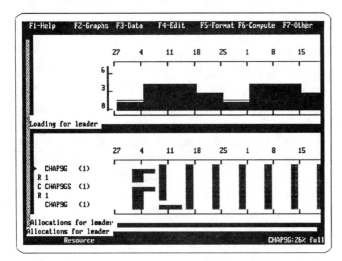

is invoked by pressing "F5 Format; 1. Split window display". By choosing to put the resource loading histogram on the top of the screen and the resource allocations Gantt on the bottom of the screen, users may get an on-line look at both views of the plan. (See Figure A1.21.) This split window may be used to display many other project views—including PERT, Gantt, and Fast Track.

It is possible to scroll the cursor through the top screen *or* the bottom screen, but not both at the same time. The active cursor choice is alternated by pressing "Control-W". When the cursor is active in the resource loading histogram, it only scrolls horizontally. When it is active in the Resource Allocations List screen, the cursor only moves vertically.

Which resource is being displayed may be changed by selecting "F4 Edit; 1. Switch resources" and entering a new name.

As soon as there are resource conflicts anywhere in the system, Harvard Project Manager 3.0 displays the message "Resource" on the bottom of the screen. (Figure A1.12) It also places an "R" on the corresponding task in the task list (See Figure A1.22.), an "R" on the corresponding task in the Task Allocations screen (Figure A1.18) and an "R" on the resource list (Figure A1.16). These flags reflect the total participation in all projects, not just the current one. This can be very helpful in a multiproject environment but

it can also be very confusing when trying to deal with leveling the current project. The tradeoffs are weighted differently, depending on the thrust of the user's needs.

The task start date and duration are changed in the Task screen, which is accessed by pressing "F3 Data; 5. Task form". (Figure A1.17) Tasks are added by pressing "F4 Edit; 2. Add task". Task-level changes to overtime, part-time, availability, resource lags, and resource reassignments are made by pressing "F3 Data; 3. Allocations list". (Figure A1.18) Deleting a resource assignment must be done from the corresponding Task Allocations screen by selecting "F4 Edit; 2. Remove allocation". Resource availability and overtime at the project level is modified with "F3 Data; 2. Resource list". (Figure A1.16) The global effects may be viewed on the bar chart by pressing "F2 Graphs; 3. Gantt chart".

Another aspect of interactive leveling is controlling the system-generated leveling by restricting which resources are subject to the automated leveling process. This restrictive leveling of tasks can be turned on or off at will—in the corresponding Task Allocations screen by changing the field for anchoring to *Yes* (if the task should be excluded from the leveling process) or *No* (if the task should be subjected to leveling). However, if this field is changed to *Yes* on every task, the leveling will be aborted. If it is changed to *Yes* on just a few tasks, leveling will proceed satisfactorily.

Appendix 1.7.12 Baseline Project Plans for Resource Leveling *(8.34)*

Harvard Project Manager 3.0 supports one version of a baseline. By saving the optimal plan as the baseline for the resource-constrained plan that is selected for implementation, users have one-half of the requirements met. This version is archived and a second version is produced. Then, by saving the resource-constrained plan as the baseline for the plan to which progress will be posted, the other half of the requirements will be met. Unfortunately, this work-around does not provide comparisons between all three versions. However, even though the process is cumbersome, users may assimilate the data by perusing both sets of reports.

Appendix 1.7.13 Resources, Multiprojects, and Project Management Software *(8.35.4)*

Since the resource list and the calendars in Harvard Project Manager 3.0 are both directory-wide, they are available to all project plans. Duplicates are not an issue.

With the file link, the whole subproject is represented by a single one-line entry in the Gantt chart and the PERT chart. The system automatically brings in all corresponding resource allocations and resource calendars.

Resource allocations are carried up one notch into the master project. Subprojects that have themselves been leveled are also reflected up one rung into the master project.

Each Resource Histogram screen in the master project will reflect the resource's commitment in every active project in the system. (Figure A1.20) Furthermore, the corresponding Resource Allocations List screen will show every task in every active project in the system to which the resource is assigned. (See Figure A1.21. Also note that CHAP9G and CHAP9GS are different projects.)

If the current master project is the only active project in the system, a split screen that shows the Resource Histogram screen and the matching Resource Allocations List screen will enable the user to easily pinpoint the sources of resource conflicts.

When there are nested subprojects, the process of visiting and returning from subprojects may be repeated until the desired subproject is reached.

In a nested multiproject environment, it is not possible to use the automatic leveling feature from the master project; system-generated leveling must be executed from the bottom up. All data is correctly rolled up from one notch in the nest to the next.

This product takes much longer to complete the leveling process than any of the other products. Three subprojects in a master project took well over one hour to complete processing—in comparison to other systems that took a few seconds to, at the longest, several minutes. (See the discussion earlier in this appendix about automatic resource leveling.) The three subprojects were:

1. A 6-month project plan with 60 activities and 4 resources;

2. A 6-month project plan with 4 different resources; and

3. A 3-month project plan in parallel with the second plan and using the same resources.

When an attempt is made to return to the master project, the system forces the user to save the subproject, whether or not modifications have been made. In this manner, all changes made in visited subprojects are automatically reflected in the master project.

Appendix 1.7.14 Guidelines and Documentation *(8.36)*

There are a few pages in Harvard Project Manager 3.0 on resource management.

APPENDIX 1.8 CALCULATING COSTS

Appendix 1.8.1 Costs and Project Management Software *(9.4)*

In addition to the code for a work breakdown structure, Harvard Project Manager 3.0 provides two levels of accounting codes: (1) the field for the name of the responsible supervisor; and (2) an additional code field. These two fields appear on the Project screen,[6] on the

---

[6]For example, they may be used to designate the name of the project champion in the responsible field and the name of the project manager in the code field.

Task and Milestone screens,[7] and in the resource list.[8]

Costs are summarized in most of the on-line screens. (Figures A1.4 and A1.17) There is also a cost histogram that shows the project-level costs. Several other screens such as the task list, the PERT chart, etc.), may also be reformatted to display costs. Finally, costs may be found on the hard copy reports.

This product supports fixed costs (called *other* costs), overhead costs, and penalty costs. The formulas for determining costs have been documented in several chapters of the user manual. These totals are seen on the Task screen *and* the Project screen. They are summarized as follows:

1. The *regular (non-overtime) cost per day* for each resource is computed by multiplying the cost per unit (from the resource list) by the work units (of the task allocation). The system insures that the working hours per day (from the task allocation) are not exceeded.

2. The *overtime cost* is determined by multiplying the overtime hours per day (from the task allocation—if it does not exceed the maximum overtime hours per day (of the resource list)) by the overtime rate (in the resource list).

3. The *resource cost per day* equals the non-overtime cost per day plus the overtime cost per day.

4. The resource's *planned* cost (in the task) is computed by multiplying the respective resource's *planned* work effort (from the task allocation) by the resource's cost per day (in the resource list).

5. The *planned* resource cost of a task equals the sum of *all* of the *planned* resource costs for the task.

6. The *planned* other cost of a task is the fixed costs associated with the task.

7. The *planned* total cost of a task is equal to the sum of the *planned* resource costs and the *planned* other costs.

8. The *projected resource* cost[9] is equal to the sum of all of the respective resource *planned* costs if actual costs have *not* been entered.

9. The *projected other* cost[10] is the same as the *planned* other costs—until the task is marked 100 percent complete.

10. The *projected* task total is equal to the *projected* resource costs plus the *projected* other costs These values are also used for the baselines (original *planned* costs—from whatever point the baseline is set!).

Harvard Project Manager 3.0 also provides additional fields that are on the Project screen but not the Task screen for the following costs:

1. *Penalty* costs may be entered at the project level (they cannot be entered at the task level). The costs will be assessed by the system for each time unit that passes until the project is designated as completed.

2. *Planned* overhead costs may also be entered at the project level. They represent allocated project-level overhead such as heat, electricity, secretarial pool.[11]

3. *Planned* other costs at the project level are computed by the system. They are equal to the sum of the *planned* other costs from the task level plus any system-calculated accrued *penalty* costs from the project level.

4. *Planned* resource costs at the project level are equal to the sum of the task-level *planned* resource costs.

5. *Planned* total costs at the project level are equal to the sum of all of the *planned* other costs from the task level plus the sum of the *planned* resource costs from the task level plus the project-level *planned* overhead.

---

[7]For example, they may be used to designate the name of the job supervisor in the responsible field and the name of the department in the code field.

[8]For example, they may be used to designate the name of the resource supervisor in the responsible field and the name of the department in the code field.

[9]Users ought to note that there is one way to compute *projected* costs for resources; another way to compute *projected* costs for *other*.

[10]Once more, users should consider that there is one way to compute *projected* costs for resources; another way to compute *projected* costs for *other*.

[11]The manual suggests that if costs will be accrued monthly and users know the monthly costs, they should multiply them by the number of months that the project lasts and enter that value.

6. *Projected* overhead at the project level is equal to the *planned* overhead—until project completion. It is not affected by any *actual* overhead costs entered during the project. At project completion, however, it is set to the value entered at that time for *actual* overhead.

7. *Projected* resource costs at the project level are equal to the sum of all of the task-level *projected* resource costs.

8. *Projected* other costs at the project level are equal to the project-level *planned* other costs—until completion.

9. *Projected* total costs at the project level are equal to the sum of all of the *projected* other costs from the task level plus the sum of all of the *projected* resource costs from the task level plus the project-level *projected* overhead.

Harvard Project Manager 3.0 allows users to export the data from the allocations list to LOTUS 1-2-3 in both Version 1A and Version 2 format. This includes data such as the planned, actual, projected, and baseline durations and costs.

APPENDIX 1.9 COMPRESSING TIME

Appendix 1.9.1 Time-Constrained Plans and Project Management Software *(10.9)*

When leveling in a Harvard Project Manager 3.0 time-constrained environment, if users want the system to do everything possible to level resources *except* extend the target date, they should set a finish date in the Project screen—before automatically leveling resources. Users may produce reports sorted on slack.

APPENDIX 1.10 ASSIGNING THE WORK

Appendix 1.10.1 The Assignment Report *(11.1)*

After selecting "7. Reports" from the Harvard Project Manager 3.0 main menu, users may choose to print the "Allocations by Resource" report. (See Figure A1.23.)

Moving the cursor to this selection in the reports list and pressing "F2 Print Options; 4. Sort/Select" will bring the user to a screen that itemizes the fields that may be displayed on the report. (See Figure A1.8. for a similar list.) There are many fields from which to choose; but, minimally, the task name, task start date, task finish date, and planned duration fields should be flagged. If the printer is wide enough, the description field (which may contain ad hoc information) may also be selected.

Pressing F10 then invokes the Sort screen. (See Figure A1.24.) The sort order should be "Resource Name = 1A, Range = *enter the name as it appears on the Resource List*" followed by "Start Date = 2A".

This format may be saved as a template, so that it may be used over and over again.

Figure A1.23

THIS IS THE ASSIGNMENT FOR THE BOSS

Allocations by Resource		21-Jan-1989			Page 1
Resource name	Task name	Task start date	Task finish date	Planned work	
boss	12	8-Jul-1988 8:00am	22-Jul-1988 4:00pm	11.00 Dys W	
boss	13	8-Jul-1988 8:00am	13-Jul-1988 4:00pm	4.00 Dys W	
boss	21	3-Aug-1988 8:00am	10-Aug-1988 4:00pm	6.00 Dys W	
boss	22	3-Aug-1988 8:00am	24-Aug-1988 4:00pm	16.00 Dys W	
boss	26	11-Aug-1988 8:00am	19-Aug-1988 4:00pm	7.00 Dys W	
boss	32	22-Aug-1988 8:00am	2-Sep-1988 4:00pm	10.00 Dys W	
boss	39	7-Sep-1988 8:00am	23-Sep-1988 4:00pm	13.00 Dys W	
boss	43	26-Sep-1988 8:00am	30-Sep-1988 4:00pm	5.00 Dys W	
boss	45	5-Oct-1988 8:00am	11-Oct-1988 4:00pm	4.00 Dys W	
boss	48	18-Oct-1988 8:00am	25-Oct-1988 4:00pm	6.00 Dys W	
boss	51	26-Oct-1988 8:00am	3-Nov-1988 4:00pm	7.00 Dys W	
boss	52	4-Nov-1988 8:00am	9-Nov-1988 4:00pm	4.00 Dys W	
boss	6	1-Jul-1988 8:00am	7-Jul-1988 4:00pm	4.00 Dys W	

Figure A1.24

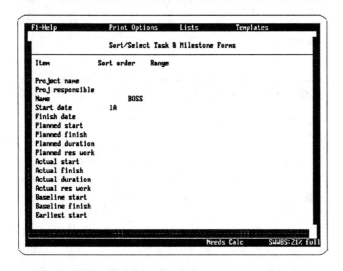

Appendix 1.10.2 The Ad Hoc Information (11.2)

The 254-character task description field in Harvard Project Manager 3.0 may have been printed as part of the assignment report. (See Figure A1.23.) If the printer wasn't wide enough to print all of the data at one time, the same operations may be repeated this time, selecting just the description field for display. (See Figure A1.25.)

If the 50-character notes fields in Fast Track mode were used, a similar "Fast Track" report may also be printed.

It is likely that these reports will need to be supplemented by output from a word processor.

Appendix 1.10.3 The Work Package Cover Sheet (11.5)

Harvard Project Manager 3.0 automatically generates a cover sheet for the "Allocations by Resource" report. The cover sheet prints the date, the project name, and the resource name.

Appendix 1.10.4 The Responsibility Grid (11.6)

In Harvard Project Manager 3.0, a word processor may be used to create the forms that meet this requirement.

Appendix 1.10.5 The Supporting Documentation (11.8)

In Harvard Project Manager 3.0, a resource Gantt and a resource histogram (Figure A1.21) may be selected from the graphics reports selection list of the reports module. The resource Gantt shows all of the resource's tasks in *all* projects to which the resource is assigned.

Figure A1.25

```
                              THESE ARE THE NOTES FOR THE BOSS

Allocations by Resource                21-Jan-1989                       Page 1

Resource name      Task name      Task description

boss               12             THIS IS THE DESCRIPTION FOR
                                  TASK 12

boss               13             THIS IS THE DESCRIPTION FOR
                                  TASK 13

boss               21
boss               22
boss               26
boss               32
boss               39
boss               43
boss               45
boss               48
boss               51
boss               52
boss               6              THIS IS THE DESCRIPTION FOR
                                  TASK 6
```

This resource histogram should be limited to the current project.

Before initiating the operations to produce either of the reports, however, the user must insure that the cursor is pointed at the correct resource name in the resource list.

Then, the "Resource Allocations" report may be invoked to print the resource Gantt. The resource histogram is produced from the "Resource Loading" report.

Both reports may be printed sideways in order to get more data on each page. They may be printed with or without the corresponding timescale and with or without a legend. Users may also reduce the image to get even more data on each page.

Harvard Project Manager 3.0 also provides a tabular loading report. (See Figure A1.26.) Users may first choose the scale for the time periods by pressing "F5 Format: 4. Timescale display" and selecting the timeframe (for example, days, weeks, or months. See Figure A1.15.) Next, from the reports subsystem, se-

lecting the "Resources by Time" report and designating "1. Loading" and "Range = *the resource name as it appears in the Resource List*" will set up the report so it can be printed. (Figure A1.24)

Appendix 1.10.6 The Problem Log *(11.10)*

In Harvard Project Manager 3.0, a word processor may be used to create the forms that meet this requirement.

Appendix 1.10.7 The Work Notes Form *(11.11)*

In Harvard Project Manager 3.0, a word processor may be used to create the forms that meet this requirement.

Appendix 1.10.8 Viewing the Data on the Screen *(11.12)*

The reports in Harvard Project Manager 3.0 may only be displayed in hard copy.

Figure A1.26

Resources by Time		20-Feb-1989				Page 1-1
	27-Jun-1988	4-Jul-1988	11-Jul-1988	18-Jul-1988	25-Jul-1988	
boss						
Resource pln cost	800.00	3600.00	5200.00	4000.00	1600.00	
Resource act cost	400.00	2000.00	1200.00	0.00	0.00	
Resource prj cost	800.00	3600.00	5200.00	4000.00	1600.00	
Resource loading	2.00	3.00	3.00	2.00	1.00	
don						
Resource pln cost	0.00	0.00	0.00	0.00	0.00	
Resource act cost	0.00	0.00	0.00	0.00	0.00	
Resource prj cost	0.00	0.00	0.00	0.00	0.00	
Resource loading	0.00	0.00	0.00	0.00	0.00	
hicost						
Resource pln cost	0.00	0.00	0.00	0.00	0.00	
Resource act cost	0.00	0.00	0.00	0.00	0.00	
Resource prj cost	0.00	0.00	0.00	0.00	0.00	
Resource loading	0.00	0.00	0.00	0.00	0.00	
leader						
Resource pln cost	300.00	1600.00	3300.00	2300.00	1400.00	
Resource act cost	200.00	1200.00	800.00	0.00	0.00	
Resource prj cost	314.29	1590.98	3326.32	2279.53	1388.89	
Resource loading	1.50	3.50	3.50	2.50	1.50	
lois						
Resource pln cost	0.00	0.00	0.00	0.00	0.00	
Resource act cost	0.00	0.00	0.00	0.00	0.00	
Resource prj cost	0.00	0.00	0.00	0.00	0.00	
Resource loading	0.00	0.00	0.00	0.00	0.00	

APPENDIX 1.11 REPORTING STATUS

Appendix 1.11.1 Baselines *(12.2)*

The Harvard Project Manager 3.0 baseline information is in fields called "planned."

Appendix 1.11.2 Extracting the Jobs for the Turn-Around Document—On a Range of Dates *(12.5)*

In Harvard Project Manager 3.0, it is easy to extract on a date range with the sort/select by entering the desired values as "From date .... Through date". (Figure A1.24)

Appendix 1.11.3 Setting Up an *As-Of* Date *(12.6)*

The Harvard Project Manager 3.0 *As-of* date is set with "F5 Format; 4. Timescale display". (Figure A1.15) New schedules are correctly computed when the directions that are outlined in the rest of this appendix are followed.

Appendix 1.11.4 Entering Percent Complete *(12.7)*

The Harvard Project Manager 3.0 field for percent complete is optional; however, if it is not entered, progress will not be reflected in the Gantt chart, the earned value feature will not be operative, and the project-level percent complete will be incorrect. (Earned value will be covered later.)

The percent field is on the Task screen (or the task list). Because the percent approach in Harvard Project Manager 3.0 is based on the theory that the amount of time expended does not necessarily equate to the percent complete (the last method described), the percent in the Task screen does not communicate with the task allocations list, and it is not automatically updated to reflect any actual time that has been entered on the Task Allocations screen. The user must manually compute (or assess) the value for percent and enter it into the Task screen (or task list).

In the same vein, normally entering a value in the percent field has no effect on the actual work field

or the remaining work field (in the Task Allocations screen). The only exception to this application is when an actual finish date and 100 % are entered into the Task screen (or task list). Then, the actuals fields (on the Task screen) and the actual work and remaining work fields (of the Task Allocations screen) are automatically updated to reflect the completion status. If the original value of planned work has not changed, no further action will be necessary. However, if the total actual work is different from the planned work, the user will need to manually rectify the actual work field.

The above application does not work in reverse. That is, when the user enters a zero in the remaining work field (of the Task Allocations screen), the system does not know that the job has been completed. The actual finish date and the 100 % must also subsequently be entered into the Task screen.

Appendix 1.11.5 Hard Copy Turn-Around Documents *(12.8)*

The architecture of Harvard Project Manager 3.0 is such that some of the required turn-around time data is on the Task Allocations screen (Figure A1.18) and some of the required turn-around time data is on the Task screen (Figure A1.17) or task list (Figure A1.22). Furthermore, the reports are designed around these forms, and there is no custom report writer. Consequently, there is no report that contains all of the data required for a turn-around document. Users may choose to invoke either the "Task and Milestone List" or the "Allocations by Resource" report.

The "Task and Milestone List". It is not possible to limit this report only to data that pertains to one resource. However, although this report cannot be filtered on resource name, it may be screened on another field, the *responsible* field.[12] Then, the user may select to display the planned start, planned finish, planned work, actual start, actual finish, and actual work fields. On a narrow-width printer, Harvard Project Manager 3.0 limits its reports to the data that can fit on an 8½ × 11 page. Therefore, several of the selected columns

---

[12]If this field is to be used to sort on resources, it will require double data entry of the resource name into two fields, the resource name *and* the responsible name.

Figure A1.27

```
Allocations by Resource                      26-Jan-1989

Resource name     Task name        Actual work        Remaining work

leader            4                0.00 Dys W          0.00 Dys W



Allocations by Resource                      26-Jan-1989

Resource name     Task name        Task start date         Task finish date          Planned work

leader            4                25-Jul-1988  8:00am      5-Aug-1988  4:00pm        10.00 Dys W



Task & Milestone List                        26-Jan-1989

Task name         Actual finish           Actual work

29                                        0.00 Dys W
31                                        0.00 Dys W



Task & Milestone List                        26-Jan-1989

Task name         Planned start           Planned finish           Planned work       Actual start

29                29-Jul-1988  8:00am      2-Aug-1988  4:00pm       0.00 Dys W
31                29-Jul-1988  8:00am      2-Aug-1988  4:00pm       0.00 Dys W
```

may be truncated or the report will be aborted. Unless a wide-carriage printer is used, it will take two different runs of the report to display all of the columns. (See Figure A1.27.) Since it is not possible to display the remaining work field with this report, team members will need to be instructed to manually write it in when they are reporting status.

The "Allocations by Resource" report. This report may be screened on resource name. However, while it does enable the user to display the task start and task finish dates, it cannot create columns for actual start and actual finish dates. These will have to be overwritten in the task date columns. Team members will need to be instructed to manually write these values in when they are reporting status. The planned work, actual work, and remaining columns may also be displayed on this report. (Figure A1.27)

There is no hours-this-period or hours-to-date field in this system. The actual work must be recomputed, each time, by the user—as the sum of the current actual work plus the new hours-this-period. Similarly, the

system will not automatically compute the remaining duration. This must also be done by the person reporting status. (See the discussion in the next section.)

Appendix 1.11.6 Entering the Status Collection Data *(12.9)*

Entering time reporting data in Harvard Project Manager 3.0 may require two different procedures: one that operates on the Task screen (or task list) and one that operates on the Task Allocations screen.

The Task screen. The Task screen (Figure A1.17) and the task list (Figure A1.22) both contain the actual start, actual finish, duration and percent complete. (See the earlier discussion on percent complete.) Since it is not possible to enter resource data on either of these screens, resource data is added in a second operation—on the Task Allocations screen. (Figure A1.18) Modifications to the fields on the Task screen should be made *before* the changes to the Task Allocations screen—since changes to the duration field of the Task screen will alter the planned work field of the Task Allocations screen. These changes may be valid, or they may need to be corrected.

When an actual finish date and 100 % are entered into the Task screen (or task list), the actuals fields of the Task screen and the actual work and remaining work fields (of the Task Allocations screen) are automatically updated to reflect the completion status. If the original estimate of the baseline planned work of the Task Allocations screen has not changed, no further action will be necessary. However, if the current estimate of the amount of actual work that will be required to complete the task is different than the originally estimated planned work, the user will need to go to the Task Allocations screen.

The Task Allocations screen. Used for resource assignment data, the Task Allocations screen contains the planned work field, the actual work field, and the remaining work field. When an entry is made into either the actual work field or the remaining work field, the system stops to recompute the whole schedule. Since this can considerably slow down response time, users are advised to turn off the calculations when doing the data entry described in this section. There is no time-this-period field. The user must compute the current total of actual work field. It is the sum of the value already in the field plus the new actual work (time-this-period). Similarly, the system will not automatically compute the remaining work field. This, too, must be calculated and entered by the user.[13]

Special processing. With the exceptions of Jobs H, I, and X of Figure 12.1, there were no special actions necessary to invoke any of the illustrated transactions—other than those just described. However, in Jobs H and I, in order to point the system towards computing the *proper finish dates* for these tasks, the user must (1) compute the new end date by adding the number of days remaining to the current date; (2) compute the elapsed days by calculating the number of days between the actual start date and the

new end date; (3) enter this value in the duration field of the Task screen (or task list); and (4) enter the correct values in the planned work, actual work, and remaining work fields (of the Task Allocations screen). When the total of the actual work field plus the remaining work field is less than the task duration, the system will not invoke any special actions.

In Job X, the new elapsed time will be less than the resource duration. In order the direct the system towards computing the proper finish dates, the directions in the previous paragraph must also be followed. However, the new resource total will be greater than the task duration and a "Problem" message will appear. This message suggests that the user either (1) lengthen the duration of the task, (2) make the task resource driven, (3) add more resources, or (4) re-enter the actual work or remaining work fields. (None of these responses are appropriate for this scenario.) The message can and should be ignored; however, it will always appear each time the plan is invoked, each time the Task Allocations screen is saved, and each time that the system recalculates the schedule.

Appendix 1.11.7 Performance Status Reporting (12.10)

The "Task Work Summary" report in Harvard Project Manager 3.0 does not report actual dates or slack.

"The Task and Milestone List" may be set up to report on early dates, late dates, planned dates, and actual dates. It also reports on planned duration, actual duration, slack and percent complete. It does not report remaining duration nor does it flag the critical path. The only way to see the successors is to print the "Task/Milestone Form" (one page for each job). There is also a Gantt chart that compares actuals to baselines. (See Figure A1.28.)

Harvard Project Manager 3.0 features sorting and selecting on many fields. (Figures A1.8 and A1.24) The sort may be in ascending or descending order. There are as many levels of the sort as there are choices. Although it is not possible to directly identify late jobs, users may select and sort by: planned, actual, early, and late start dates; planned, actual, early, and late finish dates; percent complete; remaining work greater than zero (range 1....999); and slack.

This product does not feature the ability to select jobs based on revised estimates. Similarly, users can-

---

[13]Before any status data has been entered into the system, both the actual work field and the remaining work field have been set to zero. Although it is confusing to see remaining work equal to zero, it is understandable—once the fact that the system does not automatically do any of these calculations comes to light.

Figure A1.28

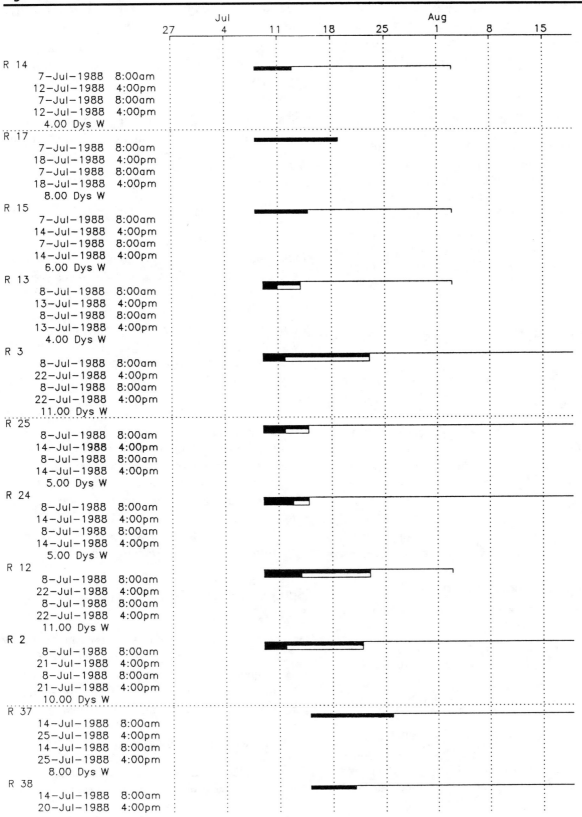

R 14		
	7–Jul–1988	8:00am
	12–Jul–1988	4:00pm
	7–Jul–1988	8:00am
	12–Jul–1988	4:00pm
	4.00 Dys W	
R 17		
	7–Jul–1988	8:00am
	18–Jul–1988	4:00pm
	7–Jul–1988	8:00am
	18–Jul–1988	4:00pm
	8.00 Dys W	
R 15		
	7–Jul–1988	8:00am
	14–Jul–1988	4:00pm
	7–Jul–1988	8:00am
	14–Jul–1988	4:00pm
	6.00 Dys W	
R 13		
	8–Jul–1988	8:00am
	13–Jul–1988	4:00pm
	8–Jul–1988	8:00am
	13–Jul–1988	4:00pm
	4.00 Dys W	
R 3		
	8–Jul–1988	8:00am
	22–Jul–1988	4:00pm
	8–Jul–1988	8:00am
	22–Jul–1988	4:00pm
	11.00 Dys W	
R 25		
	8–Jul–1988	8:00am
	14–Jul–1988	4:00pm
	8–Jul–1988	8:00am
	14–Jul–1988	4:00pm
	5.00 Dys W	
R 24		
	8–Jul–1988	8:00am
	14–Jul–1988	4:00pm
	8–Jul–1988	8:00am
	14–Jul–1988	4:00pm
	5.00 Dys W	
R 12		
	8–Jul–1988	8:00am
	22–Jul–1988	4:00pm
	8–Jul–1988	8:00am
	22–Jul–1988	4:00pm
	11.00 Dys W	
R 2		
	8–Jul–1988	8:00am
	21–Jul–1988	4:00pm
	8–Jul–1988	8:00am
	21–Jul–1988	4:00pm
	10.00 Dys W	
R 37		
	14–Jul–1988	8:00am
	25–Jul–1988	4:00pm
	14–Jul–1988	8:00am
	25–Jul–1988	4:00pm
	8.00 Dys W	
R 38		
	14–Jul–1988	8:00am
	20–Jul–1988	4:00pm

not get around the limitation by selecting on the basis of relational and arithmetic operators between current values and baseline values. Although the system does support earned value variances (See the discussion later in this appendix.), it does not report on duration variances.

Appendix 1.11.8 Highlighting Progress (12.11)

Progress in Harvard Project Manager 3.0 is not illustrated on the work breakdown structure or in Fast Track mode. Completed tasks and milestones are shown on the PERT chart in black. There is no *As-of* date line on the PERT chart or Gantt chart. Completed tasks and milestones on the Gantt are shown in black and gray. Progress on the Gantt is related to the percentage of *true work effort* that has been completed. Delays are not illustrated.

Appendix 1.11.9 Costs and Project Management Software (12.13)

In Harvard Project Manager 3.0, the costs of the tasks and of the project will be recomputed when time is reported to the task and/or when a new unit rate is assigned to a resource. There is no special field for actual-costs-this-period.

The *actual* costs are seen on the Task screen and the Project screen. The values seen at the task level are as follows:

1. The *actual* resource cost is the sum of all of the respective resource costs entered by the user for that task. (It is the sum of the non-overtime and overtime costs as described earlier in the book.)
2. The *actual* other costs are the fixed costs that are entered by the user.
3. The *actual* total task costs are the sum of the *actual* resource costs and the *actual* other costs.

The values seen at the project level are:

1. The *actual* overhead costs and penalty costs are entered by the user. These fields are intended to remain blank until the project has been completed and the actual finish date for the project has been entered.

2. The *actual* resource costs at the project level are equal to the sum of the task-level *actual* resource costs.
3. The *actual* other costs at the project level are equal to the sum of the *actual* other costs fields from the task level plus any accrued penalty costs from the project level.
4. The *actual* total costs at the project level are equal to the sum of the *actual* other costs fields from the task level plus the sum of the *actual* resource costs from the task level plus the *actual* overhead.

After actual costs have been entered, the projected costs[14] will be modified as follows:

The *projected* other costs are the same as the *planned* other costs—until a task is 100 % complete. Then, the system uses its *actual* other costs as the projected other costs.

The *projected* resource costs are equal to the sum of all of the respective resource *planned* costs—if *actual* costs have *not* been entered. Otherwise, the *projected* resource costs will be computed by adding up the new variables for the resource efforts on all of the individual tasks.

The new value will be based on the values entered for *actual* costs and remaining costs. The system multiplies the remaining work (in the task allocation form) that is entered by the user times the cost per unit (in the resource list), adding the result to the *actual* cost. This is a display-only field; it cannot be altered by the user.

The *projected* total costs are equal to the *projected* resource cost plus *projected* other costs.

Appendix 1.11.10 Cost Status Reporting (12.15)

Harvard Project Manager 3.0 is the only product that has a cost histogram that shows both bars—the originally planned costs and the current forecasted costs.

The "Task and Milestone List" can be set up to display the projected, actual, and original costs. It cannot show remaining costs. While variances may not be displayed in the task reports, they may be seen

---

[14]That is, what the project will cost if spending continues at the current rate.

in the earned value reports. (See the later discussion on earned values.)

There is no cash flow graph; however, the system does support tabular resource costs per time and project costs per time. (See Figure A1.29.)

There are two cost graphs: costs per unit of time and cumulative costs. Both are histograms. (See Figures A1.30 and A1.31.) Both show planned and actual costs, and each bar, in turn, shows three different kinds of costs: resource costs, overhead costs, and other costs.

Appendix 1.11.11 Earned Values and Project Management Software (12.17)

Harvard Project Manager 3.0 supports earned value analysis for costs.

The BAC is equal to the total baseline costs.

The BCWS is equal to:

$$\frac{\text{as of date} - \text{baseline start}}{\text{baseline finish} - \text{baseline start}} \times \text{total baseline costs}$$

The BCWP is equal to the percent complete (entered by user) × the total baseline costs.

The ACWP is equal to the actual costs The schedule variance is equal to the BCWS − the BCWP.

The cost variance is equal to the BCWP − the ACWP.

The last estimate at completion (LEC) is = to the actual resource costs + the remaining resource costs + the other costs[15] + the overhead costs.[16]

The completion variance is equal to the BAC − LEC.

In addition to the tabular earned value reports, there is an earned value by time period graph that shows earned value in each time period. (See Figure A1.32.)

Appendix 1.11.12 Reporting on Resource Availability (12.20)

The Harvard Project Manager 3.0 Resource Histogram screen that is pictured in Figure A1.20 may be printed. This is also true for the resource Gantt chart pictured in Figure A1.21, which may be set up to show baseline values as well as current values. The "Resources by Time" report pictured in Figure A1.26 is a tabular view of the resource and cost histograms.

On the other hand, the "Allocations by Resource" report pictured in Figure A1.27 may be limited to one resource and then set up to display the task name, the start and finish dates, the number of resources available (quantity) and the planned regular hours, planned overtime hours, the actual work, and the remaining work. Harvard Project Manager 3.0's reporting system cannot display overscheduled or underscheduled hours on a tabular report. Users will have to compare quantity, planned hours, and the start and finish dates to find overscheduling and underscheduling.

Appendix 1.11.13 Reporting on Resource Utilization (12.21)

In Harvard Project Manager 3.0, there is no reporting on resource utilization for period totals. The "Resources by Time" report can be set up so that it shows planned, actual, and projected dollars for each chosen period. However, it does not report actual and projected values for time. Similarly, it does not present *to-date* totals, nor are there any row and/or column totals for this report.

The "Allocations by Task" report is a variation on the "Allocations by Resource" report (Figure A1.23), except that the first column prints the task name instead of the resource name. It can provide the row totals and can be selected on resource name within a given date range. This report displays the planned, actual, and remaining dollars and the planned, actual, and remaining time.

---

[15]That is, baseline other costs if the task is not 100 percent complete or actual other costs if the task is 100 percent complete.

[16]That is, baseline overhead costs if the project is not 100 percent complete or actual overhead costs if the project is 100 percent complete.

Figure A1.29

Project Cost by Time 11-Feb-1989 Page 1

Date	Act resource cost	Act other cost	Prj overhead cost	Prj resource cost
27-Jun-1988 12:00am	1080.00	0.00	0.00	1080.00
4-Jul-1988 12:00am	4840.00	0.00	0.00	5000.00
11-Jul-1988 12:00am	2600.00	0.00	0.00	8640.00
18-Jul-1988 12:00am	0.00	0.00	0.00	5480.00
25-Jul-1988 12:00am	0.00	0.00	0.00	1400.00
1-Aug-1988 12:00am	0.00	0.00	0.00	1600.00

Project Cost by Time 11-Feb-1989 Page 1

Date	Pln overhead cost	Pln resource cost	Pln other cost	Act overhead cost
27-Jun-1988 12:00am	0.00	1080.00	0.00	0.00
4-Jul-1988 12:00am	0.00	5000.00	0.00	0.00
11-Jul-1988 12:00am	0.00	8640.00	0.00	0.00
18-Jul-1988 12:00am	0.00	5480.00	0.00	0.00
25-Jul-1988 12:00am	0.00	1400.00	0.00	0.00
1-Aug-1988 12:00am	0.00	1600.00	0.00	0.00

Figure A1.30

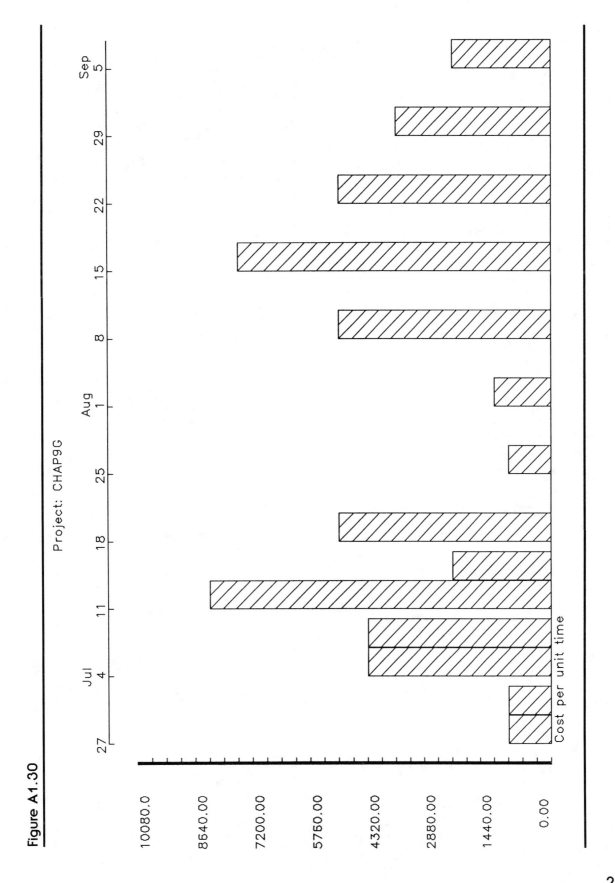

Figure A1.31

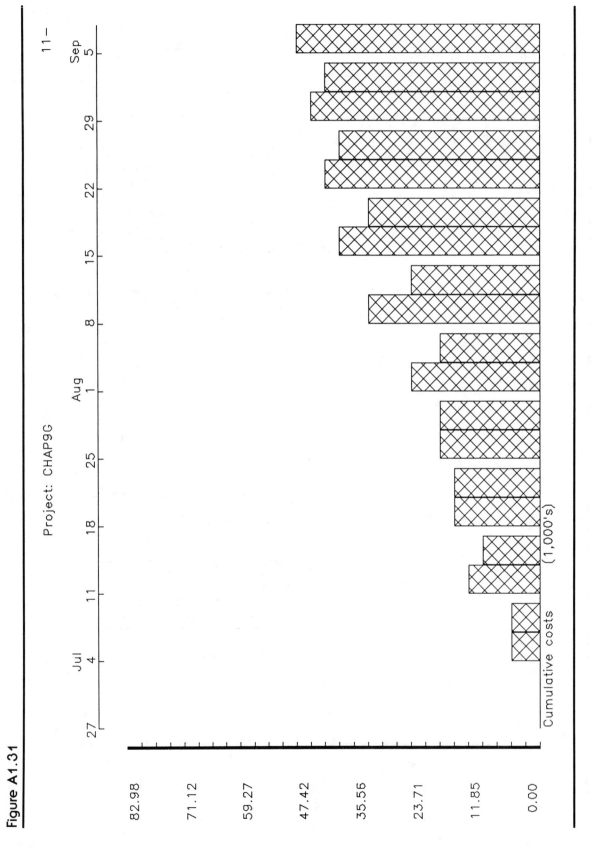

Figure A1.32

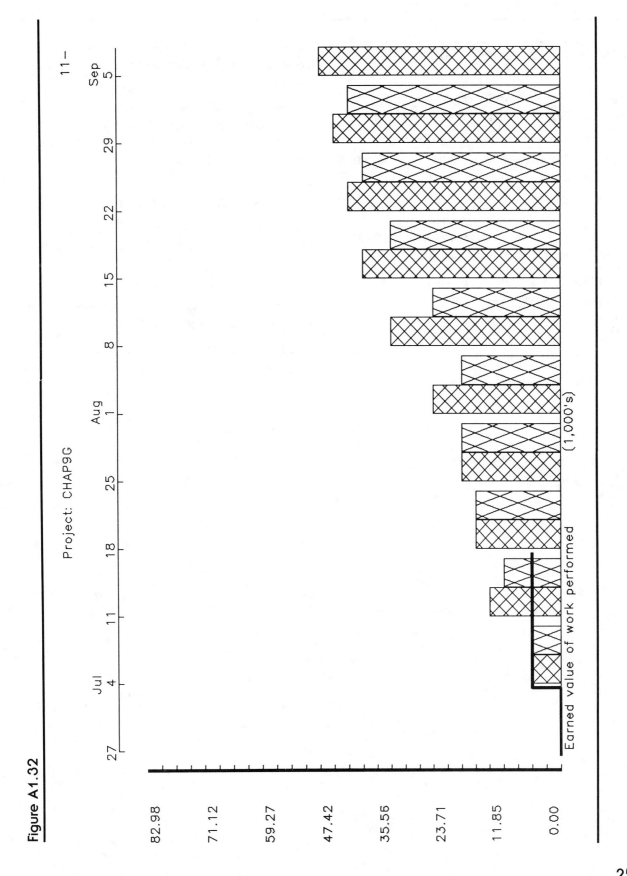

259

APPENDIX 1.12 MANAGING THE PROJECT

Appendix 1.12.1 Who Produces Perts and Gantts that May Be Restricted to Critical Path Jobs? *(13.7)*

Harvard Project Manager 3.0 will not support selecting on the critical path or on slack for either the PERT Charts or the Gantt Charts.

Appendix 1.12.2 Who Produces Reports that May Be Restricted to Fixed-Date Jobs? *(13.8)*

Harvard Project Manager 3.0 does not support extraction of report data based on fixed dates.

Appendix 1.12.3 Who Produces Perts and Gantts that May Be Restricted to Summary Jobs? *(13.9)*

Harvard Project Manager 3.0 will not support selecting on summary jobs for either the PERT Charts or the Gantt Charts. Users may apply the subproject feature to overcome this limitation.

Appendix 1.12.4 Local Area Networks *(13.14)*

Harvard Project Manager 3.0 prevents access to files when they are active. It does not provide read/write protection.

APPENDIX 1.12.5 Guidelines for Tracking and Managing the Project *(13.15)*

Harvard Project Manager 3.0 does not have tracking and plan management guidelines.

APPENDIX 2: SUPERPROJECT EXPERT 1.1

APPENDIX 2.0 INTRODUCTION

Each section in each appendix is keyed back to its corresponding introductory section in the tutorial. Readers will find that the respective tutorial section is noted in italicized parentheses at the end of each appropriate section header line.

APPENDIX 2.1 BASIC FEATURES: PRODUCTS WITH MORE THAN ONE GRAPHIC DATA ENTRY MODE

Appendix 2.1.1 Data Entry Mode (16.2.1)

This product offers many data entry choices: the user can opt for Network mode, Work Breakdown Structure mode, Gantt mode, or Outline Mode. Outline mode also permits the user to selectively single out the data entry items to be included in the outline form. SuperProject Expert is driven by the Work Breakdown Structure mode. Since planning often starts in this mode, this may turn out to be an advantage.

Appendix 2.1.2 Size and Storage Constraints (16.3.1)

SuperProject Expert loads the project data into main memory. In this *variable-length record* system, an average task in an average project requires 530 bytes.

Thus, a machine with 640K main memory provides for a project size of approximately 500 tasks. This number may be increased by

- Storing project information in several subprojects and linking them together; or
- Reducing the amount of information that is stored with each task.

With expanded memory, users may almost double the plan size, up to 2,800 tasks per project.

SuperProject Expert requires that the minimum number of buffers in the system configuration file be set to 12. Each additional buffer further reduces the memory available for project plans by 528 bytes. Thus, when an additional 10 buffers have been allocated, 5,280 bytes that would have been available for the plan are no longer present.

As projects are first loaded to memory, they are loaded into contiguous storage positions. As users continue to edit the project, it becomes more and more fragmented. This becomes important as the project approaches the memory limit, since small units of fragmented memory may not be usable. When working with large projects, users are advised to periodically save the project using the "Putaway" function under the File menu and then reload it. (See the following discussions.) This action will insure that all of the data is contiguous.

Figure A2.1

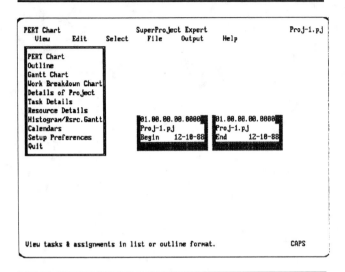

```
PERT Chart                SuperProject Expert              Proj-1.pj
    View      Edit    Select    File    Output    Help

┌─────────────────┐
│PERT Chart       │
│Outline          │
│Gantt Chart      │
│Work Breakdown Chart│
│Details of Project│
│Task Details     │
│Resource Details │
│Histogram/Rsrc.Gantt│  ▓01.00.00.00.0000▓  ▓01.00.00.00.0000▓
│Calendars        │  Proj-1.pj           Proj-1.pj
│Setup Preferences│  Begin   12-10-88    End     12-10-88
│Quit             │
└─────────────────┘




  View tasks & assignments in list or outline format.         CAPS
```

Figure A2.2

```
Preferences               SuperProject Expert              Proj-1.pj
    View      Edit    Select    File    Output    Help

      ┌─────────────────┐                 Feature Options
      │Beginner Mode    │
Auto Reca│Intermediate Mode│          esource Leveling:      Yes No
Confirm Q│Expert Mode      │          eedback Actuals:       Yes No
Confirm D│Save as Default  │          evel Using Priority First: Yes No
Auto Puta│Date & International Preferences│hou Link Type:     Yes No
Auto Posi│Advanced Scheduling Options│hou Extended Reporting: Yes No
Auto Crea└─────────────────┘          hou Subprojects:       Yes No
Sound:              Yes No      Show Task Duration Deviation: Yes No
Blink Conflict:     Yes No      Show Hour of Day:      Yes No
Date Entry on PERT/WBS:Yes No   Show Time of Day:      Yes No
Evaluation Diagnostics:Yes No   Show Costing:          Yes No
Auto Arrange on PERT:  Yes No   Show Actuals:          Yes No
         Format Options         Show Early/Late Dates & Delay:Yes No
Time Format:    12hr 24hr       Show Planned Date/Totals: Yes No
2nd Gantt Line:Actual Planned None  Show WBS and % Complete: Yes No
Screen:Monochrome Color BW graphic  Show Workday on Gantt: Yes No
Project Suffix:pj    Gantt Hrs/Day: 9  Show FinDelay/UnAsgn on Gantt:Yes No
Mark Tasks Critical with Float To: 0  Show WBS number on PERT/WBS: Yes No
Current Date:12-10-88

  Set all preferences to Beginner settings.                   CAPS
```

Appendix 2.1.3 System Structure *(16.3.2)*

At its highest level, the product is propelled by a command line at the top of the screen. The command types are View; Edit; Select; File; Output; and Help. (See Figure A2.1.) Each of these commands has its own set of subcommands, which may be accessed through pull-down menus. (See the View command in Figure A2.1.)

The View command. The View command is a very powerful command. In addition to other options, View is used to set the global system project data defaults, the project details, and the Data Entry mode.

Appendix 2.1.4 Global System Project Data Defaults *(16.3.3)*

To create the global system project data defaults, the Setup Preferences subcommand of the View command is used to access the Set Preferences screen (See Figure A2.2.).

The number and type of Preference parameters may be dependent upon the experience level of the user. Consequently, the user mode (beginner, intermediate, or expert) may also be designated at this time by selecting the Edit pull-down menu from the Set Preferences screen.

Unless the choices are finalized with the "Set Preferences; Save as default," the choices will disappear at the end of the session.

Appendix 2.1.5 New Projects *(16.3.4)*

Project-specific parameters are entered via the Project Details screen (See Figure A2.3.), which is invoked from the View pull-down menu.

Figure A2.3

```
Project Details          SuperProject Expert              Proj-1.pj
    View      Edit    Select    File    Output    Help

┌─────────────────────────────────────────────────────────────────┐
│Name:Proj-1.pj │                                                  │
│ID:P1   Directory:C:\SPJ\                                          │
│                          ─── Defaults ───    ─── Totals ───      │
│Author:              Leader:        Hours:     40   Var:     0.00  │
│WBSMask:11.22.33.44.????  Freeze:Yes No  Fixed:  0.00  Fixed:  0.00│
│Created:12-10-88  Revised:12-10-88 # 0  Rate:  25.00  Total:  0.00 │
│  Start:12-10-88+                   Rate Mult: 1.00  Actual:  0.00 │
│ Finish:12-10-88     Dur:    0 0h   Duration:    1   Hours:  0 Our: 0│
│   Late:12-10-88     Dev:0.00       Allc:dayx Pr: 50  Tasks:  0 Rsrc: 0│
├─────────────────────────────────────────────────────────────────┤
│Workday  Start  Finish Hrs 121 2 3 4 5 6a7 8 9 1011121 2 3 4 5 6p7 8 9 1011│
│                                                                   │
│Sunday   8:00a  8:00a  8  --------bb------------bb------------bb---│
│Monday   8:00a  5:00p  8  --------bb------------bb------------bb---│
│Tuesday  8:00a  5:00p  8  --------bb------------bb------------bb---│
│Wednesday 8:00a 5:00p  8  --------bb------------bb------------bb---│
│Thursday 8:00a  5:00p  8  --------bb------------bb------------bb---│
│Friday   8:00a  5:00p  8  --------bb------------bb------------bb---│
│Saturday 8:00a  8:00a  8  --------bb------------bb------------bb---│
└─────────────────────────────────────────────────────────────────┘

  Project name, used as the file name for the project.         CAPS
```

Appendix 2.1.6 Accessing Existing Plans (16.3.5)

To work with an existing project plan, it must be retrieved from storage and loaded into main memory. To accomplish this, the File command followed by the Load project subcommand and the project name must be selected. The project name is found in the Project Name window that is displayed after pressing "/; File; Load project". (See Figure A2.4.)

The slash command. For the experienced user, the two-step process of accessing the command line and the pull-down menus may be condensed with the slash command. The keyboard slash ("/") followed by the first letter of the desired command, which, in turn, is followed by the first letter of the subcommand, will reduce the effort. Thus, "/VS" will invoke the Set Preferences screen. Of course, this means the user must have memorized the options, a feat that, after some limited repetitive use of the product, is not very difficult.

Appendix 2.1.7 Immediate Processor or Batch (16.3.6)

During data entry, SuperProject Expert is an immediate processor. Automatic recalculation may be turned off in the Set Preferences screen.

Appendix 2.1.8 Adding Plan Data (16.3.7)

The four entry modes (PERT, Outline, Gantt, Work Breakdown) are also found in the View pull-down menu. (See Figure A2.5.) Similarly, plan data may be entered into the task details form which is also accessed from the View pull-down menu.

Appendix 2.1.9 Optional "What-if's" or Permanent Saves (16.3.8)

Plan data is not made permanent until the user chooses to save it and until the user designates the name under which the plan is to be saved.

Appendix 2.1.10 Ad Hoc Information Storage (16.3.9)

The description fields in the Project Details screen, the Task Details screen and the Resource Details screen are to the right of the name field, and each have 56 characters that may be used to record data. However, the system also features a miniature word processor, which may be accessed from either the Task Details screen or the Outline screen by pressing "/; Edit; View; Note text". Free-form notes may be entered for each job in the plan. Up to 5,280 characters of free-form note text may be entered for each project.

Figure A2.4

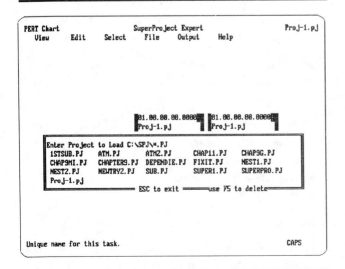

Figure A2.5

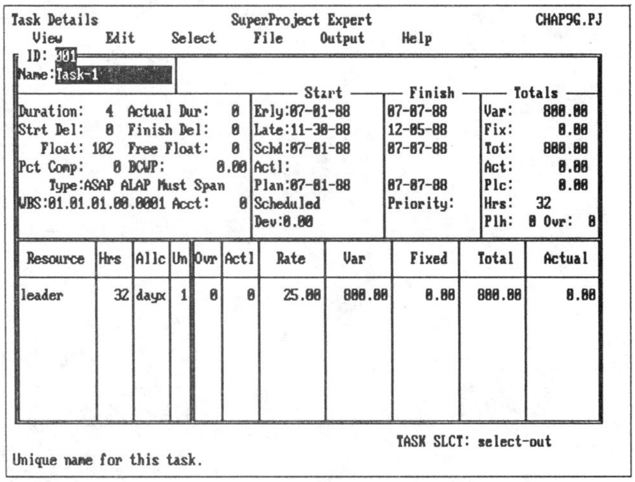

Appendix 2.1.11 Exporting Data *(16.3.10)*

SuperProject Expert also exports data to LOTUS 1-2-3, dBase III, SuperCalc4, and in Comma Separated Values.

Special features: micro-mainframe connection. SuperProject Expert interfaces with Computer Associates' mainframe product, CA—TELLAPLAN.

APPENDIX 2.2 WORK BREAKDOWN STRUCTURES

Appendix 2.2.1 Graphics Support *(4.8.2)*

SuperProject Expert supports WBS graphics. It is very easy to learn. SuperProject Expert only requires the user to select ''/; Edit; Create''—if the work unit is to be added at the same level. (See Figure A2.6.)

To start a lower level requires two actions. First, the work unit is added at the current level; then, it must be moved to a lower level by *demoting* it. A second function ''shift; down-arrow'' accomplishes the trick. The shift arrow keys easily *promote* and *demote* entries, thereby making the process of moving the entry to the correct level a very simple procedure. Once a lower level has been created, the upper level is designated as a *heading*. When the network is generated, each heading will become a beginning and ending node in the network, thus surrounding the jobs within the group. This, too, is very beneficial.

Figure A2.6

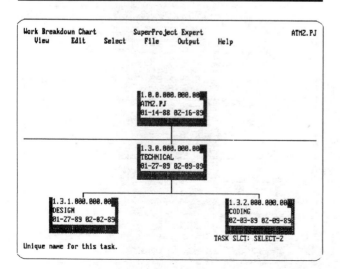

Unique name for this task.

Appendix 2.2.2 Level Support *(4.8.3)*

Since SuperProject Expert requires periods as mandatory delimiters between the levels, its number of levels is driven by the pattern of characters and periods that can be devised from 16 positions. This is not a serious limitation. SuperProject Expert will also automatically generate the WBS code (according to the user-defined WBS mask on the Project Details screen in Figure A2.3.) or will allow the user to override the code with a manually entered code.

Appendix 2.2.3 Data Entry Requirements *(4.8.4)*

In SuperProject Expert, the user may define a WBS numbering mask on the Project Details screen, which the system may subsequently use to provide automatic numbering—a very nice time saver.

Appendix 2.2.4 Durations and Dependencies *(4.8.5)*

It is not necessary to enter dependencies while creating the WBS. The Project Details default duration may be set to zero (Figure A2.3), thereby requiring no additional effort on the part of the user.

Appendix 2.2.5 Random Sequence of Data Entry *(4.8.6)*

SuperProject Expert supports WBSs, Gantts, networks, and outlines. With the exception of the networks, each of these modes allows random data entry.

Appendix 2.2.6 Using the Copy Features with the *Template* Tasks *(4.8.7)*

SuperProject Expert will allow the user to selectively take the *template* plan into other projects by using the ''File Include'' feature. This product also supports *template* tasks in subprojects that can be connected to one project as many times as required.

Appendix 2.2.7 Rollup Support *(4.8.8)*

SuperProject Expert will provide automatic rollups on many reports (e.g., the work breakdown summary), if the jobs in the project plan have been flagged for rollup levels. This is done with the '' + '' or '' — '' keys of the numeric key pad. This product also provides intermediate subtotals on time and money fields. SuperProject Expert also features the best type of duration rollup: with no extra effort on the part of the user, the rollup on the duration field computes, not the total work effort, but rather the total time span of the entries inside each header family.

Appendix 2.2.8 Guidelines and Documentation (4.8.9)

SuperProject Expert has limited WBS documentation.

APPENDIX 2.3 ESTIMATING

Appendix 2.3.1 Estimating Support and Estimating Guidelines (5.7.1)

SuperProject Expert supports the PERT method of estimating which was discussed earlier in the text. There are five and a half pages of documentation describing this approach. The product provides for two implementation alternatives: (1) Give one estimate, choose the uncertainty,[1] and let the system compute the other two estimates; or (2) give three estimates and let the system determine the uncertainty in the estimates. With the exception of situations of extreme uncertainty, it is advisable to choose the second approach—giving the three estimates. Furthermore, the second approach also supports the probability of success work that was addressed in Chapter 7.

Appendix 2.3.2 Estimates of *True Work Effort* Versus Resource-Driven Elapsed Time (5.7.4)

Until resources are assigned to activities, SuperProject Expert supports true work effort in the duration field of the Task Details screen. (Figure A2.5) After resources have been assigned to activities, true work effort might only be found in the resource hours field.

Appendix 2.3.3 Durations and Units of Measurement (5.7.6)

SuperProject Expert accepts durations in units of hours, days, and weeks. In SuperProject, the system comes with a global default duration of five days, which can be reset to the user preference at project initialization. (Figure A2.3) Within each task of SuperProject Expert, the global default may then be overridden. SuperProject Expert supports mixed units of measurement through its ''Override'' option.

Appendix 2.3.4 Zero Duration Milestones (5.7.7)

SuperProject Expert supports zero duration milestones.

Appendix 2.3.5 Lead and Lag Times with Duration but No Effort (5.7.8)

SuperProject Expert supports lag time with a two step process. First, the *Show link type* field on the intermediate or expert Set Preferences screen must be set to *Yes*. (Figure A2.2) Then, the lag time may then be entered from the Task Details screen (via selecting ''/; View; Task details'') or when in PERT mode (by selecting ''/; Edit; Link tasks; Task lag''. See the bottom of Figure A2.7.) Until a value is entered into the lag field, it will always default to zero.

Figure A2.7

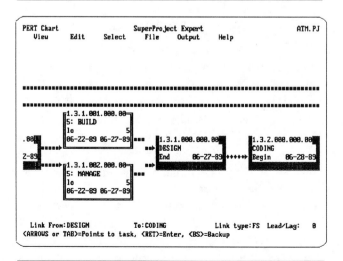

---

[1]That is, the number of standard deviations.

APPENDIX 2.4 NETWORKS

Appendix 2.4.1 Types of Networks (6.8.1)

SuperProject Expert's network is in precedence notation.

Appendix 2.4.2 Types of Relationships (6.8.2)

In SuperProject Expert, the default link is finish-to-start. When the system is in either Intermediate or Expert mode, start-to-start and finish-to-finish relationships are also available. In order to see the relationship types on the network, the "Show link type" must be set to *Yes* in Set Preferences.

Appendix 2.4.3 Number of Dependencies (6.8.3)

SuperProject Expert allows the user to designate either predecessors or successors. Their combined maximum is theoretically limited only by the total size of memory. The information needed to compute the total number of potential dependencies (etc.) is documented in an appendix.

In another vein, SuperProject Expert supports two kinds of relationships: system-generated WBS links or user-created predecessor/successor links. (Figure A2.7) The WBS links are square; the user-created links are round- or diamond-shaped. The former do not use storage while the latter are the ones to consider in size computations. These links will be discussed further in the next section.

Appendix 2.4.4 Establishing Dependencies (6.8.4)

In SuperProject Expert, of the two types of dependencies, the WBS links are automatically generated by the system, which saves time. When a WBS link goes from an upper level in the WBS to a lower level in the same WBS, this link cannot be removed. Furthermore, if the user tries to create a predecessor link where this WBS link already exists, the system will reject the predecessor link. This is a positive feature, since it prevents unwarranted use of storage.

User-created predecessor links are only legal between any two of the lowest-level WBS entries or from one WBS ending header to a second WBS beginning header. They may be set up from PERT mode by choosing "/; Edit; Link tasks". When the command line appears on the bottom of the screen (Figure A2.7), the "From" and "To" entries will be pre-filled with the name of the job in which the cursor currently resides. Move the cursor to the node required to correctly fill in the "From" entry; press return; then move the cursor to the node required to correctly fill in the "To" entry; and press return. This is definitely the way to go when there are many relationships to enter.

An alternative, albeit one with more keystrokes, is to access the Tasks Details screen by selecting "/; View; Task details" and fill in the predecessor and successor columns in the matrix that is invoked by then pressing "/; Edit; View options; Precedence".

When the start of one task may be dependent upon the completion of all of the tasks within another group of tasks, it is advisable to designate the header of the group as the predecessor rather than the last detail task in the group. In this manner, additional ending detail tasks may later be inserted into the group without the need to modify relationships.

Appendix 2.4.5 How Easy Is It to Enter Dependencies? (6.8.6)

SuperProject Expert does not require number entries to create relationships. All the user need do is position the cursor and press enter. This is definitely the way to go when there are many relationships to enter.

Unfortunately, however, in an average-sized project plan, the connecting tasks may be far apart, may not show up on the same screen, and may be hard to locate with the cursor. If this occurs when the dependencies have already been mapped out on hard copy, the user may simply key in the correct information instead of scrolling with the cursor. On the other hand, if the user is attempting to interactively lay out the schedule, establishing dependencies may become a trying experience.

While predecessor links are common between beginning and ending headers, the product also permits links from a low-level task to an upper header begin or from an upper header end to a low-level task. However, the resulting network is unpredictable, sometimes with other jobs being incorrectly linked along with the operation or, at other times, creating a network that is very difficult to interpret. Users are ad-

Figure A2.8

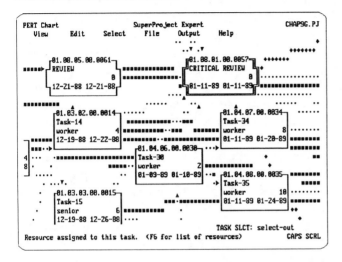

vised not to create these types of links. With all the different link types, an average plan is sometimes difficult to understand. (See Figure A2.8.)

Appendix 2.4.6 Inserting Jobs into the Middle of the Plan (6.8.7)

SuperProject Expert is basically a WBS-driven product. After getting into WBS mode, adding a new lower level from the respective upper level is accomplished by selecting "/; Edit; Create", moving the cursor to the new entry, and pressing "Shift; down-arrow". Entries at the same level are created by selecting "/; Edit; Create". From either of these approaches, additions always wind up under the correct level in the PERT, in parallel to the other first jobs in that level. Jobs added to the plan in Gantt mode or Outline mode, if they are also promoted or demoted (shift/arrow keys) to their proper levels, will wind up in the correct position in the WBS and will also usually wind up in the correct place in the network. In all of the above operations, the dependencies are *automatically* connected by the WBS link, the relationship that consumes no storage space. Furthermore, there is a fifty-fifty chance that the relationship will be correct—requiring no further action by the user. The addition simply belongs either in its parallel position at the beginning of the sequence (as earlier described) or it needs to be moved to its correct sequential position. Those that do need

fixing are easy enough to correct by entering the bona fide link as described above.[2]

On the other hand, jobs that are inserted in PERT mode will always wind up at the top of the work breakdown structure and, on the PERT, as the very first jobs in the project—no matter where they are inserted in the plan. Consequently, the largest majority of the time, corrections will have to be made with the more costly[3] predecessor/successor link.

Appendix 2.4.7 Subnetwork Dependencies (6.8.8)

In SuperProject Expert, subnetwork dependencies are no problem, except for the verification problems described later.

Appendix 2.4.8 Moving Jobs in the Network (6.8.9)

SuperProject Expert has a very easy to use "Move" feature. In PERT mode, it will move a selected task or even a group of selected tasks. All relationships are maintained. It is very helpful in purifying the aesthetics of the PERT, thus making the network increasingly more readable. The direction of movement is determined by the shift arrow keys.

In an average project with several subnetworks, many tasks, and many relationships, the "clean-up" process is time consuming. Furthermore, it should be performed only after the user is certain that no more jobs will be added to the network. Additions to the project cause the network to be recalculated. As a result, the work that has already been moved is often shifted back to undesirable locations.

Appendix 2.4.9 Removing Dependencies (6.8.10)

To delete a header or task in SuperProject Expert, simply place the cursor on the job in question and press "/; Edit; Unlink". Then, fill in the "From" and "To" entries.

---

[2]Of course, even these user-created links consume memory—there are just fewer of them this way. WBS entry mode thus increases total storage availability.

[3]In terms of memory utilization.

Appendix 2.4.10 Deleting Jobs in the Plan (6.8.11)

In SuperProject Expert, when removing headers or tasks, the system automatically connects the relationships on both sides of the deleted job. Also when deleting a header, the system gives the user the option to also delete (or save) all of the header's lower-level descendants.

Appendix 2.4.11 Lag and Lead Times (6.8.12)

SuperProject Expert supports lag time with a two-step process:

1) The show link type field on the intermediate or expert Set Preferences screen must be set to *Yes*; and

2) The lag time may then be entered in the task details form by selecting ''/; View; Task details; /; Edit; View options; Schedule'' or, when in PERT mode, by selecting ''/; Edit; Link tasks; Task lag''. (Figure A2.7)

Until a value has been entered into the lag field, it will default to zero. All three types of relationships the vendor supports may have lag times. The lag time and the relationship type may both be seen on the ''Predecessor/Successor'' report.

Appendix 2.4.12 Copying Jobs in the Plan (6.8.13)

SuperProject Expert has no feature per se to copy pieces of a plan; however, it is possible to copy whole plans and import them from one file into another by selecting ''/; File; Include''. The whole copied plan—tasks, resources, and dependencies—will be imported into the current plan.

Appendix 2.4.13 Copying the *Template* Jobs (6.8.14)

In SuperProject Expert, if inside relationships are a requirement, the user is advised to copy in the *template* tasks with the ''/; File; Include'' described in the previous copy section. This is a simple and straightfor-

ward approach to *template* implementation. Once these tasks have been imported into the master project, any changes in the *template* plan must also be done manually in every occurrence of *template* tasks in the master. The master plan will then be restricted by the size limitations described earlier in the text.

SuperProject Expert also supports the subproject link concept, a feature that may also be used for the *template* application. However, for this purpose, it is not as smooth an implementation as the ''File Include''. (It will be addressed in more detail later in this appendix in the discussion about multiproject environments.) In order to work with subprojects in SuperProject Expert, ''Show Subprojects'' in the Set Preferences screen must be set to *Yes*. Subprojects may be copied as many times as desired into any given plan. Duplicate task names are allowed. Subprojects do not allow inside dependencies, but their beginning and ending headers may be connected to other tasks that occur at the lowest level in the work breakdown structure of the master project.

There are two ways to create subprojects:

• One way is to attach the subproject to a task. This approach does not increase the size of the master project. From the Task Details screen, select ''/; Edit; Enter subproject connection''. The subproject will then be attached to the task. There will be an asterisk on the border of the corresponding box in the PERT and the WBS to indicate that the task has been attached to a subproject. The name of the attached subproject will also be noted in the Task Details screen, on the Outline screen, and on the Project Details screen.

• The second approach results in a different-shaped box (albeit still with an asterisk on the border) on both the PERT and WBS, which makes it slightly easier to identify. However, it also increases the size of the master project. After the *template* tasks have been copied into the plan with the ''/; File; Include'' as many times as necessary, each set of headers and tasks is highlighted by pressing ''/; Select; Select single object''. This is followed by selecting ''/; File; Build subproject'', an operation that gathers all of the subproject jobs into the subproject heading. Thereafter, only the heading is exhibited; the jobs inside are suppressed. Each time this operation is executed a different subproject will need to be created; therefore, the user must be prepared to provide the system with unique subproject file names.

Appendix 2.4.14 Loops in the Network (6.8.15)

SuperProject Expert will not allow loops. Whenever an attempt is made to create a loop, the system issues a "Circular Links" message.

Appendix 2.4.15 Dangling Jobs (6.8.16)

SuperProject Expert allows dangling, but any hanging jobs are automatically linked finish-to-start to the last job in the plan. This could be enhanced if the system also displayed a message when this occurs.

Appendix 2.4.16 Verifying Dependencies Are Correct (6.8.17)

SuperProject Expert allows the user to easily scroll through the network. Nevertheless, the scattered placement of jobs in combination with all of the WBS links, predecessor links, and the mysterious underlying links (described in this section) may initially make the network very difficult to verify. (Figure A2.8)

In an average-sized project with several subnetworks, many tasks, and many relationships, the system does not bundle tiers of the work breakdown structure into meaningful groups. Nodes are scattered throughout the network, causing many confusing connections. Furthermore, squares are used to illustrate WBS links, and circles or diamonds are used to illustrate predecessor links. Circles, diamonds, and squares give no indication as to their direction. Consequently, when several links between jobs cross paths, it is hard to determine their continuing directions.

The network has been developed so that when the related jobs are far apart (for example, when the predecessor is at the beginning of the project and the successor is at the end of the project), their dependencies must cross the network by hooking up to other nodes that are close to them—even if these additional nodes are not part of the dependency path. They are referred to as underlying links, and may also cause confusion during the verification process. Inserting "dummy" nodes between the distanced predecessor and its successor, and moving the predecessor and its

"dummies" away from the rest of network, works around this problem. Of course, this uses up memory.

SuperProject has a very easy-to-use "Move" feature (although it is time consuming, as are most "Move" features) that will eliminate many, but not all, of the above problems. After the user has moved all of the nodes into positions that make following the connections feasible, verification is simplified.

An alternative to verification with the network is to scroll through each Task Details screen and check the predecessor and successor columns against a hard copy of the plan.

Appendix 2.4.17 Network Aesthetics (6.8.19)

In SuperProject Expert, once the user has moved the nodes into positions that make the network readable and understandable, the network becomes significantly more acceptable. At that point, the only limitations are those caused by the circle/square confusion and any residual underlying links. (Figure A2.8)

Appendix 2.4.18 Scaled to Time? (6.8.20)

The network in SuperProject Expert is not scaled to time.

Appendix 2.4.19 Networks and Work Breakdown Structures (6.9)

Because SuperProject Expert creates beginning and ending milestones for each group of tasks, it is not necessary to undo relationships as the "latest last jobs" are added to the network. This product also allows automatic resolution of relationships when the "latest last job" is added.

Appendix 2.4.20 Limiting Relationships to the Lowest Level (6.9.1)

Although SuperProject Expert only allows user-created predecessor relationships at the current lowest level or between headers, WBS links are automatically generated at all upper levels. Whenever a lowest level node is further partitioned, it automatically gets a beginning and ending header and the appropriate internal WBS links are created. Whenever predecessor relationships are established inside the current WBS level, the linked node automatically becomes the lowest level.

The plan does not have to be completed in order to create the network and its dependencies.

Appendix 2.4.21 Dependencies in a Multiproject Environment (6.12)

In order to work with subprojects in SuperProject Expert, "Show Subprojects" in the Set Preferences screen must be set to *Yes*. There is no limit to the number of times a subproject may be used. The master project is *not* constrained by the sum of its subprojects.

The "File Include" and the "Build Subproject" should not be used for this application. (See the earlier discussion on *template* plans.)

A separate master project needs to be created, with (1) *the start date set to the start date of the earliest subproject*;[4] and (2) one task for each of the subproject plans. Then, each task ought, in turn, to be attached to its respective subproject. This is done by selecting "/; Edit; Enter subproject connection" from the corresponding Task Details screen and entering the subproject name. Dependency connections are simply made as outlined earlier in this appendix.

There are two ways to insure that the modifications that have been made to any of the subprojects are reflected in the master projects. In the first, the master project plan must be saved (using the "Putaway") and recalled in order to complete the operation. In the second method, positioning the cursor on each task entry in the outline and pressing "/; File; Update subproject" will insure that the correct durations and dates are reflected in the master project. This has implications when there are nested subprojects and will be addressed later.

Because SuperProject Expert may keep several projects in memory simultaneously, subsequent loading of any one of the attached subprojects will result in all of the subprojects being loaded—to the extent that they will fit into memory. After they have been saved, unwanted subprojects may also be discarded from memory in order to make room to load others.

The user may easily flip back and forth by moving the cursor to the corresponding task and selecting "/; File; Zoom in on subproject" or "/; File; Return to superproject". To speed things up, the calculations

may be temporarily stopped from the Set Preference menu. When there is no longer a need to flip back and forth, the calculations should be turned back on. It is not necessary to do double data entry when the subprojects have been linked. If the procedures described above are followed, changes made in the subprojects are automatically reflected in the master project.

Appendix 2.4.22 Printing and Viewing Networks (6.13)

In SuperProject Expert, viewing the network may be achieved by selecting "/; View; PERT". To print the network is also a simple process: From PERT mode, enter "/; Output; Plotter/graph" and complete the menu.

Appendix 2.4.23 Guidelines and Documentation (6.15)

In SuperProject Expert, there is one page on networks, two pages on links, and several pages on multiprojects.

APPENDIX 2.5 OPTIMAL PLANS

Appendix 2.5.1 Calendars (7.14.1)

Calendar information in SuperProject Expert is stored in two places: under the Project Details and under the Project Calendar screens. The Project Details screen (Figure A2.3) is accessed by pressing "/; View; Details of project". The starting hour and ending hour of each day of the week, as well as the number of hours worked each day, are entered in this screen. It is also here that the user tells the system when each day's breaks (for example, lunch) usually occur.

In a different vein, holidays are very easily entered into the calendar (accessed with "/; View; Calendar") by moving the cursor to the box corresponding to the date and typing "Holiday". (See Figure A2.9.)

In the project calendar, Saturdays and Sundays automatically default to be labeled *Weekends*. While they can be changed to non-weekend days by assigning hours to the corresponding field for number of hours worked that day (in the Project Details screen), none of the other weekdays may be designated a weekend day. Nevertheless, any of the other five weekdays may be made into non-work days by entering a zero into the corresponding field for number of hours worked that day.

---

[4]This will be essential for correct schedule calculations.

Figure A2.9

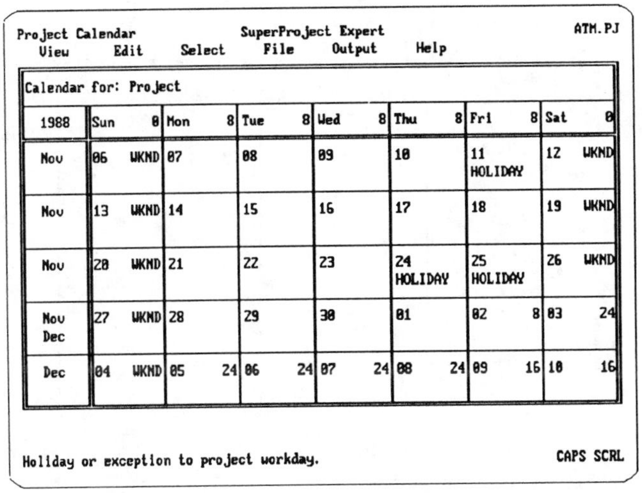

```
Project Calendar              SuperProject Expert            ATM.PJ
   View      Edit    Select     File    Output    Help

Calendar for: Project
┌──────┬──────────┬─────────┬─────────┬─────────┬─────────┬──────────┬─────────┐
│ 1988 │Sun     8 │Mon    8 │Tue    8 │Wed    8 │Thu    8 │Fri     8 │Sat    0 │
├──────┼──────────┼─────────┼─────────┼─────────┼─────────┼──────────┼─────────┤
│ Nov  │06   WKND │07       │08       │09       │10       │11        │12   WKND│
│      │          │         │         │         │         │HOLIDAY   │         │
├──────┼──────────┼─────────┼─────────┼─────────┼─────────┼──────────┼─────────┤
│ Nov  │13   WKND │14       │15       │16       │17       │18        │19   WKND│
├──────┼──────────┼─────────┼─────────┼─────────┼─────────┼──────────┼─────────┤
│ Nov  │20   WKND │21       │22       │23       │24       │25        │26   WKND│
│      │          │         │         │         │HOLIDAY  │HOLIDAY   │         │
├──────┼──────────┼─────────┼─────────┼─────────┼─────────┼──────────┼─────────┤
│ Nov  │27   WKND │28       │29       │30       │01       │02      8 │03     24│
│ Dec  │          │         │         │         │         │          │         │
├──────┼──────────┼─────────┼─────────┼─────────┼─────────┼──────────┼─────────┤
│ Dec  │04   WKND │05    24 │06    24 │07    24 │08    24 │09     16 │10     16│
└──────┴──────────┴─────────┴─────────┴─────────┴─────────┴──────────┴─────────┘

Holiday or exception to project workday.              CAPS SCRL
```

It is advisable to save the calendar as the default. Otherwise, it will need to be recreated each time the system is invoked. When the user is satisfied with the calendar, it should be saved by selecting "/; Edit; Save as default" from the Project Calendar screen.

Once the calendar has been saved as the default, it may also be used by other projects' plans as well by selecting "/; Edit; Load default" from the Project Calendar screen.

Appendix 2.5.2 Choosing the Correct Project Start Date *(7.14.2)*

In SuperProject Expert, the project start date is entered into the *start date* field on the Project Details screen, which is accessed by selecting "/; View; Details of project". It is only necessary to take this action one time—at plan initiation.

The scheduling algorithm uses the current *operating system* date. Therefore, the desired project start date must be entered into the *current date* field of the Set Preferences screen *each time the project plan is invoked*[5]. If this action is not taken, the resulting date computations will be unpredictable and undesirable. This is especially true when the current date is *later*

than the project start date.[6] The resulting date computations are based on the current date rather than the desired project start date.

Appendix 2.5.3 Insuring that the Plan Is Not Constrained by Resources *(7.14.3)*

On the SuperProject Expert Set Preferences screen, the user should say *No* to *Resource Leveling*; *Level Using Priorities First*; and *Auto Create Resources*. Finally, resources should not be entered on the Task Details screen.

Appendix 2.5.4 Avoiding Imposed Target Dates *(7.14.3)*

Superproject Expert supports four types of date entries in the type field of the Task Details screen. (Figure A2.5) The values for this field are (1) ASAP (As Soon As Possible), (2) ALAP (As Late As Possible), (3) MUST (Must Start on a Given Date), and (4) SPAN (draw out over a defined timeframe). The default is ASAP. The user should accept the default when scheduling the optimal plan.

Appendix 2.5.5 Calculating the Schedule *(7.14.4)*

In SuperProject Expert, schedules will be continuously updated when the *auto recalculation* field in the Set Preferences screen is turned on to *YES*. On the other hand, if this slows the system down, it may be set to *No*. Then, schedules may be recalculated on an ad hoc basis by pressing the "Shift" key along with *1*.

Appendix 2.5.6 The Forward Pass: Calculating the Early Dates *(7.14.5)*

Among the several sets of dates in SuperProject Expert, two are significant now: the *early* dates and the *scheduled* dates.

The dates found in the *early finish, early start* fields correspond to ending the predecessor at 5:00 P.M. and starting its successor(s) at 5:01 P.M. of the

---

[5] This field is not saved with the project data.

[6] As is often the case later in the project when doing *What-If* Analysis.

same day. Thus, the *early start* dates are confusing. The *early finish* date always corresponds to a correctly computed finish date.

The dates found in the *scheduled finish, scheduled start* fields correspond to ending the predecessor at 5:00 P.M. one day and starting its successor(s) at the start of the next business day. These dates always correctly correspond to the dates computed using the traditional scheduling algorithm.

Appendix 2.5.7 Zero Duration Milestones (7.14.8)

SuperProject Expert uses the preferred approach for scheduling zero duration milestones—it schedules the milestone at the end of the day on which all of the predecessors have finished.

Appendix 2.5.8 Retaining a Baseline Record of the Optimal Plan (7.14.11)

From SuperProject Expert's Outline mode, selecting "/; Edit; Transfer to baseline" will store the values from the scheduled date fields in the planned dates fields. The planned dates do not change until this process has been invoked again. The planned date fields become the baseline values and may then be seen in various screens and reports. In large projects, creating a baseline can consume extensive amounts of memory. If all of the available memory is consumed, some of the tasks in the plan will not have their baseline set. Furthermore, no further modifications may be made to the plan until it has been broken into subprojects. (See the multiproject discussions.)

Appendix 2.5.9 Interpreting the Dates on the Screen (7.14.12)

From the SuperProject Expert Outline mode, the user can selectively choose which columns of data are to be displayed. This is done by designating the desired fields on the Select Criteria screen, which is invoked from "/; Select; Task". There are 67 fields from which to choose, many of which are the desired dates. (See Figure A2.10.)

On the PERT chart, only the early start and finish dates are displayed. The Set Preferences documentation indicated that the user may also exhibit late dates

Figure A2.10

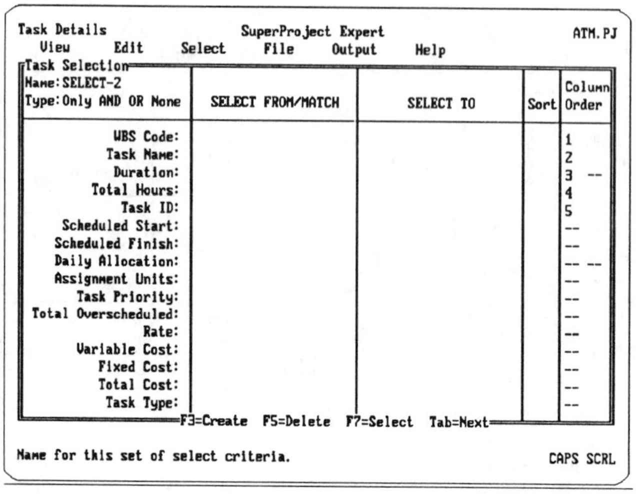

and baseline planned dates, but the product did not work as described. These dates did not show up.

On the Gantt chart, there is the standard time-scaled display of bars for each job. The bars are placed according to the *scheduled* dates. If the user chooses "2nd Gantt Line: Actual" or "2nd Gantt Line Planned" from the Set Preferences screen, a second time-scaled bar will be drawn after each job. Although the second line is confusingly labeled *scheduled*, this time-scaled bar will relate to the actual dates or the baseline planned dates respectively.

While it does display the task number and name on the Gantt chart, the system does not support columns for reporting dates—even after invoking the select criteria. There is a four-step *work-around*; however, the user is advised to use the Outline mode instead. The *work-around* involves producing a report that is then displayed on the screen rather than spooled to hard copy:

1. Invoke Gantt mode by selecting "/; View; Gantt".
2. Select the desired columns by pressing "/; Select; Task" and naming this set of select criteria.
3. Tell the system to send the report to the screen by pressing "/; Output; Screen" and selecting "Screen" for the value of the field called *output to*. (See Figure A2.11.)

Figure A2.11

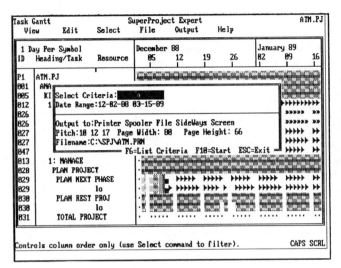

```
Task Gantt              SuperProject Expert                    ATM.PJ
   View      Edit     Select    File    Output    Help

1 Day Per Symbol              December 88            January 89
ID   Heading/Task   Resource   05   12   19   26    82   89   16

P1   ATM.PJ
001  ANA
005  XI Select Criteria:      a
012   1 Date Range:12-02-88 03-15-89
026
026    Output to:Printer Spooler File SideWays Screen
027    Pitch:18 12 17  Page Width: 88   Page Height: 66
027    Filename:C:\SPJ\ATM.PRN
047              F6=List Criteria  F10=Start  ESC=Exit
013    1: MANAGE
028    PLAN PROJECT
029    PLAN NEXT PHASE
029               lo
830    PLAN REST PROJ
830               lo
031    TOTAL PROJECT

Controls column order only (use Select command to filter).    CAPS SCRL
```

Figure A2.12

```
Task Gantt              SuperProject Expert                   CHAP9G.PJ
   View      Edit     Select    File    Output    Help

9 Hours Per Day            Jul 21 88  Jul 22  Jul 23  Jul 24  Jul 25
ID   Heading/Task  Resource  8:88a    8:88a   8:88a   8:88a   8:88a

C9   CHAP9G.PJ
864    group1
001    Task-1
001              leader
002    Task-2
002              leader
003    Task-3
003              leader
004    Task-4
004              leader
005    Task-5
005              leader
865    group2
006    Task-6
006              boss
012    Task-12
                                          TASK SLCT: select-out
Name of heading/task or resource.                          CAPS SCRL
```

4. Format the report by selecting "/; Output; View" and entering the name from Step 2 into the field called "Select Criteria". Press the F10 key to send the report to the screen.

Appendix 2.5.10 Annotating the Critical Path (7.14.13)

SuperProject Expert shows the critical path bars on the Gantt in red. In the network, the product highlights the critical path with red rectangles at the beginning and end of the project and diamonds through the rest of the project. The nodes on the critical path look like any other nodes.

Appendix 2.5.11 Gantt Chart Time Periods (7.14.15)

SuperProject Expert time periods may be in any increment from hours to years. Theoretically, there is no limit to the number of time periods that may be displayed. Once in Gantt mode, by repetitively selecting "/; Edit; Enlarge", the user may display smaller and smaller time periods until hours per day is displayed. The scheduled lunch hour will be blocked out as well. (See Figure A2.12.) Selecting "/; Edit; Reduce" causes larger and larger increments to be displayed until years is the timeframe. Finally, to go

immediately to hours per day, the user may simply select "/; Edit; Modify days per symbol" and enter *0* in the *days per symbol* field.

After turning the "Scroll Lock" key on, the user may move in any direction around the Gantt chart by pressing the arrow keys.

The bars on the Gantt chart are broken to show weekends and holidays.

Appendix 2.5.12 Scheduling in the Multiproject Environment (7.14.17)

Calendar data in SuperProject Expert is not imported into master projects from subprojects. If one of the subproject calendars has been saved as the default *and* if it meets the current requirements, it will have to be attached to the master project from the Calendar screen by selecting "/; Edit; Load default". Otherwise, a new calendar will need to be created when the master project is set up.

The schedule will be correctly computed if (1) the master project was created with a start date equal to the start date of the earliest subproject; (2) the master project has been saved with the "Putaway" and reloaded; and (3) the system date on the Set Preferences screen has been set to the date equal to the start date of the earliest subproject. Step 2 may be replaced by the Update Subprojects procedure described earlier in the book and addressed in more detail in the next section.

If the Update Subprojects procedures are followed, changes made in the subprojects are automatically reflected in the master project. Additional procedures may be required for nested subprojects and will be addressed in the next section.

Appendix 2.5.13 Nesting Subprojects in a Multiproject Environment *(7.14.18)*

In SuperProject Expert, when there are nested subprojects, the process of visiting and returning from subprojects may be repeated until the desired subproject is reached.

When nesting subprojects, using the "Putaway" and reloading causes all modifications to be reflected. On the other hand, if the master project and all of the subprojects have not been "Put away" and reloaded, the lower-level values in each subproject must be manually carried upward by the user. Starting at each task that is attached to the lowest notch at the bottom of the nest and working upwards to the highest notch in each rung, the user should press "/; File; Update subproject". When the update subproject command is issued, the system computes the total duration of the next lower project in the rung and uses it as the duration of the current task. This action will insure that the current task's dates will be computed correctly. In a complex nest of subprojects, users are advised to create a hard copy tree of the nested groups and check each one off as its schedule is computed. If only one subproject is overlooked, all of the subsequent schedules may be incorrect. Consequently, even though saving and reloading slows up processing, it may be the preferred alternative.

APPENDIX 2.5.14 Guidelines and Documentation *(7.14.20)*

There is one page of information in SuperProject Expert about the critical path and several pages on date computations.

APPENDIX 2.6 CALCULATING A FINISH DATE

Appendix 2.6.1 Products that Support the Statistical Approach *(7.26.1)*

Figure A2.13

Outline SuperProject Expert ATM.PJ
View Edit Select File Output Help

Heading/Task	Resource	Task ID	Pr	Dur	Dev	Opt Dur	Likly Dur	Pess Dur	Schd Start
ATM.PJ		P1		71	3.00				12-02-88←
ANALYSIS		001		55	0.00	5	5	5	12-02-88
KICK-OFF		005		37	0.00	5	5	5	12-02-88
1: BUILD		012		10	0.00	5	5	5	12-02-88
DO CHARTER		026		5	1.00	2	5	8	12-02-88
	boss	026	50	5					12-02-88
	leader	026	50	5					12-02-88
DO H.L.A		027		5	1.00	2	5	8	12-09-88
	boss	027	50	5					12-09-88
	leader	027	50	5					12-09-88
Task-47		047		7	2.00	1	7	13	12-02-88
1: MANAGE		013		36	0.00	5	5	5	12-03-88
PLAN PROJECT		028		36	0.00	5	5	5	12-03-88
PLAN NEXT PHASE		029		5	2.00	0	4	12	12-03-88
	boss	029	50	5					12-03-88
PLAN REST PROJ		030		37	0.00	5	5	5	12-03-88

CALC
Task priority. All assignments are set to this priority.

Computer Associates, Inc. is to be commended for their valiant attempt at implementing the PERT approach. (See Figure A2.13.) At first blush, this was a very exciting prospect but, sadly, their implementation of this feature leaves a lot to be desired. Nevertheless, it is also very important to note that this is the *only* product that even comes this close! Standard deviations are valid at the task level only. They may not be entered at any header levels.

- Users may enter values in the duration and deviation columns and the system will automatically compute the correct matching values for the optimistic, most likely, and the pessimistic estimates. In this manner, users may choose the level of uncertainty they want the task to reflect.
- Alternatively, the three estimates may be entered and the system will correctly compute the task duration and standard deviation.[7]

The standard deviation at the project level (Figure A2.3 and Figure A2.13) is a display-only field. Consequently, users cannot decide, at the project level, that they would like all of their estimates to reflect a designated degree of uncertainty and have the system accordingly compute all of the optimistic, pessimistic, and most likely estimates, as well as the corresponding duration. (Standard deviations may only be entered at the task level, as described above.)

[7]Using the formulas for the beta (β) distribution.

Furthermore, although the project-level standard deviation is indeed the standard deviation of the critical path and appears to be computed using the same formula described earlier in this appendix,[8] the system *rounds* the results! Thus, a project-level standard deviation of 2.43 is displayed as 2.00; 2.53 is represented as 3.0. What is even more disappointing is the fact that, when three inch-pebble-level estimates (4–40 hours) are entered for each task in the project, the standard deviation for the project often rounds to *0*! The bottom line is that the value that the system computes for the standard deviation of the project is not likely to be very beneficial in the computations for determining a reasonable late finish date.

Users should also be aware that, while the beauty of this product is that it does support the feature, some of the documentation that describes it is not correct!

For example, the manual *and* the help screens state that "the durations entered for the optimistic and pessimistic should be the durations likely to occur 1 percent of the time (three standard deviations)." This, of course, is not accurate. Three standard deviations reflects the 99.73 percent probability that the estimate will fall within the interval of optimistic and pessimistic. Rather than assuming that the optimistic and pessimistic estimates occur only 1 percent of the time, these estimates will be more satisfactory if they are developed using the guidelines presented in either this appendix or earlier in the book.

In another scenario, the manual talks about "entering a deviation of 5," but really means that the *range* from the most likely should be ± 5 days. Then, it gives examples:[9]

- 95, 100, and 105 days with "a 68 percent chance of taking between 95 and 105 days." Estimates of 95, 100, and 105 days yield a standard deviation of

1.67 (much greater than 68 percent). One standard deviation, (68 percent) on a most likely estimate of 100 days, results in an optimistic duration of 97 days and a pessimistic duration of 103 days.

- 90, 100, 110 days with "a 95 percent chance of taking between 90 and 110 days." Estimates of 90, 100, and 110 days yield a standard deviation of 3.33 (greater than 100 percent). Two standard deviations (95 percent) on a most likely estimate of 100 days results in an optimistic duration of 94 days and a pessimistic duration of 106 days.

- 85, 100, 115 days with "a 99 percent chance of taking between 85 and 115 days." Estimates of 85, 100, and 115 days yield a standard deviation of 5.00 (approaching 200 percent). Three standard deviations (99 percent) on a most likely estimate of 100 days results in an optimistic duration of 91 days and a pessimistic duration of 109 days.

In spite of the limitations described in this section, users will discover, when reading the next section, that this product goes a long way toward providing a foundation for a *work-around*.

Appendix 2.6.2 Using the New Reasonable Late Finish Date of the Project (7.26.3)

In SuperProject Expert, users can choose a fixed date for the start of the project *or* the finish of the project, *but not both!* (See the Project Details screen in Figure A2.3.) To retain the correct early start date in the Project Details screen, a fixed-date milestone may be added to the end of the project. The correct late dates will be computed and stored in each of the late start and late finish fields. The early finish date of the project may only be found in the early finish date of the last task(s) in the project that occurs before the fixed-date milestone. If the Set Preferences "Mark Tasks Critical With Float To" has been used, the system will recognize the new critical path.

---

[8]The vendor states that, with the exception of any tasks that have actual finish dates, all tasks on the critical path are candidates for the computations. When there are parallel tasks on the critical path, *only one of the tasks is used.*

[9]There is nothing wrong with using the values the vendor gives for optimistic and pessimistic in these examples. As a matter of fact, ranges as wide as these are fairly common at the milestone level. What is incorrect here are the probabilities that the literature assigns to these ranges.

APPENDIX 2.7 ADDING RESOURCES

Appendix 2.7.1 Creating the Resource Calendars (8.8)

In SuperProject Expert, resource calendar information is stored in two places: under the Resource Details

Figure A2.14

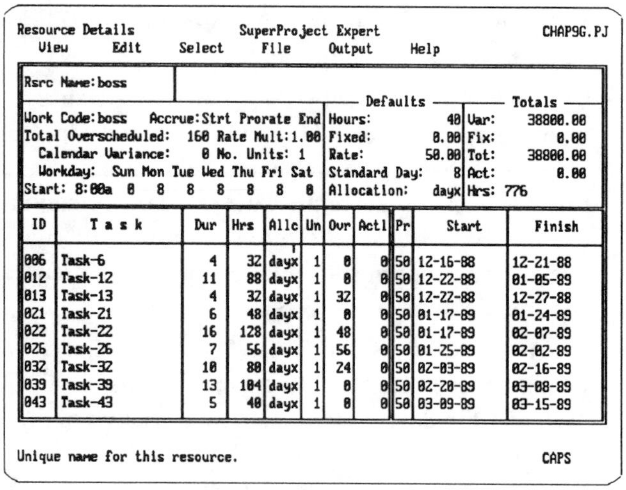

```
┌──────────────────────────────────────────────────────────────┐
│ Resource Details          SuperProject Expert        CHAP9G.PJ │
│    View      Edit    Select     File    Output    Help         │
│ ┌────────────────────────────────────────────────────────────┐ │
│ │ Rsrc Name: boss                                            │ │
│ ├────────────────────────────────┬───── Defaults ──┬─ Totals ─┤ │
│ │ Work Code: boss   Accrue: Strt Prorate End │Hours:    40│Var:  38800.00│
│ │ Total Overscheduled:  160 Rate Mult:1.00 │Fixed:   0.00│Fix:    0.00│
│ │    Calendar Variance:   0 No. Units: 1 │Rate:    50.00│Tot:  38800.00│
│ │    Workday:  Sun Mon Tue Wed Thu Fri Sat │Standard Day:  8│Act:    0.00│
│ │ Start: 8:00a  0   8   8   8   8   8   0 │Allocation:  dayx│Hrs: 776│
│ ├────┬─────────┬────┬────┬────┬──┬────┬────┬──┬─────────┬────────┤ │
│ │ ID │  Task   │Dur │Hrs │Allc│Un│Ovr │Actl│Pr│  Start  │ Finish │ │
│ ├────┼─────────┼────┼────┼────┼──┼────┼────┼──┼─────────┼────────┤ │
│ │ 006│ Task-6  │  4 │ 32 │dayx│ 1│  0 │  0 │50│12-16-88 │12-21-88│ │
│ │ 012│ Task-12 │ 11 │ 88 │dayx│ 1│  0 │  0 │50│12-22-88 │01-05-89│ │
│ │ 013│ Task-13 │  4 │ 32 │dayx│ 1│ 32 │  0 │50│12-22-88 │12-27-88│ │
│ │ 021│ Task-21 │  6 │ 48 │dayx│ 1│  0 │  0 │50│01-17-89 │01-24-89│ │
│ │ 022│ Task-22 │ 16 │128 │dayx│ 1│ 48 │  0 │50│01-17-89 │02-07-89│ │
│ │ 026│ Task-26 │  7 │ 56 │dayx│ 1│ 56 │  0 │50│01-25-89 │02-02-89│ │
│ │ 032│ Task-32 │ 10 │ 80 │dayx│ 1│ 24 │  0 │50│02-03-89 │02-16-89│ │
│ │ 039│ Task-39 │ 13 │104 │dayx│ 1│  0 │  0 │50│02-28-89 │03-08-89│ │
│ │ 043│ Task-43 │  5 │ 40 │dayx│ 1│  0 │  0 │50│03-09-89 │03-15-89│ │
│ └────┴─────────┴────┴────┴────┴──┴────┴────┴──┴─────────┴────────┘ │
│ Unique name for this resource.                          CAPS   │
└──────────────────────────────────────────────────────────────┘
```

screen (See Figure A2.14.) and under the Resource Calendar. (Figure A2.18.) The workday, workhour, and holiday values in these screens default to the project-level values, but they can be modified by the user.

The Resource Details screen is accessed by pressing "/; View; Resource details". The resource's standard workday starting hour, the default number of hours per any given workday, *and* the standard number of hours worked each day of the week that the resource is available are entered in this screen.

Part-time resources are designated at the project level using the resource daily allocation type and amount fields in this form. They will be discussed later in this appendix.

The user cannot tell the system when the resource's daily breaks (for example, lunch) usually occur. They will default to the project breaks. This may create a problem when the resource's daily workhours do not coincide with the breaktimes.

In a different vein, holidays unique to the resource are very easily entered into the resource calendar (accessed with "/; View; Calendar" and pressing the tab key to get to the corresponding resource calendar) by moving the cursor to the box corresponding to the date and typing "Holiday." This process may also be used for the number of working hours for a single specific calendar day.

Once the user is satisfied with the calendar, it should be saved by selecting "/; Edit; Save as default"

from the Calendar screen. Otherwise, the calendar settings will be gone the next time the system is invoked.

Appendix 2.7.2 Creating the Resource Pool (8.9)

In SuperProject Expert, resources may be individuals, groups of individuals, equipment, or materials. On the other hand, when the costs associated with a task's resource are *fixed* costs or onetime costs, they may be entered at the project level or at the task level in the fixed costs fields. (Figures A2.3 and A2.5)

The maximum number of resources per project is theoretically limited only by the total size of memory. The information needed to compute the total number of potential resources (etc.) is documented in an appendix in the user's manual.

After recalling the Resource Details screen by pressing "/; View; Resource details", new resources are created by pressing "/; Edit; Create". There is one screen for each resource. (Figure A2.14) In addition to the standard resource data, this screen is also used to enter resource calendar information and cost reporting information.

The standard resource data entered at this time are: the 10-character resource name, the number of available resources of this type, the standard number of workhours per any given day, the standard number of hours worked each weekday that the resource is available, the overtime multiplier (for example, 1.5 is used for time-and-a-half), and the work group category of the resource.

Two additional fields, the resource daily allocation amount field and the resource allocation type field, which are paired together, default to the values set in the Project Details screen. Users are advised to set the resource allocation type to default to "x." The default of the resource daily allocation amount field should be "full-time." (The use of these two fields will be covered in greater detail later in this appendix.)

The unit of measurement for each resource defaults to hours. A default hourly rate is set in the Project Details screen. On the other hand, the user may override the default rate and enter a unique hourly rate for each resource. It is important to note that changes to this field only affect the costs of *new* tasks to which the resource is subsequently assigned. The costs of *previously* assigned tasks will remain computed at the original rate. Although it is possible, in Outline mode, to manually correct the cost for each task, this is time consuming. Consequently, users are advised to check carefully to insure that the correct rate has been entered before assigning resources to jobs.

SuperProject Expert does not support multiple billing rates for one resource.

Appendix 2.7.3 Assigning Part-Time Resources at the Project Level (8.10)

SuperProject Expert describes the following process for creating part-time resources at the project level:

> Resources who will be part-time through the entire project may be designated in the Resource Details screen, which is invoked by pressing "/; View; Resource". (Figure A2.14) The part-time participation is indicated by modifying the resource daily allocation amount and type fields (in the default box) to show the number of hours per day that the resource is generally available. (For example, "4d" implies that the resource may work 4 hours per day until the job is done). Alternatively, this field can be set up to allocate a given percentage of the resource's day to project tasks. (For example, "50%d" means the resource may work halftime until the job is done).

This implementation does not work as the vendor states. Instead of having the effect illustrated in Example 2, a constant value of 40 hours is assigned to the resource (ignoring any values in the original duration), and the schedule is computed, using the original duration, as if the resource were available 100 percent of the time.

> Examples of other valid responses in the daily allocations and type fields are "50%x" or "4x". Or, users may alter the default working hours per day, the default standard workday, the default hours per week, or combinations thereof.

Each of these approaches has the effect of *reducing* the resource hours as a result of the multiplication of the original duration by the fractional percentage availability equivalent. This reduction is artificial and incorrect. Furthermore, the system simply ignores resource hours and keeps the original duration for scheduling. (The original duration still contains the true work effort.)

The bottom line, at the project level, is that the only way to get schedules to reflect the part-time participation scenario described in Example 2 is to enter the number of part-time *hours per day* into *each day* of the respective resource calendar. The correct schedules are computed and the true work effort remains intact in the duration field. (There will be no special field that holds the number of elapsed calendar days but this is not a serious problem.) This is a very effective way to create varying levels of part-time participation. But to perform this operation for all of the resources on all of the jobs in an average-sized project is a time-consuming and potentially error-prone exercise. Instead, users are advised to set part-time participation at the task level. (See the discussion later in this appendix.)

Appendix 2.7.4 Deleting and Changing Resources at the Project Level (8.11)

Resources in SuperProject Expert are deleted from the Resource Details screen by pressing "/; Edit; Delete resource". Deleting a resource in the pool automatically results in the project-wide removal of all corresponding resource assignments.

Names are changed in the same manner as other modifications. Changing a name results in a project-wide replacement of all occurrences of the old name with the new name.

Appendix 2.7.5 Matching Resources to Jobs (8.14)

In SuperProject Expert, resources may only be assigned to tasks. The number of allowable resource names per task is determined by the variable-length formula discussed earlier. The most direct and simple way to assign resources is to cursor through either the WBS, PERT, Gantt, or Outline screens while adding resources to tasks. This is very easy. After moving the cursor to the designated task, the return key is pressed to get to the resource field. Following this step, the F6 key is pressed to bring up a window with a list of resources. Moving the cursor to the desired resource and pressing the return key completes the job.

This operation, however, only adds the resource and any of the default values. On the other hand, it is easy to override the defaults by recalling the Resource

Details screen ("/; View; Resource details"). (Figure A2.14) At the bottom of this screen, there is a matrix that contains all task data corresponding to each resource assignment. Making additions and corrections in this matrix is very easy. Similarly, since keying in a task identification number *or* the task name onto any blank line in the matrix brings in all of the other task-related data, this screen may also be used to input resource assignments in bulk.

In addition to the task identifier and the task name, the other required fields are the assignment hours (defaults to the task duration), the number of assigned resources (defaults to one), the task priority (defaults to the value set in the Task Details screen), and the resource allocation type and daily allocation amount (used to designate task full-time or part-time; it defaults to the values set when the resource was added to the resource list).

In SuperProject Expert, the resource availability number is used for leveling. If the assigned number exceeds the available number, it will not be flagged until leveling. Leveling will then be aborted. Furthermore, a resource name may only be assigned to a task once, regardless of the availability number.

When an undefined resource is assigned to a task, the system automatically creates a corresponding entry in a Resource Details screen. All default values are automatically entered. The user must remember to enter the desired values at a later date.

At the task level, true work effort is entered into the duration field. If the integrity of this field is to be maintained, it should *not* be changed. (The use of the duration field in resource driven scheduling will be explained in greater detail later in the next section.)

Appendix 2.7.6 Assigning Part-Time Resources at the Task Or Activity Level *(8.15)*

A different and unique set of resource daily allocation amount and type fields is also part of each SuperProject Expert task assignment. (See the *Allc* field in Figure A2.5.) Part-time participation may be restricted to specific tasks by retaining the default values of "dayx" in the Resource Details screen's resource allocation fields and modifying these fields in the task assignments. These task assignments are found in either the matrix that is at the bottom of the Resource Details screen (contains all of the tasks for a given resource) or the matrix that is at the bottom of the Task Details screen (contains all of the resources for a given task). The matrix that is at the bottom of the Task Details screen is called the Task Schedule screen; and it is accessed from the Task Details screen by pressing "/; Edit; View options; Schedule data". After assigning the resource, this is a four step process:

1. The resource daily allocation type is set to "d."
2. The resource daily allocation amount is set to the percentage number (for example, "50%").
3. The task type is set to "span."
4. The task type is *reset* to "ASAP."

The correct part-time true work effort will then be in the resource hours and the correct elapsed calendar days will be in the task duration. Varying part-time within a task may be done in the resource calendar by varying the hours on any given day. (Figure A2.18)

Appendix 2.7.7 Assigning Multiple Resources to a Job *(8.16)*

Adding multiple resources at the SuperProject Expert task level is a seven-step process. This sequence of steps may not be altered. After the Task Details screen has been invoked by pressing "/; View; Task details", resources are assigned to the task following the directions described earlier in this appendix. (The assigned number of resources, of course, should not exceed the availability number in the Resource Details screen.) Then, for each of the resources on the Task Details screen, the following steps are executed:

1. The resource daily allocation type is set to "x."
2. The resource daily allocation amount is set to the percentage number (for example, "50%"—if two resources are being added; "25%"—if four resources are being added.).
3. The resource daily allocation type is *reset* to "d."
4. The corrected values for true work effort are entered into the resource hours field.
5. The corrected elapsed calendar time is computed by the user and entered into the task duration field, the field used for scheduling. (If there are different values in the resource hours field for each resource,

the longest one should be selected for the task duration field.)

6. The resource daily allocation amount is *reset* to "day."

7. Since the automatic scheduling does not work in this process, the schedule may be recomputed by pressing "Shift; 1".

The true work effort will no longer be found in the task duration field; but it will be in the resource hours field.

Appendix 2.7.8 What to do when the Resource Effort Must Be Less than the Elapsed Calendar Days (8.17)

In SuperProject Expert, when the value of the resource hours is equal to true work effort but is less than the task elapsed time, the work can be distributed anywhere within the task's duration. (See Figure A2.15.) To create the conditions illustrated in Example 1, the following steps must be executed from the Task Details screen:

1. A *dummy* no-cost resource must be added to the resource pool.

2. The dummy resource must be assigned to the task along with the real resource. All of the default values are accepted. (Since the task duration field takes on the value of the longest resource hours, this is necessary for maintaining the correct value in the task duration field.)

3. The real resource's daily allocation type is set to "d."

4. The correct hours are placed in the real resource's hours field. When the scenario illustrated in Ex-

Figure A2.15

task *candidate time slice*	= 15 days

assignment lag time	resource hours
10 days	5 days

ample 2 occurs, the user will simply need to enter the percentage in the resource allocation amount field.

The resource allocation type field should be left at "x." The system will correctly handle everything else.

The scenario in Example 3 is accomplished by delaying the resource duration with a corresponding value in the resource assignment lag start time. The resource assignment lag time field is only found in the Task Schedule screen, which is accessed by pressing "/; View; Task details; /; Edit; View options; Schedule data". Naturally, the sum of the resource hours and the resource assignment lag time may not be greater than the task *candidate time slice*. For this application, users are cautioned not to use the start delay field of the task form, since this field is used by the leveling operation and may be obliterated during that process.

Remember, also, that when these actions are taken, the original record of the true work effort is now in the resource hours field and the task duration will then contain the elapsed calendar days.

Appendix 2.7.9 Fixed Dates for Activities or Tasks (8.19)

SuperProject Expert does not use the scheduling algorithm that highlights projects that are late before they start.

Fixed dates may be entered at any level in the work breakdown structure, such as heading records[10] or task records. Although this action may create new critical paths, there is nothing unique about them.

There are two types of fixed dates: *must start* dates and *must finish* dates. Must start dates can be entered on headings but must finish dates are not allowed. Both must start dates and must finish dates may be entered at the task level.

There are four sets of dates on the task form[11]

---

[10]This product supports heading records and task records. Heading records are automatically created as soon as a lower level in the work breakdown structure is created.

[11]Accessed by pressing "/; View; Task".

and in the outline[12]: the early start and finish dates, the late start and finish dates, the scheduled start and finish dates, and the planned start and finish dates.

Headings and tasks may be modified in the Task Details screen or the Outline Screen. The must dates are entered into the early start or early finish fields.

On the other hand, the only dates seen on the PERT[13] and the WBS[14] are the scheduled dates. To be able to set must dates on the PERT and the WBS, "date entry on PERT/WBS" on the Set Preference screen must be turned on to *Yes*. Headings and tasks may then be modified in these modes.

The must dates (either start or finish) are automatically flagged with small arrows next to them wherever they are displayed.

In no case will the early dates and planned dates of any predecessors ever be changed. Likewise, the late dates are not affected by most of these operations. (See the later discussion on must finish dates.)

If the new fixed date of the affected job is the same as its system-generated dates, there will be no other effects on the schedule.

When the fixed date is earlier or later than the system-generated dates, to some degree, SuperProject Expert automatically keeps the early-date fields and the scheduled-date fields in synchronization. This will be explained in the following discussions.

When the fixed date is later than the system-generated early dates, the scheduled start and finish dates of the affected job will be recomputed. If the fixed date is a must start date, the early start date will also be kept in synchronization with the scheduled start date. However, the early finish date will not change. If the fixed date is a must finish date, the early finish date will also be kept in synchronization with the scheduled finish date. However, the early start date will not change. Finally, in the successors, both sets of early dates and scheduled dates will be modified by the system to maintain compatibility with the new dates of the fixed task.

When the fixed date is earlier than the system-generated early dates and the "musts override pred-

ecessors" in the "Advanced Scheduling Options" of the Set Preferences screen is set to *No*, only the early dates in the affected job will change. No other dates will change. However, if the fixed date can't be met, the task number will flash wherever it's displayed.

On the other hand, if this option is set to *Yes*, the system disregards the dates driven by any predecessor(s) and accepts the must date as the new scheduled date. Furthermore, new early dates and scheduled dates will be computed for the affected job as well as for any affected successors. The system will also keep the early and scheduled dates in synchronization.

If the must finish date is used on a milestone to set the late finish date of the project, the late dates of all of the predecessors will be correctly computed.

Other than the small arrows and the flashing conflicts (as described above), the system does not flag delays caused by fixed dates.

Appendix 2.7.10 Special Leveling Patterns in Project Management Software (8.29)

In SuperProject Expert, the system defaults to the first type of leveling. The vendor calls the second approach *smoothing*. It is invoked by recalling the Set Preferences screen, then by calling up the "Advanced Scheduling Options" window (accessed by pressing "/; Edit; Advanced"), and setting "Resource smoothing" to *Yes*. (See Figure A2.16.)

This product also allows the user to tell the sys-

Figure A2.16

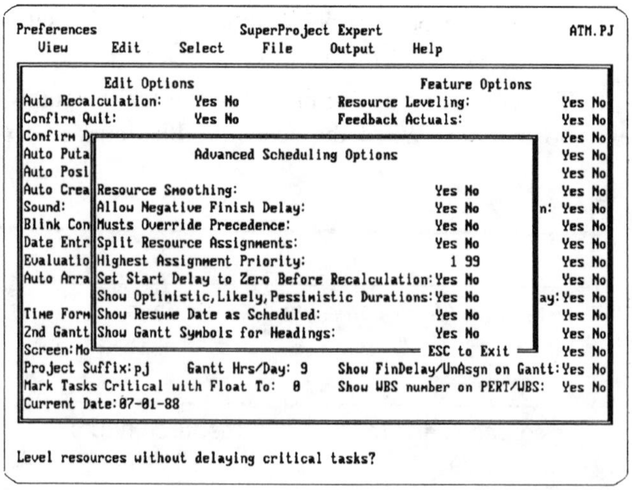

---

[12]Accessed by pressing "/; View; Outline".

[13]Accessed by pressing "/; View; PERT".

[14]Accessed by pressing "/; View; Work Breakdown". (See Figure A2.6.)

tem if, during leveling, jobs can be broken up and scheduled around other jobs. Users may indicate this choice by setting "Split resource assignments" in this "Advanced Scheduling Options" window to *Yes*.

Appendix 2.7.11 Automatic Resource Leveling (8.30)

Before any SuperProject Expert leveling operations may be performed, users must set the correct project starting date in the Set Preferences screen. Then, when the resource leveling field in the Set Preferences screen is turned on to *Yes*, when "Level using priorities first" is set to *No*, and when "Resource smoothing" in the "Advanced Scheduling Options" is turned to *No*, the first type of leveling (described in the previous section) will occur. The leveled dates will be placed in the scheduled start and scheduled finish fields. Resources will be assigned jobs by placing the values from the scheduled dates fields into the resource assignment dates.

Resource smoothing *Yes* applies the second leveling approach described above. Thus, it only levels resources for tasks with float. Tasks will not be delayed if they have no float; resource conflicts may, therefore, remain unresolved.

Setting the value of "Level using priorities" to *No* results in the amount of float being used as the prime consideration when resolving resource conflicts. This results in a tighter schedule. Setting priorities will be addressed in the next section.

All effects of leveling may be erased simply by pressing "/; View; Set Preferences" and changing resource leveling to *No*.

If "Show early/late dates & delay" of the Set Preferences screen is set to *Yes* and the "Set start delay to zero before recalculation" of the "Advanced Scheduling Options" is also set to *Yes*, the number of days the task has been delayed due to leveling will be found in the start delay field of the task details form and shown by *skid* marks on the Gantt chart. (Figure A2.12)

Appendix 2.7.12 Setting Special Leveling Priorities on Tasks Or Activities (8.31)

In SuperProject Expert, if, on the Set Preferences screen, "Resource leveling" and "Level using priorities first"

are both set to *Yes*, then the system assumes, during the leveling process, that the priority is more important than the amount of remaining float. Priorities may be assigned to headings and tasks, as well as to the individual resource assignments within a task. Priorities at the heading level override all other subordinate heading priorities, task priorities, and resource assignment priorities. Priorities at the task level override priorities at the resource assignment level. The "highest assignment priority" on the "Advanced Scheduling Options" can be used to set either 1 or 99 as the highest priority. (Figure A2.16) Heading or task priorities may only be set in Outline or Task Details screen mode. Resource assignment priorities are set on the Resource Details screen.

Appendix 2.7.13 User-Driven Interactive Leveling (8.32)

When SuperProject Expert users select "/; View; Histogram/Resource Gantt", the system automatically presents a split-screen display—with a resource-limited Gantt at the top and the corresponding resource histogram at the bottom. (See Figure A2.17.)

This resource Gantt shows any critical path tasks in red. Tasks that are delayed (either by automated or by manual leveling procedures) are shown by *skid* marks on the Gantt chart. Float is also marked. If the "2nd Gantt Line" on the Set Preferences screen is set

Figure A2.17

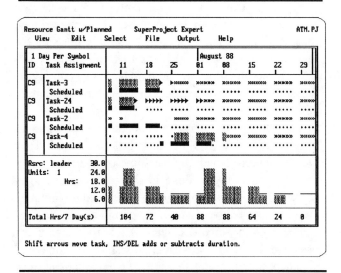

to *planned*, the Gantt will show a permanently positioned bar in the second line. This bar will be fixed with original dates so that, as modifications are made during the leveling process, users can see where the task *was* in comparison to where it currently *is*.

The height of each column in the resource histogram at the bottom of the screen shows the level of commitment. With a horizontal line drawn across the histogram at the corresponding vertical axis level, the histogram also implicitly shows available resource levels. However, this line is only visible when the corresponding resource assignment is equal to or less than the respective resource availability. There is no line when the resource is overcommitted and causes the column to extend above the level of resource availability. The numbers on the vertical axis automatically adjust so that they are always scaled to be slightly higher than the maximum resource commitment. The columns have no color differentiation between overscheduling and scheduling within limits of availability. The total number of available resources is also displayed in the units field of the histogram.

Both the Gantt chart and the histogram in SuperProject Expert show weekends and holidays.

Although the histogram changes in synchronization to modifications in the Gantt, the cursor only moves in the Gantt region. It moves both horizontally and vertically in this region.

Although the WBS cannot be modified from this split-screen mode, new tasks may be added here for split jobs (by pressing "/; Edit; Create"); new dependencies may be created and old ones deleted (by pressing "/; Edit; Link" or "/; Edit; Unlink" respectively); durations may be changed (increased or decreased, one time scale increment at a time, by simply pressing the "insert" or "delete" keys); starting and ending dates may be modified by moving the whole task simply by pressing the "right arrow" or "left arrow" cursor keys.

Changing the start and finish dates to extend over an elapsed calendar time must be done in the Task Details screen. Changing part-time or overtime hours for a specific day is done in the resource calendar. (See the later discussion on the split calendar window.) Adding new resources must be completed in the Resource Details screen. (Figure A2.14) Changing the assigned resource, modifying existing resource assignment hours, or deleting a resource assignment must

each be completed in the Resource Details screen or the Task Details screen. The resource assignment lag time field is only found in the Task Schedule screen, which is accessed by pressing "/; View; Task details; /; Edit; View options; Schedule data".

The start delay field of the Task Details screen is automatically set during the automated leveling process. However, users may take control over the start delay of each task and override this setting by modifying it during the user-driven leveling process. If "Show early/late dates & delay" of the Set Preferences screen is set to *Yes*, the delay will be shown by *skid* marks on the Gantt chart. If the modifications to the start delay field are to be permanent, the "Set start delay to zero before recalculation" of the "Advanced Scheduling Options" must also be set to *No*. (Figure A2.16) From the Task Details screen, all entries in the start delay field may be wiped out by pressing "/; Edit; zero all delay".

From the Resource Details screen, the system can be instructed to eliminate all resources that have not been assigned to tasks. This is simply accomplished by pressing "/; Edit; Erase orphan resource".

The timescale may also be modified to show hours per day when working with smaller jobs. Users may also alternate between displaying the whole Gantt or the split screen. On the other hand, while the size of the histogram can be increased to where only one or two tasks are remaining in the Gantt, it can't be increased to where the histogram covers the whole screen.[15]

If the "Blink conflicts" on the Set Preferences screen is set to *Yes*, then conflicts will blink on the resource Gantt. However, the interactive process is so easy to use that this really isn't necessary—and the blinking often only serves as a distraction. Another indication of resource conflicts is in the overscheduled hours field, found in the outline screen and in the matrix of task assignments in the Resource Details screen.

Last, the scheduled number of hours for each day shows on the Resource Calendar. (See Figure A2.18) Since the resource calendar also displays the number of hours in the standard workday, it is easy to spot the

[15]This is probably because the system is not set up to allow the cursor to move in the histogram.

Figure A2.18

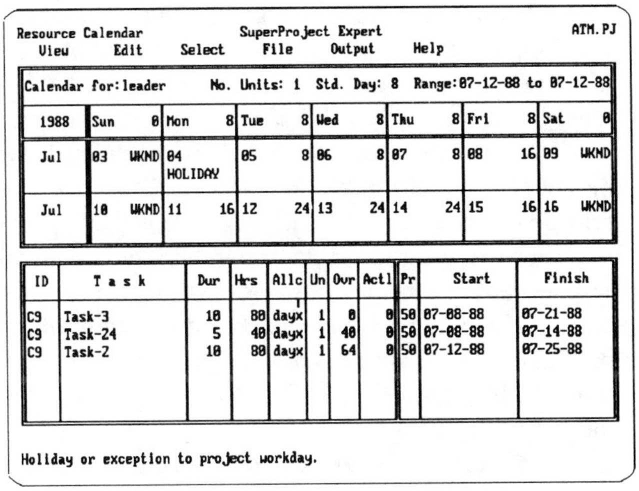

```
Resource Calendar          SuperProject Expert                    ATM.PJ
    View      Edit    Select    File    Output    Help

Calendar for: leader      No. Units: 1  Std. Day: 8  Range:07-12-88 to 07-12-88

  1988  Sun    0 Mon    8 Tue    8 Wed    8 Thu    8 Fri    8 Sat    0

  Jul   03  WKND 04        05    8 06    8 07    8 08   16 09  WKND
                  HOLIDAY

  Jul   10  WKND 11   16 12   24 13   24 14   24 15   16 16  WKND


  ID    T a s k     Dur  Hrs  Allc  Un Ovr Actl Pr   Start      Finish

  C9   Task-3       10   80 dayx  1   0    0 50 07-08-88    07-21-88
  C9   Task-24       5   40 dayx  1  40    0 50 07-08-88    07-14-88
  C9   Task-2       10   80 dayx  1  64    0 50 07-12-88    07-25-88


Holiday or exception to project workday.
```

days with overcommitments. However, it is not easy to tell what tasks are causing that day's resource conflict. Once again, the vendor has provided a split-screen feature. Pressing ''/; Edit; View options; Schedule'' will invoke a bottom window that contains a matrix listing all of the tasks to which the resource is assigned for that calendar day. (See Figure A2.18.)

SuperProject Expert is a semi-interactive leveling system. For most of the leveling operations, users will see the results of their modifications immediately and while working from one screen! (Users must only leave the leveling window to modify calendar information as well as certain nonbasic task and resource data.)

Appendix 2.7.14 Baseline Project Plans for Resource Leveling (8.34)

SuperProject Expert supports one version of a baseline. By saving the optimal plan as the baseline for the resource-constrained plan that is selected for implementation, users have one-half of the requirements met. This version is archived and a second version is produced. Then, by saving the resource-constrained plan as the baseline for the plan to which progress will be posted, the other half of the requirements will be met. Unfortunately, this *work-around* does not provide comparisons between all three versions. Although the process is cumbersome, users may assimilate the data by perusing both sets of reports.

Appendix 2.7.15 Resources, Multiprojects, and Project Management Software (8.35.4)

Template resource files in SuperProject Expert can be copied from project to project by implementing the link, a feature which is addressed in the following discussion.

By attaching the subproject to a task, as described earlier in this appendix, it may be represented in the master project by a single one-line entry in the Gantt chart and the PERT chart. This action also causes the correct dates to be reflected in the master file task, but it does not concatenate any resource data. Incorporating the resource pool and the resource assignments into a master project requires that a second connection be established between the master project and each of the subprojects. From the Project Details screen of the master project, each subproject should be linked to the master project by pressing ''/; Edit; Link'', moving the cursor to the respective subproject name, and pressing ''Enter''. This ought to be repeated for each of the subprojects that was attached in the first step, described earlier. New resources are appended to the resource details list. When there are duplicate resources in the master project and the subproject, the data in the resource record of the master project is retained and the resource data in the subproject is ignored. Consequently, users ought to choose carefully the first subproject to be linked, since that will be the source of the permanent resource data. Linked subprojects will also have access to all of the resources in the master project.

The step that is described here and the step to create dependencies in a multiproject environment, (described earlier) must both be executed because (1) attaching without linking will show the tasks and their dates but will not incorporate the resources or their assignments and (2) using the link in the master project without first attaching the subprojects to a task will not allow the subproject to be represented in the master project by a single task.

Since SuperProject Expert can keep several projects in memory simultaneously, after the projects have been connected in this manner, loading any one of the projects will also load as many of the other subprojects that memory will allow. Unwanted subprojects may be discarded from memory in order to make room to load others.

When using fixed dates with this feature, only one or the other of the must start date or the must finish date may be selected. They cannot be intermixed.

Neither of the connections imports the project calendar. Similarly, they do not incorporate the resource calendars. An acceptable calendar for each resource should be part of the default calendar. Otherwise, a new calendar for each resource will need to be created when the master project is set up.

The system also provides an attractive feature for the matrix at the bottom of the Project Details screen. By pressing ''/; Edit; View Linked Projects'', a list of all linked *and* all attached subprojects will be displayed. (See Figure A2.19.) This is true for the Project Details screens of each of the subprojects as well. Furthermore, at the master project level, the matrix at the bottom of each Resource Details screen displays *all* of the resource's task commitments in *each* of the subprojects. Next to each task is the identifier of the respective subproject.

Each resource histogram in the master project will reflect the resource's commitment in every subproject and therefore will show just where the over-scheduling occurs. Furthermore, the corresponding resource Gantt chart will show every task in every subproject to which the resource is assigned. Next to each task is the identifier of the respective subproject. Consequently, users will also be able to pinpoint easily

Figure A2.19

```
Project Details          SuperProject Expert        SUPERPRO.PJ
   View      Edit    Select    File    Output    Help

Name: SUPERPRO.PJ
ID:S1    Directory:C:\SPJ\
                                 ┌──── Defaults ────┬──── Totals ────
Author:          Leader:          Hours:      40   Var:     76776.00
WBSMask:11.22.33.44.????  Freeze:Yes No  Fixed:   0.00  Fixed:     0.00
Created:07-01-88 Revised:12-13-88 # 7  Rate:    25.00  Total:   76776.00
  Start:07-01-88+                 Rate Mult:  1.00 Actual:      0.00
 Finish:03-01-90        Dur:  429  0h  Duration:    1  Hours: 3784 Ovr: 1016
   Late:03-01-90        Dev:0.00      Allc:days Pr: 50 Tasks:    2 Rsrc:  5

ID      T a s k    Subproject   ID  Linked Projects Using Common Resources

S1  SUPERPRO.PJ                 sub C:\SPJ\SUB.PJ
001 Task-1        CHAP9G.PJ     C9  C:\SPJ\CHAP9G.PJ
002 Task-2        ATM.PJ        P1  C:\SPJ\ATM.PJ



Project name, used as the file name for the project.
```

the offending tasks that are causing the resource conflicts.

This product *does* support leveling across projects from the master project. However, all subprojects in the nest must be linked and every project in the nest must be in memory at the same time. If, as recommended, the subproject attach has also been used, the master project must be saved with the ''Putaway'' and reloaded before all of the dates are reflected correctly.

For very large projects that will not fit into memory, this approach is not possible. Starting at each task that is attached to a lowest notch at the bottom of the nest and working upwards to the highest notch in each rung, each subproject must be leveled and saved with the ''Putaway.''

On the other hand, instead of the ''Putaway,'' after leveling the subproject, users may alternatively move to the higher-level task to which the subproject is attached and press ''/; File; Update subproject''. Either action will insure that the current task's durations, dates, and resource commitments will be reflected correctly in the next higher rung of the nest. In a complex nest of subprojects, users are advised to create a hard copy tree of the nested groups and check each one off as it is leveled. If only one subproject is overlooked, all of the subsequent leveling may be incorrect.

Users may protect linked subprojects from unanticipated schedule changes by setting ''Freeze'' on their respective Project Details screen to *Yes*. This will allow their resource workloads to be considered during the updates of other parts of the master project while also maintaining the values of their plan.

When there are nested subprojects, the process of visiting and returning from subprojects may be repeated until the desired subproject is reached. Alternatively viewing the subprojects and the master project is an easy process.

If the multiproject procedures described earlier in the book are followed, changes made in the subprojects are automatically reflected in the master project.

Appendix 2.7.16 Guidelines and Documentation (8.36)

In SuperProject Expert, there are several pages on resource management.

Figure A2.20

```
Project Calendar            SuperProject Expert              CHAP9G.PJ
  View       Edit    Select    File    Output    Help

Calendar for: Project                        Range:07-05-88 to 07-05-88

 1988   Sun   0 Mon   0 Tue   0 Wed   0 Thu   0 Fri   0 Sat   0

 Jun   26 WKND 27      28      29      30      01   56 02 WKND
 Jul

 Jul   03 WKND 04      05   56 06   56 07   64 08   96 09 WKND
               holiday
```

ID	Task Assignment	Resource	Hrs	Allc	Un	Dur	Rate	Var.	Fixed	Actual
006	Task-6	boss	32	dayx	1	4	50.00	1600.0	0.00	0.00
001	Task-1	leader	32	dayx	1	4	25.00	800.00	0.00	0.00
009	Task-9	worker	16	dayx	1	2	10.00	160.00	0.00	0.00
011	Task-11	senior	24	dayx	1	3	15.00	360.00	0.00	0.00
007	Task-7	senior	56	dayx	1	7	15.00	840.00	0.00	0.00
008	Task-8	worker	32	dayx	1	4	10.00	320.00	0.00	0.00

Holiday or exception to project workday.   CAPS

Figure A2.21

```
Outline                     SuperProject Expert              CHAP9G.PJ
  View       Edit    Select    File    Output    Help
```

Heading/Task	Resource	Variable Cost	Fixed Cost	Total Cost	Task Acct
CHAP9G.PJ		71120.00	0.00	71120.00	
group1		9200.00	0.00	9200.00	
Task-1		800.00	0.00	800.00	0
	leader	800.00	0.00	800.00	
Task-2		2000.00	0.00	2000.00	0
	leader	2000.00	0.00	2000.00	
Task-3		2000.00	0.00	2000.00	0
	leader	2000.00	0.00	2000.00	
Task-4		2000.00	0.00	2000.00	0
	leader	2000.00	0.00	2000.00	
Task-5		2400.00	0.00	2400.00	0
	leader	2400.00	0.00	2400.00	
group2		39120.00	0.00	39120.00	
Task-6		1600.00	0.00	1600.00	0
	boss	1600.00	0.00	1600.00	
Task-12		4400.00	0.00	4400.00	0

TASK SLCT: Select-4
Name of heading/task or resource.   CAPS

APPENDIX 2.8 CALCULATING COSTS

Appendix 2.8.1 Costs and Project Management Software *(9.4)*

For costing, the settings for "Show costing" and "Show planned totals" on the Set Preference screen ought to be set to *Yes*. It is important to note that, in this product, if the assignment rate for a resource is modified *after* the resource has been assigned to a task, *the costs of the task will not* be readjusted—even if no time has yet to be reported to the task!

In addition to the number for the work breakdown structure, users may also enter an accounting code [ACCT]. Both are entered in the Task Details screen.

There are no cost histograms in this product. However, in addition to the task totals, users may also see rollup totals at the resource level on the Resource Details screen[16] and at the project level on the Project Details screen. A really nice touch, SuperProject Expert will show daily project totals from the Project Calendar screen. (See Figure A2.20.) Daily resource totals may also be displayed in the same manner—from the Resource Calendar screen. Furthermore, with the task select feature, users may customize the columns displayed on the Outline screen and, therefore, also see the totals of the subordinate jobs at each heading level. (See Figure A2.21.)

The term *assignment* is used to refer to resources when they are reflected in the Task Details screen. *Assignment* hours is the resource's true work effort. The *assignment* rate is the resource's *hourly* rate. This value initially defaults to the resource default rate in the Resource Details screen (which, in turn, defaults to the rate set in the Project Details screen). Thus, *assignment* cost is the *assignment* rate times the *assignment* hours. The term *variable* costs is also used to indicate resource costs. It is synonymous with resource *assignment* costs.

Fixed costs and overhead costs must be created as separate resources and assigned to the respective activity just like any other resource. *Fixed* costs are used for materials, one time, or per-use costs. *Total* costs are equal to *variable* costs plus *fixed* costs. *Actual* costs are, of course, as the name states.

The formulas for resource costs are:

1. The *assignment variable* costs are equal to the *assignment rate* times the *assignment hours*.

2. The *variable* costs are equal to the sum of the resource's *assignment variable* costs.

[16]From any of the Detail screens and Calendar screens, pressing "/; Edit; View options; Costs" will allow the user to display cost information.

3. The *fixed* costs default to the project value but users can override this value at entry time. The total is equal to the sum of the resource's *assignment fixed* costs.

4. The *total* resource costs is equal to the sum of the resource's *assignment total* costs.

At the task level, the formulas for costs are:

1. *Variable* costs are equal to the sum of the task's *assignment variable* costs.

2. *Fixed* costs are equal to the sum of the task's *assignment fixed* costs. This field cannot be edited.

3. *Total* task costs are equal to the sum of the task's *assignment total* costs.

4. *Planned* costs are equal to the total cost value in the baseline—that is, the sum of the baseline *variable* costs plus the baseline *fixed* costs.

Variable costs, *fixed* costs, *total* costs, and *actual* costs are all reported at the project level. SuperProject Expert will export any of the data found in the task selection criteria in either LOTUS 1-2-3 format or SuperCalc4 format.

APPENDIX 2.9 COMPRESSING DURATIONS

Appendix 2.9.1 Time-Constrained Plans and Project Management Software (10.9)

In the SuperProject Expert ''Advanced Scheduling Options'' of the Set Preferences screen, ''Resource smoothing'' should be set to *Yes*. (Figure A2.16) Users may produce reports sorted on float and free float.

APPENDIX 2.10 ASSIGNING THE WORK

Appendix 2.10.1 The Assignment Report (11.1)

In SuperProject Expert, reports are driven by one of the three sets of selection criteria: the resource select, the task select, or the assignment select. (Figure A2.10) Each of these transactions has its own set of fields that may be displayed. In some cases, there is field duplication from one set of criteria to another, thus facilitating certain reporting requirements. In other cases, the desired data can only be accessed from one of the

sets, thus limiting the ability to meet certain reporting requirements. When all of the desired data cannot be found in one set, users must be satisfied with a subset of the data, choosing the select view that yields the largest subset.

After completing two operations, the user may use the assignment select to produce an assignment sheet that presents all of the required data for an assignment report. In the first step, the assignment data is selected and the report columns are ordered by:

1. Pressing ''/; Select; Assignment select'';

2. Choosing to display ''task name'', ''task ID'', ''duration'', ''scheduled start'', ''scheduled finish'', ''task description'', and ''resource name'';

3. Designating ''ONLY'' and then entering the resource name as it appears on the Resource Details screen into the ''Match From'' column;

4. Choosing to sort, first on resource name and second, on start date; and

5. Giving a unique name to this set of select criteria.

In the second step, the report (See Figure A2.22.) is produced by:

1. Pressing ''/; Output; Report'' (See Figure A2.23.);

2. Choosing ''assignments'' as the report type and ''predecessor/successor'' as the matrix type;

3. Entering the name from Step 5 above in the Select-criteria field; and

4. Pressing F10.

Appendix 2.10.2 The Ad Hoc Information (11.2)

The 56-character task and resource description fields of SuperProject Expert may be printed as part of several reports. For example, both fields may be displayed on a detailed resource report. (See Figure A2.24.) This report is produced by: (1) pressing ''/; Select; Resource select'' and setting up the select criteria for a given resource (See the discussion earlier in this appendix.); (2) pressing ''/; Output; Report'' from the Outline screen (Figure A2.23); (3) choosing ''resource detail'' for the report type and ''none'' for the matrix selection; (4) entering the name of the select criteria from Step 1; and (5) pressing F10.

Figure A2.22

Page: 1-2

01-21-89 Resource Assignments Report CHAP9G.PJ

Resource Name	Predecessor	Type	Lag	Predecessor	Type	Lag	Predecessor	Type	Lag	Predecessor	Type	Lag
boss												
boss	Task-6	FS	0h									
boss	Task-6	FS	0h									
boss	CRITICAL REVIEW	FS	0h									
boss	CRITICAL REVIEW	FS	0h									
boss	Task-21	FS	0h									
boss	DUMMY2	FS	0h									
boss	Task-32	FS	0h	Task-33	FS	0h	DUMMY3	FS	0			
boss	Task-39	FS	0h									

Page: 1-1

01-21-89 Resource Assignments Report CHAP9G.PJ

Heading/Task	Task ID	Schd Start	Schd Finish	Dur	WBS Code	Task Description
Task-6	006	07-01-88	07-07-88	4	01.02.01.00.0006	this is the task description field for this job 2.
Task-12	012	07-08-88	07-22-88	11	01.02.02.00.0012	
Task-13	013	07-08-88	07-13-88	4	01.02.03.00.0013	
Task-21	021	08-03-88	08-10-88	6	01.02.04.00.0021	
Task-22	022	08-03-88	08-24-88	16	01.03.04.00.0022	
Task-26	026	08-11-88	08-19-88	7	01.02.05.00.0026	
Task-32	032	08-22-88	09-02-88	10	01.02.08.00.0032	
Task-39	039	09-07-88	09-23-88	13	01.02.10.00.0039	
Task-43	043	09-26-88	09-30-88	5	01.02.11.00.0043	
Task-45	045	10-05-88	10-11-88	4	01.02.13.00.0045	
Task-48	048	10-18-88	10-25-88	6	01.02.16.00.0048	
Task-51	051	10-26-88	11-03-88	7	01.02.17.00.0051	
Task-52	052	11-04-88	11-09-88	4	01.02.18.00.0052	

Figure A2.23

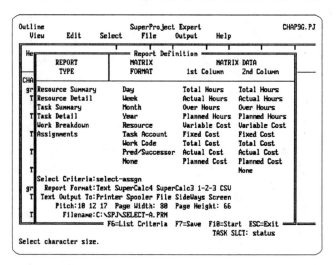

The system also features a miniature word processor, which may be accessed from either the Task Details screen or the Outline screen by pressing "/; Edit; View; Note text". Free-form notes may be entered for each job in the plan. This information may also be printed on several reports. For example, all of the note text about a given task may be reported from the Task Details screen. (See Figure A2.25.) This report is produced by: (1) pressing "/; Edit; View; Note text"; (2) pressing "/; Output; View"; (3) choosing to view the current task; and (4) pressing F10. Step 1 may be varied to report costing information, schedule information, or predecessor/successor information.

Appendix 2.10.3 The Work Package Cover Sheet (11.5)

In SuperProject Expert, a cover sheet that has all of the required data may easily be created with the note text option.

Appendix 2.10.4 The Responsibility Grid (11.6)

In SuperProject Expert, a responsibility grid that has all of the required data may easily be created with the "Note Text" option.

Appendix 2.10.5 The Supporting Documentation (11.8)

The SuperProject Expert resource Gantt and histogram (Figure A2.17) may be displayed in one report from the Histogram screen by pressing "/; Output; View" and F10. SuperProject Expert does not have a tabular loading report.

Appendix 2.10.6 The Problem Log (11.10)

In SuperProject Expert, a problem log that has all of the required data may easily be created with the "Note Text" option.

Appendix 2.10.7 The Work Notes Form (11.11)

In SuperProject Expert, a work notes form that has all of the required data may easily be created with the "Note Text" option.

Appendix 2.10.8 Viewing the Data on the Screen (11.12)

SuperProject Expert allows the user to display the reports in hard copy or on the screen.

APPENDIX 2.11 REPORTING STATUS

Appendix 2.11.1 Baselines (12.2)

The SuperProject Expert baseline information is in fields called *planned*.

Appendix 2.11.2 Extracting the Jobs for the Turn-Around Document—on a Range of Dates (12.5)

Date ranges in SuperProject Expert are designated with the Select Criteria screen by entering the values in the corresponding columns for "Select from/match" and "Select to". (Figure A2.10) There are no date options on the Resource Select. On the Assignment Select, users may choose from the scheduled start and the scheduled finish. On the Task Select, the choices are from either of the planned, actual, scheduled, early, late, and must dates.

Figure A2.24

| 01-21-89 | | | | | | Resource Detail Report | | CHAP9G.PJ |

Total Hours	Actual Hours	Ovr Hours	Rate	Variable Cost	Fixed Cost	Total Cost	Actual Cost
			50.00				
32			50.00	1600.00		1600.00	
88			50.00	4400.00		4400.00	
32		32	50.00	1600.00		1600.00	
48			50.00	2400.00		2400.00	
128		48	50.00	6400.00		6400.00	
56		56	50.00	2800.00		2800.00	
80		24	50.00	4000.00		4000.00	
104			50.00	5200.00		5200.00	
40			50.00	2000.00		2000.00	
32			50.00	1600.00		1600.00	
48			50.00	2400.00		2400.00	
56			50.00	2800.00		2800.00	
32			50.00	1600.00		1600.00	
776	0	160		38800.00	0.00	38800.00	0.00
776	0	160		38800.00	0.00	38800.00	0.00

| 01-21-89 | | Resource Detail Report | | | | | | | CHAP9G.PJ |

Resource Task/Subproject	Resource Description	Work Code	Accrual Method	Std day	Rate Mult.	Cldr Var	Start Time	Un
boss	this is the description for the boss	boss	End	8	1.00		8:00a	1
Task-6	this is the task description field for this job 2.							1
Task-12								1
Task-13								1
Task-21								1
Task-22								1
Task-26								1
Task-32								1
Task-39								1
Task-43								1
Task-45								1
Task-48								1
Task-51								1
Task-52								1

Figure A2.25

```
Task Details                                    Project: CHAP9G.PJ
01-21-89   3:08p                                     Revision:  29
                                                                       +
┌ ID: 001═══════════════════════════════════════════════════════════════┐
│Name:Task-1            this is the task description field for this job1. │
│              ──────────── Start ─────── Finish ─────── Totals ───       │
│Duration:   4   Actual Dur:   0 │Erly:07-01-88 │07-07-88 │Var:   800.00  │
│Strt Del:   0   Finish Del:   0 │Late:11-30-88 │12-05-88 │Fix:     0.00  │
│   Float: 102   Free Float:   0 │Schd:07-01-88 │07-07-88 │Tot:   800.00  │
│Pct Comp:     0 BCWP:      0.00 │Actl:         │         │Act:     0.00  │
│    Type:ASAP                   │Plan:07-01-88 │07-07-88 │Plc:     0.00  │
│WBS:01.01.01.00.0001 Acct:    0 │Scheduled     │Priority:│Hrs:    32     │
│                                │Dev:0.00      │         │Plh:  0 Ovr:  0│
├────────────────────────────────────────────────────────────────────────┤
│This is a test to try out the note text feature of this system.  This is a│
│note that goes with task-1.  IT's resource is called leader.             │
└──────────────────────────────────────────────────────────────────────────┘
```

Appendix 2.11.3 Setting up an *As-of* Date (12.6)

The SuperProject Expert *As-of* date is set by the value of *current date* in the Set Preferences screen. Users who wish to include and reflect status data for the day on which the data is being entered will need to set the value in the current date field to one day later. Each time the project plan is called up after the new *As-of* date has been set, the system will flash a message saying "There is a conflict because the first task in the plan is earlier than the project start date." The system then asks if "The project start date should be reset to the actual start date." Users should answer *Yes* and then proceed.

The "Feedback actuals" and "Show actuals" on the Set Preferences screen should be set to *Yes*. Finally, on the "Advanced Scheduling Options" window (Figure A2.16), the "Show resume date as scheduled" should be set to *No*.[17] When the above settings are in place, the system automatically and correctly recomputes the new schedule. This is a simple process, and there is practically no special effort subsequently re-

quired from the user. (See the discussions in the rest of this appendix.)

Appendix 2.11.4 Entering Percent Complete (12.7)

To use percent complete in SuperProject Expert, the "Show WBS and % Complete" on the Set Preferences screen should be set to *Yes*.

Entering an actual start date at the task level triggers the computation for the task's actual hours and the percent complete. The actual hours are automatically computed by multiplying the number of workdays between the actual start and the current date, by the standard workday length in the resource details form. The percent complete is automatically calculated by dividing the actual hours by the original hours. Users may easily override the computed value by manually entering their own assessment of completion.

Entering a value in the percent complete field does *not* conversely drive the value in the actual hours field.

When the actual finish date is entered, the system automatically marks the task 100 percent complete and recomputes the actual hours by multiplying the number of working days between the actual start date and the actual finish date, by the standard workday length in the resource details form. This, too, may be overwritten if it is not correct.

---

[17]If it is set to *Yes*, the scheduled start date of all jobs currently in progress will be set to the current date rather than the actual date they started. While this application does not negatively affect the scheduled finish date, it is confusing and obscures visibility of the actual start date.

The documentation in SuperProject Expert implies that the system also supports the Fifty-fifty percent method (described earlier). To use this method, users are instructed to enter 50 percent in the percent complete field when they enter the actual start date. The field is supposed to automatically change to 100 percent when the actual finish date is entered. This did not work as described.

Appendix 2.11.5 Hard Copy Turn-Around Documents (12.8)

In SuperProject Expert, reports are driven by one of the three sets of select criteria: the Resource Select, the Task Select, or the Assignment Select. (Figure A2.10) Each of these transactions has its own set of fields that may be displayed. In some cases, there is field duplication from one set of criteria to another, thus facilitating certain reporting requirements. In other cases, the desired data can only be accessed from one of the sets, thus limiting certain reporting requirements. When all of the desired data cannot be found in one set, users must be satisfied with a subset of the data, choosing the select view that yields the largest subset.

It is possible, using the task selection criteria, to display total hours and remaining hours. However, these fields are display-only fields where, for example, the remaining hours field is computed by the system as equal to the total hours minus the actual hours. If users wish to modify the remaining hours, they will have to recalculate a new duration and enter the new value in that field.

There are two approaches to developing a turn-around document: the "Task Details" report and the "Resource Assignment" report.

The "Task Details" Report. This approach results in a report with all of the required information, the "Task Detail" report, which has been driven by the Task Select. (See Figure A2.26.) The user may select the task name, the actual start date, the actual hours, the original duration, the actual finish date, the scheduled start date, the scheduled finish date and an optional percent complete. Although the system supports limiting the reports to a date range, the tasks on this report cannot be separated out by resource name.

Figure A2.26

01-26-89				Task Detail Report		Page: 1-1 CHAP9G.PJ	
Task Name Resource Name	Actual Start	Actl Hours	Dur	Actual Finish	Schd Start	Schd Finish	Pct Comp
Task-1	07-01-88		4	07-07-88	07-01-88	07-07-88	100
leader		32	4		07-01-88	07-07-88	

		32					
Task-2	07-08-88		10		10-13-89	10-24-89	20
leader		16	10		10-13-89	10-24-89	

		16					
Task-3	07-08-88		11		10-13-89	10-25-89	18
leader		16	11		10-13-89	10-25-89	

		16					
Task-4			10		10-26-89	11-08-89	
leader			10		10-26-89	11-08-89	

		0					

Figure A2.27

01-26-89   Resource Assignments Report

Heading/Task	Task ID	Schd Start	Schd Finish	Dur	Actl Hours	Actual Start	Actual Finish
Task-6	006	07-01-88	07-07-88	4	32		
Task-13	013	07-08-88	07-14-88	4	8		
Task-12	012	07-08-88	07-20-88	11	32		
Task-22	022	08-10-88	08-31-88	16			
Task-21	021	08-10-88	08-17-88	6			
Task-26	026	08-18-88	08-26-88	7			
Task-32	032	08-29-88	09-12-88	10			
Task-39	039	09-14-88	09-30-88	13			
Task-43	043	10-03-88	10-07-88	5			
Task-45	045	10-13-88	10-18-88	4			
Task-48	048	10-25-88	11-01-88	6			
Task-51	051	11-02-88	11-10-88	7			
Task-52	052	11-14-88	11-17-88	4			
					======		
					72		

Optionally, the user may enter the resource name data for a *second* time—as a code in either the task account field or at the end of the WBS code. Otherwise, all of the tasks for *all* of the resources are reported on each report. As a result, there will be an extra (and sometimes excessive) usage of paper, the report may be hard to follow, and the completeness of the turn-around data may be hard to verify.

The "Resource Assignments" Report. The second approach results in a resource-limited task list, but it cannot report on all of the required data. This is the "Resource Assignments" report, and it is driven by the assignment select. (See Figure A2.27.) The user may select the task ID, the scheduled start, the scheduled finish, the original duration, and the actual hours. Columns for the actual start and the actual finish will have to be written in by the resource who is reporting the status.

Appendix 2.11.6 Entering the Status Collection Data (*12.9*)

In SuperProject Expert, users may choose any *one* of several screens to enter *all* of the reporting data. For entering information about several tasks, the Outline screen that also displays the resource assignments is the easiest to work with. This is invoked from the Outline screen by pressing "/; Edit; View; Work Breakdown Outline". (Figure A2.13)

By using the Task Select, the user can set the Outline screen so that columns are displayed for actual start, actual time, duration, actual finish, scheduled start, scheduled complete and, optionally, the percent complete field.

There is no field for time-this-period. However, entering a value in the actual start date field also causes a value for actual time (to-date) to be automatically computed and entered. The actual time is automatically computed by multiplying the number of work days between the actual start date and the current date, by the workday length in the task form. If this is not the right number, the user may easily correct it by manually calculating and entering the desired value for actual time. It is important to note that actual time may only be entered into the *resource assignment line* that accompanies each task in the outline. The corresponding entry in the task line will be automatically updated.

When the actual finish date is entered, the system automatically marks the task 100 percent complete and recomputes the actual time by multiplying the number of working days between the actual start date and the actual finish date, by the workday length in the task form. This, too, may be overwritten if it is not correct.

The remaining time fields and the total time fields are display-only fields. When users wish to reflect remaining time, they will manually have to recalculate the *task duration* and enter the new value in that field.

The percent complete is automatically computed by the system; however, the user may enter an override value. (See the earlier discussion in this appendix.)

For time reporting, there are no special actions required to invoke any of the scenarios described in Figure 12.1. However, for cost reporting, additional special processing *will* be called for. These requirements will be addressed later in this appendix.

Appendix 2.11.7 Performance Status Reporting (12.10)

By using the task selection criteria in SuperProject Expert, the Outline screen may be set up to display the actual start and finish dates, the actual and remaining duration, the float, the planned hours, planned start date, and the planned finish date. (See Figure A2.28.) This "Task Details" report may be produced following the directions given earlier in the book. The "Task Summary" report lists each task along with its predecessors and successors. There is also a Gantt chart that compares actuals to baseline. (See Figure

Figure A2.28

Task Name Resource Name	Actual Start	Actual Finish	Actl Dur	Float	Plan Hours	Hours Remaining	Planned Start	Planned Finish
Task-1 leader	07-01-88	07-07-88	4	0			07-01-88	07-07-88
Task-2 leader	07-08-88		2	102		64	07-08-88	07-21-88
Task-3 leader	07-08-88		2	101		72	07-08-88	07-21-88
Task-4 leader			0	101		80	07-22-88	08-04-88
Task-5 leader			0	101		96	08-05-88	08-22-88
Task-6 boss	07-01-88	07-07-88	4	0			07-01-88	07-07-88
Task-7 senior	07-01-88	07-11-88	6	0			07-01-88	07-12-88
Task-8 worker	07-01-88		6	53		8	07-01-88	07-07-88
Task-9 worker	07-01-88		6	39		8	07-01-88	07-05-88

01-26-89   Task Detail Report   Page: 1-1   CHAP9G.PJ   01-26-89

Figure A2.29

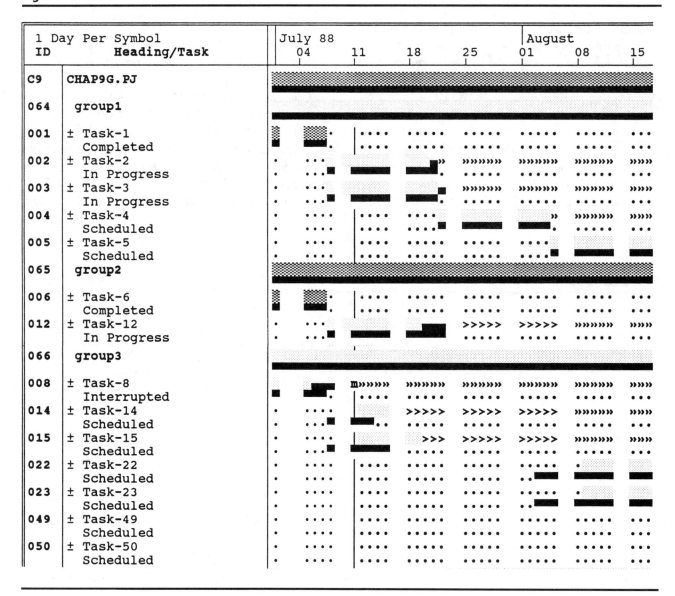

A2.29.) The columns of the Gantt chart may be customized to show any of the task selection criteria.

Also, by using the task selection criteria, users may direct the system to sort and select on many fields. The sort may only be in ascending order and is limited to three levels. Users may select by scheduled, planned, actual, early, late, and must start dates; scheduled, planned, actual, early, late and must finish dates; percent complete; float; and free float. By sorting on status,[18] users may identify jobs that are late and scheduled to finish in the next period, and jobs that are late and scheduled to start in the next period. Alternatively, it is possible to sort on hours remaining (range 1 to 999).

[18]Sorting on status can take on the values of scheduled to start, late in starting, late in finishing, in progress, interrupted, complete.

This product does not feature the ability to select jobs based on revised estimates. Similarly, users cannot get around the limitation by selecting based on relational and arithmetic operators between current values and baseline values. Although the system does support earned value variances (See the discussion later in this appendix.), it does not report on duration variances.

Appendix 2.11.8 Highlighting Progress (12.11)

In SuperProject Expert, there is no special highlighting or time line on the PERT chart to show completion. On the other hand, the Gantt chart is very helpful: the *As-of* date is shown by a vertical dashed line; progress is shown on the bars by darker hued colors; progress is related to the percentage of *true work effort* that has been completed; and delays are illustrated.

Appendix 2.11.9 Costs and Project Management Software (12.13)

''Feedback actuals'', ''Show actuals'', and ''Show costing'' on the SuperProject Expert Set Preferences screen must be set to *Yes*.

When time is reported to a task, the system does *not* correspondingly compute and insert the respective costs for that assignment. Actual costs must be calculated[19] and entered separately by the user. The vendor has indicated that, in the next release, they are seriously considering an option that will cause costs to be recalculated after entering actuals.

When the rate is changed for a given resource, the system does *not* reflect the change in any tasks to which the resource has already been assigned. Thus, the system does *not* update the total costs for a task based on a new resource rate. The new value will need to be computed by the user[20] and entered manually.

There is no special field for actual-costs-this-period.

The *actual* costs and the *total* costs are seen on the task form, the resource form, and the project form.

The values seen at the task level are:

1. The *actual* task cost is the sum of all of the respective actual resource variable costs entered by the user for that task.
2. The *actual* task-level fixed costs are entered by the user.
3. After reporting status to the project, the *total* task cost is the sum of the *actual* resource variable costs plus the *actual* task-level fixed costs plus the *remaining* task-level costs.

The values seen at the resource level are:

1. The *actual* resource cost is the sum of all of the respective actual task costs entered by the user for that resource.
2. The *actual* resource-level fixed costs are entered by the user.
3. After reporting status to the project, the *total* resource cost is the sum of the *actual* task costs and the *actual* resource-level fixed costs and the *remaining* task-level costs.

The values seen at the project level are:

1. The *actual* project costs are equal to the sum of the task-level *actual* costs.
2. The *actual* fixed costs at the project level are equal to the sum of the *actual* task-level fixed costs fields.
3. After reporting status to the project, the *total* costs at the project level are equal to the sum of the *actual* costs fields from the task level, plus the sum of the *actual* fixed costs from the task level plus the sum of the *remaining* task-level costs.

The *actual* costs, *fixed* costs, *total* costs, and *remaining* costs may also be chosen from the select criteria. The select criteria may be used to format the Outline screen and reports.

Fixed and overhead costs are added to the project by creating separate resources and then assigning them to the corresponding tasks. By entering the desired value in the accrue field of the respective Resource Details screen, the user may instruct the system on how to accrue costs on reports:

• strt = accrued at the beginning of the task (e.g., equipment leasing down payments)

---

[19]By multiplying the actual hours by the resource rate.

[20]By multiplying the task hours by the new resource rate.

Figure A2.30

```
Outline                                          Project: CHAP9G.PJ
02-17-89   6:23p                                      Revision:  41
                                                                      +
```

Heading/Task	Resource	Total Cost	Actual Cost	Cost Remaining	Variance at Completion	Planned Cost
CHAP9G.PJ		71120.00	8920.00	62200.00	0.00	71120.00
group1		9400.00	1600.00	7800.00	-200.00	9200.00
Task-1		800.00	800.00	0.00	0.00	800.00
	leader	800.00	800.00			
Task-2		2000.00	400.00	1600.00	0.00	2000.00
	leader	2000.00	400.00			
Task-3		2200.00	400.00	1800.00	-200.00	2000.00
	leader	2200.00	400.00			
Task-4		2000.00	0.00	2000.00	0.00	2000.00
	leader	2000.00	0.00			
Task-5		2400.00	0.00	2400.00	0.00	2400.00
	leader	2400.00	0.00			
group2		39120.00	4000.00	35120.00	0.00	39120.00
Task-6		1600.00	1600.00	0.00	0.00	1600.00
	boss	1600.00	1600.00			
Task-12		4400.00	1600.00	2800.00	0.00	4400.00
	boss	4400.00	1600.00			
Task-13		1600.00	800.00	800.00	0.00	1600.00
	boss	1600.00	800.00			

- prorate = accrued throughout the task (e.g., employees)
- end: = accrued when job is finished (e.g., contractors)

Appendix 2.11.10 Cost Status Reporting (12.15)

SuperProject Expert is the only product that will select jobs that are over or under budget.

The task selection criteria may be set up to display the total costs, the actual costs, the remaining costs, the variance at completion, and the original planned baseline costs. (See Figure A2.30.) The variance at completion is equal to the originally planned costs minus the current forecasted costs.

There are no cash flow reports, no reports on costs per period, no cost histogram, and no cumulative costs reports in this product.

Appendix 2.11.11 Earned Values and Project Management Software (12.17)

SuperProject Expert supports earned values. (See Figure A2.31.)

Earlier in this appendix, users were advised to set the *As-of* date to the day *following* the status date. (This is done on the Set Preferences screen.) Now, in order to help the system to compute the correct values for the earned value analysis, users must set the *As-of* date to the *same day as the status date*.[21]

---

[21] And remember to change it back to one day later for traditional status reporting!

Figure A2.31

```
Outline                                                    Project: CHAP9G.PJ
02-20-89  12:41p                                              Revision:  41

                                                                         +

Heading/Task  Resource    Earned      Bdgt.Cost    Schedule      Cost    Variance at
                          (BCWP)      Work Schd.   Variance    Variance   Completion

CHAP9G.PJ                 9245.60     4103.08      5142.52     325.60       0.00
  group1                  1564.00     1533.33        30.67     -36.00    -200.00
    Task-1                 800.00      800.00         0.00       0.00       0.00
           leader
    Task-2                 400.00      400.00         0.00       0.00       0.00
           leader
    Task-3                 360.00      400.00       -40.00     -40.00    -200.00
           leader
    Task-4                   0.00        0.00         0.00       0.00       0.00
           leader
    Task-5                   0.00        0.00         0.00       0.00       0.00
           leader
  group2                  2738.40     2256.92       481.48   -1261.60       0.00
    Task-6                1600.00     1600.00         0.00       0.00       0.00
           boss
    Task-12               1584.00      800.00       784.00     -16.00       0.00
           boss
    Task-13                800.00      800.00         0.00       0.00       0.00
           boss
```

The BCWP is equal to the planned costs times the percent complete.[22]

The BCWS is the value equal to the planned percentage complete times the planned dollars.

The schedule variance is equal to the BCWP − the BCWS.

The cost variance is equal to the BCWP − the ACWP.

The variance at completion is equal to the planned dollars minus the current total forecasted dollars.

SuperProject Expert has a unique approach to *rolling up* the earned values from the tasks into the group-level heading activities and into the project-level data. While the other products add the values from *within* the group, SuperProject Expert actually calculates the answers from the corresponding values *at* the group level.

Users should not forget to reset the current date when they are finished computing and reporting on earned values.

Appendix 2.11.12 Reporting on Resource Availability (12.20)

The SuperProject Expert resource Gantt/histogram that is pictured in Figure A2.17 may be printed. (Figure A2.29) This Gantt may be set up to show or suppress baseline values.

---

[22]This value reflects the actual percentage completed. It is either system-computed or entered by the user.

The ''Resource Assignment'' report (Figure A2.27) may be set up to display, *for each task assigned to a resource*, the total number of resources available, the total hours required, the overscheduled hours, the actual hours, and the start and finish dates. The system does not show underscheduled hours. Users will have to compare resources available, total hours required, and the start and finish dates to find underscheduling.

Appendix 2.11.13 Reporting on Resource Utilization *(12.21)*

There are no reports in SuperProject Expert that provide periodic resource utilization totals. There are two approaches to producing the required information: through the resource reports or through the task reports. Each of these reports may be *customized* by using the corresponding select criteria.

Used with the ''Task Summary'' report, the Task Select supports the display of the planned, actual, and total hours; the planned, actual, and total costs; and the cost variance.[23] Users may also choose to display the scheduled start and finish dates as well as the remaining costs and hours. (See Figure A2.32.) However, although the system supports limiting the data on this report to a date range, the tasks can*not* be separated out by resource name. Optionally, the user may enter the resource data for a *second* time—as a code in either the task account field or at the end of the WBS code—and then select on the chosen field. Otherwise, all of the tasks for *all* of the resources are reported on each report.

Used with the ''Resource Detail'' report, the Assignment Select will allow filtering on a resource name, but it does not support the display of planned hours and costs or remaining hours and costs. However, it does allow the display of total and actual hours and total and actual costs. Users may also choose to display the scheduled start and finish dates. (See Figure A2.33.) This report also groups the data by resource.

APPENDIX 2.12 MANAGING THE PROJECT

Appendix 2.12.1 Who Produces Perts and Gantts that May Be Restricted to Critical Path Jobs? *(13.7)*

In SuperProject Expert, if the selection criteria have been set up to choose only those tasks with float equivalent to the float on the critical path, the Gantt chart may be restricted to display these tasks only. This is accomplished by pressing ''/; Edit; View; Tasks only''. The system will not support restricting the PERT charts by selecting on the critical path or on float.

Appendix 2.12.2 Who Produces Reports that May Be Restricted to Fixed Date Jobs? *(13.8)*

SuperProject Expert reports may be selected based on the values in the must start or must finish dates fields.

Appendix 2.12.3 Who Produces Perts and Gantts that May Be Restricted to Summary Jobs? *(13.9)*

In SuperProject Expert, all of the data about a group of tasks may be drawn up into its summary header by placing the cursor on the summary header and pressing the ''—'' key. After this operation, both the Gantt and the PERT chart will be restricted to displaying the appropriate summary data.

Appendix 2.12.4 Local Area Networks *(13.14)*

SuperProject Expert prevents access to files when they are active. It does not provide read/write protection.

Appendix 2.12.5 Guidelines for Tracking and Managing the Project *(13.15)*

SuperProject Expert does not have tracking and plan management guidelines.

---

[23]The planned dollars minus the total dollars.

Figure A2.32

02-24-89   Task Summary Report   CHAP9G.PJ

Cost Remaining	Variance at Completion	Schd Start	Schd Finish	Task Acct
		07-01-88	07-07-88	1000
1600.00		07-12-88	07-21-88	1000
1800.00	-200.00	07-12-88	07-22-88	1000
2000.00		07-25-88	08-05-88	1000
2400.00		08-08-88	08-23-88	1000
2200.00		08-10-88	08-24-88	1000
400.00		07-12-88	07-13-88	1000
800.00		08-10-88	08-15-88	1000
1400.00		10-03-88	10-12-88	1000
1600.00		10-13-88	10-24-88	1000
600.00		11-18-88	11-22-88	1000

02-24-89   Task Summary Report   CHAP9G.PJ

Heading/Task	Plan Hours	Actl Hours	Total Hours	Hours Remaining	Planned Cost	Actual Cost	Total Cost
Task-1	32	32	32		800.00	800.00	800.00
Task-2	80	16	80	64	2000.00	400.00	2000.00
Task-3	80	16	88	72	2000.00	400.00	2200.00
Task-4	80		80	80	2000.00		2000.00
Task-5	96		96	96	2400.00		2400.00
Task-23	88		88	88	2200.00		2200.00
Task-24	40	24	40	16	1000.00	600.00	1000.00
Task-36	32		32	32	800.00		800.00
Task-44	56		56	56	1400.00		1400.00
Task-46	64		64	64	1600.00		1600.00
Task-53	24		24	24	600.00		600.00
	======	=====	======		============	==========	============
	672	88	680		16800.00	2200.00	17000.00

Figure A2.33

02-22-89		Resource Detail Report				CHAP9G.PJ

Resource Task/Subproject	Variable Cost	Total Cost	Actual Cost	Total Hours	Actual Hours	Ovr Hours
boss						
Task-6	1600.00	1600.00	1600.00	32	32	
Task-12	4400.00	4400.00	1600.00	88	32	16
Task-13	1600.00	1600.00	800.00	32	16	32
Task-21	2400.00	2400.00		48		
Task-22	6400.00	6400.00		128		48
Task-26	2800.00	2800.00		56		56
Task-32	4000.00	4000.00		80		24
Task-39	5200.00	5200.00		104		
Task-43	2000.00	2000.00		40		
Task-45	1600.00	1600.00		32		
Task-48	2400.00	2400.00		48		
Task-51	2800.00	2800.00		56		
Task-52	1600.00	1600.00		32		
	38800.00	38800.00	4000.00	776	80	176
leader						
Task-1	800.00	800.00	800.00	32	32	
Task-2	2000.00	2000.00	400.00	80	16	
Task-3	2200.00	2200.00	400.00	88	16	80
Task-24	1000.00	1000.00	600.00	40	24	40
Task-4	2000.00	2000.00		80		
Task-5	2400.00	2400.00		96		
Task-23	2200.00	2200.00		88		80
Task-36	800.00	800.00		32		32
Task-44	1400.00	1400.00		56		
Task-46	1600.00	1600.00		64		
Task-53	600.00	600.00		24		
DO CHARTER	1000.00	1000.00		40		
DO H.L.A	1000.00	1000.00		40		
	19000.00	19000.00	2200.00	760	88	232
	76376.00	76376.00	8920.00	3760	368	864

APPENDIX 3: PROJECT WORKBENCH 3.0

APPENDIX 3.0 INTRODUCTION

Each section in each appendix is keyed back to its corresponding introductory section in the tutorial. Readers will find that the respective tutorial section is noted in italicized parentheses at the end of each appropriate section header line.

APPENDIX 3.1 GANTT-DRIVEN PRODUCTS

Appendix 3.1.1 Data Entry Mode *(16.2.2)*

Whereas it is likely that the user will primarily use Project Workbench's Gantt mode to do *most* of the data entry, the system also allows *relationships* to be entered while in Dependency Definition mode.

Appendix 3.1.2 Size and Storage Constraints *(16.3.1)*

Project Workbench comes in two versions: the Standard Workbench and the Advanced Workbench. Both require a minimum of 640K of main memory.[1] Since the Standard Workbench acts on project data solely in memory, the size of its projects is limited to 300 data records.

The Advanced Workbench starts by operating on the project plan in main memory. However, if the default dependency, resource allocations and lines of text are not changed, when the number of project data records exceeds 572, the system will automatically extend the project data area by creating *spill* files on the disk drive. At that time, the size of the project is limited only by the amount of available disk space.[2]

Project Workbench has a three-level work breakdown structure. The product also has a 12-position alphanumeric identification field for each job.

When charting the project in Network mode, a path through the network is defined as a sequence of jobs that are executed one after the other. There may be many paths through the network from the start of the project to the end of the project. In Project Workbench, the longest chain in a given path is limited to 250 jobs.

Subprojects are also supported in the Advanced Workbench.

---

[1]Although it was not available for review at the time of this writing, a new feature will be included in an impending release: EMS will be supported.

[2]Projects that use spill files have slower response times than those which reside solely in memory.

Figure A3.1

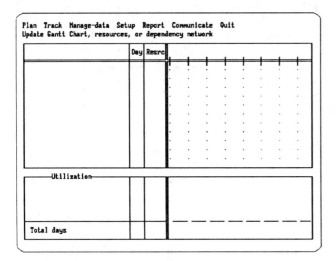

```
Plan Track Manage-data Setup Report Communicate Quit
Update Gantt Chart, resources, or dependency network
```

Figure A3.2

```
Global
Update global characteristics, global calendar, or actuals capture time periods
                           ┌─Time periods─
                       ┌─Calendar─
                   ┌─Definition─
                                                              Save
   Dates        Today: 07-01-88  Format: mm-dd-yy             Yes

   Display      Normal: 03-00   Highlighted: 05-00   Inverse: 00-05   No

   Level names  (1) PRO Project       (2)  PHA Phase        No
                (3) ACT Activity      (4)  TSK Task

   Calendar     Start day of week: Mon  Business days in week: BBBBBHH   No

                                                    Request  Used
                Resources in a single project          20      0
                Resources in a group report            20
   Limits       Dependency links (approximate)        200      0
                Lines text window 1 before overflow     21      0      No
                Lines text window 2 before overflow     21      0
                Help facility resident in memory        No
                Activities in memory before overflow    71      0
```

Appendix 3.1.3 System Structure (16.3.2)

Project Workbench is directed through a hierarchy of command lines that are found in an area at the top of the screen. Line 1 lists the options and Line 2, as the user cursors across Line 1, presents a brief description of each option. (See Figure A3.1 for the options and a description of ''Plan''.)

Appendix 3.1.4 Global System Project Data Defaults (16.3.3)

Two of the second-level options under Setup are Project and Global. The global system project data options are found in the third level—under Global. (See Figure A3.2.)

In Project Workbench, the menu hierarchies may be bypassed if the user employs the QuicKey mode. QuicKey mode is entered and exited by toggling the F2 function key. Then, each subcommand under Plan may be invoked with one keystroke or with ''Alt'' plus one key stoke. This requires memorizing 50 keyboard shortcuts, which are a combination of (1) function keys; (2) alphabet keys; (3) the ''Alt'' key plus an alphabetic key; and (4) cursor control keys. This sounds imposing—however, the more common com-

mands are not hard to remember. Consequently, researching the short-cut may only be required when accessing an infrequently used command. An excellent on-line help is also available—in QuicKey mode as well as menu mode.

Appendix 3.1.5 New Projects (16.3.4)

To choose the project start date, select ''Setup; Global; Today's date'' and enter and save the desired date. This action automatically initializes the project start date and the first day displayed on the Gantt chart to the desired date. Then, choose ''Setup; Project'' to invoke the Project Definition screen—to define other project parameters such as the start day of the week, the hours worked per day, and the resource units of measure. (See Figure A3.3.)

Appendix 3.1.6 Accessing Existing Plans (16.3.5)

The second-level options under Manage-Data (Figure A3.1) are Save, Recall, Insert, Transfer, and Options. To load a desired project, choose ''Manage-Data; Recall'' and the File Recall screen will be displayed. (See Figure A3.4.) Pressing ''Enter'' will display the file names of all of the projects in the data base.

Figure A3.3

```
Project
Enter information on Project Definition Form or Project Calendar

                          ┌──────────Calendar──────────┐
                          ├──────────Definition────────┤
Title  ·················        Project ID ··········   Version ·······
Manager name ···········        Manager ID ····         Dept ········
Description ··········································
·······················································

┌──────────────────────────┬──────────────────────────┐
│     Authorizations       │       Assumptions        │
├──────────────────────────┼──────────────────────────┤
│ Project start date  87-01-88│ Start day of week      Mon     │
│ Project end date    ········│ Business days in week  BBBBBHH │
│                            │ Start date of fiscal year 01-01-88 │
│ Baseline budget     0      │ Hours per day          8       │
│ Baseline start date ········│                                │
│ Baseline end date   ········│ Resource unit of measure Days  │
│                            │ Resource decimal places  1     │
│ Last actuals period start ··│ Resource loading pattern Contour │
│ Last actuals period end   ··│ Histogram column width   5     │
└──────────────────────────┴──────────────────────────┘
```

whenever new dependencies are added, whenever the resource loading pattern is changed, and whenever data is entered through the Tracking subsystems, Project Workbench is called a semi-immediate processor system. New schedules are computed with the autoscheduler by progressively selecting "Plan; Gantt; Autoschedule". If the project start date is different from the current date, use of this feature also requires setting the plan date as described in the discussion of new projects.

Appendix 3.1.8 Adding Plan Data (16.3.7)

The second level under Plan is Gantt, Resources, and Dependencies. If "Plan; Gantt" is selected, the third level is Insert, Change, and so on. When "Plan; Gantt; Insert" is chosen, plan data may be entered on the third-level screen. (See Figure A3.5.)

Appendix 3.1.9 Optional "What-If's" or Permanent Saves (16.3.8)

Plan data is not made permanent until the user chooses to save it and until the user designates the name under which the plan is to be saved.

Figure A3.4

```
Recall
Enter name of file to be recalled or press Enter to display directory

┌──────────────────────────────────────────────────┐
│ Filename C:\PMW3\PMW3\                             │
│                                                    │
│ ATM1     10-02-88 ATM2     12-05-88 CHAP9   09-29-88 CHAP9G  12-02-88 │
│ MOREC8   09-14-88 MOREC8B  07-07-88 MOVE    07-14-86 PROJECTA 09-08-88 │
│ PROJECTB 09-08-88 RESPATS  11-16-88 SUB     10-02-88 SUB-SUB  06-20-88 │
│ SUBNEST  09-29-88 SUP1     12-07-88 SUPERPRO 12-02-88 TEST    09-08-88 │
│ TESTSUB  08-13-88 TUTORZ   01-12-88 │
│                                                    │
└──────────────────────────────────────────────────┘
```

Figure A3.5

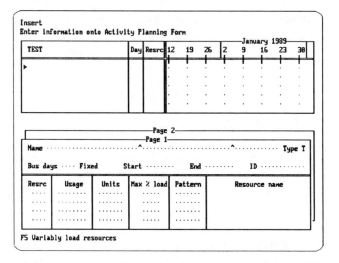

Appendix 3.1.7 Immediate Processor or Batch (16.3.6)

Project Workbench immediately updates the dates in a job whenever it is added to the plan and whenever its duration is modified. However, because the system requires a separate operation to update the schedule

Appendix 3.1.10 Ad Hoc Information Storage (*16.3.9*)

Project Workbench features a text processor in the Reports module that allows users to record up to 18,000 characters per page of information. The text data initially resides in memory, but can also be held in a disk overflow area if there is not sufficient virtual storage. Although the number of lines of text in memory initially defaults to 21, this number is ultimately controlled by the number of dependencies and resource allocations.

Information may also be stored at the activity level in the 30-character deliverable field and the 11-character short name field. (These are both on Page 2 of the Activity Planning screen. (See Figure A3.10 below.)) Data may also be entered into the 135-character project description field. The activity name field is 63 characters long and, therefore, the user may also enter data at the end of this field.

Appendix 3.1.11 Exporting Data (*16.3.10*)

Project Workbench will export data in Fixed ASCII format, Comma Separated Values, and Data Interchange format.

APPENDIX 3.2 WORK BREAKDOWN STRUCTURES

Appendix 3.2.1 Graphics Support (*4.8.2*)

Project Workbench does not provide graphic work breakdown structures. Project Workbench is Gantt-driven (that is, the bar chart controls most operations).

Appendix 3.2.2 Level Support (*4.8.3*)

Project Workbench supports a three-level work breakdown structure, which may be given any terminology for the levels that the user designates on the Global Definition screen. (Figure A3.2) The terms *phase*, *activity*, and *task* are the product's default designations. The system is told what level a job is at by the entry of a corresponding one-position value in the type field on the Activity Planning screen. (Figure A3.5) This signal causes the correct indentation in the Gantt chart outline. Without an entry in the type field, all jobs will be viewed as tasks and uniformly indented.

The system also supports a 12-position alphanumeric identification number that is user-generated. This number is not ordinarily displayed on the Gantt screen. In order to see it, the user must select "Plan; Gantt; View" and tell the system to display the activity IDs.

Appendix 3.2.3 Data Entry Requirements (*4.8.4*)

If Project Workbench users are not looking for rollup reporting, then only one entry is necessary—the user-generated activity identification number. If rollup reporting is necessary, then one (or both) of the category fields are also required.

Appendix 3.2.4 Durations and Dependencies (*4.8.5*)

It is not necessary to enter durations or dependencies when initially creating Project Workbench jobs. The system automatically defaults to durations of one day.

Appendix 3.2.5 Random Sequence of Data Entry (*4.8.6*)

Building the plan using Project Workbench is restricted to Gantt Chart Entry mode and Dependency Definition mode. However, when the type field is correctly entered, the name field on the Gantt is indented to the respective position in the WBS level. While Project Workbench does allow random entry of records, it will not sort them via the identification number or *category* code into their expected location in the Gantt outline.

Appendix 3.2.6 Using The Copy Features With The *Template* Tasks (*4.8.7*)

Project Workbench supports repetitive copying of the *template* jobs that occur within the plan. This may be accomplished by creating the *template* jobs as a separate file and *attaching* the *template* file in the project file as a subproject or through the "Manage-Data; Insert" command. Although it still has limitations, the latter is the recommended approach.

Appendix 3.2.7 Rollup Support *(4.8.8)*

Project Workbench produces standard reports on resource effort and costs, and many of their reports will break and summarize these values when an activity category code or resource category code change occurs. Although it is also displayed on reports, the activity identification number is *not* used for rollup reporting. Nevertheless, the "Activity Details" report will display total costs for the whole project, total number of resource days used by the whole project, and the length of the project.

A variation on rollup reporting can be achieved by choosing Activity as the level of reporting detail. With this choice, the reporting of *all tasks will be suppressed*, with their totals being rolled up into the activity line that *is* reported. Of course, if phase is the level of detail selected, all data will be suppressed except the one line for each phase.

On the other hand, to provide *subtotal* rollup reporting that also shows the phases, activities, *and* tasks, Project Workbench also supports two 6-position category fields (one for activities and one for resources), which *can* be used as sorting and subtotaling fields. Only one intermediate subtotal is supported, however. For example, the category codes can be used to rollup either all of the tasks within each activity *or* all of the activities within each phase *or* all of the phases within the project—but not both.

It is not possible to total all of the tasks within each activity *and then* all of the activities within each phase *and then* all of the phases within the project. However, if the activity code is set up to indicate unique phases, each report can be limited to select only the data for a given phase. Thus, several reports can be produced, rolling up the data into each phase. The phase totals will then have to be computed manually to get the project totals.

There is no customized report writer in this product.

Within the project plan itself (for example, on the Gantt or on reports), Project Workbench does not provide standard rollups on usage or business days durations for tasks within activities or activities within phases. However, it does provide the preferred duration rollup approach when incorporating subprojects. If the *template* has been imported using the subproject

approach and the subproject is created with *Display each subproject activity* set to *No*, the best type of duration rollup will be provided: with no extra effort on the part of the user, the rollup on the *business days* field computes—not the total work effort—but rather the total time span of the entries inside of the level. Furthermore, with *Include resource usage* set to *Yes*, total person effort will also be computed—rolled up into the *usage* field. Unfortunately, only the usage field is displayed on the Gantt screen. The business days field is only visible on the Activity Planning screen and certain reports. (Figure A3.5)

Appendix 3.2.8 Guidelines and Documentation *(4.8.9)*

Project Workbench has two pages of documentation on work breakdown structures.

APPENDIX 3.3 ESTIMATING

Appendix 3.3.1 Estimating Support and Estimating Guidelines *(5.7.1)*

Project Workbench has a page and a half of sensible tips on estimating that are packed with several excellent thought-provoking concepts.

Appendix 3.3.2 Estimates of *True Work Effort* Versus Resource-Driven Elapsed Time *(5.7.4)*

In Project Workbench, there are two duration/time fields: (1) usage, which is tied to entering resource names along with the *true work effort* estimate; and (2) business days, which is the number of elapsed calendar working days and may either be fixed to true work effort or variably driven by resource constraints, weekends, and holidays. These fields become increasingly more important as the planning process proceeds, providing flexibility to this product that is not found in many other products. The fact that the true work effort must be tied to a resource name may lead the user to initially believe that the system is resource driven. However, this is not so. An optimal plan (which, of course, contains true work effort) may be created by:

1. Accepting certain defaults that should be: the business days field has a matching default of "Fixed"[3]; the default resource is called "X"; and the maximum resource loading is 100 percent.

2. The default resource loading pattern is set in the Project Definition screen. "Contour" should be selected at this time. (This will be covered later in more detail.)

3. An optimal plan may be created by entering the true work effort estimates into the usage field and then choosing "NO: do not include resource constraints" in the autoscheduling feature (which will be covered later in more detail.). True work effort estimates should not be placed in the business days field. It should be left blank.

Assigning real resources to the usage field may be ignored for now; however, they *must* be entered later or there will be no costs computed for the task.

Appendix 3.3.3 Durations and Units of Measurement (5.7.6)

The shortest allowable duration in Project Workbench's business days field is one day. While the product allows the entry in the usage field of work effort in either hours or days, estimates of less than one day are rounded to the next highest whole day and put into the business days field, which is the value used when computing schedules.[4] Project Workbench defaults to "day". The minimum duration for scheduling in Project Workbench is one day. (See earlier discussion.) Project Workbench allows mixed units of measurement, but only uses whole days in scheduling.

---

[3]Although it was not available for review at the time of this writing, a new feature will be included in an impending release: the user may designate at the project level whether the default should be fixed or variable. Users are advised to choose fixed.

[4]If estimates of hours are used, this could have a very unpleasant effect on the total project duration. For example, if this happened on 20 sequential project jobs, the end result (factoring in weekends) could artificially extend the project by one month.

Figure A3.6

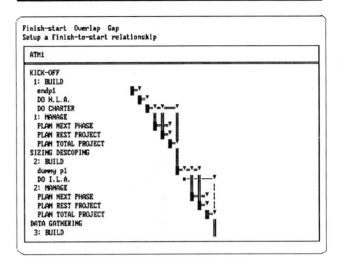

Appendix 3.3.4 Zero Duration Milestones (5.7.7)

Because Project Workbench does not support zero durations, it does not allow zero duration milestones. There is a *work-around* for this limitation, using the "Plan; Dependencies; Add-Link; Overlap", (See Figure A3.6.) that will be presented in more detail later in the appendix.

Appendix 3.3.5 Lead and Lag Times with Duration but No Effort (5.7.8)

Project Workbench provides three solutions to this problem:

1. Assign resource "X" to a separate activity or task whose corresponding business days are equal to the lead time. These activities or tasks will appear on the summary reports; or

2. Create an "Add-Link; Gap" task.[5] (Figure A3.6) With this approach, the delay time is inserted between two selected tasks and will appear on the network charts and the "Activity Dependency" report; or

---

[5]By using "Plan; Dependencies; Add-Link; Gap".

3. Shift,[6] into the future for the number of days equal to the lead time, the task(s) that will be affected by the lead time and then set the corresponding dependencies.[7]

APPENDIX 3.4 NETWORKS

Appendix 3.4.1 Types of Networks *(6.8.1)*

Project Workbench produces activity-on-a-node [AON] diagrams.

Appendix 3.4.2 Types of Relationships *(6.8.2)*

Project Workbench supports three variations on the finish-to-start relationship: (1) the traditional; (2) overlapping the start of the successor ''n'' days or ''x'' percent before the finish of the predecessor; and (3) creating a gap between the finish of the predecessor and the start of the successor. Although it was not available for review at the time of this writing, a new feature will be included in an impending release: users may also designate relationships as finish-to-finish or start-to-start.

Appendix 3.4.3 Number of Dependencies *(6.8.3)*

In Project Workbench, when the hardware has 640k or more memory, the total number of dependencies per project is 600. The default maximum is 100 dependencies and 20 resources, in which case the project size (before spill files are created) will default to 531 jobs. Users may increase the number of dependencies to 600—if they are willing to reduce the total number of jobs, resources, and text. For example, when the number of dependencies is increased to 250 along with the 20 resources, the total number of jobs that will be allowed is decreased to 413. Changes to the number of dependencies must be made *before* any project files are loaded into memory. The modification is made by selecting ''Setup; Global'', changing the number, and saving the change. (Figure A3.2)

There is no limit to the number of dependencies for any given task. Theoretically, if only one task has relationships, it could have 600.

A discussion about how many sets of parallel jobs (subnetworks) the system will support at one time will be introduced later in this appendix. In Project Workbench, the number of dependencies selected by the user will directly influence the number of subnetworks allowed per project.

When working in Network mode, each series of sequential jobs is referred to as a unique path through the network. There may be many paths through the network from the start of the project to the end of the project. In Project Workbench, the longest chain in a given path is limited to 250 jobs. This means, of course, that the length of the critical path is limited to 250 jobs.

Appendix 3.4.4 Establishing Dependencies *(6.8.4)*

Project Workbench supports a three-level work breakdown structure, breaking the project into phases, activities, and then tasks. Dependencies may only be established at the *lowest* level, the task level.

Although these *task* relationships can be viewed in the Network mode, they may only be added or modified in Gantt mode or Dependency Definition mode.

Selecting ''Plan; Dependencies; Add-Link'' will go to the Dependency screen that is used for linking. (Figure A3.6) Then, for each connection, the user must (1) select the type of link: (a) finish-start; (b) overlap; (c) gap (See the discussion on lag and lead times later in this appendix.); and (2) position the cursor to the predecessor row; press return; position the cursor to the successor row; and press ''Return.''

Since the majority of the task relationships are finish-start, and since the user is often entering many relationships at one sitting, it is advisable to learn the key combinations that enable the use of the short-cut QuicKey mode.

Alternatively, users may establish dependencies when in Gantt mode by selecting ''Plan; Gantt; Shift'' and moving a task to overlap with the preceding task or to create a gap between two tasks. Then, relationships may be confirmed by using the ''Mark'' and ''Connect'' options of the ''Shift'' feature, where the ''Mark'' is applied to the predecessor and the ''Connect'' is applied to the successor.

---

[6]By using ''Plan; Gantt; Shift''.

[7]By using the ''Mark'' and ''Connect'' options of the ''Shift'' feature.

Appendix 3.4.5 How Easy Is It to Enter Dependencies? *(6.8.6)*

Project Workbench does not require number entries to create relationships. All the user needs to do is position the cursor and press "Enter".

Appendix 3.4.6 Inserting Jobs into the Middle of the Plan *(6.8.7)*

In Project Workbench, selecting "Plan; Gantt; Insert" allows the addition of new jobs; but the user must then manually resolve all the new relationships in the separate procedures for entering dependencies, described above.

Appendix 3.4.7 Subnetwork Dependencies *(6.8.8)*

In Project Workbench, the Network screen default is 7 rows and 250 columns. This means that the project is also limited to 7 subnetworks—unless the user is willing to (1) increase the number of dependencies that reside in main memory[8] or (2) to accept a network where subnetworks nodes are mixed together in each of the levels. The first option is definitely preferable and easy to implement. First, this process must be initiated as soon as the system is invoked. No project files may be in memory. Then, selecting "Setup; Global" (Figure A3.2) and increasing the number of dependencies will increase the number of subnetworks. Each project may have from 5 to 15 subnetworks, depending on the global number of relationships. For example, 200 dependencies will support 14 subnetworks. The project values for subnetworks are set by selecting "Plan; Dependencies; Network; Configure" and selecting the number of subnetworks and the number of parallel paths for each subnetwork.

In an average-sized project with several subnetworks, many tasks, and many dependencies, the system-generated network may be very tangled. Even the vendor acknowledges this problem.

Relationships are established using "Plan; Dependencies; Add-Link" and may be shown on the Project Workbench Dependency Diagram. (See Figure A3.7.) When entering the network that is reported in

Figure A3.7

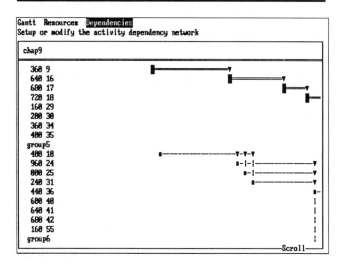

Figure A3.8

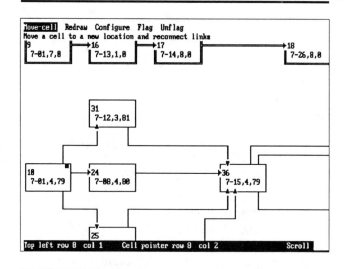

Figure A3.7., the network that is illustrated in Figure A3.8 was expected. Instead, the network that is illustrated in Figure A3.9 was produced. To get the network Figure A3.8, the "Plan; Dependency; Network; Move-Cell" function was used. This small plan required moving five boxes with a dozen or more keystrokes.[9] It will not be unusual, furthermore, to need

---

[8]And, of course, reduce other factors, such as total jobs.

[9]The "Redraw" function does not perform this objective.

Figure A3.9

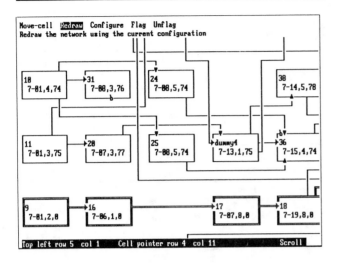

to flip back to the "Dependency Add-Link" screen to make additional modifications.

In the case study—a project with 7 subnetworks and a total of 60 tasks, no subnetwork of which had more than three additional parallel paths—similar difficulties were encountered. Even after changing the number of subnetworks to 14 and the number of parallel paths to four, the network was still very tangled. The "Redraw" function did not fix this problem either. However, when using the "Move-Cell" function to reposition the nodes in the network so that they could be followed, the network was more than satisfactory. This is true—even though the clean-up job took several hours.

In an average plan with several subnetworks, many tasks, and many relationships, this operation can become difficult and time consuming. Therefore, it may be advisable to enter only a small portion of the plan at a time and fix the network diagram before proceeding on to the next batch.

Appendix 3.4.8 Moving Jobs in the Network (6.8.9)

Project Workbench has a perfect move for "cleaning up" the network: it moves the job and carries the relationships with it. Press "Plan; Dependencies; Network; Move-Cell" then (1) move the highlighted box

to the task to be moved; press "Return"; and (2) move the highlighted box to the new position; press "Return". In an average project with several subnetworks, many tasks, and many relationships, the "clean-up" process is time-consuming. (See the earlier discussion.) To some degree, this process can be speeded up with the QuicKey process, using the combinations of "Alt-F" followed by the "Alt-M".

Appendix 3.4.9 Removing Dependencies (6.8.10)

In Project Workbench, selecting "Plan; Dependencies; Remove-Link" takes the user to the linkage Gantt screen. (Figure A3.6) Then (1) position cursor at the row of the predecessor task; press "Return"; and (2) position the cursor at the row of the successor task; press "Return". Alternatively, positioning the cursor at a task and selecting "Plan; Dependency; Disconnect" will delete all of its links.

Appendix 3.4.10 Deleting Jobs in the Plan (6.8.11)

In Project Workbench, selecting "Plan; Gantt; Delete" eliminates the job and leaves dangling tasks.

Appendix 3.4.11 Lag and Lead Times (6.8.12)

In Project Workbench, by using "Plan; Dependencies; Add-Link; Gap", lag time may be inserted between two tasks and will appear on the network charts and on the "Dependency Definition" report. (a hard copy of Figure A3.6) To have these activities or tasks appear on the summary reports, attach resource "X" to a separate activity or task whose corresponding business days are equal to the lead time.

Appendix 3.4.12 Copying Jobs in the Plan (6.8.13)

Project Workbench's internal copy does indeed replicate tasks, and it carries relationships as well. The range copy allows users to flag and then copy one job or a whole group of jobs. Users may also apply "Plan; Gantt; Range; Extract" to a portion of a plan, save it to disk, and then bring it into a second plan. (See the discussion later in this appendix on *templates*. Entire plans are copied by saving the original plan under a new name.

Appendix 3.4.13 Copying the *Template* Jobs (6.8.14)

The *template* file in Project Workbench may be a separately created file or it may be "lifted" from within an existing plan. The second type is set up from the original plan from "Plan; Gantt; Range" by flagging the desired set of jobs, pressing "Extract" and naming the *template* file. *Template* files may be brought into a master plan through the use of the "Manage-Data; Insert" or through a subproject connect.

Because of the subproject limitations (described later in this section), the user may be well advised not to use subprojects for getting *template* jobs into the master plan. An alternative is to use the "Insert" function. This approach supports internal relationships and automatically determines the new dates. However, once the tasks have been imported into the master project, any changes in the *template* plan must also be done manually in every occurrence of *template* tasks in the master.

Alternatively, subprojects may be "attached" to any task in the master file via the Page 2 form that is "hidden" behind the Activity Planning screen for that job. (Figure A3.5) This form is easily accessed with the "page down" key. (See Figure A3.10.) Note that there are three important parameters in this form: "Include resource usage;" "Summarize by resource category;" and "Display each subproject activity." These are used in two separate processes, each of which must be executed correctly to attach a subproject for use in the *template* application. After each of the two processes has been completed, the master project must be saved and recalled at least once before the procedure is considered wrapped up.

1. If all three parameters are set to *No* and the masterproject has been saved and recalled, the spanned duration of all of the jobs within the subproject project will be correctly computed and entered into the business days field of the task to which the subproject is attached.

2. Next, to get the correct value for total work effort into the usage field, the master project must be

Figure A3.10

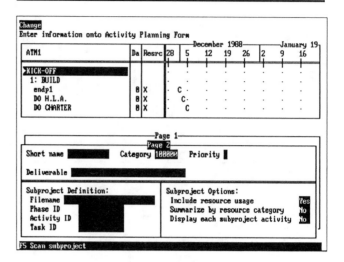

saved and recalled with a value of *Yes* for "Include resource usage." However, the task to which the subproject has been attached will be locked into position whenever the master project is invoked. If correct schedules are to be reflected, these tasks will have to be unlocked individually each time the project is invoked. Although it is necessary, this, unfortunately, can become very tiresome.[10]

If both procedures have been done correctly and the autoscheduler is executed (with resources equal *No*), the corrected work effort, dates, and durations *will* be shown on the Gantt. The original subproject dates will remain as the start and finish dates on Page 1 of the Activity Planning screen, as the "Planned Dates" on the "Activity Dependency" report, and shown with milestone markers on the Gantt chart. (They may be ignored.) The new dates will also be in the "Revised Dates" of the "Activity Dependency" report.

Whole phases and/or activities may also be linked to a master project by using "Y" in "Display each subproject activity."

In certain cases, these procedures will not work unless both the master project and *the subproject have*

---

[10]The process may be somewhat speeded up by using the QuicKey "L".

been set up following the directions described later for choosing the correct project start date.

Attached subprojects suffer from the common restriction of prohibiting relationships between jobs in the master plan and any detail tasks inside the subproject. Sadly, they also will not allow dependency links to be established between any jobs in the master plan and the detail tasks at the beginning or ending of the subproject group. The product documentation did describe a *work-around* for this problem; it will be addressed in the multiproject discussion later in this appendix.

Finally, when nesting subprojects, only the dates in the first level into the nest are updated automatically with the autoscheduler. The lower levels must be done manually by the user. This limitation restricts the potential of nested *template* plans.

Appendix 3.4.14 Loops in the Network *(6.8.15)*

Project Workbench prevents loops and displays a message at the bottom of the screen: ''link invalid''.

Appendix 3.4.15 Dangling Jobs *(6.8.16)*

Project Workbench allows dangling.

Appendix 3.4.16 Verifying Dependencies Are Correct *(6.8.17)*

In Project Workbench, dependencies may be connected only at the task level. Dependency corrections may be made only in Gantt mode or Dependency Definition mode; they may not be made in Network mode. If the user is comfortable with verification of relationships while in Gantt mode or Dependency Definition mode, no further action is necessary. However, in projects with many tasks and many relationships, visually verifying dependencies in either of these modes may become very difficult. Consequently, the user will have to flip back and forth between (1) the Network screen to confirm the relationships and (2) the Gantt or the Dependency Definition screens to correct the relationships, alternating the steps described above for establishing dependencies and below for viewing networks.

In an average-sized project, system creation of

Figure A3.11

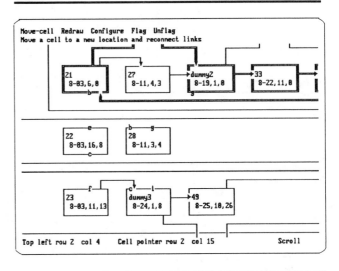

the network does not usually result in a chart that is easy to read.

- The system-created network often results in a tangled mix-up. Consequently, jobs that ought to follow one another sequentially are often scattered around the network.

- If the nodes are far apart, no attempt is made to connect them. Instead, letters which have been inserted into the borders of the node are used as ''on-page'' connectors. It is not unusual to see several unconnected nodes (with letters on their borders) suspended in midair on the network. (See Figure A3.11.) Fortunately, using the ''Move-Cell'' feature described earlier to reposition the jobs to their approximately correct locations causes the connections to reappear.

- With so many scattered and suspended nodes, the whole network will usually need to be improved with the ''Move-Cell'' feature before verification can take place. Dependency modifications cannot be made on the Network screen; therefore, flipping between the ''Dependency; Add-Link'' screen and the Network screen will be required. Although time consuming, this is not a hard operation. The user may also wish to use the ''Dependency Diagram'' report, shown in Figure A3.16 below.

Figure A3.12

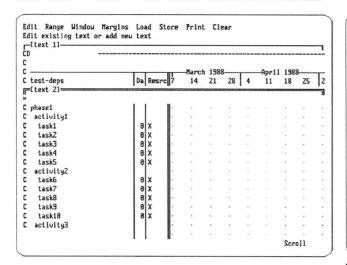

Figure A3.13A

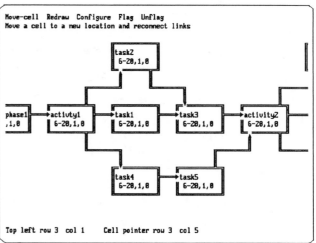

Figure A3.13B

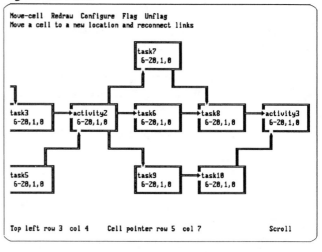

Dependencies may only be set at the task level. The Gantt chart report in Figure A3.12 indicates that Phase 1 has three activities, with Activity 1 partitioned into 5 tasks and Activity 2 similarly partitioned into 5 tasks. Activity 3 has not been partitioned yet. Their relationships are illustrated in Figures A3.13A and A3.13B, although these diagrams have been "forged" in order to illustrate the example.

• In reality, Project Workbench only puts jobs at the task level on the network. The actual network that was produced did not have nodes for Phase1 or any of the three activities. Without these entries and their dependencies, the network (after clean-up with the "Move-Cell") looked like Figure A3.14. With the dependencies added at the task level, the network in Figure A3.15 resulted. Neither of these last two networks gives a complete picture of the plan (as illustrated in Figures A3.13A and A3.13B). Consequently, it is not possible to verify all of the plan. Since dependencies in Project Workbench are only allowed at the lowest level, additional dummy overlapping tasks had to be added for "Phase 1, Activity 1, and Activity 2" to the task level in the Gantt (as illustrated in the Project Workbench dependency diagram in Figure A3.16) in order to get the networks in Figures A3.13A and A3.13B.

Appendix 3.4.17 Network Aesthetics (6.8.19)

In Project Workbench, once the user has moved the nodes into positions that make the network readable and understandable, it is a rather pleasing network.

Appendix 3.4.18 Scaled to Time? (6.8.20)

The network in Project Workbench is not scaled to time.

Figure A3.14

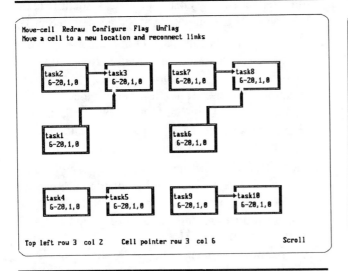

Figure A3.16

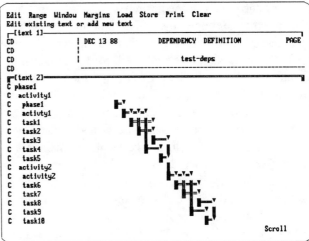

Figure A3.15

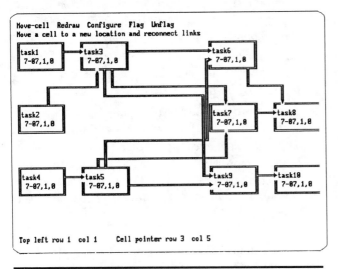

Appendix 3.4.19 Networks and Work Breakdown Structures (6.9)

Project Workbench does not create beginning and ending nodes and, consequently, requires reestablishing dependencies while moving down in the WBS. Nevertheless, adding in a duplicate ending job is very easy. Similarly, it does not support automatic resolution of relationships when adding the "latest last job."

Furthermore, Project Workbench's restriction that only allows dependencies at the task level forces the user to work around this limitation when creating the inexact plan. In order to create dependencies at the activity level in the inexact plan, the user must create "dummy" tasks inside those later activities that have not, as yet, been partitioned.

Appendix 3.4.20 Limiting Relationships to the Lowest Level (6.9.1)

Project Workbench is a product with a three-level work breakdown structure (phase, activity, task). In this system, dependencies are only allowed at the lowest level, i.e., the task level. This is true even when the activity has not yet been partitioned and there are no tasks under it. Consequently, there may be limited value to operating on the network until all of the tasks have been identified. (See the *work-around* described in the introduction to this section.)

Appendix 3.4.21 Dependencies in a Multiproject Environment (6.12)

There is no limit to the number of times a subproject may be used in Project Workbench. The master project is *not* constrained by the sum of its subprojects.

A separate master project is to be created, with one task for each of the subproject plans. Then, each task should, in turn, be "attached" to its respective subproject.[11] This is very simply accomplished by moving the cursor to the desired task, selecting "Plan; Gantt; Change; page down" and entering the subproject name[12] and *No* for the other parameters. (Figure A3.10) Users should be advised *not* to set "Display each subproject activity" to *Yes* and then attempt to autoschedule with resources. This will cause some very undesirable results after adding resources to the plan.[13] Similarly, the "Manage-Data; Insert" and "Plan; Gantt; Range; Extract" should not be used for this application. (See the earlier discussion in this appendix on *template* plans.) The master project plan must then be saved and recalled in order to complete the operation.

When the multiproject scenario equates to the set of subprojects illustrated in Figure 6.17 (that is, there is no interdependency between the projects other than shared resources), the operation may be considered finished for the time being.

On the other hand, when there are subproject interdependencies, there may be several more operations that must be performed before the corresponding schedules will be automatically computed. For example, if the only relationship between Subproject 1 and Subproject 2 in Figure 6.18 is that Subproject 2 cannot start until Subproject 1 finishes, the tasks in the master project (that represent the subprojects themselves) must also be connected—or the master project will not have the correct dates. This is simply done in the same manner described for standard intraproject dependencies that was described earlier in this appendix.

However, if there are interdependencies between the subprojects—such as illustrated between Task C in Start # 2 and Task D in Start #1 in Figure 6.18, dummy tasks that are attached to the subprojects must be inserted:

1. Users must insure that all tasks involved in the interdependency scenario have task identification numbers. These numbers will be needed in Step 3.

2. Add a dummy before Task D in Start # 1. Give it a unique task identifier and assign it to the dummy resource "X". Create the correct dependency (for example, finish-to-start) between the new dummy task and Task D in Start # 1. (Now, Task D is dependent on *both* Task C in Start # 1 and the new dummy task in Start # 1.)

3. Go to Page 2 of the dummy task Activity Planning screen (Figure A3.10), and enter the correct subproject name in the file entry field and the unique task identification number of Task C in Start # 2 in the task ID field. Users may choose *No* to all of the parameters or may choose *Yes* to "Include resource usage" and *No* to the other parameters. (See the discussions above.)

4. After Start # 1 has been saved and recalled, the dummy task will have the correct duration of Task C in Start # 2, and it will be locked into place. *In this scenario, the lock should NOT be removed!* After the autoscheduler has been executed, Task D will have a start date that reflects its dependency on both of its predecessors.

5. A superproject master plan may also be created with one task for Start # 1 and one task for Start # 2, etc. This master plan then represents a set of nested subprojects. If the directions for nested subprojects that were described earlier in the book are followed, the master plan will also have the correct dates.

This approach works when creating all of the interdependencies illustrated in Figure 6.18.

In certain cases, the procedures described in this section will not work unless both the master project and *the subproject have been set up following the proper directions for choosing the correct start date for projects as well as for the subprojects and their dates.* For example, when the first day displayed in the master project is later than the dates from the subproject, the dates in the subproject will be ignored. Furthermore, if today's date is later than the first day displayed, the autoscheduler will start the subproject on today's date rather than the first day displayed. Users will need to

---

[11]Subprojects should not be linked to phases or activities in the master project.

[12]Alternatively, users may press the F5 key to get a list of file names and then point the cursor to the appropriate name.

[13]The system ignored dependencies and scheduled the tasks wherever there was resource availability—at best, by scheduling tasks from *succeeding* subprojects at the *beginning* of the master project; at worst, by scheduling the *last* task in a subproject on day *one* of the master project.

check (and, perhaps, correct) both of these conditions while flipping between subprojects.

The user may flip back and forth between the master plan and the subprojects by placing the cursor on the subproject name (Page 2 of the Activity Planning screen) and hitting the F5 key.

There is no need to do double data entry with this approach. When there are just two levels of projects (that is, a master project level and one level of subprojects), changes made in the subprojects are automatically reflected upward into the master project. Additional procedures are required for nested subprojects, which will be addressed later.

Appendix 3.4.22 Printing and Viewing Networks (6.13)

In Project Workbench, the network cannot be viewed until the dependencies have been entered into the system. Until this process has been completed, there will be a blank Network screen. Once there are entries in the plan, selecting "Plan; Dependencies; Network" will get the user to the Network screen. To scroll through the network, press the "Scroll Lock" key and then use the arrow keys. To print, press "Reports; Create; CPM Network", select "Memory; Printer" as the defaults, and press F10.

Appendix 3.4.23 Guidelines and Documentation (6.15)

There are two pages of documentation on networks. There is also one chapter on subprojects in Project Workbench, which does describe some multiproject applications.

APPENDIX 3.5 OPTIMAL PLANS

Appendix 3.5.1 Calendars (7.14.1)

Project Workbench features a global system calendar that contains holidays, the default starting day of the business week, and the business days of the week. Users enter a "B" for each work day and an "H" for each weekend day. Holidays may be set by moving the cursor to the desired date and pressing the space bar to toggle it on or off. Alternatively, by pressing

the F3 key, the holiday window is invoked. (See Figure A3.17.) This window is used to enter a range of dates, rather than having to enter each date individually. The information for each holiday may then be entered. Pressing the F10 key permanently records the holiday data.

Calendar information for the project is stored under "Setup; Project". Initially, these values default to the global calendar settings. There are two pages on project calendar information: (1) the Project Definition screen (Figure A3.3) and (2) the Project Calendar screen, which is identical in format to the Global Calendar screen. On Page 1 of the Project Definition screen, the user tells the system on which day to start the work week, designates work days and weekend days as described above, enters the fiscal year that the project starts, and enters the number of workhours per day. Although the system allows entries into the resource usage field in hours, it does not support scheduling true work effort of less than one day and, therefore, doesn't support scheduling around lunch and other nonworking hours. As a consequence, these values cannot be entered into the calendar.

The project calendar is invoked with the "Page Down" key. Holidays are set as described above. Once the plan has been saved, the project calendar will override the global calendar during all scheduling computations.

Figure A3.17

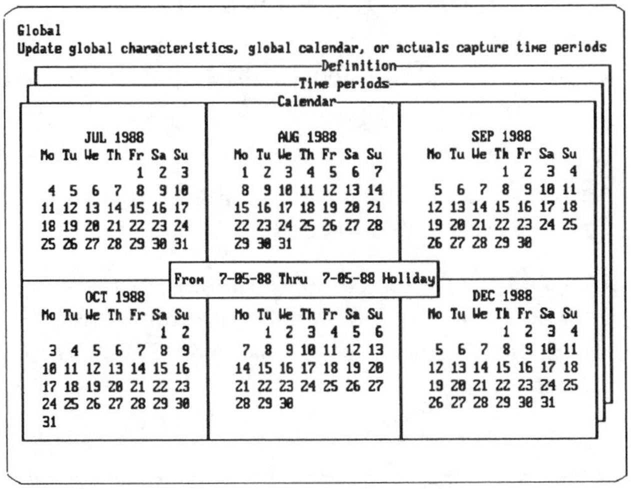

Appendix 3.5.2 Choosing The Correct Project Start Date *(7.14.2)*

In Project Workbench, the project start date is entered into the *project start date* under "Setup; Project". It is only necessary to take this action one time—at plan initiation. Scheduling computations are based on the following rules:

1. The autoscheduler ignores any tasks that occur before the first day displayed on the Gantt chart. (Figure A3.12) Therefore, if for any reason (for example, *attached* subprojects), any tasks that occur before this date must be reflected in the scheduling, the first day displayed on the Gantt chart must be modified. This is done by selecting "Plan; Gantt; View" and entering the correct date.

2. Today's date in "Setup; Global" is always automatically initialized to the current operating system date. (Figure A3.2) It may be changed by entering and saving the desired date to be used during the current terminal session. If this date is earlier than the first day displayed in the Gantt chart, it will be ignored during the autoscheduling. However, if it is later than the first day displayed in the Gantt chart, *it* will be used as the start of the project and all dates will be reflected accordingly. For all jobs without a date and that are not linked to another job that will drive their dates, the system assumes their start dates to be equal to this value of today's date. (Basically, the project start date under "Setup; Project" is ignored.) Consequently, except for the first date that the project data is entered, *each time the system is invoked*, it will be necessary to adjust the global value of today's date to match the start date of the project currently being planned.[14]

Appendix 3.5.3 Insuring that the Plan Is Not Constrained by Resources *(7.14.3)*

To insure that the plan is not constrained by resources, users are advised to follow the directions presented earlier under "Estimates of True Work Effort Versus Resource-driven Elapsed Time."

---

[14]This field is not saved with the project data.

Appendix 3.5.4 Avoiding Imposed Target Dates *(7.14.3)*

In Project Workbench, the user may enter designated dates into the *start* or *end* fields. (Figure A3.5) It is advisable to leave these fields blank when calculating the optimal plan.

Appendix 3.5.5 Calculating the Schedule *(7.14.4)*

A semi-immediate scheduling system, Project Workbench computes schedules from "Plan; Gantt" when either "Autoschedule" or "F2; A" is pressed. At this time, users should say *No* to "Include resource constraints." If the QuicKey process, "F2; A", was pressed, the menu will no longer be displayed. Pressing F2 a second time will restore the menu display.

Appendix 3.5.6 The Forward Pass: Calculating the Early Dates *(7.14.5)*

Project Workbench defaults to the traditional scheduling algorithm.

Appendix 3.5.7 Zero Duration Milestones *(7.14.8)*

Project Workbench does not allow zeros as a value for durations. However, if the milestone is (1) created with the default duration of one day, (2) assigned to the dummy resource "X", and (3) linked to *each* of its predecessors with an overlap of one day, it will be scheduled with the same date as the finish of its predecessors.

Appendix 3.5.8 Verifying Schedules with Units of Measurement Less Than One Day *(7.14.9)*

Although Project Workbench does allow hours as a unit of measurement in the resource usage field, it will not allow units of measurement of less than one day in the business days field. Since this is the field used for scheduling, durations of less than one day were not checked at this time.

Appendix 3.5.9 Retaining a Baseline Record of the Optimal Plan (7.14.11)

The baseline in Project Workbench may be saved by pressing ''Plan; Gantt; Range; Baseline'' or the QuicKey, ''Alt-B''. There are four dates on the ''Activity Dependency'' reports: early, late, planned, revised. Set to the early dates, the planned dates may temporarily be regarded as baseline dates. Until progress is posted to the task, the early and late dates are set to the baseline dates as well. After progress is posted, the value of these fields may vary.

Appendix 3.5.10 Interpreting the Dates on the Screen (7.14.12)

Along with its time-scaled matrix, the Project Workbench Gantt chart gives the job identification number, job name (either long or short), usage days, and the resource name. While these fields may be controlled with the View command, the system does not provide a way of displaying columns of dates. For each task in the network display, the system shows the scheduled start date but no other dates. In the plotted version of the network, the early and late dates are displayed along with the whole name.

Appendix 3.5.11 Annotating The Critical Path (7.14.13)

Project Workbench draws double lines around the network nodes on the critical path and also uses double lines to connect these nodes. (Figure A3.8) On the Gantt, Project Workbench initiates each time-scaled bar that is on the critical path with the letter ''C''. (See Figure A3.18.)

Although it was not available for review at the time of this writing, a new feature will be included in an impending release: the user may designate whether the determination of the critical path should be based on the current status of the plan (that is, the revised dates) or the baseline dates. At this point in the planning process, this is not an important consideration. However, it will become meaningful later on when managing the project (or phase).

Figure A3.18

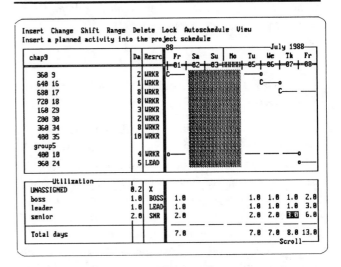

Appendix 3.5.12 Gantt Chart Time Periods (7.14.15)

The Project Workbench Gantt chart shows time in days, weeks, months, quarters, semiannual, and annual periods. This increment is chosen and/or reconfigured from the *period duration* field, which is found in the screen invoked after selecting ''Plan; Gantt; View''.

Then, starting with the first day displayed field, the Gantt will show 9 periods at a time on each screen and allow the user to scroll through a total of 45 periods. Projects with more than 45 time periods are legitimate and may be seen by changing the first day displayed. However, the user is cautioned to remember the effects that changing the value of this field will have on the autoscheduler. (See the earlier discussion about the project start date.)

After turning on the ''Scroll Lock'' key, the user may move in any direction around the Gantt chart by pressing the arrow keys.

Finally, the width of each time period may be changed by entering a new value in the periods field, which is also found in the screen invoked after selecting ''Plan; Gantt; View''. As this value is increased, the total number of periods displayed will decrease. For example, when the periods duration is days and periods is increased from 5 to 8, the number of time frames decreases from 45 to 28.

When the timescale has been set to days, the bars on the Gantt chart show weekends and holidays. (Figure A3.18) For all other timescales, the bar is continuous.

Appendix 3.5.13 Scheduling in the Multiproject Environment (7.14.17)

The project calendar of the master file in Project Workbench becomes the ruling calendar. Its data is retained, and the calendar data in subsequent subprojects is dropped. The master file must be saved and recalled whenever modifications are made to it. Since Project Workbench is a semi-immediate processing system, the new schedule is not computed until the user executes the autoscheduler. Once the master file has been saved and recalled, each task may need to be unlocked before the schedule will be correctly computed by the autoscheduler. There is no need to do double data entry with this approach. When there are just two levels of projects (that is, a master project level and one level of subprojects), changes made in the subprojects are automatically reflected upward into the master project. Additional procedures are required for nested subprojects and will be addressed in the next section.

Group processing in Project Workbench. There is a property of Project Workbench, called the ''Group'' feature, that allows users to combine several projects into a group heading, which may be used for Autoscheduling by group and for reporting by group. *(All group operations may only be invoked when there are NO projects in memory!)*[15] By selecting ''Report; Group'', the user may invoke the Group Definition screen. (See Figure A3.19.) The priority column in this screen is used to (1) indicate the order in which the autoscheduler should process each of the subprojects within the group as well as (2) the order in which the subproject detail should be printed on the reports.

In Group mode, when the autoscheduler is subsequently invoked, the ''Group'' option will be displayed. (See Figure A3.20.) In Group Autoschedule, the system will use the calendar of the Project Workbench *template* project in memory *or* the calendar from

---

[15]There is an exception to this rule: when a Project Workbench *template* project (which has no activities in it) is residing in memory.

Figure A3.19

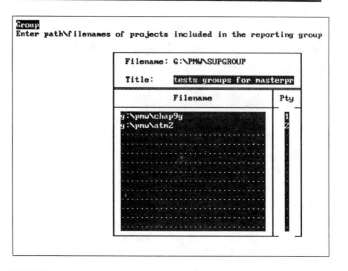

Figure A3.20

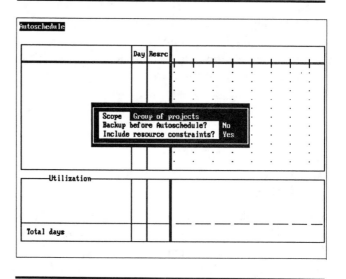

the *first* project to be autoscheduled. If the multiproject scenario matches the illustration in Figure 6.17 (that is, there is no dependency between the subprojects—other than shared resources), there is no more work to be done for the time being.

On the other hand, the Group facility has no way of defining dependencies. Therefore, when there is an interdependency between subprojects (for example, when Subproject 2 in Figure 6.18 cannot start until

Subproject 1 has finished), the "Group" facility will have no way of recognizing these relationships. Users will need to first complete the nongroup scheduling described in the beginning of this section. The correct start date for the successor subproject(s) will have to be noted. Then, the user will need to go into each of the individual subproject files and *manually* change its starting date to the correct date. After completion of these operations, any group processing will be correct.

Appendix 3.5.14 Nesting Subprojects in a Multiproject Environment *(7.14.18)*

When nesting subprojects in Project Workbench, only the dates in the first level into the nest are automatically reflected upward with the autoscheduler. (This is true for normal mode as well as Group mode.) To bring the dates in the lower levels upwards in the nest is a manual process. Starting at each task that is attached to a lowest notch at the bottom of the nest and working upwards to the highest notch in each rung, each project must be autoscheduled and then saved. In a complex nest of subprojects, users are advised to create a hard copy tree of the nested groups and check each one off as its schedule is computed. If only one subproject is overlooked, all of the subsequent schedules may be incorrect. There is no other *work-around* to this procedure.

Appendix 3.5.15 Subprojects and Their Dates *(7.14.19)*

In Project Workbench, subprojects *attached* to Page 2 (Figure A3.10) are always initially brought into the master project at the subproject dates, regardless of their dependencies in the master project. Remember that there are three important parameters in this Page 2: "Include resource usage;" "Summarize by resource;" and "Display each subproject activity."

1) If all three parameters are set to *No* and the masterproject has been saved and recalled, then the details of the subproject will *not* be seen and each task to which the subproject has been attached will be locked in place every time the master project is invoked. However, in some scenarios, these tasks will need to be unlocked *before* the autoscheduler is executed. Furthermore, if these tasks initially

occur *after* the first day displayed, *and* if today's date is correct, after the autoscheduler is executed, the correct spanned durations and corresponding dates will be reflected on the Gantt chart and found in the revised date field of the "Activity Dependency" report.

2) After the master project has been saved and recalled with a value of *Yes* for "Include resource usage," each task to which a subproject has been attached will still always be locked whenever the master project is invoked. If correct schedules are to be reflected, the tasks may once more have to be individually unlocked each time the project is invoked. (See Chapter 6.) Although it is sometimes necessary, this, unfortunately, can become very tiresome.

If both procedures have been done correctly and the autoscheduler is executed, the corrected work effort, dates, and durations *will* be shown on the Gantt. The original subproject dates will remain as the start and finish dates on Page 1 of the Activity Planning screen (Figure A3.5), as the planned dates field on the "Activity Dependency" report, and may be shown with milestone markers on the Gantt chart. The new dates will also be in the revised dates field of the "Activity Dependency" report.

In certain cases, these procedures will not work unless both the master project and the subproject have been set up following the earlier directions in this appendix for choosing the correct project start date.

Appendix 3.5.16 Guidelines and Documentation *(7.14.20)*

Project Workbench does not have guidelines for developing schedules.

APPENDIX 3.6 CALCULATING A FINISH DATE

Appendix 3.6.1 Using the New Reasonable Late Finish Date of the Project *(7.26.3)*

In Project Workbench, all the user needs to do is enter the desired end date in the *project finish* date of the Project Definition screen. (Figure A3.3) The correct late dates are computed and stored in each of the late

Figure A3.21

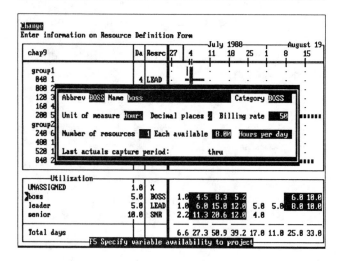

Figure A3.22

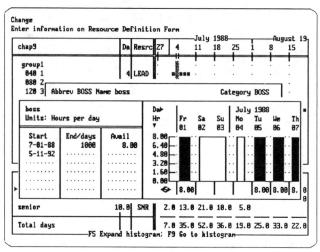

start and late finish fields. The early finish date of the project may only be found in the early finish date of the last task(s) in the project. This product always highlights the critical path of the project—regardless of the amount of slack.

APPENDIX 3.7 ADDING RESOURCES

Appendix 3.7.1 Creating the Resource Calendars (8.8)

In Project Workbench, at the project level, resource calendar information is in three places: the resource calendar (Figure A3.17), the resource pool that is created with the resource form (See Figure A3.21.), and the project-level resource availability profile (See Figure A3.22.). There is also a loading profile for each task (described later). Since these are one of the most important features of Project Workbench, they will be addressed separately later in this appendix.

The resource calendar automatically carries all of the project-level workdays and nonworkdays. This calendar may be accessed by pressing "Plan; Re-source; Resource-calendar". Then, moving the cursor in the spreadsheet to the desired resource name and pressing "Enter" will invoke the Resource Calendar screen. Modifications may be made to this calendar by moving the cursor to the desired date and pressing the spacebar to toggle it on or off. On the other hand,

pressing the F3 key invokes the holiday window. (Figure A3.17) This window may be used to enter a range of dates, rather than having to enter the date individually. The information for each holiday may then be entered. Pressing the F10 key permanently records the holiday data.

In addition to the standard resource pool information, the resource form also requires the user to specify the resource availability, expressed in the same units of measurement that the user stipulated when creating the resource. For example, if the unit of measurement is days, assigning a value of 1.0 day per day sets the resource at full-time availability. Setting part-time resources at the project level will be addressed later in this appendix.

Project workbench does support unique working hours for a single specific calendar day. The project-level resource availability profile is accessed by pressing "Plan; Resource; Change", moving the cursor to the desired resource, pressing "Enter", and pressing F5. (Figure A3.22) The information in the matrix on the left of the screen is called the resource availability table and may be filled in with the date(s) of the affected day(s) and the modified number of available hours. The chart on the right is called a histogram. Since the height of each column in the histogram shows the level of commitment, changes to the number of available hours may also be made in the histogram itself.

Even though it also supports estimates in hours in the usage field, the system does not support daily breaks (for example, lunch) or any workday starting and ending times.

Appendix 3.7.2 Creating the Resource Pool (8.9)

Project Workbench resources may be individuals, groups of individuals, equipment, or materials. Although an earlier version of this product had a field for nonstaff costs, there is no longer a separate operation for *fixed* costs. Rather, it is one of the options in *units of measurement*.

Although Project Workbench supports a maximum of 200 resources per project, the system defaults to 20. This can easily be changed on the Global parameters screen (accessed by "Setup; Global") Users may increase the number of resources to 200—if they are willing to reduce the total number of jobs, dependencies, and text. For example, when the number of dependencies is increased to 250 along with the 20 resources, the number of jobs (before spill files are created) is decreased to 413. With 50 resources and 200 dependencies, the total number of jobs is 452. Changes to the number of resources must be made *before* any project files are loaded into memory. The modification is made by selecting "Setup; Global", changing the number, and saving the change. (Figure A3.2)

Resources are listed in the utilization spreadsheet at the bottom of each screen. (Figure A3.18) They are added to the system in a resource form that is called up by pressing "Plan; Resource; Insert". (Figure A3.21) The required information is: the 4-character resource code name (to be used when assigning the resource to a task), the full resource name (used for display), the number of available resources of this type, the units in which the resource is measured (hours, days, etc.), the work group category of the resource, and the resource billing rate.

Units of measurement must match the value entered into the usage field when durations were added to the plan. Furthermore, if the unit of measurement is hours, the normal number of workhours per day the resource is available must also be designated. On the other hand, if the unit of measurement is days, the normal number of days per week the resource is avail-

able must be entered. Project Workbench does not support multiple billing rates for one resource.

Appendix 3.7.3 Assigning Part-Time Resources at the Project Level (8.10)

As described in the previous section, the resource form in Project Workbench also requires that the user specify the resource availability, expressed in the same units of measurement that the user stipulated when creating the resource. At the project level, a part-time resource is designated using this field. For example, if the unit of measurement is days, assigning a value of 0.5 day per day sets the resource at halftime availability. The system will automatically distribute the true work effort across the correct number of elapsed calendar days. This is true regardless of whether the business days field is fixed or variable. True work effort will be in the usage field, and elapsed calendar days will be in the business days field.

Project Workbench is unique in that it allows varying levels of part-time participation at different periods during the project. Using the resource calendar along with the project-level resource availability profile, the product supports unique working hours for a specific range of calendar days. This project-level resource availability profile is modified as described earlier. The integrity of true work effort will be maintained in the usage field, and the elapsed calendar days will be in the business days field.

Users ought to be cognizant of using the two processes described here (that is, modifying resource availability in the resource form and in the resource availability profile) at the same time. The availability in the profile will override the availability in the form, placing a "v" in the field in the form.

Appendix 3.7.4 Deleting and Changing Resources at the Project Level (8.11)

Resources in Project Workbench may not be deleted from the resource pool until all corresponding commitments have either been deleted or reassigned. Then, resources are deleted from the pool by pressing "Delete".

Names are changed in the same manner as other modifications. Both the four-character resource code name and the full resource name may be changed.

Changing either name results in a project-wide replacement of all occurrences of the old name with the new name.

Appendix 3.7.5 Matching Resources to Jobs (8.14)

Resources may only be assigned at the task level. Although Project Workbench supports a maximum of 200 resource names per project, the system defaults to 20. This can easily be changed on the Global parameters screen (accessed by "Setup; Global"). Since there is no limit to the number of resource names for any given task, it is possible to assign all of the resources to any one task. Theoretically, if only one task has resource names, it could have 200. (See earlier discussion.)

Resources may be assigned on the Activity Planning screen, which is recalled by pressing "Plan; Gantt", moving the cursor to the desired task, and pressing "Change". (Figure A3.5) Pressing the "Enter" key twice will position the cursor for the first resource assignment.

The 4-character name code is entered into the first field. There is no way to recall a list of valid name codes. Although the list is displayed in the resource spreadsheet at the bottom of the Gantt chart, the display is obscured when the Activity Planning screen is invoked. A list in a window would be very helpful here. In lieu of the list, users are advised to note the valid code *before* recalling the Activity Planning screen.

Defaults are filled in by the system for the other resource fields. However, the user may override these entries. The data to be entered now is the unit of measurement (defaults to the value in the resource form. See Figure A3.21.), the resource loading pattern (defaults to the value set up in the Project Definition screen[16]), and the maximum percentage of time the resource may be assigned to work on the task (must be entered in the same scale as the unit of measurement in the resource form; defaults to 100 percent). The maximum percentage will be important when doing

resource leveling and will be addressed in more detail later. The resource's full name (from the resource form) is also displayed, but cannot be modified.

There is no place to enter the number of resources being assigned to the task; therefore, there is no need to check for excessive assignments.

Each of the names of the resources assigned to the task may be displayed optionally in one of the Gantt chart columns. How many resource names are displayed is related to the width of this column. This width is determined in the View screen, which is accessed by pressing "Plan; Gantt; View".

When an undefined resource is assigned to a task, the system automatically invokes a resource form. The user must then proceed in the usual fashion for entering a new resource.

In Project Workbench, the resource number is used for leveling. Furthermore, a resource name may only be assigned to a task once—regardless of the number in the resource form.

The usage field (which contains the true work effort) has already been entered when adding durations to the optimal plan. In order to maintain the integrity of true work effort, this field should *not* be modified. When the resource effort is different from the task duration, special actions are required, which will be addressed later in this appendix.

Appendix 3.7.6 Assigning Part-Time Resources at the Task or Activity Level (8.15)

In Project Workbench, by keeping the true work effort in the usage field and modifying the business days field, users may make the resource part-time. For example, 5 days in the usage field may be spread over 10 days in the business days field.

Part-time resources may also be set at the task level in the maximum percent load field of the Activity Planning screen. (Figure A3.5) The transaction is not complete until the business days field in each respective task is set to variable. This is accomplished either by default at the project level[17] or on a task-by-task

---

[16]Before any resources are assigned to tasks, this default value in the Project Definition screen should be set to "Contour". This will be discussed in more detail later in this appendix.

[17]Although it was not available for review at the time of this writing, a new feature will be included in an impending release: the user may designate at the project level whether the default should be fixed or variable. Users are advised to choose fixed.

basis, through manual intervention. Then, after autoscheduling with resources, the system provides the best of all worlds. The correct scheduling is performed; the business days field contains the correct elapsed calendar days; and the usage field maintains the integrity of the true work effort.

When a resource will only be available a limited number of days per week *and* a limited number of hours per day, the user is advised to enter the number of days per week in the resource form. (Figure A3.21) Part-time hours per day may later be controlled at the task level with a separate entry:

1. One way of setting part-time at the task level is with the maximum loading percent, as just described. This field allocates the *same number of hours per day for each day of the task*.

2. Another way is with the task-level resource loading profile. This profile enables the user to designate a *different number of part-time hours for each day of the task*. (It is also very helpful in the process of user-driven interactive leveling and will be discussed later in this appendix.) From the Activity Planning screen, moving the cursor to the desired resource, pressing enter and pressing F5 will invoke the task's resource loading profile. (See Figure A3.23.) The information in the matrix to the left of the histogram is called the task loading table and may be filled in with the date(s) of the affected day(s) and the distribution of the usage hours. Since the height of each column in the histogram shows the level of commitment, these changes may also be made in the histogram itself. At the conclusion of this operation, the system will compute the total number of usage hours in the profile and replace the original usage hours with this new value. Because this is a process of redistribution of usage hours, the process must be applied *very carefully*, insuring that the total number of hours entered across each day of the loading histogram does not exceed or fall short of the intended true work effort. Since the loading histogram has precedence over the usage value in the Activity Planning screen, the desired true work effort may be obliterated by changes to the loading histogram.

Users ought also to be cognizant of using the two processes described here at the same time—for example, modifying resource availability in the resource form to show one version of availability and modifying the assigned hours in the task's resource loading profile to show resources working when they are not available. Using both processes in concert may produce results that were not intended.

Appendix 3.7.7 Assigning Multiple Resources to a Job (8.16)

Tasks in Project Workbench become resource driven by changing the business days field on the Activity Planning screen from fixed to variable. In order to complete the multiple resource entry, users must manually compute the true work effort for each resource and enter the value in the corresponding usage field. Executing the autoscheduler with resource leveling set to *No* will get the correct number of calendar days into the *business* days field. True work effort remains untouched in the usage field.

Appendix 3.7.8 What to Do when the Resource Effort Must Be Less than the Elapsed Calendar Days (8.17)

In Project Workbench, when the usage hours are equal to true work effort but less than the task elapsed time, the work can be distributed anywhere within the business days field. To create the conditions illustrated in Example 1, the user simply enters the task starting and ending dates along with the true work effort in the usage field. (The business days field may be left at fixed.)

Project Workbench cannot compute percentages and enter the corresponding value in the usage field. When the scenario illustrated in Example 2 occurs, the user will need to compute manually the hours or days that equate to the percentage level and then proceed as in Example 1.

The scenario in Example 3 may be implemented by entering the true work effort in the usage field and entering the elapsed calendar days in the business days field, The operation is completed with the task-level resource loading profile. (Figure A3.23) This profile enables the user to designate a *different number of usage hours for each day of the task*. From the Activity Planning screen, moving the cursor to the desired resource, pressing enter and pressing F5 will invoke the

Figure A3.23

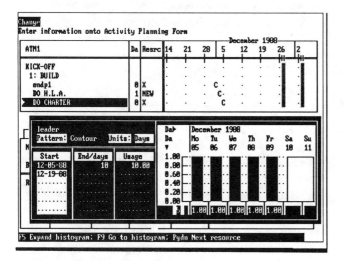

respective task-level resource loading profile. The information in the matrix to the left of the histogram is called the task loading table and may be filled in with the date(s) of the affected day(s) and the distribution of the usage hours. Since the height of each column in the histogram shows the level of commitment, these changes may also be made in the histogram itself.

Users ought also to remember that when these actions are taken, the original record of the true work effort is now in the resource usage field, and the business days field will then contain the elapsed calendar days.

Appendix 3.7.9 Fixed Dates for Activities or Tasks (8.19)

Project Workbench does not use the scheduling algorithm that highlights projects that are late before they start.

Fixed dates may be entered at any level in the work breakdown structure. The business days field should be set to *fixed* before starting these operations. (Otherwise, changing dates may change the elapsed calendar days of the task.)

Project Workbench reports four sets of dates: the revised dates, the planned dates, the early dates, and the late dates. The early and late dates of all jobs in the plan are never affected by the following operations. Similarly, the dates of any jobs that are predecessors

to the affected jobs are not altered by the following operations.

Fixed dates are entered on the Activity Planning screen, which is invoked by pressing "Plan; Gantt; Change". This is followed by moving the cursor to the desired activity and pressing the "Enter" key. The fixed date may then be entered into the start field of the screen. Fixed end dates are not supported by this product—a date entered into the end date field only serves to alter the business days value. The operation is completed by insuring that the cursor is pointing to the correct activity and pressing "Lock". (If the "Lock" is *not* invoked, the fixed start date will be ignored by the autoscheduler.)

When the fixed date of the affected activity is the same date as its system-generated dates, there are no changes to the schedule.

When the fixed date of the affected activity is earlier or later than its system-generated dates, its revised and planned dates are modified accordingly. The planned and revised fields of any affected successors are modified as well.

Fixed dates are marked with an "L" on the Gantt chart.

If the late finish date of the project is entered onto the project finish date field of the Project Definition screen (Figure A3.3), the late dates of all of the predecessors will be correctly computed.

Appendix 3.7.10 Special Leveling Patterns in Project Management Software (8.29)

With respect to leveling patterns, Project Workbench is not like the other products. In describing how to establish the resource pool earlier in this appendix, users were informed that Project Workbench supports variable resource availabilities at the project level—that is, available resource hours may be different on different days. Later, in the discussion about assigning resources to jobs, users were informed that this product also supports variable resource assignments at the task level—that is, it allows resources to be assigned to tasks by varying the hours per day on each day of any given task. Now it is time to address the fact that Project Workbench also supports variable loading patterns for resource leveling.

There are five different loading patterns that may be used for leveling. Using the Project Definition screen

(Figure A3.3), any one of these five can be set up as the resource assignment default pattern. At any later time, users may also override this default by keying in an alternate value in the pattern field of the Activity Planning screen. The five patterns are:

- Contour—this is the pattern of choice. *The vendor advises that users make this the default loading pattern* because it allows the autoscheduler to load resources as evenly as possible. If there are no resource conflicts, the system uses the uniform pattern (described below); otherwise the system uses any remaining resource hours in the most efficient manner possible.
- Uniform—allocates the same amount of resource time to each day of a task, subject to the resource's availability and maximum percentage loading.
- Front—schedules resources for as many hours per day as possible (subject to the resource's availability and maximum percentage loading) as soon as possible in order to finish the job as soon as possible.
- Back—schedules resources for as many hours per day as possible (subject to the resource's availability and maximum percentage loading) as late as possible in order to finish the job as late as possible. The end date of the project may be extended.
- Fixed—is a user-determined loading pattern. On the task-level resource loading profile (Figure A3.23), users enter the desired number of resource hours to be assigned *each day*.

All of these patterns (but especially Front and Back) only become meaningful when the true work effort in the usage field is less than the elapsed calendar days in the business days field. When that is the case, the manner in which the true work effort is distributed across the elapsed calendar days becomes significant. Similarly, when the business days field is set to variable, the patterns also have a meaningful effect on the loading. (See the discussion later in this section.)

Furthermore, the patterns are not fully applied until the autoscheduler has been invoked. For example, after resources have first been assigned to jobs, but before the autoscheduler has been run, Uniform and Contour are identical in the manner in which the system assigns available resource hours. This is also true after modifications have been made to the Activity

Planning screen[18] but before the schedule has been rerun.

Use of these leveling patterns works best if the business days field is generally set to fixed.[19] When it is set to variable with tasks that have (1) one resource only;[20] or (2) all resources with the same loading pattern, the autoscheduler will load Uniform, Front, and Back identically.

The vendor suggests the tightest fit schedule will usually be obtained when most of the tasks are Contour loaded with fixed business days. These values should be selected as the defaults and an initial schedule should be created. Then, the vendor suggests that users limit the use of variable business days to a relatively small number of noncritical background tasks and also to use Contour loading for these tasks.[21] A limited number of tasks may then be Front-loaded—if that is truly the requirement. Fixed loading should only be used in exceptional circumstances—such as putting in a long task where there will be a four-hour meeting every Monday morning for three months. Uniform loading is not recommended if a tight fit schedule is to be generated by the autoscheduler.

When tasks are in competition for the same resources, the resources are assigned to the tasks using the following pattern priorities: first by tasks with Contour loading, then by Uniform loading, then by Front loading or Back loading, and last by Fixed loading. Since, during the Autoscheduling, tasks with Fixed loading patterns get the last resource allocations (when there is a conflict between Contour and Fixed), the

---

[18] For example, if either of the dates or the maximum percentage fields have been changed in a Contour-loaded task.

[19] Although it was not available for review at the time of this writing, a new feature will be included in an impending release: the user may designate at the project level whether the default should be fixed or variable. Users are advised to choose fixed.

[20] As will most often be the case.

[21] When tasks are in competition for the same resources, using variable in the business days field of a task allows the autoscheduler to split up its hours, thus scheduling the task around other tasks and extending the elapsed calendar days in the business days field of the variable task. Although the duration of the project (or phase) may ultimately be extended, using variable business days judiciously and carefully can significantly improve resource utilization.

system shifts the Fixed job to an entirely different time slice. Because the allocated work time moves to different days, the shift may not match the user's originally intended pattern of work. In another scenario, when there's a conflict between tasks with Contour loading and tasks with Front or Back loading, the tasks with Front or Back loading are shifted. Finally, when there is a conflict between tasks with Front or Back loading and tasks with Fixed loading, the task with Fixed loading is shifted once more.

When these patterns are used, if the tasks to which they're applied are *locked* into place, they will not be shifted during subsequent leveling with the autoscheduler. (To read about locking, see the discussion on fixed dates earlier in this appendix.)

Appendix 3.7.11 Automatic Resource Leveling (8.30)

Before any Project Workbench leveling operations may be performed, users must set the correct project starting date by pressing ''Setup; Global'' and entering the start date in the ''today's date'' field. (Figure A3.2) Then, leveling may be simply invoked by pressing ''Plan; Gantt; Autoscheduling'' and answering *Yes* to resource leveling. (See Figure A3.24.)

The leveled dates will be in the start date and end date fields. When two or more tasks have the same starting dates, and there are available resources for these tasks, but there are no priorities assigned to these

Figure A3.24

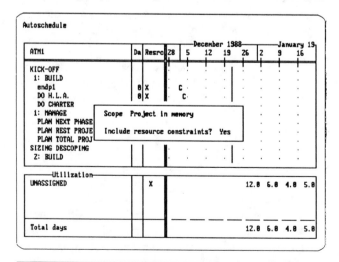

tasks, resources are assigned to the tasks in the order that they appear on the Gantt chart. Setting priorities will be addressed in the next section.

Unless the project plan has been saved under a different name, there will be no record of the original dates.

All effects of leveling may be erased simply by executing the autoscheduler with leveling turned to *No*.

The system provides no flags to indicate leveling delays.

Appendix 3.7.12 Setting Special Leveling Priorities on Tasks Or Activities (8.31)

A one-character priority code is found on Page 2 of the Activity Planning screen of Project Workbench. (Figure A3.10) During the leveling process, jobs with priority codes are scheduled first. They are scheduled according to the value of the priority field—the lower the value, the higher the priority. Zero has the highest priority. Then, the order of importance goes from 1 to 9, followed by a blank, which is, is turn, followed by the alphabet, from A to Z. Z has the lowest priority. The system insures that predecessor jobs have a priority at least as high as that of their successors. Priorities set at higher levels in the work breakdown structure are assigned to their subordinate levels but can also be overridden at the lower levels.

Appendix 3.7.13 User-Driven Interactive Leveling (8.32)

Project Workbench features a resource utilization spreadsheet, a matrix that is comparable to a numeric histogram and is always present at the bottom of the Gantt screen. (Figure A3.18) The time periods in the spreadsheet are equal to the Gantt timescale. Updates to the spreadsheet are immediate; they occur without the need to run the autoscheduler. As soon as resource overscheduling occurs, it is immediately flagged with a reverse video highlighting of the spreadsheet resource total for that period. This indicates that the resource is overscheduled somewhere in the plan during that time period.

Keeping in mind that a bar on a Gantt chart shows elapsed time, and not necessarily the amount of true work effort that is being done on each day of a task, Project Workbench's resource spreadsheet can be set up to overcome this problem. It can be adjusted to show the daily total of assigned hours for each resource. First, the spreadsheet may be laid out to display one of three types of data: the cumulative resource utilization, the starting total of available resource units, or the remaining unassigned resource units. Next, spreadsheet units may be displayed in hours, days, costs or percent. These two choices are made by pressing "Plan; Resource; View" and choosing the desired options. To simplify interactive leveling, "Utilization" and "Days" ought to be selected.

Furthermore, during the leveling process, interpreting the source of the conflict is facilitated when the Gantt timescale is set to days. This is done by pressing "Plan; Gantt; View" and selecting "Days" for the period duration. Additionally, when "Days" has been selected, the Gantt will show weekends and holidays.

Although this product has two histograms (the project-level resource availability profile shown in Figure A3.22 and the task-level resource loading profile shown in Figure A3.23), and although they both show weekends and holidays, neither shows cumulative resource utilization for all of the tasks to which the resource has been assigned. Instead, these histograms are intended for use in assignment (or reassignment) of resources to one task at a time.

Much as Project Workbench features reports that may be limited to one resource (for example, the "Gantt" or the "Activity Detail," both of which also contain the respective resource spreadsheet entry), and whereas these reports can be displayed on the screen, there is no way to limit the Gantt that is displayed on the screen with the resource spreadsheet to just the tasks for one resource. Consequently, without a hard copy of the report, users need to scroll through the whole plan looking for the offending tasks.

Modifications are made in the three subsystems. New tasks are added; resource assignments are added, changed or deleted; and dates, task-level resource availability, and task loading patterns are changed in the Gantt subsystem ("Plan; Gantt". Figure A3.5). Relationships are added or changed in the Dependency subsystem ("Plan; Dependency". See Figure A3.7.). Resources are added, and project-level resource availabilities are changed in the Resource subsystem ("Plan; Resource". See Figures A3.21 and A3.22.).

Project Workbench provides a feature that is very helpful in eliminating resource conflicts. Using "Plan; Gantt; Shift", the start and/or end date of a single task may be moved forward or backward in time. As the job is moved, the changes in resource allocations are respectively reflected in the resource spreadsheet. While tasks with Fixed loading are shifted intact, the system adjusts the tasks with the other four loading patterns according to the resource availability. Whole groups of jobs may also be moved with "Plan; Gantt; Range; Flag; Shift".

Because the Gantt-Resource Spreadsheet window is always displayed while making the necessary modifications, Project Workbench might be called a fully-interactive leveling system. Furthermore, date changes, resource assignments, resource loading, and resource availabilities can be entered from this screen and are reflected as soon as they are entered. On the other hand, since the autoscheduler is a separate process, some of the modifications (for example, new dependencies and loading patterns) are not reflected until the project is rescheduled. Therefore, Project Workbench is classified as a semi-interactive leveling system.

Appendix 3.7.14 Baseline Project Plans for Resource Leveling (8.34)

Project Workbench supports one version of a baseline. By saving the optimal plan as the baseline for the resource-constrained plan that is selected for implementation, users have half of the requirements met. This version is archived, and a second version is produced. Then, by saving the resource-constrained plan as the baseline for the plan to which progress will be posted, the other half of the requirements will be met. Unfortunately, this *work-around* does not provide comparisons between all three versions. However, albeit the process is cumbersome, users may assimilate the data by perusing both sets of reports.

Appendix 3.7.15 Resources, Multiprojects, and Project Management Software (8.35.4)

In Project Workbench, a *template* project file may be created and saved under a special name—a file that contains the project calendar, the resource forms data, the resource availability profile, and the resource calendars. (It should have no activities in it.) After this file has been recalled and saved under a new name (in order to preserve the *template*), project-specific resource data, activities, and tasks may be added to it. In this manner, the common resource data may be imported from one project to another. Later, if and when the project calendar and/or the resource data has been changed, users must remember to reflect the changes in the *template* and all in projects that use the *template*.[22]

When subprojects have been attached to a task with ''Include resource usage'' set to *Yes*, all of the associated resource assignments will be imported into the project. However, if users have not started with a *template*, it is not possible to import any resource pool, resource availability, or resource calendar information from one project to another.

On the other hand, if a subproject is attached to a task, and the resources in the subproject are not part of the master project resource pool, the system prompts the user to enter the correct pool and the correct resource availability histogram data for the resource. New resources are appended to the resource pool. (Users will also be required to remember to add the resource calendar information.) When there are duplicate resources in the master project and the incoming subproject, the resource record in the master project is retained and the resource data in the subproject is ignored.

In a multiproject scenario similar to the one illustrated in Figure 6.17 (that is, where the only dependency between subprojects is the sharing of resources), the Group Autoschedule will level resources from a master project across its subprojects.

Conversely, when there are subproject interdependencies such as those illustrated in Figure 6.18, the Group Autoschedule will not reflect the correct dates or the correct leveling across projects from the master project.

Users ought to be advised never to attach a subproject with ''Display each subproject activity'' equal to *Yes* and then attempt to autoschedule with resources. This will cause undesirable results.

In one scenario, the system ignored dependencies and scheduled jobs wherever there was resource availability—at best by scheduling tasks from *succeeding* subprojects at the *beginning* of the master project; at worst by scheduling the *last* task in a subproject on Day *1* of the master project.

Page 1 of the task to which the subproject is attached shows the total commitment for each resource assigned the subproject. (Figure A3.5) When the data in the resource spreadsheet is highlighted in reverse video, the resource may be overcommitted. (See the earlier discussion on interactive leveling.) If the resource column in the Gantt has been set up to be wide enough to display all of the resource identifiers, the resource name in each Gantt line will also be highlighted in reverse video. (See Figure A3.25.) Consequently, users may easily trace the Gantt to pinpoint the subproject where the overscheduling is occurring. If the cause of the spreadsheet highlight is just due to one project, the resource name will be highlighted only on one Gantt line. On the other hand, when two or more Gantt lines are highlighted, the overcommitment can be inside both subprojects and/or between the subprojects.

When nesting subprojects, only the resource requirements in the first level into the nest are automatically reflected upward with the autoscheduler. To bring the assignments in the lower levels upwards in the nest is a manual process that has been described

Figure A3.25

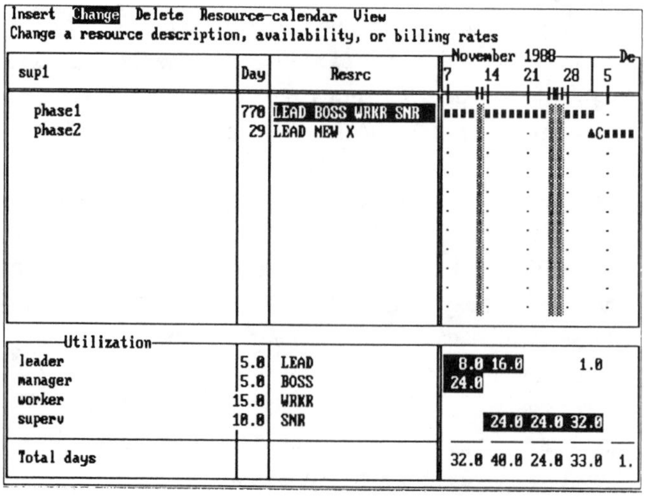

---

[22]The system does not tell the user what projects use which templates; therefore, it is a good idea to make a text file with this data.

earlier. If this process is followed, changes made in the subprojects are automatically reflected in the master project.

Appendix 3.7.16 Guidelines and Documentation (8.36)

In Project Workbench, there is one chapter on resource management and several pages in a chapter on project management that pertain to scheduling resources.

APPENDIX 3.8 CALCULATING COSTS

Appendix 3.8.1 Costs and Project Management Software (9.4)

In Project Workbench, there is a category code on Page 2 of the Activity Planning screen. (Figure A3.10) This code may be used as a field for a work breakdown structure or as an accounting code. From the Gantt subsystem, the View command can be used to display costs. (The reports, many of which show costs, can also be designated to be displayed on the screen.) The system will report on total costs per resource, total costs per resource category (for example, all programmers), etc. By designating the level of detail, users can report on total costs per task, total costs per resource, total costs per activity category (if all of the tasks within the activity have been given the same activity category code), total costs per phase, and total costs per project. If the user invokes the sort reports (Page 3 of the report create), various subtotals may also be reported.

This system supports fixed costs if users create a resource called *fixed*—at a dollar rate that can then be used in multiples when assigning it to each task. In addition to the regular reporting of costs per task, this also allows the user to subsequently report on the sum of all fixed costs.

Project Workbench will export data in Fixed AS-CII format, Comma Separated Values (CSV), and Data Interchange Format (DIF).

APPENDIX 3.9 COMPRESSING TIME

Appendix 3.9.1 Time-Constrained Plans and Project Management Software (10.9)

In Project Workbench, other than fixing the end date of the project, there are no special requirements for leveling in a time-constrained environment. Users may produce reports sorted on float.

APPENDIX 3.10 ASSIGNING THE WORK

Appendix 3.10.1 The Assignment Report (11.1)

There are two standard reports in Project Workbench that may be used as assignment reports. In the first report, selected by pressing "Report; Create; Activity Status—Time and Usage" (See Figure A3.26.), the data that is displayed is the activity name, the short activity name, the deliverables description, the planned/revised start date,[23] the planned/revised end date, the resource name, the usage (true work effort) forecasted to complete, and the original usage time. The "Activity Details" report, which is invoked by pressing "Report; Create; Activity Details" (See Figure A3.27.) displays the activity name, the short activity name, the deliverables description, a start date, an end date, the business days (elapsed days), the resource name, the usage days (true work effort), cost, float, and the activity category. The costs disclosure may be suppressed by choosing *No* from the "Display Costs" option on the report select.

A third report, selected by pressing "Report; Create; Activity Dependency" (See Figure A3.28.), will print a list of activities with their predecessors and successors. However, this report only displays business days; it does not show usage. This report also displays four sets of dates: the revised dates, the planned dates, the early dates, and the late dates.

To limit any of these reports to just printing the data for a given resource, the user may direct the system to "Select On Resource ID = *the resource name as it appears in the resource pool*" and to sort on "Resource ID = 1 (1 is the highest)" and "Start Date = 2". (See Figures A3.29 and A3.30.)

Appendix 3.10.2 The AD HOC Information (11.2)

The short name field and the deliverables description in Project Workbench are automatically printed as part of the assignment reports. (Figures A3.26 and A3.27)

---

[23]These are the date fields that also reflect the results of any fixed dates.

Figure A3.26

chap9

Name	Start Planned Rev/act	End Planned Rev/act	Status	CP	Resrc	Actual (+) To-Date	Fcst (=) To-Cmpl	Latest (=) Estimate	Orig (vs) Plan	Ahead (=) (Behind)
								Usage		
group2										
240 6	7-01-88	7-07-88			BOSS	0.0	4.0	4.0	4.0	0.0
480 12	7-08-88	7-22-88			BOSS	0.0	11.0	11.0	11.0	0.0
520 13	7-08-88	7-13-88			BOSS	0.0	4.0	4.0	4.0	0.0
group2										
840 21	8-03-88	8-10-88		Y	BOSS	0.0	6.0	6.0	6.0	0.0
group3										
880 22	8-03-88	8-24-88			BOSS	0.0	16.0	16.0	16.0	0.0

Resource summary

Name	Units									
boss	hour				BOSS	0.0	776.0	776.0	776.0	0.0
Total project	7-01-88	12-01-88	Total hours			0.0	776.0	776.0	776.0	0.0

Figure A3.27

chap9

Original dates and Usage

------Name------	Start	End	Duration Bus days	Status	------Resource assignments------ Name	Usage	Cost	Float	Pty Category
group2									
240 6	7-01-88	7-07-88	4		boss	4.0	1,600	7	
480 12	7-08-88	7-22-88	11		boss	11.0	4,400	7	
520 13	7-08-88	7-13-88	4		boss	4.0	1,600	14	
group2									
840 21	8-03-88	8-10-88	6		boss	6.0	2,400	0	
group3									
880 22	8-03-88	8-24-88	16		boss	16.0	6,400	8	G3
Total project	7-01-88	12-01-88			Total hours	776.0			
					Total cost		38,800		

Resource summary

Name	Units	Rate Amt Start	Start	End		Usage	Cost		Category
boss	hours	50	7-01-88	12-01-88	BOSS	776.0	38,800		BOSS
Total project			7-01-88	12-01-88	Total hours	776.0			
					Total cost		38,800		

Figure A3.28

Name	Float	Dates	Start	End	Status	Duration Bus days	Revised vs Late	------Who------
240 6	7	Revised:	7-01-88	7-07-88		4	51	boss
		Planned:	7-01-88	7-07-88		4		
		Early:	9-02-88	9-08-88				
		Late:	9-14-88	9-19-88				

Successors:
12   7   Finish/Start
13   14   Finish/Start

480 12	7	Revised:	7-08-88	7-22-88		11	51	boss
		Planned:	7-08-88	7-22-88		11		
		Early:	9-09-88	9-23-88				
		Late:	9-20-88	10-04-88				

Predecessors:
6   7   Finish/Start
Successors:
dummy1   Critical   Overlap   1 Days

520 13	14	Revised:	7-08-88	7-13-88		4	58	boss
		Planned:	7-08-88	7-13-88		4		
		Early:	9-09-88	9-14-88				
		Late:	9-29-88	10-04-88				

Predecessors:
6   7   Finish/Start
Successors:
dummy1   Critical   Overlap   1 Days

Figure A3.29

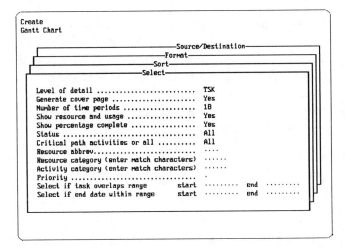

Figure A3.30

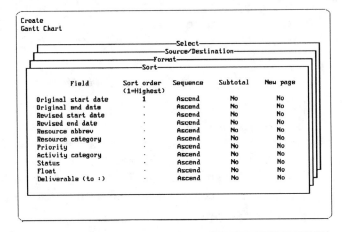

Appendix 3.10.3 The Work Package Cover Sheet *(11.5)*

The Project Workbench text processor may be used to create the forms that meet this requirement. (See Figure A3.31.)

Appendix 3.10.4 The Responsibility Grid *(11.6)*

The Project Workbench text processor may be used to create the forms that meet this requirement.

Appendix 3.10.5 The Supporting Documentation *(11.8)*

In Project Workbench, by selecting "Report; Create; Gantt" and directing the system to "Select On Resource ID = *the resource name as it appears in the resource pool*" (Figure A3.29) and to sort on "Resource ID = 1" and "Start Date = 2" (Figure A3.30), the user may print a Gantt chart that is limited to just the data for a given resource.

If the user has a printer that will capture screen images, the task-level resource loading histogram (Figure A3.23) may be captured after pressing "Plan; Gantt; Change; F5 Variably load resource; F5 Expand histogram". Completing these steps for each task and then pressing the "Print Screen" key will wrap up the operation.

Although there are no special tabular loading reports in Project Workbench, most report types display the corresponding resource spreadsheet at the end of the report.

Figure A3.31

```
this is a sample report of the text data for the cover letter:

PROJECT NAME:_____

DATE:        _____

SIGNOFF 1:   _____

SIGNOFF 2:   _____

SIGNOFF 3:   _____
```

Figure A3.32

```
 Global
 Update global characteristics, global calendar, or actuals capture time periods
                            ─Calendar─
                         ─Definition─
                      ─Time periods─

 Start of first actuals capture period  7-01-88  Period duration  Week

     1   7-01-88    2   7-08-88    3   7-15-88    4   7-22-88    5   7-29-88
     6   8-05-88    7   8-12-88    8   8-19-88    9   8-26-88   10   9-02-88
    11   9-09-88   12   9-16-88   13   9-23-88   14   9-30-88   15  10-07-88
    16  10-14-88   17  10-21-88   18  10-28-88   19  11-04-88   20  11-11-88
    21  11-18-88   22  11-25-88   23  12-02-88   24  12-09-88   25  12-16-88
    26  12-23-88   27  12-30-88   28   1-06-89   29   1-13-89   30   1-20-89
    31   1-27-89   32   2-03-89   33   2-10-89   34   2-17-89   35   2-24-89
    36   3-03-89   37   3-10-89   38   3-17-89   39   3-24-89   40   3-31-89
    41   4-07-89   42   4-14-89   43   4-21-89   44   4-28-89   45   5-05-89
    46   5-12-89   47   5-19-89   48   5-26-89   49   6-02-89   50   6-09-89
    51   6-16-89   52   6-23-89   53   6-30-89   54   7-07-89   55   7-14-89
    56   7-21-89   57   7-28-89   58   8-04-89   59   8-11-89   60   8-18-89
    61   8-25-89   62   9-01-89   63   9-08-89   64   9-15-89   65   9-22-89
 ▼  66   9-29-89   67  10-06-89   68  10-13-89   69  10-20-89   70  10-27-89
```

Appendix 3.10.6 The Problem Log (11.10)

The Project Workbench text processor may be used to create the forms that meet this requirement.

Appendix 3.10.7 The Work Notes Form (11.11)

The Project Workbench text processor may be used to create the forms that meet this requirement.

Appendix 3.10.8 Viewing the Data on the Screen (11.12)

The Project Workbench text processor may be used to create the forms that meet this requirement.

APPENDIX 3.11 REPORTING STATUS

Appendix 3.11.1 Baselines (12.2)

The Project Workbench baseline information is in fields called planned.

Although it was not available for review at the time of this writing, a new feature will be included in an impending release: the user may designate whether the determination of the critical path should be based on the current status of the plan (that is the revised dates) or on the original baseline dates.

Appendix 3.11.2 Frequency of Reporting (12.3)

Project Workbench has three tracking subsystems. One of these three subsystems, the Capture-Actuals subsystem, is driven by reporting periods. These reporting periods are set up in the third page behind the Global screen. (See Figure A3.32.) When the user selects the period duration (for example, days or weeks) and enters the starting date of the first period, the system automatically generates a list of all of the periods. Conversely, if users choose variable period durations, they may enter each reporting period manually.

Appendix 3.11.3 Extracting the Jobs for the Turn-Around Document—on a Range of Dates (12.5)

In each Project Workbench reporting submenu, the range of dates may be entered into the "Select if task overlaps range: start. . . . end. . . ." or "Select if end date within range range: start. . . . end. . . ." fields. (Figure A3.29)

Appendix 3.11.4 Setting Up an *As-of* Date (12.6)

If the first type of status gathering technique is used, the Project Workbench *As-of* date is set in the today field of the Global screen. (Figure A3.2) Users who wish to include and reflect status data for the day on which the data is being entered will need to set this value to one day later.

Appendix 3.11.5 Entering Percent Complete (12.7)

The percent field in Project Workbench appears on the screen of two of the three tracking subsystems: the Status subsystem and the Replan subsystem. (See the detailed subsystems discussion later in this appendix.)

The system automatically computes the percentage value as soon as actual effort is entered into the system. The formula for percentage is:

$$\frac{\text{Actuals times 100}}{\text{Actuals + Estimate-To-Complete}}$$

The percentage value is, therefore, *correctly* tied to the true work effort and not to the elapsed time. Furthermore, as soon as any actuals are reported, the percentage field reverts to a display-only field. On the other hand, if the user chooses to start off by entering a value for the percentage complete, the system will accept it—*but it will not update any of the pertinent fields!* Although the status field will reflect changes to the percentage value, the actuals to date, and the estimates to complete remain unchanged.

Any data entered as actuals will automatically override all data entered as percentages.

Finally, users are advised against entering both actuals and percentages. If they alternate between sometimes entering their own percentage and letting the system calculate the percentage other times, the summary report percentages may be incorrect. Users are advised to enter actuals, to leave the percentage field alone, and to let the system do the job it does so well.

Appendix 3.11.6 Hard Copy Turn-Around Documents (12.8)

Project Workbench provides an excellent standard turn-around document that displays the task name, the original estimate, the hours to date, the estimate to complete, and the planned start and finish dates. (See Figure A3.33.) This report also provides space for the resource, when reporting status, to enter the hours this period, the new estimate to complete, and the actual or revised start and/or finish dates, as well as the status.

Appendix 3.11.7 Entering the Status Collection Data (12.9)

Project Workbench status data may be entered from one of three subsystems: the Status subsystem, the Replan subsystem, and the Capture-actuals subsystem. They are each invoked from the "Tracking" option on the main menu. (Figure A3.1) The system automatically keeps the data in all three subsystems synchronized.

The Status subsystem is used to enter cursory status information, without really requiring data about the actual resource effort expended. It will not be covered here.

Of the other two subsystems, one is used to enter data by resources within a given reporting period (Capture-Actuals), and the other is used to enter data at the task level (Replan). If it is necessary to change the resource loading histogram (Figure A3.23), it may be accessed from either of these two subsystems.

The Capture Actuals subsystem. The Capture-Actuals subsystem is the more rigorous status gathering approach. It presents a screen with all of the tasks for a selected resource within a given reporting period. (See Figure A3.34 and the earlier discussions on types of status reporting approaches and establishing reporting periods.)

Using this subsystem, the user may enter the actual work effort to date, the estimate of the true work effort required to complete the task,[24] the actual (or revised) start and finish dates, and the status. This screen also enables the user to add new tasks to the plan if they are necessary.

When the job has been completed during the reporting period, the system wants to make the completion date equal to the last date of the period—even when the planned completion date falls within the middle of the period. To keep the original date, the user must override a warning message.

Also, with this approach status may only be entered for work that was done in that period. The system will reject time and dates that are outside of the period or force new dates that wrap around the period. Thus, if data collection and/or entry is delayed, and more than one reporting period needs to be entered, the reported time will need to be divided into separate periods and entered accordingly. If, as a result of the current status, the elapsed business days field[25] also needs to be changed, the user will have to switch to the Replan subsystem to complete the data entry.

The Replan subsystem. The Replan subsystem is not bound by any reporting periods but it requires the user to save and recall each task separately—task by task by task. (See Figure A3.35.) In spite of this small obstacle:

• The corresponding screens have all of the pertinent data on them;

---

[24]This value should relate to true work effort and *not* elapsed time, since this field is used to compute the forecasted costs to completion. (See the discussion later in this appendix.)

[25]The field that drives the date computations.

Figure A3.33

| JUL 12 88 | | | | ACTUALS CAPTURE WORKSHEET | | | | | | PAGE | 1 |
| | | | | 7-01-88 thru 7-15-88 | | | | | | | |

| ------ Name ------ | | | ------ Status as of 6-30 ------ | | | | ---- New actuals/estimates (Hrs) ---- | | | |
	Planned	Actual	Estimate to cmpl	Start Plan/rev	End Plan/rev	Status	Actual usage	Estimate to cmpl	Start	End	Status
worker (WRKR)											
chap9											
group3											
320 8	32.0	0.0		7-01-88 7-01-88	7-07-88 7-12-88	Strt	16.0	___	7-01-88	___	___
400 10	32.0	0.0		7-01-88	7-07-88	Cmpl	32.0	___	7-01-88	___	___
group3											
560 14	32.0	0.0	32.0	7-08-88 7-13-88	7-13-88 7-18-88		___	___	___	___	

Unplanned activities:

Total usage for period   56.0

Comments/outstanding or anticipated problems:

Figure A3.34

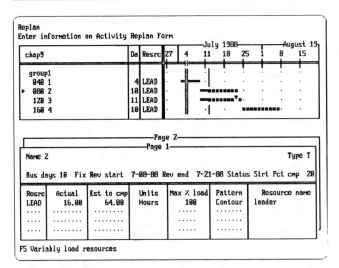

```
/‾‾‾‾‾‾‾‾‾‾‾‾‾‾‾‾‾‾‾‾‾‾‾‾‾‾‾‾‾‾‾‾‾‾‾‾‾‾‾‾‾‾‾‾‾‾‾‾‾‾
Capture-actuals
Enter actuals for designated resource

Project chap9                    Period  7-08-88  thru  7-14-88
Resource WRKR worker             Units   Hours

      Activity        | Period | Estimate| Forecast| Forecast| Stat
                      | actual | to cmpl | start   | end     |
 group3
  328 8               | ...... |   8.88  | 7-01-88 | 7-12-88 | Strt
  568 14              | ...... |  32.88  | 7-13-88 | 7-18-88 |
 group4
  368 9               | ...... |   8.88  | 7-01-88 | 7-12-88 | Strt
  648 16              | ...... |   8.88  | 7-13-88 | 7-13-88 |
  688 17              | ...... |  64.88  | 7-14-88 | 7-25-88 |
  728 18              | ...... |  64.88  | 7-26-88 | 8-84-88 |
 group5
  688 48              | ...... |  24.88  | 7-21-88 | 7-25-88 |
  648 41              | ...... |  32.88  | 7-21-88 | 7-26-88 |
▼
 Totals              |  8.88  | 248.88  |         |         |

F5 Histogram for resource/activity
```

Figure A3.35

```
/‾‾‾‾‾‾‾‾‾‾‾‾‾‾‾‾‾‾‾‾‾‾‾‾‾‾‾‾‾‾‾‾‾‾‾‾‾‾‾‾‾‾‾‾‾‾‾‾‾‾
Replan
Enter information on Activity Replan Form
                             ┌─July 1988─────────August 19┐
 chap9          | Da|Resrc|27  4   11  18  25  1   8   15
 group1
  848 1         |  4|LEAD |·──├─·──·
▸ 888 2         | 18|LEAD |·  ──▬▬▬▬▬▬▬·
  128 3         | 11|LEAD |·  ──▬▬▬▬▬▼·
  168 4         | 18|LEAD |·  ·│·  ·▬▬▬▬▬▬▬▬·

──────────────────────Page 2─
──────────────────────Page 1─
 Name Z                                          Type T

 Bus days 18  Fix Rev start  7-88-88 Rev end  7-21-88 Status Strt Pct cmp  28

 Resrc| Actual | Est to cmp| Units | Max % load| Pattern | Resource name
 LEAD |  16.88 |   64.88   | Hours |    188    | Contour | leader
 .... | ...... | ........  |       |  .....    | ......  |
 .... | ...... | ........  |       |  .....    | ......  |
 .... | ...... | ........  |       |  .....    | ......  |

F5 Variably load resources
```

- They do not require switching to another screen to complete the data entry;
- Each transaction is not bound by periods; and
- The user has the most control over the data entry.

Completing the data entry via this subsystem is the recommended data entry approach.

The data in the Replanning screen is practically identical to the data in the Activity Planning screen.

Now the fields are the business days, the revised (or actual) start, the revised (or actual) finish, the status, the percent complete, the actual time to date, the estimated time to completion, and the other standard fields from the Activity Planning screen.

The Replan subsystem is the system to use when it is necessary to change estimates, dates, and so on.

Entering the data. Users are advised to let the system compute the percentage complete. (See the earlier discussion.) As soon as actual data has been entered for a task, the status changes to started. It remains at started and does not automatically change to *completed*—even when there is no remaining time and the percentage complete is equal to 100 percent. At the appropriate time, the user must toggle the value in the status field to *complete*. When a value for the actual time to date is entered, the system automatically computes the estimated time to completion. If the resource loading histogram has not been invoked, the user may modify the estimated time to completion if it has changed. When the resource loading histogram has been invoked, the modifications must be made there. The other fields are entered or modified in the normal fashion.

Special processing. For certain of the transactions illustrated in Figure 12.1, special handling is necessary.

- With today's date set to July 12, 1988 and Jobs H and I having eight hours estimated to completion, the system asked if the end date should be extended to July 12. Answering *Yes* completed the transaction correctly.

The following transactions were not completed correctly:

- Job S (which, following the original direction, was set at *fixed business days*) also had eight hours estimated to completion but the system did not recognize it and ask if the date should be shortened to July 12. The system assumes that the remaining true work effort in the usage field should be spread across the remaining business days. Changing the task to *variable business days* and using "Recalc" will establish the correct business days and dates.

- Job X only had 16 hours estimated to completion; but the system did not recognize it and asked if the

Figure A3.36

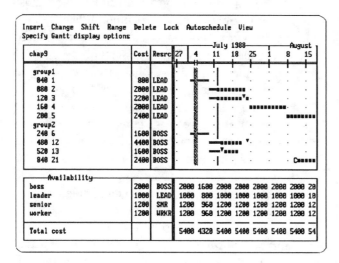

date should be shortened to July 13. The new date was not computed correctly after the autoscheduler was invoked either. The new end date had to be entered manually.

- Job L only had 56 hours estimated to completion; but the system did not recognize it and ask if the date should be shortened to July 20. The new date was not computed correctly after the autoscheduler was invoked either. (See the following discussion.) The new end date had to be entered manually.

Updating the schedule computations. Many of the date changes that are required as a result of the tracking modifications are not rippled through the rest of the plan until the autoscheduler has been invoked. Users should not forget to complete this important part of the procedure.

Understanding the reported dates. In another vein, users need to know that there are some variations on dates that are reported in the system. On the ''Activity Dependency'' report, there are four sets of dates: the revised dates, the planned dates, the early dates, and the late dates. The only dates that reflect progress reporting are the revised dates. The planned dates, the early dates, and the late dates all reflect the original baseline dates. The revised dates may be entered by the user or updated by using the Autoscheduler or Recalc. The start and end dates on the other reports are also the original baseline dates. On the other hand,

the scheduled dates in the CPM network are the revised dates.

Appendix 3.11.8 Performance Status Reporting (12.10)

The Project Workbench ''Activity Status — Actual Vs. Plan'' report (Figure A3.26) may now be used for status reporting. All jobs, not just those for a selected resource, may now be printed. Jobs that are on the critical path are marked with a ''Y'' in the CP column.[26] The status column is either blank, marked complete, or has the value for percentage complete that was computed by the system.

The ''Activity Dependency'' report may also be used for status reporting. (Figure A3.28) Optionally, it may be limited to just jobs on the critical path. This report also lists the successors and their relationship to the critical path.

The Gantt chart shows a vertical line that represents today's date. The original baseline start date is indicated by an upright triangle. The original baseline finish date is indicated by an inverted triangle.

Project Workbench features sorting and selecting on many fields. (Figures A3.29 and A3.30) For example, users may select only those jobs that are on the critical path. While the system will optionally display percent complete, it will not select on percent complete. Although it is not possible to directly identify the late jobs, users may select on other values for status.[27] The sort may be in ascending or descending order. There are as many levels of the sort as there are choices. Users may sort by: original and revised start dates; original and revised finish dates; status; and float. While percent complete may be displayed on reports, it is not possible to sort on this field. It is also not possible to sort or select on remaining duration.

There are two variance-type fields in this system: the *Ahead (Behind)* field on the ''Activity Status''

---

[26] Although it was not available for review at the time of this writing, a new feature will be included in an impending release: the user may designate whether the determination of the critical path should be based on the current status of the plan (that is the revised dates) or the baseline dates.

[27] Which may take on the values of: started; not started; complete; or not complete.

report (Figure A3.26) and the *Revised Vs. Late* field found on the "Activity Dependency" report. (Figure A3.28) The Ahead (Behind) field represents the variance (in time units) between the baseline resource usage and the projected resource usage. This data is helpful when the resource usage is the same as the business days. However, if the resource usage is less than the business days, schedule slippages may not be readily apparent. The Revised Vs. Late field does not serve the purposes described in this section. Furthermore, it is not possible to sort or select based on either of these fields. There are no other fields for reporting variances on revised estimates.

Appendix 3.11.9 Highlighting Progress (12.11)

On the Project Workbench network, completed jobs have a small, solid square in the upper right-hand corner. There is no time line on the PERT. On the Gantt chart, the bar for completed is based on percentage, and that portion of the bar is respectively transformed into two parallel lines. The *As-of* line on the Gantt is a solid vertical line. Delays are also illustrated.

Appendix 3.11.10 Costs and Project Management Software (12.13)

In Project Workbench, the costs of the tasks and of the project will be recomputed when time is reported to the activity and/or when a new unit rate is assigned to a resource. There is no special field for displaying actual-costs-this-period.

By pressing "Plan; Resources; View" and choosing "costs" for the display units, the user may set the Gantt screen up so that it shows the latest total costs for each entry in the Gantt and for each entry in the resource spreadsheet.

The *original* cost is equal to the baseline stored cost.

The *actual cost to date* reflects the accumulated activity and project expenditures for the particular resource and cost account to date.

The *forecast to complete* is an estimate of the cost remaining to complete a particular activity or task. It is computed by multiplying the estimated resource usage time to completion by the resource unit rate. If

no time has been reported to the job, the original resource usage is used.

The *latest costs* are computed by adding the *actual costs to date* plus the *forecast to complete*.

The *variance* is called Ahead (Behind). It is the difference between the *latest costs* and the *original* cost amount.

Appendix 3.11.11 Cost Status Reporting (12.15)

After selecting "Plan; Resources; View" in Project Workbench, if the user sets the system to show cost units, the resource spreadsheet shows costs by period, by resource and totals for each period, and the Gantt chart shows the costs for each task. (See Figure A3.36.)

There is one cost report, the "Activity Status— Time and Costs" report. It is modeled on the report shown in Figure A3.26, except that, instead of time, it shows the actual costs to date, the forecasted costs to completion, the latest estimated total costs, the original baseline costs, and the variances in dollars. There is no cost histogram and no cumulative costs graph or report in Project Workbench.

Appendix 3.11.12 Earned Values and Project Management Software (12.17)

Project Workbench does not support earned value computations. On the other hand, the system does report variances. The variance on the "Activity Dependency" report (Figure A3.28) is called Revised Vs. Late. On the "Status" report (Figure A3.26), it is called Ahead (Behind).

Appendix 3.11.13 Reporting on Resource Availability (12.20)

In Project Workbench, the project-level resource availability profile that is pictured in Figure A3.22 and the task-level resource loading histogram that is pictured in Figure A3.23 may both be printed with the "Print Screen" key.

The Gantt chart pictured in Figure A3.18 may also be printed for a given resource. This Gantt chart may show the baseline start and end dates along with the revised start and end dates. At the end of the Gantt chart report, there will always be a copy of the resource summary spreadsheet that is seen on the screen. This spreadsheet shows the required resources and the available resources. The period length is determined by the periods set up in the Gantt chart. While the screen version will flag overscheduling, it will not show underscheduling. On the hard copy version, neither overscheduling nor underscheduling will be flagged. Users will have to scan across the line, mentally computing the results.

Appendix 3.11.14 Reporting on Resource Utilization *(12.21)*

There are no reports in Project Workbench that provide periodic totals on resource utilization. The resource dollars by time may be seen on the "Activity Status —Time and Cost" report. The resource hours by time may be seen on the "Activity Status—Time and Usage" report.

APPENDIX 3.12 MANAGING THE PROJECT

Appendix 3.12.1 Who Produces Perts and Gantts that May Be Restricted to Critical Path Jobs? *(13.7)*

The Project Workbench network cannot be restricted to just the jobs on the critical path. On the other hand, this product always recognizes the critical path—even if slack is greater than zero. It is possible to limit the Gantt report to just the critical path.

Appendix 3.12.2 Who Produces Reports that May Be Restricted to Fixed-Date Jobs? *(13.8)*

Although, in Project Workbench, it is not possible to select data based on jobs that have been *Locked*, if any positions in either the activity code or the priority code have been used to indicate a fixed task, then this requirement may be met.

Appendix 3.12.3 Who Produces Perts and Gantts that May Be Restricted to Summary Jobs? *(13.9)*

In Project Workbench, by entering the desired type value for phase or activity into the level of detail in the report selection criteria, the Gantt may be restricted to any of these WBS levels. A wild-card character string may also be used to match and extract on other designated summary activity identification numbers. Since the network only displays the task level, the issue of summaries on the PERT is not applicable here.

Appendix 3.12.4 Local Area Networks *(13.14)*

Project Workbench prevents access to files when they are active. It does not provide read/write protection.

Appendix 3.12.5 Guidelines for Tracking and Managing the Project *(13.15)*

Project Workbench has an excellent chapter on controlling projects.

APPENDIX 4: TIME LINE 3.0

APPENDIX 4.0 INTRODUCTION

Each section in each appendix is keyed back to its corresponding introductory section in the tutorial. Readers will find that the respective tutorial section is noted in italicized parentheses at the end of each appropriate section header line.

APPENDIX 4.1 GANTT-DRIVEN PRODUCTS

Appendix 4.1.1 Data Entry Mode (16.2.2)

Gantt-driven Time Line 3.0 has expanded their product by also allowing data entry while in Network mode, and has enhanced their networking capabilities by interfacing the product with Time Line Graphics. While Time Line Graphics does not support project data entry, it does have full graphics project reporting capabilities. Operating in either Plotter or Printer mode, Time Line Graphics uses files from the Time Line 3.0 database.

Appendix 4.1.2 Size & Storage Constraints (16.3.1)

Time Line 3.0 calculates limits based on schedule units rather than by project plans. For example, Time Line 3.0 allows linking or combining more than one project within a schedule (similar to subprojects within a proj-

ect). All of the projects within the schedule are added up, along with the master schedule size, to be considered as one schedule unit. Each schedule unit is limited to the extents described in the following paragraph.

Time Line 3.0 initially works on schedules when they are in main memory. Requiring 640K RAM, the product will support schedules with up to 1,000 tasks. If the hardware configuration also features expanded memory specification (EMS), the product will support schedules with up to 1,600 tasks.[1] When the schedule size exceeds the total of main memory plus EMS,[2] the system will create overflow files on the hard disk. Of course, response times will suffer when this occurs. Actually, for best performance, the vendor recommends using EMS for plans with more than 400 tasks.

While the product requires 640K RAM and the vendor specifies a minimum of 640K, the documentation also states that the system will run with 512K memory—if the user is willing to accept reduced functionality. This is referred to as a low memory condition. Low memory conditions are also caused as the numbers of dependencies, reporting filters, Gantt chart/report layouts, and permissible undo/redo steps per

---

[1] An alternative to EMS, albeit one that will moderately slow down response times, is to create a "RAM disk" on the hard drive.

[2] Or the "RAM disk".

Figure A4.1

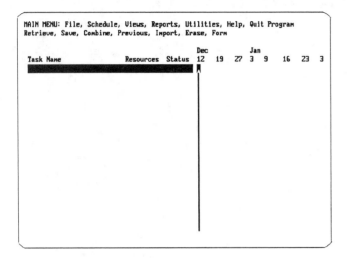

Figure A4.2

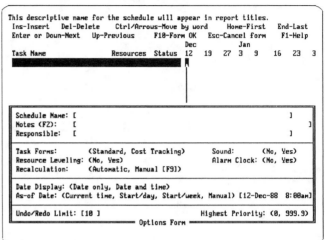

schedule are increased. The type of task form selected will also affect memory usage. The first feature that is affected and ultimately eliminated when approaching low memory conditions is the graphic networking feature.

Appendix 4.1.3 System Structure (16.3.2)

Time Line 3.0 is managed through a hierarchy of menu lines at the top of the screen. (See Figure A4.1.)

Appendix 4.1.4 Global System Schedule Data Defaults (16.3.3)

This product does not support global system schedule parameters.

Appendix 4.1.5 New Schedules (16.3.4)

New schedule information is entered with the Options screen (See Figure A4.2.), which is accessed with ''/; Schedule; Options'' or by saying *Yes* to the fifth question, ''Do you want to enter schedule information or change options?'', under ''/; Schedule; New''. This function ''walks'' users through the setup process, helping them to designate the desired parameters for the new schedule.

Appendix 4.1.6 Accessing Existing Plans (16.3.5)

An existing file is loaded by choosing ''/; File; Retrieve'' and selecting the desired schedule from the Retrieve menu that is subsequently displayed. (See Figure A4.3.)

Figure A4.3

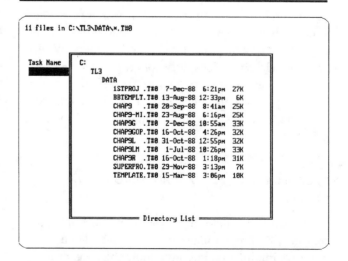

Appendix 4.1.7 Immediate Processor or Batch (16.3.6)

Time Line 3.0 is an immediate processor system. The automatic recalculation may be turned off by setting Recalc to manual on the Options screen. (Figure A4.2)

Appendix 4.1.8 Adding Plan Data (16.3.7)

The level under "/; Schedule; Tasks" is Add, Edit, Copy, Notes, Search, Indent, Outdent, Delete, and Form. If Add or Edit is selected, schedule data may be entered or modified with the tracking Detail Task screen which is consequently invoked. (See Figure A4.4.)

Appendix 4.1.9 Optional "What-if's" or Permanent Saves (16.3.8)

Plan data is not made permanent until the user chooses to save it and until the user designates the name under which the plan is to be saved.

Appendix 4.1.10 Ad Hoc Information Storage (16.3.9)

Each tracking Detail Task screen, Resource/Cost List screen, Project Options screen, Layout screen, Filter screen, and Reports form has a notes field. Users may also create a journal file to store these notes or to independently save the ad hoc information. In screen mode, the corresponding notes entry screen is invoked by moving the cursor to the notes field and pressing the F2 key. At the journal level, pressing "/; Schedule; Journal" will bring up the journal list. Pressing the F2 key will then bring up a blank journal form. Time Line 3.0 provides a miniature word processor that allows the user to enter up to 6,000 characters of free-form data for each notes field. (There is no limit to the number of notes fields per schedule.)

Appendix 4.1.11 Exporting Data (16.3.10)

Time Line 3.0 will export data to LOTUS 1-2-3.

APPENDIX 4.2 WORK BREAKDOWN STRUCTURES

Appendix 4.2.1 Graphics Support (4.8.2)

Time Line 3.0 does not provide graphic work breakdown structures. Time Line 3.0 is Gantt-driven. (That is, the bar chart controls most operations.)

Appendix 4.2.2 Level Support (4.8.3)

Time Line 3.0 has two fields for breakdowns, a field for a work breakdown structure and one for an organizational breakdown structure. In the WBS, it is possible to create as many levels as can fit the pattern of characters and periods that can be devised from 15 positions. Although it is only 10 positions, the same is true for the OBS. For the majority of schedules, the number of levels that can be derived from the WBS will be more than adequate.

Appendix 4.2.3 Data Entry Requirements (4.8.4)

In Time Line 3.0, the number of entries depends on the use of the WBS and the OBS. The standard Task screen does not exhibit the WBS or OBS. Selecting the tracking Detail Task screen (Figure A4.4) from the Options screen (Figure A4.2) will display the proper task form.[3] Similarly, the Standard layout for display-

Figure A4.4

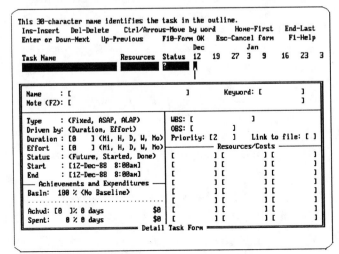

---

[3]This form uses more main memory.

Figure A4.5

```
                                        Press [/] for Main Menu
milestone for start          Resource:
ALAP MILESTONE, 12-Dec-88  8:00am.  Future.

                                           Start    End
Task Name                    WBS Code   Dur Date     Date       EAC
   milestone for start                  0.0 12-Dec-88 12-Dec-88  0.00
   project milestones                  31.0  5-Jan-89 16-Feb-89  0.00
      finish analysis                   0.0  5-Jan-89  5-Jan-89  0.00
      finish impl. modeling             0.0 17-Jan-89 17-Jan-89  0.00
      finish tech                       0.0  8-Feb-89  8-Feb-89  0.00
      finish project                    0.0 17-Feb-89 17-Feb-89  0.00
   PROJECT ATM            0.0.0.000.000 47.0 12-Dec-88 16-Feb-89 ********
      ANALYSIS            1.0.0.000.000 16.0 12-Dec-88  4-Jan-89 ********
         KICK-OFF         1.1.0.000.000  4.0 12-Dec-88 15-Dec-88 ********
            1: BUILD      1.1.1.000.000  2.0 12-Dec-88 13-Dec-88 ********
               DO H.L.A.  1.1.1.001.000  1.0 12-Dec-88 12-Dec-88 ********
               DO CHARTER 1.1.1.002.000  2.0 12-Dec-88 13-Dec-88   16.00
            1: MANAGE     1.1.2.000.000  4.0 12-Dec-88 15-Dec-88 ********
               NEXT       1.1.2.001.000  2.0 12-Dec-88 13-Dec-88 ********
               REST       1.1.2.002.000  2.0 12-Dec-88 13-Dec-88   16.00
               TOTAL      1.1.2.003.000  2.0 14-Dec-88 15-Dec-88 ********
         SIZING DESCOPING 1.2.0.000.000  4.0 16-Dec-88 21-Dec-88 ********
            2: BUILD      1.2.1.000.000  2.0 16-Dec-88 19-Dec-88 ********
               DO I.L.A.  1.2.1.001.000  2.0 16-Dec-88 19-Dec-88 ********
                     1STPROJ  End: 16-Feb-89  5:00pm
```

ing and reporting the Gantt chart only exhibits the task name, resources, status, and the graphic Gantt chart. With "/; Schedule; Layout;" (or "/; Schedule; Layout; F2") followed by pressing the "Insert" key, a new display with the WBS field will appear.[4] (See Figure A4.5.)

Time Line 3.0 also supports outlining of task names when entering schedule data in Gantt mode. (See Figure A4.16 below.) After the task data is keyed in, the tasks themselves are easily indented or outdented with "Shift/right arrow" or "Shift/left arrow".[5] It is *very easy* to enter an outline that corresponds to just about any WBS. A task that has one or more tasks indented beneath it is called a summary task. A lowest-level task with no tasks indented beneath it is called a detail task. Indenting or outdenting a summary task correspondingly moves all levels beneath it. This may be troublesome if the user is trying to reorganize only a part of the outline (and its corresponding WBS). Similarly, a task under one summary task may not simply be moved to under another summary task; it

must be outdented to the same level as its summary task before it may be moved. This last feature may become tiresome when trying to reorganize even an average-sized schedule. This is discussed in greater detail later in this appendix.

Nevertheless, entering the schedule data in the Time Line 3.0 Outline mode greatly simplifies verification of the WBS. Furthermore, when the data has been entered in Outline mode, the system automatically does an excellent job of summarization. Given this fact, it becomes questionable if, in many cases, entering a WBS number is even needed. On the other hand, in certain uses with the reporting filter, the WBS may come in handy. (See the discussion later in this appendix.)

Appendix 4.2.4 Durations and Dependencies (4.8.5)

Time Line 3.0 does not require durations and dependencies to initialize a project plan. Although Time Line Graphics creates networks that are scaled to time, this is not a problem because the data is printed above and below the node.

Appendix 4.2.5 Random Sequence of Data Entry (4.8.6)

Although in Time Line 3.0, the tracking Detail Task screen (Figure A4.4) may be accessed from either Gantt or Network mode, random entries made in Network mode may be hard to reconcile with the correct WBS. When using the Outline mode, it is essential that the task be placed in the correct place; therefore, random entry is unacceptable. On the other hand, it is very easy to insert a new task in Gantt mode (by positioning the cursor on the task above the place where the new task is to be entered and pressing the "Insert" key to get the task form). The challenge comes when trying to use the new task to create a different arrangement of the WBS. This may require several extra steps of outdents, moves, and indents.

Appendix 4.2.6 Using the Copy Features with the *Template* Tasks (4.8.7)

Time Line 3.0 has a "Task Copy" function for duplicating pieces of the plan within the project. Sum-

---

[4]Although the task name field allows 30 characters to be entered, 28 characters is the maximum number of characters that can be displayed on the screen

[5]Although the documentation does not state as much, the "Shift/arrow" will only work with the arrows on the numeric keypad and not with the cursor movement arrows.

mary tasks cannot be copied. The function will copy one lowest-level detail task at a time, with all of its corresponding data. At a minimum, the name of the old task will have to be changed to the name of the new task. Generally speaking, the Time Line 3.0 "Copy" function is not practical for copying the *template* tasks.

The product does support a "File Combine" or a "File Link" function, both of which will import other schedules into the master schedule. In either case, if using WBS numbers and part of the number will remain constant, that part may be entered into the WBS field of the tracking Detail Task screen of each job in the *template* plan. After these tasks have been imported into the master schedule with the "File Combine", each of the WBS numbers may be expanded by editing the WBS field in the tracking Detail Task screen while in Cursor Insert mode.

Appendix 4.2.7 Rollup Support (4.8.8)

In Time Line 3.0, if the schedule data is entered in Outline mode, the system will automatically perform most of the desired rollups (on time, resources, and dollars). This product also features the best type of duration rollup: with no extra effort on the part of the user, the rollup on the duration field computes—not the total work effort—but rather the total time span of the entries inside of each outline family. Consequently, activating a WBS code may be superfluous, unless the user wants to select (called filtering), sort, and/or report by WBS code on pieces of the schedule. Even then, filtering on WBS code is a cumbersome affair. Jobs may only be selected on an individual basis or for all candidates that *start* with a certain number (e.g. all jobs that start with 3 or even with 3.1.1). There is no way to filter on a range of codes (e.g. all of the 3s *and* 4s); and, therefore, a new filter must be created for each entry in the WBS. This is not only tiresome; but each additional filter designation also consumes precious main memory.

Appendix 4.2.8 Guidelines and Documentation (4.8.9)

Time Line 3.0 has two pages of WBS information.

APPENDIX 4.3 ESTIMATING

Appendix 4.3.1 Estimating Support and Estimating Guidelines (5.7.1)

Time Line 3.0 does not provide guidelines that support the estimating techniques described in this book. They assume the estimating has been completed and the duration is known. (Instructions on how to use the system to achieve the implementation of a feature are not considered guidelines.)

Appendix 4.3.2 Estimates of *True Work Effort* versus Resource-Driven Elapsed Time (5.7.4)

Time Line 3.0 supports *true work effort* in the effort field of the tracking Detail Task screen. When *driven by duration* is selected from the tracking Detail Task screen (this is also the default selection), *true work effort* is also in the duration field.

Appendix 4.3.3 Durations and Units of Measurement (5.7.6)

Time Line 3.0 allows the user to choose between minutes, hours, days, weeks, and months. Minutes and hours have limited use, however. In most projects, they will generate more time periods than the system can handle; therefore, they can only be used in short projects or phases. The default duration in Time Line 3.0 is 0 days. Time Line 3.0 supports mixed units of measurement and will make the consistency adjustments. This product provides a precision feature that will round any in-between estimates to the nearest hour, half-hour, quarter-hour, six minutes, five minutes, or one minute. The precision default is "hour," the choice of which is more than adequate for the majority of projects. Choosing a smaller precision will limit the total size of the project. In a two to three month project, 15 to 30 minutes is the smallest precision that can be invoked—or the schedule size will be exceeded.

Appendix 4.3.4 Zero Duration Milestones (5.7.7)

Time Line 3.0 supports zero duration milestones.

Figure A4.6

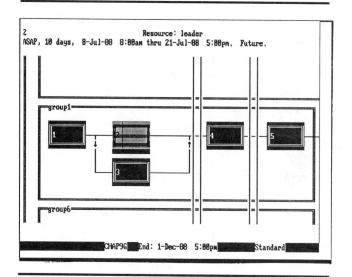

```
Should dependency be attached to the beginning or end of the predecessor?
Arrows-Change selection    First Letter-Change selection      Enter-Select
Enter or Down-Next    Up-Previous      F10-Form OK    Esc-Cancel form    F1-Help
                                                       Start    End
Task Name                      WBS Code     Dur   Date    Date         EAC
   milestone for start                      0.0  12-Dec-88 12-Dec-88   0.00
   project milestones                      31.0   5-Jan-89 16-Feb-89   0.00
     finish analysis                        0.0   5-Jan-89  5-Jan-89   0.00
     finish impl. modeling                  0.0  17-Jan-89 17-Jan-89   0.00
     finish tech                            0.0   8-Feb-89  8-Feb-89   0.00
     finish project                         0.0  17-Feb-89 17-Feb-89   0.00
   PROJECT ATM              0.0.0.000.000  47.0  12-Dec-88 16-Feb-89  xxxxxxxx
     ANALYSIS               1.0.0.000.000  16.0  12-Dec-88  4-Jan-89  xxxxxxxx
       KICK-OFF             1.1.0.000.000   4.0  12-Dec-88 15-Dec-88  xxxxxxxx
         1: BUILD           1.1.1.000.000   2.0  12-Dec-88 13-Dec-88  xxxxxxxx
P          DO H.L.A.        1.1.1.001.000   1.0  12-Dec-88 12-Dec-88  xxxxxxxx
           DO CHARTER       1.1.1.002.000   2.0  12-Dec-88 13-Dec-88    16.00

From the (Start, End) of the Predecessor: DO H.L.A.

        (Add, Subtract) [0  ] (Minutes, Hours, Days, Weeks, Months)

    then (Start, End)  the Successor  : DO CHARTER
                       Dependency Form
       1STPROJ    End: 16-Feb-89  5:00pm
```

Figure A4.7

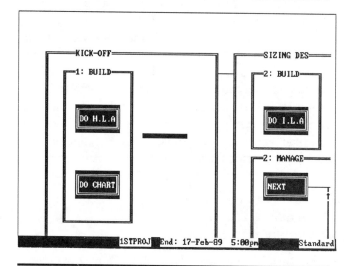

```
2                             Resource: leader
ASAP, 10 days,  8-Jul-88  8:00am thru 21-Jul-88  5:00pm.  Future.

 group1

   1        2              4        5

            3

 group6

                    CHAP9G  End: 1-Dec-88  5:00pm      Standard
```

Appendix 4.3.5 Lead and Lag Times with Duration but No Effort *(5.7.8)*

Time Line 3.0 allows the user to show lag time with the use of the dependency form. (See Figure A4.6.) This process is referred to as creating a "partial dependency." While partial dependencies are noted in (1) the status code field or (2) the dependency list (See Figure A4.9 below.) with a "p" (when the delay time is from the predecessor) or an "s" (when the delay time is to the successor) the amount of lag time is not shown on the Gantt or the PERT.[6] The lag time, however, is displayed in the message line at the top of the dependency list.

APPENDIX 4.4 NETWORKS

Appendix 4.4.1 Types of Networks *(6.8.1)*

Time Line Graphics produces precedence diagrams. Time Line 3.0 produces a variation on an activity-on-a-node network. (See Figure A4.7.) The task information is indeed inside the node. If Outline mode has

---

[6]A better approach is to create a separate task with the corresponding duration and then enter a dummy resource whose cost is zero. Of course, this does consume precious memory.

been used to create the schedule, the groups will be nested one within another. (See Figure A4.8.) Tasks cannot be further indented or outdented while in Network mode. The display of the inside tasks of any summary group may be suppressed or reopened by pressing the "—" or "+" keys respectively.

Appendix 4.4.2 Types of Relationships *(6.8.2)*

In Time Line 3.0, the default relationship is finish-to-start. The other three relationships are created with a

Figure A4.8

```
 KICK-OFF                            SIZING DES

  1: BUILD                            2: BUILD

   DO H.L.A                            DO I.L.A

   DO CHART                           2: MANAGE

                                       NEXT

                  1STPROJ  End: 17-Feb-89  5:00pm      Standard
```

second transaction, the dependency form. (Figure A4.6) These additional relationship types will then be displayed in the fifth and sixth positions of the status code field (which may be seen on the Gantt screen and reports), but the time difference is not displayed anywhere.

Appendix 4.4.3 Number of Dependencies (6.8.3)

The number of dependencies in Time Line 3.0 is only limited by the size of the hard disk.

Appendix 4.4.4 Establishing Dependencies (6.8.4)

To establish Time Line 3.0 dependencies, a separate transaction is required. In either Gantt or Network mode, position the cursor on the predecessor and press the spacebar (a "P" will appear next to the task). To complete the connection, position the cursor on the successor and press the F3 key. This may be done as many times as necessary.

When working in Outline mode, dependencies between a given summary task and the first tasks within its group are automatically assumed; therefore, since they are not necessary, the user will be prohibited from entering these types of relationships and wasting memory. All tasks in the first level under a summary task are assumed to start at the same time as the summary task—unless they are designated as a successor to some other task, either inside or out of the group.

Time Line 3.0 also provides default dependencies. During any entry of tasks, the system assumes the position of the cursor when the new task form is invoked, signifies the predecessor, and automatically enters the "P" at that task. Consequently, only one key stroke is necessary for linking the tasks—pressing the F3 key. This is a time saver, especially if the whole work breakdown structure and the correct dependencies are known at data entry time. Otherwise, the user may need to undo some of the relationships and redo them at their proper positions. In spite of this, since jobs that are entered sequentially are often similarly dependent, the default usually turns out to be a time saver.

When the start of one task may be dependent upon the completion of all of the tasks within another group of tasks, it is advisable to designate the summary task of the group as the predecessor rather than the last detail task in the group. In this manner, additional ending detail tasks may later be inserted into the group without the need to modify relationships.

Appendix 4.4.5. How Easy Is it to Enter Dependencies? (6.8.6)

Time Line 3.0 does not require number entries to create relationships. The system sets the user up so that if the relationship is correct all the user need do is position the cursor to the successor and press the F3 key.

Appendix 4.4.6 Inserting Jobs into the Middle of the Plan (6.8.7)

Plan data in Time Line 3.0 is added with the tracking Detail Task screen. Tasks may be inserted in either Gantt or Network mode, but the cursor must always be on an existing task before the "Add" can be invoked successfully.

If the outline has been implemented, tasks will always automatically be added at the same level as that of the current cursor position. Therefore, regardless of the mode in which the insert is invoked, the cursor must first be positioned correctly on an equivalent outline level. Then, pressing the "Insert" key will invoke the form and insert the task correctly.

The system will automatically designate the original task, in the position of the cursor at the time the add function was invoked—as the predecessor to the new task. If this is acceptable, all the user need do after entering the completed task form is press F3. New (or different) dependencies will have to be resolved in the separate procedures for entering dependencies, described above.

If there is no outline work breakdown structure and a task is inserted somewhere in the middle of the plan, it will be placed in the corresponding spot on the Gantt, but it will wind up suspended in midair at the very start of the network, with no dependencies of any kind.

Appendix 4.4.7 Subnetwork Dependencies (6.8.8)

Time Line 3.0 also supports subnetwork dependencies —even when the relationships are in outline groups that are nested within one another. (Figure A4.8) However, if the display of a group that has internal relationships (See "1: Build (Do H.L.A.)" and "2: Build (Do I.L.A.)" in Figure A4.8.) is suppressed with the "–" key, the dependency lines between the internal nodes will also disappear as well. This is not a good feature.

Appendix 4.4.8 Moving Jobs in the Network (6.8.9)

There is no way to move nodes when in the Network mode of Time Line 3.0. The user must accept the placement of jobs on the network. In Gantt mode, positioning the cursor on a task and pressing "shift/up arrow" or "shift/down arrow" will move it up or down to the next equivalent level in the outline.[7] The move carries all relationships. Indenting or outdenting a summary task correspondingly moves all of the levels beneath it. This may be troublesome if the user is trying to reorganize only part of the outline group. Similarly, a task within one summary task may not simply be moved to an equivalent level within another summary task. It must be outdented to the same level as its summary task before it may be moved, repositioned as just described, and then indented once more after it has reached its new destination. This last feature may also become tiresome when trying to reorganize even an average-sized schedule.

Appendix 4.4.9 Removing Dependencies (6.8.10)

In Time Line 3.0, position the cursor on the predecessor and press the spacebar; position the cursor on the successor and press "Control/F3". Alternatively, dependencies may easily be eliminated from the dependency list by positioning the cursor and pressing the "Delete" key. (See Figure A4.9.)

When a relationship is eliminated between two tasks within the same outline group, they become parallel instead of sequential—with the successor being moved to the start date of the whole group and the

---

Figure A4.9

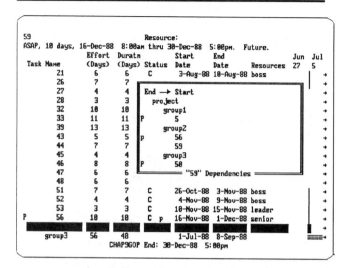

predecessor left dangling. If the connected tasks are at different outline levels, the predecessor is left dangling and the successor is moved to the start date of its corresponding outline group.

Appendix 4.4.10 Deleting Jobs in the Plan (6.8.11)

When there is an undertaking to eliminate a task in the middle of a schedule, Time Line 3.0 asks the user if the system should "attempt to bridge the connected tasks." When the answer is *Yes*, the system automatically joins dependent jobs on either side of the deleted job. Usually this is completed correctly but not invariably. The highlight feature described later should always be invoked at the completion of the operation to check for accuracy. If any corrections are necessary, they may be done using the "Establish" or "Delete" functions earlier described.

Appendix 4.4.11 Lag and Lead Times (6.8.12)

Time Line 3.0 allows the user to show lead time with the use of the dependency form. (Figure A4.6) Since this form allows the creation of all four types of relationships, the lag or lead can also be applied to all of the types. Remember, however, that although lead times may be seen in the dependency list (Figure A4.9), these items do not show up on any reports. A better approach is to create the task with the corresponding duration and then enter a dummy resource whose cost is zero.

Appendix 4.4.12 Copying Jobs in the Plan (6.8.13)

In Time Line 3.0, the "Task Copy" function will copy one lowest-level detail task at a time and carry all of the corresponding task data. The "Copy" function does not carry any of the original tasks relationships; therefore, they will have to be separately established. Summary tasks cannot be copied at all. Whole plans are copied by saving the original plan under a new name.

Appendix 4.4.13 Copying the *Template* Jobs (6.8.14)

While the Time Line 3.0 "Task Copy" function can duplicate one task at a time, this feature is not generally useful for copying *template* plans. There is also a "Link" function that may be used for multiproject requirements; however, since it does not import or show the tasks *or* allow dependencies, it will not be addressed at this time. (See the discussion later in this appendix for multiproject applications.)

The product does have a very easy-to-use "File Combine" function that will import the *template* tasks if they have been saved in a separate file. Selecting "/; File; Combine" (followed by choosing the options to combine the "tasks/resources/costs" and to preserve the "durations") will import the *template* tasks as often as desired. Furthermore, duplicate names are no problem and there is no restriction on internal *template* dependencies.

When the group of *template* tasks has been successfully included in the current schedule, they will be found at the bottom of the Gantt under a heading that has been positioned at the highest outline level. This heading is named "Summary of," and is followed by the *template* plan name. Moving this group of tasks to the proper position in the schedule will require several combinations of indents and moves.

When originally creating the *template* plan, the tasks should not be given fixed dates.

Once these tasks have been imported into the master project, any changes in the *template* plan must also be done manually in every occurrence of *template* tasks in the master.

Appendix 4.4.14 Loops in the Network (6.8.15)

Time Line 3.0 signals loops, and the offending action can then quickly be undone by pressing "Shift/F10". For the rare cases where this does not eliminate the problem, when "Control/F4" is pressed, the system will display a very nice network view of just the tasks involved in the loop. The violating relationships may then be eliminated as described earlier.

Appendix 4.4.15 Dangling Jobs (6.8.16)

Time Line 3.0 allows dangling.

Appendix 4.4.16 Verifying Dependencies are Correct (6.8.17)

Verification of dependencies on the printed hard copy of the Time Line 3.0 network is not difficult at all. However, in an average-sized schedule, the network is usually too big to be displayed on one screen. Furthermore, since the network in Time Line 3.0 is drawn with nested summary boxes, this often causes a widely spaced arrangement. (Figure A4.8) As a result, it is sometimes hard to follow dependencies from one screen to another. As a vendor-suggested alternative, Time Line 3.0's excellent dependency highlighting feature (described at the end of this section) does aid in the screen verification of relationships.

Appendix 4.4.17 Highlighting Dependency Paths (6.8.18)

Time Line 3.0 has a special feature that allows the user to highlight the immediate predecessors and successors of any designated task. It works in both Gantt and Network mode. Pressing the F4 key will highlight all of the tasks that are related to the appointed one. If the highlighted tasks are spread apart, the user may have to scroll through the Gantt or network to view them.

On the other hand, pressing "Shift/F4" will display a window with the respective dependency list.

(Figure A4.9) This list shows the name of the outline group of each related task as well as specifically designating which tasks are predecessors and which tasks are successors. Partial dependencies are also displayed, along with the corresponding amount of lead time, if present.

Relationships may be deleted, changed, and added from within the dependency list. It is also possible to review the dependencies for another task in the list by positioning the cursor on the desired task and pressing the "Enter" key.

Appendix 4.4.18 Network Aesthetics (6.8.19)

Time Line Graphics produces precedence diagrams. Time Line 3.0 produces a variation on an activity-on-a-node network. The task information is indeed inside the node; however, the outline groups are nested one within another. (Figure A4.8)

In the section on establishing dependencies, the user was advised that, when the start of a task may be dependent upon the completion of all of the tasks within a group, it is a good idea to designate the summary task of the group as the predecessor rather than the last detail task in the group. In this manner, additional ending detail tasks may be inserted without the need to modify relationships. This is still true. However, whenever this approach is implemented, the internal tasks have no dependency lines and appear to be suspended in midair. (See "2: Build" in Figure A4.8.)

The amount of data that is displayed on each node may be varied from no data at all (only a very small node) or a truncated task name (10 characters for summary tasks and 8 characters for detail tasks), to other variations with full names, dates, durations, dollars, and so on.

Appendix 4.4.19 Scaled to Time? (6.8.20)

Time Line 3.0 is not scaled to time but Time Line Graphics is.

The units of measurement in the Time Line Graphics PERT are days, weeks, months, and years. (The Time Line 3.0 product also supports durations in minutes and hours.) Users who wish to enter estimates in minutes or hours into Time Line 3.0 may find this limitation a disadvantage when the durations are converted by Time Line Graphics. The corresponding node may be represented by a mere vertical line or a box that equates to one day's length. Time Line Graphics, however, does print the task data above and below the node. Therefore, the network is still readable and useful.

Appendix 4.4.20 Networks and Work Breakdown Structures (6.9)

Since internal entries of the Time Line 3.0 outline groups are clustered within boxes, there is no need for beginning and ending nodes. Similarly, when the start of a task may be dependent upon the completion of all of the tasks within a group, it is advisable to designate the summary task of the group as the predecessor rather than the last detail task in the group.

Appendix 4.4.21 Dependencies in a Multiproject Environment (6.12)

In Time Line 3.0, a project schedule may be used as a subschedule as often as required. There are two ways to create subschedules; both have advantages and disadvantages. In the first alternative, the master schedule is *not* constrained by the sum of its subschedules. It is implemented by linking a file to a task. The second approach may not be used with very large projects. Furthermore, the second approach does not lend itself gracefully to the order in which the multiproject topics will be addressed in this text. The second approach uses the "File Combine". Although, at first blush, the "File Link" appeared to satisfy the multiproject requirements, it turns out that it is not at all useful when trying to identify resource conflicts. This is a serious enough drawback to eliminate it from the ensuing discussions. In spite of the disadvantages of Alternative 2 (the "File Combine"), it is the approach of choice.

In starting, the "File Combine" should not be used to import subschedule jobs until the proper project calendar has been invoked.

Subschedule jobs are imported by selecting "/; File; Combine; Tasks/Resources/Costs". The user will then be asked to choose between preserving durations or dates. Durations ought to be chosen. All of the jobs from the subschedule will be imported into the master schedule.

Dependency connections are simply made as outlined earlier in this appendix.

To speed things up, the calculations may be temporarily stopped from the "/; Schedule; Options" screen. (Figure A4.2) When there is no longer a need for faster response times, the calculations should be turned back on.

This approach may also require the maintenance of the original and the merged copies of subproject plans.

Appendix 4.4.22 Printing and Viewing Networks (6.13)

To view the network on the Time Line 3.0 screen, press "/; View; Network". To print, press "/; Reports; Network; Go". To increase or decrease the amount of information that is displayed inside the node, press "/; Reports; Network; Change layout".

Appendix 4.4.23 Guidelines and Documentation (6.15)

Time Line 3.0 has a chapter on implementing dependencies in the product. This chapter contains several pages of useful information and hints on network implementation. Although the documentation does contain a whole appendix dedicated to implementing multiprojects in Time Line 3.0, there are no conceptual guidelines on multiprojects.

APPENDIX 4.5 OPTIMAL PLANS

Appendix 4.5.1 Calendars (7.14.1)

There is always a calendar present in a Time Line 3.0 schedule—even when it is blank. The resident calendar is always the calendar that belonged to the last project that was in memory when the user last quit the system.

New calendar settings are entered in any of the three data entry screens that are invoked by selecting one of "Workhours; Dates; Settings". They are all accessed under "/; Schedule; Calendar". The hours worked (or, for lunch, etc., the hours *not* worked) each day are set by selecting "Workhours", moving the cursor to the corresponding day and hour, and pressing the spacebar to toggle the field to a *Yes* or

Figure A4.10

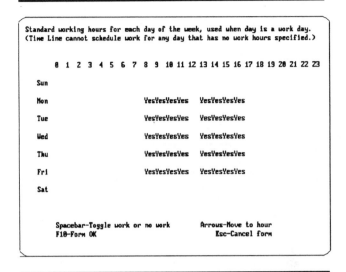

No value. (See Figure A4.10.) The holidays are set by selecting "Dates", moving the cursor to the designated date, and pressing the spacebar to toggle the field to a *no work* value. (See Figure A4.11.) Finally, by selecting "Settings", the user may then designate the standard workday, the standard workweek, the day the work week begins, the year the project begins, the precision, and whether to set the finish dates at the end of the current workday or the beginning of the next workday. (See Figure A4.12.) Once the calendar

Figure A4.11

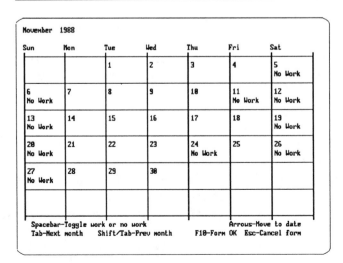

Figure A4.12

```
The number of hours in your standard work day.
  Enter a number (no fractions).
  Enter or Down-Next    Up-Previous      F10-Form OK    Esc-Cancel form    F1-Help




  ┌──────────────────────────────────────────────────────────────────────┐
  │ Standard Workday: [8 ] hours      Standard Workweek: [5] days          │
  │──────────────────────────────────────────────────────────────────────│
  │ Standard Week Begins: (Sun, Mon, Tues, Wed, Thurs, Fri, Sat)          │
  │ Standard Year Begins: [January ]                                       │
  │──────────────────────────────────────────────────────────────────────│
  │ Precision: (Hour, Half-Hour, 15 Minutes, 6 Minutes, 5 Minutes, 1 Minute) │
  │──────────────────────────────────────────────────────────────────────│
  │ Format End Dates: (End of the day, Start of the next day)             │
  └═══════════════════════ Calendar Settings Form ═══════════════════════┘
```

has been created, it may be copied into other plans by selecting "/; File; Combine; Calendar". However, this action will only be successful if it is implemented *before* any other data has been entered into the schedule. The schedule must be empty or the action will be rejected! Furthermore, in an empty schedule, the "Calendar Combine" may be executed repetitively. *The incoming calendar data always overwrites the existing calendar data.*

Appendix 4.5.2 Choosing the Correct Project Start Date (7.14.2)

In Time Line 3.0, the project start date is determined by the date of the first scheduled task. Therefore, a single, fixed milestone task is created at the beginning of the project. The date of this task is set to the project start date. To complete the process, this milestone task is made a predecessor to each of the first tasks in the schedule.

Before the first job is added to the plan, it is a good idea to scroll the cursor so that the first day displayed on the Gantt chart corresponds to the first day of the project. This simple process is completed by pressing the "Right Arrow" or "Left Arrow" key until the proper date is displayed. If this step is omitted, the first jobs in the plan may be created with the incorrect start date and all subsequent dates may be incorrect, as well.

Appendix 4.5.3 Insuring that the Plan Is Not Constrained by Resources (7.14.3)

In Time Line 3.0, *driven by duration* is the default selection. For this application, the default should be retained. (Figure A4.4) The user ought also to (1) refrain from adding resources to the task form; (2) select "Status" equals "Future" on the task form; and (3) answer *No* to "/; Schedule; Options; Resource leveling". (Figure A4.2)

Appendix 4.5.4 Avoiding Imposed Target Dates (7.14.3)

In Time Line 3.0, there are three possible values for the type field in the task form: ALAP, ASAP, and fixed. (Figure A4.4) The default is ASAP. The user should accept the default when scheduling the optimal plan.

Appendix 4.5.5 Calculating the Schedule (7.14.4)

In Time Line 3.0, automatic calculations may be turned on by setting "/; Schedule; Options; Recalculation" to "Automatic". (Figure A4.2) On the other hand, if this slows the system down, it may be set to "Manual." Then, schedules may be recalculated on an ad hoc basis by pressing the F9 key.

Appendix 4.5.6 The Forward Pass: Calculating the Early Dates (7.14.5)

Time Line 3.0 allows the user to select which one of the two scheduling algorithms to apply. The choice is made by selecting "/; Schedule; Calendar; Setting" and choosing the desired alternative (*end of the day* or *start of the next day*) from the *format end dates* parameter. (Figure A4.12) The end of the day choice invokes the traditional scheduling algorithm.

Appendix 4.5.7 Zero Duration Milestones (7.14.8)

In Time Line 3.0, even with *format end dates* of the Calendar Settings screen set to *end of the day*, Time Line 3.0 schedules zero duration milestones at the start of the next business day following the completion of all of its predecessors. This can be offset with the following *work-around*:

1. Create finish-to-finish dependencies between the zero duration milestone and *each* of its predecessors. (Figure A4.6) Subtract the amount equal to the precision selected from the Calendar Settings screen[8] from the end of *each* of the predecessors. Although the time of day for the milestone will not be scheduled correctly, the correct date will be reported.

2. Because Step 1 will cause the successor(s) of the zero duration milestone to be scheduled incorrectly, this must be offset by creating start-to-start relationships between the milestone and *each* of its successor(s), adding the precision amount from Step 1 to the start of the successor(s).

Appendix 4.5.8 Retaining a Baseline Record of the Optimal Plan *(7.14.11)*

A Time Line 3.0 baseline plan may be set by selecting "/; Schedule; Baseline". To see the baseline dates and bars displayed on a second line for each entry on the Gantt screen, the user should say *Yes* to "Show Baseline" after selecting "/; Schedule; Layout". (See Figure A4.13.) Set to the original early dates, the baseline dates do not change until this process has been invoked again. The baseline fields are also displayed on several reports.

Appendix 4.5.9 Interpreting the Dates on the Screen *(7.14.12)*

With the "Layout" option, Time Line 3.0 allows the user to choose the layout of columns to be displayed on the Gantt chart and the network. The Gantt may have up to 16 columns reported in addition to the time-scaled matrix. It may display the early and late dates for both the current and the baseline plans. The network allows up to six columns reported for each network node. In both Gantt and Network mode, there are 65 different columns to choose from, many of which are the desired date columns. Time Line Graphics shows the early dates on the network. However,

---

Figure A4.13

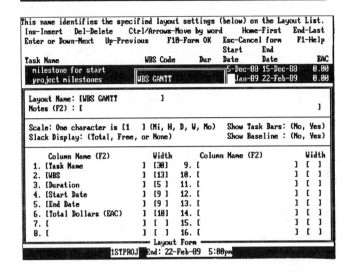

it only produces hard copy reports. The graphics cannot be viewed on the screen.

Appendix 4.5.10 Annotating the Critical Path *(7.14.13)*

In Gantt mode, Time Line 3.0 allows the user to select and display only those jobs on the critical path. The display of jobs that are not on the critical path is suppressed. This is done by selecting "/; Schedule; Filter; Select" and choosing *Critical Path* from the select criteria. On the other hand, the user may elect instead to display all jobs in the plan and highlight those jobs on the critical path in any preferred color. This is accomplished for Gantt or Network mode by selecting "/; Schedule; Filter; Highlight" and choosing *Critical Path* from the select criteria.

Appendix 4.5.11 Verifying Lag and Lead Time *(7.14.14)*

In Time line 3.0, using the example in Figure 7.6, from the end of the finish of Job 1 (February 3, 1988 at 5:00 P.M.), the system was instructed to add 10 days (See the dependency form, Figure A4.6.), then to start Job 2. Job 2 was scheduled to start on February 19, 1988 at 8:00 A.M.

Appendix 4.5.12 Gantt Chart Time Periods (7.14.15)

The timeframes in the Time Line 3.0 Gantt display are affected by entering two values: the precision setting and the character scale.

Accessed by selecting "/; Schedule; Calendar; Setting", the *Precision* field may be set to 1 minute, 5 minutes, 6 minutes, 15 minutes, half-hour, or hours. (In an average two to three month project, the smallest precision that can be invoked is 15 minutes to a half-hour.)

Next, the character scale is chosen by selecting "/; Schedule; Layout; F2 Edit" and choosing minutes, hours, days, weeks, or months. (Figure A4.13) As long as the choice is larger than the precision selection, it will determine the intervals displayed on the bar chart. But no matter what value is selected for the character scale, if it is smaller than the value selected for the precision field, the character scale will have no effect on the display. In other words, the smallest time period that can be displayed may not be less than the precision value.

The user may move in any direction around the Gantt chart by pressing the arrow keys.

The bars on the Gantt chart are continuous; they are not broken by weekends or holidays. (See Figure A4.16 below.)

Appendix 4.5.13 Scheduling in the Multiproject Environment (7.14.17)

The Time Line 3.0 master project calendar is the ruling calendar. Its data is retained and the calendar data in the subprojects is dropped. The corresponding schedules will be computed automatically. Because this is a merge process, maintaining the original *and* merged copies of the subprojects may later require double data entry.

Appendix 4.5.14 Nesting Subprojects in a Multiproject Environment (7.14.18)

Since Time Line 3.0 melds the subproject plans together, the nested issue is inapplicable.

Appendix 4.5.15 Guidelines and Documentation (7.14.20)

Time Line 3.0 does not have guidelines for developing schedules.

APPENDIX 4.6 CALCULATING A FINISH DATE

Appendix 4.6.1 Using the New Reasonable Late Finish Date of the Project (7.26.3)

In Time Line 3.0, to create a fixed late finish date *and* get the correctly computed late dates requires two steps: (1) users may create a milestone with a fixed date that is one day *later* than the fixed date; and (2) the milestone is joined to each of its predecessors in an end-to-end relationship, *subtracting* one day from the end of each predecessor. (Figure A4.6) The correct late dates are computed and stored in each of the late total start and late total finish fields. The early finish date of the project may only be found in the early finish date of the last task(s) in the project that occur before the fixed-date milestone. The highlights of the critical path are lost. The system will not recognize a critical path of greater than zero.

APPENDIX 4.7 ADDING RESOURCES

Appendix 4.7.1 Creating the Resource Calendars (8.8)

Time Line 3.0 does not support resource calendars. Setting part-time resources at the project level will be addressed later.

Appendix 4.7.2 Creating the Resource Pool (8.9)

In Time Line 3.0, resources may be individuals or groups of individuals. Costs are defined as equipment or materials. Both are created using the same form, the Resource/Cost List screen. (See Figure A4.14.) The user must designate which choice is being made. Once the choice has been made, it is locked in as soon as resources have been assigned to jobs. Then, the choice may not be changed without first deleting *all* assignments. When the costs that are associated with

Figure A4.14

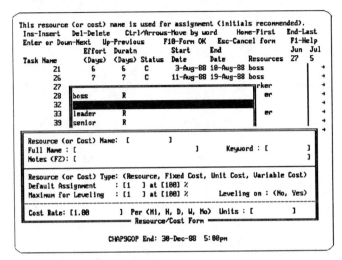

```
This resource (or cost) name is used for assignment (initials recommended).
Ins-Insert   Del-Delete   Ctrl/Arrows-Move by word     Home-First   End-Last
Enter or Down-Next  Up-Previous    F10-Form OK   Esc-Cancel form      F1-Help
                   Effort  Duratn          Start      End              Jun  Jul
Task Name          (Days)  (Days) Status   Date       Date  Resources  27   5
         21          6       6      C      3-Aug-88 10-Aug-88 boss            >
         26          7       7      C     11-Aug-88 19-Aug-88 boss            >
         27                                                   rker            >
         28 │boss         R                                   er              >
         32 │                                                                 >
         33 │leader       R                                   er              >
         39 │senior       R                                                   >

Resource (or Cost) Name: [          ]
Full Name : [                   ]       Keyword : [         ]
Notes (FZ): [                                                ]

Resource (or Cost) Type: (Resource, Fixed Cost, Unit Cost, Variable Cost)
Default Assignment    : [1  ] at [100] %
Maximum for Leveling  : [1  ] at [100] %       Leveling on : (No, Yes)

Cost Rate: [1.00     ] Per (Mi, H, D, W, Mo) Units : [       ]
───────────────────── Resource/Cost Form ─────────────────────

                  CHAP9GOP End: 30-Dec-88 5:00pm
```

a task are fixed costs or onetime costs, they may be entered as *fixed* costs, *unit* costs, or *variable* costs.

Time Line 3.0 allows 300 resources per project.

Resources are stored in the Resource/Cost List, which is accessed by pressing "/; Schedule; Resources; List". Then, the resource setup form is invoked by pressing the "Insert" key. The standard resource information to be entered at this time is: the 10-character resource code (to be used when assigning the resource to a phase, activity, or task), the full resource name, the units in which the resource is measured (hours, days, pounds), the cost per unit,[9] the work group category of the resource, and descriptive notes.

There are two resource availability numbers: the number of resources to automatically assign to a job (to be used later when assigning resources to jobs) and the maximum number of available resources of this type (to be used later during leveling). Although the default assignment number may be less than the leveling number, it can never be the other way around—the system will always raise the leveling number to be at least as high as the default assignment number.

The normal number of workhours per day that

the resource is available may also be entered in the resource form; however, it is entered as a percentage of each workday that the resource is available. If there is more than one resource in the group, this percentage will apply to the whole group, not just to one resource in the group.

Once the list has been completed, it may be reviewed at any time by pressing "/; Schedule; Resource; List". Resource data may be viewed by then moving the cursor to the designated resource and pressing the F2 key.

In addition to the standard resource data, this screen is also used to enter resource leveling directions.

Time Line 3.0 does not support multiple billing rates for one resource.

Appendix 4.7.3 Assigning Part-Time Resources at the Project Level (8.10)

In Time Line 3.0, part-time participation may be entered at the project level in the default assignment percentage of the Resource/Cost List screen. (Figure A4.14)

However, if, as recommended earlier, the task is *driven by duration*, the duration field of the corresponding tracking Detail Task screen will be multiplied by this fraction and the results will be placed in the effort field of the tracking Resource Assignment screen. (See Figure A4.15.) While the duration field stays the same, this operation *reduces* the resource effort, the opposite and incorrect result. Consequently, in this scenario, *driven by duration* is not the appropriate choice. Users will then need to override this value at each task level by making the task *effort driven* and then rekeying the correct *true work effort* into the effort field of the tracking Detail Task screen. (See the discussion on part-time at the task level later in this appendix.)

At the conclusion of the operation, the *true work effort* will be in the effort field of the tracking Detail Task screen and in the effort field of the tracking Resource Assignment screen. The correct elapsed calendar days will be in the duration field of the tracking Detail Task screen.

Because the system does not support resource calendars, it does not support varying levels of part-time participation.

---

[9]Based on the resource type selection (described above), the unit and cost per unit values may only be entered if resource type is *resource*, *unit cost*, or *variable cost*.

Figure A4.15

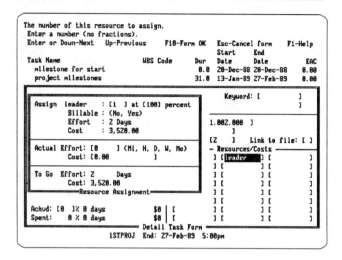

```
The number of this resource to assign.
Enter a number (no fractions).
Enter or Down-Next   Up-Previous      F10-Form OK   Esc-Cancel form    F1-Help
                                        Start    End
Task Name                  WBS Code   Dur   Date    Date          EAC
    milestone for start               8.0  20-Dec-88 20-Dec-88    0.00
    project milestones               31.0  13-Jan-89 27-Feb-89    0.00

                                          Keyword: [        ]
  Assign leader    : [1 ] at [100] percent              ]
         Billable : (No, Yes)
         Effort   : 2 Days                  1.002.000  ]
         Cost     : 3,528.00                          ]
                                           [2   ]   Link to file: [ ]
  Actual Effort: [0     ] (Mi, H, D, W, Mo)  - Resources/Costs
         Cost: [0.00          ]             ] [leader  ] [        ]
                                            ] [        ] [        ]
  To Go Effort: 2   Days                    ] [        ] [        ]
         Cost: 3,528.00                     ] [        ] [        ]
             Resource Assignment            ] [        ] [        ]
                                            ] [        ] [        ]
  Achvd: [0  ]% 0 days      $0  [           ] [        ] [        ]
  Spent:   0 % 0 days       $0  [           ] [        ] [        ]
                               Detail Task Form
                      1STPROJ  End: 27-Feb-89  5:00pm
```

Appendix 4.7.4 Deleting and Changing Resources at the Project Level (8.11)

Time Line 3.0 resources may not be deleted from the resource pool until all corresponding commitments have either been deleted or reassigned. Then, resources are deleted from the Resource/Cost List by pressing the "Delete" key. Before the removal is completed, the system asks the user for confirmation.

Names are changed in the same manner as other modifications. Changing a name results in a project-wide replacement of all occurrences of the old name with the new name.

Appendix 4.7.5 Matching Resources to Jobs (8.14)

Time Line 3.0 is unique in that it also allows the user to assign resources to summary jobs in the work breakdown structure as well as to tasks.

Time Line 3.0 allows 24 resource names or costs to be assigned to each task. Resource names are assigned on the tracking Detail Task screen (Figure A4.4), which must be accessed each time by pressing "/; Schedule; Task; Edit"[10]. Once the task form has been

called up, the "Tab" key is pressed twice (if using the standard Task screen) or four times (if using the tracking Detail Task screen) to get to the first resource field. Then, pressing the F2 key will call up a list of resource names. Moving the cursor to the desired resource and pressing the "Return" key completes the first half of the transaction. At this point, the tracking Resource Assignment screen will pop up and it is time for the second operation. The tracking Resource Assignment screen only requires the completion of two fields—if the standard Task screen is in use. In this window, the number of assigned resources and the percentage of available time are both entered. These default to the values defined in the Resource/Cost List, and they must not exceed the numbers in the Resource/Cost List or they will be rejected.

These fields are also in the tracking Resource Assignment screen that accompanies the tracking Detail Task screen. (Figure A4.15) Additionally, with this expanded tracking Resource Assignment screen, the user may tell the system if this resource on this task should be billable.

Displayed at the top of the Gantt chart is a list of the resources who are assigned to the job that is designated by the current cursor position.

In the Time Line 3.0 resource pool (Figure A4.14), there are two resource availability numbers: one for the default number to assign to a task and one for the leveling number.[11] In this product, if the assignment number in the task form exceeds the leveling number from the resource pool, it will be rejected with an error message. The user will be required to correct the assignment number in the task form or to change the leveling number in the resource pool.

Whenever users try to assign a resource name to a task for a second time, the system asks them if they really want to do it. To the extent that the entry does not exceed the leveling number, users may then override the assignment number from the pool.

Resources may not be assigned unless they have first been entered into the Resource/Cost List. When an undefined resource is assigned to a task, the system automatically invokes the Resource/Cost List. The user

---

[10]It would be nice if there were some way to scroll through these forms instead of repeating the four key strokes each time a new task needs to be recalled.

[11]Although the default assignment number may be less than the leveling number, it can never be the other way around —the system will always raise the leveling number to be at least as high as the default assignment number.

must then proceed in the usual fashion for entering a new resource.

At the project level, duration defaults should have been set to *driven by duration* (*true work effort*). If the integrity of the duration field is to be maintained, this setting should *not* be changed. When the resource effort is different than the task duration, special actions are required, which will be addressed later in this appendix.

Appendix 4.7.6 Assigning Part-Time Resources at the Task or Activity Level (8.15)

With *driven by* in the Time Line 3.0 tracking Detail Task screen set to *effort*, this system supports part-time at the task level. (Figure A4.4) The respective percentage value may be entered in the tracking Resource Assignment screen that pops up during resource assignment. The user will also need to key the correct *true work effort* into the *effort* field of the tracking Detail Task screen.

At the conclusion of the operation, the *true work effort* will also be in the *effort* field of the tracking Resource Assignment screen. The correct elapsed calendar days will be in the *duration* field of the tracking Detail Task screen.

Appendix 4.7.7 Assigning Multiple Resources to a Job (8.16)

In Time Line 3.0, additional resources are assigned to jobs following the directions described earlier in the appendix. (The assigned number of resources, of course, should not exceed the availability number in the Resource/Cost List. See Figure A4.14.)

If *driven by* in the tracking Detail Task screen is set to *duration*, parallel multiple resources require no special handling. However, *doubling up* calls for a new approach.

First, *driven by* in the tracking Detail Task screen must be set to *effort*. Then, adding multiple resources automatically results in the task duration being equally distributed between all resources. The right touch, the result is, for example, that a four-day duration will result in two days per resource *and* two elapsed calendar days in the duration field. (Time Line 3.0 automatically calculates the duration of the job from the number of resources assigned to it.) Thus, the system

automatically adjusts the effort fields to allow the job to get finished sooner. This greatly simplifies the implementation of Example 5.

In Example 6, the work for each resource cannot be evenly distributed. Time Line 3.0 does not support this case. Although there is a *work-around* for it, adding multiple resources in this situation is not a straightforward exercise:

> To start, *driven by* in the tracking Detail Task screen must be set to *duration*. The user must next compute the elapsed calendar days and enter the value in the duration field. After the multiple resources have been assigned, the value for their effort must be corrected by altering their percentage participation in the tracking Resource Assignment screen. (Figure A4.15) However, this approach can only be used when the number of new elapsed calendar days is an even integer and the percentage values break into an even number of segments. When this is not true, the resulting effort for the resource may wind up a fractional value.

In the above examples, the *true work effort* for each resource will be in the effort field of the tracking Resource Assignment screen. (Figure A4.15) The effort field in the tracking Detail Task screen will contain the total of all of the resource efforts. The correct elapsed calendar days will be in the duration field of the tracking Detail Task screen.

Appendix 4.7.8 What To Do When the Resource Effort Must Be Less than the Elapsed Calendar Days (8.17)

In Example 1, the *true work effort* must be distributed across an elapsed calendar time. Time Line 3.0 does not support this case. Although there is a *work-around* for it, it is not a straightforward exercise nor does it work in all cases:

> To start, *driven by* in the tracking Detail Task screen must be set to *duration*. The user must next compute the elapsed calendar days and enter the value in the duration field. After the resource has been assigned, the value for his or her effort must be corrected by altering the corresponding percentage participation in the tracking Resource Assignment screen. (Figure A4.15) However, this approach can only be used when

the number of new elapsed calendar days is an even integer and the percentage value breaks into an even number of segments. When this is not true, the resulting effort for the resource may wind up a fractional value.

Conversely, the scenario in Example 2 is very simple to implement. Leaving the *driven by* field set to *duration*, the user must only change the corresponding percentage field in the tracking Resource Assignment screen.

Time Line 3.0 does not support Example 3.

Appendix 4.7.9 Fixed Dates for Activities Or Tasks *(8.19)*

Time Line 3.0 does not use the scheduling algorithm that highlights projects that are late before they start.

Fixed dates may be entered at any level in the work breakdown structure. They are entered on the tracking Detail Task screen which is invoked by pressing "/; Schedule; Task, Edit". Task types in this form may be fixed, ASAP (as soon as possible), or ALAP (as late as possible). The system defaults to ASAP. If ALAP is selected, this action will cause the task to be scheduled at the very end of the candidate time slice. While this does not extend the project end date, it can easily create a new critical path.

If fixed is selected, the user may enter either the fixed start date or the fixed end date. The system computes the alternate.

Time Line 3.0 reports one set of early dates, the start and end dates; it also reports two sets of late dates, depending on free slack or total slack. (See the discussion later in this appendix.) There is also one field for reporting fixed start dates. Whenever a fixed date is entered into a task, the early dates and both sets of late dates will be set to the same value, creating a zero slack status for the task. The late dates of the affected task's predecessors are also recalculated. As a result of these operations, the task with a fixed date and *all* of its predecessors are forced onto the critical path, resulting in what may appear to be a *dangling* piece of the critical path.

During scheduling, fixed dates will be set at either their designated date or after the latest finish date of their predecessors, whichever is later.

If the new fixed date of the affected task is the same as its system-generated dates, all of its dates will be set to the system-generated dates. The dates of its successors will remain unchanged. The late dates of its predecessors will be recomputed, but their early dates will remain unchanged. This may change the slack of the predecessors as well as the status of the critical path.

If the new fixed date of the affected task is earlier than its system-generated dates, its dates will *not* be changed to the earlier value, but they will all be set to the original system-generated early dates. Furthermore, the late dates of its predecessors may be recomputed, but their early dates will remain unchanged. This may change the slack of the predecessors as well as the status of the critical path. The dates of its successors will remain unchanged.

If the new fixed date of the affected task is later than its system-generated dates, all of its dates will be set based on this value. The late dates of its predecessors will be recomputed, but their early dates will remain unchanged. Likewise, all of the dates of any affected successors will be recomputed. These operations may change the slack of all of the affected jobs as well as the status of the critical path.

Inside the Gantt chart, the system flags fixed jobs where they are delayed by their predecessor(s). The flag is scaled to show the amount of delay. Since the date changes result in the affected tasks being set to zero slack, all fixed-date tasks are automatically considered part of the critical path. Similarly, any predecessor that delays a fixed job automatically is considered part of the critical path.

If the late finish date of the project is entered into a fixed-date milestone, the late dates of all of the predecessors will be correctly computed.

Appendix 4.7.10 Automatic Resource Leveling *(8.30)*

Before Time Line 3.0 leveling can be called in, each resource must have leveling set to *Yes* on the respective Resource/Cost List screen. (See Figure A4.14. This value may safely be entered when establishing the resource pool; it will have no effect on schedules until the next step is executed.) The leveling process itself may be invoked by pressing "/, Schedule; Option" and setting resource leveling to *Yes*. (Figure A4.2)

The system checks the number of times the same

Figure A4.16

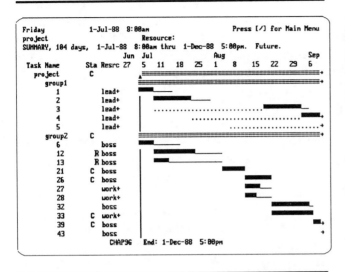

Figure A4.17

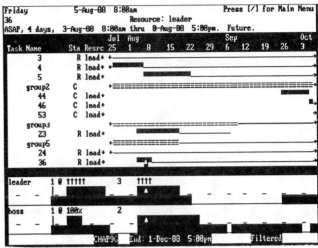

resource name has been assigned to a task. If that number exceeds the maximum number for leveling that was entered into the Resource/Cost List screen, leveling will be aborted and the user will be requested to change either the tracking Detail Task assignment or the Resource/Cost List.

Time Line 3.0 schedules critical tasks and critical milestones before tasks with slack. The leveled dates will be in the start date and end date fields. All effects of leveling may simply be erased by returning to the Options screen and turning leveling to *No*.

Tasks that have been delayed as a result of leveling will have a small letter "r" in the fourth position of the status code field. They will also have a dotted line to the left of the Gantt chart task bar, starting at the date on which the job could have started had there not been a resource conflict. (See Figure A4.16.)

Appendix 4.7.11 Setting Special Leveling Priorities on Tasks Or Activities (8.31)

In Time Line 3.0, priorities are only used whenever two are more tasks are competing for the same resource(s). When there are resource conflicts, the system checks the priority code in the tracking Detail Task screen and schedules the task with the highest priority first. (Figure A4.4) The highest priority field in the Project Options screen (Figure A4.2) may be used to set either 0 or 999.9 as the highest priority. Task-level

priorities are set in the priorities field of the tracking Detail Task screen. Time Line 3.0 does not support priorities at the higher levels in the work breakdown structure.

Appendix 4.7.12 User-Driven Interactive Leveling (8.32)

Resource histograms in Time Line 3.0 may be displayed by pressing ''/; Schedule; Resource; Histogram'' and selecting the desired resource name. To help find available time on another resource, up to five histograms can be displayed at one time. (See Figure A4.17.)

The vertical axis on the histogram relates to the number of assigned resources; the scale on the horizontal axis is connected to the Gantt chart scale. The height of each column in the histogram shows the level of commitment. With a horizontal line drawn across the histogram at the corresponding vertical axis level, the histogram also implicitly shows available resource levels.

Users may choose their own color schemes for the histogram. For example, resource utilization that stays within limits of availability may be displayed in red, underutilization may be blank, and overscheduling may be displayed in orange.

The vertical axis scale of the Time Line 3.0 histogram often does not go all the way up to the maximum overutilization number. However, as the user horizontally moves the cursor through the histogram, Time Line 3.0 displays a resource utilization number that is equivalent to the exact amount of resource scheduling (over, equal, under) for that date.

Histograms always share the screen with the Gantt chart. So that users may later evaluate the impacts of their leveling process, they are advised to suppress as much of the columnar data and display as much of the Gantt as possible. This is an easy operation:

> For example, creating a user-driven leveling layout ("/; Schedule; Layout") by only selecting a short name field plus a 3-position status field provides the necessary columnar data and also allows the majority of the screen for the Gantt task bars. Resource conflicts are illustrated with a capital "R" in the third column of the status field. The "Layout" options ought to also be set up to position the task bars at the original dates and to display the slack. It is not possible to show leveling delays on the Gantt chart unless the automatic leveling has been executed.

Similarly, the critical path should be highlighted with a special filter. This is done by pressing "/; Schedule; Filter; Highlight; Critical path".

The actual number of tasks that can be seen in the Gantt chart will depend, not on the layout, but on how many histograms are being displayed—the more histograms, the fewer tasks displayed on the Gantt.

When the histogram is being displayed along with the Gantt, there are two cursors (one in the Gantt and one in the histogram), and they both move horizontally in synchronization. On the other hand, the cursor in the Gantt chart is the only one that can be moved vertically.

Time Line 3.0 is one of the products that allows users to limit the tasks displayed in the Gantt chart to those relating to just one resource. This requires that a second filter be invoked, a process that is completed by pressing "/; Schedule; Filter; Select" and entering the resource name in the keyword field.

This histogram does not show weekends and holidays.

Time Line 3.0 is a fully-interactive leveling system. Tasks can be shifted in the Gantt chart simply by changing the predecessor/successor relationships. Other types of date changes, durations, resource reas-

signments, resource assignment deleting[12] and job splitting are made in the tracking Detail Task screen. New tasks and their resource assignments are added by pressing "/; Schedule; Task; Add". Overtime and part-time changes at the task level are made in the tracking Resource Assignment screen. (Figure A4.15) Project-level resource availability may be changed in the Resource/Cost List screen. (Figure A4.14) Resources may be added to the Resource/Cost List by pressing "/; Schedule; Resources; List; Insert". Time Line 3.0 does not support resource lags.

Sometimes, while working in one resource mode, it will be necessary to get a global view of the whole project. The filters will then need to be removed (by pressing "/; Schedule; Filter; Clear"). To get back to one resource mode, both of the filters will need to be reinstituted.

Another aspect of interactive leveling is to control the system-generated leveling by restricting which resources are subject to the automated leveling process. This restrictive leveling of resources can be turned on or off at will in the corresponding Resources/Cost List by toggling the field for leveling to *on* (if the resource should be subject to leveling) or to *Off* (if the resource should be excluded from the leveling process).

Appendix 4.7.13 Baseline Project Plans for Resource Leveling (8.34)

Time Line 3.0 supports one version of a baseline. By saving the optimal plan as the baseline for the resource-constrained plan that is selected for implementation, users have half of the requirements met. This version is archived, and a second version is produced. Then, by saving the resource-constrained plan as the baseline for the plan to which progress will be posted, the other half of the requirements will be met. Unfortunately, this *work-around* does not provide comparisons between all three versions. However, albeit the process is cumbersome, users may assimilate the data by perusing both sets of reports.

---

[12]The original resource name must be deleted before a new resource assignment can be made.

Appendix 4.7.14 Resources, Multiprojects, and Project Management Software (8.35.4)

There are no resource calendars in Time Line 3.0. *Template* resource files can be copied from schedule to schedule by pressing "/; File; Combine; Resources/Costs". This action may also be used to import resources from several subschedules into a master schedule, adding them to the master schedule Resource/Cost List—if they are not already present. When there are duplicate resources in both the master schedule and the subschedule, users will be asked to specify whether the *combine* policy is to keep the existing resource or to overwrite the original with the new. This is a personal preference.

Combining subschedules, as opposed to *linking* them, brings in all of the jobs from a plan, merging them into the master schedule. When they have been successfully imported into the master schedule, the subschedule will be found at the bottom of the Gantt under a heading that is at the highest outline level. This heading is "Summary of", followed by the subschedule name. Moving the cursor to the heading and pressing the "—" key will close the outline and cause the whole subschedule to be represented by a single one-line entry in the Gantt chart and the PERT chart.

Filters, layouts, and journal notes may also be imported with the "File Combine". If the filter references a resource and there is no corresponding resource in the Resource/Cost List, the system will drop the resource from the filter. Consequently, filters should be only combined *after* the resources have been imported.

Because this is a merge process, maintaining the original *and* merged copies of the subschedules may later require double data entry.

Since all of the subschedules are merged into one project, the other issues in this section are inapplicable.

Using the Time Line 3.0 "File Link". With the "File Link", the whole subschedule is represented by a single one-line entry in the Gantt chart and the PERT chart. It also brings in resources, adding them to the master schedule Resource/Cost List—if they are not already present. When there are duplicate resources in both the master schedule and the subschedule, the resource record in the master schedule is retained and the resource data in the subschedule is ignored. Consequently, users ought to choose carefully the first subproject to be linked—since that may be the source of permanent resource data.

Each resource commitment is *averaged* across each day of the master schedule. In other words, the resource commitment is spread evenly across the total number of working days in the master schedule. Furthermore, the master schedule histogram will *not* show any overcommitment—no matter how much overcommitment occurs in the subschedules.

Since no overscheduling is established, there is no value to performing automatic leveling from the master schedule in an attempt to level the resources across all subschedules. On the other hand, subschedules that have themselves been leveled are reflected up one rung into the master schedule. (This is not true with nested subschedules.) Resource commitments are also carried up one notch; but interpreting overcommitment is meaningless.

There is no need to do double data entry with the "File Link". Changes made in the subschedules are automatically reflected in the master schedule.

Appendix 4.7.15 Guidelines and Documentation (8.36)

Time Line 3.0 has a few pages on resource management.

APPENDIX 4.8 CALCULATING COSTS

Appendix 4.8.1 Costs and Project Mangement Software (9.4)

In addition to the codes for a work breakdown structure and an organizational breakdown structure that are found on the tracking Detail Task screen, Time Line 3.0 also supports reporting on a keyword field.

There are four types of costs that may be entered into the Resource/Cost List screen: *resource* cost, *variable* cost, *unit* cost, *fixed* cost. (Figure A4.14) Depending on the type selected from the list, a different assignment form will be invoked. When resource or variable is chosen, the tracking Resource Assignment screen is displayed. (Figure A4.15) For fixed costs, a fixed cost assignment form is called up. Unit costs also have their own assignment form. These forms are similar to the tracking Resource Assignment screen.

Fixed costs are entered as a dollar amount. The type is defined in the Resource/Cost List screen, but the value may be different in each task.

Unit costs are entered in the Resource/Cost List screen with a unit cost rate, unit metric value, default number, and maximum number.

Variable costs are entered just like resource costs.

Once assignments have been made, the cost type can't be changed until all assignments have been deleted.

There are no on-line cost graphics in this product. However, the Gantt layout can be customized to many views of costs. Since cost data is found in the layout fields and the fields for the "Cross Tab" reports, almost any view can be seen, depending on how the user formats the corresponding reports.

Task-level data and resource data are accessible on cross tab reports. All costs are rolled up into the summary level tasks so the summary reflects the costs of its children (plus any of its own associated costs). Thus, the column totals reflect the sum of the costs reported at the summary levels. When users wish to be able to enter costs but not have them included as part of the total project costs, this product allows the assignment to be designated as nonbillable.

The system also reports on baseline data such as the *baseline billable* (if the resource was assigned as billable in the baseline) and the *baseline total dollars* (the total dollars assigned in the baseline for the resource or cost).

Time Line 3.0 will export project data to LOTUS 1-2-3.

Appendix 4.8.2 Costs in a Multiproject Environment (9.5)

Time Line 3.0 costs are carried up from all levels of subschedules. However, if the resource is defined in different schedules at different rates, the system offers the option to specify if the first definition should rule or should be overwritten. This may mean that, as a consequence, the cost information may not be summarized accurately. If the rates must be different, users should avoid using the same name for resources in two schedules.

APPENDIX 4.9 COMPRESSING TIME

Appendix 4.9.1 Time-Constrained Plans and Project Management Software (10.9)

In Time Line 3.0, other than fixing the end date of the project, there are no special requirements for leveling in a time-constrained environment. Users may produce reports sorted on free slack and total slack.

APPENDIX 4.10 ASSIGNING THE WORK

Appendix 4.10.1 The Assignment Report (11.1)

Although Time Line 3.0 provides a standard report, called the "Status" report that contains all of the columns necessary for the resource assignment report, it cannot select the data so that it is limited to a given resource. It can only print all of the jobs for all of the resources.

This is not a serious problem, however. Time Line 3.0 makes it very easy to develop customized reports. (See Figure A4.18.)

1. The Gantt chart screen should first be filtered so that it only displays the jobs for the selected resource. This is done by pressing "/; Schedule; Filter; Select; Insert", moving the cursor to the resources field, pressing F2, and selecting the *resource name as it appears in the Resources/Cost List*.

2. The Gantt chart layout may then be set up for the assignment report by pressing "/; Schedule; Layout; Insert" and choosing the required columns. From among the choices, the user may select the task name, the task identifier, the start date, the finish date, and the duration. The layout may (or may not, depending on the printer paper width) be set up to display (or repress) the task bars.

3. This report may be printed by pressing "/; Reports; Gantt".

Appendix 4.10.2 The Ad Hoc Information (11.2)

The system supports several 6,000 character notes fields and journal entries that may be edited with the Time Line 3.0 mini word processor.

Figure A4.18

Schedule Name : chap9
Responsible   :
As-of Date   : 1-Jul-88 8:00am   Schedule File : C:\TL3\DATA\CHAP9G

this is the notes field for the project.

Select filter : boss

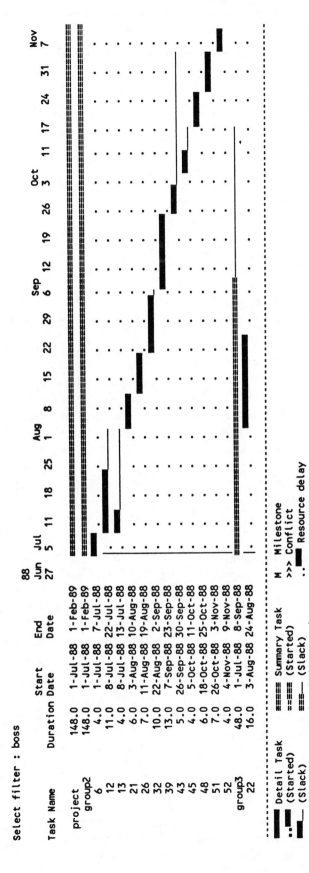

Task Name	Duration	Start Date	End Date
project	148.0	1-Jul-88	1-Feb-89
group2	148.0	1-Jul-88	1-Feb-89
6	4.0	1-Jul-88	7-Jul-88
12	11.0	8-Jul-88	22-Jul-88
13	4.0	8-Jul-88	13-Jul-88
21	6.0	3-Aug-88	10-Aug-88
26	7.0	11-Aug-88	19-Aug-88
32	10.0	22-Aug-88	2-Sep-88
39	13.0	7-Sep-88	23-Sep-88
43	5.0	26-Sep-88	30-Sep-88
45	4.0	5-Oct-88	11-Oct-88
48	6.0	18-Oct-88	25-Oct-88
51	7.0	26-Oct-88	3-Nov-88
52	4.0	4-Nov-88	9-Nov-88
group3	48.0	1-Jul-88	8-Sep-88
22	16.0	3-Aug-88	24-Aug-88

▆▆ Detail Task   ▦▦▦ Summary Task   M Milestone
▪▪▪ (Started)   =▦▦ (Started)   >>> Conflict
▪▄ (Slack)   ▦▦ (Slack)   ▪▪ ▆ Resource delay
------- Scale: 1 day per character

TIME LINE Gantt Chart Report, Strip 1, Page 1

Figure A4.19

```
Schedule Name : chap9
Responsible   :
As-of Date    : 1-Jul-88  8:00am    Schedule File : C:\TL3\DATA\CHAP9G

this is the notes field for the project.


Select filter : boss


Task Name  Notes

  project  this is the notes field for the project.
    group
        6  this is the free form notes field for job 6.  it has an
       12  this is the free form notes field for job 12.  all of the
       13  all of the resources in this exercise are the "BOSS".  this


TIME LINE Gantt Chart Report, Strip 1, Page 1
```

A layout may be defined to print a report that displays the notes fields. In the Layout screen, however, the maximum number of characters for this field is limited to 80 characters. (See Figure A4.19.) The number of characters actually printed on the report is further constrained by the number of print positions on the page and how many other fields are also being printed on the report. (The maximum number of print positions, in Compressed mode, is 150.)

These journal notes may be saved to an ASCII file and subsequently edited with a word processor.

Appendix 4.10.3 The Work Package Cover Sheet (11.5)

In Time Line 3.0, a word processor may be used to edit and print the notes and journals that meet this requirement.

Appendix 4.10.4 The Responsibility Grid (11.6)

In Time Line 3.0, a word processor may be used to edit and print the notes and journals that meet this requirement.

Appendix 4.10.5 The Supporting Documentation (11.8)

After setting up the Time Line 3.0 filter criteria as described earlier in this appendix, the user may print a resource-limited Gantt by pressing "/; Reports; Gantt". (Figure A4.16)

The resource histogram may also be printed. (Figure A4.17) However, while the amount of resource utilization will be displayed, the number of actual available resources will not.

There are several standard "Cross Tab" reports. Initially, the user may be drawn to using one of these reports, the "Resources vs. Time" report. However, this report does not respond to filtering. (See the earlier discussion.) It will print *all* of the jobs for all of the resources in the schedule. This is not a problem, because another report, the "Task vs. Time" report, does respond to filtering. (See Figure A4.20.) It may be used to produce a tabular resource loading report by pressing "/; Report; Cross Tab" and then choosing "Task vs. Time" twice in succession. The operation is completed by choosing "Report on: Resources" and entering "Total man days" in the report data field.

Appendix 4.10.6 The Problem Log (11.10)

In Time Line 3.0, a word processor may be used to edit and print the notes and journals that meet this requirement.

Appendix 4.10.7 The Work Notes Form (11.11)

In Time Line 3.0, a word processor may be used to edit and print the notes and journals that meet this requirement.

Figure A4.20

```
Schedule Name : chap9
Responsible   :
As-of Date    : 1-Jul-88  8:00am     Schedule File : C:\TL3\DATA\CHAP9G
```

	8-Aug-88	9-Aug-88	10-Aug-88	1-Sep-88	Total
project	2	2	2	1	57 *
group2	1	1	1	1	41
6					4
12					11
13					4
21	1	1	1		6
26					7
32				1	9
39					0
43					0
45					0
48					0
51					0
52					0
group3		1	1	1	16
22		1	1	1	16
Total	2	2	2	1	57 *

TIME LINE Task vs Time Report showing Total ManDays, Strip 4

Appendix 4.10.8 Viewing the Data on the Screen (11.12)

Time Line 3.0 allows the user to display the reports in hard copy or on the screen.

APPENDIX 4.11 REPORTING STATUS

Appendix 4.11.1 Baselines (12.2)

In Time Line 3.0, the baseline information is in fields called baseline.

Appendix 4.11.2 Extracting the Jobs for the Turn-around Document—on a Range of Dates (12.5)

Each Time Line 3.0 report has a report form that allows the user to select on a range of dates. (See Figure A4.21.) When attempting to display the Gantt report, the layout must have "Show task bars = yes" in order for the report form to allow the option of date ranges.

Appendis 4.11.3 Setting Up an As-Of Date (12.6)

The Time Line 3.0 As-of date in the Project Options screen (Figure A4.2) may be modified to choose "Manual" and then to show the current status date. However, if this field is changed before entering the progress data, all kinds of strange modifications to the task date fields results. Users are advised to enter their status data first and then bring this field up to date by setting this value to one day later.

Appendix 4.11.4 Entering Percent Complete (12.7)

The percentage fields in Time Line 3.0 are directly linked to the baseline values. This means that any percentages reflect the percent of the amount originally planned. For example, if the duration of a task needs to be changed, and then time is subsequently reported to that task, the percentage will not reflect a value

Figure A4.21

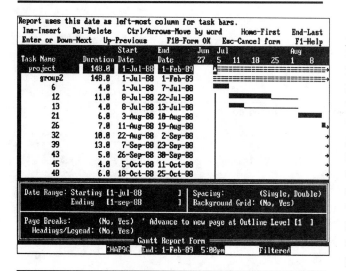

```
Report uses this date as left-most column for task bars.
Ins-Insert   Del-Delete   Ctrl/Arrows-Move by word   Home-First   End-Last
Enter or Down-Next   Up-Previous   F10-Form OK   Esc-Cancel form   F1-Help
                             Start      End      Jun  Jul               Aug
Task Name       Duration Date        Date      27    5   11  18  25   1    8
  project          148.0  1-Jul-88  1-Feb-89
    group2         148.0  1-Jul-88  1-Feb-89
      6              4.0   1-Jul-88  7-Jul-88
      12            11.0   8-Jul-88  22-Jul-88
      13             4.0   8-Jul-88  13-Jul-88
      21             6.0   3-Aug-88  10-Aug-88
      26             7.0  11-Aug-88  19-Aug-88
      32            10.0  22-Aug-88   2-Sep-88
      39            13.0   7-Sep-88  23-Sep-88
      43             5.0  26-Sep-88  30-Sep-88
      45             4.0   5-Oct-88  11-Oct-88
      48             6.0  18-Oct-88  25-Oct-88
Date Range: Starting [1-jul-88    ]  Spacing:          (Single, Double)
            Ending   [1-sep-88    ]  Background Grid: (No, Yes)
Page Breaks:        (No, Yes)  ' Advance to new page at Outline Level [1  ]
Headings/Legend: (No, Yes)
                          Gantt Report Form
            CHAP9G  End: 1-Feb-89  5:00pm        Filtered
```

based on how much progress has been made against the new duration but, rather, how much progress has been made against the old duration. This is very helpful in earned value analysis. On the other hand, if the user is trying to measure *actual progress* by percentages, the system is limited in its ability to aid in the management of the project. Yet, from the perspective of the zero percent—one hundred percent status philosophy presented in this text, Time Line's application of this feature is not a serious detriment.

Furthermore, in addressing status reporting (later in this appendix), another use of percentage will be presented. This additional application will require the use of the percentage *or* the remaining duration. By allowing the user to choose remaining duration, this product supports *effort to go* and any residual objection to percentage concepts have been removed.

There are two percentage fields: the percent of the *spent resource effort* and the percent of the *duration achieved*. While the percent of the spent resource effort is automatically computed by the system as soon as any actual time is reported to the task, the percent of duration achieved is treated differently. Values may be entered by the user in this field—or it may be left blank until the task is completed. The system does nothing with this field until the job is done. Then, it is automatically set to 100 percent. In the meantime, users may enter a number that reflects one of the percent methods described earlier in this section.

Appendix 4.11.5 Hard Copy Turn-around Documents *(12.8)*

A Time Line 3.0 layout for a turn-around document may be created. This layout may easily be filtered on resource name and extracted on a range of dates. The report may display the name, the original duration, the start date, the finish date, and the resource effort. (See Figure A4.22.) Then, the spent duration and to go duration fields may also be displayed. Since the resource may have to enter data in these last two fields, the layout should be set up so the columns are wide enough for write-ins. Finally, a large column of spaces will have to be inserted in the report to enable the resource who is reporting status to write in the actual start date and actual finish date. (The layout doesn't provide for selection on these fields.)

Appendix 4.11.6 Entering the Status Collection Data *(12.9)*

Time Line 3.0 has a unique feature called the *alarm clock*. It is set in the Options screen. (Figure A4.2) The alarm clock frees the user from searching for all of the tasks that need status updates. When the schedule has been saved and retrieved with the alarm clock set to *On*, each task that should have been started or finished by the *As-of* date will be displayed one at a time. The user may bypass updating the task or may invoke the tracking Detail Task screen to enter the status information. (Figure A4.4)

Progress data is entered task by task by task from the tracking Detail Task screen. First, the status field is changed to either *started* or *done*.

If *done* is entered into the status field, the system will automatically enter the actual start date and the actual finish date. Each of these fields will be filled in with their original start and finish values. The user may override these values. The percent of the duration achieved will be set to 100 percent. Entering *done* does not update the spent resource effort and the percentage of the spent resource effort. This will have to be done by the user.

If *started* is entered into the status field, the system will automatically enter the actual start date with the original start value. The user may override this value. The percent of the duration achieved will not be touched. Similarly, entering *started* does not update

Figure A4.22

Schedule Name : chap9
Responsible :
As-of Date : 12-Jul-88 8:00am   Schedule File : C:\TL3\DATA\CHAP9GBA

this is the notes field for the project.

Select filter : worker

Task Name	Dur	Start Date	End Date	Eff Days	Spent Duration	To Go Duration
project	****	1-Jul-8	1-Feb-8	****	6.0	142.0
group2	****	1-Jul-8	1-Feb-8	****	6.0	142.0
27	4.0	18-Aug-8	23-Aug-8	4	0.0	4.0
28	3.0	18-Aug-8	22-Aug-8	3	0.0	3.0
33	****	29-Aug-8	13-Sep-8	****	0.0	11.0
47	6.0	13-Oct-8	20-Oct-8	6	0.0	6.0
group3	****	1-Jul-8	15-Sep-8	****	6.0	47.0
8	2.0	1-Jul-8	5-Jul-8	2	2.0	0.0
8 1/2	1.0	12-Jul-8	12-Jul-8	1	0.0	1.0
14	4.0	13-Jul-8	18-Jul-8	4	0.0	4.0
49	****	1-Sep-8	15-Sep-8	****	0.0	10.0
group4	****	1-Jul-8	22-Aug-8	****	6.0	30.0
9	1.0	1-Jul-8	1-Jul-8	1	1.0	0.0
9 1/2	1.0	12-Jul-8	12-Jul-8	1	0.0	1.0
16	1.0	13-Jul-8	13-Jul-8	1	0.0	1.0
17	8.0	14-Jul-8	25-Jul-8	8	0.0	8.0

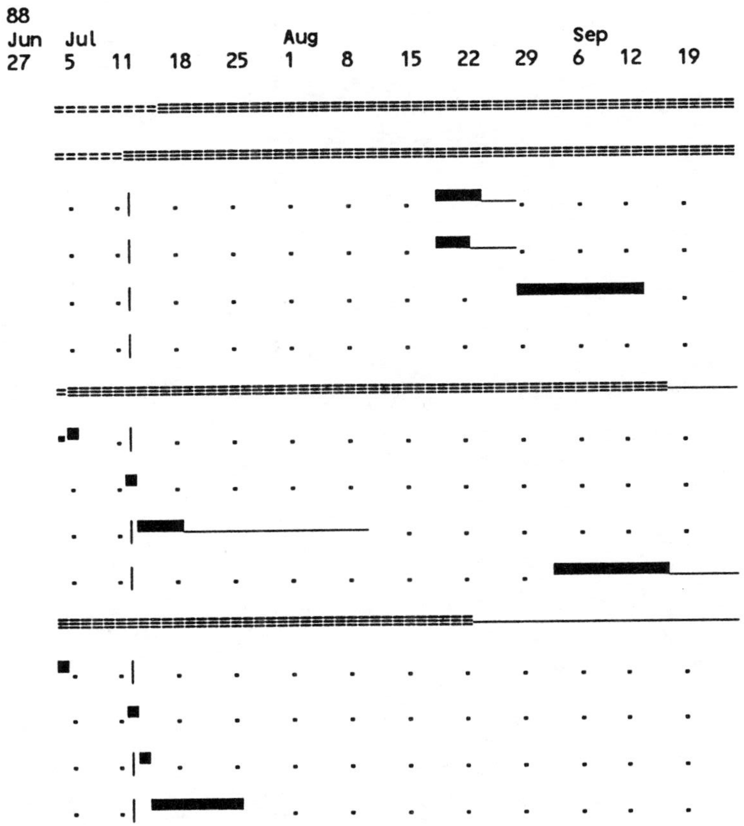

Timescale: 88 Jun 27 | Jul 5 | 11 | 18 | 25 | Aug 1 | 8 | 15 | 22 | 29 | Sep 6 | 12 | 19

Legend:
Detail Task   ===== Summary Task   M Milestone
.:= (Started)   ==== (Started)   >>> Conflict
(Slack)   === (Slack)   . Resource delay
-------- Scale: 1 day per character

TIME LINE Gantt Chart Report, Strip 1, Page 2

367

the spent resource effort and the percentage of the spent resource effort. This will have to be done by the user. (See the following discussion.)

The system does not support time-this-period. The *actual spent resource effort* represents the total time-to-date and must be manually computed by the user. To enter actual spent resource effort, the tracking Resource Assignment screen will need to be invoked. (Figure A4.15) An entry in the actual effort field causes the percentage of the spent resource effort field to be automatically updated.

For most of the transactions illustrated in Figure 12.1, three actions were required: entering a status of *started*, invoking the tracking Resource Assignment screen, and entering actual spent resource effort. Occasionally a start or finish date must be changed or a duration must be modified.

Special processing. For certain of the transactions illustrated in Figure 12.1, special handling is necessary.

Because the system cannot always handle situations in which the elapsed time is greater than the *true work effort*, three jobs (H, I, and X) each had to be split into *two smaller tasks*—with the first task representing the part of the work that had been completed and the second task representing the unfinished work. Furthermore, it was not possible to get all of the correct dates entered for these three jobs.

- In Job H, the duration was changed to 2. The actual start date was correct (July 1) but the actual finish date was not (July 5). It is not possible to mark this task *done* because the system will credit it with the original four days of effort. As it stands, the job is credited with 50 percent of the spent resource effort. It is not possible to enter 100 percent for the achieved percentage because the system will again credit the whole four days.

- A second job needed to be created for the rest of Job H. This task had a one-day duration. Next, the dependency between the first H task and the second H task had to be set up so that the second started four days after the first. In this way, the start and finish date of the second was correct (July 12).

- Finally, in order that the correct dates be computed for the rest of the schedule, the original relationships between H and its successors must be deleted. These

relationships must now be between the new job and the old H's successors.

This same process must be repeated for I and X.

A similar situation also existed for L. However, the relationship between the two jobs must be set up so that from the finish of the original L, one day is subtracted and then the new second half of L is started. The finish date of the new job will be correct (July 20), but its start date will be wrong (July 6).

A similar situation also existed for M. However, it could be handled with the *work-around* described earlier in this appendix for situations when the elapsed time is greater than the *true work effort* and the resource effort is an exact percentage of the original duration.[13]

- In Job M, the duration was changed to 8, the resource percentage was changed to "1 @ 50%", and the actual effort of two days was entered. The correct start and finish dates were computed and the correct percentages were computed.

Appendix 4.11.7 Performance Status Reporting (12.10)

A Time Line 3.0 layout may be created that displays the name, the original duration, the start and finish date, the late dates, spent effort, the to go effort, and the total slack. (See Figure A4.23.) Optionally, the percentage fields may also be displayed. The layout can be saturated with columnar data, or it can be set up to show the Gantt as well. Since this system does not distinguish between start dates and actual dates, there is no selection for these fields. Successors may only be seen on the network chart.

Time Line 3.0 features filtering and sorting on many fields. The sort may be in ascending or descending order. There is only one level of the sort. If a

---

[13]H, I, and X cannot be handled with this approach because the duration is not an even number of days and/or the resource percentage is not an exact portion of the duration. For example, in Job I, 2 days of effort doesn't divide evenly into seven elapsed days (28.57 percent). $7 \times 28\% = 1.96$ resource effort days and $7 \times 29\% = 2.03$ resource days. Using either of these makes the costs to the project inaccurate.

Figure A4.23

Schedule Name : chap9
Responsible   :
As-of Date   : 12-Jul-88 8:00am   Schedule File : C:\TL3\DATA\CHAP9GBA

this is the notes field for the project.

Select filter : worker

Gantt chart timeline scale (Scale: 1 day per character), year 88:

Jun 27 | Jul 5 | 11 | 18 | 25 | Aug 1 | 8 | 15 | 22 | 29

Task Name	Dur	Start Date	End Date	Eff Spen Days	To G Dur	LtTotl Dur	LtTotl End	TlSlack (Days)	Baseline End Date
project	****	1-Jul-8	1-Feb-8	****	6.0	****	1-Feb-8	0	1-Feb-89
group5	****	1-Jul-8	24-Aug-8	****	6.0	****	18-Jan-8	100	17-Aug-88
40	3.0	16-Aug-8	18-Aug-8	0.0	3	3.0	13-Jan-8	101	11-Aug-88
41	4.0	16-Aug-8	19-Aug-8	0.0	4	4.0	13-Jan-8	100	12-Aug-88
10	4.0	1-Jul-8	7-Jul-8	4	4.0	0.0	7-Jul-8	0	7-Jul-88
group4	****	1-Jul-8	22-Aug-8	****	6.0	****	13-Jan-8	99	15-Aug-88
34	8.0	9-Aug-8	18-Aug-8	8	8.0	0.0	13-Jan-8	101	11-Aug-88
35	****	9-Aug-8	22-Aug-8	****	0.0	****	13-Jan-8	99	15-Aug-88
30	2.0	5-Aug-8	8-Aug-8	2	2.0	0.0	30-Dec-8	99	1-Aug-88
29	3.0	5-Aug-8	9-Aug-8	3	3.0	0.0	4-Oct-8	39	2-Aug-88
18	8.0	26-Jul-8	4-Aug-8	8	8.0	0.0	29-Sep-8	39	28-Jul-88
17	8.0	14-Jul-8	25-Jul-8	8	8.0	0.0	19-Sep-8	39	18-Jul-88
16	1.0	13-Jul-8	13-Jul-8	1	1.0	0.0	7-Sep-8	39	6-Jul-88
9 1/2	1.0	12-Jul-8	12-Jul-8	1	1.0	0.0	6-Sep-8	39	6-Jul-88
9	1.0	1-Jul-8	1-Jul-8	1	1.0	0.0	26-Aug-8	39	5-Jul-88
group3	****	1-Jul-8	15-Sep-8	****	6.0	****	21-Dec-8	65	8-Sep-88
49	****	1-Sep-8	15-Sep-8	****	0.0	****	21-Dec-8	65	8-Sep-88

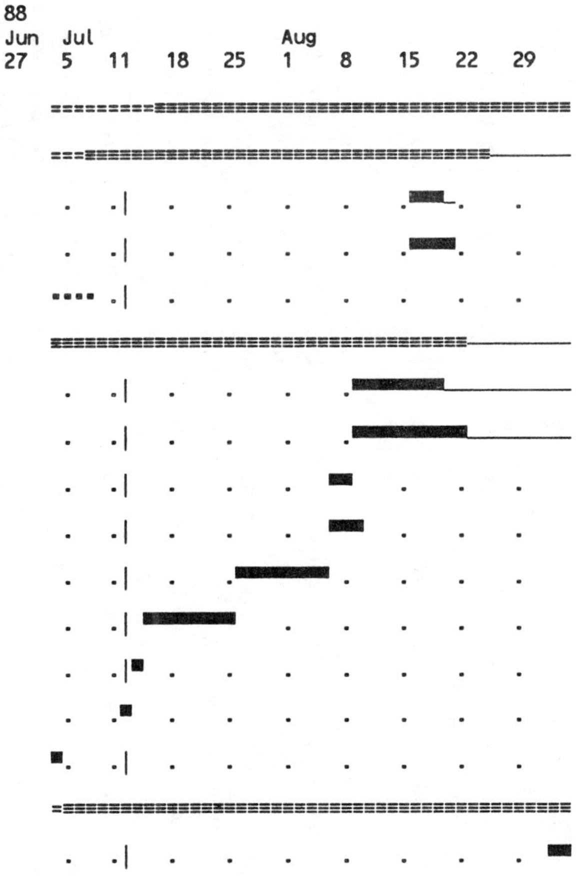

Legend:

```
------ Detail Task        ===== Summary Task      M   Milestone
       (Started)          ====  (Started)         >>> Conflict
       (Slack)            ===   (Slack)           ..  Resource delay
--------------- Scale: 1 day per character ---------------
```

TIME LINE Gantt Chart Report, Strip 1, Page 2

baseline schedule has been saved, it is possible to use the "Filter" option to select all tasks that are ending later than planned. Users may also select and sort by: fixed dates; late free dates; baseline dates; early and late dates for both the start and finish of each task; percent achieved (but not percent of spent resource effort); several percents in relationship to the baseline; to go effort; free slack; and total slack.

This product does not feature the ability to select jobs based on revised estimates. Similarly, users cannot get around the limitation by selecting based on relational and arithmetic operators between current values and baseline values. Although the system does support earned value variances (See the discussion later in this appendix.), it does not report on duration variances.

Appendix 4.11.8 Highlighting Progress (12.11)

In Time Line 3.0, there is no special marking that shows progress nor is there an *As-of* line on the network. On the Gantt chart, there *is* an *As-of* line. Progress is shown in half-height squares and remaining work is shown in full-height rectangles. Delays are also illustrated. There is also a baseline-to-actuals comparison bar chart, which shows originals as a series of circles.

Appendix 4.11.9 Costs and Project Management Software (12.13)

In Time Line 3.0, the costs of the tasks and of the project will be recomputed when time is reported to the activity and/or when a new unit rate is assigned to a resource. There is no special field for actual-costs-this-period.

Costs are seen on the tracking Detail Task screen, the tracking Resource Assignment screen, and on the Gantt screen. Two *earned value* costs and the *actual spent* costs are seen on the tracking Detail Task screen. The values for *total*, *actual*, and *to go* are seen on each of the tracking Resource Assignment screens. Any of the many costs fields may be displayed on the Gantt screen using the "Layout" option.

The *total* dollars are equal to the originally estimated cost of the task or the project. The *spent* dollars are equal to the actual cost of work performed to date. The *to go* dollars are the current forecasted estimate

of the cost to completion. The *estimate at completion* is equal to the *spent* dollars plus the *to go* dollars. The *estimate at completion variance* is the difference between the *total* dollars and the *estimate at completion*.

Appendix 4.11.10 Cost Status Reporting (12.15)

The Time Line 3.0 Gantt "Layout" option may be set up to display the total dollars, the spent dollars, the to go dollars, the original baseline dollars, and the variances. (See Figure A4.24.)

Although there is no graphic view of cash flow reporting in Time Line 3.0, the system does provide a "Tabular Period" report for cash. (See Figure A4.25.) The user may choose the date ranges of the report, the period length (hours, days, weeks, months, years), and the type of cash field (Baseline totals, projected totals, to go totals, or spent totals). Users may also designate row totals and/or column totals.

There is no cost histogram, nor is there a cumulative costs report.

Appendix 4.11.11 Earned Values and Project Management Software (12.17)

Time Line 3.0 supports earned value analysis for costs. (See Figure A4.26.) The system has many earned value fields.

The field for total baseline dollars is the amount Budgeted At Completion [BAC].

The field for total dollars Estimated At Completion [EAC] has two sources: for the baseline, it is the BAC; for the current schedule, it is the sum of the money spent plus the sum of the money yet to be spent.

The field for achieved dollars [BCWP] is computed by multiplying the percent achieved[14] by the baseline dollars.

The elapsed baseline dollars field is equal to the Budgeted Cost of Work Scheduled [BCWS]. It is the value of work, in dollars, which should be completed to date.

The spent dollars field is the Actual Costs for Work Performed [ACWP]. The field for spent dollars as a % of the baseline is equal to [ACWP] $\div$ [BCWS].

---

[14]The percent achieved is the actual percent value entered by the user.

Figure A4.24

```
Schedule Name : chap9
Responsible   :
As-of Date    : 12-Jul-88  8:00am    Schedule File : C:\TL3\DATA\CHAP9GBA

this is the notes field for the project.
```

Task Name	Total $ (EAC)	Spent $ (ACWP)	To Go $	Total BL $ (BAC)	EAC Variance	Cost Variance
project	71,120.00	8,920.00	62,200.00	71,120.00	0.00	88.40
group1	9,400.00	1,600.00	7,800.00	9,200.00	-200.00	-40.00
1	800.00	800.00	0.00	800.00	0.00	0.00
2	2,000.00	400.00	1,600.00	2,000.00	0.00	0.00
3	2,200.00	400.00	1,800.00	2,000.00	-200.00	-40.00
4	2,000.00	0.00	2,000.00	2,000.00	0.00	0.00
5	2,400.00	0.00	2,400.00	2,400.00	0.00	0.00
group2	39,120.00	4,000.00	35,120.00	39,120.00	0.00	-16.00
6	1,600.00	1,600.00	0.00	1,600.00	0.00	0.00
12	4,400.00	1,600.00	2,800.00	4,400.00	0.00	-16.00
13	1,600.00	800.00	800.00	1,600.00	0.00	0.00
21	2,400.00	0.00	2,400.00	2,400.00	0.00	0.00
26	2,800.00	0.00	2,800.00	2,800.00	0.00	0.00
27	320.00	0.00	320.00	320.00	0.00	0.00
28	240.00	0.00	240.00	240.00	0.00	0.00
32	4,000.00	0.00	4,000.00	4,000.00	0.00	0.00
33	880.00	0.00	880.00	880.00	0.00	0.00
39	5,200.00	0.00	5,200.00	5,200.00	0.00	0.00
43	2,000.00	0.00	2,000.00	2,000.00	0.00	0.00
44	1,400.00	0.00	1,400.00	1,400.00	0.00	0.00
45	1,600.00	0.00	1,600.00	1,600.00	0.00	0.00
46	1,600.00	0.00	1,600.00	1,600.00	0.00	0.00
47	480.00	0.00	480.00	480.00	0.00	0.00
48	2,400.00	0.00	2,400.00	2,400.00	0.00	0.00
51	2,800.00	0.00	2,800.00	2,800.00	0.00	0.00
52	1,600.00	0.00	1,600.00	1,600.00	0.00	0.00
53	600.00	0.00	600.00	600.00	0.00	0.00
56	1,200.00	0.00	1,200.00	1,200.00	0.00	0.00
fixed e	0.00	0.00	0.00	0.00	0.00	0.00
group3	11,280.00	160.00	11,120.00	11,360.00	80.00	54.40
8	160.00	160.00	0.00	320.00	160.00	54.40
8 1/2	80.00	0.00	80.00			
14	320.00	0.00	320.00	320.00	0.00	0.00
15	720.00	0.00	720.00	720.00	0.00	0.00

```
TIME LINE Gantt Chart Report, Strip 1, Page 1
```

The field for to go dollars is the amount of money predicted to completion. It is equal to the [BAC] minus the [BCWP].

The schedule variance field is equal to the [BCWP] minus the [BCWS] The cost variance field is equal to the [BCWP] minus the [ACWP]. The field for variance at completion is equal to the [BAC] minus the [EAC]. The cost variance % field is equal to the cost variance ÷ the [BCWP]. The EAC variance % field is equal to the EAC variance as a component of the total budget.

The system also computes two other variance fields: duration as % of baseline[15] and to go duration as % of baseline.[16]

---

[15](actual duration ÷ baseline duration) × 100.

[16](to go duration ÷ baseline duration) × 100.

Figure A4.25

Schedule Name : chap9
Responsible :
As-of Date : 12-Jul-88 8:00am   Schedule File : C:\TL3\DATA\CHAP9GBA

this is the notes field for the project.

	Jul-88	Aug-88	Sep-88	Oct-88	Nov-88	Dec-88	Total
project	21,600.00	23,800.00	10,040.00	9,080.00	5,880.00	720.00	71,120.00 *
group1	6,000.00	3,400.00					9,400.00
1	800.00						800.00
2	2,000.00						2,000.00
3	2,200.00						2,200.00
4	1,000.00	1,000.00					2,000.00
5		2,400.00					2,400.00
group2	7,600.00	7,200.00	8,640.00	9,080.00	5,880.00	720.00	39,120.00
6	1,600.00						1,600.00
12	4,400.00						4,400.00
13	1,600.00						1,600.00
21		2,400.00					2,400.00
26		2,800.00					2,800.00
27		320.00					320.00
28		240.00					240.00
32		1,200.00	2,800.00				4,000.00
33		240.00	640.00				880.00
39			5,200.00				5,200.00
43				2,000.00			2,000.00
44				1,400.00			1,400.00
45				1,600.00			1,600.00
46				1,600.00			1,600.00
47				480.00			480.00
48				2,000.00	400.00		2,400.00
51					2,800.00		2,800.00
52					1,600.00		1,600.00
53					600.00		600.00
56					480.00	720.00	1,200.00
fixed end							0.00
group7	840.00						600.00
7	840.00						840.00
milestones							840.00
d4							0.00
d1							0.00
d2							0.00
d3							0.00
Total	21,600.00	23,800.00	10,040.00	9,080.00	5,880.00	720.00	71,120.00 *

TIME LINE Task vs Time Report showing Total Dollars, Page 2

Figure A4.26

```
Schedule Name : chap9
Responsible   :
As-of Date    : 12-Jul-88  8:00am   Schedule File : C:\TL3\DATA\CHAP9GBA

this is the notes field for the project.
```

Task Name	Elpsd BL $ (BCWS)	Achieved $ (BCWP)	Spent $ (ACWP)	Schedule Variance	Cost Variance	Total $ (EAC)	Pct Achvd	Spent Dur as % BL	Spent $ as % BL
project	8,760.00	9,008.40	8,920.00	248.40	88.40	71,120.00	13	4	13
group1	1,600.00	1,560.00	1,600.00	-40.00	-40.00	9,400.00	17	17	17
1	800.00	800.00	800.00	0.00	0.00	800.00	100	100	100
2	400.00	400.00	400.00	0.00	0.00	2,000.00	20	20	20
3	400.00	360.00	400.00	-40.00	-40.00	2,200.00	18	20	20
4	0.00	0.00	0.00	0.00	0.00	2,000.00	0	0	0
5	0.00	0.00	0.00	0.00	0.00	2,400.00	0	0	0
group2	3,200.00	3,984.00	4,000.00	784.00	-16.00	39,120.00	10	4	10
6	1,600.00	1,600.00	1,600.00	0.00	0.00	1,600.00	100	100	100
12	800.00	1,584.00	1,600.00	784.00	-16.00	4,400.00	36	36	36
13	800.00	800.00	800.00	0.00	0.00	1,600.00	50	50	50
21	0.00	0.00	0.00	0.00	0.00	2,400.00	0	0	0
26	0.00	0.00	0.00	0.00	0.00	2,800.00	0	0	0
27	0.00	0.00	0.00	0.00	0.00	320.00	0	0	0
28	0.00	0.00	0.00	0.00	0.00	240.00	0	0	0
32	0.00	0.00	0.00	0.00	0.00	4,000.00	0	0	0
33	0.00	0.00	0.00	0.00	0.00	880.00	0	0	0
39	0.00	0.00	0.00	0.00	0.00	5,200.00	0	0	0
43	0.00	0.00	0.00	0.00	0.00	2,000.00	0	0	0
44	0.00	0.00	0.00	0.00	0.00	1,400.00	0	0	0
45	0.00	0.00	0.00	0.00	0.00	1,600.00	0	0	0
46	0.00	0.00	0.00	0.00	0.00	1,600.00	0	0	0
47	0.00	0.00	0.00	0.00	0.00	480.00	0	0	0
48	0.00	0.00	0.00	0.00	0.00	2,400.00	0	0	0
51	0.00	0.00	0.00	0.00	0.00	2,800.00	0	0	0
52	0.00	0.00	0.00	0.00	0.00	1,600.00	0	0	0
53	0.00	0.00	0.00	0.00	0.00	600.00	0	0	0
56	0.00	0.00	0.00	0.00	0.00	1,200.00	0	0	0
fixed	0.00	0.00	0.00	0.00	0.00	0.00	0	0	0
group3	720.00	214.40	160.00	-505.60	54.40	11,280.00	2	13	1
8	320.00	214.40	160.00	-105.60	54.40	160.00	67	50	50
8 1/2			0.00			80.00	0		
14	160.00	0.00	0.00	-160.00	0.00	320.00	0	0	0
15	240.00	0.00	0.00	-240.00	0.00	720.00	0	0	0

```
TIME LINE Gantt Chart Report, Strip 1, Page 1
```

The field for mathematical EAC also has two values. For the baseline, it is the BAC; for the current schedule, it is the money actually spent to date plus the baseline estimate of unfinished work (spent dollars [ACWP] plus total baseline dollars [BAC] minus achieved dollars [BCWP]).

The field for productivity cost ratio is equal to the ratio of work accomplished to work scheduled to be accomplished ([BCWP] ÷ [BCWS]). The spending rate ratio field is equal to the ratio of dollars spent to date to dollars planned to be spent ([ACWP] ÷ [BCWS]).

Appendix 4.11.12 Reporting on Resource Availability (12.20)

The Time Line 3.0 resource histogram that is pictured in Figure A4.17 may be printed. The resource Gantt chart pictured in Figure A4.16 may be printed, with or without the baseline values.

After the schedule has been filtered to limit the data to one resource, the "Task vs. Time" report will show resource allocations by periods for a given resource. (Figure A4.20) It does not show the available number of resources. Users will need to work with a copy of the "Resource Details" report in order to know the available number. Similarly, they will need to mentally calculate overscheduling and underscheduling.

Appendix 4.11.13 Reporting on Resource Utilization *(12.21)*

Although Time Line 3.0 features several types of cross tab reports that give totals per period and totals to date, it is not possible to combine planned, actual, and projected values on one report. They may be produced separately, however, and then compared manually. (See Figure A4.27.[17]) These reports may be supplemented with the status reports, which, in turn, have been filtered on a designated resource name. (Figures A4.23 and A4.24)

Appendix 4.11.14 Earned Value Productivity Reporting *(12.22)*

In Time Line 3.0, the SPI is called the productivity time ratio; the CPI is called the productivity cost ratio. These values may be chosen with the layout and then displayed on a report.

APPENDIX 4.12 MANAGING THE PROJECT

Appendix 4.12.1 Who Produces Perts and Gantts that May Be Restricted to Critical Path Jobs? *(13.7)*

The Time Line 3.0 filter may be set up to select on recognition of the critical path but *not* on slack. There-

---

[17]This report may also be structured to show time instead of dollars.

fore, the Gantt may be filtered on the critical path. However, this application only works if the critical path has *zero* slack. The system does not recognize any jobs of greater than zero slack as being on the critical path. Therefore, if users have entered a reasonable late finish date based on the probability techniques described earlier, they will *not* be able to select based on the critical path. The network function will undo any filters before the nodes can be displayed; therefore, it is not possible to produce a network limited to the critical path.

Appendix 4.12.2 Who Produces Reports that May Be Restricted to Fixed-Date Jobs? *(13.8)*

Time Line 3.0 reports may be selected based on the values in the *Fixed Start* field.

Appendix 4.12.3 Who Produces Perts and Gantts that May Be Restricted to Summary Jobs? *(13.9)*

All of the Time Line 3.0 data about a group of lower-level tasks may be drawn up into its summary task by placing the cursor on the summary task and pressing the "—" key. After this operation, both the Gantt and the network will be restricted to displaying the appropriate summary data. Because the network does *not* display connecting lines between summary tasks, many summary nodes will be suspended in midair. Therefore, the value of a summary network for the purpose described in this section is questionable.

Appendix 4.12.4 Local Area Networks *(13.14)*

Time Line 3.0 prevents access to files when they are active. It does not provide read/write protection.

Appendix 4.12.5 Guidelines for Tracking and Managing the Proejct *(13.15)*

Interspersed in the several pages of Time Line 3.0 documentation for using the system are some hints on how to track projects.

Figure A4.27

Schedule Name : chap9
Responsible :
As-of Date : 12-Jul-88 8:00am   Schedule File : C:\TL3\DATA\CHAP9GBA

this is the notes field for the project.

	1-Jul-88	5-Jul-88	6-Jul-88	7-Jul-88	8-Jul-88	11-Jul-88	Total
project	200.00	200.00	200.00	200.00	700.00	700.00	2,200.00 *
group1	200.00	200.00	200.00	200.00	400.00	400.00	1,600.00
1	200.00	200.00	200.00	200.00			800.00
2					200.00	200.00	400.00
3					200.00	200.00	400.00
4							0.00
5							0.00
group2							0.00
44							0.00
46							0.00
53							0.00
group3							0.00
23							0.00
group5					300.00	300.00	600.00
24					300.00	300.00	600.00
24 1/2							0.00
36							0.00
Total	200.00	200.00	200.00	200.00	700.00	700.00	2,200.00 *

TIME LINE Task vs Time Report showing Spent Dollars

APPENDIX 5: MICROSOFT PROJECT 4.0

APPENDIX 5.0   INTRODUCTION

Each section in each appendix is keyed back to its corresponding introductory section in the tutorial. Readers will find that the respective tutorial section is noted in italicized parentheses at the end of each appropriate section header line.

APPENDIX 5.1 GANTT-DRIVEN PRODUCTS

Appendix 5.1.1 Data Entry Mode *(16.2.2)*

Microsoft Project allows project data entry while in Gantt mode and Network mode.

Appendix 5.1.2 Size and Storage Constraints *(16.3.1)*

Also working on project data in main memory, Microsoft Project supports plans of up to 200 activities in 256K and 999 activities in 640K. These limits go down as the number of dependencies and resources per activity goes up. Larger projects may be created by linking several smaller projects together under a master project.

Appendix 5.1.3 System Structure *(16.3.2)*

Microsoft Project is managed through a hierarchy of menu lines at the bottom of the screen. Each menu line in the lower level also states the name of the upper-level menu from which it descended. (See Figure A5.1.)

Appendix 5.1.4 Global System Project Data Defaults *(16.3.3)*

There is no function in this system for entering global system project data defaults.

Figure A5.1

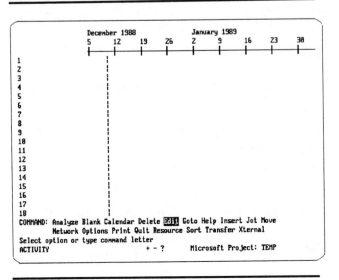

Figure A5.2

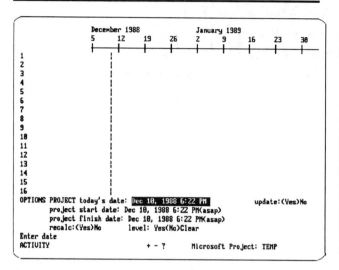

Figure A5.3

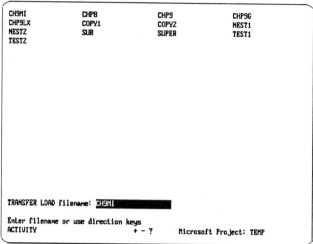

Appendix 5.1.5 New Projects (16.3.4)

To enter a new project, select "Options; Project" and the Project Options screen will appear at the bottom of the screen. (See Figure A5.2.)

Appendix 5.1.6 Accessing Existing Plans (16.3.5)

The second level under Transfer is Load, Save, Clear, Delete, Import, Export, Forecast, Options, and Rename. Existing project data is loaded into main memory by choosing "Transfer; Load" and the Filename screen will appear. Pressing a cursor arrow key will cause a list of valid files names to be displayed. (See Figure A5.3.) Moving the cursor to the desired name and pressing "Enter" will load the project.

Appendix 5.1.7 Immediate Processor Or Batch (16.3.6)

Microsoft Project is an immediate processor system. The automatic recalculation may be turned off by setting Recalc to *No* on the Project Options screen.

Appendix 5.1.8 Adding Plan Data (16.3.7)

The Edit command (Figure A5.1) is used to enter new activity data or modify existing data. Selecting Insert

from the command line will introduce additional blank records at a designated place in the Gantt chart. After the desired number of blank records has been entered, the Edit command may be used to summon an Activity Details screen for each respective new record. (See Figure A5.4.)

Figure A5.4

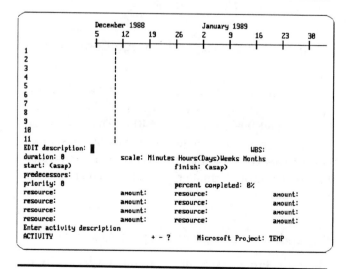

Appendix 5.1.9 Optional "What-If's" Or Permanent Saves (16.3.8)

Plan data is not made permanent until the user chooses to save it and until the user designates the name under which the plan is to be saved.

Appendix 5.1.10 Ad Hoc Information Storage (16.3.9)

By invoking the "JOT" option on the Activity Details screen menu, the user may add up to 200 characters of information about each activity.

Appendix 5.1.11 Exporting Data (16.3.10)

Microsoft Project exports data to SYLK, LOTUS 1-2-3, dBase—and in Data Interchange Format.

APPENDIX 5.2 WORK BREAKDOWN STRUCTURES

Appendix 5.2.1 Graphics Support (4.8.2)

Microsoft Project does not provide graphic work breakdown structures. Microsoft Project is Gantt driven. (That is, the bar chart controls most operations.)

Appendix 5.2.2 Level Support (4.8.3)

In Microsoft Project, the user-devised permutations of nine positions in the identification number determine the number of levels.

Appendix 5.2.3 Data Entry Requirements (4.8.4)

Microsoft Project also only requires one identification number to be entered by the user. In addition, this product automatically generates a separate task identification field, a process that requires no extra action on the part of the user. Determined by the sequential row position on the Gantt Chart screen, these numbers are not permanently assigned. They are internal Microsoft Project placement keys and are updated with every sequential schedule modification.

Appendix 5.2.4 Durations and Dependencies (4.8.5)

Microsoft Project does not require durations and dependencies to initialize a project plan.

Appendix 5.2.5 Random Sequence of Data Entry (4.8.6)

Microsoft Project, a system that supports Gantt and Network data entry modes, also allows random entry.

Appendix 5.2.6 Using the Copy Features with the *Template* Tasks (4.8.7)

If the *template* tasks have been stored in a separate plan, Microsoft Project will allow the user to selectively take the *template* plan into other projects. Microsoft Project supports two ways to import a *template* plan: the "External Copy" option and the "External Link" option. Microsoft Project limits importing a *template* plan to only once per project but this can be overcome by making duplicate copies of the *template* plan before starting the operation. Furthermore, Microsoft Project does not allow duplicate activity names between plans. Although some products provide an automated feature that helps to create unique names in each plan, users must complete this process manually.

Appendix 5.2.7 Rollup Support (4.8.8)

Rollup reports[1] may be easily customized in Microsoft Project using the "Options, Filter, Edit, WBS" commands to select and the "Print, Utilities, Report" commands to produce. With wild-card filtering, the user

---

[1] Common groups of reports may be produced. As an example, one group of reports with totals of each of the Phase 1 intermediate deliverables within the Phase 1 major deliverables may be generated. Then, these reports may be followed by a second group of reports showing totals of all of the Phase 1 major deliverables. The second group may then be followed by like reports for Phase 2 and so on. The production of each individual report is a separate process. These reports may then be visually analyzed and manually reconciled. At times, this is complex and time consuming, but it is better than no reports at all.

may select all of the occurrences of a work-type (e.g., testing) that occurs anywhere in a Microsoft Project plan, as long as the code for that type of work is always in the same position of the WBS.

Appendix 5.2.8 Guidelines and Documentation *(4.8.9)*

The Microsoft Project documentation has a chapter on work breakdown structures.

APPENDIX 5.3   ESTIMATING

Appendix 5.3.1 Estimating Support and Estimating Guidelines *(5.7.1)*

Microsoft Project does not provide guidelines that support the estimating techniques described in this text. They assume the estimating has been completed and the duration is known. (Instructions on how to use the system to achieve the implementation of a feature are not considered guidelines.)

Appendix 5.3.2 Estimates of *True Work Effort* Versus Resource-Driven Elapsed Time *(5.7.4)*

Until resources are added to the plan, Microsoft Project supports *true work effort*. Under certain circumstances, when resources are to be assigned to jobs, the value of *true work effort* will need to be overlaid by the value of the resource effort.

Appendix 5.3.3 Durations and Units of Measurement *(5.7.6)*

Microsoft Project allows the user to choose between minutes, hours, days, weeks, and months. Minutes and hours have limited use, however. In most projects, they will generate more time periods than the system can handle; therefore, they can only be used in short projects or phases. There is no default duration in Microsoft Project. The system supports mixed units of measurement and will make the consistency adjustments.

Appendix 5.3.4 Zero Duration Milestones *(5.7.7)*

Microsoft Project supports zero duration milestones.

Appendix 5.3.5 Lead and Lag Times with Duration but No Effort *(5.7.8)*

Microsoft Project supports lead and lag times in the following manner: (1) identify the two jobs that need to be separated by the lead time; (2) pick the latest of the two; (3) choose the Edit command; and (4) modify the predecessor field of the latest job by adding "/N"[2] after the predecessor number. (Figure A5.4) The *Predecessor lead/lag* time may be displayed using the product's custom report writer.

APPENDIX 5.4   NETWORKS

Appendix 5.4.1 Types of Networks *(6.8.1)*

Microsoft Project's network is in precedence notation.

Appendix 5.4.2 Types of Relationships *(6.8.2)*

Microsoft Project's default relationship is finish-to-start. It also supports start-to-start (with the letter "s" entered after the predecessor number); or finish-to-finish (with the letter "f" entered after the predecessor number).

Appendix 5.4.3 Number of Dependencies *(6.8.3)*

The system allows for a maximum of 16 predecessors per activity. There are 104 characters per set of relationships. The vendor suggests that, if more than 16 predecessors are needed, each group ought to be brought to a milestone, with all of the milestones then being brought to the successor. Of course, this reduces the total number of available activities.

Appendix 5.4.4 Establishing Dependencies *(6.8.4)*

Data entry may be made in Gantt or Network mode. To create dependencies, simply complete the predecessor entry in the Activity Details screen. (Figure A5.4)

---

[2]Where "N" equals the lag/lead time.

Appendix 5.4.5 How Easy Is it to Enter Dependencies? (6.8.6)

In Microsoft Project, the user must add the system-generated number to the predecessor entry on the Activity Details screen. This is easy to find by scrolling up and down the screen. However, in a very large plan, it is helpful to have a hard copy of the plan in hand when entering the dependencies, unless changes to the plan have occurred since the report was produced.

Appendix 5.4.6 Inserting Jobs into the Middle of the Plan (6.8.7)

To insert a job when in Microsoft Project's Network mode: (1) move the cursor to a blank spot in the network; (2) select ''Details'' from the submenu; and (3) complete the Activity Details screen. All of the affected Activity Detail screens will then need to be reedited as described above to correct the predecessors.

Appendix 5.4.7 Subnetwork Dependencies (6.8.8)

In Microsoft Project, subnetwork dependencies are no problem.

Appendix 5.4.8 Moving Jobs in the Network (6.8.9)

Activities may be moved around in Gantt mode. This move is used to change row placement of the job on the Gantt. During this process, relationships are maintained even though the system-generated identification numbers are updated to reflect the new position. The move in Microsoft Project is not intended to be used to clean up aesthetics of PERT (e.g., crossed lines). There is no way to move nodes in Network mode. The user must accept the placement of jobs on the PERT.

Appendix 5.4.9 Removing Dependencies (6.8.10)

In Microsoft Project, simply change the predecessor field on the Activity Details screen.

Appendix 5.4.10 Deleting Jobs in the Plan (6.8.11)

Microsoft Project has two commands that remove activities: Delete and Blank. They can only be executed from Gantt mode. The former removes all traces of the activity. The latter eliminates the activity, leaving a blank Gantt chart line in its place, allowing room for reentry of additional activities. Both leave dangling activities. Removing a task in PERT mode will also eliminate the task from the WBS; however, removing a milestone in PERT mode will not eliminate it from the WBS.

Appendix 5.4.11 Lag and Lead Times (6.8.12)

Microsoft Project supports lead times in the following manner: (1) identify the two jobs that need to be separated by the lead time; (2) pick the latest of the two; (3) choose the Edit command; and (4) modify the predecessor field of the latest job by adding ''/N''[3] after either the predecessor number or, if there is one, the relationship type. (Figure A5.4) All three types of relationships that the vendor supports can have lag times. This does not appear on any reports. A better approach is to create the task with the corresponding duration and then enter a dummy resource whose cost is zero. Of course, this also consumes precious memory.

Appendix 5.4.12 Copying Jobs in the Plan (6.8.13)

There is no way in Microsoft Project to duplicate parts of a plan within the same plan. However, Microsoft Project does support an ''External Copy'', which will include all or part of a second plan into the current plan. Additionally, the external plan's ''Options; Project'' must set Update and Recalc to *Yes*. (Figure A5.2) The ''Copy'' is only accessible in Gantt mode, and any given file may only be copied into a plan one time.

There is additional information the user must know in order to effectively use this feature—information that is not documented in the user manual. The ''External Copy'' will only work, however, if the activity

---

[3]Where ''N'' equals the lag/lead time.

names in the external plan are totally different from those in the current plan. If task names in the current file have been duplicated in the external file, Microsoft Project gives a "Duplicate activity" message and only inserts a blank Gantt line (in the current plan) in place of the copied entries. A *work-around* for this problem will be presented in the next section.

Appendix 5.4.13 Copying the *Template* Jobs (6.8.14)

Microsoft Project supports subprojects, a feature that may also be used for the *template* application. The *template* plan is brought into the current project with either the "External Link" or the "External Copy" operation.

The "External Link" is not a feature that lends itself gracefully to the *template* application:

- A subproject may only be linked to a project one time. This can be overcome by saving multiple copies of the *template* subproject under different names.

- The activity names in a subproject may not duplicate any of the activity names in the master project or any other subproject. If there are duplicates, they will not be linked. To work around this problem, the name fields in each subproject must be edited.

- The date of the subproject must closely follow the end date of its predecessor in the master project. If it does not, the system will signal an error message stating that the subproject scheduled date is too early.

- The "External Link" only creates a one-line entry in the master project Gantt and Network modes to represent the subproject. The internal tasks are not expanded and consequently there can be no inside links.

To overcome the above limitations, the user is advised to employ the "External Copy" feature. This operation will simply copy all of the activities into the plan in the designated position. Once these tasks have been imported into the master project, any changes in the *template* plan must also be done manually in every occurrence of *template* tasks in the master. The master plan will then be restricted by the size limitations.

Although duplicate subproject names and duplicate task names are still prohibited, even with the "External Copy" feature, date conflicts do not occur, the subproject is expanded into its tasks, and internal links are supported.

Last, neither the "External Link" nor the "External Copy" options will work unless the "Options; Project" in the *template* plan has had Update and Recalc set to *Yes*.

Few of these requirements have been documented in the user manual.

Appendix 5.4.14 Loops in the Network (6.8.15)

Microsoft Project prevents loops. The message "Circular references" also includes the identification numbers of the activities in the loop. This is a helpful advantage in resolving the reference.

Appendix 5.4.15 Dangling Jobs (6.8.16)

Microsoft Project allows dangling.

Appendix 5.4.16 Verifying Dependencies Are Correct (6.8.17)

If the plan has been entered in Gantt mode, Microsoft Project provides a network whose subnetworks are vertically elongated on both paper and the monitor. The illustrated subnetworks have a large blank horizontal space in the middle of the diagram. (See the vertical lines in the middle of Figure A5.5.) As a consequence, often only one subnetwork at a time can be viewed on the screen. To verify the lower subnetwork, the user must scroll down the screen. After doing so, the view of the upper subnetwork is lost. Unfortunately, this problem cannot be rectified with a "Move" feature that enables shifting of nodes. Because of this repetitive up and down scrolling, verification is frustrating and not very easy. This is further complicated by confusing stemming from crossed lines and not being able to follow them.

Microsoft Project does have another feature, however, that helps to diffuse this problem. It will be discussed in the next section.

When the plan is being created in Network mode, the user has more control over placement of the nodes. By positioning the cursor so that the nodes will not be vertically elongated, the subnetworks can be closer

Figure A5.5

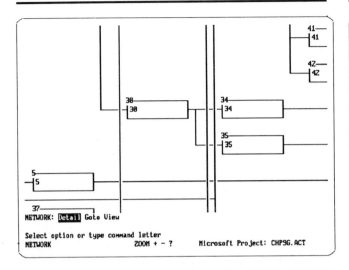

Figure A5.6

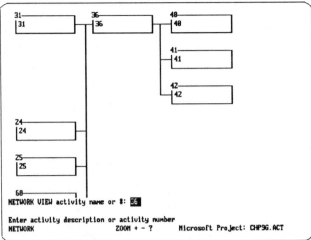

together.[4] As a consequence, the network is more readable and, therefore, more easily verifiable. If they are concerned about the readability of their networks, users are advised to enter plan data in Network mode.

Appendix 5.4.17 Highlighting Dependency Paths (6.8.18)

Microsoft Project also provides an excellent implementation of this feature. It is very easy to use—from either Gantt mode or Network mode. First, position the cursor on the designated activity. From Gantt mode, simply select "Network; View". Once in View mode, the user can scroll piecemeal through the whole network, highlighting only those designated activities in the desired chain. This feature significantly reduces the problems with verification that were described above. (See the trace for Number 36 in Figure A5.6.)

Appendix 5.4.18 Network Aesthetics (6.8.19)

When the plan has been entered in Gantt mode, Microsoft Project does not have an aesthetically pleasing

network. As discussed earlier, the Microsoft Project network is vertically elongated in both hard copy and on the monitor. There is a great deal of wasted space (and therefore paper) when printing the network. Both viewing the network on the screen and reading the hard copy are complicated because of this distancing. Similarly, the usual problems with difficulty in interpreting overlapping lines may be exacerbated in this type of network implementation. (Figure A5.5) Although there may still be a few oddly placed nodes, some small degree of elongation, and some crossed dependency lines, plans that are entered while in Network mode are much more aesthetically pleasing than those entered in Gantt mode.

Appendix 5.4.19 Scaled to Time? (6.8.20)

The network in Microsoft Project is not scaled to time.

Appendix 5.4.20 Networks and Work Breakdown Structures (6.9)

Microsoft Project does not create beginning and ending nodes and, consequently, requires reestablishing dependencies while moving down in the WBS. Nevertheless, adding in a duplicate ending job is very easy. Similarly, it does not support automatic resolution of relationships when adding the "latest last job."

---

[4]The user only has control over some of the vertical elongation. In spite of this semblance of control, the system still takes over and places the nodes where it wants to—only they're not as far apart. Also, dependency connections may still be crossed, but not as hard to follow.

Appendix 5.4.21 Dependencies in a Multiproject Environment *(6.12)*

In Microsoft Project, subprojects can never be used more than one time. There can be no duplicate names in the plans or the process will be aborted. The user must manually rectify this problem. (See the discussion under *template* tasks earlier in this appendix.) The master project is *not* constrained by the sum of its subprojects.

A separate master project needs to be created, with one activity for each of the subproject plans. The master project start date will need to be reentered in the Project Options screen. (Figure A5.2) Each activity will, in turn, be linked to its respective subproject. This is done by selecting "External; Link" from the Activity Details screen and entering the subproject name. The "External Copy" should not be used for this application. To speed things up, the calculations may be temporarily stopped from the Project Options screen. When there is no longer a need for faster response times, the calculations ought to be turned back on. Dependency connections are simply made as outlined earlier in this appendix.

Other than invoking the normal procedure for accessing plan data, there is no way to flip back and forth between plans.

There is no need for double data entry when the subprojects have been linked. Changes made in the subprojects are automatically reflected in the master project.

Appendix 5.4.22 Printing and Viewing Networks *(6.13)*

Viewing the network in Microsoft Project is very simple: just select "Network" from the main command line. (Figure A5.1) To print, select "Print; Printer; Network". To print the network sideways, first set "Options; Display; Style:graphics".

Appendix 5.4.23 Guidelines and Documentation *(6.15)*

Microsoft Project has two pages of documentation on types of relationships. For help in a multiproject environment, the manual also has several pages in a chapter on how to work with large projects.

APPENDIX 5.5 OPTIMAL PLANS

Appendix 5.5.1 Calendars *(7.14.1)*

Microsoft Project supports two types of calendar entry: days of the week and hours per day. The default days of the week are set by pressing "Calendar; Standard; Days". (See Figure A5.7.) The days of the week will then be displayed at the bottom of the screen. Pressing the "Tab" key moves the cursor to a selected day of the week (for example, *Monday*). Then, pressing the spacebar turns the day on to a workday or off to a rest day. Finally, pressing the "Return" key sets the standard workdays.

The standard hours worked per day are set by pressing "Calendar; Standard; Hours". (See Figure A5.8.) Pressing the "Tab" key moves the cursor to the status field. In Microsoft Project, the workday is divided into 15-minute increments. Using the cursor keys moves the highlight to a different 15-minute segment. Pressing the spacebar turns the highlighted 15-minute segment to either a working segment or a rest segment. In this way, the daily starting and ending time, standard breaktimes, lunch time, and nonworking time may be set. Finally, pressing the "Return" key completes the operation.

Holidays are designated under "Calendar; Edit; Days" by pressing the "Tab" key to get to the status

Figure A5.7

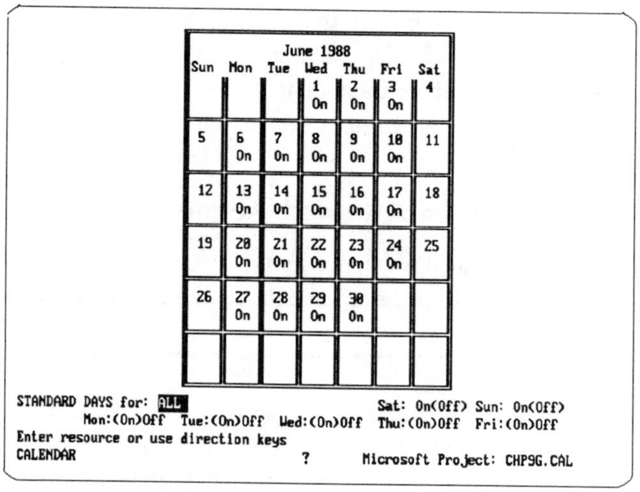

Figure A5.8

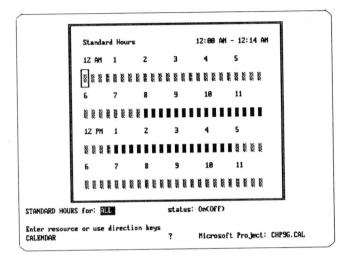

```
Standard Hours                  12:00 AM - 12:14 AM

12 AM  1      2      3      4      5

6      7      8      9      10     11

12 PM  1      2      3      4      5

6      7      8      9      10     11


STANDARD HOURS for: ALL            status: On(Off)

Enter resource or use direction keys
CALENDAR                    ?      Microsoft Project: CHP9G.CAL
```

field, moving the cursor to the designated month and day, pressing the spacebar to toggle the workday to *Off*, and pressing the "Return" key to complete the operation.

Once the calendar has been created, it may be copied into other plans by pressing "Transfer; Load" from the Calendar screen and selecting the desired calendar.

Appendix 5.5.2 Choosing the Correct Project Start Date (7.14.2)

In Microsoft Project, the start date of the project may be controlled through the *project start date* in the Project Options screen which is accessed by selecting "Options; Project". It is only necessary to take this action one time—at plan initiation. However, the today's date field controls subsequent scheduling; often this may only be effectively changed by altering the operating system date. (See the later discussions on the "Update" option.)

Appendix 5.5.3 Insuring that the Plan Is Not Constrained by Resources (7.14.3)

In Microsoft Project's "Options; Project", the user should say *No* to "Level" and should not add resources to the Activity Details screen.

Appendix 5.5.4 Avoiding Imposed Target Dates (7.14.3)

In Microsoft Project, the start and finish field of the Activity Details screen can each be left blank with ASAP or ALAP selected in the type field. Alternatively, if a date is keyed into either of these fields, it is considered a fixed date. If no action is taken at all, the system assumes the default to be ASAP. For optimal plans, the user is advised to accept the default.

Appendix 5.5.5 Calculating the Schedule (7.14.4)

In Microsoft Project, automatic calculations may be turned on by setting "Options; Project; Recalc" to *Yes*. On the other hand, if this slows the system down, it may be set to *No*. Then, schedules may be recalculated on an ad hoc basis by pressing the F4 key.

Appendix 5.5.6 The Forward Pass: Calculating the Early Dates (7.14.5)

Microsoft Project defaults to the traditional scheduling algorithm.

Appendix 5.5.7 Zero Duration Milestones (7.14.8)

Microsoft Project uses the preferred approach for scheduling zero duration milestones—it schedules the milestone at the end of the day on which all of the predecessors have finished.

Appendix 5.5.8 Retaining a Baseline Record of the Optimal Plan (7.14.11)

The baseline plan is called the "Forecast" plan by Microsoft Project. It may be saved by selecting "Transfer; Forecast". Unlimited versions of the plan may be saved and recalled from the Forecast screen under different names. Consequently, this product allows more baselines than most of the other products. The early dates are saved in the forecast fields. The forecast dates do not change until this process has been invoked again. A split screen comparison between forecast dates and actuals may be invoked by selecting Analyze from the main menu. (See Figure A5.9.) There

Figure A5.9

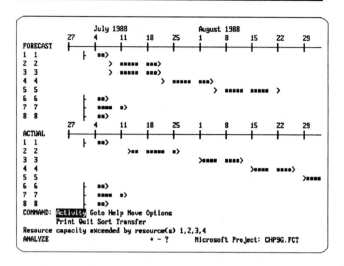

Figure A5.10

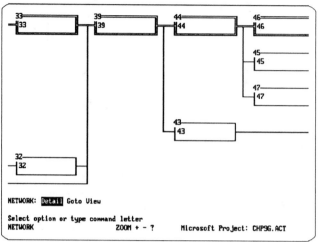

are several reports that compare forecast figures with actuals.

Appendix 5.5.9 Interpreting the Dates on the Screen (7.14.12)

Other than the timescale at the top of the Microsoft Project Gantt chart, there are no date columns in this mode. (Figure A5.1) The time-scaled bars are drawn to correspond to the early dates. The network only displays the name and number of each job. It does not show any dates. (Figure A5.5)

Appendix 5.5.10 Annotating the Critical Path (7.14.13)

Microsoft Project draws double lines around the network nodes on the critical path and also uses double lines to connect these nodes. (See Figure A5.10.) On the Gantt, Microsoft Project highlights those jobs that are on the critical path with a different color than the other jobs.

Appendix 5.5.11 Gantt Chart Time Periods (7.14.15)

Time periods in Microsoft Project may range from 15 minutes to 6 months. By pressing the ''—'' key, the user may cause smaller and smaller intervals to be

Figure A5.11

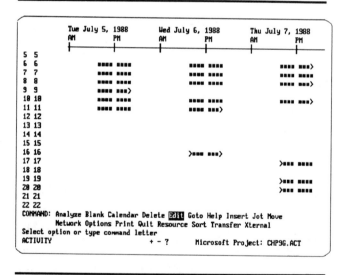

displayed until hours per day—in 15-minute intervals—is displayed.[5] (See Figure A5.11.) The opposite effect is achieved by pressing the '' + '' key.

The user may move in any direction around the Gantt chart by pressing the arrow keys.

The bars on the Gantt chart are broken to show weekends and holidays.

---

[5]Lunch is also blocked out.

Appendix 5.5.12 Scheduling in the Multiproject Environment *(7.14.17)*

Calendars in Microsoft Project are not imported with the subproject. Nor will the master project read calendar information from a subproject. However, the appropriate data is easily brought in from the Calendar screen by pressing "Transfer; Load" and selecting the desired calendar file. Since incoming data will always overwrite existing data, if more than one file will be involved, the file that contains the permanent values should be transferred last.

The start date in the subproject file should be set to be the same as or earlier than the end date of its latest predecessor in the master project. If it is not, the start date of the subproject will be used, throwing off the subsequent dates in the master project. On the other hand, if these instructions are followed, the system will signal messages stating that (1) the subproject scheduled date is too early; (2) the correct date will be placed in the master; but (3) the subproject date will not be changed. Users may ignore these messages.

Finally, the order in which the subprojects are modified and saved is important. To insure that the latest modifications in the subprojects are reflected in the master project, they must each be reloaded and resaved from the bottom up.

Appendix 5.5.13 Nesting Subprojects in a Multiproject Environment *(7.14.18)*

In Microsoft Project, if the instructions in the previous section are followed, all date changes are reflected in each rung of the nest. In a complex nest of subprojects, users are advised to create a hard copy tree of the nested groups and check each one off as its schedule is computed. If only one subproject is overlooked, all of the subsequent schedules may be incorrect. There is no other *work-around* to this procedure.

Appendix 5.5.14 Guidelines and Documentation *(7.14.20)*

Microsoft Project does not have guidelines for developing schedules.

APPENDIX 5.6 CALCULATING A FINISH DATE

Appendix 5.6.1 Using the New Reasonable Late Finish Date of the Project *(7.26.3)*

In Microsoft Project, users can choose a fixed date for the start of the project *or* the finish of the project, *but not both!* (See the Project Options screen in Figure A5.2.) To create a fixed late finish date *and* get the correctly computed late dates requires that a milestone be created with a fixed date that is one day *later* than the fixed date. The correct late dates are computed and stored in each of the late start and late finish fields. The early finish date of the project may only be found in the early finish date of the last task(s) in the project that occur before the fixed-date milestone. Unless the user is willing to manually enter a "c" after the number in the duration field of *every* job on the critical path, the highlights of the critical path are lost.

APPENDIX 5.7 ADDING RESOURCES

Appendix 5.7.1 Creating the Resource Calendars *(8.8)*

Microsoft Project supports two types of calendar entry: days of the week and hours per day.

The resource's nonworking days are designated under "Calendar; Standard; Days". (Figure A5.7) From there, the resource calendar is accessed by pressing the right cursor key to invoke a list of resources, moving the cursor key to the desired resource, and pressing the "Tab" key to return to the calendar. All of the project-level holidays and weekend designations are automatically carried into each resource calendar. However, these dates may be modified by pressing the "Tab" key to get to the status field, moving the cursor to the designated weekday or month and day and pressing the spacebar to toggle the value to *Off* or *On*. Finally, pressing the "Return" key completes the operation.

The resource's working hours per day are designated under "Calendar; Standard; Hours". (Figure A5.8) From there, the resource workhours matrix is accessed by pressing the right cursor key to invoke a list of resources, moving the cursor key to the desired resource, and pressing the "Tab" key to return to the matrix. (In Microsoft Project, the workday is divided into 15-minute increments.) The hours from the project-level workday are automatically carried into the resource workhours matrix. However, they may be modified. First, the ''Tab'' key must be pressed again to move the cursor to the status field. Using the cursor keys moves the highlight to a different 15-minute segment. Pressing the spacebar turns the highlighted 15-minute segment to either a working segment or a rest segment. In this way, each resource's unique starting and ending time, breaktimes, lunch time, and non-working time may be set. Finally, pressing the ''Return'' key completes the operation.

Microsoft Project cannot set unique workhours for a single specific calendar day. Part-time resources are also designated at the project level using the resource calendar. This will be discussed later.

Appendix 5.7.2 Creating the Resource List *(8.9)*

In Microsoft Project, resources may be individuals, groups of individuals, equipment, or materials. There is no separate operation for *fixed* costs. Rather, it is one of the options in *units of measurement*, described below.

There may be 255 resources per project.

Resources are added to the Resource List screen (See Figure A5.12.), which is invoked by pressing

Figure A5.12

Resource	Capacity	Unit Cost	Per	Days to Complete	Cost to Complete
1 leader	1	25.00	Hour	0.00	0.00
2 boss	1	50.00	Hour	0.00	0.00
3 senior	2	15.00	Hour	0.00	0.00
4 worker	3	10.00	Hour	0.00	0.00
5					
6					
7					
8					
9					
10					
11					
12					
13					
14					
15					

Cost to complete 0.00 Total cost of project 71120.00

EDIT resource: boss ID: boss capacity: 1
cost: 50.00 per:(Hour)Day Week Month Use Fixed
Enter resource description
RESOURCE ? Microsoft Project: CHP9G.RES

''Resource'' in the main menu. (Figure A5.1) There is one line in this list for each resource. Resources are added to this list by entering data into a form that appears when ''Edit'' is pressed. The information to be entered is: the 15-character resource name, the number of available resources of this type, the units in which the resource is measured (hours, days, etc.), and the cost per unit. The normal number of workhours per day the resource is available is entered into the calendar.

It is not possible to group several resources of the same type (for example, programmers) under one entry, and then, later, to assign this entry more than once per activity. This will be discussed in more detail later in this appendix.

Microsoft Project does not support multiple billing rates for one resource.

Appendix 5.7.3 Assigning Part-Time Resources at the Project Level *(8.10)*

It is possible, in Microsoft Project, to designate part-time resource participation at the project level by adjusting the number of standard workhours per day in the respective resource calendar. For every activity that the resource is assigned to, the correct scheduling will occur and the *true work effort* will remain in the activity duration field. There is no special field containing the number of elapsed calendar days, but this is not a serious problem. The system does not support varying levels of participation at the project level.

Appendix 5.7.4 Deleting and Changing Resources at the Project Level *(8.11)*

Resources in Microsoft Project are deleted from the Resource List screen by pressing ''Delete''. Deleting a resource in the list automatically results in the project-wide removal of all corresponding resource assignments.

Names are changed in the same manner as other modifications. Changing a name results in a project-wide replacement of all occurrences of the old name with the new name.

Appendix 5.7.5 Matching Resources to Jobs (8.14)

In Microsoft Project, the assignments are entered into the Activity Details screen and may be made at any level in the work breakdown structure. (Figure A5.4) There may be eight resource names assigned to each activity. The first Activity Details screen is recalled by pressing "Edit" from the main menu. Thereafter, subsequent forms may easily be brought to the screen by simply pressing the "Up Arrow" or "Down Arrow" keys to scroll through the activity list.

Once the Activity Details screen has been invoked, pressing the "Tab" key nine or more times will position the cursor at a blank resource name field. At this point, pressing the "Right Arrow" key will invoke a window with the list of available resources. Then, positioning the cursor on the name of a desired resource and pressing the "Return" key will complete the first part of the process.

A resource name may only be assigned to an activity once—regardless of the availability number in the resource list. According to the documentation, this restriction has been implemented in order to help the user to avoid assigning the same resource to an activity more than once. However, when teams need to be used and it is likely that more than one member (but not all members) of the team will need to be assigned to an activity, it will be necessary to create a separate entry for each team participant.

The assignment number is also entered in the Activity Details screen. In Microsoft Project, the availability number is used for leveling. The system will allow the user to enter an assignment number into the Activity Details screen that is greater than the availability number set in the resource list. The system simply assumes two parallel resources of the same duration and effort and processing continues as usual.

When an undefined resource is assigned to a task, the system automatically creates a corresponding entry in the resource list. No values, however, are entered. The user must remember to enter the desired values at a later date.

Microsoft Project only has one duration field. If the integrity of the duration field is to be maintained, this setting should *not* be changed. When the resource effort is different than the task duration, special actions are required, which will be addressed later in the appendix.

Appendix 5.7.6 Assigning Part-Time Resources at the Task or Activity Level (8.15)

While it is possible to designate part-time resource participation at the project level (by adjusting the number of standard workhours per day in the respective resource calendar), it is not possible to override this value at the activity level. This is true, in spite of the fact that, in the Activity Details screen, the assignment number of resources may be entered as a fraction. Fractional entries have no effect on scheduling.

Appendix 5.7.7 Assigning Multiple Resources to a Job (8.16)

Microsoft Project supports multiple resources— as long as all of the resources will be working for the same length of time and the time is equal to the *true work effort* (as in Example 5). For *doubling up* as illustrated in Example 6, the user will simply need to recompute the new duration and enter the value into the duration field of the Activity Details screen.

For using resources that each have different durations, separate parallel activities that are dependent on the same predecessor will need to be created, one for each unique duration.

Appendix 5.7.8 What to Do when the Resource Effort Must be Less than the Elapsed Calendar Days (8.17)

Microsoft Project does not support any of the three scenarios described. On the other hand, the system does allow the user to enter an "e" with the duration in the Activity Details screen to signal elapsed time rather than *true work effort*. (When the system schedules dates, it then ignores nonworking days and holidays.) However, users are cautioned not to use this feature for the examples described. The cost is computed at the elapsed calendar time and *not* the *true work effort*, a process that increases the costs of the job!

Appendix 5.7.9 Fixed Dates for Activities Or Tasks (8.19)

Microsoft Project does not use the scheduling algorithm that highlights projects that are late before they start.

This product does not make distinctions between summary records and lower levels in the WBS.

There are three sets of dates reported in Microsoft Project: the early dates, the late dates, and the scheduled dates. The dates found in the Activity Details screen are the scheduled dates. (Figure A5.4) If left blank, these dates default to ASAP scheduling (as soon as possible).

The system also accepts ALAP (as late as possible) in either the start date or the finish date field. This action will cause the task to be scheduled at the very end of the *candidate time slice*. While this does not extend the project end date, it can easily create a new critical path.

On the other hand, a date entered into the start date or finish date fields acts as a fixed date. When a value is entered into either of these two date fields, the system will automatically put the corrected date (based on durations) in the alternate field. These new dates are reported in the scheduled date fields. The early date and late date fields will still contain the original values.

The system schedules activities that have fixed dates first, then schedules by ALAP, and, last of all, schedules by ASAP.

If the fixed dates are the same as the current system-generated dates of the affected activity, there is no change to the schedule. The system will not accept fixed dates that are earlier than the current system-generated dates of the affected activity.

If the fixed dates are later than the current system-generated dates of the affected activity, the new dates will be in the scheduled date fields. The early and late date fields will contain the original values. The system will leave all of the dates of all of the predecessors alone but it will modify the early, late, and scheduled dates of any affected successors.

Only activities with zero slack are considered to be on the critical path. In order to accommodate the fixed date, the system may need to add slack to the job. As a consequence, activities that have fixed dates and that are also on the critical path will not always show up on the critical path. To force a job to the critical path, users must add ''c'' after the duration number in the Activity Details screen.

Microsoft Project produces no special flags to indicate fixed dates or delays due to fixed dates.

If the late finish date of the project is entered into a fixed date milestone, the late dates of all of the predecessors will be correctly computed.

Appendix 5.7.10 Automatic Resource Leveling (8.30)

Microsoft Project only supports the second leveling approach. Before any leveling operations may be performed, users must insure that the operating system date is set to a value that is either on or before the project starting date. Then, leveling is invoked by pressing the F3 key or by setting the level field in the Project Options screen to *Yes*. (Figure A5.2) Microsoft Project uses the following rules and sequence of execution for resolving leveling conflicts:

- First, if there is slack time *and* there is a nonzero priority *and* there are no fixed dates *and* there is a start date later than today's date, the job may be shifted within the candidate time frame.

- Next, resources are assigned by the lowest priority number first, then by early start time, then by slack time, then by smallest duration, then by highest resource requirements and, finally, by activity number.

For the control sample, priorities were all set to 1. Setting priorities will be addressed in the next section.

Leveling does not affect the project end date and, therefore, may leave some resources overscheduled.

The leveled dates will be in the scheduled start and the scheduled finish fields.

Delays due to resource leveling are shown with dotted lines between the original starting date symbol and the new starting date symbol. (See Activities 3 and 5 in Figure A5.13.)

All effects of leveling may easily be erased by pressing ''Options; Project'' and setting leveling to ''Clear''.

Figure A5.13

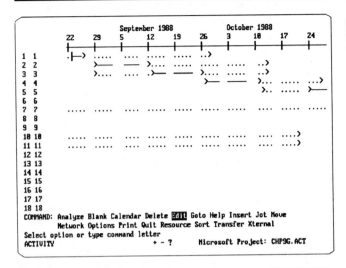

Figure A5.14

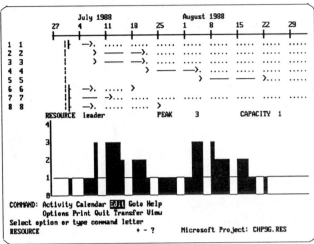

Appendix 5.7.11 Setting Special Leveling Priorities on Tasks Or Activities (8.31)

During the leveling process, when there is a nonzero entry in the priorities field of the Activity Details screen, Microsoft Project automatically uses priorities above any other criteria. The priority may be any number between 1 and 100—the lower the number, the higher the priority. Priorities set at higher levels in the work breakdown structure have no effect on their subordinate levels.

Appendix 5.7.12 User-Driven Interactive Leveling (8.32)

In Microsoft Project, resource conflicts are flagged with a message that names the resources that have been overscheduled. This message is found at the bottom of the screen. (Figure A5.9) However, like most products, the system does not use this message to tell the user where the overscheduling takes place. This is done with the resource histograms.

In Microsoft Project, there are three split windows for viewing resource histograms: a resource histogram with a project-level activity Gantt (See Figure A5.14.), a resource histogram along with a window that lists the corresponding resource assignments (See

Figure A5.15.), and two different resources in a histogram comparison (See Figure A5.16.).

The height of each column in the histogram shows the level of commitment. With a horizontal line drawn across the histogram at the corresponding vertical axis level, the histogram also implicitly shows available resource levels. Underutilization and overutilization

Figure A5.15

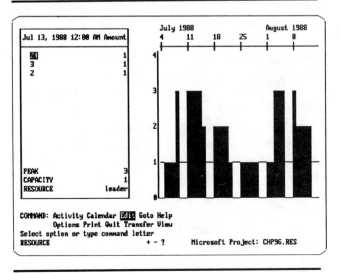

Figure A5.16

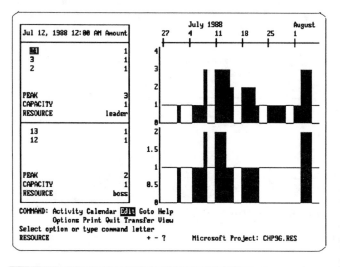

are both the same color. Where there is no utilization, the column is blank.

Both the Gantt chart and the histogram in Microsoft Project show weekends and holidays.

The resource histogram with the project-level activity Gantt (which is accessed by pressing "Resource; View; Activity". See Figure A5.14.) is a split screen with the project Gantt at the top of the screen and a single designated resource histogram at the bottom. The Gantt, naturally, is scaled to time and can be scrolled using the arrow cursor keys. The cursor does not operate in the histogram at the bottom. There are also two figures present: the *capacity*, which is the number of available resources and the *peak*, which tells the highest number of assignments this resource reached during the entire project.

The activity Gantt display may also be limited to only those activities that relate to a given resource. This is done by pressing "Options; Filter; Edit" and entering the resource name in the corresponding field. This filter may be saved and easily recalled at any time.

The Resource Histogram and Assignment window (Figure A5.15), a powerful leveling tool accessed by pressing "Resource; View; Histogram", has a time scaled resource histogram on the right side of the screen and a window that displays a list of the resource's assignments on the left side of the screen. The cursor

is active in both displays. By moving the "Right Arrow" and "Left Arrow" keys, the user can shift the cursor to any given day in the histogram (for example, to a day where the resource is heavily overscheduled).

As the cursor moves from day to day in the histogram, *the list of the activities to which the resource is assigned on that day changes accordingly in the Activity Details window.* This is the only product that lists, on a daily basis, the offending activities that are contributing to resource overscheduling. The user does not have to go poking through the Gantt to find them. Furthermore, those activities that are on the critical path are highlighted in the Assignment window. In addition to this information, the date is displayed in the Assignment window, along with the capacity number (the number of available resources) and the peak number (the number of resources actually assigned that day). As the cursor moves through the histogram, this peak number changes to reflect the number of resources assigned that day.

By moving the "Up Arrow" and "Down Arrow" keys, the user may position the Activity Details window cursor on a specific activity.

Last, the user may display and compare two sets of Resource Histogram and Assignment windows—one set for one resource on the top of the screen and a second set for a second resource on the bottom of the screen. (Figure A5.16) This is done by pressing "Resource; View; Comparison". The cursor is only active in one set at a time; but the active set can easily be changed by pressing the F1 key.

Microsoft Project is a semi-interactive leveling system. Most resource conflicts are resolved from any of the above split screens by moving the cursor to the activity in question and pressing "Activity; Edit" or "Resource; Edit". The Activity Details screen is used to change the dates, the durations, and the relationships, and to add, change, or delete the resource assignments. The Resource List screen (Figure A5.12) is used to change the availability in the resource list.

Although most modifications may be made from any of these three displays, users must leave the Leveling window to add new activities and resources or to modify calendar information. Activities may be added from the Activity Details screen by pressing "Insert". Similarly, resources are added from the Resource List screen by pressing "Insert". Data is changed in the resource calendar by pressing "Calendar; Days" or

"Calendar; Hours". Resource lags are not supported in this product.

Appendix 5.7.13 Baseline Project Plans for Resources Leveling (8.34)

Microsoft Project supports one version of a baseline. By saving the optimal plan as the baseline for the resource-constrained plan that is selected for implementation, users have one-half of the requirements met. This version is archived and a second version is produced. Then, by saving the resource-constrained plan as the baseline for the plan to which progress will be posted, the other half of the requirements will be met. Unfortunately, this *work-around* does not provide comparisons between all three versions. However, although the process is cumbersome, users may assimilate the data by perusing both sets of reports.

Appendix 5.7.14 Resources, Multiprojects, and Project Management Software (8.35.4)

From the Microsoft Project Resource List screen, the *template* resource files can be copied from project to project by pressing "Transfer; Load", moving the cursor to the name of the desired resource filename and pressing "Enter". (Figure A5.12)

The "External Link" brings in subproject resources, adding them to the master project's resource list—if they are not already present. When there are duplicate resources in the master project and the subproject, the data in the resource record of the master project is retained and the resource data in the subproject is ignored. Consequently, users ought to carefully choose the *first* subproject to be loaded, since that will be the source of the permanent resource data.

The link does not bring in project-level calendar information, nor does it bring in the resource calendars. However, this is easily done from the Calendar screen by pressing "Transfer; Load" and selecting the desired calendar file. (Figures A5.7 and A5.8) In this case, since incoming data will always overwrite existing data, if more than one file will be involved, the file that contains the permanent values should be transferred *last*.

Resource assignments are carried up one notch into the master project. Subprojects that have themselves been leveled are also reflected up one rung into

the master project. (This is not true with nested subprojects.) Below the first level, the histograms will show capacity fixed to 1.

The whole subproject is represented by a single one-line entry in the Gantt chart and the PERT chart. The system automatically names the activity using the original subproject file name plus the extension ".ACT". This is a very meaningful feature, especially since it will also be shown in all of the Resource Histogram windows with that same name. (See the earlier discussion in this appendix on interactive leveling for a description of the histograms.) As a result, it is very easy to determine which project within a group of several subprojects is causing the overcommitment. On the other hand, it is impossible to determine what activities within that subproject are the offenders. That information is only available at the subproject level. Other than the normal procedure for changing back and forth between plans, there is no way to alternatively view the subprojects and the master project.

It is not possible to perform automatic leveling from the master schedule in an attempt to level the resources across all subprojects.

When the "External Link" option is used, the act of transferring resources consumes extra main memory. Needless to say, increased memory use will slow down response times during subsequent calculations.

The order in which the subprojects are modified and saved is also important. To insure that the latest modifications in the subprojects are reflected in the master project, they must each be reloaded and resaved from the bottom up.

Appendix 5.7.15 Guidelines and Documentation (8.36)

Microsoft Project has a few pages on resource management.

APPENDIX 5.8 CALCULATING COSTS

Appendix 5.8.1 Costs and Project Management Software (9.4)

Other than the code for a work breakdown structure, Microsoft Project does not provide any additional accounting codes. From this perspective, accounting codes may only be entered at the activity level. On the other hand, rollup reports may also be generated by sorting on resource name.

Although there is a hard-copy cost histogram, there is no on-line graphical presentation of costs. The Resource List screen (Figure A5.12) does list the total project costs and the total costs to completion for each resource. (See the following discussion on formulas.) Using the "Print; Display" command, the user may also view several of the hard-copy reports on the screen. Many of these reports contain costs figures.[6]

Fixed costs and overhead costs must be created as separate resources and assigned to the respective activity just like any other resource. They may be created as *fixed* or per *use*. (Figure A5.12) When the resource has been established as a *fixed* resource, all costs are considered paid for on the first day an activity uses that resource. *Usage* costs are each time costs. Unless a separate activity has been created to represent the whole project, there is no way to enter project-level fixed or overhead costs. (In the following formulas, references to today's date mean the operating system date.) The formulas for *resource costs per day* are:

• The hourly rate × hours per day; or
• The weekly rate ÷ the number of defined days per week; or
• The defined daily cost.

Resource costs are computed as:

1. The *cost per resource day per activity* is equal to the resource cost per day times the daily amount of the resource used by that activity.

2. The *total resource costs per day* are equal to the sum of all of the values from Item 1 for the resource on the given day.

3. The *total project cost for a resource* is equal to the sum of all of that resource's costs for each day of the project.

4. The *total costs to completion* for each resource are equal to the sum of the total resource costs per day for each day in the project beyond (and including)

today's date. At the beginning of the project, this is equal to the total project cost for a resource. After the beginning of the project, this is driven by the choices in the "Update" option. (See the discussions later in this appendix.)

The formulas for activity costs are:

1. The total activity cost per day is equal to the sum of all of the daily costs of each of the resources assigned to the activity for that day. (See Item 1 in the previous section.)

2. The total activity cost for the project is equal to the sum of the costs of each of the resources assigned to the activity for each day of the activity.

3. The *cost to completion* for *each* activity (for each day in the project beyond (and including) today's date) is determined two ways: at the beginning of the project, this is equal to the cost for each of the resources for that activity times the duration of the activity; after the beginning of the project, this is driven by the choices in the "Update" option. (See the discussion later in this appendix.)

4. The *total* activity *costs to completion* (for each day in the project beyond (and including) today's date) is determined two ways: at the beginning of the project, this is equal to the sum of all of the resource costs in all of the activities for each day of the project; after the beginning of the project, this is driven by the choices in the "Update" option. (See the discussion later in this appendix.)

The formulas for total costs are:

1. The total cost of the project[7] is determined from the sum of the total cost of all resources used for each day of the project.

2. The total cost of the project per day is equal to the total resource cost per day or the total activity cost per day.

Microsoft Project will export all project data in LOTUS 1-2-3 format.

---

[6]For example, total costs for each activity in the project.

[7]This value stays fixed once users have entered the unit cost of the resources, but will be readjusted if they reassign the resources or modify the unit cost!

Appendix 5.8.2 Costs in a Multiproject Environment (9.5)

In Microsoft Project, with the "External Link", users can indicate how they want to bring in costs: *none* means no; *fixed* means all costs will be brought in as though they occurred on the first day; and *actual* means the costs will be charged to the project as they are accrued. Costs are rolled up several levels; but only the first level can be designated as *actual*; below that, all levels will roll up costs as *fixed* rather than *actual*—regardless of how they were invoked at the "sub-subproject" level. *Actual* costs consume substantially more memory and cause response time to slow down.

APPENDIX 5.9 COMPRESSING TIME

Appendix 5.9.1 Time-Constrained Plans and Project Management Software (10.9)

The automatic leveling in Microsoft Project only levels within a time-constrained plan. Other than setting the desired end date, users do not have to take any special action. Users may produce reports sorted on slack.

APPENDIX 5.10 ASSIGNING THE WORK

Appendix 5.10.1 The Assignment Report (11.1)

Microsoft Project features several standard reports that may be used for assignment (for example, the "Activity Detail" report and the "Activity Table" report). However, these reports display several sets of dates as well as costs. For this reason, users may prefer to customize their own reports. Report customization is very easy. To create an assignment report (See Figure A5.17.):

1. Start from the Activity Details screen;

2. Choose all of the activity records for a given resource by pressing "Options; Filter; Edit" (See Figure A5.18.) and marking "Select = On", "Match On = All", and "Resource Name = *enter the resource name as it appears in the resource list*".

3. Choose "Print; Utilities; Report" and choose the desired fields. For example, users may choose columns for activity description, scheduled start date, scheduled finish date, duration, and predecessors.

4. Pressing "Print; Printer; Return" will complete the process. Before pressing the "Return" key in the last step, the user may enter up to three lines of data that will be used as a report title.

Appendix 5.10.2 The Ad Hoc Information (11.2)

The 200-character activity notes field in Microsoft Project may be displayed on the standard "Activity Detail" report. However, this report also displays several dates and costs. It is very easy to customize a report that will display only the activity name and identifier along with the corresponding notes. (See Figure A5.19.) If the activity list has been filtered to select only the data for a given resource, a simple and straightforward report is obtained. (See the earlier discussions on filtering and customizing.)

It is likely that these reports will need to be supplemented by output from a word processor.

Appendix 5.10.3 The Work Package Cover Sheet (11.5)

In Microsoft Project, a word processor may be used to create the forms that meet this requirement.

Appendix 5.10.4 The Responsibility Grid (11.6)

In Microsoft Project, a word processor may be used to create the forms that meet this requirement.

Appendix 5.10.5 The Supporting Documentation (11.8)

The Microsoft Project resource histogram (Figure A5.15) may be reported from the Resource List screen by pressing "Print; Printer; Histogram; Resource". After filtering (See the earlier discussion.), the resource Gantt (Figure A5.14) may be produced from the Activity Details screen by pressing "Print; Printer; Schedule". A tabular resource loading report may be produced from the Resource List screen by pressing "Print; Printer; Period; Demand". The user may choose the periods (for example: days, weeks or months).

Figure A5.17

```
                              custom

Project: TEMP                           Date: Jul  1, 1988   7:29 PM
--------------------------------------------------------------------
            Activity                    Scheduled
            Description                 Start Date
--------------------------------------------------------------------
6                                  Jul  1, 1988   8:00 AM
12                                 Jul  8, 1988   8:00 AM
13                                 Jul  8, 1988   8:00 AM
21                                 Aug  3, 1988   8:00 AM


       ------------------------------------------------------------

   Project: TEMP                          Date: Jul  1, 1988   7:29 PM
   -----------------------------------------------------------------
         Scheduled              Total
         Finish Date            Duration
   -----------------------------------------------------------------
   Jul  7, 1988   5:00 PM   4.00 Days
   Jul 22, 1988   5:00 PM   11.00 Days
   Jul 13, 1988   5:00 PM   4.00 Days
   Aug 10, 1988   5:00 PM   6.00 Days


       ------------------------------------------------------------

   Project: TEMP                          Date: Jul  1, 1988   7:29 PM
   -----------------------------------------------------------------

                 Predecessors
   -----------------------------------------------------------------

       6
       6

       21
   -----------------------------------------------------------------


   -----------------------------------------------------------------
   Notes:

     6
       this is the note for 6

     12
       this is the note for 12

     13
       this is the note for 13
```

Figure A5.18

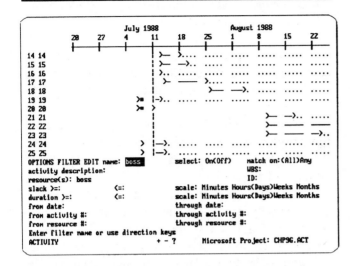

Appendix 5.10.6 The Problem Log *(11.10)*

In Microsoft Project, a word processor may be used to create the forms that meet this requirement.

Appendix 5.10.7 The Work Notes Form *(11.11)*

In Microsoft Project, a word processor may be used to create the forms that meet this requirement.

Appendix 5.10.8 Viewing the Data on the Screen *(11.12)*

While not all of the reports in Microsoft Project may be displayed on the screen, many of the popular reports can be viewed on-line.

Figure A5.19

```
                  THIS IS THE REPORT TO PRINT
                  THE AD HOC INFORMATION

Project: TEMP                              Date: Jan 21, 1989  3:17 PM
---------------------------------------------------------------------
Activity                    Activity
Number                      Description
---------------------------------------------------------------------
        1     6 THIS IS THE DESCRIPTION FOR 6
        2    12 THIS IS THE DESCRIPTION FOR 12
        3    13 THIS IS THE DESCRIPTION FOR 13
        4    21
        5    22
        6    26
        7    32
        8    39
        9    43
       10    45
       11    48
       12    51
       13    52
---------------------------------------------------------------------


---------------------------------------------------------------------
  Notes:

  6
    this is the note for 6

 12
    this is the note for 12

 13
    this is the note for 13
```

APPENDIX 5.11 REPORTING STATUS

Appendix 5.11.1 Baselines *(12.2)*

In Microsoft Project, the baseline information is in the forecast fields.

Appendix 5.11.2 Extracting the Jobs for the Turn-Around Document—on a Range of Dates *(12.5)*

Date ranges in Microsoft Project may be designated on the options filter form by entering the values for "from date through date". (Figure A5.18)

Appendix 5.11.3 Setting Up an *As-Of* Date *(12.6)*

The Microsoft Project *As-of* date is set in the today's date field on the Project Options screen. In order for this to work correctly, users must insure that the operating system date is on or before the *As-of* date. New schedules are then correctly computed when the directions that are outlined in the rest of this appendix are followed.

Appendix 5.11.4 Entering Percent Complete *(12.7)*

Once the project is under way, Microsoft Project assumes all activities will stay on time. The user may then direct the system to maintain this approach and automatically compute percent complete—or to ignore the percent field and give control of the status to the user. The desired alternative is recorded by setting the update field on the Project Options screen to *Yes* or *No* respectively.

When "Update" equals *Yes*, the system has control of percentage status and one of three conditions occurs:

- If the start date of the activity is later than the setting for today's date, percent complete will be 0 percent;
- If the setting for today's date is later than the finish date of the activity, percent complete will be 100 percent; or
- If the setting for today's date is between the start and the finish date of the activity, the percentage is computed by dividing the number of working days between the start date of the activity and today's date by the activity duration.

When "Update" equals *Yes*, users may also override percent complete.[8] Changing the percent in this mode will cause a corresponding change in the *duration* of the activity.

When "Update" equals *No*, the status of percent is controlled by the user. Changing the percent in this mode will *not* cause a corresponding change in the duration of the activity.

In either mode, changes to percent alter the dates of the activity; therefore, caution should be exercised when entering a new value. When "Update" equals *Yes*, a change to the percent will change the duration and adjust the finish date accordingly. When "Update" equals *No*, a change to the percent will adjust the start date accordingly.

The bottom line is that, for better control of status reporting, the "Update" option should be set to *No*.

Appendix 5.11.5 Hard Copy Turn-Around Documents *(12.8)*

In Microsoft Project, it is very easy to produce a customized turn-around document that displays the activity name, the scheduled start date, the scheduled finish date, the total duration, the duration to date, the duration to complete, the percent complete, the predecessors, and the notes fields. (See Figure A5.20.) If the turn-around document is customized from the Forecast screen, actual dates may also be printed along with forecasted dates (used to represent scheduled dates).

Appendix 5.11.6 Entering the Status Collection Data *(12.9)*

Updating the activities in Microsoft Project is done in the Activity Details screen. The bulk of the modifications may be achieved by manipulating the percent complete field. (See the earlier discussion.) Of course, if the value is anything other than the system-computed

---

[8]They may want to do it for any and every activity that doesn't match up to the system computations. They may need to do it every time they invoke the project.

Figure A5.20

```
                      THIS IS A SAMPLE TURN-AROUND
                              DOCUMENT

Project: TEMP                              Date: Jul 11, 1988  5:00 PM
----------------------------------------------------------------------
Activity        Scheduled             Scheduled            Total
Number         Start Date           Finish Date          Duration
----------------------------------------------------------------------
       1  Jul  1, 1988  8:00 AM   Jul  7, 1988  5:00 PM   4.00 Days
       2  Jul  8, 1988  8:00 AM   Jul 22, 1988  5:00 PM  11.00 Days
       3  Jul 11, 1988  8:00 AM   Jul 14, 1988  5:00 PM   4.00 Days
       4  Aug 10, 1988  8:00 AM   Aug 17, 1988  5:00 PM   6.00 Days
       5  Aug 10, 1988  8:00 AM   Aug 31, 1988  5:00 PM  16.00 Days
       6  Aug 18, 1988  8:00 AM   Aug 26, 1988  5:00 PM   7.00 Days
       7  Aug 29, 1988  8:00 AM   Sep 12, 1988  5:00 PM  10.00 Days
       8  Sep 14, 1988  8:00 AM   Sep 30, 1988  5:00 PM  13.00 Days
----------------------------------------------------------------------
                      THIS IS A SAMPLE TURN-AROUND
                              DOCUMENT

Project: TEMP                              Date: Jul 11, 1988  5:00 PM
----------------------------------------------------------------------
   Duration          Duration
    to Date          to Complete            Predecessors
----------------------------------------------------------------------
4.00 Days          0.00 Days
2.00 Days          9.00 Days       6 THIS IS THE DESCRIPTION FOR 6
1.00 Day           3.00 Days       6 THIS IS THE DESCRIPTION FOR 6
0.00 Days          6.00 Days
0.00 Days         16.00 Days
0.00 Days          7.00 Days       21
0.00 Days         10.00 Days
0.00 Days         13.00 Days       32
----------------------------------------------------------------------


----------------------------------------------------------------------
  Notes:

  6
    this is the note for 6

 12
    this is the note for 12

 13
    this is the note for 13
```

percent complete, the user will need to manually calculate the correct number. This is easily done by dividing the known days-to-date by the duration days. (Caution should be exercised when changing the percentage values. See the earlier discussion in this appendix.)

There is no time-this-period field in this system. Furthermore, although several reports will display the duration-to-date and the duration-to-complete, there is no way to enter these values. They must be driven by the values entered for the activity duration and the percent complete.

Figure A5.21

```
                        THIS IS A SAMPLE
                        STATUS REPORT

Project: CHP9G                        Date: Jul 11, 1988  5:00 PM
------------------------------------------------------------------
Activity:

  1 6 THIS IS THE DESCRIPTION FOR 6

              Planned duration: 4.00 Days    Duration to date: 4.00 Days
              Slack avail: 52.00 Days        % Complete: +100.00%

                     Start                         Finish
      Sched:  Jul  1, 1988  8:00 AM       Jul  7, 1988  5:00 PM
      Actual: Jul  1, 1988  8:00 AM       Jul  7, 1988  5:00 PM

      Early:  Jun 30, 1988  8:00 AM       Jul  6, 1988  5:00 PM
      Late:   Sep 14, 1988  8:00 AM       Sep 19, 1988  5:00 PM

  ----------------------------------------------------------------
  Notes:

      this is the note for 6

  ----------------------------------------------------------------
  Predecessors:

      NONE

  ----------------------------------------------------------------
  Successors:

  2 12 THIS IS THE DESCRIPTION FOR 12      Slack avail: 51.00 Days

     Sched  Start: Jul  8, 1988  8:00 AM
     Early  Start: Jul  8, 1988  8:00 AM
     Late   Start: Sep 20, 1988  8:00 AM

  3 13 THIS IS THE DESCRIPTION FOR 13      Slack avail: 58.00 Days

     Sched  Start: Jul  8, 1988  8:00 AM
     Early  Start: Jul  8, 1988  8:00 AM
     Late   Start: Sep 29, 1988  8:00 AM


------------------------------------------------------------------
Resources used to date:
                  FORECAST            ACTUAL           VARIANCE
*  1 boss
     Amount            1.00              1.00            0.00%
     Duration     4.00 Days         4.00 Days           0.00%
     Cost          $1600.00          $1600.00           0.00%

Activity total:
     Duration     4.00 Days         4.00 Days           0.00%
     Cost          $1600.00          $1600.00           0.00%
```

Figure A5.22

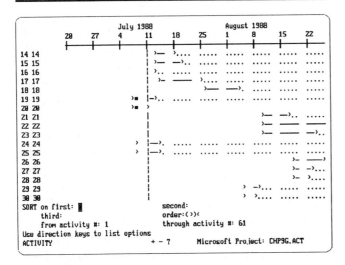

Special processing. Sometimes, the duration and the finish date must be modified. (For example, see C and S in Figure 12.1) In Microsoft Project, the scenarios in G, H, I, and M may *not* be implemented as illustrated. The start dates must be *reset* to 6/30, 7/8, 7/11, and 7/14, respectively—or the durations will be incorrect.[9] These new dates must be computed manually. Example X may not be implemented at all, unless the dependency with J is eliminated and the start date is changed to 7/7, implying an overlap of X with J.

Appendix 5.11.7 Performance Status Reporting (*12.10*)

From the Forecast screen (Figure A5.9), pressing "Print; Printer; Activity; Summary" will cause a very comprehensive status report to be produced. (See Figure A5.21.) It contains the planned duration; the duration to Date; the slack; the percent complete; the scheduled, actual, early, and late dates; the notes; several resource utilization fields; a list of predecessors and successors and their slack; and their scheduled, early, and late dates. From this screen, it is also possible to print a Gantt chart that compares actuals to the baseline.

Microsoft Project features sorting and selecting on several fields. (See Figures A5.18 and A5.22.) With the exception of the parameter for jobs that are *critical*, the sort may only be in ascending order. The parameter for *critical* sorts jobs with least slack first. There are three levels of the sort. Although it is not possible to directly identify late jobs, users may select by: actual, early, and late start dates; actual, early, and late finish dates; and by activities that are critical. While percent complete may be displayed on the report, it is not possible to sort or select on this field. Similarly, these operations may not be performed on remaining duration.

This product does not feature the ability to select jobs based on revised estimates. Similarly, users cannot get around the limitation by selecting based on relational and arithmetic operators between current values and baseline values. Microsoft Project *does* report on duration variances—both on the number of days and on the percent by which the original deviates from the projected. Unfortunately, it is not possible to sort or select on variances.

Appendix 5.11.8 Highlighting Progress (*12.11*)

In Microsoft Project, there is no special highlighting or time line on the PERT chart to show completion. On the other hand, the Gantt chart is very helpful: the *As-of* date is shown by a vertical dashed line; progress is shown on the bars by solid squares; progress is related to the percentage of the duration that has been completed; and delays are not illustrated.

Appendix 5.11.9 Costs and Project Management Software (*12.13*)

In Microsoft Project, the costs of the activities and of the project will be recomputed when time is reported to the activity and/or when a new unit rate is assigned to a resource. There is no special field for actual-costs-this-period.

The *total* cost of the project, the *cost to complete* of the project, and the *cost to complete* for each resource are computed by the system and are seen on the Resource List screen. (Figure A5.12) To see the activity costs that are computed by the system, the user must invoke one of the on-line reports.

When a separate *fixed* resource has been added

---

[9]Incorrect durations, in turn, will cause the project costs to be computed incorrectly.

to the resource list and then assigned to an activity, all costs will be accrued on the first day an activity uses that resource. When a separate *usage* resource has been added to the resource list and then assigned to an activity, costs are accrued each time the resource is used.

If the "Update" option equals *Yes* (Figure A5.2), the duration of the activity may be affected when the user enters a corrected percentage value. (See the earlier time tracking discussion and the discussion later in this appendix on percents and costs.) If the duration of the activity is affected, the *total costs to completion* will be correspondingly affected. Naturally, this will also affect the total costs of the project.

As the project progresses, the system will compute the *cost to completion for* each *activity* based on the activity's remaining business days that are beyond *(and including)* today's date. The remaining business days are based on the current forecasted duration of the activity.

As the project progresses, the system will compute the *activity's* total *costs to completion* as the sum of the daily costs of each of the resources assigned to each activity for each day in the project beyond *(and including)* today's date.

As the project progresses, the system will compute the *total cost to completion for* each *resource* as the sum of the total resource costs per day for each day in the project beyond *(and including)* today's date.

As the project progresses, the system will compute the *total* project *costs to completion* as the activity costs to completion or the resource costs to completion.

Appendix 5.11.10 Percentages and Their Effects on Costs *(12.14)*

When "Update" equals *Yes* in the Microsoft Project Options screen, users may override the percent complete. In this mode, changing the percent will cause a corresponding change in the duration of the activity. This change will, in turn, affect the costs of the project. If the duration is increased, the costs of the activity (and thus the project, since they are now computed on elapsed time rather than *true work effort*) will be incorrectly inflated, or vice versa. When "Update equals No", the system does not change durations.

Appendix 5.11.11 Cost Status Reporting *(12.15)*

By using the Microsoft Project custom report writer from the Analyze screen (Figure A5.9), it is possible to display total forecasted costs, actual costs to date, the costs to completion, the total projected costs, the cost variance, and the percentage of the cost variance. (See Figure A5.23.)

The "Cost Envelope" report will display a graphic view of cash flows for early, late, and scheduled dates. (See Figure A5.24.) The system automatically makes the timeframes on this graph the size necessary to fit the whole project on one page. This report will also show all costs in a multiproject scenario.

There is a "Cost Histogram" report; however, it only shows total revised costs for each period. There is no graphic view of cumulative costs.

Appendix 5.11.12 Earned Values and Project Management Software *(12.17)*

From the Analyze screen (Figure A5.9), Microsoft Project supports a variation of an earned value report. Although it cannot compute the BCWP and the BCWS, the custom report writer allows the user to display several comparisons between the baseline forecasted dollars and the current forecasted dollars. (See Figure A5.25.)

Because of the special processing that was necessary to implement various transactions illustrated in Figure 12.1, several of the actual costs to date were incorrect. (Also, see the discussion on percentages earlier in this appendix.)

Appendix 5.11.13 Costs in a Multiproject Environment *(12.18)*

The Microsoft Project "External Link" asks the user to choose whether the resource costs are to be accrued as if they are all being paid on the first day of the master project (called *fixed*) or if the costs should be charged to the master project as they occur in the subproject (called *actual*).

If the *actual* costs option has been selected, expenditures will be carried up one rung in the nest; below that, the costs will be represented as fixed costs,

Figure A5.23

```
                           SAMPLE
                        COST PROGRESS
                           REPORT

Project: TEMP                           Date: Jul 11, 1988 10:33 PM
-------------------------------------------------------------------
Activity       Total              Cost              Cost to
Number        Cost (F)          to Date (A)       Complete (A)
-------------------------------------------------------------------
   1           $800.00           $800.00             $0.00
   2          $2000.00           $400.00          $1600.00
   3          $2000.00           $400.00          $1800.00
   4          $2000.00             $0.00          $2000.00
   5          $2400.00             $0.00          $2400.00
   6          $1600.00          $1600.00             $0.00
   7           $840.00           $840.00             $0.00
   8           $320.00           $160.00            $80.00
   9           $160.00            $80.00            $80.00


-------------------------------------------------------------------
             $71120.00          $7400.00         $63720.00
```

```
                           SAMPLE
                        COST PROGRESS
                           REPORT

Project: TEMP                           Date: Jul 11, 1988 10:33 PM
-------------------------------------------------------------------
              Total             Cost                %
             Cost (A)         Variance        Cost Variance
-------------------------------------------------------------------
             $800.00            $0.00             0.00%
            $2000.00            $0.00             0.00%
            $2200.00          $200.00           +10.00%
            $2000.00            $0.00             0.00%
            $2400.00            $0.00             0.00%
            $1600.00            $0.00             0.00%
             $840.00            $0.00             0.00%
             $240.00           -$80.00          -25.00%
             $160.00            $0.00             0.00%


-------------------------------------------------------------------
           $71120.00            $0.00
```

regardless of how they were invoked at the sub-sub-project level.

When the "External Link" option is used, the act of transferring resources consumes extra main memory. This is especially true if the *actual* costs options is selected. Needless to say, increased memory use will slow down response times during subsequent calculations.

Appendix 5.11.14 Reporting on Resource Availability *(12.20)*

A Microsoft Project resource histogram that is similar to those pictured in Figures A5.14, A5.15, and A5.16 may be printed. The resource Gantt chart may also be printed. There is also a Gantt that shows actuals to be forecasted (baseline).

Figure A5.24

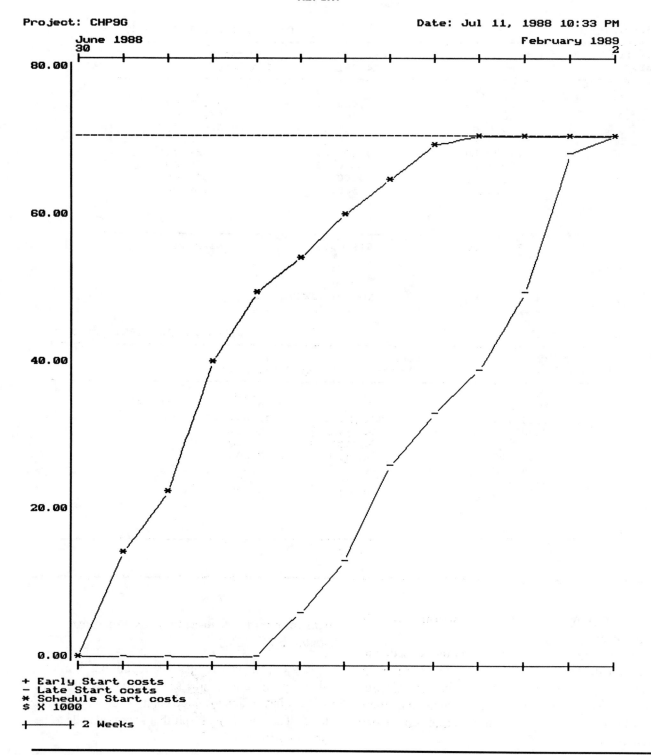

Figure A5.25

```
                          SAMPLE
                          EARNED
                          VALUE

Project: TEMP                         Date: Jul 11, 1988 10:33 PM
-----------------------------------------------------------------
Activity        Total            Cost              Cost
Number          Cost (F)         to Date (A)       to Date (F)
-----------------------------------------------------------------
   1            $800.00          $800.00           $800.00
   2            $2000.00         $400.00           $400.00
   3            $2000.00         $400.00           $400.00
   4            $2000.00         $0.00             $0.00
   5            $2400.00         $0.00             $0.00
   6            $1600.00         $1600.00          $1600.00
   7            $840.00          $840.00           $720.00
   8            $320.00          $160.00           $320.00
   9            $160.00          $80.00            $160.00


-----------------------------------------------------------------
             $71120.00          $7400.00          $8760.00
```

The tabular "Resource Loading by Periods" report shows the resource commitments across a user-designated timeframe. The "Resource Assignment" report (Figure A5.17) may be set up to display the number of resources available (capacity), the number required (allocation), the duration to date, the duration to completion, the percentage of duration to date, the percentage of duration to completion, and the peak resource usage. The user will need to compare the capacity, allocation, and peak usage fields to find overscheduling and underscheduling.

Appendix 5.11.15 Reporting on Resource Utilization (12.21)

Although Microsoft Project does support periodic reporting for resource utilization, the reports only show columns for the current values. (See Figure A5.26.[10]) There are no columns for planned values. Furthermore, the period reports only produce one summary line for each resource; they do not break the resource infor-

mation into tasks by resource. Although there are no row totals for each resource, the report does show column totals for each period.

Summary resource reports are also available that compare planned (forecast) to actuals and variances. (See Figure A5.27.) This report may be produced for costs or for time.

APPENDIX 5.12 MANAGING THE PROJECT

Appendix 5.12.1 Who Produces Perts and Gantts That May Be Restricted to Critical Path Jobs? (13.7)

The Microsoft Project network cannot be restricted to just the jobs on the critical path. On the other hand, the Gantt Charts can be limited to just those activities selected if slack is less than an established lowest value.

Appendix 5.12.2 Who Produces Reports That May Be Restricted to Fixed-Date Jobs? (13.8)

Microsoft Project does not support extraction of report data based on fixed dates.

---

[10]The current value reflects *actuals* when work has been done and *projected to completion* when the activity has not been started or completed.

Figure A5.26

```
                          SAMPLE
                    RESOURCE PERIOD
                         REPORT

Project: CHP9G                          Date: Jul 11, 1988 10:33 PM
Time scale: Week

Period ending          Jul  7, 1988     Jul 14, 1988      Jul 21, 1988


*  1 leader                 $600.00         $2600.00          $2200.00

*  2 boss                  $1200.00         $2000.00          $3600.00

*  3 senior                 $840.00         $1800.00          $1920.00

*  4 worker                 $240.00          $640.00           $640.00
                       ------------     ------------      ------------
Total:                     $2880.00         $7040.00          $8360.00
```

Appendix 5.12.3 Who Produces Perts and Gantts That May Be Restricted to Summary Jobs? *(13.9)*

The Microsoft Project network cannot be restricted to just the summary jobs. On the other hand, by creatively setting up the WBS number and using wild-cards for filtering, the Gantt Charts can be limited to just the desired summary activities.

Appendix 5.12.4 Local Area Networks *(13.14)*

Microsoft Project prevents access to files when they are active. It also provides read/write protection.

Appendix 5.12.5 Guidelines for Tracking and Managing the Project *(13.15)*

Interspersed among the several pages of Microsoft Project documentation for using the system are some hints on how to track projects.

Figure A5.27

```
                                SAMPLE
                           RESOURCE COST
                                REPORT

                                       Date: Jul 11, 1988 10:33 PM
  Project: CHP9G                       Report type: COST
  -----------------------------------------------------------------
                    FORECAST          ACTUAL          VARIANCE
     Resource                                     Difference    Percent
  -----------------------------------------------------------------

*  1 leader
     Cost per Hour:    $25.00          $25.00          $0.00      0.00%
     Amount Used:   84.00 Days      85.00 Days       1.00 Day    +1.19%
     Total Cost:    $16800.00       $17000.00        $200.00     +1.19%

*  2 boss
     Cost per Hour:    $50.00          $50.00          $0.00      0.00%
     Amount Used:   97.00 Days      97.00 Days      0.00 Days     0.00%
     Total Cost:    $38800.00       $38800.00         $0.00       0.00%

*  3 senior
     Cost per Hour:    $15.00          $15.00          $0.00      0.00%
     Amount Used:   66.00 Days      65.00 Days      -1.00 Day    -1.52%
     Total Cost:    $7920.00        $7800.00        -$120.00     -1.52%

*  4 worker
     Cost per Hour:    $10.00          $10.00          $0.00      0.00%
     Amount Used:   95.00 Days      94.00 Days      -1.00 Day    -1.05%
     Total Cost:    $7600.00        $7520.00        -$80.00      -1.05%
  -----------------------------------------------------------------
  Total Project Cost:
                   $71120.00       $71120.00         $0.00       0.00%

                                SAMPLE
                          RESOURCE DURATION
                                REPORT

                                       Date: Jul 11, 1988 10:33 PM
  Project: CHP9G                       Report type: DURATION
  -----------------------------------------------------------------
                    FORECAST          ACTUAL          VARIANCE
     Activity:                                    Difference    Percent
  -----------------------------------------------------------------

*  1 leader
                   84.00 Days      85.00 Days       1.00 Day    +1.19%

*  2 boss
                   97.00 Days      97.00 Days      0.00 Days     0.00%

*  3 senior
                   66.00 Days      65.00 Days      -1.00 Day    -1.52%

*  4 worker
                   95.00 Days      94.00 Days      -1.00 Day    -1.05%
  -----------------------------------------------------------------
  Total Project Duration:
                  149.00 Days     150.00 Days       1.00 Day    +0.67%
```

APPENDIX 6: VIEWPOINT 2.52

APPENDIX 6.0 INTRODUCTION

Each section in each appendix is keyed to its corresponding introductory section in the tutorial. Readers will find that the respective tutorial section is noted in italicized parentheses at the end of each appropriate section header line.

APPENDIX 6.1 NETWORK-DRIVEN PRODUCTS

Appendix 6.1.1 Data Entry Mode *(16.2.3)*

ViewPoint mandates that jobs may be added to the plan only while in network mode. On the other hand, it will also allow modifications to be made while in Gantt mode. The system works through keyboard selection, a mouse, and a combination of both.

Appendix 6.1.2 Size and Storage Constraints *(16.3.1)*

Initially, ViewPoint works on projects in main memory. The minimum requirement for skeletal project information is 17,375 bytes. A project with 100 activities will consume approximately 60,000 bytes.

ViewPoint's foundation is based on leveled sets of networks that are represented as branches of the Network Tree. Because ViewPoint works in main memory on only a branch of the plan at a time, the vendor suggests that the size of the branch be kept to 40 activities and 80 connections. If a branch is allowed to get much larger than this, the overflow will be held in a disk buffer and response time will slow down significantly. The number of branches in the combination of main memory, buffers, and hard disk is limited only by the amount of available storage.

Appendix 6.1.3 System Structure *(16.3.2)*

At its highest level, ViewPoint is driven by a main menu. (See Figure A6.1.) The majority of work, however, is done on the Network Planning screen (See Figure A6.2.) which is accessed from the main menu and is drawn scaled to time. There are several windows that can be accessed from the Network Planning screen. (See the planning menu in Figure A6.3.)

Appendix 6.1.4 Global System Project Data Defaults *(16.3.3)*

This product does not have a function for entering global system project data defaults. However, there is a configuration form that does address dependencies, slack, and scheduling algorithms.

Appendix 6.1.5 New Projects *(16.3.4)*

New projects are created first by selecting the New Project choice on the main menu. The Project Direc-

Figure A6.1

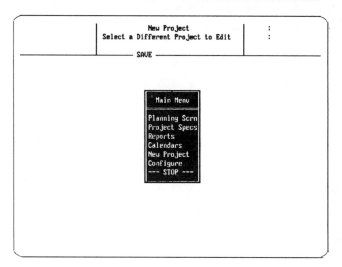

Figure A6.2

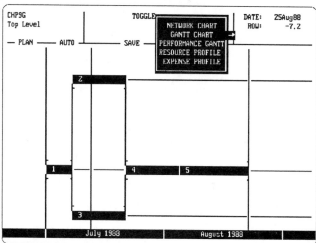

Figure A6.3

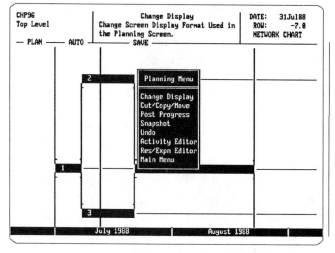

Figure A6.4

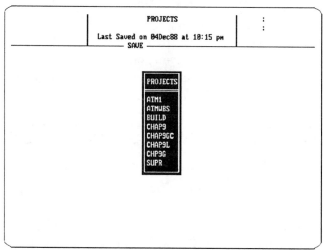

tory window is then displayed. (See Figure A6.4.) Electing the system-provided Build file will create a skeleton set of project data which can then be modified according to the user's requirements. After returning to the main menu, picking out Project Specs will access the Project Specification screen (See Figure A6.5.), whereupon the project data may be entered.

Appendix 6.1.6 Accessing Existing Plans
(16.3.5)

There are two steps for designating which plan data the user wants to access. First, selecting New Project from the main menu will bring up the Project Directory. Then, pointing the mouse at the name of the desired project plan will set the necessary pointers.

Figure A6.5

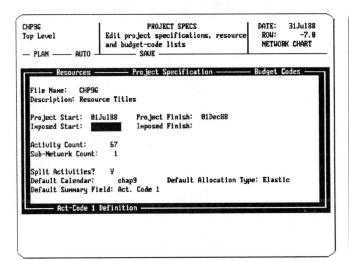

Figure A6.6

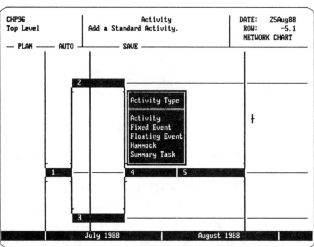

Appendix 6.1.7 Immediate Processor or Batch (16.3.6)

ViewPoint is an immediate processor system. The automatic recalculation may be turned off by toggling the ''Auto'' switch at the top of the Network Planning screen. (Figure A6.2)

Appendix 6.1.8 Adding Plan Data (16.3.7)

To start, the Network Planning screen must be selected from the main menu. Since project data may only be entered when in Network Edit mode, the Network Chart must be selected from the Mode window. The cursor must then be moved to the place on the screen that corresponds to the date when the activity will start. Pointing the mouse will summon the Activity Type window (See Figure A6.6.) Selecting the desired activity type will bring up the corresponding Activity window. (See Figure A6.7.)

Appendix 6.1.9 Optional "What-If's" or Permanent Saves (16.3.8)

Plan data is not made permanent until the user chooses to save it and until the user designates the name under which the plan is to be saved.

Figure A6.7

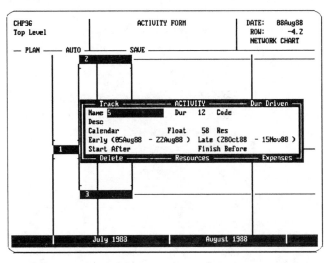

Appendix 6.1.10 Ad Hoc Information Storage 16.3.9)

The description fields in the Project Specification screen, the Activity window, the Event window, the Hammock window, and the Summary window hold 47, 48, 48, 49, and 47 characters respectively. The Resource window holds 29 characters. (Several of these windows will be addressed later in the text.)

Appendix 6.1.11 Exporting Data *(16.3.10)*

Viewpoint will export data to LOTUS-123, Version 1A and Version 2, dBase III, and in Comma Separated Values format.

APPENDIX 6.2 WORK BREAKDOWN STRUCTURES

Appendix 6.2.1 Graphics Support *(4.8.2)*

ViewPoint features a Network Tree that strongly resembles a work breakdown structure; however, it is not a fully functional WBS graphic. For example, at any given level, it suppresses visualization of all lower levels except one branch. The Network Tree is accessed from the Network Planning screen by pressing the F5 key. Then, the user may vary which lower level is displayed by moving the cursor to the desired node and pressing a "Cursor arrow" key. Accordingly, the entire tree may be scanned by alternating which lower level(s) are viewed. (See Figure A6.8.)

A feature of the package, ViewPoint's Network Tree is more a hierarchical representation of a leveled set of networks, with each set depicting a subnetwork or subproject of the total project. Rather than using the WBS to initiate the planning process, the ViewPoint documentation directs the user to start with a network and then employ the network to drive the development of the tree. Hammocks and summary tasks may be used at the upper levels, and the corresponding activity groups should be placed in the lower levels.

In another vein, it is important to note that entries put under one of the nodes in Viewpoint's Network Tree are not automatically carried over into the node's corresponding network. Therefore, though starting in Network Tree mode may simulate the WBS (albeit limited in nature), it will also require double data entry to create a network that corresponds to the lower-level nodes. Switching back and forth between the branches may also become confusing, especially if the nodes have not been meaningfully named. To use this approach *and* the WBS satisfactorily, it is likely that some (or all) of the WBS will have to be drawn manually first.

Like other work breakdown features, it is not mandatory to use the ViewPoint Network Tree mode for this application. The Network Tree is very useful when the size limitations of a branch have been reached. It is also of great value in a multiproject environment.

Appendix 6.2.2 Level Support *(4.8.3)*

ViewPoint has three activity code fields (Activity Codes 1, 2, and 3), each 16 positions long. Since the first code field may also be divided into 8 subfields (across 16 characters), there are a total of ten levels.

Appendix 6.2.3 Data Entry Requirements *(4.8.4)*

ViewPoint, as noted earlier, has been designed to use the network to drive the Network Tree. Using the Network Tree to start the planning process opposes the ViewPoint philosophy. As a result, the WBS approach will require double data entry for each job created in Network Tree mode. When initiating the planning process in Network mode, the user can opt to limit the WBS number to Activity Code 1, in which case, there is only one number to enter. If Codes 2 and 3 are also used, they cannot be entered in Network mode. They must be entered with a second process, in Table mode.

Appendix 6.2.4 Durations and Dependencies *(4.8.5)*

ViewPoint's Network Tree can be created without durations and dependencies. On the other hand, when

Figure A6.8

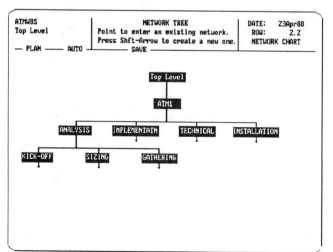

using their Network Planning mode to initiate the planning process, each work unit must be placed on the screen relative to its position in the plan. Therefore, dependencies must be known first. Furthermore, since ViewPoint's network is drawn scaled to time, work units that are entered without durations create fractional nodes on the network. The nodes, since plan data is placed inside them, appear to be unnamed, and it is difficult to distinguish one from the other. Consequently, estimates should also be completed in order to initiate the planning process, or *fake estimates* must be used as a *work-around*.

Appendix 6.2.5 Random Sequence of Data Entry (4.8.6)

ViewPoint supports random entry in the Network Trees; however, the networks must then be linked into the Network Trees, and the networks, of course, are structured.

Appendix 6.2.6 Using the Copy Features with the *Template* Tasks (4.8.7)

ViewPoint supports *cut and paste* of activities within the plan, and the *template* tasks may easily be stored in and retrieved from a library.

Appendix 6.2.7 Rollup Support (4.8.8)

ViewPoint provides rollup support on money, duration and resource fields. Specification of the rollup view is determined by either (1) a summary task rollup record (Figure A6.6) which identifies the summary selection field[1] and the code field values[2] to select for rollup;[3] or (2) a hammock rollup record, which affords no selection criteria, but simply captures the durations between the designated starting and ending points of the hammock. (The data is entered into windows that are similar to the Activity window pictured in Figure A6.7.) If the summary task record is used in order to

get the rollup, the exact same code must be used in the starting positions of the lower-level activities. Rollups will still not occur, however, unless there is a matching event at the beginning and ending of each group of jobs, and unless these beginning and ending events also have identical code numbers. Using wild-card filtering, the user may select all of the occurrences of a work type (e.g., testing) that occurs anywhere in a ViewPoint project plan—as long as the code for that type of work is always in the same position of the WBS. Further report customization is possible—using an assembly-language-type report writer.

Appendix 6.2.8 Guidelines and Documentation (4.8.9)

ViewPoint has limited WBS documentation.

APPENDIX 6.3 ESTIMATING

Appendix 6.3.1 Estimating Support and Estimating Guidelines (5.7.1)

ViewPoint does not provide guidelines that support the estimating techniques described in this book. They assume that the estimating has been completed and that the duration is known. ViewPoint has an entire chapter on estimating but it is a chapter on estimating costs, not time. (Instructions on how to use the system to achieve the implementation of a feature are not considered guidelines.)

Appendix 6.3.2 Estimates of *True Work Effort* Versus Resource-Driven Elapsed Time (5.7.4)

Durations may only be entered into ViewPoint when in planning mode. Furthermore, ViewPoint defaults to duration-driven estimating. Until resources have been assigned to activities, *true work effort* will be found in the activity duration field. After resources have been assigned, *true work effort* might only be found in the respective resource duration field.

Appendix 6.3.3 Durations and Units of Measurement (5.7.6)

In ViewPoint, the only unit of measurement supported is days. Since the only choice in ViewPoint is days,

---

[1]Choose one of Activity Codes 1, 2 or 3 (See the earlier discussion on Level support.)

[2]Indicating the value(s) Activity Codes 1, 2 or 3 may take.

[3]These two fields may also be used in conjunction with wild-card filtering masks.

the issue of default durations is not applicable. Again, because ViewPoint only supports days, the issue of mixed measurements is not applicable.

Appendix 6.3.4 Zero Duration Milestones (5.7.7)

ViewPoint has special milestone windows called Event windows. They are similar to the Activity window pictured in Figure A6.7, containing fields for the name, duration, code, description, calendar, float, and the two sets of dates.

Appendix 6.3.5 Lead and Lag Times with Duration but No Effort (5.7.8)

ViewPoint's Connection window allows lag times. (See Figure A6.9.) However, the lag time does not show up as a separate item on any report.[4]

APPENDIX 6.4 NETWORKS

Appendix 6.4.1 Types of Networks (6.8.1)

The network in ViewPoint is a Precedence diagram.

Appendix 6.4.2 Types of Relationships (6.8.2)

ViewPoint supports finish-to-start, finish-to-finish, and start-to-start relationships. The relationship type is established during the dependency connect. (Figure A6.9) For example, in a finish-to-finish relationship, the mouse is pointed at the end of each activity bar. In start-to-start, the mouse is pointed at the beginning of each bar.

In another vein, for jobs with small estimates, it is often hard to point with accuracy to the end or beginning of the bar. In such cases, it will be necessary to change the activity estimate to one that is large enough to create a longer activity bar. When the connections have been made, the estimate should be corrected. The risk here is that the user will forget to amend the estimate and the plan will be wrong.

---

[4]A better approach is to create a separate task with the corresponding duration and then enter a dummy resource whose cost is zero. Of course, this does consume precious memory.

Figure A6.9

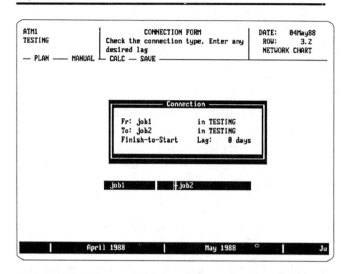

ViewPoint provides a special feature to allow the work to be interrupted during activities that have finish-to-finish relationships. If the *split activities* field in the Project Specification screen is set to *Yes*, the system will allow the interruptions. (Figure A6.5) Otherwise, a finish-to-finish relationship that delays the completion of one of the activities will also drag its early start to maintain the correct duration. Thus, if the activity's finish is delayed, it will also start later.

Appendix 6.4.3 Number of Dependencies (6.8.3)

The foundation of ViewPoint is the Network Tree. In order to make the best use of the product, the sub-networks ought to be portioned across branches of the Network Tree. Since branches of the Network Tree are processed in main memory, there is a limit to the size of each branch. The vendor suggests that a branch be constrained to approximately 40 activities and 80 relationships. If the branch becomes much larger than this, the overflow will be processed in a disc buffer and response time will suffer.

Appendix 6.4.4 Establishing Dependencies (6.8.4)

All data is entered in Network mode. To create relationships in ViewPoint, four steps are required: (1)

move the cursor to the predecessor and point the mouse; (2) move the cursor to the successor and point the mouse; (3) point the mouse again to get the Connection window; and (4) fill in the window.

Setting up the dependencies between branches of the Network Tree requires six steps: (1) point the mouse to the end of the last job in the predecessor subproject; (2) press F5 to go to the Network Tree; (3) move the cursor to the branch designating the successor subproject; (4) confirm the selection; (5) point the mouse to the beginning of the first job in the successor subproject; and (6) fill in the Connection window.

When connecting activities, the mouse is pointed at the activity bar. Summary activities or tasks may not be connected. When connecting events, the mouse is pointed at the symbol. There are no restrictions on multiple relationships.

Appendix 6.4.5 How Easy Is it to Enter Dependencies? (6.8.6)

Creating relationships in ViewPoint is very simply accomplished by pointing the mouse three times and then entering the relationship type.

Appendix 6.4.6 Inserting Jobs into the Middle of the Plan (6.8.7)

The main feature of ViewPoint is that it allows the user to ''draw'' the network on the screen. Although plan modifications may also be made in Gantt mode, additions are restricted to the Network Planning screen. Jobs may be added anywhere in the plan by choosing a blank spot on the Network Planning screen and pressing the mouse.[5] The Activity Type window will then appear. (Figure A6.6) Choosing a type will invoke the proper window. (Figure A6.7) Summary activities must always be accompanied by beginning and ending events. Even though users are able to place the job in almost

---

[5]The rows in the Network Planning screen are grouped in sets of five and are numbered 0 through 4. Activity bars always go in Row 2, the middle row. If the user points the mouse at any of the other rows, the activity will always shift to the closest Row 2. Event symbols are always placed in Row 1. The connection lines will be generated by the system and put in the other rows.

the exact spot they choose, an insert between two activities will still require dependencies to be reestablished as described above.

Appendix 6.4.7 Subnetwork Dependencies (6.8.8)

ViewPoint's subnetwork dependencies within the *same* branch of the Network Tree are easily added as described above. However, if the subnetwork connections are not close together, the system sometimes draws part of the connection at each dependent activity and doesn't connect them. (See Figure A6.10. Documentation is a successor to Conversion. Note the trace message.) A couple of these in one branch may cause some confusion.

More often than not, subnetworks will be in different branches of the Network Tree. Adding relationships between them is a slightly more complicated procedure and was also described above. At the conclusion of this operation, each branch has an arrow pointing to the connection point. (See Testplan in Figure A6.10.) When connections are to be made between two branches at the *same* level on the Network Tree, this is called a horizontal connection:

- First, an ending event or milestone is placed on the predecessor of the first branch.
- Then, it is copied into the second branch and placed as the beginning event or milestone of the successor.

Figure A6.10

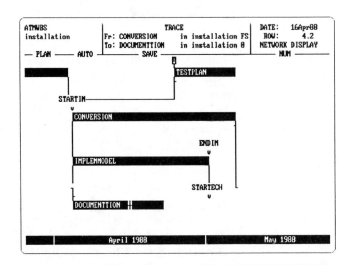

(See the discussion on how to copy later in this appendix.) Once again, the connections are illustrated as arrows.

Users are advised to restrict the use of connections between branches to only once between branch levels. Otherwise, the differentiation between the arrows may become difficult.

Appendix 6.4.8 Moving Jobs in the Network (6.8.9)

There are three functions in ViewPoint that are grouped together: the "Move," the "Cut/paste," and the "Copy/paste." The "Move" and the "Cut/paste" are used to shift entries in the network. The "Copy/paste" will be discussed later in this appendix. The "Move" only allows the user to vertically shift activities. It will not allow horizontal movement. The "Move" maintains all relationships. Horizontal and vertical shifts are both possible with the "Cut/paste" feature. However, in the course of this application, all relationships outside of the "cut" area are dropped. Since the network is drawn scaled to time, only the "Move" may be used for clean-up. The "Cut/paste" is used to change positions of jobs within the plan.

During either operation, the cursor must be used to highlight the designated area. However, there are times that, for some unexplained reason, the cursor just doesn't want to do its job. The operation must then be aborted and tried again. Sometimes, it even takes several tries to get the highlight to work.

Appendix 6.4.9 Removing Dependencies (6.8.10)

Removing dependencies in ViewPoint is very easy. Repeating the procedure for establishing dependencies will recall the Connection window. (Figure A6.9) When an existing connection is invoked, the word "Delete" will appear as an option on the border of the window. Pointing the cursor at "Delete" will remove the relationship.

Appendix 6.4.10 Deleting Jobs in the Plan (6.8.11)

In ViewPoint, removing jobs is easily accomplished by pointing the cursor at the activity bar and then pointing the cursor at the delete field in the Activity window. The "Delete" leaves dangling jobs.

Appendix 6.4.11 Lag and Lead Times (6.8.12)

ViewPoint's Connection window allows lag times. On the network, double connection lines are drawn to represent the length of the lag. All three types of relationships can have lag times. Remember, the lag time does not show up as a separate item on any report. A better approach is to create the task with the corresponding duration and then enter a dummy resource whose cost is zero. Of course, this also consumes precious memory. Hammock activities may have no lag time associations.

Appendix 6.4.12 Copying Jobs in the Plan (6.8.13)

The "Copy/paste" function in ViewPoint will copy any number of highlighted jobs while maintaining all relationships within the highlighted region. (See the earlier discussion under "Move" about the temperamentality of this function.)

Appendix 6.4.13 Copying the *Template* Jobs (6.8.14)

ViewPoint's "Copy/paste" feature will allow users to carve out pieces of a plan for reproduction of the *template* tasks. This may be done as often as necessary. All relationships within the copied area are maintained and new relationships are simply added as usual. This product also provides a feature that allows a library to be created for each set of repetitively used activities. This *template* library entry is easy to save from the Network Planning screen by pressing the F8 key. It may later be retrieved with the F7 key. Whole project plans or "carved out pieces" may easily be stored and retrieved from the library.

Appendix 6.4.14 Loops in the Network (6.8.15)

ViewPoint documentation states that loops will be signaled, that a message will be displayed, and that the system will help the user debug the loop. Unfortunately, the Loop Message window obscures the network and makes the debugging process very difficult. A better solution would simply be to prevent the loop in the first place. A second, albeit not as good, alternative would be putting the loop message into the Message window.

Appendix 6.4.15 Dangling Jobs *(6.8.16)*

ViewPoint allows dangling.

Appendix 6.4.16 Verifying Dependencies Are Correct *(6.8.17)*

In even an average-sized project, the ViewPoint network is not always easy to interpret. Since the network is drawn scaled to time, the system will pull two sequential tasks together if there is no lead or lag time between them. If they are on the critical path, they will be separated by a thin yellow line. Otherwise, the system will leave a thin black space between the two activities. The net result is that a group of sequential jobs is suddenly represented by a long bar. (See the small activity to the right of Test2 in Figure A6.11.) This is sometimes disconcerting, but it goes away if the successor has multiple relationships, one of which affects its start date.

ViewPoint's network can be created without durations or with durations of less than five days (4 to 40 hours). However, since the network is drawn scaled

to time, work units that are entered with short or no durations create fractional nodes on the network. Since plan data is placed inside the nodes, they appear to be unnamed, and it is difficult to distinguish one from the other. Consequently, estimates must be longer (and thus in conflict with the estimating approach), or the user must be willing to work with a cryptic network. In another vein, the fractional nodes almost make it impossible to connect dependency types.

Another source of scaled-to-time frustration occurs when the system automatically chooses to overlap an ending event or milestone of one activity with the beginning event or milestone of the next activity. The first gets obscured, the other gives up access to its window, and sometimes the name on the screen is a mystifying contraction of the two names.

To help the user interpret the directions of the relationships, the system generates little "ticks" in the connection lines. (Figure A6.11) These can be very helpful in the verification process. However, when there are multiple relationships, the network may be drawn with a series of overlapping lines which may subsequently be difficult to interpret.

- In Figure A6.11, Preparefor2 is only connected to Test2 and Planrest is only connected to Plannext. However, these relationships are difficult to verify.

- In Figure A6.12, Activities 2 and 3 are dependent on Activity 1 but Activities 4 and 5 have no con-

Figure A6.11

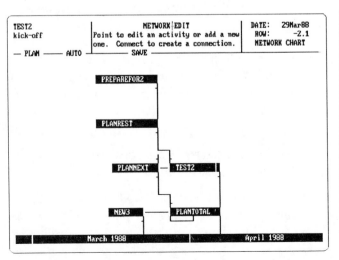

Figure A6.12

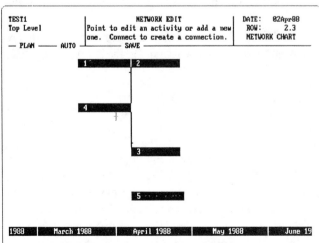

Figure A6.13

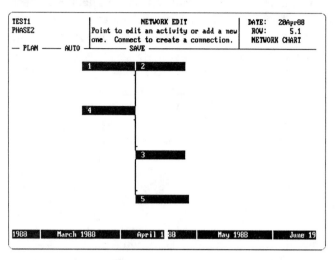

nection. When a connection is then made between Activities 4 and 5 (See Figure A6.13.), the dependencies become difficult to verify.

Vertically moving the offending jobs (for example, moving Test2 to the same row as Preparefor2 in Figure A6.11) often eliminates the problem.

Sometimes, if the connections are far apart, the connections will be open-ended. (Figure A6.10) In this illustration, Documentation cannot start until Conversion has finished. If this situation occurs more than once in a branch, it will again be hard to verify the connections.

The problems with connection verification are somewhat alleviated when using the "Trace" facility.

Appendix 6.4.17 Highlighting Dependency Paths (6.8.18)

ViewPoint features an excellent "Trace" function. After pointing the cursor at the designated job, pressing "T" will flash all of the connections of that job's immediate predecessors and successors. If there are multiple relationships, pressing the spacebar will scroll through each set of connections, telling the relationship type and lag time (if any) for each connection.

Appendix 6.4.18 Network Aesthetics (6.8.19)

At first blush, the ViewPoint network was aesthetically pleasing and easy to work with. However, after entering an average-sized project with several subnetworks and multiple relationships, several problems surfaced:

- When the subnetwork connections are not close together, the connections may be open-ended.
- Since the network is drawn scaled to time, work units that are entered with short or no durations create fractional nodes on the network. Since plan data is placed inside the nodes, they appear to be unnamed, and it is difficult to distinguish one from the other.
- Sometimes, the system automatically chooses to overlap an ending event or milestone of one activity with the beginning event or milestone of the next activity.
- When there are multiple relationships, the network may be drawn with a series of overlapping lines which may subsequently be difficult to interpret.
- In jobs with small estimates, it is often hard to point with accuracy to the end or beginning of the bar when trying to make connections.

Appendix 6.4.19 Scaled to Time? (6.8.20)

ViewPoint is scaled to time. The network may be scaled to weeks, months, quarters of a year, and years by pressing the F3 key along with the "Right Arrow" or "Left Arrow" keys.

Although the length and position of the node is automatically generated by the system, at times the pictured beginning or end of the node does not exactly correspond with the start and finish dates.

When 4–40 hour estimates are used, the node all but disappears, and connecting the dependencies correctly becomes almost impossible.

Appendix 6.4.20 Networks and Work Breakdown Structures (6.9)

Using the Network Tree in ViewPoint accomplishes the same result as beginning and ending nodes. Therefore, it will not be necessary to undo relationships as the "latest last jobs" are added to the network. On the other hand, adding the "latest last job" will require reestablishing the dependencies.

Appendix 6.4.21 Setting Up Hammocks (6.11)

ViewPoint hammocks are one of the choices that can be made when users invoke the "Add activity" process. Until the dependency connections have been made, the hammock is of zero duration. A start-to-start relationship is established between the hammock and the first activity in the group and a finish-to-finish relationship is established between the hammock and the last activity in the group. Then, the length of the hammock will automatically extend to equal the duration of the group. The Hammock window will similarly contain the total duration of the group. Because of this feature, when they are used in the upper levels of the Network Tree, hammocks are extremely useful for illustrating the global view of the lower levels. The lowest level in the Network Tree may be set up as the activity level. Small groups of activities may be represented as hammocks in the next higher level. (Relationships between the branches are established as described earlier in this appendix.) These hammocks may be grouped into larger hammocks in the next higher level and so on—up to a single hammock that represents the entire project at the top level.

Appendix 6.4.22 Dependencies in a Multiproject Environment (6.12)

In ViewPoint, each of the subproject plans is entered into one branch of the Network Tree and, as such, are part of one plan. Each branch may be developed from scratch, copied from another branch, or copied from the library. (See the *template* discussion earlier in this appendix.) Moving from branch to branch is accomplished by selecting the F5 key, moving the cursor to the designated branch, and confirming the selection.

There is no limit to the number of times a subproject may be copied with the library function. However, this plan may be constrained by the size limitations described earlier.

The top level of the master project Network Tree may set up so that it contains only a hammock for the entire master project. The next level may contain the hammocks of each subproject. At this level, users have a network and a Gantt chart, both of which have a single, one-line entry for each of the subprojects.

Setting up the subproject-to-subproject or subproject-to-hammock interdependencies is completed as described earlier. Similarly, flipping back and forth between subprojects is as easy as changing branches of the Network Tree.

If the subprojects have been imported from the library, the maintenance of the original and the merged copies of the subproject plans may require double data entry.

Appendix 6.4.23 Printing and Viewing Networks (6.13)

In ViewPoint, the Network Planning screen is where most of the data entry occurs. It is selected through the Network Display window. ViewPoint's print function only prints one screen at a time— either with the "Print Screen" key or "ALT-P".

Appendix 6.4.24 Guidelines and Documentation (6.15)

In ViewPoint, there are two pages describing the types of relationships and a few pages on multiprojects.

APPENDIX 6.5 OPTIMAL PLANS

Appendix 6.5.1 Calendars (7.14.1)

ViewPoint stores calendar information under "Calendars" which is accessed from the main menu. Pointing the mouse to the date which corresponds to the holiday will turn it on. (See Figure A6.14.) The project start date and days worked per week are designated in a second screen, the Calendar window. (See Figure A6.15.) Since they only support durations in increments of days, these systems do not support scheduling lunch and other nonworking hours into the calendar.

From the corresponding Calendar screen, the calendar must be saved in the library by pressing F8 or the data will be lost. Furthermore, the name of the calendar must also be entered into the default calendar field of the Project Specification screen. Once a calendar has been saved in the library, it is available to any project.

Figure A6.14

```
CHAP9GC              EDIT DATES           DATE:   31Jul88
Top Level      Point to toggle the work/holiday   ROW:      2.2
chap9          status of a day.                NETWORK CHART
— PLAN ——— AUTO ——— SAVE ————————————— CAPS -

        Jul  1988            Aug  1988            Sep  1988
   S  M  T  W  T  F  S    S  M  T  W  T  F  S    S  M  T  W  T  F  S

                  1  2       1  2  3  4  5  6                1  2  3
   3  4  5  6  7  8  9    7  8  9 10 11 12 13    4  5  6  7  8  9 10
  10 11 12 13 14 15 16   14 15 16 17 18 19 20   11 12 13 14 15 16 17
  17 18 19 20 21 22 23   21 22 23 24 25 26 27   18 19 20 21 22 23 24
  24 25 26 27 28 29 30   28 29 30 31            25 26 27 28 29 30
  31

        Oct  1988            Nov  1988            Dec  1988
   S  M  T  W  T  F  S    S  M  T  W  T  F  S    S  M  T  W  T  F  S

                     1       1  2  3  4  5                   1  2  3
   2  3  4  5  6  7  8    6  7  8  9 10 11 12    4  5  6  7  8  9 10
   9 10 11 12 13 14 15   13 14 15 16 17 18 19   11 12 13 14 15 16 17
  16 17 18 19 20 21 22   20 21 22 23 24 25 26   18 19 20 21 22 23 24
  23 24 25 26 27 28 29   27 28 29 30            25 26 27 28 29 30 31
  30 31
```

Figure A6.15

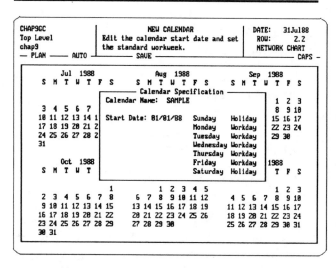

```
CHAP9GC              NEW CALENDAR         DATE:   31Jul88
Top Level      Edit the calendar start date and set   ROW:      2.2
chap9          the standard workweek.          NETWORK CHART
— PLAN ——— AUTO ——— SAVE ————————————— CAPS -

        Jul  1988            Aug  1988            Sep  1988
   S  M  T  W  T  F  S    S  M  T  W  T  F  S    S  M  T  W  T  F  S
                        ┌─── Calendar Specification ───┐
                        │ Calendar Name:  SAMPLE        │     1  2  3
   3  4  5  6  7        │                               │     8  9 10
  10 11 12 13 14 1      │ Start Date: 01/01/88   Sunday    Holiday   15 16 17
  17 18 19 20 21 2      │              Monday    Workday   22 23 24
  24 25 26 27 28 2      │              Tuesday   Workday   29 30
  31                    │              Wednesday Workday
                        │              Thursday  Workday
        Oct  1988       │              Friday    Workday  1988
   S  M  T  W  T        │              Saturday  Holiday   T  F  S
                        └───────────────────────────────┘
                     1       1  2  3  4  5                   1  2  3
   2  3  4  5  6  7  8    6  7  8  9 10 11 12    4  5  6  7  8  9 10
   9 10 11 12 13 14 15   13 14 15 16 17 18 19   11 12 13 14 15 16 17
  16 17 18 19 20 21 22   20 21 22 23 24 25 26   18 19 20 21 22 23 24
  23 24 25 26 27 28 29   27 28 29 30            25 26 27 28 29 30 31
  30 31
```

Appendix 6.5.2 Choosing the Correct Project Start Date (7.14.2)

Creating a ViewPoint starting event that has been placed at the exact starting date of the project is the first step in managing the correct starting date. The second step is also simple: create finish to start dependencies from the starting event to the first activity in each of the

subnetworks. It is only necessary to take this action one time—at plan initiation. From then on, modifying the project start date is easily accomplished by changing the target date in the Event window.

Appendix 6.5.3 Insuring that the Plan Is Not Constrained by Resources (7.14.3)

ViewPoint allows the user to designate the manner in which resources will be allocated to the plan. This choice is made in the "Define allocation type" of the Project Specification screen. It is important to state, at this time, that the ViewPoint documentation initially gives the user the impression that the system is resource-driven. Fortunately, this is not so. Until resources are assigned to the plan, these fields will have no effect on the schedule. ViewPoint defaults to *duration driven*, which will drive the optimal plan.

Appendix 6.5.4 Avoiding Imposed Target Dates (7.14.3)

In ViewPoint, if "Constraints" is set to *No* on the configuration form under the main menu, the Activity window will have two fields: *target start* and *target finish*.

If "Constraints" is set to *Yes* on the configuration form under the main menu, Field 1 on the Activity window is divided into two parts. The first part can have three values: start after; finish after; and start on. (The default is start after.) Field 2 is also divided into two parts. The first part can have two values: finish before and start before. (The default is finish before.)

When developing the optimal plan, the constraints field should be set to *No* and the target date fields should be left blank.

Appendix 6.5.5 Calculating the Schedule (7.14.4)

Calculations in ViewPoint may be controlled from the Network Planning screen by pointing the mouse at the choice in "Auto/Manual". When the system is turned on to "Manual", schedules may be recalculated on an ad hoc basis by pointing the mouse at the *calc* field at the top of the screen.

Appendix 6.5.6 The Forward Pass: Calculating the Early Dates (7.14.5)

ViewPoint defaults to the traditional scheduling algorithm.

Appendix 6.5.7 Zero Duration Milestones (7.14.8)

ViewPoint uses the preferred approach for scheduling zero duration milestones—it schedules the milestone at the end of the day on which all of the predecessors have finished.

Appendix 6.5.8 Retaining a Baseline Record of the Optimal Plan (7.14.11)

Baseline plans in ViewPoint may only be stored from the Gantt screens that are selected from the Network Planning screen by choosing ''Gantt'' or ''Performance Gantt''. Then, pressing ''F9; Snapshot'' will store a baseline plan. The early dates are stored as the snapshot dates. They are called *original start* and *original finish* on many reports. The snapshot dates do not change until this process has been invoked again.

Appendix 6.5.9 Interpreting the Dates on the Screen (7.14.12)

In ViewPoint, both the network and the Gantt charts are drawn with time-scaled bars. The dates may not be separately displayed on the screen.

Appendix 6.5.10 Annotating the Critical Path (7.14.13)

ViewPoint shows the Gantt time-scaled bars and the network nodes in red. It also shows the node connectors on the network in red.

Appendix 6.5.11 Gantt Chart Time Periods (7.14.15)

By pressing F3 in concert with the ''Left Arrow'' key, the time between the intervals gets smaller in ViewPoint. By pressing F3 in concert with the ''Right Arrow''

key, the time between the intervals gets larger. The timeframes may be weeks, months, quarters, or years.

The user may move in any direction around the Gantt chart by pressing the arrow keys or moving the mouse.

The bars on the Gantt chart are continuous; they are not broken by weekends or holidays. (See Figure A6.16.)

Appendix 6.5.12 Scheduling in the Multiproject Environment (7.14.17)

In ViewPoint, when subprojects are imported into the master project, the system checks to see if its calendar is currently in the master project's calendar collection. If not, the calendar is added to the list. The maximum number of calendars in the collection is 10.

In spite of the fact that the calendars have been imported, the calendar that was originally set as the default calendar in the Project Specification screen is not replaced. On the other hand, a different default calendar is easily brought in to the Project Specification screen by pointing the mouse at the field and picking the name of the desired calendar file from the list in the calendar collection. The corresponding schedules will be automatically computed.

Users ought to also be advised that there can only be one default calendar per project plan. If each of the subprojects must have a separate calendar, the default

Figure A6.16

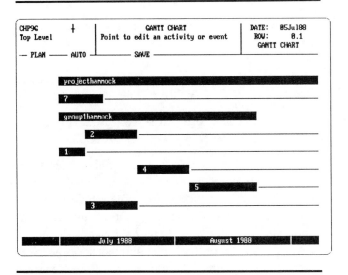

calendar must be ignored, and the calendar name must be entered into the calendar field of *every* job in the subproject. Fortunately, this may be performed en masse in the Activity Editor screen, which is invoked from the planning menu, by pressing "Activity Editor; Activity Schedule".

The correct calendar name is entered in each job by pointing the mouse at the field and picking the name of the desired calendar file from the list in the calendar collection. The corresponding schedules will be automatically computed.

Because this is a merge process, maintaining the original *and* merged copies of the subprojects may later require double data entry.

The top level of the master project Network Tree may be set up so that it contains only the hammocks of each subproject. Then, users may have a network and a Gantt chart, both of which have a single, one-line entry for each of the subprojects. Each hammock's early and late start as well as its early and late finish dates will represent the respective dates of the first and last activity in the corresponding subproject branch.

Appendix 6.5.13 Nesting Subprojects in a Multiproject Environment *(7.14.18)*

Since each rung of the nest must be part of the Viewpoint Network Tree, this issue is inapplicable.

Appendix 6.5.14 Guidelines and Documentation *(7.14.20)*

ViewPoint does not have guidelines for developing schedules.

APPENDIX 6.6 CALCULATING A FINISH DATE

Appendix 6.6.1 Using the New Reasonable Late Finish Date of the Project *(7.26.3)*

In ViewPoint, to create a fixed late finish date *and* get the correctly computed late dates requires that a fixed event be created with a *start on* date that is one day *later* than the fixed date. The correct late dates are computed and stored in each of the late start and late finish fields. If a project-level hammock has been created, the early *and* late start dates of the hammock will be set to the *early* start date of the project, and

the early *and* late finish dates of the hammock will be set to the *late* finish date of the project. The early finish date of the project may be found in the project finish date of the Project Specification screen. The highlights of the critical path are lost.

APPENDIX 6.7 ADDING RESOURCES

Appendix 6.7.1 Creating the Resource Calendars *(8.8)*

ViewPoint stores calendar information under Calendars (Figure A6.15), which is accessed from the main menu. Unique resource calendars may be created in exactly the same way as the project calendar. Pointing the mouse to the date that corresponds to the holiday will turn it on. The project start date and days that the resource works each week are designated in a second screen, the Calendar window. The calendar must be saved under a special resource name or the data will be lost. Each calendar collection in a project is limited to 10.

Before the resource calendar will have any affect on schedules, its name will need to be entered into the calendar field of the Activity window of all activities to which the resource will be assigned. (Figure A6.7) Pointing the mouse at this field will invoke a list of names from the calendar collection. Moving the cursor to the desired calendar name and pressing "Enter" completes the transaction.

Part-time participation is not supported at the project level. The system does not support daily breaks (for example, lunch), unique working hours for a single specific calendar day, or any workday starting and ending times.

Appendix 6.7.2 Creating the Resource Pool *(8.9)*

Resources in ViewPoint may be individuals, groups of individuals, equipment, or materials. A *fixed* cost category may be added to the resource pool just like any other resource. Later, when assigning this resource to a job, a fixed value may be entered into the Expense window.

Project data is managed in a combination of main memory, buffers, and hard disk. The number of activities, dependencies, resources, and tree branches in this combination is limited only by the total amount

Figure A6.17

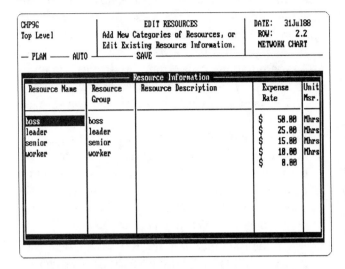

Figure A6.18

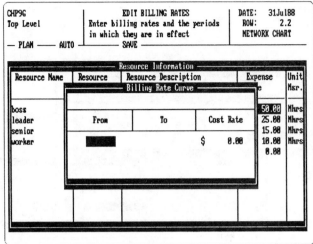

of available storage. The vendor suggests that projects be limited to 40 activities and 80 dependencies. While there is no specific limit on the number of resources per project, once a project gets large enough, the system will use disk buffering and response time will notably slow down.

Resource information is stored in the Resource Information Editor (See Figure A6.17.), which is accessed by pointing to the word ''Resources'' on the border of the Project Specification screen. (See Figure A6.5.) The data to be entered consists of the 16-character resource name, the units in which the resource is measured (hours, days, pounds), the cost per unit, the work group category of the resource, and descriptive notes.

ViewPoint supports an unlimited number of billing rates for each resource. The dates and variable rates may be entered using a window that is called up by pointing the mouse to cost per unit field in the Resource Information Editor screen. (See Figure A6.18.)

Until the user is ready to level resources, there is no way to enter the number of working hours per day for an individual resource. The system assumes the normal work day for all participants. (Overtime hours may also be set at leveling time.) The number of available resources is implicitly designated in the Resource Usage window, which is used to allocate resource availability at the activity level and will be covered later in this appendix.

Appendix 6.7.3 Assigning Part-Time Resources at the Project Level *(8.10)*

In ViewPoint, part-time participation is not supported at the project level—it is only supported at the activity level. (See the discussion later in this appendix.)

Appendix 6.7.4 Deleting and Changing Resources at the Project Level *(8.11)*

Resources in ViewPoint may not be deleted from the Resource Information Editor screen until all corresponding commitments have either been deleted or reassigned. Then, resources are deleted from the pool by pressing ''ALT-D''.

Names are changed in the same manner as other modifications. Changing a name results in a project-wide replacement of all occurrences of the old name with the new name.

Appendix 6.7.5 Matching Resources to Jobs *(8.14)*

In ViewPoint, resources may only be assigned to activities; they may not be assigned to events or summary activities. There may be up to three resource names per activity. People are assigned to jobs using the Resource Usage window (See Figure A6.19.) that is

Figure A6.19

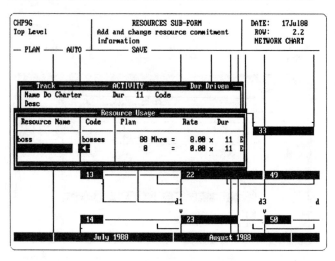

called up by pressing "Resource" on the border of the Activity window. Resources may not be assigned until they are defined in the Resource Information Editor. Then, the corresponding resource name and the resource code will be very easily entered into the Resource Usage window.

> After pointing the mouse at either column, the system displays a second window with a list of possible choices. It is only necessary to point the mouse at the correct selection and the field will be automatically filled in.

New terms, *elastic* and *fixed*, are found in two places: in the "Define allocation type" on the Project Specification screen and in the last column of the Resource Usage window. Elastic means that the schedule will be driven by the duration of the activities, while fixed means that the schedule may become resource driven. Furthermore, a second set of new terms, either *duration driven* or *resource driven*, is found on the border of the Activity window. These two values drive the scheduling algorithms.

The value chosen for "Define allocation type" will determine the default value ("E" or "F" for "elastic" and "fixed" respectively) in the last column of the Resource Usage window. Initially, these values do not affect schedules. Until resources have actually been assigned to the plan, all activities default to *duration driven* scheduling.

Users ought to initially set the "Define allocation type" to "E". Unless a counter action is taken, all dates will remain activity driven and the *true work effort* in the activity duration field will be preserved.

The plan (also *true work effort*), rate (hours per day), and duration (value from the activity duration) fields are also entered in the Resource Usage window. Basically, they are used in two different ways.

1. When the last column in the Resource Usage window equals "E" (*duration driven*), these fields are used for the third leveling pattern for distribution of *true work effort*. This will be addressed again under resource leveling in this appendix. In "E" mode, plan and rate may be modified.

2. When the last column in the Resource Usage window is equal to "F" (*resource driven*), the entries are used for resource-driven scheduling and will be addressed later in this appendix. In "F" mode, all three fields may be modified.

In spite of the fact that plan and rate may be modified in "E" mode, if integrity of the original duration is important, the user is advised *not to tamper with these fields at this time*. The system ought to be allowed to do its job in the distribution of *true work effort*.

Unknown resources cannot be assigned to an activity until they have been entered into the resource pool. All three resources assigned in the Resource Usage window may be the same resource name. The available number of resources being applied to the task is implicitly related to the assigned number of entries in the Resource Usage window. Furthermore, there is no available value defined in the resource pool. Consequently, there is no need to check for excessive assignments.

Appendix 6.7.6 Assigning Part-Time Resources at the Task or Activity Level (8.15)

There are three fields in the ViewPoint Resource Usage window: the resource duration field (called *plan*, equivalent to *true work effort*), rate (hours per day), and duration (the value from the activity duration, used for scheduling). The last column in the window contains the default value ("E" or "F") from the "Define allocations type" in the Project Specification screen.

When the value of this field is "E", only the plan and rate fields may be modified. The activity will always remain duration driven and will never become resource driven.

In order to designate part-time participation, the user must toggle this last column to "F".[6] Now, the duration *may also* be modified and the activity may become resource driven.

Of the three variables, any last two that are modified will determine the value of the third. The rate field of this window is now changed to reflect the part-time hours per day. This last action causes the resource duration field (plan) to be multiplied by the rate, thus reducing the resource effort. This is artificial and incorrect. However, it has no effect on scheduling. Re-keying the plan field to the original value completes the transaction properly. Similarly, users ought also to be aware that:

- The name in the Activity window border will change from duration driven to resource driven;

- The duration in the Activity window will change to the value (elapsed calendar days) in the duration field of the Resource Usage window;

- The duration field in the Activity window may no longer be modified;

- The *true work effort* will be in the resource plan field of the Resource Usage window; and

- The name of the resource that's driving the activity will appear in the resource field of the Activity window.

Appendix 6.7.7 Assigning Multiple Resources to a Job (8.16)

In ViewPoint, at the project level resource-constrained plans are put into effect when there is an "F" in the "Define allocations type" of the Project Specification screen and the value in the last column of the Resource Usage window (Figure A6.19) has *not* been changed to the alternate value. Similarly, at the activity level, activity-driven jobs may also be transformed into re-source-driven jobs by toggling the last column in the Resource Usage window.

Multiple resources are added to this window following the guidelines for assigning resources that were presented earlier in this appendix.

As explained in the prior section, in addition to plan and rate in the Resource Usage window, now the activity duration *may also* be modified. Of the three variables, any last two that are modified will determine the value of the third. Values for rate, plan, and duration are now entered for each of the resources. ViewPoint uses the longest resource duration for the activity duration. A resource-driven activity is created. The guidelines that were described in the prior section hold true here as well.

Appendix 6.7.8 What to Do when the Resource Effort Must Be Less Than the Elapsed Calendar Days (8.17)

In ViewPoint, when the resource plan value is equal to the *true work effort* but is less than the activity elapsed time, the resource plan value can be distributed anywhere within the activity *candidate time slice*. (See Figure A6.21 below.)

There are three fields in the Resource Usage window: the resource duration field (called *plan*, equivalent to *true work effort*), rate (hours per day), and duration (the value from the activity duration, used for scheduling). Of the three variables, any last two that are modified will determine the value of the third.

To create the conditions illustrated in Example 1, the last column must also be toggled to "F". Then, the *true work effort* must be entered into the plan field, and the elapsed calendar days must be entered into the duration field.

ViewPoint cannot compute percentages. When the scenario illustrated in Example 2 occurs, the user will need to compute the hours or days that equate to the percentage level manually and then proceed as in Example 1.

The scenario in Example 3 is implemented by delaying the resource plan value with a corresponding value in the resource delay time. In ViewPoint, this is accomplished by calling up the Resource Budget Distribution window (see Figure A6.20.) by pointing to the corresponding plan entry in the Resource Usage window.

---

[6]Alternatively, these changes may also be made en masse in the Activity Resource Plan Usage Table, a screen which is invoked by selecting "Res/Exp Editor; Resource-Planned" from the planning menu.

Figure A6.20

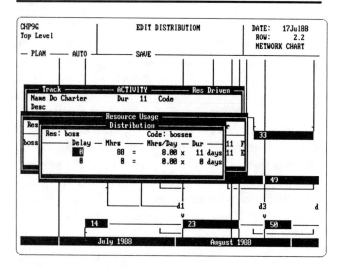

Figure A6.21

activity *candidate time slice* = 15 days

resource delay time	resource plan
10 days	5 days

Naturally, the sum of the resource plan and the resource delay time may not be greater than the activity *candidate time slice*.

The guidelines that are described in the section about assigning part-time resources at the activity level hold true here also.

Appendix 6.7.9 Fixed Dates for Activities Or Tasks *(8.19)*

ViewPoint uses the scheduling algorithm that highlights projects that are late before they start.

Fixed dates may be entered at any level in the work breakdown structure. They may be entered into the Activity windows and Event windows. (Figure A6.7)

The system flags all fixed activities with a tab column marker.

The product also provides three sets of dates: early dates, late dates and constrained dates. ViewPoint supports start on, start after, start before, finish before, and finish after. Start on was evaluated.

If the new fixed date of the affected activity is the same as its system-generated dates, its late start date is set equal to the fixed date, but there are no changes to its other dates. Nor are there any changes to any dates in the successors. On the other hand, the system computes new late dates for the predecessors, thereby causing them to have zero slack and forcing them onto the critical path.

If the new fixed date of the affected activity is later than its system-generated dates, the system replaces the early start and early finish dates *and* its late start date with this new fixed date. It also recomputes early dates for successors, but not late dates. Finally, the system recomputes late dates for predecessors but not early dates.

If the new fixed date of the affected activity is earlier than its system-generated dates, the system keeps the same early dates on the job. Continuing on, it changes the late start of the affected activity, but leaves its late finish alone. On the other hand, the system does nothing to any of the dates in the successors. Finally, it leaves the early dates on the predecessors alone, but modifies both late dates. This creates negative slack, showing when the project should have started. This is an excellent signal that the project is late before it starts! (The date that the project should have started is in the late start date of the first job(s) in the project.)

If the late finish date of the project is entered into a fixed-date event, the late dates of all of the predecessors will be correctly computed.

Appendix 6.7.10 Special Leveling Patterns in Project Management Software *(8.29)*

In ViewPoint, the first type of leveling is called *Constrain*; the second is called *Level*. The user decides which of the two types of leveling is to be used during the leveling process. This choice is made at leveling time.

This product also supports activity splitting but this feature is not related to leveling. It relates to establishing dependencies and was addressed earlier.

Appendix 6.7.11 Automatic Resource Leveling (8.30)

ViewPoint is another one of the products that support both types of leveling. However, the vendor has switched the terminology. Here the term *leveling* really means the second type of leveling. It adjusts resource constraints where there is slack but it does not remove all resource conflicts, nor does it extend the project. On the other hand, *constraining* is the term used to refer to the first type of leveling. These operations are performed in the Resource Profile screen, a histogram that is built using the early dates of the plan. (See Figure A6.22.) The height of each column in the histogram shows the level of commitment for the resource on each day.

The Resource Profile screen in ViewPoint. After selecting the Resource Profile screen from the display toggle in the upper right corner of the Network Planning screen, a blank histogram will be presented to the user. Toggling a resource name in the upper left corner of this screen will invoke the corresponding resource histogram. The vertical axis of this histogram always automatically adjusts to a number of hours that is about a third higher than the greatest resource requirement. Next, the resource profile schedule menu is invoked by pointing the mouse. The second type of leveling is simply performed by selecting "Level" from this menu. To execute the first type of leveling,

on the other hand, requires a bit of user ingenuity. To begin, "Constrain" is selected from the resource profile schedule menu.

The normal number of workhours per day. A line must then be drawn across the graph at the level that indicates the proper number of hours. This is easily accomplished by pointing the mouse at the respective hours on the vertical axis, pulling the line across the horizontal axis at the vertical axis level, and pointing the mouse again. (See Figure A6.23.) Initially, the gradient markers on the vertical axis are not always scaled to match multiples of eight hours. For example, only 15 or 17 hours may be toggled. However, since the vertical axis automatically adjusts itself, the correct scaling occurs after executing the operation once or twice. Although it is troublesome to have to perform this operation twice to get the desired result, a second execution usually does correct the problem.

Overtime hours. Because the vertical axis on the histogram goes higher than the number of hours in one day, this same process can be used to indicate the maximum number of workhours per day (including overtime) the resource is available.

Multiple resources per job classification. There is no place to indicate that one of the resources actually is a job classification representing a variable number of available resources. Once the user is at the stage where individual resources are being assigned to jobs, this is not a problem. On the other hand, when trying

Figure A6.22

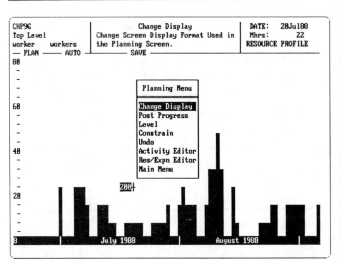

Figure A6.23

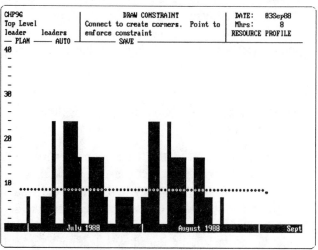

Figure A6.24

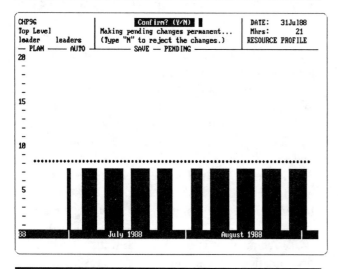

to start with job classifications only, the operation requires a little ingenuity. For example, a pool of three programmers may be entered as one resource. Since the vertical axis on the histogram is so flexible, the group may then be scheduled by simulating overtime as described in the previous paragraph.

Saving the leveled or constrained plans. The results of these operations are temporary—unless the user consciously chooses to make them permanent. *Leveling* and *constraining* become a permanent part of the plan only if the user points the mouse to the word "Pending" (in the Message window) and then replies *Yes* to the questions that asks if the changes should be saved. (See Figure A6.24.) Finally, the plan should also be saved using the general save procedures.

Delayed activities are flagged with a blinking pointer symbol. Delayed events are flagged with a set of *skid* marks.

Appendix 6.7.12 User-Driven Interactive Leveling *(8.32)*

ViewPoint is a semi-interactive leveling system. Gantt charts of the whole project may be viewed on the screen by selecting "Gantt Chart" from the display toggle in the upper right corner of the Network Planning screen. (Figure A6.16) Hard copy reports of the same Gantt may be produced by selecting "Schedule Gantt Chart" from the report selection menu. There

is no way to produce a Gantt chart of activities limited to one resource.

The first type of automatic leveling that was described earlier in this appendix is the type that may extend the project end date. It is performed by *constraining*. The process is executed in the Resource Profile screen. (Figure A6.22) The height of each column in the histogram shows the level of commitment.

In this histogram:

- Both the weekends and holidays are reflected.
- Moving the cursor to the highest point in any column will display the number of required resource units in the Message window at the top middle of the screen.
- Pointing the mouse anywhere in the histogram shows the cumulative total of resources used through that point.
- Moving the cursor to a point in any column and pressing "ALT-F" will cause a shift to the Network Planning screen. (Figure A6.2) The cursor will be positioned on the first offending activity. Pressing "ALT-N" will move the cursor to the next offending activity until there are no more candidates. There will be no way to return to the Resource Profile screen.
- Moving the cursor to a point in the column and pressing "T" will display the name plus all of the resource usage information of the first offending activity in the Message window at the top middle of the screen. Pressing the spacebar will scroll through all of the offending activities. On the other hand, before pressing the spacebar, pressing F2 will invoke a corresponding Activity window. Modifications may be made to dates or activity duration in this Activity window—or the Resource Usage window may subsequently be called up and modifications made to resource assignments.[7]

Following the directions for leveling resources, users may restrict the leveling to different levels on

---

[7]To delete a resource assignment, the cursor must be placed on the respective resource and the "ALT-D" key must be pressed. This action eliminates both the resource name and the resource code.

different days during the project rather than *constrain* the whole project at the same level. The line that's pulled across the horizontal axis at the vertical axis level may be placed at different levels of the vertical axis on each selected day. (See Figure A6.25.) This is accomplished by clicking the mouse whenever the direction of the constraining line needs to be changed. For example, click to go up and down; then click to go back and forth, or vice versa. The rest of the procedure is completed as described earlier.

The Resource Profile screen may be printed by pressing the ''Print Screen'' key.

Finally, wholesale resource usage modifications may be made to the Activity Resource Plan Usage Table, a screen which is invoked by selecting ''Res/Exp Editor; Resources-Planned'' from the planning menu.

Appendix 6.7.13 Baseline Project Plans for Resource Leveling (8.34)

ViewPoint supports one version of a baseline. By saving the optimal plan as the baseline for the resource-constrained plan that is selected for implementation, users have half of the requirements met. This version is archived and a second version is produced. Then, by saving the resource-constrained plan as the baseline for the plan to which progress will be posted, the other half of the requirements will be met. Unfortunately,

this *work-around* does not provide comparisons between all three versions. However, albeit the process is cumbersome, users may assimilate the data by perusing both sets of reports.

Appendix 6.7.14 Resources, Multiprojects, and Project Management Software (8.35.4)

In ViewPoint, if the *template* resource pool has been stored in a separate library, it may be copied from project to project by simply retrieving it from the library with the F7 key.

When subprojects are imported from the library, the system automatically brings in all corresponding resource assignments. New resources are appended to the resource pool. When there are duplicate resources in both the master project and the subproject, the resource record in the master project is retained and the resource data in the subproject is ignored. Consequently, users ought to carefully choose the first subproject in the list of projects to be merged, since that will be the source of the permanent resource data.

Because the resource calendars have been entered into each respective Activity window, they are automatically imported with the subproject. This is a merge process, so maintaining the original *and* merged copies of the subprojects may later require double data entry. Since all of the subprojects are merged into one project, the other issues in this section are inapplicable.

Appendix 6.7.15 Guidelines and Documentation (8.36)

There are several pages in ViewPoint on resource management as well as several more pages on managing resources in a multiproject environment.

APPENDIX 6.8 CALCULATING COSTS

Appendix 6.8.1 Costs and Project Management Software (9.4)

Resources in ViewPoint may be individuals, groups of individuals, equipment or materials.

Cost information is entered in the Budget Code Information screen (See Figure A6.26.) which is accessed by pressing ''Budget Codes'' on the border of the Project Specification screen. These budget codes may easily be saved in and retrieved from the library.

Figure A6.25

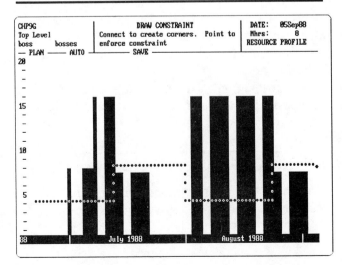

Figure A6.26

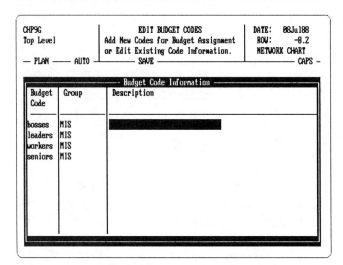

Figure A6.27

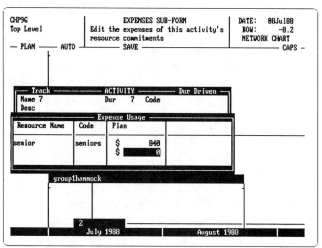

The Expense Profile screen (a cost histogram) in ViewPoint looks just like the resource histogram—except that the vertical axis is scaled to costs. (Figure A6.22) This Expense Profile screen can show the costs for one resource across a set of activities or the costs for all of the resources within an accounting group. By combining all of the categories, the user may view the Expense Profile screen for the entire project. Other cost information is also available in many reports as well as most of the windows (described below).

• Total expenses for all resources allotted to an activity are found in several reports.

• Total costs for all resources in that branch of the Network Tree are also found in these reports.

• Total costs for all resources in the project are also found in these reports.

A *fixed* cost category may be added to the resource pool just like any other resource—choosing 1 for the cost per unit. Later, when assigning this resource to a job, a value may be entered into the Expense Usage window. (See Figure A6.27.)

Hammocks do not reflect cost data.

The system calculates expenses based on rates entered for each resource in the Resource Information Editor screen. (Figure A6.17) To see the total resource assignments for an activity, users only need to point the mouse to the word "Expenses" on the border of

the Activity window (See Figure A6.7. and Figure A6.27.)

Fixed expenses and/or *overhead* may also be added with this Expense window. Similarly, this window may also be used to override the expense that the system computes for the activity. *Overtime* effects are calculated manually and entered into the Expense window as an override.

Total costs for each resource in each of the activities can be seen in the Activity Expense Plan Usage screen (See Figure A6.28.)

The system distributes the expenses evenly across the duration of the activity. However, users may gain control over the way in which expenses are distributed by using the Expense Usage Distribution window—which looks like the Resource Usage Distribution window in Figure A6.20, except that dollars are used instead of hours.

ViewPoint will export data to LOTUS 1-2-3 in Version 1A and Version 2, dBase III, and in Comma Separated Values.

APPENDIX 6.9 COMPRESSING TIME

Appendix 6.9.1 Time-Constrained Plans and Project Management Software *(10.9)*

In ViewPoint, choosing *leveling* instead of *constraining* will result in a time-constrained, leveled plan. Users may produce reports sorted on float.

Figure A6.28

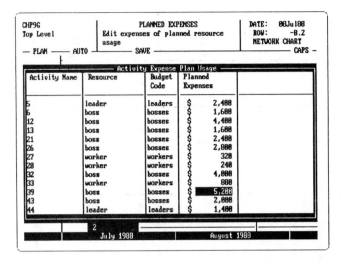

APPENDIX 6.10 ASSIGNING THE WORK

Appendix 6.10.1 The Assignment Report (11.1)

Along with the activity name and description fields in ViewPoint, the "Project Schedule" report displays several sets of dates: the baseline dates, the early dates, the late dates, the fixed dates, and the actual dates.

This product also features an assembly-language-type report writer. Actually, all of the standard reports have been defined in this language. Outside of the system, each report file may easily be duplicated with the operating system "Copy" command. Then, the copied report may be modified with a word processor or the operating system's Line Editor. At first, this may appear like an overwhelming process. However, when the documentation is used in conjunction with working on an existing report file, the exercise was not difficult at all.

With this in mind, the standard "Project Schedule" report may be modified to display only the desired date information. (See Figure A6.29.)

There is also a standard predecessor/successor report, called the "Dependency" report. This report may be limited to printing only the data pertaining to a given resource, accomplished by choosing selection

criteria where "Select Field = Resource Name"; "Test" is set to " = to"; and low value is set to "*the resource name as it appears in the resource pool.*" (See Figure A6.30.) Then, the sort criteria are set up so that the data is sorted on "Sort Field Name = Early Start" and "Sort Order = Ascending". (See Figure A6.31.)

Appendix 6.10.2 The Ad Hoc Information (11.2)

The ViewPoint description fields are automatically printed as part of the assignment reports. (Figure A6.29)

It is likely that these reports will need to be supplemented by output from a word processor.

Appendix 6.10.3 The Work Package Cover Sheet (11.5)

In ViewPoint, a word processor may be used to create the forms that meet this requirement.

Appendix 6.10.4 The Responsibility Grid (11.6)

In ViewPoint, a word processor may be used to create the forms that meet this requirement.

Appendix 6.10.5 The Supporting Documentation (11.8)

In ViewPoint, after setting up the sort and select criteria as described earlier in this appendix, the user may print a resource-limited Gantt (Figure A6.16) by choosing the standard report called "Activity/Resource Gantt."

If the user has a printer that will capture screen images, the resource histogram may be printed by pressing the "Print Screen" key.

There are no tabular loading reports in ViewPoint.

Appendix 6.10.6 The Problem Log (11.10)

In ViewPoint, a word processor may be used to create the forms that meet this requirement.

Figure A6.29

Project Name: CHP9G
Network Name: Top Level

ViewPoint
Project Schedule Report

Status Date: July 1, 1988
Run Date: January 21, 1989
Finish Date: February 2, 1989
Page 1

P L A N N E D   S C H E D U L E

Activity Name and Description	Activity Code	Org & Rem Dur	Original Start & Finish							
9		2	01Jul88							Activity
		2	05Jul88							
6		4	01Jul88							Activity
		4	07Jul88							
13		4	08Jul88							Activity
		4	13Jul88							
12		11	08Jul88							Activity
		11	22Jul88							
21		6	03Aug88							Activity
		6	10Aug88							
22		16	03Aug88							Activity
		16	24Aug88							
26		7	11Aug88							Activity
		7	19Aug88							
32		10	22Aug88							Activity
		10	02Sep88							
39		13	07Sep88							Activity
		13	23Sep88							

Figure A6.30

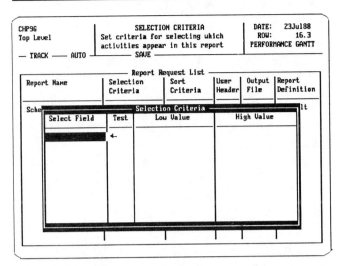

Figure A6.31

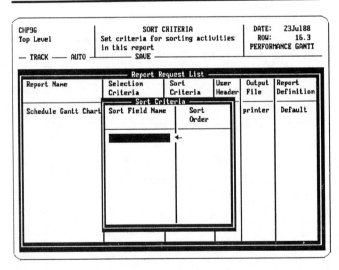

Appendix 6.10.7 The Work Notes Form (11.11)

In ViewPoint, a word processor may be used to create the forms that meet this requirement.

Appendix 6.10.8 Viewing the Data on the Screen (11.12)

The reports in ViewPoint may only be displayed in hard copy.

APPENDIX 6.11 REPORTING STATUS

Appendix 6.11.1 Baselines (12.2)

The ViewPoint baseline information is in the "original" fields.

Appendix 6.11.2 Extracting the Jobs for the Turn-Around Document—on a Range of Dates (12.5)

ViewPoint's reporting periods may easily be set up in the Report Selection Criteria window by setting the select field to one of the early, late, actual, or original (baseline) dates, setting the test field to "Range", and entering the dates in the low value and high value fields. (Figure A6.30)

Appendix 6.11.3 Setting Up an As-Of Date (12.6)

ViewPoint works in two modes: Planning mode and Status mode. When in Status mode, the system automatically draws an As-of line vertically on the screen at the position of the designated status date. From then on, the plan is divided into "work that has been done" and "work that has yet to be done", and the colors of the activity bars are changed accordingly. After the status data has been entered, this feature provides an excellent visual aid to assessing progress. With one glance up and down this line, the user can easily spot the problem areas. However, the progress that is noted depicts progress based on *elapsed time* and not *true work effort*. (See the discussion on percent complete in the next section.) This means that sometimes the progress may be reported too optimistically and sometimes too pessimistically. Setting the As-of date requires two procedures:

- Status mode is called *Tracking* and is invoked by pointing the mouse at the word "Plan" at the upper left hand corner of the screen. (Figure A6.2)

- From the planning menu (Figure A6.3), pointing the mouse at "Post Progress" will invoke a screen into which the As-of date is entered. (See Figure A6.32.) The name of the field is called the *proposed status date*. None of the other fields in that screen are modified at this time.

Figure A6.32

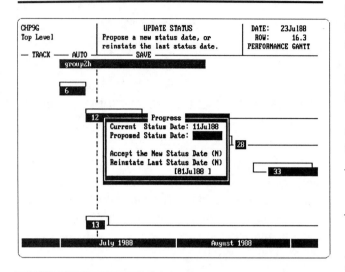

After the status data has been entered (See the discussions later in this appendix.), one final operation is necessary:

• From the planning menu, the Status screen is invoked once more and *Yes* is entered in response to the question "Accept the new status date". None of the other fields in that screen are modified. When this operation is completed, the system will calculate a new schedule, taking into account the remaining work to be completed as of the new status date.

Appendix 6.11.4 Entering Percent Complete (*12.7*)

In ViewPoint Status mode there are companion windows to the Activity windows and Resource Usage windows that are used in planning mode. However, the entry fields in the bottom line of the Activity window are now changed to actual start, actual finish, percent complete, and remaining duration. Similarly, the entry columns in the Resource Usage window have now been changed to actual hours, remaining hours, and percent complete.

It is important to note that the percent complete on the Activity window represents the percentage of *elapsed time* and not the percentage of *true work effort*. The percentage of *true work effort* is found in the Resource Usage window. Yet, it is the percentage

complete in the Activity window that is used to show progress on the network. This means that sometimes the progress may be reported too optimistically and sometimes too pessimistically.

The percent complete field may be entered by the user, or the user may enter other values and let the system compute it.

Percent in the Activity window. When the user enters *remaining duration* on the Activity window, the system computes percent complete by:

$$\frac{\text{Duration} - \text{Remaining Duration}}{\text{Duration}} \text{ times } 100.$$

When the user enters *percent complete* on the Activity window, the system automatically computes the remaining duration. If this is the first time data has been entered for the activity, the system also enters the actual start date, using the value from the early start date. If 100 percent is entered, the system will also enter the finish date using the early finish date[8] and set the remaining duration to zero.

Percent in the Resource Usage window. When the user enters *actual hours* on the Resource Usage window, the system *does not automatically compute remaining hours!* The remaining hours are not changed until the user manually computes the correct value and enters it. The formula for percent complete is:

$$\frac{\text{Actual Hours}}{\text{Actual Hours} + \text{Remaining Hours}} \times 100.$$

When the user enters *percent complete* on the Resource Usage window, the system automatically computes the actual hours and the remaining hours.

Appendix 6.11.5 Hard Copy Turn-Around Documents (*12.8*)

A standard ViewPoint report, the "Project Schedule" report, displays the activity name, the activity code, the original and remaining durations, the original (baseline) start and finish dates, the earliest (scheduled)

---

[8]This value can *not* be set by the user. If the finish date is not the same date as the early finish date, the early finish date must be changed.

start and finish dates, the latest start and finish dates, the target (fixed) start and finish dates, the actual start and finish dates, the percent complete, the float, and the type of job. (See Figure A6.33.) If some of the standard columns may be sacrificed, this report may be modified to show the planned resource hours, the remaining resource hours, the actual resource hours, and/or the predecessors.

Appendix 6.11.6 Entering the Status Collection Data (12.9)

Entering time reporting data in ViewPoint may require three different procedures: one on the Activity window, one on the Resource Usage window, and one on the Resource Usage Distribution window.

The Activity window. The status fields in the companion status-reporting Activity window are the actual start and actual finish, the percent complete, and the remaining duration. Alternatively, this data may be entered in table mode—in the Activity Progress Editor screen.

The actual start date may be entered by the user, or it will be computed by the system as soon as a value for percent complete or remaining duration is entered. The system uses the early date.

When the percent complete is entered, the system automatically updates the remaining duration. Conversely, entering the remaining duration automatically updates the percent complete. (See the earlier discussion.)

The actual finish date may *not* be entered by the user. The system controls the value of the actual finish. If 100 percent is entered into the Activity window, the system will enter the finish date using the original early finish date. If the finish date is not the same date as the original early finish date, the early finish date should be changed before entering the 100 percent. This is done by (1) pressing "Plan" on the border of the companion status-reporting Activity window (this invokes the original Activity window), and (2) modifying the early finish date. Then, the companion Status Reporting window may be invoked and the 100 percent may be entered.

It is important to note that the progress indicated on the network depicts progress based on the percent value of this window. Frequently, the duration in this window represents elapsed time and not *true work effort*. *True work effort* is entered in the Resource Usage window. (See the earlier discussion on percent complete, the following discussion on the Resource Usage window, and the following discussion on special processing.) This means that sometimes, the progress may be reported too optimistically or too pessimistically.

In activities that are resource-driven, when the hours are changed on the Resource Usage window, the duration on the Activity window may be affected. This is not true for duration-driven activities.

The ViewPoint Resource Usage window and Usage Distribution window. The status reporting fields on this window are the actual time, the remaining time and the percent complete. Alternatively, this data may be entered in table mode—in the Resource Progress Editor screen.

There is no time-this period field in this system. If the percent is entered, the system automatically computes the actual time (to date) and the remaining time. (See the earlier discussion.) On the other hand, the actual time may be entered by the user. However, the system does *not* automatically compute the remaining time—but rather leaves the value that was originally there. The user must enter the correct value.

By pointing the mouse at the remaining time column of the Resource Usage window, the user can access the Usage Distribution window. Even though it is accessed from Status mode, the window does not change. If the Usage Distribution window has been used during the planning stage, entries now made in this window will automatically recompute the remaining time.

Special processing. While most of the scenarios in Figure 12.1 can be implemented simply as described above, other scenarios require special handling. This refers to the situations when the activity's duration must be changed (as illustrated in Example C); when the elapsed time must be longer than the resource *true work effort* (as illustrated in Examples H, I and M); and when the elapsed time must be shorter than the resource *true work effort* (as illustrated in Examples G, S, and X).

These changes are made after (1) pressing "Plan" on the border of the companion status-reporting Activity window (this invokes the original Activity window) and (2) modifying the original duration. Then,

Figure A6.33

Project Name: CHP9G
Network Name: Top Level

ViewPoint
Project Schedule Report

Status Date: July 11, 1988
Run Date: January 28, 1989
Finish Date: February 2, 1989
Page 1

Activity Name and Description	Activity Code	Org & Rem Dur	Original Start & Finish	Earliest Start & Finish	Latest Start & Finish	Target Start & Finish	Actual Start & Finish	Pct. Comp	Float	
		PLANNED SCHEDULE					ACTUAL SCHEDULE			
10		4	01Jul88	01Jul88	01Jul88	AS	01Jul88	100	0	Activity
		0	07Jul88	07Jul88	07Jul88	AF	07Jul88			
9		7	01Jul88	11Jul88	06Sep88	AS	01Jul88	86	40	Activity
		1	05Jul88	11Jul88	06Sep88					
8		7	01Jul88	11Jul88	26Sep88	AS	01Jul88	86	54	Activity
		1	07Jul88	11Jul88	26Sep88					
16		1	06Jul88	12Jul88	07Sep88			0	40	Activity
		1	06Jul88	12Jul88	07Sep88					
14		4	08Jul88	12Jul88	29Sep88			0	56	Activity
		4	13Jul88	15Jul88	04Oct88					
17		8	07Jul88	13Jul88	08Sep88			0	40	Activity
		8	18Jul88	22Jul88	19Sep88					
18		8	19Jul88	25Jul88	20Sep88			0	40	Activity
		8	28Jul88	03Aug88	29Sep88					
29		3	29Jul88	04Aug88	30Sep88			0	40	Activity
		3	02Aug88	08Aug88	04Oct88					
30		2	29Jul88	04Aug88	29Dec88			0	100	Activity
		2	01Aug88	05Aug88	30Dec88					

the other companion windows may be invoked and the rest of the data may be entered.

When, with respect to *true work effort* in the Resource Usage window, the elapsed time in the Activity window is lengthened, the result is that the percent complete will be too optimistic. In illustration, the actual progress in Example I was only 50 percent, while the system showed 86 percent.

When, with respect to *true work effort* in the Resource Usage window, the elapsed time in the Activity window is shortened, the result is that the percent complete will be too pessimistic. In illustration, the actual progress in Example X was 60 percent, while the system only showed 50 percent.

Appendix 6.11.7 Performance Status Reporting (12.10)

The ViewPoint ''Project Schedule'' report that was used for the turn-around document (Figure A6.33) may also be used for status reporting. The successors may be found on the ''Dependency'' report. There are two Gantt chart reports, but neither of them show the baseline values, nor can they be customized to shows these values. On the other hand, the on-line Performance Gantt screen does show the baseline values compared to the current values. If a graphics printer is available, this screen may be printed with the ''Print Screen'' key. (See Figure A6.34.)

Figure A6.34

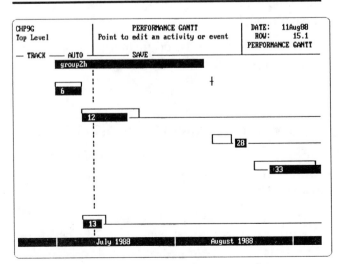

This product features sorting and selecting on many fields. (Figures A6.30. and A6.31) The sort and select are two separate processes, each with its own set of parameters. The sort may be in ascending or descending order. There are more than nine levels of the sort. Although it is not possible to directly identify late jobs, users may select by: original, actual, early, and late start dates; original, actual, early, and late finish dates; and slack. They may sort on early and late dates, percent complete, and float. While it is possible to select on remaining duration (1 to 999), reports may not be sorted on this field.

This product does feature the ability to select jobs based on revised estimates. Although the system does support earned value variances (See the discussion later in this appendix.), it does not report on duration variances.

Appendix 6.11.8 Highlighting Progress (12.11)

ViewPoint progress is illustrated on the PERT chart and the Gantt chart in white. Since the PERT is a time-scaled network, the last accepted *As-of* date is shown by a vertical dashed line. The proposed *As-of* date line is shown by a vertical dotted line. Progress is related to the elapsed duration and not necessarily to the *true work effort*. Delays are also illustrated.

Appendix 6.11.9 Costs and Project Management Software (12.13)

In ViewPoint, the costs of the activities and of the project will be recomputed when time is reported to the activity and/or when a new unit rate is assigned to a resource. There is no special field for actual-costs-this-period.

By pointing the mouse at ''Update expenses'' on the border of the companion status-reporting Activity window, the companion status-reporting Expense window (Figure A6.27) will be invoked. Now, the window will contain fields for actual and remaining expenses. These fields are also on the companion status-reporting Activity Expense Usage screen. (Figure A6.28) Cost accrual may be controlled with the Expense Usage Distribution form. Hammocks do not reflect cost data.

The Expense Profile screen can show the costs for one resource across a set of activities or the costs for all of the resources within an accounting group.

By combining all of the categories, the user may view the Expense Profile screen for the entire project. Other cost information is also available in many reports.

- Total expenses for all resources allotted to an activity are found in several reports.
- Total costs for all resources in that branch of the Network Tree are also found in these reports.
- Total costs for all resources in the project are also found in these reports.

Appendix 6.11.10 Cost Status Reporting (12.15)

There are two tabular cash flow reports in ViewPoint: the weekly and monthly "Tabular Costs by Resource and by Activity." They can be selected to show the costs for either the early schedule or the late schedule. They show the planned, actual, and remaining costs for each resource on each activity and also the totals for each activity. (See Figure A6.35.) The on-line Cost Profile screen is a cost histogram that can be printed on a graphics printer by pressing the "Print Screen" key. It only shows the current total forecasted costs per period; it does not also show the original baseline costs. There is no "Cumulative Cost Profile" report.

Appendix 6.11.11 Earned Values and Project Management Software (12.17)

ViewPoint supports earned value analysis. (See Figure A6.36.)

The value for the BCWP is computed as the planned cost times [the actual cost amount divided by (the actual cost amount plus the remaining cost amount)].

The value for the BCWS is computed as the planned cost times the percent of the elapsed planned time. The percent of the elapsed time is derived from subtracting the planned start time from either the planned finish or the "Time — Now"[9] (whichever is less), and dividing that answer by the planned finish minus the planned start.

The ACWP is, of course, the actual cost for work performed.

ViewPoint also reports on schedule variance, which is defined as (the baseline finish minus the baseline start) minus (the actual finish minus the actual start) on the "Earned Value" report.

While the BCWS and the ACWP were correctly computed, the results for the BCWP were not.

Appendix 6.11.12 Reporting on Resource Availability (12.20)

Before constraining the ViewPoint resource profile histogram that is pictured in Figure A6.23, it may be printed using the "Print Screen" key. Similarly, residual overscheduling that remains after constraining may also be printed. The resource Gantt chart pictured in Figure A6.16 may be printed with one of the standard reports. The performance Gantt pictured in Figure A6.34 shows the baseline values. It may be printed with the "Print Screen" key.

The "Weekly Resource & Expense" report may be selected on a given resource name and on a range of dates. Other than the line drawn on the resource profile histogram (Figure A6.23), the total number of available resources is not available anywhere in the system. Users will be required to keep a handwritten report of this data.

Appendix 6.11.13 Reporting on Resource Utilization (12.21)

The ViewPoint weekly or monthly "Resource/Expense" reports show *all* of the desired data.

APPENDIX 6.12 MANAGING THE PROJECT

Appendix 6.12.1 Who Produces Perts and Gantts that May Be Restricted to Critical Path Jobs? (13.7)

The ViewPoint PERT chart cannot be limited to just those jobs on the critical path. The Gantt chart may be selected on activities whose total float is less than an established lowest value.

---

[9]A ViewPoint term. This value (or its source) is not defined anywhere in the documentation.

Figure A6.35

Project Name: CHP9G
Network Name: Top Level

ViewPoint
Activity Resource & Expense Report

Status Date: July 11, 1988
Run Date: February 11, 1989
Page 1

Activity Name and Description	Activity Code	Org & Rem Dur	Resource Name and Budget Code	PLAN ACTUAL REMAINING	Total Resources	Total Expenses
1		4	leader	PLAN	32 Mhrs	800
		0	leaders	ACTUAL	32 Mhrs	800
				REMAINING	0 Mhrs	0
1			Activity Totals:	PLAN	32	800
				ACTUAL	32	800
				REMAINING	0	0
10		4	worker	PLAN	32 Mhrs	320
		0	workers	ACTUAL	32 Mhrs	320
				REMAINING	0 Mhrs	0
10			Activity Totals:	PLAN	32	320
				ACTUAL	32	320
				REMAINING	0	0
11		3	senior	PLAN	24 Mhrs	360
		0	seniors	ACTUAL	24 Mhrs	360
				REMAINING	0 Mhrs	0
11			Activity Totals:	PLAN	24	360
				ACTUAL	24	360
				REMAINING	0	0

Figure A6.36

Project Name: CHP9G
Network Name: Top Level

ViewPoint
Earned Value Report
Project To Date

Status Date: July 11, 1988
Run Date: July 11, 1988
Page 1

Actual Activity Start Date	Activity Name and Description	Resource Name and Budget Code	Budgeted Cost Of Work Scheduled	Budgeted Cost Of Work Performed	Actual Cost of Work Performed	Variance Schedule & Cost
01Jul88	1	leader leaders	800	800	800	0 0
01Jul88	1	Activity Totals:	800	800	800	0 0
01Jul88	10	worker workers	320	320	320	0 0
01Jul88	10	Activity Totals:	320	320	320	0 0
01Jul88	11	senior seniors	360	360	360	0 0
01Jul88	11	Activity Totals:	360	360	360	0 0
		Project Totals:	8249	9022	8920	773 102

Appendix 6.12.2 Who Produces Reports that May Be Restricted to Fixed-Date Jobs? *(13.8)*

ViewPoint reports may be selected based on the values in the *constrained* dates or *constrained* types fields.

Appendix 6.12.3 Who Produces Perts and Gantts that May Be Restricted to Summary Jobs? *(13.9)*

If all of the ViewPoint hammocks have been set up in one branch of the Network Tree, the PERT chart can be limited to just those jobs. The Gantt chart may be restricted to summary activities, events, or hammocks.

Appendix 6.12.4 Local Area Networks *(13.14)*

ViewPoint gives the user who is *opening* the files control over the lock/protection. The file can be opened as read only or as read/write. Aside from this difference, the file protection works like all other products do. The system also keeps other users out of an active file.

Appendix 6.12.5 Guidelines for Tracking and Managing the Project *(13.15)*

Interspersed in the several pages of ViewPoint documentation for using the system are some hints on how to track projects.

APPENDIX 7: PRIMAVERA PROJECT PLANNER 3.1

APPENDIX 7.0 INTRODUCTION

Each section in each appendix is keyed back to its corresponding introductory section in the tutorial. Readers will find that the respective tutorial section is noted in italicized parentheses at the end of each appropriate section header line.

APPENDIX 7.1 FULL-SCREEN, FORMS-DRIVEN PRODUCTS

Appendix 7.1.1 Data Entry Mode (16.2.4)

Although it does have bar charts, Primavera Project Planner does not support network graphics. It is a full-screen, forms-driven product. The optional Primavision software is a plotter package that does not support project data entry but does have full graphics project reporting capabilities. Primavision works on files that are stored in Primavera format in the Primavera Project Planner database. Primavision produces its plots on laser printers, dot matrix printers, and, of course, plotters.

Appendix 7.1.2 Size & Storage Constraints (16.3.1)

Primavera Project Planner operates on data that is stored on the hard disk; therefore, the size of the project is only limited by the amount of remaining disk space. On the other hand, Primavision is limited to 500 activities. (It points to excluded activities with off-page connectors.) Thus, if the user wishes to employ Primavision for plotting the network, the project size is constrained by this boundary. Projects larger than that will have to be culled for a subset of activities that can be graphed. On the other hand, when drawing bar charts with Primavision, the project size may go up to 10,000 activities. Not including the hard drive storage requirements for Primavision, the requirements for Primavera Project Planner are approximately three megabytes.

Appendix 7.1.3 System Structure (16.3.2)

Primavera Project Planner is made up of ten subsystems that are accessed from the Primavera Utilities screen. (See Figure A7.1.) Choosing ''Select an existing project....1'' will ultimately take the user to the Project Data Menu screen (See Figure A7.2.), the place where the majority of the work is selected. The lowest-level screens are combinations of a stationary data area at the top, a dynamically changing window area in the middle, and two menu lines at the bottom—one for commands and one for window selection. (See Figure A7.3.)

Figure A7.1

```
                    PRIMAVERA UTILITIES
                    ~~~~~~~~~~~~~~~~~~~

        The following projects are contained in the directory:
        ADM1  ATM1  BAS1  BH9G  CH9G  CH9L  CHP9  OPT9
        SUB1  SUPR


                SELECT an existing project.......1
                LIST project names and titles....2
                ADD a new project................3
                DELETE a project.................4
                DUPLICATE and rename project.....5
                MERGE several projects...........6
                MAINTAIN target plans............7
                BACKUP one or more projects......8
                RESTORE one or more projects.....9
                SUMMARIZE projects into master...0

                    PRIMAVISION.....................P
                    CONFIGURE PRIMAVERA.............C
                    EXIT...........................X

        Press selection
```

Figure A7.2

```
                    PROJECT DATA MENU                     CHP9
                    ~~~~~~~~~~~~~~~~~
        Project data:
            Calendar.........................1
            Activity data....................2

        Dictionaries:
            Activity codes...................3
            Resource.........................4
            Cost accounts....................5

        Calculations:
            Scheduling.......................6
            Leveling.........................7

        Reports:
            Execution........................8
            Specification....................9

        PRIMAVISION..........................P

                Return to PRIMAVERA utility menu.......R
                Exit...................................X

        Press selection
```

Figure A7.3

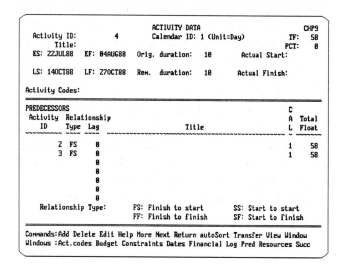

Figure A7.4

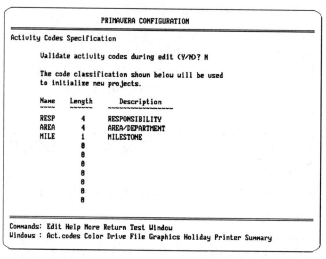

Appendix 7.1.4 Global System Project Data Defaults (16.3.3)

Global system project data defaults may be set with the "Configure Primavera....C" on the Primavera Utilities screen. (See Figure A7.4.)

Appendix 7.1.5 New Projects (16.3.4)

New Projects are added to the system with "Add a new project....3" on the Primavera Utilities screen, which in turn invokes the Add a New Project screen. (See Figure A7.5.)

Figure A7.5

```
                    ADD a new project
                    ~~~~~~~~~~~~~~~~~~

Name of new project:

Project Title:

Company/Client Name:

Report Center Heading:

Network Type (PDM or ADM): PDM

Planning Unit (Day, Week, Month):   = Not defined

Project will Start:        Project must finish no later than:

Week starts on: MON

Number of Workdays per Week: 5



Commands: Advance Edit Help Return eXecute
```

Appendix 7.1.6   Accessing Existing Plans (16.3.5)

To work with an existing project (or a new project that has just been added to the system): (1) pick out "Select an existing project....1" from the Primavera Utilities screen; (2) enter the project name; (3) choose Advance from the commands at the bottom of the Confirm Selection screen (See Figure A7.6.); (4) and choose from one of the options on the Project Data Menu screen.

Figure A7.6

```
                    CONFIRM selection
                    ~~~~~~~~~~~~~~~~~

                  Project name is CHP9

Project Title:
Company Name:

Report Center Heading:

Network Type (PDM or ADM): PDM    Calendar ID: 1

Planning Unit: D = Day

Project Start Date: 01JUL88     Project must Finish no later than:

Schedule data date: 01JUL88     Early Finish Date: 01DEC88

          TARGET #    TARGET PROJECT      DATA DATE
          --------    --------------    -----------
             1            OPT9           01JUL88
             2


Commands: Advance Edit Help Return
```

Appendix 7.1.7   Immediate Processor or Batch (16.3.6)

New schedules are computed in a separate operation by invoking "Scheduling....6", under the Project Data Menu screen. A new feature, pressing the F9 key will invoke the scheduling algorithms. In this sense, Primavera has become a semi-immediate processor system.

Appendix 7.1.8   Adding Plan Data (16.3.7)

Data is added to the system on the screen that is invoked when "Activity data....2" is selected from the Project Data Menu screen. (See Figure A7.3.) There will be discussions on planning units and calendars later in this appendix.

Appendix 7.1.9.   Optional "What-If's" Or Permanent Saves (16.3.8)

Project Plans are permanently updated as soon as data is entered into a record. If they are doing *What-If* analysis, users are advised to make a backup copy of the plan *before* they start working. (There is no limit to the number of plans that may be saved for comparison.)

Appendix 7.1.10   Ad Hoc Information Storage (16.3.9)

Information may be entered at the activity level by selecting the "Log" option on the Activity screen. Then, the user may enter nine lines of data, where each line holds 48 characters. The lines do not automatically wrap. The user must manage the amount of data and the spacing in each log line.

Appendix 7.1.11   Exporting Data (16.3.10)

This product will export data to LOTUS 1-2-3, dBASE III, and in ASCII format.

APPENDIX 7.2 WORK BREAKDOWN STRUCTURES

Appendix 7.2.1   Graphics Support (4.8.2)

Primavera Project Planner does not provide graphic work breakdown structures. Primavera Project Planner is forms driven (that is, activity data is entered in screens that have been formatted like forms).

Appendix 7.2.2   Level Support *(4.8.3)*

In Primavera Project Planner, the number of WBS levels is related to how many combinations the user can devise from four levels of an activity identification number, 20 activity codes, 26 cost categories, and an unlimited total of cost account numbers. Primavera Project Planner supports two kinds of networks: ADM and PDM. They will be discussed later on in greater detail. In ADM, the activity number is divided into two parts, each 5 positions long. The activity number is 10 positions in PDM.

Appendix 7.2.3   Data Entry Requirements *(4.8.4)*

In Primavera Project Planner, there is only one number field to enter in PDM mode and two numbers to enter in ADM mode—if the WBS is restricted to the activity identification number. On the other hand, if the activity codes are also used, there may be 2 to 21 additional fields to enter for each activity record entered. (The calendar identification defaults to the first user-defined calendar—Calendar 1.)

Appendix 7.2.4   Durations and Dependencies *(4.8.5)*

Primavera Project Planner does not require durations and dependencies to initialize a project plan.

Appendix 7.2.5   Random Sequence of Data Entry *(4.8.6)*

Primavera Project Planner has only one form of entry, the Activity Data screen, and thus supports random entry.

Appendix 7.2.6   Using the Copy Features with the *Template* Tasks *(4.8.7)*

Although it does support duplication of a total project plan, Primavera Project Planner is unable, with one direct operation, to selectively copy jobs within the plan. However, the *template* tasks may be "filtered

out" with the AutoSort and then stored in a separate project file using the "Duplicate" function. (Figure A7.1) During the "Duplicate" process, the system asks users if unique character strings should be appended to the activity identifiers. If users say *Yes*, they will then be able to later use the "Merge" function to bring these jobs into the current plan.

Appendix 7.2.7   Rollup Support *(4.8.8)*

Primavera Project Planner will provide standard reporting by resource and cost. While it is not possible to produce subtotals on breaks between activity codes, the system *will* break and subtotal on values from the cost accounts dictionary. By using the many available parameter codes and ranges in conjunction with the sort and selection criteria of the "Customizing Reports" function, various types of rollup summaries may be produced.[1]

Rollups on duration are not provided as a standard Primavera feature. However, a hammock record will provide this information.

Appendix 7.2.8   Guidelines and Documentation *(4.8.9)*

Primavera Project Planner has limited WBS documentation.

APPENDIX 7.3   ESTIMATING

Appendix 7.3.1   Estimating Support and Estimating Guidelines *(5.7.1)*

Primavera Project Planner does not provide guidelines that support the estimating techniques described in this

---

[1]Common groups of reports may be produced. As an example, one group of reports with totals of each of the Phase 1 intermediate deliverables within the Phase 1 major deliverables may be generated. Then, these reports may be followed by a second group of reports showing totals of all of the Phase 1 major deliverables. The second group may then be followed by like reports for Phase 2 and so on. The production of each individual report is a separate process. These reports may then be visually analyzed and manually reconciled. At times, this is complex and time consuming, but it is better than no reports at all.

book. It assumes the estimating has been completed and the duration is known. (Instructions on how to use the system to achieve the implementation of a feature are not considered guidelines.)

Appendix 7.3.2 Estimates of *True Work Effort* Versus Resource-Driven Elapsed Time *(5.7.4)*

In Primavera Project Planner, the *original duration* field supports *true work effort*. (Figure A7.3)

Appendix 7.3.3 Durations and Units of Measurement *(5.7.6)*

Primavera Project Planner supports days, weeks, and months. There is no default at project initialization. The planning units may not be mixed but they can be changed at any time. The system will make the correct translations.

Appendix 7.3.4 Zero Duration Milestones *(5.7.7)*

In Primavera Project Planner, a zero duration activity may be made into a milestone through a designation in the Constraints window. (See Figure A7.7.)

Appendix 7.3.5 Lead and Lag Times with Duration but No Effort *(5.7.8)*

Primavera Project Planner also uses lag times—in the Predecessor and/or Successor windows of the Activity Data screen. (Figure A7.3) Lag relationships may also be seen in any customized report that displays the detailed predecessor/successor lines and/or the predecessor/successor analysis lines.[2]

APPENDIX 7.4 NETWORKS

Appendix 7.4.1 Types of Networks *(6.8.1)*

Although it does support a bar chart display, the basic Primavera Project Planner has no network graphics capabilities.

----

[2]An alternative approach is to create a separate task with the corresponding duration and then enter a dummy resource whose cost is zero.

Figure A7.7

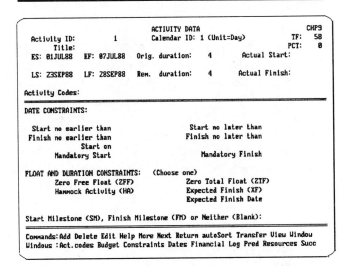

The companion product, Primavision, provides a feature for network logic plotting to hard copy. It uses the Primavera Project Planner files to plot networks in activity-on-a-node form. Primavision plots to hard copy, or the graphics may be viewed and modified on the screen.

The basic Primavera Project Planner supports two kinds of networks in Forms-Entry mode: the Precedence Diagramming Method (PDM) and the Arrow Diagramming Method (ADM). Requiring "I-J" nodes, the ADM is actually an activity-on-the-arrow network. A project must be permanently defined as one of these two types. Once declared, the network type may be changed, using a free vendor-supplied routine that has been designed for moving P3 projects into Microsoft Project.

Primavera Project Planner also provides a graphic "Network Logic" report of certain selected paths but this report is intended as a supplement to a graphic network such as the one produced by Primavision.

Appendix 7.4.2 Types of Relationships *(6.8.2)*

Primavera Project Planner allows start-to-finish, finish-to-finish; start-to-start; and finish-to-start dependencies for the PDM mode. In ADM, only the conventional finish-to-start is allowed.

Appendix 7.4.3 Number of Dependencies (6.8.3)

Primavera Project Planner allows the user to designate either predecessors or successors. There is no limit to the number of predecessors and successors. In a multiple predecessor relationship, the system will flag the job(s) that drive(s) the date of the successor. In the PDM, seven relationships at a time may be added in either the Predecessor or the Successor window. If more are required, pressing "M" for "More" will bring up a new blank window with an additional seven fields. In the ADM, relationships are established with the "I-J" nodes.

Appendix 7.4.4 Establishing Dependencies (6.8.4)

Data is entered in forms mode.

ADM networks. In Primavera Project Planner's ADM mode, the nodes define the relationships between the activities. (Figure A7.8) The *Activity ID* (in the top part of the form) is divided into two fields: an "I" node field and a "J" node field. The identification number of the "J" node field—of the activity that precedes the new activity—is entered into the "I" node field of the new Activity Data screen. The identification number of the "I" node field—of the activity that follows the new activity—is entered into the "J" node field of the new Activity Data screen.

Figure A7.8

```
                        ACTIVITY DATA                      ADM1
  I node: 10000   J node: 11000   Calendar ID: 1 <Unit=Day>     TF:    0
           Title: ATM PROJECT                              PCT:   0
  ES: 01JUL88   EF: 01JUL88   Orig. duration:   1    Actual Start:

  LS: 01JUL88   LF: 01JUL88   Rem. duration:   1    Actual Finish:

 Activity Codes:

 SUCCESSORS
                                                          Total
  I Node   J Node   Title                          CAL   Float
  ~~~~~~   ~~~~~~   ~~~~~~~~~~~~~~~~~~~~~~~~~~~~~~~  ~~~   ~~~~~
  11000    20000                                     1     1
  11000    30000                                     1     0




 Commands:Add Delete Edit Help More Next Return autoSort Transfer View Window
 Windows :Act.codes Budget Constraints Dates Financial Log Pred Resources Succ
```

PDM networks. In PDM mode, the relationships are established by either entering:

1. The Activity ID of the preceding activity into one of the seven fields in the Predecessor window (Figure A7.3); or
2. The Activity ID of the succeeding activity into one of the seven fields in the Successor window.

Either of these windows may be invoked from the command line at the bottom of the screen. An entry into a predecessor automatically resolves the references in the successor field and vice versa. Furthermore, if the Activity ID of any job is modified, the system will automatically resolve any references to it.

Appendix 7.4.5 Special Considerations for Primavera Project Planner's Multiple Relationships (6.8.5)

All types of multiple relationships are supported in PDM.

Parallel multiple relationships are prohibited in Primavera Project Planner's ADM; therefore, "dummies" are a must in that situation. However, since there are no storage limitations on plans, this is not too terrible a problem. In ADM mode, the Predecessor and Successor windows may not be modified. They are for viewing only. (Figure A7.8)

Appendix 7.4.6 How Easy Is it to Enter Dependencies? (6.8.6)

In Primavera Project Planner, for both ADM and PDM, the Activity IDs for predecessors and successors must be entered. When the cursor is positioned on a blank predecessor or successor field, the user may then press the F1 key to invoke a list of valid activities. Moving the cursor (which is now positioned in the list) to the desired activity and pressing "Enter" will cause the correct value to be transferred to the dependency field. Since the network is not displayed on the screen, it may be helpful to have a hard copy of the plan when entering dependencies.

Appendix 7.4.7 Inserting Jobs into the Middle of the Plan *(6.8.7)*

In Primavera Project Planner, plan data is added with the Activity Data screen. Inserted activities will require that new dependencies be resolved manually as described earlier.

Appendix 7.4.8 Subnetwork Dependencies *(6.8.8)*

In Primavera Project Planner, subnetwork dependencies are no problem.

Appendix 7.4.9 Moving Jobs in the Network *(6.8.9)*

Primavera Project Planner does not have a "Move" feature. Jobs are moved by changing the dependency fields.

Appendix 7.4.10 Removing Dependencies *(6.8.10)*

In Primavera Project Planner's ADM, the "I" node and the "J" node fields must be deleted or modified. In the PDM, the changes are made in the Predecessor and Successor windows.

Appendix 7.4.11 Deleting Jobs in the Plan *(6.8.11)*

Primavera Project Planner has a Delete command on the main command line. The system asks for a confirmation before the delete is actually completed. Deleting an activity leaves dangling activities (which may be reported in the schedule report diagnostics). Since there is no network to illustrate where the dangling jobs are, it is advisable to note the predecessors and successors of the delete candidate before performing the operation.

Appendix 7.4.12 Lag and Lead Times *(6.8.12)*

Primavera Project Planner allows lag times in the PDM only—in the Predecessor and/or Successor windows of the Activity Data screen. (Figure A7.3) All types of PDM relationships that the vendor supports can have lag times. Lag relationships may be seen in any customized report that displays the detailed predecessor/successor lines and/or the predecessor/successor analysis lines. In an alternative approach to creating lags, users may opt to create a new activity with the corresponding duration and then enter a dummy resource whose cost is zero. Of course, a new activity also consumes precious memory.

Finish-to-start lag time may be inserted in the ADM network with "dummy" activities.

Appendix 7.4.13 Copying Jobs in the Plan *(6.8.13)*

Primavera Project Planner can duplicate whole project plans with the "Duplicate and rename project" function. The AutoSort may be used to "filter out" selected parts of a plan before duplication. If the activity identifiers are unique in both plans, it is possible to import whole plans from one file into another when selecting the "Merge several projects" function. The product also provides a feature to automatically make the names in a plan unique. This will be discussed in greater detail in the next section.

Appendix 7.4.14 Copying the *Template* Jobs *(6.8.14)*

From the Primavera Project Planner Primavera Utilities screen, the "Merge several projects....6" feature will support the *template* plan replication. (Figure A7.1) The system does not allow duplicate names of jobs with one plan. However, it does provide a feature to allow the user to indicate an uncommon character string to be used to make the activity identifiers in the *template* plan unique. The user simply (1) enters the name of the *template* plan; (2) enters the character string; and (3) tells the system if the character string is to be placed at the beginning or end of the current activity identifier. The system nicely completes the process.

Appendix 7.4.15 Loops in the Network *(6.8.15)*

During Primavera Project Planner's data entry, the system will permit looping conditions to be entered. When the schedule is calculated in the second step, whether in straight batch or with the F9 key, the system checks for loops. If any are detected, a "Loop Diagnostic" report is produced and the schedule calculations are aborted. This report lists all activities in each loop and notes whether the loop is a closed loop (goes back into itself) or a segmented loop (a piece of the plan goes into a closed loop). The user may then use the report to edit the offending activities. The loop must be corrected before the schedule computations can be completed. Sometimes, the "Network Logic" report of certain selected activities within a designated slack path may be printed, and this will help to visualize the problem. Other times, the solution will require manually drawing the portion of the PERT chart that is effected by the loops before the loop can be debugged.

Appendix 7.4.16 Dangling Jobs (6.8.16)

Primavera Project Planner allows dangling.[3]

Appendix 7.4.17 Verifying Dependencies Are Correct (6.8.17)

Because, without a screen or hard copy network, it is hard to get an overview of the project and actually see the relationships in their setting, verification is somewhat difficult in Primavera Project Planner.

This is true in spite of the new feature that lets the user follow a path through the plan. (See the discussion in the next section.)

For those users who also have Primavision and will integrate it with Primavera Project Planner, verification and correction may be done by flipping between Primavision and Primavera Project Planner. This is done through the Project Data Menu screen. (Figure A7.2) Primavision's hierarchical "PDM Network Logic Diagram" report, an activity-on-a-node network, is very pleasing to read and makes the effort worthwhile. Primavision also produces ADM, or activity-on-the-arrow, networks.

---

[3]Although the vendor believes it is considered to be a benefit to permit danglers, the system does flag open-ended activities.

Appendix 7.4.18 Highlighting Dependency Paths (6.8.18)

Primavera Project Planner's path tracing is accomplished while in Activity Screen mode, by pressing the *Next* command, pressing the "Down Arrow" key to get to the Predecessor or Successor window, moving the cursor to choose the dependency entry to follow, and pressing "Enter". These steps are repeated for each activity visited.

In addition to this trace feature, Primavera Project Planner has a report called the "Network Logic Diagram" that will chart all of the activities in a given slack path.

Another alternative path tracing approach is to use "The Project Schedule With Predecessors and Successors" report, a standard linear report in which each activity is printed with its immediate predecessors and successors.

In even an average-sized project, path tracing is only valuable when there is a hard copy network with which to compare the Activity screens or the report. Otherwise, it may be necessary to manually draw the network as the verification operation progresses.

Appendix 7.4.19 Network Aesthetics (6.8.19)

Primavision will plot networks that are scaled to time or networks that are driven purely by the logical relationships between the jobs. While the time-scaled networks are certainly respectable, the hierarchical "PDM Network Logic Diagram" report is truly aesthetically gratifying. ADM networks, in general, are not attractive but Primavision's "ADM Logic Network" report is easy to read.

Appendix 7.4.20 Scaled to Time? (6.8.20)

There is no network in Primavera Project Planner. Primavision is scaled to time. Since the system prints the activity data above and below the node, the network is still readable and useful.

Appendix 7.4.21 Networks and Work Breakdown Structures (6.9)

Primavera Project Planner does not create beginning and ending nodes and, consequently, requires reestablishing dependencies while moving down in the WBS. Nevertheless, adding in a duplicate ending job is very easy. Similarly, it does not support automatic resolution of relationships when adding the "latest last job."

Appendix 7.4.22 Setting Up Hammocks *(6.11)*

In Primavera Project Planner, after creating an activity record that will represent the hammock, a start-to-start predecessor relationship is established between the hammock and the first activity in the group. Then, a finish-to-finish successor relationship is established between the hammock and the last activity in the group. Entering "HA" in the duration calculation code field after pressing "Window; Constraints" completes the operation. The total duration of the group will be in the hammock. (Figure A7.7)

Appendix 7.4.23 Dependencies in a Multiproject Environment *(6.12)*

At first blush, it appears that Primavera Project Planner provides two approaches for implementing multiprojects—summarizing or merging. In scenarios equivalent to Figure 6.17, the "Summarize" feature will suffice. The more complex implementation is the one that is equivalent to Figure 6.18. In this case, the "Merge" facility should be used. There is no limit to the number of times a subproject may be used during the "Merge". The master project is *not* constrained by the sum of its subprojects.

Primavera Project Planner melds the subproject plans into *one* plan. Maintaining the original *and* merged copies of the subprojects may later require double data entry.

After the user has selected "Merge several projects....6" from the Primavera Utilities screen, the system will prompt for the name of the subprojects. (Figure A7.1) If there are duplicate activity names in any of the subprojects, the procedure will be aborted. However, the "Merge" process does ask the user to optionally designate uncommon character strings that can be affixed to the beginning or ending of each of the

activities in a subproject, thus giving them unique names. (See the discussion under *template* tasks earlier in this appendix.) Merged projects must also be defined in the same planning unit.

The system does *not* set up the dependencies between each subproject plan. This must be done manually by the user. Therefore, before starting the "Merge" operation, it is advisable to create a single beginning and ending node for each subproject, making note of their names. Dependency connections are then simply made as outlined earlier in this appendix.

Users should take note that the activity codes dictionary and the cost accounts dictionary are *not* brought in with the "Merge". If rollup reporting is to be maintained, this data will need to be reentered.

A subset consisting only of hammocks may be extracted from the merged master project by executing the AutoSort with selection criteria of "CON EQ HA". Bar charts (which may be displayed on screen) will then have a single, one-line entry for each of the subprojects. Similarly, this selection criteria may be used in Primavision to plot networks and bar charts consisting exclusively of hammocks.

Appendix 7.4.24 Printing and Viewing Networks *(6.13)*

Although it does support bar charts, Primavera Project Planner has no network graphics. Its companion product, Primavision, is a plotter product. It also supports on-screen network viewing. (Because of the sizable differences in proportions between the way plotter driver and the screen driver work, the network on the screen may appear very small. This is not a handicap, however, since the system provides users with a feature that enables them to zoom in on any part of the network and then pan (move) the zoom around the network.) To initialize the printing of a "Network Logic Diagram" report in Primavision, there is a nine-step process. Some of the steps include transactions for specifying the content of the network, selecting the activities to be plotted, and tailoring the output. Seven out of the nine steps are usually only executed once —at network initialization. The last two steps, "Executing a diagram plot" and "Terminating a diagram plot" are used to plot the output. Pressing "X" on the Plot Specification screen will start the plotter.

Appendix 7.4.25 Guidelines and Documentation (6.15)

In Primavera Project Planner, there are several very good pages on networks and relationship types. There are no guidelines on multiprojects.

APPENDIX 7.5   OPTIMAL PLANS

Appendix 7.5.1   Calendars (7.14.1)

The number of working days per week and the starting day of the week are defined at project initiation in the Add Project screen. (Figure A7.5)

In addition to a system-controlled continuous calendar, Primavera Project Planner supports three user-defined calendars. Each project *must* have at least one user-defined calendar.

Choosing "Calendar....1" under the Project Data Menu screen (Figure A7.2) will invoke a calendar screen into which the user may enter the calendar information. (See Figure A7.9.) Holidays are called *nonworking periods*. After moving the cursor to a selected date field, the holiday date may be keyed in. Alternatively, the user may press the F1 key and invoke a Calendar window. (See Figure A7.10.) Moving the cursor to the desired date and pressing the "Return key will cause the designated date to be placed in the chosen field.

Since the smallest unit of measurement is in in-

Figure A7.9

```
          GLOBAL CALENDAR INFORMATION              CHP9

 Planning Unit: D = Day              Week starts on: MON
 Start date: 01JUL88   Data date: 01JUL88  Finish date:


 ┌─────────────────────────┬─────────────────────────┐
 │  Calendar ID specified  │  Calendar ID available  │
 │           1             │          2, 3           │
 ├─────────────────────────┼─────────────────────────┤
 │ Nonwork periods  Page: 1│ Exceptions      Page:  1│
 │                         │                         │
 │ Start  Period  End Period│ Start  Period  End Period│
 │ ~~~~~~~~~~~~~~  ~~~~~~~~~~│ ~~~~~~~~~~~~~~  ~~~~~~~~~~│
 │     04JUL88             │                         │
 │     05SEP88             │                         │
 │     10OCT88             │                         │
 │     11NOV88             │                         │
 │     24NOV88             │                         │
 │     25NOV88             │                         │
 │     Scroll using Home, End│   Scroll using PgUp, PgDn│
 └─────────────────────────┴─────────────────────────┘
 Commands: Add Delete Edit Help More Next Print Return Transfer View Window
 Windows : Calendar Global List
```

Figure A7.10

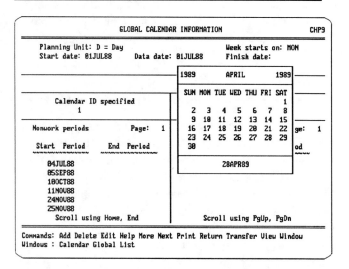

```
          GLOBAL CALENDAR INFORMATION              CHP9

 Planning Unit: D = Day              Week starts on: MON
 Start date: 01JUL88   Data date: 01JUL88  Finish date:

                          ┌────────────────────────────┐
                          │ 1989        APRIL      1989 │
 ┌────────────────────────┤                            │
 │  Calendar ID specified │ SUN MON TUE WED THU FRI SAT │
 │           1            │                          1  │
 │                        │  2   3   4   5   6   7   8  │
 │                        │  9  10  11  12  13  14  15  │
 │ Nonwork periods  Page: 1 16  17  18  19  20  21  22 ge:  1
 │                        │ 23  24  25  26  27  28  29  │od
 │ Start  Period  End Period 30                        │
 │ ~~~~~~~~~~~~~~  ~~~~~~~~└────────────────────────────┘~~
 │     04JUL88
 │     05SEP88                       28APR89
 │     10OCT88
 │     11NOV88
 │     24NOV88
 │     25NOV88
 │     Scroll using Home, End        Scroll using PgUp, PgDn

 Commands: Add Delete Edit Help More Next Print Return Transfer View Window
 Windows : Calendar Global List
```

crements of days, the system does not support scheduling lunch and other nonworking hours into the calendar.

Once the calendar has been created, it may be copied into other project plans by choosing the *transfer* command from the Calendar Dictionary screen and entering the name of the original plan.

Appendix 7.5.2 Choosing the Correct Project Start Date (7.14.2)

In Primavera Project Planner, the starting date of the project may be set in the *start date* on the calendar, the *project will start date* on the Add a New Project screen or the *project start date* on the Confirm Selection screen. It is only necessary to take this action one time—at plan initiation. The system will automatically keep these dates in synchronization.

During the planning stage (before progress is reported to the plan), this date will also be entered into the *schedule data date* field of the Confirm Selection screen, a protected field that may not be modified on that screen. (Figure A7.6) Later, during progress reporting, the important date is the *current project data date*, which may be changed by invoking the scheduling algorithm (for example, by pressing the F9 key) and then changing the *current project data date* field before the schedule is computed. Alternatively, the *current project data date* on the scheduling screen may be updated. (See Figure A7.27 below.) At the activity level, if the calendar for that given activity is not equal to the default calendar (Calendar 1), the user will need to remember to make the necessary updates.

Appendix 7.5.3 Insuring that the Plan Is Not Constrained by Resources (7.14.3)

In Primavera Project Planner, the *remaining duration* field will drive the optimal plan. Since the presence (or absence) of resources in a plan will not drive the schedule unless the user chooses to level the plan, it is not necessary to add resources at this time.

Appendix 7.5.4 Avoiding Imposed Target Dates (7.14.3)

In Primavera Project Planner, there are seven date constraint choices accessed by selecting "Windows; Constraints" from the Activity Data screen. (Figure A7.7) For the optimal plan, the user is advised to leave *all* of these blank.

Appendix 7.5.5 Calculating the Schedule (7.14.4)

A semi-immediate processing system, Primavera Project Planner computes schedules when "Scheduling....6" is selected from the Project Data Menu screen. A shortcut to scheduling is invoked from the Activities screen by pressing F9 and entering the *current project data date*. Before progress is posted to the plan, this date is the same date as the project start date.

Appendix 7.5.6 The Forward Pass: Calculating the Early Dates (7.14.5)

Primavera Project Planner defaults to the traditional scheduling algorithm.

Appendix 7.5.7 Zero Duration Milestones (7.14.8)

Primavera Project Planner supports milestones that have been designated as starting milestones, ending milestones, or stand-alone milestones. (The stand-alone milestone may, for example, be used for the dummy job illustrated in Figure 6.16.) The designation is made

through the Constraints window. Starting milestones will have early start and late start dates, but no finish dates. Ending milestones will have early finish and late finish dates, but no start dates. The value of the milestone's date is driven by the default Calendar 0 or by one of the three user calendars. It is possible to set the system so that ending milestones will fall at the preferred time—the close of the business day on which all of the predecessors have finished.

Appendix 7.5.8 Retaining a Baseline Record of the Optimal Plan (7.14.11)

In Primavera Project Planner, unlimited versions of the plan (called *target* plans) may be saved as baseline versions by selecting "Maintain target plans....7" from the utilities menu. Since there can be two active target plans per project, this product allows one more baseline than most of the other products. (Figure A7.6) The original early dates are used for the target dates. The target dates can be viewed on several reports. For each activity, the target early and late dates and the current early and late dates may be viewed together in the Dates window.

Each target plan is saved as a duplicate of the original plan. It may then also be viewed as an individual project and can be accessed from the project names on the utilities menu. In this manner, the target dates may be viewed on the screen.

Since they are complete stand-alone plans, the target plans can be modified without limitation. (Users should be cautioned to apply this feature judiciously, since modifications may affect the target plan's usefulness as a baseline plan.)

Appendix 7.5.9 Interpreting the Dates on the Screen (7.14.12)

The bar chart in Primavera Project Planner allows the early and late dates of the current and/or the target plan to be displayed. (See Figure A7.11.) This product does not graphically show the network. However, in the Primavision network logic diagrams, the early dates and the late dates are both displayed. The network diagrams do not show both the current and the target plan dates. Primavision produces hard copy reports; or the network can be viewed on the screen.

Figure A7.11

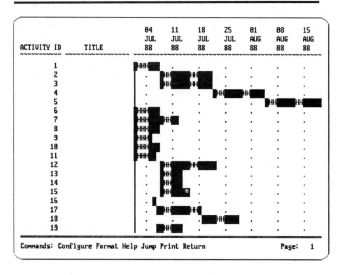

```
                         04    11    18    25    01    08    15
                         JUL   JUL   JUL   JUL   AUG   AUG   AUG
ACTIVITY ID   TITLE      88    88    88    88    88    88    88
~~~~~~~~~~~   ~~~~~       ~~~~~~~~~~~~~~~~~~~~~~~~~~~~~~~~~~~~~~~
        1                 HH
        2                    HH   HH
        3
        4                          HH   HH
        5                                   HH
        6                 HH
        7                 HH   H
        8                 HH
        9                 HH
       10                 HH
       11                 HH
       12                    HH   HH
       13
       14                    H
       15                      H
       16                 H
       17                 HH   HH
       18                 HH   HH
       19                   HH   H

Commands: Configure Format Help Jump Print Return          Page:   1
```

Appendix 7.5.10 Annotating the Critical Path (7.14.13)

If plotting in Primavision, the critical path may be highlighted in the user's choice of color. Otherwise, the critical path is highlighted in bolder graphics.

Appendix 7.5.11 Gantt Chart Time Periods (7.14.15)

Time periods in Primavera Project Planner may be in increments from days to weeks to months. Theoretically, there is no limit to the number of time periods that may be displayed. By pressing the arrow keys, the user may move in any direction around the Gantt chart by pressing the arrow keys.

The bars on the Gantt chart may be broken by holidays and by weekends. To get more data on the screen, the vendor suggests only using workdays, excluding the nonworking days.

Appendix 7.5.12 Scheduling in the Multiproject Environment (7.14.17)

Calendars in Primavera Project Planner are not imported with the subproject. However, they are easily brought in from the calendar dictionary by pressing "Transfer" and entering the name of the project from

which to retrieve the calendar. Because incoming data will always overwrite existing data, if more than one file will be involved, the file that contains the permanent values should be transferred last.

Since Primavera Project Planner is a semi-immediate processing system, the new schedule is not computed until the user executes this operation (for example, by pressing the F9 key).

Because this is a "Merge" process, maintaining the original *and* merged copies of the subprojects may later require double data entry.

A subset consisting only of hammocks may be extracted from the merged master project by executing the AutoSort with selection criteria of "CON EQ HA". Bar charts (which may be displayed on screen) will then have a single, one-line entry for each of the subprojects. Similarly, this selection criteria may be used in Primavision to plot networks and bar charts consisting exclusively of hammocks. Each hammock's early and late start dates, as well as its early and late finish dates, will represent the respective dates of the first and last activity in the corresponding subproject.

Appendix 7.5.13 Nesting Subprojects in a Multiproject Environment (7.14.18)

Since using the Primavera Project Planner "Merge" function melds the subproject plans together, the nested issue is inapplicable.

Appendix 7.5.14 Guidelines and Documentation (7.14.20)

There are several very good pages in Primavera Project Planner showing the basis for scheduling calculations.

APPENDIX 7.6 CALCULATING A FINISH DATE

Appendix 7.6.1 Using the New Reasonable Late Finish Date of the Project (7.26.3)

In Primavera Project Planner, all the user need do is enter the new, desired late end date in the *project must finish no later than* field of the Project Confirm Selection screen. (Figure A7.6) The correct late dates are computed and stored in each activity's late start and late finish fields. If a hammock has been created that spans the entire project, the correct early start and finish dates and the correct late start and finish dates of the project will both be displayed in the hammock record. If no hammock has been created, the early finish date of the project may only be found in the early finish date of the last task(s) in the project or in the early finish field of the Project Confirm Selection screen. Other than providing a report that flags the zero slack path(s), this product will not flag critical paths with float greater than zero.

APPENDIX 7.7 ADDING RESOURCES

Appendix 7.7.1 Creating the Resource Calendars *(8.8)*

Primavera Project Planner does not support resource calendars, nor does it support part-time resources at the project level. However, if there are only one or two unique resource calendars, they may be entered in one of the user-generated calendars.

Appendix 7.7.2 Creating the Resource Pool *(8.9)*

Resources in Primavera Project Planner may be individuals, groups of individuals, equipment, or materials. Since the vendor proposes that *fixed* costs need no special treatment, Primavera Project Planner has no separate operation for them. Rather, they are added just like any other resource.[4]

There is no limit to the number of resources in a project.

"Resources are entered in the Resource Dictionary screen (See Figure A7.12.), which is accessed from the Project Data Menu screen by pressing "Resources....4". There is one screen for each resource. The standard resource information to be entered at this time is: the eight-character resource name, the normal number of available resources of this type, the maximum number of available resources of this type, the units in which the resource is measured (hours, days, etc.), and the cost per unit. Both fields for numbers of resources must be in multiples that correspond to units of measurement. (For example, if units of measurement is hours, and two resources are normally available eight hours per day, the entry is 16.)

The system also supports multiple billing rates for each resource: optionally, the user may indicate the effective dates for the number of resources and/or the cost per unit.

[4]The vendor suggests that users may create zero duration activities or set the resource duration equal to zero.

Figure A7.12

RESOURCE DICTIONARY CH9G

Resource: BOSS Units: hour
Description:

RESOURCE LIMITS AND PRICES:

Normal limit	Max limit	Through	Price/unit	Through
8	8		50.00	
0	0		0.00	
0	0		0.00	
0	0		0.00	
0	0		0.00	
0	0		0.00	

Commands: Add Delete Edit Help List Next Print Return Transfer Usage

Appendix 7.7.3 Assigning Part-Time Resources at the Project Level *(8.10)*

In Primavera Project Planner, part-time participation is not supported at the project level—it is only supported at the activity level. (See the discussion later in this appendix.)

Appendix 7.7.4 Deleting and Changing Resources at the Project Level *(8.11)*

Resources in Primavera Project Planner are deleted from the Resource Dictionary screen by pressing "Delete". Deleting a resource in the pool automatically results in the project-wide removal of all corresponding resource assignments. Before deleting a resource, the system asks for confirmation of the delete request.

Names are changed in the same manner as other modifications. Changing a name results in a project-wide replacement of all occurrences of the old name with the new name.

Appendix 7.7.5 Matching Resources to Jobs (8.14)

In Primavera Project Planner, resources may be assigned at any level in the work breakdown structure; however, if they are assigned to hammocks, they will not be affected by the leveling and smoothing algorithms described later. There is no limit to the number of allowable resource names that can be assigned to a given activity. They are allocated to an activity record through the Resource window, which is accessed by pressing ''Windows; Resources'' from the Activity screen. (See Figure A7.13.)

Minimally, the eight-character resource name, the number of resource units assigned per day, and the total amount of resource effort must be entered for each resource. A work category code is also optional. The scale for the assigned units must match the scale in the resource's dictionary entry (for example, with a dictionary scale of hours, one full-time resource would have an assigned resource unit of eight hours per day). (Figure A7.12) Furthermore, if the quotient—when the resource effort is divided by the total number of assigned resource units—exceeds the activity duration, the number of assigned resource units will be increased to insure that the activity duration will remain constant.

The same resource may be assigned to an activity as often as necessary. However, if duplicate resource names are entered, the system requires a single character *tie-breaker* code to be entered into each resource

Figure A7.13

```
                           ACTIVITY DATA                        CHP9
    Activity ID:      1         Calendar ID: 1 (Unit=Day)    TF:  58
       Title:                                                PCT:   0
    ES: 01JUL88   EF: 07JUL88   Orig. duration:   4    Actual Start:

    LS: 23SEP88   LF: 28SEP88   Rem. duration:    4    Actual Finish:

    Activity Codes:

    RESOURCE SUMMARY:      Resource  1       Resource  2      Resource  3
                          ~~~~~~~~~~~~~~~   ~~~~~~~~~~~~~~~  ~~~~~~~~~~~~~~~
    Resource               WORKER   1        WORKER   2
    Cost Acct/type        TEST1             TEST2
    Units per time period           1.00              1.00             0.00
    Budget quantity                 1                 1                0
    Resource Lag/Duration  0                 0                 0
    Percent Complete
    Actual qty this Period          0                 0                0
    Actual qty to date              0                 0                0
    Quantity to complete            1                 1                0
    Quantity at completion          1                 1                0
    Variance (units)                0                 0                0

    Commands:Add Delete Edit Help More Next Return autoSort Transfer View Window
    Windows :Act.codes Budget Constraints Dates Financial Log Pred Resources Succ
```

assignment (for example: (a) Programmer 1 and Programmer 2; or (b) when the user wants to represent two different profiles of usage for the same resource.).

If the number of resources being applied to the task exceeds the maximum resource availability in the resource pool, it will not be flagged until leveling. Leveling, however, will not abort but there will be an error message for each affected activity on the ''Leveling Diagnostic'' report that automatically prints at the end of the operation.

Resources may be randomly added to the project. When an undefined resource is assigned to a task, the system will briefly give a message indicating that an unknown resource has been entered. It will then automatically create a corresponding entry in the resource pool. No values, however, are entered. The user must remember to enter the desired values at a later date, or no costs will be computed for the jobs associated with the new resource.

The *true work effort* is in the original duration field and the remaining duration field. If the integrity of the duration field is to be maintained, these settings should *not* be changed at this time.[5] When the resource effort is different from the task duration, special actions are required, which will be addressed later in this appendix.

Appendix 7.7.6 Assigning Part-Time Resources at the Task or Activity Level (8.15)

In Primavera Project Planner, part-time participation is supported at the activity level. If the user assigns a number in the assigned units per day of the Resource window (Figure A7.13) that reflects the part-time participation, the quantity fields in the Resource window, the Budget window (See Figure A7.19 below.), and the Financial window (See Figure A7.20 below.) will be multiplied by the corresponding fractional percentage value, thus reducing the total resource effort. This is artificial and incorrect. Therefore, in order to complete the part-time designation, users must also manually compute the number of elapsed calendar days that will be required to reflect the part-time participation in the job and enter this value in the remaining

---

[5]Of course, when progress is later posted to the activity, the remaining duration may need to be changed.

duration field of the Activity screen. Then, they must rekey the *true work effort* back into the quantity fields. (These operations must be performed in this order, or incorrect values will be the result.)

Appendix 7.7.7 Assigning Multiple Resources to a Job *(8.16)*

Resource information is entered in the Primavera Project Planner Resource window. (Figure A7.13) If duplicate resource names are entered, the system requires a single-character *tie-breaker* code to be entered into each resource assignment (for example, Worker 1 and Worker 2).

By design, Primavera Project Planner is not intended to support resource-driven scheduling. On the other hand, users may easily add more people to a job. In order to complete the multiple resource entry, users must manually compute the number of elapsed calendar days that will be required to reflect each resource's level of participation, and enter this value in the remaining days field of the Activity screen. Then, for each resource, they must key the desired *true work effort* values into the quantity fields of the Resource window.

Appendix 7.7.8 What to Do when the Resource Effort Must Be Less than the Elapsed Calendar Days *(8.17)*

In Primavera Project Planner, when the total number of units equals the *true work effort*, but is less than the activity elapsed time, the work can be distributed anywhere within the activity *candidate time slice*. (See Figure A7.14 below.) To create the conditions illustrated in Example 1, if the user puts the *true work effort* in the *quantity to complete* and the *quantity at completion* fields (found in the Resource window), this will reduce the corresponding assigned units per day to reflect the correct distribution of effort.

Primavera Project Planner cannot compute percentages. When the scenario illustrated in Example 2 occurs, the user will need to manually compute the hours or days that equate to the percentage level and then proceed as in Example 1.

The scenario in Example 3 is accomplished by delaying the resource duration with a corresponding value in the resource lag/duration fields.

Figure A7.14

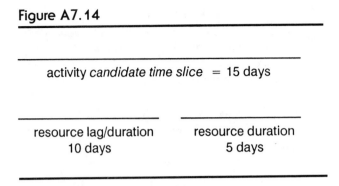

activity *candidate time slice* = 15 days

| resource lag/duration 10 days | resource duration 5 days |

Naturally, the sum of the resource duration and the resource lag/duration may not be greater than the activity *candidate time slice*.

Remember, also, that when these actions are taken, the record of the *true work effort* is now in the quantity to complete and the quantity at completion fields (found in the Resource window). The original duration and remaining duration will then contain the elapsed calendar days.

Appendix 7.7.9 Fixed Dates for Activities Or Tasks *(8.19)*

Primavera Project Planner uses the scheduling algorithm that highlights projects that are late before they start.

Fixed dates may be entered at any level in the work breakdown structure. They are entered on the Constraint window, which is accessed from the Activity screen by pressing "Window;Constraint". (Figure A7.7)

Constraint types in this form fall into three categories: those that affect only early dates, those that affect only late dates, and those that affect both the early and late dates. Those that affect only early dates are called CES (Constrained Early Start: Start No Earlier than) and CEF (Constrained Early Finish: Finish No Earlier Than). Those that affect only late dates are called CLS (Constrained Late Start: Start No Later Than) and CLF (Constrained Late Finish: Finish No Later Than). Both sets of dates are affected by *start on*, *mandatory start*, and *mandatory finish*.

Three parameters were evaluated: start on, mandatory start, and start no later than.

If the new fixed date of the affected activity is the same as its system-generated dates, all three of the evaluated constraint types produce the same results:

The late date of the affected activity is set to match its early date. The late dates of the predecessor activities are modified to retain compatibility with the new late date in the affected activity. There is no change to the dates in the successors.

If the new fixed date of the affected activity is later than its system-generated dates, mandatory start and start on produced the same results:

The new dates are in both the early and late fields of the affected activity. The early dates of the successors are modified to maintain compatibility with the affected activity. The late dates of the successors are untouched. The early dates of the predecessors are untouched. The late dates of the predecessors are modified to maintain compatibility with the affected activity.

In start no later than, if the new fixed date of the affected activity is later than its system-generated dates:

The new dates are in the late date fields of the affected activity. The early date fields of the affected activity are untouched. The dates of the successors are untouched; the early dates of the predecessors are untouched. The late dates of the predecessors are modified to maintain compatibility with the affected activity.

If the new fixed date of the affected activity is earlier than its system-generated dates, start no later than and start on produced the same results:

The late date of the affected activity is modified to reflect the new date. There is no change to the dates in the successors. There is no change to the early dates of the predecessors. The late finish date of the immediate predecessors is modified to reflect the new late date in the affected activity. All of the other late dates in the predecessors are left blank.

In mandatory start, if the new fixed date of the affected activity is earlier than its system-generated dates:

Both sets of dates in the affected activity are set to the new dates. A new set of early dates is computed for the successors. There is no change to the late dates of the successors. There is no change to the early dates of the predecessors. The late finish date of the immediate predecessors is modified to reflect the new late date in the affected activity. All of the other late dates in the predecessors are left blank.

There are no special flags to indicate activities that are delayed due to fixed dates.

If the late finish date of the project is entered onto the project must finish no later than field of the Project Confirm Selection screen, the late dates of all of the predecessors will be correctly computed.

Appendix 7.7.10 Special Leveling Patterns in Project Management Software (8.29)

Primavera Project Planner calls the second approach *smoothing*. The user decides which of the two types of leveling is to be used during the leveling process. This choice is made at leveling time. (See the discussion later in this appendix.)

Appendix 7.7.11 Automatic Resource Leveling (8.30)

The Primavera Project Planner Resource Leveling screen (See Figure A7.15.) is invoked from the Project Data Menu screen by selecting ''Leveling....7''. This product supports what may be called *selective* leveling: the user may enter the name of each resource to be included in the leveling operation or one easy stroke

Figure A7.15

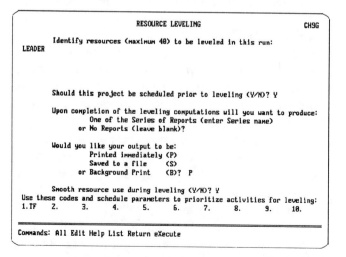

("A" for "All"), selects the first 40 resources in the resource dictionary.

At this time, the system must also be told whether or not it should run a new schedule before leveling. This option automatically defaults to *No*. However, since leveling is more frequently going to be run repetitively than for the first time, the default ought to be the other way around. The way it is now, the user can easily forget to say *Yes* and then get unexpected scheduling results.[6]

With the leveling run, the system also allows the user to produce a whole host of any selected reports.

Next, the user must choose whether or not to smooth resources during the operation (that is, to choose one of the two types of leveling).

Finally, leveling may be driven by up to 10 user-directed priorities. The default is to prioritize by total float; however, users may alternatively choose free float.[7] Total float was retained for the control sample. Setting priorities will be addressed in the next section.

Naturally, dates may change because activities may be delayed either as a result of resource constraints or because a predecessor was delayed. The original early dates in the schedule may be replaced by either of these two dates. A nice touch, a hard copy "Resource Leveling Analysis" report may be produced at the end of every leveling run. This reports lists the delays according to these two categories.

Similarly, if the new project finish date is later than the old finish date, a new backward pass will also be computed and the dates will be placed in the late date fields. Primavera Project Planner is a permanent save system; therefore the original early and late dates will only be present in one of the baselines. However, to remove the leveled dates and retrieve the original

dates, the user only needs to recalculate the schedule.

If the results of leveling and smoothing are acceptable, the user must manually enter *each* of the acceptable leveled dates into the date constraints field of the Constraints window for each activity. (See the earlier discussion on fixed dates.)

Other than on the "Resource Leveling Analysis" report, the system does not flag delays due to leveling.

Appendix 7.7.12 Setting Special Leveling Priorities on Tasks or Activities *(8.31)*

Primavera Project Planner uses priorities at the project level to drive the scheduling algorithms. The leveling initiation screen accepts a hierarchy of 10 priorities. (Figure A7.15) There are designated abbreviations for many of the fields in the activity record. By using these abbreviations in the priority fields of the leveling screen, users can tell the system the order in which to schedule resources. The default is by total slack.

Appendix 7.7.13 User-Driven Interactive Leveling *(8.32)*

For this application, Primavera Project Planner offers two graphs: the Gantt screen and the Resource Histogram screen. (See Figures A7.11 and A7.16.) They may be displayed on the screen or easily printed as well. These graphics default to text displays (that is, they are represented by letters and not by solid bars). However, at system installation, the user may reconfigure the display formats to exhibit graphics rather than text. This operation is completed by entering the ASCII code equivalents for the defaults. The correct ASCII code values are displayed when the user presses the F1 key.[8]

Although the Gantt and Resource Histogram are easily viewed on two separate screens, there is no split-window facility that allows the user to see them together. Furthermore, Primavera Project Planner is a manual leveling system. These are display-only screens; there is no way, from these screens, to interactively make changes to the plan and immediately see the results.

---

[6]The vendor disagrees with this premise. It is assumed that, whenever users make changes to the schedule, they will systematically rerun the schedule process so that they can see the effects of the modifications. The leveling default is *No*, so that these users will be saved the time of running a new schedule before they can level. Both sides of this issue are valid. An added feature would be one in which the user could choose the default.

[7]Primavera Project Planner is the only product that allows the user to choose between using *free* float or *total* float during leveling.

---

[8]However, the vendor suggests that "if users want meaningful report data, they should use letters and not symbols."

Figure A7.16

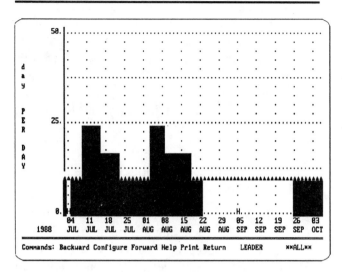

The Gantt chart is invoked from the Activity screen by pressing "View; Bar", choosing days, weeks, or months as the scale, and, finally, choosing the starting month of the Gantt. All of the activities in the plan will be charted. On the other hand, the AutoSort may be executed to restrict the Gantt to display only the activities for a single resource. (To get back the display of the whole plan, a second sort must be executed.) The Gantt chart shows the early dates, the late dates, and the slack.

The resource histogram is invoked from the Activity screen in a series of steps that are initiated by pressing "View; Resource". A format screen is then presented to the user. This screen requests directions about whether to display the histogram or a cumulative usage curve; about whether to use early dates, late dates, or both dates; about whether to display effort or cost; about whether to scale the display to days, weeks, or months; and about what month the display should start with. After editing this screen, the user is then required to press "Window; Select" and enter the name of the designated resource.

The height of each column in the histogram shows the level of commitment. With a horizontal line drawn across the histogram at the corresponding vertical axis level, the histogram also implicitly shows available resource levels. The usage columns are all one color. Nonutilization is left blank.

While the Gantt chart shows holidays (albeit not weekends—when activities are more than a week long), the histogram shows neither weekends nor holidays.

Modifying the plan to eliminate resource conflicts is done in the Activity screen and the Resource Dictionary screen. The Activity Data screen is easily invoked by pressing "Return" from either one of the graphic displays. The activity slated for change is reached by pressing "Next" and entering the name of the desired activity. To make changes in the Resource Dictionary screen, the user must exit activity mode, go back to the Project Data Menu screen and select the Resource Dictionary screen. The Activity screen is used to add or split jobs; to add, change, or delete the resource assignments; and to change the dates, the durations, the relationships, and the resource lags. The Resource Dictionary screen is used to change resource availability. There are no resource calendars in this product.

Appendix 7.7.14 Baseline Project Plans for Resource Leveling (8.34)

Primavera Project Planner is the only product that supports two baseline versions within the same plan.

Appendix 7.7.15 Resources, Multiprojects, and Project Management Software (8.35.4)

From the Primavera Project Planner resource dictionary, *template* resource files can be copied from project to project by pressing "Transfer", entering the name of the desired resource filename, and pressing "Enter." With this "Transfer" feature, incoming data will always overwrite existing data. If more than one file will be involved, the file that contains the permanent values should be transferred *last*.

On the other hand, with the file "Merge", the system automatically brings in all corresponding resource assignments, and new resources are also added to the resource dictionary. However, when there are duplicate resources in both the master project and the subproject, the resource record in the master project is retained, and the resource data in the subproject is ignored. Consequently, users ought to choose carefully the *first* subproject in the list of projects to be merged, since that will be the source of the permanent resource data.

This product does not support resource calendars. Hammocks do not reflect resource data.

Because this is a "Merge" process, maintaining the original *and* merged copies of the subprojects may later require double data entry.

Since all of the subprojects are merged into one project, the other issues in this section are inapplicable.

Appendix 7.7.16 Guidelines and Documentation *(8.36)*

There are two very comprehensive chapters in Primavera Project Planner on resource management and a third chapter on adding fixed dates to the project plan.

Figure A7.17

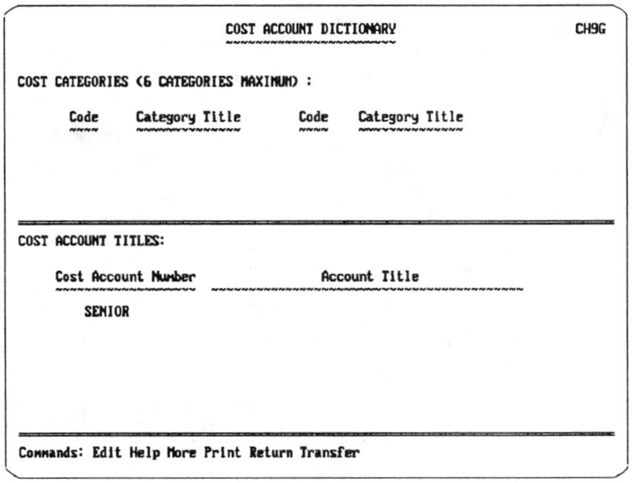

COST ACCOUNT DICTIONARY CH9G

COST CATEGORIES (6 CATEGORIES MAXIMUM) :

Code Category Title Code Category Title

COST ACCOUNT TITLES:

Cost Account Number Account Title

SENIOR

Commands: Edit Help More Print Return Transfer

APPENDIX 7.8 CALCULATING COSTS

Appendix 7.8.1 Costs and Project Management Software *(9.4)*

In Primavera Project Planner, cost categories may be set up in a work breakdown structure code that is entered into the activity indentifier field of the Activity Data screen. This form may also be used to enter up to 20 activity codes. In addition to these fields, users may also enter cost categories into the Cost Accounts Dictionary screen—which may be accessed from the Project Data Menu screen by selecting "Cost Accounts....5". (See Figure A7.17.) There are up to 26 one-position cost category codes. A longer descriptive category title may be associated with each of any 6 of the 26 codes. Users may also enter an unlimited number of 11-position cost account numbers, along with a corresponding account title description field for longer information. These codes may be used for rolling up cost data that can, in turn, be used to track budgets and accumulate resource usage, actual costs, and estimates of costs to completion. The 11-position cost account number and the one-position category code go in the Resource window.

In Primavera Project Planner, the hardest part of maintaining cost control is establishing an effective correspondence between the activity codes that are used for scheduling and the codes used for cost accumulation. However, since, in most software projects, the work breakdown structure code can be placed in the activity identification number, it may not be necessary to use the activity code fields. Thus, this problem is usually trivial for software projects. The vendor suggests that, if cost codes are to be used, they ought to be set up so that they relate to the distribution of a work package.

The cost histogram in Primavera Project Planner looks just like the resource histogram—except that the vertical axis is scaled to costs. In addition to the cost histogram, this product also provides a cumulative cost curve. (See Figure A7.18.) There is no on-line display of total project costs anywhere in the system!

Primavera Project Planner processes cost data according to a set of global cost rules that may be used as is or modified at the project level. These rules are called AutoCost rules and will be covered later. The AutoCost rules control the data during the management of the project. There may be up to six billing rates per resource. *Fixed* costs are entered just like any other resource. This system uses the current unit prices to calculate the *budgeted* cost, *actual* costs to date; and *cost to completion* (from the current data date to the project end).

In Primavera Project Planner, *quantity* refers to resources; *cost* refers to financial data; and *estimates* refers to both units (quantity) and costs. The *budgeted cost* is equal to the *original* or *latest revised* budget for a particular resource and/or cost account. The *budgeted quantity* is equal to the total resource units required by an activity—that is, the units per day times

Figure A7.18

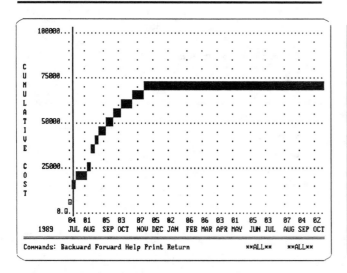

```
 100000...|
         .|   .  .  .  .  .  .  .  .  .  .  .  .  .  .  .
C        .|   .  .  .  .  .  .  .  .  .  .  .  .  .  .  .
U  75000...|
M        .|   .  .  .  .  .  .  .  .  .  .  .  .  .  .  .
U        .|   .  .  .  .  .  .  .  .  .  .  .  .  .  .  .
L        .|   .  .  .  .  .  .  .  .  .  .  .  .  .  .  .
A        .|   .  .  .  .  .  .  .  .  .  .  .  .  .  .  .
T  50000...|
I        .|   .  .  .  .  .  .  .  .  .  .  .  .  .  .  .
V        .|   .  .  .  .  .  .  .  .  .  .  .  .  .  .  .
E        .|   .  .  .  .  .  .  .  .  .  .  .  .  .  .  .
C  25000...|
O        .|   .  .  .  .  .  .  .  .  .  .  .  .  .  .  .
S        .|   .  .  .  .  .  .  .  .  .  .  .  .  .  .  .
T        .|
     0.0  .|
          |  04 01 05 03  07 05 02  06 06 03  01 05 03  07 04 02
     1989    JUL AUG SEP OCT NOV DEC JAN FEB MAR APR MAY JUN JUL AUG SEP OCT

Commands: Backward Forward Help Print Return        **ALL**   **ALL**
```

Figure A7.20

```
                          ACTIVITY DATA                           CH9G
Activity ID:      14      Calendar ID: 1 (Unit=Day)        TF:  55
     Title:                                                PCT:   0
ES: 13JUL88  EF: 18JUL88  Orig. duration:   4      Actual Start:

LS: 29SEP88  LF: 04OCT88  Rem.  duration:   4      Actual Finish:

Activity Codes:

FINANCIAL SUMMARY:       Resource  1        Resource  2        Resource  3
                         ~~~~~~~~~~~~       ~~~~~~~~~~~~       ~~~~~~~~~~~~
Resource                 WORKER
Cost Acct/type
Budgeted cost               320.00              0.00               0.00
Actual cost this period       0.00              0.00               0.00
Actual cost to date           0.00              0.00               0.00
Percent expended                 0                 0                  0
Percent complete
Earned value                  0.00              0.00               0.00
Cost to complete            320.00              0.00               0.00
Cost at completion          320.00              0.00               0.00
Variance                      0.00              0.00               0.00

Commands:Add Delete Edit Help More Next Return autoSort Transfer View Window
Windows :Act.codes Budget Constraints Dates Financial Log Pred Resources Succ
```

the remaining duration. The system estimates costs based on resource price per unit (as defined in the resource dictionary) and quantities (as defined in the resource pool). They are kept in synchronization with the displays in the Budget window and the Financial window. (See Figures A7.19 and A7.20.)

Primavera Project Planner will export project data in LOTUS 1-2-3 format for Releases 1A and 2.

Figure A7.19

```
                          ACTIVITY DATA                           CH9G
Activity ID:      14      Calendar ID: 1 (Unit=Day)        TF:  55
     Title:                                                PCT:   0
ES: 13JUL88  EF: 18JUL88  Orig. duration:   4      Actual Start:

LS: 29SEP88  LF: 04OCT88  Rem.  duration:   4      Actual Finish:

Activity Codes:

BUDGET SUMMARY:                                    | Total of all  1 Resources
Resource    1  WORKER      Units       Cost        |    Units        Cost
Cost Acct                ----------  ----------    | ----------  ----------
Units per time              8.00                   |
Resource Lag / Duration  0                         |
Percent Complete / Expended              0         |       0          0
Budget Amount               32      320.00         |      32       320.00
Scheduled Budget  (BCWS)    16      160.00         |      16       160.00
Earned Value      (BCWP)     0        0.00         |       0         0.00
Actual to Date    (ACWP)     0        0.00         |       0         0.00
Estimate to Complete        32      320.00         |      32       320.00
Estimate at Completion      32      320.00         |      32       320.00
Variance                     0        0.00         |       0         0.00

Commands:Add Delete Edit Help More Next Return autoSort Transfer View Window
Windows :Act.codes Budget Constraints Dates Financial Log Pred Resources Succ
```

APPENDIX 7.9 COMPRESSING TIME

Appendix 7.9.1 Time-Constrained Plans and Project Management Software (10.9)

In Primavera Project Planner resource-constrained projects, the values for normal and maximum should be the same. In time-constrained plans, users may keep raising the value for the maximum until the desired date is reached. Smoothing should also be set to *Yes*. (Figure A7.15) Reports may be produced that are sorted on total float and free float.

APPENDIX 7.10 ASSIGNING THE WORK

Appendix 7.10.1 The Assignment Report (11.1)

Primavera Project Planner comes with an easy-to-use custom report writer. Although the system also comes with a set of default reports, many of them are set up to be used with the tutorial project data and may not be applied to live project data. These default reports, on the other hand, are very helpful as guidelines for developing the customized reports.

Customized reports are created in the reports specification subsystem, which is accessed by pressing "Specification....9" from the Project Data Menu screen. Using the corresponding windows, each report needs

Figure A7.21

```
                    SCHEDULE REPORT                    CH9G

Ref.No.: SR-01   Title: CLASSIC SCHEDULE REPORT - SORTED BY ES,

SELECTION CRITERIA:  Four successive levels of screening are available.

Level 1: Meet (All/Any)      selection criteria listed below:

                 SPC      CC       LOW           HIGH

       Select if        is
       Select if        is
       Select if        is
       Select if        is
       Select if        is
       Select if        is
       Select if        is
Schedule Parameter Codes: ACT PNO SNO ES EF LS LF AS AF TF PCT OD RD RES FFL CAL
                          ED LD AD CON V1E V1L V2E V2L
                          RESP AREA MILE

      Criteria Codes (CC): EQ NE GT LT WR NR

Commands: Add Del Edit Help Level More Next Return Save Transfer Window eXecute
Windows : Content Format List Order Selection Target
```

Figure A7.22

```
                    SCHEDULE REPORT                    CH9G

Ref.No.: SR-01   Title: CLASSIC SCHEDULE REPORT - SORTED BY ES,

ORDER(SORT) ACTIVITY DATA for presentation using schedule parameter codes:

   Sort by:  1.  ES        2.  TF       3.          4.

             5.            6.           7.          8.

             9.           10.          11.         12.

            13.           14.          15.         16.

            17.           18.          19.         20.

Schedule Parameter Codes: ACT PNO SNO ES LS EF LF AS AF TF PCT OD RD DES FFL CAL
                          MIL V1E V1L V2E V2L
                          RESP AREA MILE

Commands: Add Del Edit Help Level More Next Return Save Transfer Window eXecute
Windows : Content Format List Order Selection Target
```

Figure A7.23

```
                                              CH9G
          Types of Reports

   Schedule (tabular) reports.......1

   Barchart schedule...............2

   Network logic diagram...........3

   Resource reports................4

   Cost reports....................5

   Export data files...............6

   Import data files...............7

   Resource loading reports........8

          Help.............................H
          Return to Project Data Menu........R

   Press selection
```

to be set up so that it selects *all* records that meet the criteria "RES EQ *resource name as it appears in the Resource Dictionary screen*" (See Figure A7.21.) and is ordered on "ES" (early start). (See Figure A7.22.)

An assignment report may be created by selecting "Schedule (Tabular) Reports....1" from the Types of Reports Menu screen. (See Figure A7.23.) The process is completed by then selecting "Window; Content; ACL", where ACL is the activity detail line containing the activity identifier, the activity description, the original duration, the remaining duration, the calendar id,

the scheduled early start date, the scheduled early finish date, and the percent complete. (See Figure A7.24.) The "Resource Loading" report pictured in Figure A7.26 below may also be included in the assignment package.

While the users cannot choose the *placement* of the fields in the detail lines of the reports, they can *prevent* various selected fields from being printed on certain reports. In the report format window, placing an "M" (for mask) next to the candidate field will prevent its display. If the user masks float and the late dates in the "Tabular Schedule" report described above, the system will automatically print the early dates under a heading relabeled as scheduled dates.

Appendix 7.10.2 The Ad Hoc Information (11.2)

The ad hoc information in Primavera Project Planner may be reproduced on hard copy following almost the same directions as for the assignment report. The only difference is that, in addition to the ACL detail line in "Window; Content" a second line called LCL is also selected. (See Figure A7.25.) It is likely that these reports will need to be supplemented by output from a word processor.

Figure A7.24

PRIMAVERA PROJECT PLANNER

REPORT DATE 28APR89 RUN NO. 6
7:14
TURNAROUND DOCUMENT FOR SCHEDULE BY FIRS

START DATE 1JUL88 FIN DATE 1DEC88
DATA DATE 1JUL88 PAGE NO. 1

ACTIVITY ID	ORIG DUR	REM DUR	CAL	%	CODE	ACTIVITY DESCRIPTION	SCHEDULED START	FINISH
6	4	4	1	0		THIS IS THE DESCRIPTION FOR JOB 6	1JUL88	7JUL88
12	11	11	1	0		THIS IS THE DESCRIPTION FOR JOB 12	8JUL88	22JUL88
13	4	4	1	0		THIS IS THE DESCRIPTION FOR JOB 13	8JUL88	13JUL88
21	6	6	1	0		THIS IS THE DESCRIPTION FOR JOB 21	3AUG88	10AUG88
22	16	16	1	0			3AUG88	24AUG88
26	7	7	1	0			11AUG88	19AUG88
32	10	10	1	0			22AUG88	2SEP88
39	13	13	1	0			7SEP88	23SEP88
43	5	5	1	0			26SEP88	30SEP88
45	4	4	1	0			5OCT88	11OCT88
48	6	6	1	0			18OCT88	25OCT88
51	7	7	1	0			26OCT88	3NOV88
52	4	4	1	0			4NOV88	9NOV88

Figure A7.25

PRIMAVERA PROJECT PLANNER

REPORT DATE 28APR89 RUN NO. 5 START DATE 1JUL88 FIN DATE 1DEC88
7:11
TURNAROUND DOCUMENT FOR SCHEDULE BY FIRS DATA DATE 1JUL88 PAGE NO. 1

ACTIVITY ID	ORIG DUR	REM DUR	CAL	%	CODE	ACTIVITY DESCRIPTION	SCHEDULED START	SCHEDULED FINISH
6	4	4	1	0		THIS IS THE DESCRIPTION FOR JOB 6 THIS IS THE LOG INFORMATION FOR JOB 6. THE RESOURCE IS CALLED BOSS.	1JUL88	7JUL88
12	11	11	1	0		THIS IS THE DESCRIPTION FOR JOB 12 THIS IS THE LOG INFORMATION FOR JOB 12. IN THIS CASE, THE RESOURCE IS ALSO THE BOSS.	8JUL88	22JUL88
13	4	4	1	0		THIS IS THE DESCRIPTION FOR JOB 13	8JUL88	13JUL88
21	6	6	1	0		THIS IS THE DESCRIPTION FOR JOB 21	3AUG88	10AUG88
22	16	16	1	0			3AUG88	24AUG88
26	7	7	1	0			11AUG88	19AUG88
32	10	10	1	0			22AUG88	2SEP88
39	13	13	1	0			7SEP88	23SEP88
43	5	5	1	0			26SEP88	30SEP88
45	4	4	1	0			5OCT88	11OCT88

Figure A7.26

```
                          PRIMAVERA PROJECT PLANNER

REPORT DATE 20JAN89  RUN NO.  14     RESOURCE LOADING REPORT        START DATE  1JUL88   FIN DATE 1FEB89

resource loading for boss                                          DATA DATE   1JUL88   PAGE NO.   1

                          TOTAL USAGE FOR  DAY
```

ACTIVITY ID	ACTIVITY DESCRIPTION	1 JUL	4 JUL	5 JUL	6 JUL	7 JUL	8 JUL	11 JUL	12 JUL	13 JUL	14 JUL	15 JUL
	1988											
							UNITS = hour					
	BOSS -											
6		8		8	8	8						
12							8	8	8	8	8	8
13							8	8	8	8		
21												
22												
TOTAL BOSS		8	0	8	8	8	16	16	16	16	8	8
REPORT TOTAL		8	0	8	8	8	16	16	16	16	8	8

Appendix 7.10.3 The Work Package Cover Sheet *(11.5)*

In Primavera Project Planner, a word processor may be used to create the forms that meet this requirement.

Appendix 7.10.4 The Responsibility Grid *(11.6)*

In Primavera Project Planner, a word processor may be used to create the forms that meet this requirement.

Appendix 7.10.5 The Supporting Documentation *(11.8)*

The Primavera Project Planner Resource Histogram screen (Figure A7.16) may be printed by customizing the "Resource Profile" report under "Resource Reports....4" in the Types of Reports Menu screen. A weekly resource Gantt may be printed by customizing the "Weekly Barchart" report under "Barchart Schedule....2" in the Types of Reports Menu screen. A periodic tabular report may be printed by customizing the "Resource Loading" report under "Resource Loading Reports....8" in the Types of Reports menu. (See Figure A7.26.)

Appendix 7.10.6 The Problem Log *(11.10)*

In Primavera Project Planner, a word processor may be used to create the forms that meet this requirement.

Appendix 7.10.7 The Work Notes Form *(11.11)*

In Primavera Project Planner, a word processor may be used to create the forms that meet this requirement.

Appendix 7.10.8 Viewing the Data on the Screen *(11.12)*

The reports in Primavera Project Planner may only be displayed in hard copy.

APPENDIX 7.11 REPORTING STATUS

Appendix 7.11.1 Baselines *(12.2)*

In Primavera Project Planner, the baseline fields are called target.

Appendix 7.11.2 Extracting the Jobs for the Turn-Around Document—on a Range of Dates *(12.5)*

From each respective report in the Primavera Project Planner report module pressing "Window; Select; Select all if ef wr low high" will designate the date ranges. (Figure A7.21)

Appendix 7.11.3 Setting Up an *As-Of* Date *(12.6)*

From the Primavera Project Planner Activity window, pressing F9 will invoke the scheduling process. The system asks for a current project data date. The *As-of* date is entered into this field. Alternatively, selecting "Schedule....6" from the Project Data Menu screen will invoke a Scheduling Parameters screen. (See Figure A7.27.) One of the entries is the "current project data date". The *As-of* date is entered into this field. Users who wish to include and reflect status data for the day on which the data is being entered will need to set the new value to one day later.

Appendix 7.11.4 Entering Percent Complete *(12.7)*

There are three percentage values in Primavera Project Planner: the percentage for the *elapsed time* of the

Figure A7.27

```
               SCHEDULING COMPUTATION                        CH9G


    Upon completion of the scheduling computations will you want to produce:
             One of the Series of Reports (enter Series name)
         or No Reports (leave blank)?

    Would you like your output to be:
                 Printed immediately (P)
                 Saved to a file     (S)
             or Background Printed   (B)?  P

    Current project Data Date is 1ZJUL88

    Schedule Calculation Logic - Retained or Progress override (R/P): R

    List constraints (Y/N)? Y                    List open ends (Y/N)? Y

    List activities with out of sequence progress (Y/N)? Y



  Commands: Edit Help List Return eXecute
```

Figure A7.28

```
               AUTOMATIC COST/RESOURCE CALCULATION RULES          CH9G

SET: CH9G        DATE:  1JUL88

During update, the following rules will apply to on-screen calculations:

  1 Link remaining duration and schedule percent complete (Y/N)...........Y
  2 Freeze resource units per day (Y/N)....................................Y
  3 Add actual to estimate to complete or
    Subtract actual from estimate at completion (A/S)....................A
    Allow "negative estimate to complete" (Y/N)..........................N

  4 When quantities change, use the current unit prices to recompute costs
    Budget (Y/N)..Y    Actual (Y/N)..Y   Estimate to Complete (Y/N)..Y

  5 Use the update percent complete against budget to estimate actual
    Quantity (Y/N).....Y              Cost (Y/N).....Y

  6 Calculate variance as Budget-EAC or EAC-Budget (B/E)...................B

During every schedule computation, recalculate and store cost (Y/N)..........N
Master project rules are: Y N SN YYY YY B N

Commands: Default Edit Help Return Transfer
```

activity,[9] the percentage of the *original budget* that has been spent,[10] and the percentage for the amount of resource effort that has been expended.[11] All three of these fields may assume different values. The first two percentage values are calculated by the system. The third defaults to blank; however, it may optionally be entered by the user. When the third *has* been entered, and it conflicts with the first, the third takes precedence.

Primavera Project Planner controls the effects of progress reporting through the use of rules called AutoCost rules. These rules may be set at a global level or at a project level. (See Figure A7.28.) At the project level, they are set in a screen that is invoked by pressing "Control-R" from any of the project detail screens—for example, the Activity screen. One of the AutoCost rules, Rule 1, tells the system how to deal with the relationship between the activity percent complete and the remaining duration. Users may link these two fields or keep them isolated from each other. If they are linked:

---

[9]In this text, called *activity percentage* and seen on the upper right corner of the Activity screen.

[10]In this text, called *budget percentage* and seen in the Financial and Budget windows.

[11]In this text, called *resource percentage* and seen in the Resource and Budget windows.

- An entry into one will correspondingly effect the other
- The activity percentage complete reflects the percentage of elapsed time that has passed and not the percentage of *true work effort* that has been earned. That is because the formula for percentage complete is :

$$\frac{\text{Original Duration} - \text{Remaining Duration}}{\text{Original Duration}} \times 100$$

(Since it is one of the fields used for scheduling, original duration represents the elapsed time not *true work effort*.)

The activity percentage field has no relationship whatsoever to the budget percentage expended![12] The budget percentage percentage represents the amount of *original costs* that have been spent to date. It is computed as:

$$\frac{\text{Actual Dollars}}{\text{Original Budgeted Dollars}} \times 100$$

Appendix 7.11.5 Hard Copy Turn-Around Documents (12.8)

In Primavera Project Planner, a standard schedule report that also displays the update line may be used for a turn-around document. This update line may be customized with a standard Line Editor. (See Figure A7.29.) The report may be limited to a selected resource and to the activities within a range of dates. There is an optional percentage field. Finally, the update line can be customized so that there is a place to enter the actual start date and the actual finish date. The report is set up so that the resource may also enter the remaining duration. Although it is not shown, the update line may also be customized to allow the resource to change the original duration.

---

[12]Seen, for example, in the Budget window.

Appendix 7.11.6 Entering the Status Collection Data *(12.9)*

For general processing in Primavera Project Planner, the AutoCost Rule 2, "Freeze resource units per day", should be set to "Y". This prevents the system from forcing unwanted overtime.

Progress data may be entered in the Budget window, which is invoked from the Activity Data screen by pressing "Window; Budget". This window contains most of the fields that are necessary for data entry: the actual start date, the actual finish date, the remaining duration, the activity percentage, the resource percentage, the actual resource time to date and the estimated resource time to completion. The actual resource time this period may be entered using the products import or batch function; otherwise, this field is a display-only field.

Entering a value for remaining duration causes corresponding values to be entered into the actual resource time to date and the estimated resource time *to* completion. If these are unsatisfactory, they may be modified by the user. The system also automatically updates the estimate *at* completion and the variance. The variance is a display-only field.

The value for the estimated resource time *to* completion is determined by multiplying the remaining duration by the resource units per day.

The variables in this formula are interchangeable. For example, if the user enters the remaining duration and the estimated time *to* completion, the system may adjust the resource time per day. If the AutoCost Rule 3, "Add actuals to estimate to complete", is set to "A" (Figure A7.28), the value for the estimate *at* completion is determined by adding together the estimated resource time *to* completion and the actual resource time to date.[13] Otherwise, the value for the estimate *at* completion is fixed to the original duration and the estimate *to* completion is determined by subtracting the actual resource time to date from the value for the estimate *at* completion.

Entering an actual finish date causes the remaining duration to change to zero and the activity percentage to change to 100 percent. Conversely, entering

zero for the remaining duration does *not* cause the actual start and finish dates to be filled in.

If the activity percentage is linked to the remaining duration, (See the earlier discussion.), an entry into one will update the other. Entering 100 percent complete does *not* cause the actual start and finish dates to be filled in.

If users wish to apply the resource percentage, they will have to enter the value manually. (See the following discussion.)

The impacts of the progress modifications are not fully rippled through the plan until the new schedule is computed. After the scheduling operations, all dates in the sample exercise illustrated in Figure 12.1 were correctly computed. Both sets of the early and late dates are blanked out on the jobs that are 100 percent completed and the start dates are blanked out on those jobs with actual start dates. Users may later find these dates displayed in the Dates Window.

Special processing. Since the activity percentage is linked to the original duration, these percentages reflect the amount of elapsed time that has been expended. Sometimes this is acceptable; sometimes it is misleading. As an illustration:

- In Example H of Figure 12.1, the activity percentage was reported at 75 percent.[14] The budget costs must be 50 percent, and the resource percent must be 67 percent.
- Because of the activity percentage formula, its value in Example M was reported as *0 percent* instead of 50 percent. The budget and resource percents must be 50 percent.
- Because of the activity percentage formula, its value in Example C was reported as 10 percent instead of 20 percent. The budget percent and the resource percent are 20 and 18 percent, respectively.
- Because of the activity percentage formula, its value in Example S was reported as 80 percent instead of 75 percent. The budget percent and the resource percent are 60 and 75 percent, respectively.

The system automatically computes the correct budget percent.[15] The value for the actual dollars in

---

[13]This rule particularly affects the costing. (See the discussion later in this appendix.)

[14]See the formula in the earlier percentage discussion.
[15]See the earlier percentage discussion and definitions.

Figure A7.29

PRIMAVERA PROJECT PLANNER

REPORT DATE 28APR89 RUN NO. 8   START DATE 1JUL88 FIN DATE 1DEC88
            7:29
TURNAROUND DOCUMENT FOR THE BOSS   DATA DATE 1JUL88 PAGE NO.   1

ACTIVITY ID	ORIG DUR	REM DUR	CAL	%	CODE	ACTIVITY DESCRIPTION	SCHEDULED START	FINISH
6	4	4	1	0		THIS IS THE DESCRIPTION FOR JOB 6	1JUL88	7JUL88

TP_____ RD_____ %_____ ACTUAL START_____ ACTUAL FINISH_____
WORK COMPLETED_____
WORK TO DO_____
COMMENTS OR PROBLEMS_____

| 12 | 11 | 11 | 1 | 0 | | THIS IS THE DESCRIPTION FOR JOB 12 | 8JUL88 | 22JUL88 |

TP_____ RD_____ %_____ ACTUAL START_____ ACTUAL FINISH_____
WORK COMPLETED_____
WORK TO DO_____
COMMENTS OR PROBLEMS_____

the budget percent formula is driven by the costs that correspond to the entry in the resource column for actuals to date. (Figure A7.19)

On the other hand, to retain consistency, the correct resource percentage value must be computed manually by the user and entered into the corresponding percentage field.[16]

Sometimes, entering several variables at the same time causes contradictions in the potential results. For the times when this occurs, the system has been set up with a group of default field priorities:

- 1 = Remaining duration;
- 2 = Resource units per day;
- 3 = Actual resource time to date; and
- 4 = Estimate *to* completion and Estimate *at* completion.

Appendix 7.11.7 Performance Status Reporting (12.10)

There are several preformatted reports in Primavera Project Planner that may be used for status reporting. One report includes all of the data associated with a given resource. (See Figure A7.30.) There is another report that includes all of the successors for a given activity. A Gantt report compares actuals to baselines. There are other Gantts that compare early dates to late dates.

Primavera Project Planner features sorting and selecting on many fields. (Figures A7.21. and A7.22) The sort may be in ascending or descending order. There are seven selection fields and 16 levels of the sort. Users may select and sort by: actual, early, and

late start dates; actual, early, and late finish dates; percent complete; total float and free float; remaining duration (1 to 999); and the variance from the target baseline start or finish. This last parameter acts as a flag for late activities.

For resource reporting, there is a variance field that represents the variance (in time units) between the baseline resource effort and the projected resource effort. This data is helpful when the resource effort is the same as the calendar effort. However, if the resource effort is less than the calendar effort, schedule slippages may not be readily apparent. The system *does* support selection on four different time variances: the variance between the projected and the target 1 early date, the variance between the projected and the target 1 late date, the variance between the projected and the target 2 early date, and the variance between the projected and the target 2 late date. The system also supports earned value variances. (See the discussion later in this appendix.)

Appendix 7.11.8 Highlighting Progress (12.11)

There are no special markings that show progress on the Primavera Project Planner network. The Primavision network shows activities that are in progress with a diagonal slash across the node. Completed activities have two diagonal slashes, which form an "X" in the node. The Primavision time scaled diagrams show a solid line for the *As-of* date. The Primavera Project Planner Gantt chart may be configured by the user to show the *As-of* data date, the early dates, the late dates, and the actual dates. The markings are chosen by entering the ASCII values for the printer symbols. If they want to use special symbols (other than alphanumerics), users may press the F1 key to get a listing of the correct symbols.

Appendix 7.11.9 Costs and Project Management Software (12.13)

In Primavera Project Planner, the costs of the activities and of the project will be recomputed when time is reported to the activity.

When a new unit rate is assigned to a resource, the system gives the user the option to recalculate the costs of all the activities to which the resource is assigned. A message is displayed asking if the system

[16]When the correct resource percentage is entered, it may cause the values in the other fields to be incorrectly altered. Therefore, it will also be necessary to check and, perhaps, correct the other fields in the window as well. This product also allows the user to press "Control-X" from an Activity screen to cause the system to automatically recompute the costs for that activity. "Control-X" invokes AutoCost for that activity alone. If the resource percentage and the budget percentage are not equal, users MUST NOT INVOKE THIS FUNCTION in this application! If they do, the system will replace the budget percent with the resource percent, and the costs values will then be incorrect!

Figure A7.30

PRIMAVERA PROJECT PLANNER

REPORT DATE 31JAN89 RUN NO. 24   RESOURCE CONTROL ACTIVITY REPORT   START DATE 1JUL88 FIN DATE 1FEB89*

RESOURCE CONTROL REPORT ORGANIZED BY ACTIVITY   DATA DATE 12JUL88   PAGE NO. 2

ACTIVITY ID RESOURCE	COST ACCOUNT	ACCOUNT CATEGORY	UNIT MEAS	BUDGET	PCT CMP	ACTUAL TO DATE	ACTUAL THIS PERIOD	ESTIMATE TO COMPLETE	FORECAST	VARIANCE
10										
RD 0 AS 1JUL88 AF 7JUL88										
WORKER			hour	32	100	32	0	0	32	0
TOTAL :				32	100	32	0	0	32	0
11										
RD 0 AS 1JUL88 AF 6JUL88										
TOTAL :				0	0	0	0	0	0	0
12 this is the description for job 12										
RD 7 AS 8JUL88 EF 20JUL88 LF 4OCT88 TF 53										
TOTAL :				0	0	0	0	0	0	0

should "Compute costs now based on displayed prices for this resource: Y or N". The results of the *Yes* response are obvious. On the other hand, if the user selects *No*, the costs may be selectively recomputed, on an individual activity basis, from the corresponding Activity screen, by pressing "Control-X". *Caution* should be exercised using this function, however. (See the earlier discussion on special processing.)

Costs are seen in the Budget window and the Financial window.

The *budgeted cost* is the baseline cost. It is equal to the original or latest revised budget for a particular resource and/or cost account. Once the budget has been stored, it is not recalculated.

The field for *actual costs this period* is used to display the project expenditures for a particular resource and cost account for the current period. Users may enter data into this field; however, the entry operation may only be completed through the product's import or batch functions. It cannot be entered in online mode.

The *actual cost to date* reflects the accumulated activity and project expenditures for the particular resource and cost account to date. The system computes this field, or it may be entered by users in the Financial or Budget window. Alternatively, the user can designate that it be computed according to the AutoCost Rules 4 and 5.[17] This field may also be used during earned value analysis to measure cost performance.

The *costs to completion* are seen in the Budget window and the Financial window. The *cost to complete* is an estimate of the cost remaining to complete a particular activity. It is the difference between the *cost at completion* and the *actual cost to date*. The use of this field is affected by AutoCost Rule 3.[18] If the AutoCost Rule 3 for "Add actuals to estimate to complete" is set to "A", the costs will totally reflect

the current forecasts on what it will take to finish the project. Otherwise, the value for the number of days *at* completion will be fixed to the *original* duration and the days *to* completion will be determined by subtracting the actual resource hours to date from the original value for the days *at* completion.

The *cost at completion* is the accumulated cost of the resource or cost account at the completion of the associated activity. It is equal to the *actual costs to date* plus the *cost to complete*. The *costs at completion* are seen in the Budget window and the Financial window.

The *variance* is the difference between the *cost at completion* and the *original budgeted* amount. The *variance* is seen on the Budget, Financial, and Resource windows.

Appendix 7.11.10 Cost Status Reporting (12.15)

Primavera Project Planner is the only product that displays actual costs this period[19] and shows the early date costs, the late date costs, and the target costs on the Cumulative Cost Curve.

The "Cost Control Activity" report will display the target budget, the percent complete, the actual costs to date, the actual costs this period,[20] the estimated costs to completion, the forecasted total costs, and the variance in dollars. (See Figure A7.31.) Although this system allows users to select activities for reporting based on time variances, it does not support selection on dollar variances. There is a tabular "Cash Flow" report (See Figure A7.32.) and a "Cumulative Cost Curve" report similar to the screen pictured in Figure A7.18. To print the cost profile histogram for the whole project, users must select the data on "Cost Account = ????????????". The Cost Profile graph shows the current total forecasted costs but it does not show the target costs.

Appendix 7.11.11 Earned Values and Project Management Software (12.17)

Primavera Project Planner supports earned values for costs and times. The two earned value analysis fields

---

[17](Figure A7.28) Rule 4 says that this value is computed using the *actual time* worked times the unit price of the resource. On the other hand, Rule 5 says use the percentage times the *budget* cost. If both rules are invoked, Rule 4 governs.

[18]Part of this rule allows this value to also be computed so that negative costs to completion will be valid, a scenario commonly required in fixed-price construction projects, but not often found in systems projects.

---

[19]If it has been entered through Batch or Import mode.

[20]If it has been entered through Batch or Import mode.

Figure A7.31

```
                                    PRIMAVERA PROJECT PLANNER

REPORT DATE 11JUL88 RUN NO.  28    COST CONTROL ACTIVITY REPORT        START DATE 1JUL88  FIN DATE 1FEB89*

SUMMARY COST CONTROL ACTIVITY REPORT                                   DATA DATE 12JUL88  PAGE NO.   1
```

ACTIVITY ID RESOURCE	COST ACCOUNT	ACCOUNT CATEGORY	UNIT MEAS	BUDGET	PCT CMP	ACTUAL TO DATE	ACTUAL THIS PERIOD	ESTIMATE TO COMPLETE	FORECAST	VARIANCE
1										
RD 0 AS 1JUL88 AF 7JUL88										
TOTAL :				800.00	100	800.00	.00	.00	800.00	.00
2										
RD 8 AS 8JUL88 EF 21JUL88				LF 19DEC88 TF 102						
TOTAL :				2000.00	20	400.00	.00	1600.00	2000.00	.00
3										
RD 9 AS 8JUL88 EF 22JUL88				LF 19DEC88 TF 101						
TOTAL :				2000.00	20	400.00	.00	1800.00	2200.00	-200.00
REPORT TOTALS				71120.00	13	8920.00	.00	62200.00	71120.00	.00

Figure A7.32

```
                                    PRIMAVERA PROJECT PLANNER

REPORT DATE 28APR89  RUN NO.  6              TABULAR COST REPORT - MONTHLY         START DATE 1JUL88  FIN DATE 1FEB89*
            8:22
MONTHLY CASH FLOW FOR PROJECT                                                      DATA DATE 12JUL88  PAGE NO.   1

  PERIOD      ---AVAILABLE---      --EARLY SCHEDULE---      ---LATE SCHEDULE----      --TARGET 1 SCHEDULE--
 BEGINNING   NORMAL   MAXIMUM      USAGE    CUMULATIVE      USAGE    CUMULATIVE       USAGE    CUMULATIVE

  COST ACCOUNT = ??????????? -                                                             TARGET = EARLY

 1JUL88         0        0      21600.00    21600.00      8920.00     8920.00      22400.00     22400.00
***DATA DATE***
 1AUG88         0        0      23800.00    45400.00          .00     8920.00      26400.00     48800.00
 1SEP88         0        0      10040.00    55440.00      4773.33    13693.33       9640.00     58440.00
 1OCT88         0        0       9080.00    64520.00     14386.67    28080.00       8080.00     66520.00
 1NOV88         0        0       5880.00    70400.00     11680.00    39760.00       4480.00     71000.00
 1DEC88         0        0        720.00    71120.00     14880.00    54640.00        120.00     71120.00
```

475

are the scheduled budget field (BCWS) and the earned value field itself (BCWP). The BCWS is calculated strictly on the basis of the target budget for the activity. If there is no target, this entry will be zero. If there is a target, the BCWS is equal to

$$\frac{\text{the data date} - \text{target start}}{\text{target finish} - \text{target start}} \times \text{the total target costs.}$$

The BCWP is calculated on the activity's target budget or, if there is no target, the activity's current forecasted budget—based on the system configuration directions.[21] The designated budget value is multiplied by the resource percent,[22] if present; otherwise, it is multiplied by the activity percent. The actual quantity to date is called ACWP.

There are two variances that are displayed on the system's standard "Earned Value" report: the schedule variance and the cost variance. The value for the schedule variance is derived as the difference between the BCWS and the BCWP. The value for the cost variance is derived as the difference between the ACWP and the BCWP.

There is also another field called *variance* that is displayed on the screens and on several reports. The value for this "variance" is determined by the response to AutoCost Rule 6, "Calculate variance." In one case, the response makes overruns show as a negative value; and, in the alternate case, the response makes overruns show as a positive value. In either case, the answer is the difference between the activity budget and the estimate at completion.

In scenarios where the remaining elapsed time in the activity is greater than the remaining *true work effort* (for example, in H and M of Figure 12.1), in spite of the fact that the budget percent has been calculated by the system, users must also be sure to enter the resource percent complete[23] or the BCWP will be

---

[21]From the Primavera Utilities screen, pressing "Configure; Window; Summary" and entering "C" for current or "T" for target in the question for "Use current or target in earned value" will drive the results in the BCWP.

[22]Using the percentage definitions introduced earlier.

[23]And check the other fields in the window, too.

incorrect. Earned values may be reported on costs or on times. (See Figure A7.33.)

Appendix 7.11.12 Reporting on Resource Availability (12.20)

The Primavera Project Planner resource histogram that is pictured in Figure A7.16 may be printed. This is also true for the weekly resource Gantt chart pictured in Figure A7.11. Gantts may also show target values.

The "Resource Loading" report shows resource allocations by periods. (Figure A7.26) It does not show the available number of resources. Users will need to work with a copy of the resource dictionary in order to know the available number. Similarly, they will need to mentally calculate overscheduling and underscheduling.

Appendix 7.11.13 Reporting on Resource Utilization (12.21)

Although Primavera Project Planner does feature a "Tabular Resource Loading" report (Figure A7.26), it cannot display data for actuals. Primavera Project Planner also features periodic reporting on time and dollars. (See Figure A7.34.) All of the information above the *data date* line represents actuals; data below the line represents futures.

APPENDIX 7.12   MANAGING THE PROJECT

Appendix 7.12.1   Who Produces Perts and Gantts that May Be Restricted to Critical Path Jobs? (13.7)

The Primavera Project Planner "Network Logic Diagram" report will display a network that is limited to just those activities on the critical path. The Bar Charts can also be limited to just those activities selected where total float is less than the established lowest value.

Appendix 7.12.2 Who Produces Reports that May Be Restricted to Fixed-Date Jobs? (13.8)

Primavera Project Planner reports may be selected based on the values in the Constraints window.

Figure A7.33

PRIMAVERA PROJECT PLANNER

EARNED VALUE REPORT - COST

START DATE 1JUL88   FIN DATE 1FEB89*

DATA DATE 12JUL88   PAGE NO. 1

EARNED VALUE REPORT

COST ACCOUNT	RESOURCE	ACTIVITY ID	PCT CMP	CUMULATIVE TO DATE ACWP	BCWP	BCWS	VARIANCE COST	SCHEDULE	AT COMPLETION BUDGET	ESTIMATE
	BOSS -									
	BOSS	6	100	1600.00	1600.00	1600.00	.00	.00	1600.00	1600.00
	BOSS	12	36	1600.00	1584.00	800.00	-16.00	784.00	4400.00	4400.00
	BOSS	13	50	800.00	800.00	800.00	.00	.00	1600.00	1600.00
	BOSS	21	0	.00	.00	.00	.00	.00	2400.00	2400.00
	BOSS	22	0	.00	.00	.00	.00	.00	6400.00	6400.00
	BOSS	26	0	.00	.00	.00	.00	.00	2800.00	2800.00
	BOSS	32	0	.00	.00	.00	.00	.00	4000.00	4000.00
	BOSS	39	0	.00	.00	.00	.00	.00	5200.00	5200.00
	BOSS	43	0	.00	.00	.00	.00	.00	2000.00	2000.00
	BOSS	45	0	.00	.00	.00	.00	.00	1600.00	1600.00
	BOSS	48	0	.00	.00	.00	.00	.00	2400.00	2400.00
	BOSS	51	0	.00	.00	.00	.00	.00	2800.00	2800.00
	BOSS	52	0	.00	.00	.00	.00	.00	1600.00	1600.00
	BOSS TOTAL		10	4000.00	3984.00	3200.00	-16.00	784.00	38800.00	38800.00
	LEADER -									
	LEADER	1	100	800.00	800.00	800.00	.00	.00	800.00	800.00
	LEADER	2	20	400.00	400.00	400.00	.00	.00	2000.00	2000.00
	LEADER	3	18	400.00	360.00	400.00	-40.00	-40.00	2000.00	2200.00
	LEADER	4	0	.00	.00	.00	.00	.00	2000.00	2000.00
	LEADER	5	0	.00	.00	.00	.00	.00	2400.00	2400.00
	LEADER	23	0	.00	.00	.00	.00	.00	2200.00	2200.00
	LEADER	24	60	600.00	600.00	400.00	.00	200.00	1000.00	1000.00
	LEADER	36	0	.00	.00	.00	.00	.00	800.00	800.00
	LEADER	44	0	.00	.00	.00	.00	.00	1400.00	1400.00
	LEADER	46	0	.00	.00	.00	.00	.00	1600.00	1600.00
	LEADER	53	0	.00	.00	.00	.00	.00	600.00	600.00
	LEADER TOTAL		13	2200.00	2160.00	2000.00	-40.00	160.00	16800.00	17000.00
REPORT	TOTALS		13	8920.00	9008.40	8760.00	88.40	248.40	71120.00	71120.00

477

Figure A7.34

PRIMAVERA PROJECT PLANNER

REPORT DATE 28APR89 RUN NO.   3   TABULAR COST REPORT - DAILY   START DATE 1JUL88 FIN DATE 1FEB89*
            7:39
DAILY CASH FLOW FOR RESOURCES   DATA DATE 12JUL88 PAGE NO.   1

PERIOD BEGINNING	---AVAILABLE--- NORMAL MAXIMUM		--EARLY SCHEDULE--- USAGE CUMULATIVE		---LATE SCHEDULE--- USAGE CUMULATIVE		--TARGET 1 SCHEDULE-- USAGE CUMULATIVE	
	LEADER -				UNIT OF MEASURE = COST		TARGET = EARLY	
1JUL88	0	0	200.00	200.00	200.00	200.00	200.00	200.00
2JUL88	0	0	.00	200.00	.00	200.00	.00	200.00
3JUL88	0	0	.00	200.00	.00	200.00	.00	200.00
4JUL88	0	0	.00	200.00	.00	200.00	.00	200.00
5JUL88	0	0	200.00	400.00	200.00	400.00	200.00	400.00
6JUL88	0	0	200.00	600.00	200.00	600.00	200.00	600.00
7JUL88	0	0	200.00	800.00	200.00	800.00	200.00	800.00
8JUL88	0	0	700.00	1500.00	700.00	1500.00	600.00	1400.00
9JUL88	0	0	.00	1500.00	.00	1500.00	.00	1400.00
10JUL88	0	0	.00	1500.00	.00	1500.00	.00	1400.00
11JUL88	0	0	700.00	2200.00	700.00	2200.00	600.00	2000.00
DATA DATE								
12JUL88	0	0	600.00	2800.00	.00	2200.00	600.00	2600.00
13JUL88	0	0	600.00	3400.00	.00	2200.00	600.00	3200.00
14JUL88	0	0	400.00	3800.00	.00	2200.00	600.00	3800.00

478

Figure A7.35

```
                              PRIMAVERA PROJECT PLANNER

REPORT DATE 28APR89  RUN NO.   2                              START DATE 1JUL88  FIN DATE 1FEB89*
            10:54
SUMMARY WEEKLY BAR CHART BY FIRST ID COD                      DATA DATE 12JUL88  PAGE NO.  1

                                                                        WEEKLY-TIME PER.   1

......ACTIVITY DESCRIPTION......                     04  01  05  03  07  05  02  06  06  03  01  05  03  07  04  02
ACTIVITY ID  OD  RD  PCT   CODES   FLOAT   SCHEDULE   JUL AUG SEP OCT NOV DEC JAN FEB MAR APR MAY JUN JUL AUG SEP OCT
---- --- --- ---  --- ----   -----   --------         88  88  88  88  88  88  89  89  89  89  89  89  89  89  89  89

CH9GJOS  109 103   6              39     EARLY        AAEEEEEEEEEEEEEEEEE      .   .   .   .   .   .   .   .   .   .
AS = 1JUL88        EF = 8DEC88           LATE         AA*          .          LLLLLLLLL.
                                                      LF = 1FEB89

SUB1JOS   19  19   0               0     EARLY        EEEEE.    .   .   .   .   .   .   .   .   .   .   .   .   .   .
ES = 1JUL88        EF = 28JUL88   LS = 1JUL88  LATE   LLLLL.    .
                                                      LF = 28JUL88
```

479

Appendix 7.12.3 Who Produces Perts and Gantts that May Be Restricted to Summary Jobs? (13.9)

The Primavision networks, the Primavera Project Planner and Primavision bar charts can all be limited to just those activities designated as hammocks. A very nice feature, Primavera Project Planner has a "Summarize projects into master" utility. If it has been applied, both Primavera Project Planner and Primavision will produce summary reports and bar charts showing each of the subprojects. (See Figure A7.35.) Primavision will also produce summary networks.

Appendix 7.12.4 Local Area Networks (13.14)

Primavera Project Planner does not support LANs.

Appendix 7.12.5 Guidelines for Tracking and Managing the Project (13.15)

Interspersed in the several pages of Primavera Project Planner documentation for using the system are some hints on how to track projects.

Bibliography

A.J. Albrecht, "*Measuring Applications Development Productivity*," Proceedings, Joint Guide/Share/IBM Applications Development Symposium October, 1979 Pp. 83-92.

C.W. Axelrod, "*Getting A Clear Picture Of Costs and Benefits*," ComputerWorld, July, 1982.

B. Block, *Politics Of Projects* (New York: Yourdon Press, 1983).

B.W. Boehm, *Software Engineering Economics* (New Jersey: Prentice-Hall, 1981).

F.P. Brooks, Jr., *Mythical Man Month* (Massachusetts: Addison-Wesley Company, 1975).

C. Burrill and L. Ellsworth, *Modern Project Management* (New Jersey: Burrill-Ellsworth Associates, Inc., 1980).

T. DeMarco, *Controlling Software Projects* (New York: Yourdon Press, 1982).

G.F. Hice, W.S. Turner, and L.F. Cashwell, *System Development Methodology* (New York: North-Holland Press, 1974).

R.W. Jensen, "*An Improved Macrolevel Software Development Resource Estimation Model*," Internal Paper: Hughes Aircraft Company Defense Systems Division Space and Communications Group, Los Angeles, CA.

R.W. Jensen, S. Lucas, "*Sensitivity Analysis Of The Jensen Software Model*," Proceedings Of The Fifth International Society Of Parametric Analysts Conference, St. Louis, Missouri April, 1983.

R.W. Jensen, "*A Comparison Of The Jensen and Cocomo Schedule and Cost Estimation Models*," Proceedings Of The Fifth International Society Of Parametric Analysts Conference, St. Louis, Missouri April, 1983.

T.C. Jones, "*Software Value Analysis: A Survey Of The State Of The Art*," A Tutorial Conducted For The ACR Conference On Improving Productivity In Systems Development, Phoenix, January 1987.

C.H. Kepner and B.B. Tregoe, *The New Rational Manager* (London: John Martin Publishing, Ltd., 1981).

B.P. Lientz and E.B. Swanson, *Software Maintenance Management* (Massachusetts: Addison-Wesley, 1980).

J. Martin, *Application Development Without Programmers* (New Jersey: Prentice-Hall, 1982).

J. Martin and C. McClure, *Software Maintenance* (New Jersey: Prentice-Hall, 1983).

J. Martin, *An Information Systems Manifesto* (New Jersey: Prentice-Hall, 1984).

P.W. Metzger, *Managing A Programming Project* (New Jersey: Prentice-Hall, 1973).

J.J. Moder, C.R. Phillips, E.W. Davis, *Project Management with CPM, PERT, and Precedence Diagramming* (New York: Van Nostrand Reinhold Company, 1983).

G.J. Myers, *The Art Of Software Testing* (New York: John Wiley and Sons, 1979).

P.V. Norden, "*Curve Fitting For A Model Of Applied Research and Development Scheduling*," IBM Journal Of Research and Development, Vol. 2, No. 3 July, 1958.

P.V. Norden, "*Project Life Cycle Modeling: Background*

and Application Of Life Cycle Curves," Software Life Cycle Management Workshop, Sponsored By USACSC, Airlie, Va. 1977.

M. Page-Jones, *Practical Project Management: Restoring Quality To DP Projects and Systems* (New York: Dorset House Publishing, 1985).

S. Plotkin, *"The Real Cost Of The D.P. Professional,"* Computerworld, July 19, 1982.

L.H. Putnam, *"A Macro-Estimating Methodology For Software Development,"* Proceedings, IEEE CompCon 76, Fall, September, 1976.

L.H. Putnam and R.W. Wolverton, *"Quantitative Management: Software Cost Estimating,"* IEEE Computer Society First International Computer Software and Applications Conference, Chicago, IL. November, 1977.

L.H. Putnam and A. Fitzsimmons, *"Estimating Software Costs,"* Datamation, September, 1979.

C.R. Symons, *"Function Point Analysis: Difficulties and Improvements,"* IEEE Transactions On Software Engineering, Vol. 14 No 1. January, 1988.

C.E. Walston and C.P. Felix, *"A Method Of Programming Measurement and Estimation,"* IBM Systems Journal, Volume 16, Number 1, 1977.

J.D. Wiest and F.K. Levy, *A Management Guide to PERT/CPM* (New Jersey: Prentice-Hall, 1977).

E. Yourdon, *Managing The System Life Cycle* (New York: Yourdon Press, 1982).

E. Yourdon, (Editor) *Writings Of The Revolution: Selected Readings On Software Engineering* (New York: Yourdon Press, 1982).

L. Zells, *"A Practical Approach To A Project Expectations Document,"* ComputerWorld, August 29, 1983.

L. Zells, *"Hobbling Productivity,"* ComputerWorld, October 28, 1985.

L. Zells, *"Project Success,"* Government Data Systems, Special FCC Supplement, August, 1985.

Index[1]

[1]Terms unique to each of the seven products will be found in this index. References to other generic terms in the appendices may be found by tracing the respective term through the corresponding tutorial section.